1968

ok may be kept

ography Past and Present

EDITED

William H. Daven

Harvey Mud

Ben Siegel

California State Polytechnic College

Biography
Past and Present

SELECTIONS AND CRITICAL ESSAYS

Charles Scribner's Sons   *New York*

FOREWORD

Of the editing of anthologies there is no end. All the more reason, we believe, that each new anthology justify its existence. Our justification has been made somewhat easier by two significant factors.

First, the time seems especially propitious for an anthology of biography. Always popular, biography of late has been flourishing. Sales lists, book awards, and rental libraries indicate growing interest in the various forms of life writing. The trend is reflected on the campus as well—not only in the familiar types courses (which include biography) but in composition and literary survey courses. In these, biography is proving an effective and stimulating means of teaching the principles of writing and the major themes of literary history. Specialized courses in biography also are increasing, and there are even departments of biography (as at Dartmouth).

Second, to the best of our knowledge this anthology is the first to combine not only selections from classical and modern biographies and autobiographies but also critical and historical essays on biography. (Autobiography here has been treated merely as another form of biography; it has been singled out only by a separate table of contents as a convenience for instructor and student.) Only modest use, however, has been made of diaries, journals, and letters; most such writings (with the usual few notable exceptions) have proved on rereading to be too fragmentary and self-conscious to be considered more than fringe materials.

Biography Past and Present is intended to be functional and is aimed primarily at teachers and students. The special needs of the classroom have done much to determine the general format of the book. We might point out, however, that an anthology of this kind is at best but a guided tour to scattered points of interest in one literary area. As in all tours, the traveler will find his tastes and time schedules do not coincide always with the guide's; inevitably, he will mark points to visit again—more leisurely and on his own. The veteran traveler in biography will look here in vain for some familiar landmarks. But he must realize that like all great currents, that of biography is constantly shifting its course and reshaping its topography. At the same time he will note that continual compass readings have been provided in the exercises and questions accompanying each selection; these should make broader exploration much easier.

Our view of biography is a broad one; it includes history, scripture, and hagiography, as well as essay, diary, profile, memoir, apologia, news report, panegyric, and eulogy. We have sought always the readable, lively, representative, and varied. No attempt was made to compile an anthology of masterpieces. There were no *a priori* musts; that which seemed to us to arouse little response from students today (many selections were classroom-tested) was rejected. Many selections have been included complete; others have been abridged—some little, some much.

This volume, then, is not meant to be in any *strict* sense a historical survey of biography; the table of contents reveals that modern selections outnumber classical. We have tried, however, to suggest the evolution of biography as a literary genre; we have moved from Biblical and ancient times through the Renaissance and the Enlightenment down to the present—including selections from the most representative, rather than the most familiar or conventional, writers.

We have tried to include all levels of writing—formal, informal, and popular. Questions and exercises, as already mentioned, focus attention upon style, organization, and tone, as well as upon literary history. These should prove instructional conveniences for teachers of composition and literature who wish to use them. Those who do not will find them easy to skip, or perhaps modify.

Authoritative texts have been used for all selections; and pre-twentieth-century selections have been modernized in spelling, capitalization, and punctuation. British spelling is retained in British selections.

It has become fashionable to scoff at the thanks expressed in most introductions. Having ignored the fashionable whenever we felt the need, we shall do so once more. For we wish to thank those colleagues and friends who examined and commented on sections of this work in progress. (Some were kind enough to try various selections on their students and then report the reactions.) The list is a long one. To mention some by name and not the others would be unfair; hence we thank them all, collectively. On the home front, Isobel Davenport and Ruth Siegel kept wheels turning by clearing rooms and tables, providing unscheduled meals, typing—and never offering advice.

At this point it is customary for editors to accept full responsibility for errors of commission or omission; so we do so . . . reluctantly!

Claremont, California   WILLIAM H. DAVENPORT
April 1, 1964.   BEN SIEGEL

CONTENTS

FOREWORD   *v*

BIOGRAPHY PAST

INTRODUCTORY ESSAY   John A. Garraty, Biography in the
                          Ancient World   3
SELECTIONS
  Biblical   The Book of Ruth   18
  Classical   Plutarch, from The Life of Julius
                          Caesar   24
  Renaissance   William Roper, from *Life of Sir
                          Thomas More*   39
                          John Foxe, Bishop Ridley and
                          Bishop Latimer   52
CRITICAL ESSAY   W. S. Lewis, The Difficult Art of
                          Biography   59

SELECTIONS
  Seventeenth Century   John Aubrey, Shakespeare ·
                          Suckling · Davenant   67
                          John Bunyan, from *Grace
                          Abounding*   77
                          Samuel Pepys, from *Diary*   87
CRITICAL ESSAY   Leon Edel, [The Subject Matter
                          of Biography]   116
SELECTIONS
  Eighteenth Century   Samuel Johnson, Gray   132
                          James Boswell, from *Life of
                          Johnson*   143
CRITICAL ESSAY   Virginia Woolf, The Art of
                          Biography   164
SELECTION
  Nineteenth Century   John Gibson Lockhart, from *Life
                          of Sir Walter Scott*   172

BIOGRAPHY PRESENT

CRITICAL ESSAY   Edward Hayes O'Neill, from The
New Biography   *191*

MODERN SELECTIONS   William Butler Yeats, from *Autobiographies*   *199*

Lytton Strachey, Florence Nightingale   *207*

André Maurois, from *Disraeli*   *250*

H. G. Wells, from *Experiment in
Autobiography*   *262*

CRITICAL ESSAY   Bernard De Voto, The Skeptical
Biographer   *276*

CONTEMPORARY SELECTIONS   Thomas Sancton, The Silver Horn   *293*

Dylan Thomas, from *Portrait of
the Artist as a Young Dog*   *303*

Alfred Kazin, from A *Walker in
the City*   *313*

Catherine Drinker Bowen, [Oliver
Wendell Holmes]   *321*

James Baldwin, Notes of a Native
Son   *339*

Moss Hart, from *Act One*   *355*

CRITICAL ESSAY   Iris Origo, Biography, True and
False   *368*

CONTEMPORARY SELECTIONS   Gertrude Stein, [Ernest Heming-
way]   *380*

Robert Rice, [Mort Sahl]   *388*

Louis Untermeyer, [Amy Lowell]   *404*

James Thurber, My Friend
McNulty   *419*

Deems Taylor, The Monster   *428*

Harry Golden, Mayor William J.
Gaynor   *433*

W. A. Swanberg, from *Citizen
Hearst*   *439*

John Dos Passos, [Thorstein
Veblen]   *450*

Time Magazine, [Niels Bohr]   *459*

New York *Times,* [Monty
Woolley]   *463*

ON BIOGRAPHY: A SELECTED BIBLIOGRAPHY
A *selected list of 20th-century books and essays dealing with
biography.*   *467*

ALTERNATE TABLE OF CONTENTS   *471*

Biography Past

BIOGRAPHY
IN THE
ANCIENT
WORLD

John A. Garraty

John A. Garraty (1920–   ), *born in Brooklyn, saw wartime service as a United States Maritime instructor and received a Ph.D. in history from Columbia (1948). After many years on the Michigan State University faculty, he returned to Columbia as professor of history. A specialist in the history of the United States and in the history of biography, Garraty has written, among other works,* Henry Cabot Lodge: A Biography *(1953),* Woodrow Wilson: A Great Life in Brief *(1956), and* The Nature of Biography *(1957).*

The Nature of Biography evolved from Garraty's study of psychology at Harvard during 1952–53 on a Ford Foundation Fellowship. In the book he decided to show "how much a biographer's success depends upon his understanding of human motivation." The first part of the book—from which the following selection is taken—traces the history of biographical writing from ancient times to the present. The second part centers on the methods of writing biography. The original footnotes for this selection have been omitted.

✶ ✶ ✶ ✶ ✶

The roots of biography lie buried in man's search for immortality. Five thousand years ago Egyptian kings left in their tombs records of their fame along with the symbols of their wealth in order to insure their safe passage to eternity. These first crude accounts were not biographies by the standards of modern times, for they made no pretense at describing either the careers or the characters of their subjects. But their purposes were biographical—they sought to preserve, on earth and in heaven, the reputations of individual men.

Though they were autobiographical in form, their almost total lack of individuality makes it clear that they were actually biographies prepared as part of burial ceremonies. The "biography" of the magnate Inni, dating from the era of the New Kingdom (B.C. 1580–1350), represents the type in its most complete form. Inni was a functionary under four pharaohs. His tomb contained an account, carved on stone, of his services, and its walls were decorated with pictures showing him superintending a harvest, visiting his estate, receiving gifts from the king, and performing other functions. From these remains, one learns little of Inni, but a great deal about life in the New Kingdom.

While all the early biographical fragments portrayed types rather than men, they nonetheless displayed a flamboyant egotism. "Self-glorification has never since appeared with such naïveté," Georg Misch remarked in his comprehensive survey of ancient autobiography. "Some of the documents confront us with immoderate, even brutally vigorous, self-glorification, to a degree unique in history." By depicting themselves only at the high points of their careers, by idealizing their achievements, the Egyptians produced images as flat and distorted as their pictographs. Of the judge it is said that he "excelled the tongue of the balance in accuracy," of the slave-owner that he was kindly and tolerant. "I went forth from the door of my house with benevolent heart," one potentate of the twelfth dynasty declared. "I stood there with benevolent hand." How gullible they must have thought the deity they sought to supplicate!

In Assyria and Babylonia the development of biography followed a more secular path than in Egypt. By B.C. 1400 it had become customary there to record the deeds of kings in the form of chronicles. As in Egypt, these records were phrased in the first person, as though the king was telling his own story, but it is almost certain that they were not actually autobiographical. Etched on clay tablets, or chiseled on stone slabs, these accounts are full of blood and battle and the vain vaporizings of absolute potentates. Pride, hatred, and brutality run through them endlessly, but behind the bombast looms the primitive terror of the unknown that characterizes the human animal scarcely removed from the stone ax and the cave. "I am the king, I am the lord, I am the exalted, the great, the strong; I am famous, I am prince, I am the noble, the powerful in war; I am a lion, I am a hero of youthful strength; Assurnasirpal, the mighty king." Shelley caught the spirit of these ancient records in "Ozymandias"—"Look on my works, ye Mighty, and despair!"

But with the passage of time, these ancient biographies grew more sophisticated. The egotism remained, but virtues other than courage and strength assumed more importance, and development as well as mature power was occasionally described. By the time of Darius the Great, after the Persian conquest of the Middle East, the records had begun to deal with the constructive as well as the destructive side of leadership, and to show some sign of the ruler's concern for the ruled. The imposing monument that Darius carved beside the road that ran from Babylon to the East to commemorate one of his triumphs was full of the conventional self-glorification. "I am Darius, the great king, king of kings, king in Persia, king of the lands." And the bulk of the record consisted of a routine description of his heroic accomplishments. But there were glimmerings of a more mature view. "These lands gave me service and tribute. . . . I cherished him who was friendly to me, punished him who was hostile to me. Ahuramazda granted me dominion, gave me help."

One might expect Greek civilization to have produced a great corpus of outstanding biographies. After all, it was the Greeks who supposedly liberated the individual from the mass and gave him a real awareness of himself and his limitless potentialities. The rationality, subtlety, and curiosity of the Greeks would seem to have provided an ideal breeding ground for biography; so would their secular spirit and their interest in history. But the Greek lives that have come down through the ages are few, fragmentary, and disappointing.

Of course, Greek biography went well beyond the naïve vainglory of Egyptian and Babylonian lives. But the Greeks simply were not interested in writing biography. For one thing, although they believed in the worth of the individual man and in the importance of developing his talents fully, they were also preoccupied with the idea of man's helplessness before the mysterious force of Fate, as a reading of any of their great tragic poets makes clear. Some Greek writers also depreciated man's ability to rise above his environment. Hippocrates, for example, explained the physical and mental differences between Asiatics and Europeans in terms of varying climatic conditions. "The human body and character," he wrote, "vary in accordance with the nature of the country." People who lived in well-watered, mountainous regions where the extremes of temperature were wide—people, that is, like the Greeks—tended, according to Hippocrates, to be physically powerful and courageous to the point of ferocity and brutality. Those who inhabited temperate lands where the seasonal variations were small usually suffered from a "deficiency of spirit and courage." Herodotus was expressing a similar view when he praised the Persian King Cyrus for discouraging those of his subjects who wished to migrate to the rich lands of a conquered foe. "Soft countries," Cyrus said, "invariably breed soft men." Such a philosophy, discounting the importance of individuals, naturally discouraged the writing of biography.

In addition, the Greeks were not particularly concerned with the perpetuation of the self beyond death. Until relatively late in the development of their civilization, they did not produce formal prose memorials of individual heroes. The Athenians memorialized soldiers who fell in battle, but they did so collectively—the band was praised, not the single patriot. It was part of their view of virtue that, as Aristotle said, the "magnanimous" man was sufficient unto himself; he neither talked about himself nor expected others to speak in his behalf.

Consider Pericles' eulogy of the Athenians killed in the Peloponnesian War, as recorded by Thucydides. The orator begins by disparaging the very idea of using mere words to commemorate worthy actions. "Worth which has displayed itself in deeds would be sufficiently rewarded by honors also shown by deeds." And when he nonetheless conforms to custom and delivers his speech, he speaks chiefly of the virtues of Athenian democracy and of the value of courage, not of the individual merits of the fallen.

Further, Hellenic civilization valued "ideal" men. Just as (at least until the time of Praxiteles) Greek sculpture strove to fabricate perfect types rather than individuals, so Greek biography was concerned with the question of how well individuals conformed to a preconceived pattern of ideal behavior. Similarly, the biographers were aiming at the perfect form of *biography*. They tested their subjects against a rigid standard of values and they did so in a standardized manner. They were more eager to produce a perfectly organized and polished essay than to achieve a truthful portrait; indeed, they might deliberately sacrifice accuracy to make their prose conform to the "ideal." For example, Isocrates, who developed the *encomium* with his speech in praise of Evagoras, King of Salamis, ignored the fact that Evagoras was assassinated and implied that he died a happy death, simply because he believed that the "form" required it. Encomiasts also frankly adopted the role of advocate. They were out to make a plausible case, not necessarily to tell the whole truth. *Encomia* were sometimes written about purely legendary characters. Polycrates even wrote one on mice. Inaccuracies aside, a great emphasis on form meant that the biographies were incomplete. In his *encomium* on Agesilaus, Xenophon considered his subject's character under the headings of piety, justice, self-control, courage, wisdom, urbanity, and patriotism; he ignored other aspects of the man because they were not required by the form with which he dealt.

Finally, to the Greeks, the ideal man was the mature man. They were aware that character developed over time, but felt that the development itself was unimportant. Like the Egyptians, who pictured their heroes at the peaks of their careers, ignoring their failures and the dull routine of life, the Greeks studied man only in maturity, discarding as trivial the steps which led to his "final" form.

The earliest Greek biographical fragments to have survived are the memoirs of the poet Ion of Chios, dating from the fifth century before Christ. These were casual sketches of such famous men of that day as Pericles, Sophocles, and Aeschylus. Ion portrayed his subjects wholly from the outside, catching their impact on society rather than their personal points of view, but adding descriptive details, such as personal appearance, that were new to biography at the time. Early in the next century Xenophon attached biographical appendices to his epic account of the Persian Wars in the *Anabasis*. He also wrote a defense of his friend Socrates (the *Memorabilia*) and the already mentioned *encomium* on Agesilaus. But even the most elaborate of these works, the *Memorabilia*, was far from being a complete biography. It was not written as a single work, being rather a collection of separate pieces dealing with Socrates which were brought together and named by later scholars. The first section was produced as a reply to the accusations that had led to Socrates' condemnation and to slurs against the master's character made after his death by his enemies. In another part, written about B.C. 385, Xenophon assumed the offensive with a series of Socratic dialogues. "In order to support my opinion that he benefited his companions, alike by actions that revealed his own character and by his conversation, I will set down what I recollect of these," Xenophon wrote. The third part, a loosely connected collection of dialogues and aphorisms, and the fourth, dealing with Socrates' educational views, were also separately written. Taken all in all, the *Memorabilia* summarized Socrates' philosophy, and contained many vivid personal anecdotes (of dubious authenticity, however). But it lacked a connecting narrative, and there were vast gaps in the story. "I have described him as he was," Xenophon boasted at the end of the last section, but he did not actually make good this boast.

Yet, however disjointed and incomplete, the *Memorabilia* was the most elaborate biographical work produced up to that time. The intellectual ferment begun by Socrates and carried on by Plato and Aristotle was developing a climate favorable to biographical writing. The controversy that raged for generations over the execution of Socrates produced a great deal of literature about the man and stimulated interest in his emphasis on close, rational self-examination. Plato's effective use of concrete illustrations to "prove" generalizations (as when he justified his argument that Athens had never possessed a "good" statesman by describing the careers of Pericles and other prominent leaders) also played a part. By the middle of the fourth century, although interest in form, types, and argument for its own sake had not disappeared, writers were beginning to feel that an individual was worthy of study in his own right. Even the *encomium*, although excessively formal, abounded in graphic detail. It introduced anecdotes of the subject's childhood in order to demonstrate the seeds of his future greatness, and it established firmly the idea that a great man's deeds should be preserved in words. Significantly, Isocrates was the first Greek to write a real autobiography (the *Antidosis*), designed, he said, to "serve as a monument . . . more noble than statues of bronze."

Aristotle provided another important stimulus to biography. From Plato's postulate that the only true reality was the ideal, he conceived the theory that the ideal could be observed and understood perfectly only in action, that is, while performing its proper function. A man's life could be described, Aristotle said, not by listing his "characteristics" but by placing "the man's acts . . . on record so that his character and nature were revealed by them." This idea led Aristotle's protégé, Theophrastus, to write his famous *Characters*, which, while still designed to illustrate "types," did so by piling up examples of specific behavior. Consider, for example, this delightful picture of vanity:

> When ambition is the ruling passion of a vulgar mind, it shows itself in the eager pursuit of frivolous distinctions. The vain and vulgar man strives always to gain a place at table next to the master of the feast. . . . He takes vast pains to be provided with a black servant, who always attends him in public. If he has a considerable sum of money to pay, he provides himself with new coin for the purpose. . . . When his favorite dog dies, he deposits the remains in a tomb, and erects a monument over the grave. . . .

Theophrastus was not describing a particular person, but he was developing a technique that others were to adopt for biographical purposes. Instead of forcing a man into a preconceived mold, he proved that a man's actions could be used to generalize about his personality. "I have long been an attentive observer of Human Nature," he wrote in his introduction to the *Characters*. "I am now in the ninety-ninth year of my age; and during the whole course of my life I have conversed familiarly with men of all classes. . . . With these qualifications I have thought myself fitted for the task of describing those habitual peculiarities by which the manners of every one are distinguished."

Theophrastus became, after Aristotle's death, the leader of the so-called Peripatetic school, which Aristotle had founded. Angered by Theophrastus' success, another Peripatetic named Aristoxenus of Tarentum turned to biography for revenge, and produced what were probably the first "debunking" lives ever written. Little of Aristoxenus' work has been preserved, but references to it in the works of later writers make it obvious that his role in the development of biography was important. He attacked not only Aristotle, but also Socrates and Plato. According to Aristoxenus, Socrates was sensual, ignorant, selfish, temperamental, and a bigamist. Aristoxenus had been influenced early in his career by a follower of Pythagoras named Xenophilus; in his life of Plato he claimed that the *Republic* had been plagiarized from Pythagoras. He also wrote lives of Pythagoras and some of his disciples, these in a friendly vein. The quality of his biographical work was probably poor (certainly it was completely subjective), but its significance is clear. Aristoxenus was the first biographer to write unified treatises on particular individuals designed to defend or attack a particular point of view by exemplifying it in the person of one man.

A whole school of Peripatetic biographers developed from Aristoxenus. Little of their work remains, but its basic nature can be reconstructed from fragments and commentaries. These writers thought of themselves primarily as biographers. They were professional compilers and critics, and placed great emphasis on telling their stories in readable form. They sought to present their subjects from as many points of vantage as possible. Peripatetic biographies, in addition to dealing with the mature man, described his origins, family background, and education. Besides discussing his career, they dealt with his appearance, mannerisms, and disposition. They began with birth and ended with death.

It is true that most of the Peripatetics were poor critics. They indulged in the traditional Greek disregard for accuracy, and, either out of naïveté or out of an understandable desire to tell a good story, they did not hesitate to make use of legends and other unreliable sources. Sometimes they deliberately falsified facts, and they reveled in sensationalism. One of the later Peripatetics, Hermippus of Smyrna, who wrote a huge work on famous writers and philosophers, made a specialty of graphic death scenes, which he evidently composed entirely out of his imagination when the truth was not known, prosaic, or difficult to come by. The Peripatetic method was also discursive and anecdotal. But if their works were second rate, these writers were important in the development of biography. Hermippus, for example, influenced Plutarch. They made biography a literary genre, and a popular one. They advanced the methods and polished the style of biographical writing, even though they did so carelessly and with little regard for truth.

The most extensive example of Peripatetic biography that has survived is a life of Euripides by a Greek named Satyrus. This work shows that Peripatetic biography had not entirely escaped from the Greek emphasis on form and patterned arrangement. The beginning and the end are chronological, but the body of the life is broken down under broad captions dealing with Euripides' career as a dramatist, his personality, and his philosophy. The emphasis is on the mature man considered topically. The work has unity and organization, but little consciousness of development except in the first section dealing with the early years.

The line of Peripatetic biographers had died out by the third century before Christ. Greek writers in succeeding generations, chiefly scholars working in the great libraries of Alexandria, reacted against the slipshod inaccuracies of the Peripatetics, but in doing so they also lost the Peripatetic concern for literary artistry. Antigonus of Carystus, writing his popular *Lives of the Philosophers* about B.C. 240, evidently combined reliability with a good style, but most of the Alexandrian biographers were merely pedantic. They devoted themselves to correcting the factual errors of Peripatetic biographers like Satyrus, and to writing routine introductions to the works of the great Greek authors. Where the Peripatetics had been artistic but inaccurate, the Alexandrians were exact but dull and disorganized.

The Roman conquest of the Mediterranean world meant, of course, the spread of Greek culture westward, but the Romans had biographical traditions of their own that also influenced the writing of lives. The early Roman nobility had a vast respect for ancestors. The typical upper-class home contained portrait masks of the owner's forebears and inscriptions describing the offices and honors each had held. The traditional Roman funeral oration, the *laudatio funebris*, delivered by a close relative or friend of the deceased was also well established long before Greek literature was known in Italy.

When a member of an important family died, the body was borne in a great procession to the Forum. Actors impersonated the famous ancestors of the deceased. In the Forum the body was placed on a pyre, but before the torch was applied, the orator mounted the rostra. The "ancestors" sat on ivory seats facing the corpse, but the speaker addressed himself to the populace, gathered around the pyre. Typically his speech was full of ancestor-worship, and was of course completely uncritical, but it also dealt in detail with the official career of the subject, and sometimes contained a narrative account of important events in his life. It was common for prominent families to preserve written copies of these speeches, which they used both to recall past glories and as source material when later funerals required a repeat performance. Since these orations were usually prepared by amateurs, and prejudiced amateurs at that, they were seldom accurate. Cicero said of them: "By these laudatory speeches our history has become quite distorted; for much is set down in them that never occurred—false triumphs, too large a number of consulships, false relationships. . . . [It is] as if I, for example, should say that I was descended from Manius Tullius the patrician, who was Consul . . . ten years after the expulsion of the kings."

Roman pride in family and love of fame, so clearly reflected in the funeral orations, also led to the writing of "authorized" lives of powerful magnates by slaves or retainers. The life of the dictator Sulla was fabricated by one of his freedmen, and Tiro prepared a life of Cicero. Such works were common throughout the late Republic, and became formalized under the Empire. While purely Roman in origin, they were of course influenced by Greek biography. Cornelius Nepos, whom Gibbon praised highly, wrote a life of the wealthy art patron, Pomponius Atticus, in the first century before Christ, which dealt with Atticus' character in a topical fashion quite similar to the *encomia* of Isocrates and Xenophon. Indeed, by the time of Nepos the distinction between Greek and Roman biography was rapidly disappearing.

The supreme figure of ancient biography was Plutarch, who was born about the middle of the first century of the Christian era in Boeotia. Plutarch represented the blending of Greek and Roman culture at the apex of its development, and his *Lives of the Noble Grecians and Romans* was in many ways a summary of that culture. He wrote his biographies in pairs, always matching a Greek with a Roman. Thus he compared great generals like Alexander and Caesar, and great orators like Demosthenes and Cicero. His impartiality is attested by the fact that it is still doubtful whether he was trying to convince the Greeks that there had been Romans who were their equals, or to convince the Romans that they were no better than the Greeks. The organization of Plutarch's biographies was not unusual. Most of them dealt first with the ancestry, birth, and early life of the subject, then outlined his character, and then considered his career, which was used to illustrate in concrete terms the operation of his personality. Like Theophrastus and the Peripatetics, Plutarch used the specific to prove the general, and placed great stress on personal anecdotes. He made little contribution to the form or technique of biography, although he excelled all his predecessors in his masterful execution of traditional methods. But he was the first great exponent of a new point of view.

First of all, he escaped almost completely from the argumentative element of Greek biography and the panegyrical element of Greek *encomium* and Roman *laudatio* alike. It was not that he was coldly objective. "It was for the sake of others that I first commenced writing biographies," he admitted in a famous passage in his life of Timoleon. "But I find myself proceeding and attaching myself to it for my own; the virtues of these great men serving me as a sort of looking-glass, in which I may see how to adjust and adorn my own life." Neither was he strictly impartial. He was a hero-worshipper who looked upon the great Greeks and Romans as a race apart from the general run of mankind, and a moralist who sought to model his own life on those of his heroes and to teach others to do likewise. But his ultimate goal was always *understanding*, and he realized that it could be achieved only by sympathy, insight, and hard work.

Plutarch explained his point of view clearly in writing of the Roman General, Lucullus. Lucullus had, before Plutarch's time, been instrumental in saving Plutarch's native city, Chaeronea, from being charged by the authorities with harboring an outlaw who had murdered a Roman officer. In gratitude the Chaeroneans had erected a statue of Lucullus in the market place. In writing his biography, Plutarch wished to defend himself against the charge that personal feeling would make him overly friendly to Lucullus. He frankly admitted that he was prejudiced in favor of the General, but, he added, he would not consider "swerving from the truth." Lucullus himself, Plutarch went on:

> . . . would not thank us, if in recompense for a service which consisted in speaking the truth, we should abuse his memory with a false and counterfeit narration. For as we would wish that a painter who is to draw a beautiful face, in which there is yet some imperfection, should neither wholly leave out, nor yet too pointedly express what is defective, because this would deform it, and that spoil the resemblance; so since it is hard, or indeed impossible, to show the life of a man wholly free from blemish, in all that is excellent we must follow truth exactly, and give it fully; any lapses or faults that occur . . . we may regard rather as the shortcomings of some particular virtue, than as the natural effects of vice. . . .

Similarly, in his life of Alcibiades, Plutarch, while leaving no doubt that he abhorred and condemned his subject, also described his charm, brilliance, and military skill, and explained his weaknesses in terms of these very virtues, which brought success to him too easily. He offered a wonderful anecdote pointing up the complex character of Alcibiades, which is worth repeating, for it illustrates Plutarch's approach perfectly:

> Alcibiades had a dog which cost him seventy minas, and was a very large one, and very handsome. His tail, which was his principal ornament, he caused to be cut off, and his acquaintances exclaiming at him for it, and telling him that all Athens was sorry for the dog, and cried out upon him for this action, he laughed, and said, "Just what I wanted has happened then. I wished the Athenians to talk about this, that they might not say something worse of me."

Plutarch also excelled other classical biographers in the profundity of his scholarship. One authority counted two hundred and fifty Greek authors among the writers quoted by him, some eighty of whom are known today only through Plutarch's references. Plutarch was not always accurate; modern biographers of many of his subjects have found dozens of errors in his work. Indeed, he lacked the modern scholar's concern for tracing information back to its ultimate source. Sometimes he made use of secondary accounts even when primary sources were readily available to him, and he did not always try to distinguish between fact and hearsay, or reality and legend. But he usually made it clear what his sources were, and he readily admitted his doubts when evidence was missing or contradictory.

Plutarch always emphasized character over career. He was weak when he tried to explain the political significance of the events in his narratives. Though his knowledge of the past was encyclopedic, he was interested in people rather than in history. While from the modern point of view this approach makes his lives incomplete, it would be wrong to criticize him for it. He was conscious of what he was doing. "As portrait-painters are more exact in the lines and features of the face, in which the character is seen, so I must be allowed to give my more particular attention to the marks and indications of the souls of men," he explained.

His method was to describe his characters in action. No other biographer, not even Boswell, has excelled him in the masterly handling of anecdotal material. His stories are more than merely clever or interesting; like the incident of Alcibiades' dog, they never lack a point and always illuminate the personality. In his life of Alexander, he placed great stress on what he called Alexander's "passion for pre-eminence." Time after time, in a dozen different circumstances, he illustrated this characteristic with telling anecdotes. He recounted, for instance, the story of how Alexander, campaigning in Asia, learned that his teacher, Aristotle, had published some philosophical treatises. "Alexander to Aristotle, greeting," the hero wrote at once. "You have not done well to publish your books of oral doctrine, for what is there now that we excel others in, if those things which we have been particularly instructed in be laid open to all?" Later in his narrative, Plutarch described an incident between Alexander and one of his lieutenants, Parmenio. It was during the Persian campaign, after Alexander had defeated the army of Darius and captured most of the Persian ruler's family. Darius sent intermediaries offering a vast ransom and a section of his kingdom if Alexander would free the captives and make peace. "These propositions," Plutarch wrote, "[Alexander] communicated to his friends, and when Parmenio told him that, for his part, if he were Alexander, he should readily

embrace them, 'So would I,' said Alexander, 'if I were Parmenio.'"
Whether the prize was knowledge, wealth, or power, Plutarch made
clear that Alexander must possess it wholly.

Finally, Plutarch was startlingly "modern" in his techniques for
catching and holding the interest of his readers. A contemporary writer
of profiles, Lincoln Barnett, has claimed that there is nothing in that
type of sketch that Plutarch did not anticipate. He made brilliant use of
the clever introduction, or "lead." Sometimes he began with a broad
generalization, setting the theme of his interpretation:

> It is no great wonder if in long process of time, while fortune takes
> her course hither and thither, numerous coincidences should spon-
> taneously occur. (Sertorius)

On other occasions he began with a provocative anecdote:

> Caesar once, seeing some wealthy strangers at Rome, carrying up
> and down with them in their arms and bosoms young puppy-dogs
> and monkeys, embracing and making much of them, took occasion
> not unnaturally to ask whether the women in their country were
> not used to bear children: by that prince-like reprimand gravely
> reflecting upon persons who spend and lavish upon brute beasts
> that affection and kindness which nature has implanted in us to be
> bestowed on those of our own kind. (Pericles)

Or with a tantalizing suggestion:

> What Titus Quintius Flamininus . . . was in personal appearance,
> those who are curious may see by the brazen statue of him, which
> stands in Rome. (Flamininus)

Or with a clever quotation:

> Cato Major, hearing some commend one that was rash and in-
> considerately daring in battle, said, "There is a difference between
> a man's prizing valor at a great rate, and valuing life at little"; a
> very just remark. (Pelopidas)

Or with some personal reference, as in the already quoted passage from
his Timoleon.

Plutarch was one of the greatest biographers of all time, and one of
the most influential. His influence, however, was not really felt until the
Renaissance. In the centuries immediately following his death, his work
had little impact. As with his contemporary, Tacitus, whose life of
Agricola was the first biography in which the discussion of the hero's
personality was effectively fused with the chronological account of his
career, his reputation became established only long after his passing. The
"important" biographer during the period of Rome's decline was Gaius
Suetonius Tranquillus.

Suetonius was Plutarch's contemporary, and his *Lives of the Caesars* was packed with anecdotes. There, however, the similarity ends. Where Plutarch was an artist, Suetonius was a compiler. He recounted the lives of the first twelve Caesars, recording their deeds, personal and professional, with little comment or inspiration. He followed the traditional pattern of the Alexandrian scholars, dividing his chronological narrative into two parts separated by what Professor Duane Reed Stuart has called "a huge parenthesis" which described the character of each subject.

Suetonius crammed a great deal of information into his works. As secretary to the Emperor Hadrian, he had access to the official records of the early Empire. But he had all of the vices and few of the virtues of the closet scholar. He grubbed for facts, seldom stopping to consider what the facts meant. On the surface at least, his biographies were impartial; good qualities were listed along with bad. But through all the wealth of anecdote and graphic detail, no consistent portrait ever emerged.

Nothing points up Plutarch's genius so well as a comparison of his sketch of Julius Caesar with Suetonius'. Both writers drew upon essentially the same sources, and there is relatively little difference between them so far as facts are concerned. But how different their treatment of these facts! Suetonius, the pedant, often parades his sources before the reader in dull and repetitious quotations of the authorities. Plutarch usually indicates the specific origin of his information only where the evidence is doubtful or contradictory. Both men record tales of miraculous and supernatural events in Caesar's life; yet where Suetonius credulously parrots every legend he has heard, Plutarch more often than not prefaces his account with "It is said" or with such a comment as: "This Livy positively states for truth."

Frequently, in dealing with the same event, Plutarch shows vastly greater insight into the situation than Suetonius. Both men, in discussing Caesar's divorce of Pompeia, recount the story of her suspected liaison with Publius Clodius. Disguised in female attire, Clodius had stolen into Caesar's house during the celebration of the rites of the goddess of fertility, from which all men were barred. He had been apprehended, but when he was brought to trial Caesar refused to testify against him on the ground that there was no evidence of wrongdoing. When questioned as to why, then, he had divorced Pompeia, Caesar replied with the famous remark that *Caesar's* wife must be above even suspicion. Suetonius treats this incident as an example of Caesar's mercy and self-restraint, but Plutarch comments shrewdly: "Some say that Caesar spoke this as his real thought; others, that he did it to gratify the people, who were very earnest to save Clodius. Clodius, at any rate, escaped."

But Plutarch is most obviously superior in his handling of dramatic incidents. Here is what Suetonius makes of Caesar's decision to cross the Rubicon:

Overtaking his cohorts at the river Rubicon . . . he paused for a while, and realizing what a step he was taking, he turned to those about him and said: "Even yet we may turn back; but once cross yon little bridge, and the whole issue is with the sword." As he stood in doubt, this sign was given him. On a sudden there appeared hard by a being of wondrous stature and beauty, who sat and played upon a reed. And when . . . many of the soldiers left their posts, and among them some of the trumpeters, the apparition snatched a trumpet from one of them, rushed to the river, and sounding the warnote with one mighty blast, strode to the opposite bank. Then Caesar cried: "Take we the course which the signs of the Gods and the false dealings of our foes point out. The die is cast."

Plutarch's story is both more credible and more exciting:

When he came to the river Rubicon . . . his thoughts began to work, now [that] he was just entering upon the danger, and he wavered much in his mind, when he considered the greatness of the enterprise into which he was throwing himself. He checked his course, and ordered a halt, while he revolved with himself [sic], and often changed his opinion one way and the other, without speaking a word. This was when his purposes fluctuated most; presently he also discussed the matter with his friends . . . computing how many calamities his passing that river would bring upon mankind, and what a relation of it would be transmitted to posterity. At last, in a sort of passion, casting aside calculation, and abandoning himself to what might come, and using the proverb frequently in their mouths who enter upon dangerous and bold attempts, "The die is cast," with these words he took the river.

Caesar's murder is so inherently dramatic that any account of it would be exciting, but Plutarch provides extra touches and insights that Suetonius misses. When Casca strikes the first blow, Suetonius carefully describes exactly where the blade enters Caesar's body. Plutarch, although less definite, remarks that the wound was not serious, "coming from one who at the beginning of such a bold action was probably very much disturbed." Then he puts the reader inside Casca's heart in that brief moment when the conspirator stands alone committed before the outraged symbol of the majesty of Rome. As Caesar, grasping the offending dagger by the hilt, shouts: "Vile Casca, what does this mean?" his terrified assailant cries out: "Brother, help!"

The murderers close in, and the moment passes. Then, after describing Caesar's fall before the massed attack of the conspirators, Plutarch adds without further comment: "The conspirators themselves were many of them wounded by each other, whilst they all leveled their blows at the same person." Without denying Caesar's faults or the patriotism of his attackers, Plutarch thus points up the discreditable side of the action—a score of armed men against a lone and unsuspecting victim.

Yet if he was no Plutarch, Suetonius was always immensely popular, and the reason is not hard to come by. He told all, and the "all" of the early Roman emperors was both fascinating and titillating. Suetonius' *Lives* were saturated with tales of lust, brutality, and perversion. Consider this passage from his *Tiberius*:

> In his retreat at Capri there was a room devised by him dedicated to the most arcane lusts. Here he had assembled from all quarters girls and perverts, whom he called *Spintriae*, who invented monstrous feats of lubricity, and defiled one another before him, interlaced in series of threes, in order to inflame his feeble appetite.

Sex and scandal made the *Lives of the Caesars* popular, and the formula was adopted repeatedly in later ages with the same success.

But if Suetonius had little that was original to offer aside from sensationalism, he was at least hard-working and honest. Those Roman recorders of emperors' lives who took him as a model (men like Marius Maximus and Junius Cordus, whose works are now lost, and the various authors of the still-extant *Scriptores Historiae Augustae*) had neither of these virtues. The *Historiae Augustae* were composed about the year 300 by half a dozen authors. These men adopted whole Suetonius' scheme of organization, but possessed neither his interest nor his access to the sources. Where they lacked facts they filled their pages with trivial anecdotes. Suetonius had occasionally included letters and documents from the imperial archives in his *Lives*; his successors, unable to tap such sources, simply manufactured documents to fill up space and to disguise their ignorance. They often strung their materials together without art or reason, and with equal frequency they permitted their narratives to degenerate into servile flattery and uncritical panegyric. Biography flourished under the later emperors as never before, but along with the rest of classical culture it lost all originality and vitality as a once great civilization crumbled into the depths of the Dark Ages.

✓ Suggestions for Reading and Writing

1. Read Shelley's poem "Ozymandias" to see if you find it as revealing as Garraty does. What does the poem convey of this ancient king's character?
2. Early Greek writers are said in this selection to have been little interested in biography because they felt the individual to be the victim of fate and of environment. Has modern thought completely rejected this attitude? Do Plato's essays on Socrates contradict this attitude?

3. Egyptians and Greeks preferred accounts emphasizing their heroes' mature years and virtues and ignoring their immature years and vices. Is there anything to be said for so one-sided a view? Explain.
4. Many modern fiction writers (Ernest Hemingway, for one) stress action rather than analysis. Are they proving Aristotle's contention that a man's acts best reveal his character and nature? Can you think of any arguments against this approach?
5. Are there any similarities between the funeral of an important personage today and that of an ancient Roman nobleman? (For background, see Ruth M. Harmer's *The High Cost of Dying* [1963].)
6. Evaluate Garraty's comments on Plutarch after reading the selection included in this anthology from the latter's "The Life of Julius Caesar."

T H E
B O O K
O F R U T H

The book of Ruth is one of the most effective stories ever written. This brief pastoral romance relates how, during the period of Judges (about the twelfth century B.C.), Ruth the Moabitess became the wife of Boaz and great-grandmother to the illustrious King David. Thus Ruth and Boaz were, through Joseph, progenitors of Jesus. The historical tradition behind this claim is now hard to trace; much more clear is its implied protest against a too-unyielding nationalism.

The anonymous author is believed to have lived near the end of the fifth century B.C. The Jews, led by Ezra and Nehemiah, were then fresh from Babylonian exile and were reshaping their national life by insisting upon racial purity. Moabites especially were hated, for Deuteronomy (XXIII. 3) had declared that no Moabite was to enter the Lord's assembly.

Yet the author focuses sympathetically upon an im-

poverished Moabite stranger who embraces the Hebrew law and receives its protection. Indeed, Ruth's eloquent vows to her Hebrew mother-in-law that "thy God shall be my God and thy people my people" foreshadow the attitude of the prophet Isaiah (XL–LXVI).

Noteworthy is the author's presentation of the mother-in-law, that traditional figure of domestic discord, as the very key to family loyalty and unity.

1   1   1   1   1

CHAPTER 1

Now it came to pass in the days when the judges ruled, that there was a famine in the land. And a certain man of Beth-lehem-judah went to sojourn in the country of Moab, he, and his wife, and his two sons. And the name of the man was Elimelech, and the name of his wife Naomi, and the name of his two sons Mahlon and Chilion, Ephrathites of Beth-lehem-judah. And they came into the country of Moab, and continued there. And Elimelech Naomi's husband died; and she was left, and her two sons. And they took them wives of the women of Moab; the name of the one was Orpah, and the name of the other Ruth: and they dwelled there about ten years. And Mahlon and Chilion died also both of them; and the woman was left of her two sons and her husband. Then she arose with her daughters in law, that she might return from the country of Moab: for she had heard in the country of Moab how that the LORD had visited his people in giving them bread. Wherefore she went forth out of the place where she was, and her two daughters in law with her; and they went on the way to return unto the land of Judah. And Naomi said unto her two daughters in law, "Go, return each to her mother's house: the LORD deal kindly with you, as ye have dealt with the dead, and with me. The LORD grant you that ye may find rest, each of you in the house of her husband." Then she kissed them; and they lifted up their voice, and wept. And they said unto her, "Surely we will return with thee unto thy people". And Naomi said, "Turn again, my daughters: why will ye go with me? are there yet any more sons in my womb, that they may be your husbands? Turn again, my daughters, go your way; for I am too old to have an husband. If I should say, I have hope, if I should have an husband also to night, and should also bear sons; would ye tarry for them till they were grown? would ye stay for them from having husbands? nay, my daughters; for it grieveth me much for your sakes that the hand of the Lord is gone out against me." And they lifted up their voice, and wept again: and Orpah kissed her mother in law; but Ruth clave unto her. And she said, "Behold, thy sister in law is gone back unto her people, and unto her gods: return thou after thy sister in law". And Ruth said, "Intreat me not to leave thee, or to return from following after thee: for whither thou goest, I will go; and where thou lodgest, I will lodge: thy people shall be my people, and thy God my God: where thou diest, will I die, and there will I be buried: the Lord do so to me, and more also, if aught but death part thee and me". When she saw that she was stedfastly minded to go with her, then she left speaking unto her. So they two went until they came to Beth-lehem. And it came to pass, when they were come to Beth-lehem, that all the city was moved about them, and they said, "Is this Naomi?" And she said unto them, "Call me not Naomi, call me Mara: for the Almighty hath dealt very bitterly with me. I went out full, and the Lord hath brought me home again empty: why then call ye me Naomi, seeing the Lord hath testified against me, and the Almighty hath afflicted me?" So Naomi returned, and Ruth the Moabite, her daughter in law, with her, which returned out of the country of Moab: and they came to Beth-lehem in the beginning of barley harvest.

CHAPTER 2

And Naomi had a kinsman of her husband's, a mighty man of wealth, of the family of Elimelech; and his name was Boaz. And Ruth the Moabitess said unto Naomi, "Let me now go to the field, and glean ears of corn after him in whose sight I shall find grace". And she said unto her, "Go, my daughter". And she went, and came, and gleaned in the field after the reapers: and her hap was to light on a part of the field belonging unto Boaz, who was of the kindred of Elimelech. And, behold, Boaz came from Beth-lehem, and said unto the reapers, "The Lord be with you". And they answered him, "The Lord bless thee". Then said Boaz unto his servant that was set over the reapers, "Whose damsel is this?" And the servant that was set over the reapers answered and said, "It is the Moabitish damsel that came back with Naomi out of the country of Moab: and she said, 'I pray you, let me glean and gather after the reapers among the sheaves': so she came, and hath continued even from the morning until now, that she tarried a little in the house". Then said Boaz unto Ruth, "Hearest thou not, my daughter? Go not to glean in another field, neither go from hence, but abide here fast by my maidens: let thine eyes be on the field that they do reap, and go thou after them: have I not charged the young men that they shall not touch thee? and when thou art athirst, go unto the vessels, and drink of that which the young men have drawn." Then she fell on her face, and bowed herself to the ground, and said unto him, "Why have I found grace in thine eyes, that thou shouldest take knowledge of me, seeing I am a stranger?" And Boaz answered and said unto her, "It hath fully been shewed me, all that thou hast done unto thy mother in law since the death of thine husband: and how thou hast left thy father and thy mother, and the land of thy nativity, and art come unto a people which thou knewest not heretofore. The LORD recompense thy work, and a full reward be given thee of the LORD God of Israel, under whose wings thou art come to trust." Then she said, "Let me find favour in thy sight, my lord; for that thou hast comforted me, and for that thou hast spoken friendly unto thine handmaid, though I be not like unto one of thine handmaidens". And Boaz said unto her, "At mealtime come thou hither, and eat of the bread, and dip thy morsel in the vinegar". And she sat beside the reapers: and he reached her parched corn, and she did eat, and was sufficed, and left. And when she was risen up to glean, Boaz commanded his young men, saying, "Let her glean even among the sheaves, and reproach her not: and let fall also some of the handfuls of purpose for her, and leave them, that she may glean them, and rebuke her not". So she gleaned in the field until even, and beat out that she had gleaned: and it was about an ephah of barley. And she took it up, and went into the city: and her mother in law saw what she had gleaned: and she brought forth, and gave to her that she had reserved after she was sufficed. And her mother in law said unto her, "Where hast thou gleaned to day? and where wroughtest thou? blessed be he that did take knowledge of thee". And she shewed her mother in law with whom she had wrought, and said, "The man's name with whom I wrought to day is Boaz". And Naomi said unto her daughter in law, "Blessed be he of the LORD, who hath not left off his kindness to the living and to the dead". And Naomi said unto her, "The man is near of kin unto us, one of our next kinsmen". And Ruth the Moabitess said, "He said unto me also, 'Thou shalt keep fast by my young men, until they have ended all my harvest' ". And Naomi said unto Ruth her daughter in law, "It is good, my daughter, that thou go out with his maidens, that they meet thee not in any other field". So she kept fast by the maidens of Boaz to glean unto the end of barley harvest and of wheat harvest; and dwelt with her mother in law.

CHAPTER 3

Then Naomi her mother in law said unto her, "My daughter, shall I not seek rest for thee, that it may be well with thee? And now is not Boaz of our kindred, with whose maidens thou wast? Behold, he winnoweth barley to night in the threshingfloor. Wash thyself therefore, and anoint thee, and put thy raiment upon thee, and get thee down to the floor: but make not thyself known unto the man, until he shall have done eating and drinking. And it shall be, when he lieth down, that thou shalt mark the place where he shall lie, and thou shalt go in, and uncover his feet, and lay thee down; and he will tell thee what thou shalt do." And she said unto her, "All that thou sayest unto me I will do". And she went down unto the floor, and did according to all that her mother in law bade her. And when Boaz had eaten and drunk, and his heart was merry, he went to lie down at the end of the heap of corn: and she came softly, and uncovered his feet, and laid her down. And it came to pass at midnight, that the man was afraid, and turned himself: and, behold, a woman lay at his feet. And he said, "Who art thou?" And she answered, "I am Ruth thine handmaid: spread therefore thy skirt over thine handmaid; for thou art a near kinsman". And he said, "Blessed be thou of the LORD, my daughter: for thou hast shewed more kindness in the latter end than at the beginning, inasmuch as thou followedst not young men, whether poor or rich. And now, my daughter, fear not; I will do to thee all that thou requirest: for all the city of my people doth know that thou art a virtuous woman. And now it is true that I am thy near kinsman: howbeit there is a kinsman nearer than I. Tarry this night, and it shall be in the morning, that if he will perform unto thee the part of a kinsman, well; let him do the kinsman's part: but if he will not do the part of a kinsman to thee, then will I do the part of a kinsman to thee, as the LORD liveth: lie down until the morning." And she lay at his feet until the morning: and she rose up before one could know another. And he said, "Let it not be known that a woman came into the floor". Also he said, "Bring the veil that thou hast upon thee, and hold it". And when she held it, he measured six measures of barley, and laid it on her: and she went into the city. And when she came to her mother in law, she said, "Who art thou, my daughter?" And she told her all that the man had done to her. And she said, "These six measures of barley gave he me; for he said to me, 'Go not empty unto thy mother in law' ". Then said she, "Sit still, my daughter, until thou know how the matter will fall: for the man will not be in rest, until he have finished the thing this day".

CHAPTER 4

Then went Boaz up to the gate, and sat him down there: and, behold, the kinsman of whom Boaz spake came by; unto whom he said, "Ho, such a one! turn aside, sit down here". And he turned aside, and sat down. And he took ten men of the elders of the city, and said, "Sit ye down here". And they sat down. And he said unto the kinsman, "Naomi, that is come again out of the country of Moab, selleth a parcel of land, which was our brother Elimelech's: and I thought to advertise thee, saying, Buy it before the inhabitants, and before the elders of my people. If thou wilt redeem it, redeem it: but if thou wilt not redeem it, then tell me, that I may know: for there is none to redeem it beside thee; and I am after thee." And he said, "I will redeem it". Then said Boaz, "What day thou buyest the field of the hand of Naomi, thou must buy it also of Ruth the Moabitess, the wife of the dead, to raise up the name of the dead upon his inheritance". And the kinsman said, "I cannot redeem it for myself, lest I mar mine own inheritance: redeem thou my right to thyself; for I cannot redeem it". Now this was the manner in former time in Israel concerning redeeming and concerning changing, for to confirm all things; a man plucked off his shoe, and gave it to his neighbour: and this was a testimony in Israel. Therefore the kinsman said unto Boaz, "Buy it for thee". So he drew off his shoe. And Boaz said unto the elders, and unto all the people, "Ye are witnesses this day, that I have bought all that was Elimelech's, and all that was Chilion's and Mahlon's, of the hand of Naomi. Moreover Ruth the Moabitess, the wife of Mahlon, have I purchased to be my wife, to raise up the name of the dead upon his inheritance, that the name of the dead be not cut off from among his brethren, and from the gate of his place: ye are witnesses this day." And all the people that were in the gate, and the elders, said, "We are witnesses. The Lord make the woman that is come into thine house like Rachel and like Leah, which two did build the house of Israel: and do thou worthily in Ephratah, and be famous in Beth-lehem: and let thy house be like the house of Pharez, whom Tamar bare unto Judah, of the seed which the Lord shall give thee of this young woman." So Boaz took Ruth, and she was his wife: and when he went in unto her, the Lord gave her conception, and she bare a son. And the women said unto Naomi, "Blessed be the Lord, which hath not left thee this day without a kinsman, that his name may be famous in Israel. And he shall be unto thee a restorer of thy life, and a nourisher of thine old age: for thy daughter in law, which loveth thee, which is better to thee than seven sons, hath borne him." And Naomi took the child, and laid it in her bosom, and became nurse unto it. And the women her neighbours gave it a name, saying, "There is a son born to Naomi"; and they called his name Obed: he is the father of Jesse, the father of David.

Now these are the generations of Pharez: Pharez begat Hezron, and Hezron begat Ram, and Ram begat Amminadab, and Amminadab begat Nahshon, and Nahshon begat Salmon, and Salmon begat Boaz, and Boaz begat Obed, and Obed begat Jesse, and Jesse begat David.

╭ Suggestions for Reading and Writing

1. Does the book of Ruth fit any of the categories of ancient biography given in Garraty's "Biography in the Ancient World"? Which statements

in Garraty's discussion have relevance to a consideration of the book of Ruth as a representative biography?

2. Does the story meet modern expectations of so-called romantic love?
3. What is revealed here of ancient Hebrew social, legal, and marital customs?
4. The story of Ruth has been cited through the centuries as a supreme expression of selfless devotion. Do you agree? What motivates the behavior of the two women?
5. Why does the story end by mentioning not Ruth's happiness but Naomi's?
6. Without further research, write brief character sketches of Ruth, Naomi, and Boaz.
7. Read the Old Testament episodes dealing with such women as Eve, Tamar, Miriam, Bathsheba, and Esther. Are the authors' attitudes similar to our author's? If different, explain in what ways.

from

THE
LIFE OF
JULIUS
CAESAR

Plutarch

Study of the essay traditionally begins with Montaigne and Bacon; of English prose fiction, with Defoe and Richardson. A corresponding study of biography usually begins with Plutarch of Chaeronea (c. 46–c. 120). His Lives of the Noble Grecians and Romans, better known as the Parallel Lives, consists of twenty-three paired studies of soldiers and statesmen; each balances an outstanding Greek's life with an outstanding Roman's.

Plutarch conscientiously consulted the best of ancient historians. He was not confined, however, by their writings, for he was less interested in history than in personality and character. He chose his heroes as exemplars of specific virtues and vices to be emulated or avoided by the young. Yet he tempered his moralizing. He underscored instead for later biographies the value of small anecdotes and the seemingly trivial details of physical appearance, diet, gestures, and speech in illuminating personality and character. He also established the chronological, rather than the topical or thematic, approach to biography. Many biographers down to the present have followed his lead.

The first English translation of Plutarch's Greek did not appear until 1579. Sir Thomas North (basing his work on Jacques Amyot's sound French version) produced a translation that proved both a model of Elizabethan prose and an invaluable historical source. Shakespeare used it for his historical dramas Coriolanus and Antony and Cleopatra, as well as Julius Caesar.

The following selection consists of the last eight sections of Plutarch's "The Life of Julius Caesar." North's annotations have been omitted from the text.

↑ ↑ ↑ ↑ ↑

· · · · ·

Caesar, being now returned out of Africa, first of all made an oration to the people wherein he greatly praised and commended this his last victory, declaring unto them that he had conquered so many countries unto the Empire of Rome that he could furnish the commonwealth yearly with two hundred thousand bushels of wheat and twenty hundred thousand pound weight of oil. Then he made three triumphs, the one for Egypt, the other for the kingdom of Pont, and the third for Africa. . . .

After these three triumphs ended, he very liberally rewarded his soldiers; and to curry favor with the people, he made great feasts and common sports. For he feasted all the Romans at one time, at two and twenty thousand tables, and gave them the pleasure to see divers sword-players to fight at the sharp, and battles also by sea, for the remembrance of his daughter Julia, which was dead long before.

Then after all these sports, he made the people (as the manner was) to be mustered; and where there were, at the last musters before, three hundred and twenty thousand citizens, at this muster there were only but a hundred and fifty thousand. Such misery and destruction had this civil war brought unto the commonwealth of Rome, and had consumed such a number of Romans, not speaking at all of the mischiefs and calamities it had brought unto all the rest of Italy, and to the other provinces pertaining to Rome.

After all these things were ended, he was chosen consul the fourth time, and went into Spain to make war with the sons of Pompey: who were yet but very young, but had notwithstanding raised a marvelous great army together, and showed to have had manhood and courage worthy to command such an army, insomuch as they put Caesar himself in great danger of his life. The greatest battle that was fought between them in all this war was by the city of Munda. For then Caesar, seeing his men sorely distressed, and having their hands full of their enemies, he ran into the press among his men that fought, and cried out unto them: 'What, are ye not ashamed to be beaten and taken prisoners, yielding yourselves with your own hands to these young boys?' And so, with all the force he could make, having with much ado put his enemies to flight, he slew above thirty thousand of them in the field, and lost of his own men a thousand of the best he had.

After this battle he went into his tent and told his friends that he had often before fought for victory, but, this last time now, that he had fought for the safety of his own life. He won this battle on the very feast day of the Bacchanalians, in the which men say that Pompey the Great went out of Rome, about four years before, to begin this civil war. For his sons, the younger escaped from the battle; but within few days after, Didius brought the head of the elder.

This was the last war that Caesar made. But the triumph he made into Rome for the same did as much offend the Romans, and more, than anything that ever he had done before: because he had not overcome captains that were strangers, nor barbarous kings, but had destroyed the sons of the noblest man of Rome, whom fortune had overthrown. And because he had plucked up his race by the roots, men did not think it meet for him to triumph so for the calamities of his country, rejoicing at a thing for the which he had but one excuse to allege in his defense unto the gods and men: that he was compelled to do that he did. And the rather they thought it not meet, because he had never before sent letters nor messengers unto the commonwealth at Rome for any victory that he had ever won in all the civil wars, but did always for shame refuse the glory of it.

This notwithstanding, the Romans, inclining to Caesar's prosperity and taking the bit in the mouth, supposing that to be ruled by one man alone, it would be a good mean for them to take breath a little, after so many troubles and miseries as they had abidden in these civil wars, they chose him perpetual dictator. This was a plain tyranny; for to this absolute power of dictator, they added this, never to be afraid to be deposed.

Cicero propounded before the Senate that they should give him such honors as were meet for a man; howbeit others afterwards added to, honors beyond all reason. For, men striving who should most honor him, they made him hateful and troublesome to themselves that most favored him, by reason of the unmeasurable greatness and honors which they gave him. Thereupon, it is reported, that even they that most hated him were no less favorers and furtherers of his honors than they that most flattered him, because they might have greater occasions to rise, and that it might appear they had just cause and color to attempt that they did against him.

And now for himself, after he had ended his civil wars, he did so honorably behave himself that there was no fault to be found in him; and therefore methinks, amongst other honors they gave him, he rightly deserved this, that they should build him a temple of clemency, to thank him for his courtesy he had used unto them in his victory. For he pardoned many of them that had borne arms against him, and further-more, did prefer some of them to honor and office in the common-wealth: as, amongst others, Cassius and Brutus, both the which were made praetors. And, where Pompey's images had been thrown down, he caused them to be set up again; whereupon Cicero said then, that Caesar setting up Pompey's images again, he made his own to stand the surer. And when some of his friends did counsel him to have a guard for the safety of his person, and some also did offer themselves to serve him, he would never consent to it, but said: 'It was better to die once, than al-ways to be afraid of death.'

But to win himself the love and good will of the people, as the honorablest guard and best safety he could have, he made common feasts again and general distributions of corn. Furthermore, to gratify the soldiers also, he replenished many cities again with inhabitants, which before had been destroyed, and placed them there that had no place to repair unto: of the which the noblest and chiefest cities were these two, Carthage and Corinth; and it chanced so, that like as aforetime they had been both taken and destroyed together, even so were they both set afoot again, and replenished with people, at one self time. And as for great personages, he won them also, promising some of them to make them praetors and consuls in time to come, and unto others honors and preferments; but to all men generally good hope, seeking all the ways he could to make every man contented with his reign. Insomuch as one of his consuls called Maximus, chancing to die a day before his consulship ended, he declared Caninius Rebilius consul only for the day that remained. So, divers going to his house (as the manner was) to salute him, and to congratulate with him of his calling and preferment, being newly chosen officer, Cicero pleasantly said, 'Come, let us make haste, and be gone thither before his consulship come out.'

Furthermore, Caesar being born to attempt all great enterprises, and having an ambitious desire besides to covet great honors, the prosperous good success he had of his former conquests bred no desire in him quietly to enjoy the fruits of his labors; but rather gave him hope of things to come, still kindling more and more in him thoughts of greater enterprises and desire of new glory, as if that which he had present were stale and nothing worth. This humor of his was no other but an emulation with himself as with another man, and a certain contention to overcome the things he prepared to attempt. For he was determined, and made preparation also, to make war with the Persians. Then, when he had overcome them, to pass through Hyrcania (compassing in the sea Caspium and Mount Caucasus) into the realm of Pontus, and so to invade Scythia; and, overrunning all the countries and people adjoining unto high Germany, and Germany itself, at length to return by Gaul into Italy, and so to enlarge the Roman Empire round, that it might be every way compassed in with the great sea Oceanum.

But whilst he was preparing for this voyage, he attempted to cut the bar of the strait of Peloponnesus, in the place where the city of Corinth standeth. Then he was minded to bring the rivers of Anienes and Tiber straight from Rome unto the city of Circees, with a deep channel and high banks cast up on either side, and so to fall into the sea at Terracina, for the better safety and commodity of the merchants that came to Rome to traffic there. Furthermore, he determined to drain and sew all the water of the marshes betwixt the cities of Nomentum and Setium, to make it firm land, for the benefit of many thousands of people; and on the seacoast next unto Rome, to cast great high banks, and to cleanse all the haven about Ostia of rocks and stones hidden under the water, and to take away all other impediments that made the harbor dangerous for ships, and to make new havens and arsenals meet to harbor such ships, as did continually traffic thither. All these things were purposed to be done, but took no effect.

But the ordinance of the calendar and reformation of the year, to take away all confusion of time, being exactly calculated by the mathematicians and brought to perfection, was a great commodity unto all men. For the Romans, using then the ancient computation of the year, had not only such uncertainty and alteration of the month and times that the sacrifices and yearly feasts came, by little and little, to seasons contrary for the purpose they were ordained: but also, in the revolution of the sun (which is called *annus solaris*) no other nation agreed with them in account; and, of the Romans themselves, only the priests understood it. And therefore when they listed, they suddenly (no man being able to control them) did thrust in a month above their ordinary number, which they called in old time *Mercedonius, mensis intercularis*.

Some say that Numa Pompilius was the first that devised this way, to put a month between; but it was a weak remedy, and did little help the correction of the errors that were made in the account of the year, to frame them to perfection.

But Caesar, committing this matter unto the philosophers and best expert mathematicians at that time, did set forth an excellent and perfect calendar, more exactly calculated than any other that was before: the which the Romans do use until this present day and do nothing err as others in the difference of time. But his enemies notwithstanding, that envied his greatness, did not stick to find fault withal. As Cicero the orator, when one said, 'Tomorrow the star Lyra will rise': 'Yea,' said he, 'at the commandment of Caesar,' as if men were compelled so to say and think by Caesar's edict.

But the chiefest cause that made him mortally hated was the covetous desire he had to be called king: which first gave the people just cause, and next his secret enemies honest color, to bear him ill will. This notwithstanding, they that procured him this honor and dignity gave it out among the people that it was written in the Sibylline prophecies, 'how the Romans might overcome the Parthians if they made war with them and were led by a king, but otherwise that they were unconquerable.' And furthermore they were so bold besides, that, Caesar returning to Rome from the city of Alba, when they came to salute him, they called him king. But the people being offended, and Caesar also angry, he said he was not called king, but Caesar. Then every man keeping silence, he went his way heavy and sorrowful.

When they had decreed divers honors for him in the Senate, the consuls and praetors, accompanied with the whole assembly of the Senate, went unto him in the marketplace, where he was set by the pulpit for orations, to tell him what honors they had decreed for him in his absence. But he, sitting still in his majesty, disdaining to rise up unto them when they came in, as if they had been private men, answered them: 'that his honors had more need to be cut off than enlarged.'

This did not only offend the Senate, but the common people also, to see that he should so lightly esteem of the magistrates of the commonwealth: insomuch as every man that might lawfully go his way departed thence very sorrowfully. Thereupon also Caesar rising, departed home to his house, and tearing open his doublet collar, making his neck bare, he cried out aloud to his friends, 'that his throat was ready to offer to any man that would come and cut it.'

Notwithstanding, it is reported that afterwards, to excuse his folly, he imputed it to his disease, saying, 'that their wits are not perfect which have this disease of the falling evil, when standing on their feet they speak to the common people, but are soon troubled with a trembling of their body and a sudden dimness and giddiness.' But that was not true, for he would have risen up to the Senate, but Cornelius Balbus, one of his friends (but rather a flatterer), would not let him, saying: 'What, do you not remember that you are Caesar, and will you not let them reverence you and do their duties?'

Besides these occasions and offenses, there followed also his shame and reproach, abusing the tribunes of the people in this sort. At that time the feast Lupercalia was celebrated, the which in old time men say was the feast of shepherds or herdmen, and is much like unto the feast of the Lycaeans in Arcadia. But howsoever it is, that day there are divers noblemen's sons, young men (and some of them magistrates themselves that govern them), which run naked through the city, striking in sport them they meet in their way with leather thongs, hair and all on, to make them give place. And many noblewomen, and gentlewomen also, go of purpose to stand in their way, and do put forth their hands to be stricken, as scholars hold them out to their schoolmaster to be stricken with the ferula: persuading themselves that, being with child, they shall have good delivery; and also, being barren, that it will make them to conceive with child.

Caesar sat to behold that sport upon the pulpit for orations in a chair of gold, apparelled in triumphing manner. Antonius, who was consul at that time, was one of them that ran this holy course. So when he came into the marketplace, the people made a lane for him to run at liberty, and he came to Caesar, and presented him a diadem wreathed about with laurel. Whereupon there rose a certain cry of rejoicing, not very great, done only by a few appointed for the purpose. But when Caesar refused the diadem, then all the people together made an outcry of joy.

Then Antonius offering it him again, there was a second shout of joy, but yet of a few. But when Caesar refused it again the second time, then all the whole people shouted. Caesar having made this proof, found that the people did not like of it, and thereupon rose out of his chair, and commanded the crown to be carried unto Jupiter in the Capitol.

After that, there were set up images of Caesar in the city, with diadems upon their heads like kings. Those, the two tribunes Flavius and Marullus went and pulled down, and furthermore, meeting with them that first saluted Caesar as king, they committed them to prison. The people followed them rejoicing at it, and called them *Bruti*, because of Brutus, who had in old time driven the kings out of Rome, and that brought the kingdom of one person unto the government of the Senate and people. Caesar was so offended withal that he deprived Marullus and Flavius of their tribuneships, and accusing them, he spoke also against the people, and called them *Bruti* and *Cumani*, to wit, beasts and fools.

Hereupon the people went straight unto Marcus Brutus, who from his father came of the first Brutus, and by his mother, of the house of the Servilians, a noble house as any was in Rome, and was also nephew and son-in-law of Marcus Cato. Notwithstanding, the great honors and favors Caesar showed unto him kept him back that of himself alone he did not conspire nor consent to depose him of his kingdom. For Caesar did not only save his life after the battle of Phaisalia, when Pompey fled, and did at his request also save many more of his friends besides; but furthermore, he put a marvelous confidence in him. For he had already preferred him to the praetorship for that year, and furthermore was appointed to be consul the fourth year after that, having through Caesar's friendship obtained it before Cassius, who likewise made suit for the same; and Caesar also, as it is reported, said in this contention, 'Indeed Cassius hath alleged best reason, but yet shall he not be chosen before Brutus.'

Some one day accusing Brutus while he practiced this conspiracy, Caesar would not hear of it, but, clapping his hand on his body, told them, 'Brutus will look for this skin': meaning thereby, that Brutus for his virtue deserved to rule after him, but yet that, for ambition's sake, he would not show himself unthankful nor dishonorable.

Now they that desired change, and wished Brutus only their prince and governor above all other, they durst not come to him themselves to tell him what they would have him to do, but in the night did cast sundry papers into the praetor's seat, where he gave audience, and the most of them to this effect: 'Thou sleepest, Brutus, and art not Brutus indeed.' Cassius, finding Brutus' ambition stirred up the more by these seditious bills, did prick him forward and egg him on the more, for a private quarrel he had conceived against Caesar: the circumstance whereof we have set down more at large in Brutus' life.

Caesar also had Cassius in great jealousy, and suspected him much; whereupon he said on a time to his friends, 'What will Cassius do, think ye? I like not his pale looks.' Another time when Caesar's friends complained unto him of Antonius and Dolabella, that they pretended some mischief towards him, he answered them again: 'As for those fat men and smooth-combed heads,' quoth he, 'I never reckon of them; but these pale-visaged and carrion-lean people, I fear them most,' meaning Brutus and Cassius.

Certainly destiny may easier be foreseen than avoided, considering the strange and wonderful signs that were said to be seen before Caesar's death. For, touching the fires in the element, and spirits running up and down in the night, and also these solitary birds to be seen at noondays sitting in the great marketplace: are not all these signs perhaps worth the noting, in such a wonderful chance as happened?

But Strabo the philosopher writeth that divers men were seen going up and down in fire: and furthermore, that there was a slave of the soldiers that did cast a marvelous burning flame out of his hand, insomuch as they that saw it thought he had been burnt; but when the fire was out, it was found he had no hurt.

Caesar self also doing sacrifice unto the gods, found that one of the beasts which was sacrificed had no heart; and that was a strange thing in nature, how a beast could live without a heart. Furthermore, there was a certain soothsayer that had given Caesar warning long time afore, to take heed of the day of the Ides of March (which is the fifteenth of the month), for on that day he should be in great danger. That day being come, Caesar going unto the Senate-house and speaking merrily unto the soothsayer, told him, 'The Ides of March be come': 'So be they,' softly answered the soothsayer, 'but yet are they not past.'

And the very day before, Caesar, supping with Marcus Lepidus, sealed certain letters, as he was wont to do, at the board; so, talk falling out amongst them, reasoning what death was best, he, preventing their opinions, cried out aloud, 'Death unlooked for.' Then going to bed the same night, as his manner was, and lying with his wife, Calpurnia, all the windows and doors of his chamber flying open, the noise awoke him, and made him afraid when he saw such light; but more, when he heard his wife, Calpurnia, being fast asleep, weep and sigh, and put forth many fumbling lamentable speeches: for she dreamed that Caesar was slain, and that she had him in her arms.

Others also do deny that she had any such dream, as, amongst other, Titus Livius writeth that it was in this sort. The Senate having set upon the top of Caesar's house, for an ornament and setting forth of the same, a certain pinnacle, Calpurnia dreamed that she saw it broken down and that she thought she lamented and wept for it. Insomuch that, Caesar rising in the morning, she prayed him, if it were possible, not to go out of the doors that day, but to adjourn the session of the Senate until another day. And if that he made no reckoning of her dream, yet that he would search further of the soothsayers by their sacrifices, to know what should happen him that day. Thereby it seemed that Caesar likewise did fear and suspect somewhat, because his wife Calpurnia until that time was never given to any fear or superstition; and for then that he saw her so troubled in mind with this dream she had. But much more afterwards, when the soothsayers having sacrificed many beasts one after another, told him that none did like them, then he determined to send Antonius to adjourn the session of the Senate.

But in the meantime came Decius Brutus, surnamed Albinus, in whom Caesar put such confidence that in his last will and testament he had appointed him to be his next heir, and yet was of the conspiracy with Cassius and Brutus; he, fearing that if Caesar did adjourn the session that day, the conspiracy would out, laughed the soothsayers to scorn and reproved Caesar, saying, 'that he gave the Senate occasion to mislike with him, and that they might think he mocked them, considering that by his commandment they were assembled, and that they were ready willingly to grant him all things, and to proclaim him king of all his provinces of the Empire of Rome out of Italy, and that he should wear his diadem in all other places, both by sea and land. And furthermore, that if any man should tell them from him, they should depart for that present time and return again when Calpurnia should have better dreams: what would his enemies and ill-willers say, and how could they like of his friends' words? And who could persuade them otherwise, but that they would think his dominion a slavery unto them and tyrannical in himself? And yet if it be so,' said he, 'that you utterly mislike of this day, it is better that you go yourself in person, and, saluting the Senate, to dismiss them till another time.' Therewithal he took Caesar by the hand and brought him out of his house.

Caesar was not gone far from his house, but a bondman, a stranger, did what he could to speak with him; and when he saw he was put back by the great press and multitude of people that followed him, he went straight into his house and put himself into Calpurnia's hands, to be kept till Caesar came back again, telling her that he had greater matters to impart unto him.

And one Artemidorus also, born in the isle of Gnidos, a doctor of rhetoric in the Greek tongue, who by means of his profession was very familiar with certain of Brutus' confederates and therefore knew the most part of all their practices against Caesar, came and brought him a little bill written with his own hand, of all that he meant to tell him. He, marking how Caesar received all the supplications that were offered him, and that he gave them straight to his men that were about him, pressed nearer to him, and said: 'Caesar, read this memorial to yourself, and that quickly, for they be matters of great weight, and touch you nearly.'

Caesar took it of him, but could never read it, though he many times attempted it, for the number of people that did salute him: but holding it still in his hand, keeping it to himself, went on withal into the Senate-house.

Howbeit other are of opinion that it was some man else that gave him that memorial, and not Artemidorus, who did what he could all the way as he went to give it Caesar, but he was always repulsed by the people. For these things, they may seem to come by chance; but the place where the murder was prepared, and where the Senate were assembled, and where also there stood up an image of Pompey dedicated by himself amongst other ornaments which he gave unto the theatre, all these were manifest proofs, that it was the ordinance of some god that made this treason to be executed, specially in that very place.

It is also reported that Cassius (though otherwise he did favor the doctrine of Epicurus) beholding the image of Pompey, before they entered into the action of their traitorous enterprise, he did softly call upon it to aid him. But the instant danger of the present time, taking away his former reason, did suddenly put him into a furious passion and made him like a man half besides himself.

Now Antonius, that was a faithful friend to Caesar, and a valiant man besides of his hands, him Decius Brutus Albinus entertained out of the Senate-house, having begun a long tale of set purpose.

So Caesar coming into the house, all the Senate stood up on their feet to do him honor. Then part of Brutus' company and confederates stood round about Caesar's chair, and part of them also came towards him, as though they made suit with Metellus Cimber, to call home his brother again from banishment; and thus prosecuting still their suit, they followed Caesar till he was set in his chair. Who, denying their petitions and being offended with them one after another, because the more they were denied the more they pressed upon him and were the earnester with him, Metellus at length, taking his gown with both his hands, pulled it over his neck, which was the sign given the confederates to set upon him.

Then Casca, behind him, struck him in the neck with his sword; howbeit the wound was not great nor mortal, because it seemed the fear of such a devilish attempt did amaze him and take his strength from him, that he killed him not at the first blow. But Caesar, turning straight unto him, caught hold of his sword and held it hard; and they both cried out, Caesar in Latin: 'O vile traitor Casca, what doest thou?' and Casca, in Greek, to his brother: 'Brother, help me.'

At the beginning of this stir, they that were present, not knowing of the conspiracy, were so amazed with the horrible sight they saw, that they had no power to fly, neither to help him, not so much as once to make an outcry. They on the other side that had conspired his death compassed him in on every side with their swords drawn in their hands, that Caesar turned him nowhere but he was stricken at by some, and still had naked swords in his face, and was hacked and mangled among them, as a wild beast taken of hunters. For it was agreed among them that every man should give him a wound, because all their parts should be in this murder; and then Brutus himself gave him one wound about his privities.

Men report also that Caesar did still defend himself against the rest, running every way with his body; but when he saw Brutus with his sword drawn in his hand, then he pulled his gown over his head, and made no more resistance, and was driven either casually or purposedly, by the counsel of the conspirators, against the base whereupon Pompey's image stood, which ran all of a gore-blood till he was slain. Thus it seemed that the image took just revenge of Pompey's enemy, being thrown down on the ground at his feet, and yielding up his ghost there, for the number of wounds he had upon him. For it is reported that he had three and twenty wounds upon his body; and divers of the conspirators did hurt themselves, striking one body with so many blows.

When Caesar was slain, the Senate (though Brutus stood in the midst amongst them as though he would have said something touching this fact) presently ran out of the house, and flying, filled all the city with marvelous fear and tumult. Insomuch as some did shut to their doors, others forsook their shops and warehouses, and others ran to the place to see what the matter was; and others also that had seen it ran home to their houses again. But Antonius and Lepidus, which were two of Caesar's chiefest friends, secretly conveying themselves away, fled into other men's houses and forsook their own.

Brutus and his confederates on the other side, being yet hot with this murder they had committed, having their swords drawn in their hands, came all in a troop together out of the Senate and went into the marketplace, not as men that made countenance to fly, but otherwise boldly holding up their heads like men of courage, and called to the people to defend their liberty, and stayed to speak with every great personage whom they met in their way. Of them, some followed this troop and went amongst them, as if they had been of the conspiracy, and falsely challenged part of the honor with them: among them was Caius Octavius and Lentulus Spinther. But both of them were afterwards put to death for their vain covetousness of honor by Antonius and Octavius Caesar the Younger; and yet had no part of that honor for the which they were put to death, neither did any man believe that they were any of the confederates or of counsel with them. For they that did put them to death took revenge rather of the will they had to offend than of any fact they had committed.

The next morning, Brutus and his confederates came into the marketplace to speak unto the people, who gave them such audience that it seemed they neither greatly reproved nor allowed the fact; for by their great silence they showed that they were sorry for Caesar's death and also that they did reverence Brutus.

Now the Senate granted general pardon for all that was past, and, to pacify every man, ordained besides that Caesar's funerals should be honored as a god, and established all things that he had done, and gave certain provinces also and convenient honors unto Brutus and his confederates, whereby every man thought all things were brought to good peace and quietness again.

But when they had opened Caesar's testament, and found a liberal legacy of money bequeathed unto every citizen of Rome, and that they saw his body (which was brought into the marketplace) all bemangled with gashes of swords, then there was no order to keep the multitude and common people quiet; but they plucked up forms, tables, and stools, and laid them all about the body, and setting them afire, burnt the corpse.

Then when the fire was well kindled, they took the firebrands, and went unto their houses that had slain Caesar, to set them afire. Other also ran up and down the city to see if they could meet with any of them, to cut them in pieces; howbeit they could meet with never a man of them, because they had locked themselves up safely in their houses.

There was one of Caesar's friends called Cinna, that had a marvelous strange and terrible dream the night before. He dreamed that Caesar bade him to supper, and that he refused and would not go; then that Caesar took him by the hand, and led him against his will. Now Cinna, hearing at that time that they burnt Caesar's body in the marketplace, notwithstanding that he feared his dream, and had an ague on him beside, he went into the marketplace to honor his funerals.

When he came thither, one of the mean sort asked him what his name was. He was straight called by his name. The first man told it to another, and that other unto another, so that it ran straight through them all, that he was one of them that murdered Caesar (for indeed one of the traitors to Caesar was also called Cinna as himself); wherefore taking him for Cinna the murderer, they fell upon him with such fury that they presently despatched him in the marketplace.

This stir and fury made Brutus and Cassius more afraid than of all that was past, and therefore within few days after they departed out of Rome; and touching their doings afterwards, and what calamity they suffered till their deaths, we have written it at large in the life of Brutus. Caesar died at six and fifty years of age, and Pompey also lived not passing four years more than he. So he reaped no other fruit of all his reign and dominion, which he had so vehemently desired all his life and pursued with such extreme danger, but a vain name only and a superficial glory that procured him the envy and hatred of his country.

But his great prosperity and good fortune that favored him all his lifetime did continue afterwards in the revenge of his death, pursuing the murderers both by sea and land, till they had not left a man more to be executed, of all them that were actors or counselors in the conspiracy of his death. Furthermore, of all the chances that happen unto men upon the earth, that which came to Cassius above all other is most to be wondered at; for he, being overcome in battle at the journey of Philippi, slew himself with the same sword with the which he struck Caesar.

Again, of signs in the element, the great comet which seven nights together was seen very bright after Caesar's death, the eighth night after was never seen more. Also the brightness of the sun was darkened, the which all that year through rose very pale and shined not out, whereby it gave but small heat; therefore the air being very cloudy and dark, by the weakness of the heat that could not come forth, did cause the earth to bring forth but raw and unripe fruit, which rotted before it could ripe.

But above all, the ghost that appeared unto Brutus showed plainly that the gods were offended with the murder of Caesar. The vision was thus. Brutus being ready to pass over his army from the city of Abydos to the other coast lying directly against it, slept every night (as his manner was) in his tent; and being yet awake, thinking of his affairs (for by report he was as careful a captain and lived with as little sleep as ever man did), he thought he heard a noise at his tent-door, and looking towards the light of the lamp that waxed very dim, he saw a horrible vision of a man, of a wonderful greatness and dreadful look, which at the first made him marvelously afraid. But when he saw that it did him no hurt, but stood by his bedside and said nothing, at length he asked him what he was.

The image answered him: 'I am thy ill angel, Brutus, and thou shalt see me by the city of Philippi.'

Then Brutus replied again, and said, 'Well, I shall see thee then.' Therewithal the spirit presently vanished from him.

After that time Brutus, being in battle near unto the city of Philippi against Antonius and Octavius Caesar, at the first battle he won the victory, and overthrowing all them that withstood him, he drove them into young Caesar's camp, which he took. The second battle being at hand, this spirit appeared again unto him, but spoke never a word. Thereupon Brutus, knowing that he should die, did put himself to all hazard in battle, but yet fighting could not be slain. So seeing his men put to flight and overthrown, he ran unto a little rock not far off, and there setting his sword's point to his breast, fell upon it and slew himself; but yet, as it is reported, with the help of his friend that despatched him.

◂ Suggestions for Reading and Writing

1. Summarize Plutarch's view of Caesar's character. Is it essentially sympathetic or essentially hostile?
2. How does Plutarch interpret the motives of Cassius and Brutus? Does he have anything to say here in their favor? (For fuller portraits of the principal figures involved, see also Plutarch's lives of Pompey, Brutus, and Antony.)
3. W. S. Lewis, in "The Difficult Art of Biography" (see p. 65), quotes Plutarch on the problems facing the biographer. How well does Plutarch meet these problems in the foregoing selection?
4. An interesting term paper should result from a comparison of the different biographical approaches embodied in Plutarch's polite character portraits, Boswell's "warts and all" presentations, and Strachey's "Satanic" debunking of established historical figures. (See "On Biography: Essays," p. 468, for essays on this topic by Samuel M. Crothers and Hesketh Pearson.)
5. See G. B. Harrison, ed., *Julius Caesar in Shakespeare, Shaw and the Ancients* (1960), for the cross-relationships between Plutarch and historians of his own time—as well as for his influence on two great dramatists.
6. Compare Plutarch's Caesar with Suetonius' in *Lives of the Caesars* and Appian's in *The Civil Wars*.
7. Write a succinct analysis of Shakespeare's *Julius Caesar* to explain Shakespeare's use of Plutarch's materials. (For background, see C. F. Tucker Brooke's *Shakespeare's Plutarch* [1909].)

from

LIFE OF
SIR
THOMAS
MORE

William Roper

William Roper (1496–1578) shares with George Cavendish the distinction of having launched modern English biography. His Life of Sir Thomas More (1626) exemplifies the eye-witness biography that became extremely popular in sixteenth-century England. In its length and specific detail, Roper's biography reflects the then-growing Renaissance fascination with the individual personality.

As Sir Thomas More's son-in-law and trusted secretary, Roper not only observed but participated in the events he describes. And notable events they were, for More (1478–1535) was not only Henry VIII's powerful chancellor but the intellectual interpreter in England of the Reformation, a significant man of letters, and a devout son of the Church (he was canonized in 1935).

Roper's admiration for his subject, revealed on every page, gives the narrative a special charm. Still, critical opinion as to its merits is divided. Scholar R. W. Chambers has called it "probably the most perfect little biography in the English language." But others have pointed to Roper's weak grasp of organization, his partisan desire to clear his father-in-law's reputation of the slightest stain, his lack of concern for major

Reformation events, and his failure to mention More's important friends (such as the great Dutch scholar Erasmus) or More's famous work Utopia (Latin, 1516; English, 1551).

Few, however, deny the historical significance of this little narrative to modern biography.

*   *   *   *   *

. . . . .

This Sir Thomas More, among all other his virtues, was of such meekness that if it had fortuned him with any learned men resorting to him from Oxford, Cambridge, or elsewhere (as there did divers, some for desire of his acquaintance, some for the famous report of his wisdom and learning, and some for suits of the universities) to have entered into argument (wherein few were comparable unto him) and so far to have discoursed with them therein that he might perceive they could not, without some inconvenience, hold out much further disputation against him; then, lest he should discomfort them (as he that sought not his own glory, but rather would seem conquered than to discourage students in their studies, ever showing himself more desirous to learn than to teach), would he by some witty device courteously break off into some other matter and give over.

Of whom, for his wisdom and learning, had the King such an opinion that at such time as he attended upon his highness, taking his progress either to Oxford or Cambridge, where he was received with very eloquent orations, his grace would always assign him (as one that was prompt and ready therein) extempore to make answer thereto. Whose manner was, whensoever he had occasion, either here or beyond the sea, to be in any university, not only to be present at the reading and disputations there commonly used, but also learnedly to dispute among them himself.

Who, being chancellor of the duchy, was made ambassador twice, joined in commission with Cardinal Wolsey; once to the Emperor Charles into Flanders, the other time to the French king into France.

. . . . .

As Sir Thomas More's custom was daily (if he were at home), besides his private prayers with his children, to say the Seven Psalms, the litany and suffrages following, so was it his guise nightly before he went to bed, with his wife, children, and household to go to his chapel, and there upon his knees ordinarily to say certain psalms and collects with them. And because he was desirous for godly purposes sometime to be solitary and sequester himself from worldly company, a good distance from his mansion-house builded he a place called the New Building, wherein was a chapel, a library, and a gallery; in which, as his use was upon other days to occupy himself in prayer and study together, so on the Friday there usually continued he from morning till evening, spending his time only in devout prayers and spiritual exercises.

And to provoke his wife and children to the desire of heavenly things, he would sometimes use these words unto them: 'It is now no mastery [merit] for you children to go to heaven, for everybody giveth you good counsel, everybody giveth you good example; you see virtue rewarded and vice punished, so that you are carried up to heaven even by the chins. But if you live the time that no man will give you good counsel, nor no man give you good example, when you shall see virtue punished and vice rewarded, if you will then stand fast and firmly stick to God, upon pain of my life, though you be but half good, God will allow you for whole good.'

If his wife or any of his children had been diseased or troubled, he would say unto them: 'We may not look at our own pleasure to go to heaven in featherbeds: it is not the way. For our Lord Himself went thither with great pain and by many tribulations, which was the path wherein He walked thither; for the servant may not look to be in better case than his Master.'

. . . . .

Now while Sir Thomas More was chancellor of the duchy, the see of Rome chanced to be void, which was cause of much trouble. For Cardinal Wolsey, a man very ambitious, and desirous (as good hope and likelihood he had) to aspire unto that dignity, perceiving himself of his expectation disappointed, by means of the Emperor Charles so highly commending one Cardinal Adrian, sometime his schoolmaster, to the cardinals of Rome, in the time of their election, for his virtue and worthiness, that thereupon was he chosen Pope; . . . Cardinal Wolsey, I say, waxed so wood therewith, that he studied to invent all ways of revengement of his griefs against the Emperor; which, as it was the beginning of a lamentable tragedy, so some part of it, as not impertinent to my present purpose, I reckoned requisite here to put in remembrance.

This Cardinal therefore, not ignorant of the King's inconstant and mutable disposition, soon inclined to withdraw his devotion from his own most noble, virtuous, and lawful wife, Queen Katherine, aunt to the Emperor, upon every light occasion; and upon other, to her in nobility, wisdom, virtue, favour, and beauty far incomparable, to fix his affection, meaning to make this his so light disposition an instrument to bring about his ungodly intent, devised to allure the King (then already, contrary to his mind, nothing less looking for, falling in love with the Lady Anne Boleyn) to cast fantasy unto one of the French king's sisters.

Which thing, because of the enmity and war that was at that time between the French king and the Emperor (whom, for the cause afore remembered, he mortally maligned), he was very desirous to procure. And for the better achieving thereof requested Longland, Bishop of Lincoln and ghostly father to the King, to put a scruple into his grace's head, that it was not lawful for him to marry his brother's wife. Which the King, not sorry to hear of, opened it first to Sir Thomas More, whose counsel he required therein, showing him certain places of Scripture that somewhat seemed to serve his appetite. Which, when he had perused, and thereupon, as one that had never professed the study of divinity, himself excused to be unmeet many ways to meddle with such matters, the King, not satisfied with this answer, so sore still pressed upon him therefore, that in conclusion he condescended to his grace's motion. And further, forasmuch as the case was of such importance as needed great advisement and deliberation, he besought his grace of sufficient respite advisedly to consider of it. Wherewith the King, well contented, said unto him that Tunstal and Clarke, Bishops of Durham and Bath, with other learned of his privy council, should also be dealers therein.

So Sir Thomas More, departing, conferred those places of the Scripture with expositions of divers of the old holy doctors; and at his coming to the Court, in talking with his grace of the aforesaid matter, he said: 'To be plain with your grace, neither my Lord of Durham nor my Lord of Bath, though I know them both to be wise, virtuous, learned, and honourable prelates, nor myself, with the rest of your council, being all your grace's own servants, for your manifold benefits daily bestowed on us so most bounden to you, be in my judgment meet counsellors for your grace herein. But if your grace mind to understand the truth, such counsellors may you have devised, as neither for respect of their own worldly commodity, nor for fear of your princely authority, will be inclined to deceive you.' To whom he named St. Jerome, St. Augustine, and divers other old holy doctors, both Greeks and Latins; and moreover showed him what authorities he had gathered out of them. Which, although the King (as disagreeable with his desire) did not very well like of, yet were they by Sir Thomas More (who in all his communication with the King in that matter had always most discreetly behaved himself) so wisely tempered, that he both presently took them in good part, and oftentimes had thereof conference with him again.

. . . . . .

It fortuned, before the matter of the said matrimony brought in question, when I, in talk with Sir Thomas More, of a certain joy commended unto him the happy state of this realm: that had so catholic a prince that no heretic durst show his face, so virtuous and learned a clergy, so grave and sound a nobility, and so loving, obedient subjects, all in one faith agreeing together. 'Troth it is indeed, son Roper,' quoth he, and in commending all degrees and estates of the same went far beyond me. 'And yet, son Roper, I pray God,' said he, 'that some of us, as high as we seem to sit upon the mountains, treading heretics under our feet like ants, live not the day that we gladly would wish to be at a league and composition with them, to let them have their churches quietly to themselves, so that they would be contented to let us have ours quietly to ourselves.' After that I had told him many considerations why he had no cause so to say: 'Well,' said he, 'I pray God, son Roper, some of us live not till that day,' showing me no reason why he should put any doubt therein. To whom I said: 'By my troth, sir, it is very desperately spoken.' That vile term, I cry God mercy, did I give him. Who, by these words perceiving me in a fume, said merrily unto me: 'Well, well, son Roper, it shall not be so, it shall not be so.' Whom in sixteen years and more, being in [his] house conversant with him, I could never perceive as much as once in a fume.

But now to return again where I left. After the supplying of the imperfections of the dispensation sent (as is before rehearsed) to the commissioners into England, the King, taking the matter for ended, and then meaning no farther to proceed in that matter, assigned the Bishop of Durham and Sir Thomas More to go ambassadors to Cambray, a place neither Imperial nor French, to treat a peace between the Emperor, the French king, and him. In the concluding whereof Sir Thomas More so worthily handled himself, procuring in our league far more benefits unto this realm than at that time by the King or his council was thought possible to be compassed, that for his good service in that voyage, the King, when he after made him Lord Chancellor, caused the Duke of Norfolk openly to declare unto the people (as you shall hear hereafter more at large) how much all England was bound to him.

Now upon the coming home of the Bishop of Durham and Sir Thomas More from Cambray, the King was as earnest in persuading Sir Thomas More to agree unto the matter of his marriage as before, by many and divers ways provoking him thereunto; for the which cause, as it was thought, he the rather soon after made him Lord Chancellor.

· · · · ·

Now shortly upon his entry into the high office of the chancellorship, the King eftsoons again moved him to weigh and consider his great matter. Who, falling down upon his knees, humbly besought his highness to stand his gracious sovereign, as he ever since his entry into his gracious service had found him; saying there was nothing in the world had been so grievous unto his heart as to remember that he was not able (as he willingly would with the loss of one of his limbs), for that matter anything to find, whereby he could with his conscience safely serve his grace's contentation. As he that always bare in mind the most godly words that his highness spake unto him at his first coming into his noble service, the most virtuous lesson that ever prince taught his servant, willing him first to look unto God, and after God to him; as in good faith, he said, he did, or else might his grace well account him his most unworthy servant. To this the King answered, that if he could not therein with his conscience serve him, he was content to accept his service otherwise; and using the advice of other of his learned council whose consciences could well enough agree therewith, would nevertheless continue his gracious favour towards him, and never with that matter molest his conscience after.

But Sir Thomas More in process of time seeing the King fully determined to proceed forth in the marriage of Queen Anne; and when he, with the bishops and nobles of the higher house of the Parliament were, for the furtherance of that marriage, commanded by the King to go down unto the Common House, to show unto them both what the universities, as well of other parts beyond the seas as of Oxford and Cambridge, had done in that behalf, and their seals also testifying the same—all which matters, at the King's request, not showing of what mind himself was therein, he opened to the lower house of the Parliament—nevertheless, doubting lest further attempts after should follow, which, contrary to his conscience, by reason of his office, he was likely to be put unto, he made suit . . . [to] be discharged of that chargeable room of the chancellorship, wherein, for certain infirmities of his body, he pretended himself unable any longer to serve.

. . . . . .

When the King saw that he could by no manner of benefits win him to his side, then lo, went he about by terrors and threats to drive him thereunto. The beginning of which trouble grew by occasion of a certain nun dwelling in Canterbury, for her virtue and holiness of life among the people not a little esteemed; unto whom, for that cause, many religious persons, doctors of divinity, and divers others of good worship of the laity used to resort. Who, affirming that she had revelations from God to give the King warning of his wicked life, and of the abuse of the sword and authority committed unto him by God, and understanding my lord of Rochester, Bishop Fisher, to be a man of notable virtuous living and learning, repaired to Rochester, and there disclosed to him all her revelations, desiring his advice and counsel therein. Which the bishop perceiving might well stand with the laws of God and His holy Church, advised her (as she before had warning and intended) to go to the King herself, and to let him understand the whole circumstance thereof. Whereupon she went to the King and told him all her revelations, and so returned home again. And in short space after, she, making a voyage to the nuns of Sion, by means of one Master Reynolds, a father of the same house, there fortuned, concerning such secrets as had been revealed unto her (some part whereof seemed to touch the matter of the King's supremacy and marriage, which shortly thereupon followed), to enter into talk with Sir Thomas More. Who, notwithstanding he might well at that time without danger of any law (though after, as himself had prognosticated before, those matters were stablished by statutes and confirmed by oaths) freely and safely have talked with her therein, nevertheless in all the communication between them (as in process it appeared) had always so discreetly demeaned himself that he deserved not to be blamed, but contrariwise to be commended and praised.

. . . .

At the Parliament following was there put into the Lords' House a bill to attaint the nun and divers other religious persons of high treason, and the Bishop of Rochester, Sir Thomas More, and certain others of misprision of treason; the King presupposing of likelihood that this bill would be to Sir Thomas More so troublous and terrible that it would force him to relent and condescend to his request—wherein his grace was much deceived. To which bill Sir Thomas More was a suitor personally to be received in his own defence to make answer. But the King, not liking that, assigned the Bishop of Canterbury, the Lord Chancellor, the Duke of Norfolk, and Master Cromwell, at a day and place appointed, to call Sir Thomas More before them. At which time I, thinking that I had a good opportunity, earnestly advised him to labour unto those lords for the help of his discharge out of that Parliament bill. Who answered me he would.

And at his coming before them according to their appointment, they entertained him very friendly, willing him to sit down with them, which in no wise he would. Then began the Lord Chancellor to declare unto him how many ways the King had showed his love and favour towards him; how fain he would have had him to continue in his office; how glad he would have been to have heaped more benefits upon him; and finally how he could ask no worldly honour nor profit at his highness' hands that were likely to be denied him; hoping, by the declaration of the King's kindness and affection towards him, to provoke him to recompense his grace with the like again, and unto those things that the Parliament, the Bishops, and the universities had already passed, to add his consent.

To this Sir Thomas More mildly made answer, saying: 'No man living is there, my lords, that would with better will do the thing that should be acceptable to the King's highness than I, which must needs confess his manifold goodness and bountiful benefits most benignly bestowed upon me. Howbeit, I verily hoped that I should never have heard of this matter more, considering that I have, from time to time, always from the beginning, so plainly and truly declared my mind unto his grace, which his highness to me ever seemed, like a most gracious prince, very well to accept, never minding, as he said, to molest me more therewith. Since which time any further thing that was able to move me to any change could never I find; and if I could, there is none in all the world that would have been gladder of it than I.'

Many things more were there of like sort uttered on both sides. But in the end, when they saw they could by no manner of persuasions remove him from his former determination, then began they more terribly to touch him, telling him that the King's highness had given them in commandment, if they could by no gentleness win him, in his name with his great ingratitude to charge him, that never was there servant to his sovereign so villainous, nor subject to his prince so traitorous as he. For he, by his subtle sinister sleights most unnaturally procuring and provoking him to set forth a book of the assertion of the seven sacraments and maintenance of the Pope's authority, had caused him, to his dishonour throughout all Christendom, to put a sword in the Pope's hand to fight against himself.

When they had thus laid forth all the terrors they could imagine against him: 'My lords,' quoth he, 'these terrors be arguments for children, and not for me. But to answer to that wherewith you do chiefly burden me, I believe the King's highness of his honour will never lay that to my charge; for none is there that can in that point say in my excuse more to me than his highness himself, who right well knoweth that I never was procurer nor counsellor of his majesty thereunto, but after it was finished, by his grace's appointment and consent of the makers of the same, only a sorter out and placer of the principal matters therein contained. Wherein when I found the Pope's authority highly advanced, and with strong arguments mightily defended, I said unto his grace: "I must put your highness in remembrance of one thing, and that is this. The Pope, as your grace knoweth, is a prince as you are, and in league with all other Christian princes. It may hereafter so fall out that your grace and he may vary upon some points of the league, whereupon may grow breach of amity and war between you both. I think it best therefore that that place be amended, and his authority more slenderly touched." "Nay," quoth his grace, "that shall it not. We are so much bounden unto the see of Rome that we cannot do too much honour unto it." Then did I further put him in remembrance of the Statute of Praemunire, whereby a good part of the Pope's pastoral cure here was pared away. To that answered his highness: "Whatsoever impediment be to the contrary, we will set forth that authority to the uttermost. For we received from that see our crown imperial"; which till his grace with his own mouth told it me, I never heard of before. So that I trust when his grace shall be once truly informed of this and call to his gracious remembrance my doing in that behalf, his highness will never speak of it more, but clear me thoroughly therein himself.' And thus displeasantly departed they.

Then took Sir Thomas More his boat towards his house at Chelsea, wherein by the way he was very merry; and for that I was nothing sorry, hoping that he had got himself discharged out of the Parliament bill. When he was landed and come home, then walked we twain alone in his garden together; where I, desirous to know how he had sped, said: 'I trust, sir, that all is well, because that you be so merry.' 'It is so indeed, son Roper, I thank God,' quoth he. 'Are you then put out of the Parliament bill?' said I. 'By my troth, son Roper,' quoth he, 'I never remembered it!' 'Never remembered it, sir!' said I, 'a case that toucheth yourself so near, and us all for your sake! I am sorry to hear it; for I verily trusted, when I saw you so merry, that all had been well.' Then said he: 'Wilt thou know, son Roper, why I was so merry?' 'That would I gladly, sir,' quoth I. 'In good faith, I rejoiced, son,' quoth he, 'that I had given the devil a foul fall, and that with those lords I had gone so far as without great shame I could never go back again.' At which words waxed I very sad, for though himself liked it well, yet liked it me but a little.

Now upon the report made by the Lord Chancellor and the other lords to the King of all their whole discourse had with Sir Thomas More, the King was so highly offended with him, that he plainly told them he was fully determined that the foresaid Parliament bill should undoubtedly proceed forth against him.

· · · · ·

So fell it out, within a month or thereabouts after the making of the statute for the Oath of the Supremacy and Matrimony, that all the priests of London and Westminster, and no temporal men but he, were sent for to appear at Lambeth before the Bishop of Canterbury, the Lord Chancellor, and Secretary Cromwell, commissioners appointed there to tender the oath unto them.

Then Sir Thomas More, as his accustomed manner was always ere he entered into any matter of importance—as when he was first chosen of the King's privy council, when he was sent ambassador, appointed Speaker of the Parliament, made Lord Chancellor, or when he took any like weighty matter upon him—to go to the church and be confessed, to hear mass and be houseled, so did he likewise in the morning early the selfsame day that he was summoned to appear before the lords at Lambeth. And whereas he evermore used before, at his departure from his wife and children, whom he tenderly loved, to have them bring him to his boat, and there to kiss them all, and bid them farewell, then would he suffer none of them forth of the gate to follow him, but pulled the wicket after him, and shut them all from him; and with a heavy heart, as by his countenance it appeared, with me and our four servants there took his boat towards Lambeth. Wherein sitting still sadly awhile, at the last he suddenly rounded me in the ear and said: 'Son Roper, I thank our Lord the field is won.' What he meant thereby I then wist not, yet loath to seem ignorant, I answered: 'Sir, I am thereof very glad.' But, as I conjectured afterwards, it was for that the love he had to God wrought in him so effectually that it conquered all his carnal affections utterly.

Now at his coming to Lambeth, how wisely he behaved himself before the commissioners, at the ministration of the oath unto him, may be found in certain letters of his, sent to my wife, remaining in a great book of his works. Where, by the space of four days, he was betaken to the custody of the Abbot of Westminster, during which time the King consulted with his council what order were meet to be taken with him. And albeit in the beginning they were resolved that with an oath, not to be acknowen, whether he had to the supremacy been sworn, or what he thought thereof, he should be discharged; yet did Queen Anne by her importunate clamour so sore exasperate the King against him, that, contrary to his former resolution, he caused the said Oath of the Supremacy to be ministered unto him. Who, albeit he made a discreet qualified answer, nevertheless was forthwith committed to the Tower.

Who as he was going thitherward wearing, as he commonly did, a chain of gold about his neck, Sir Richard Southwell, that had the charge of his conveyance thither, advised him to send home his chain to his wife or to some of his children. 'Nay, Sir,' quoth he, 'that will I not; for if I were taken in the field by my enemies, I would they should somewhat fare the better by me.'

At whose landing Master Lieutenant at the Tower gate was ready to receive him, where the porter demanded of him his upper garment. 'Master porter,' quoth he, 'here it is,' and took off his cap and delivered it to him, saying, 'I am very sorry it is no better for you.' 'No, sir,' quoth the porter, 'I must have your gown.'

. . . . .

Not long after came there to him the Lord Chancellor, the Dukes of Norfolk and Suffolk, with Master Secretary and certain other of the privy council, at two several times, by all policies possible procuring him either precisely to confess the Supremacy, or precisely to deny it; whereunto, as appeareth by his examination in the said great book, they could never bring him.

Shortly hereupon Master Rich, afterwards Lord Rich, then newly made the King's Solicitor, Sir Richard Southwell, and one Master Palmer, servant to the Secretary, were sent to Sir Thomas More into the Tower, to fetch away his books from him. And while Sir Richard

Southwell and Master Palmer were busy in the trussing up of his books, Master Rich, pretending friendly talk with him, among other things of a set course, as it seemed, said thus unto him: 'Forasmuch as it is well known, Master More, that you are a man both wise and well learned as well in the laws of the realm as otherwise, I pray you therefore, sir, let me be so bold as of good will to put unto you this case. Admit there were, sir,' quoth he, 'an act of Parliament that all the realm should take me for king. Would not you, Master More, take me for king?' 'Yes, sir,' quoth Sir Thomas More, 'that would I.' 'I put the case further,' quoth Master Rich, 'that there were an act of Parliament that all the realm should take me for pope. Would not you then, Master More, take me for pope?'

'For answer, sir,' quoth Sir Thomas More, 'to your first case: the Parliament may well, Master Rich, meddle with the state of temporal princes. But to make answer to your other case, I will put you this case: suppose that the Parliament would make a law that God should not be God. Would you then, Master Rich, say that God were not God?' 'No, sir,' quoth he, 'that would I not, sith no Parliament may make any such law.' 'No more,' said Sir Thomas More, as Master Rich reported of him, 'could the Parliament make the King supreme head of the Church.' Upon whose only report was Sir Thomas More indicted of high treason upon the statute whereby it was made treason to deny the king to be supreme head of the Church; into which indictment were put these heinous words—'maliciously, traitorously, and diabolically.'

. . . . .

When Sir Thomas More came from Westminster to the Tower-ward again, his daughter, my wife, desirous to see her father, whom she thought she should never see in this world after, and also to have his final blessing, gave attendance about the Tower Wharf, where she knew he should pass by, before he could enter into the Tower, there tarrying for his coming. As soon as she saw him, after his blessing upon her knees reverently received, she hasting towards him, and without consideration or care of herself, pressing in among the midst of the throng and company of the guard that with halberds and bills went round about him, hastily ran to him, and there openly, in the sight of them all, embraced him, took him about the neck, and kissed him. Who, well liking her most natural and dear daughterly affection towards him, gave her his fatherly blessing and many godly words of comfort besides. From whom after she was departed, she, not satisfied with her former sight of him, and like one that had forgotten herself, being all ravished with the entire love of her dear father, having respect neither to herself, nor to the press of the people and multitude that were there about him, suddenly turned back again, ran to him as before, took him about the neck, and divers times together most lovingly kissed him; and at last, with a full heavy heart, was fain to depart from him: the beholding whereof was to many of them that were present thereat so lamentable that it made them for very sorrow thereof to mourn and weep.

So remained Sir Thomas More in the Tower more than a seven-night after his judgement.

. . . .

And so upon the next morrow, being Tuesday, Saint Thomas even, and the Utas of Saint Peter, in the year of our Lord 1535 (according as he in his letter the day before had wished) early in the morning came unto him Sir Thomas Pope, his singular friend, on message from the King and his council, that he should before nine of the clock the same morning suffer death.

. . . . . .

And so was he by Master Lieutenant brought out of the Tower, and from thence led towards the place of execution. Where, going up the scaffold, which was so weak that it was ready to fall, he said merrily to the lieutenant: 'I pray you, Master Lieutenant, see me safe up, and for my coming down let me shift for myself.'

Then desired he all the people thereabout to pray for him, and to bear witness with him that he should now there suffer death in and for the faith of the holy Catholic Church. Which done, he kneeled down, and, after his prayers said, turned to the executioner, and with a cheerful countenance spake thus to him: 'Pluck up thy spirits, man, and be not afraid to do thine office; my neck is very short, take heed, therefore, thou strike not awry, for saving of thine honesty.'

So passed Sir Thomas More out of this world to God, upon the very same day in which himself had most desired.

Soon after whose death intelligence came thereof to the Emperor Charles. Whereupon he sent for Sir Thomas Eliot, our English ambassador, and said unto him: 'My Lord Ambassador, we understand that the King, your master, hath put his faithful servant and grave, wise counsellor, Sir Thomas More, to death.' Whereunto Sir Thomas Eliot answered that he understood nothing thereof. 'Well,' said the Emperor, 'it is too true. And this will we say, that if we had been master of such a servant, of whose doings ourself have had these many years no small experience, we would rather have lost the best city of our dominions, than have lost such a worthy counsellor.' . . .

ᚹ Suggestions for Reading and Writing

1. Does More here seem guilty of the sin of pride? Would a truly loyal civil servant have found some means of reconciling his conscience and his king's wishes? What portrait of Henry VIII emerges?

2. Does More here seem as heroic as such earlier saints as Antony and Augustine?

3. Does Roper's More square with the man depicted in such modern studies as R. W. Chambers' *Thomas More* (1935), John Farrow's *The Story of Thomas More* (1954), Ernest E. Reynolds' *Saint Thomas More* (1954), and Leslie A. Paul's *Sir Thomas More* (1959)?

4. More has proved of interest to modern dramatists. Write a brief profile of the politician-saint-scholar who appears in Maxwell Anderson's *Anne of the Thousand Days* (1948) and Robert Bolt's *A Man for All Seasons* (1961).

5. For another contemporary eye-witness biography, see George Cavendish's *Life of Cardinal Wolsey* (1667). How do Roper and Cavendish differ in attitude toward subject and treatment of materials? (See Donald Stauffer's *English Biography Before 1700* [1930] for a detailed discussion of early English biography.)

6. John Gibson Lockhart, in his biography of Sir Walter Scott, proved to be—like Roper—a devoted son-in-law as biographer. After reading the selection from the *Life of Sir Walter Scott* (1838), p. 172, would you say that Lockhart's was a more, or less, balanced study than Roper's?

7. More was preceded into religious martyrdom by Thomas à Becket, Archbishop of Canterbury and chancellor to Henry II. In 1171 Becket was murdered by Henry's knights and became a saint, a culture hero, and the protagonist in a series of literary dramas. A fascinating characterization should emerge from a comparative study of Tennyson's *Becket* (1879), T. S. Eliot's *Murder in the Cathedral* (1935), and Jean Anouilh's *Becket* (1959).

BISHOP RIDLEY AND BISHOP LATIMER

John Foxe

In sixteenth-century England the fledgling Protestant church faced constant Catholic gibes: unlike the older faith, it lacked martyrologies or saints' lives to convince and inspire the flock to imitation and worship. It remained for John Foxe (1516–1587) —Oxford graduate, strict Calvinist, Church of England priest, and Protestant exile—to meet the challenge with his lengthy but biased History of the Acts and Monuments of the Church (1563).

Known then and later as Foxe's "Book of Martyrs," it presented a virulent account of religious persecution in England under the Catholic queen, Bloody Mary Tudor. Not surprisingly, Foxe's ghoulish descriptions of persecution and torture caught public imagination, and his account in abridged form found steady acceptance in Sunday-school libraries and among the pious. If it furthered English Protestantism, the "Book of Martyrs" also generated and prolonged religious animosities and encouraged those with a taste for martyrdom to acts of foolishness.

Foxe was neither a literary stylist nor a reliable historian. Yet his emotional involvement, command of documentary detail, and homely, energetic prose produced a narrative of power and effectiveness. Despite its shortcomings, the "Book

of Martyrs" has found its way into the general stream of
English biography.

The graphic description of the deaths of Latimer and
Ridley (who had ordained Foxe), although presenting material
not mentioned elsewhere, still has a decidedly authentic ring.
Modern editors have tended to paraphrase Foxe's text freely;
the following version of the text (Philadelphia: E. Claxton,
1881) is one of the most dramatically coherent treatments.

✓   ✓   ✓   ✓   ✓

These reverend prelates suffered October 17, 1555, at Oxford, on the
same day Wolsey and Pygot perished at Ely. Pillars of the church and
accomplished ornaments of human nature, they were the admiration of
the realm, amiably conspicuous in their lives, and glorious in their
deaths.

Dr. Ridley was born in Northumberland, was first taught grammar
at Newcastle, and afterward removed to Cambridge, where his aptitude
in education raised him gradually till he came to be the head of
Pembroke college, where he received the title of Doctor of Divinity.
Having returned from a trip to Paris, he was appointed Chaplain to
Henry VIII. and Bishop of Rochester, and was afterwards translated to
the see of London in the time of Edward VI.

His tenacious memory, extensive erudition, impressive oratory, and
indefatigable zeal in preaching, drew after him not only his own flock,
but persons from all quarters, desirous of godly exhortation or reproof.
His tender treatment of Dr. Heath, who was a prisoner with him during
one year, in Edward's reign, evidently proves that he had no Catholic
cruelty in his disposition. In person he was erect and well proportioned;
in temper forgiving; in self-mortification severe. His first duty in the
morning was private prayer: he remained in his study till 10 o'clock, and
then attended the daily prayer used in his house. Dinner being done, he
sat about an hour, conversing pleasantly, or playing at chess. His study
next engaged his attention, unless business or visits occurred; about five
o'clock prayers followed; and after he would recreate himself at chess for
about an hour, then retire to his study till eleven o'clock, and pray on his
knees as in the morning. In brief, he was a pattern of godliness and virtue, and such he endeavored to make men wherever he came.

His attentive kindness was displayed particularly to old Mrs.
Bonner, mother of Dr. Bonner, the cruel bishop of London. Dr. Ridley,
when at his manor at Fulham, always invited her to his house, placed her
at the head of his table, and treated her like his own mother; he did the

same by Bonner's sister and other relatives; but when Dr. Ridley was under persecution, Bonner pursued a conduct diametrically opposite, and would have sacrificed Dr. Ridley's sister and her husband, Mr. George Shipside, had not Providence delivered him by the means of Dr. Heath, bishop of Worcester. Dr. Ridley was first in part converted by reading Bertram's book on the sacrament, and by his conferences with archbishop Cranmer and Peter Martyr. When Edward VI. was removed from the throne, and the bloody Mary succeeded, bishop Ridley was immediately marked as an object of slaughter. He was first sent to the Tower, and afterward, at Oxford, was consigned to the common prison of Bocardo, with archbishop Cranmer and Mr. Latimer. Being separated from them, he was placed in the house of one Irish, where he remained till the day of his martyrdom, from 1554, till October 16, 1555. It will easily be supposed that the conversations of these chiefs of the martyrs were elaborate, learned, and instructive. Such indeed they were, and equally beneficial to all their spiritual comforts. Bishop Ridley's letters to various Christian brethren in bonds in all parts, and his disputations with the mitred enemies of Christ, alike prove the clearness of his head and the integrity of his heart. In a letter to Mr. Grindal, (afterward archbishop of Canterbury,) he mentions with affection those who had preceded him in dying for the faith, and those who were expected to suffer; he regrets that popery is re-established in its full abomination, which he attributes to the wrath of God, made manifest in return for the lukewarmness of the clergy and the people in justly appreciating the blessed light of the reformation.

Bishop Latimer was the son of Hugh Latimer, of Turkelson, in Leicestershire, a husbandman of repute, with whom he remained till he was four years old. His parents, finding him of acute parts, gave him a good education, and then sent him at fourteen to the university of Cambridge, where he entered into the study of the school divinity of that day, and was from principle a zealous observer of the Romish superstitions of the time. In his oration, when he commenced bachelor of divinity, he inveighed against the reformer Melancthon, and openly declaimed against good Mr. Stafford, divinity lecturer in Cambridge.

Mr. Thomas Bilney, moved by a brotherly pity towards Mr. Latimer, begged to wait upon him in his study, and to explain to him the groundwork of his (Mr. Bilney's) faith. This blessed interview effected his conversion: the persecutor of Christ became his zealous advocate, and before Dr. Stafford died he became reconciled to him.

Once converted, he became eager for the conversion of others, and commenced public preacher, and private instructor in the university. His sermons were so pointed against the absurdity of praying in the Latin tongue, and withholding the oracles of salvation from the people who were to be saved by belief in them, that he drew upon himself the pulpit animadversions of several of the resident friars and heads of houses, whom he subsequently silenced by his severe criticisms and eloquent arguments. This was at Christmas, 1529. At length Dr. West preached against Mr. Latimer at Barwell Abbey, and prohibited him from preaching again in the churches of the university, notwithstanding which, he continued during three years to advocate openly the cause of Christ, and even his enemies confessed the power of those talents he possessed. Mr. Bilney remained here some time with Mr. Latimer, and thus the place where they frequently walked together obtained the name of Heretics' Hill.

Mr. Latimer at this time traced out the innocence of a poor woman, accused by her husband of the murder of her child. Having preached before king Henry VIII. at Windsor, he obtained the unfortunate mother's pardon. This, with many other benevolent acts, served only to excite the spleen of his adversaries. He was summoned before Cardinal Wolsey for heresy, but being a strenuous supporter of the king's supremacy, in opposition to the pope's, by favour of lord Cromwell and Dr. Buts, (the king's physician,) he obtained the living of West Kingston, in Wiltshire. For his sermons here against purgatory, the immaculacy of the Virgin, and the worship of images, he was cited to appear before Warham, archbishop of Canterbury, and John, bishop of London. He was required to subscribe certain articles, expressive of his conformity to the accustomed usages; and there is reason to think, after repeated weekly examinations, that he did subscribe, as they did not seem to involve any important article of belief. Guided by Providence, he escaped the subtle nets of his persecutors, and at length, through the powerful friends before mentioned, became bishop of Worcester, in which function he qualified or explained away most of the papal ceremonies he was for form's sake under the necessity of complying with. He continued in this active and dignified employment some years, till the coming in of the Six Articles, when, to preserve an unsullied conscience, he, as well as Dr. Shaxton, bishop of Salisbury, resigned. He remained a prisoner in the Tower till the coronation of Edward VI. when he was again called to the Lord's harvest in Stamford, and many other places: he also preached at London in the convocation house, and before the young king; indeed he lectured twice every Sunday, regardless of his great age (then above sixty-seven years,) and his weakness through a bruise received from the fall of a tree. Indefatigable in his private studies, he rose to them in winter and in summer at two o'clock in the morning. By the strength of his own mind, or of some inward light from above, he had a prophetic view of what was to happen to the church in Mary's reign, asserting that he was doomed to suffer for the truth, and that Winchester, then in the Tower, was preserved for that purpose. Soon after queen Mary was proclaimed, a messenger was sent to summon Mr. Latimer to town, and there is reason to believe it was wished that he should make his escape. On entering Smithfield, he jocosely said, that the place had long groaned for him. After being examined by the council, he was committed to the Tower, where his cheerfulness is displayed in the following anecdote. Being kept without fire in severe frosty weather, his aged frame suffered so much, that he told the lieutenant's man, that if he did not look better after him he should deceive his master. The lieutenant, thinking he meant to effect his escape, came to him, to know what he meant by this speech; which Mr. Latimer replied to, by saying, "You, Mr. Lieutenant, doubtless suppose I shall *burn*; but, except you let me have some fire, I shall deceive your expectation, for here it is likely I shall be *starved with cold*."

Mr. Latimer, after remaining a long time in the Tower, was transported to Oxford, with Cranmer and Ridley, the disputations at which place have been already mentioned in a former part of this work. He remained imprisoned till October, and the principal objects of all his prayers were three—that he might stand faithful to the doctrine he had professed, that God would restore his gospel to England once again, and preserve the Lady Elizabeth to be queen; all which happened. When he stood at the stake without the Bocardo-gate, Oxford, with Dr. Ridley, and fire was putting to the pile of fagots, he raised his eyes benignantly towards heaven, and said, "God is faithful, who doth not suffer us to be tempted above our strength." His body was forcibly penetrated by the fire, and the blood flowed abundantly from the heart; as if to verify his constant desire that his heart's blood might be shed in defence of the gospel. His polemical and friendly letters are lasting monuments of his integrity and talents. It has been before said, that public disputation took place in April, 1554; new examinations took place in Oct. 1555, previous to the degradation and condemnation of Cranmer, Ridley, and Latimer. We now draw to the conclusion of the lives of the two last.

Dr. Ridley, the night before execution, was very facetious, had himself shaved, and called his supper a marriage feast; he remarked upon seeing Mrs. Irish (the keeper's wife) weep, "though my breakfast will be somewhat sharp, my supper will be more pleasant and sweet." The place of death was on the north side of the town opposite Baliol College:—Dr. Ridley was dressed in a black gown furred, and Mr. Latimer had a long shroud on, hanging down to his feet. Dr. Ridley, as he passed Bocardo, looked up to see Dr. Cranmer, but the latter was then engaged in disputation with a friar.—When they came to the stake, Dr. Ridley embraced Latimer fervently, and bid him be of good heart. He then knelt by the stake, and after earnestly praying together, they had a short private conversation. Dr. Smith then preached a short sermon against the martyrs, who would have answered him, but were prevented by Dr. Marshal, the vice-chancellor. Dr. Ridley then took off his gown and tippet, and gave them to his brother-in-law, Mr. Shipside. He gave away also many trifles to his weeping friends, and the populace were anxious to get even a fragment of his garments. Mr. Latimer gave nothing, and from the poverty of his garb, was soon stripped to his shroud, and stood venerable and erect, fearless of death. Dr. Ridley being unclothed to his shirt, the smith placed an iron chain about their waists, and Dr. Ridley bid him fasten it securely; his brother having tied a bag of gunpowder about his neck, gave some also to Mr. Latimer. Dr. Ridley then requested of Lord Williams, of Fame, to advocate with the queen the cause of some poor men to whom he had, when bishop, granted leases, but which the present bishop refused to confirm. A lighted fagot was now laid at Dr. Ridley's feet, which caused Mr. Latimer to say, "Be of good cheer, Ridley; and play the man. We shall this day, by God's grace, light up such a candle in England, as, I trust, will never be put out." When Dr. Ridley saw the flame approaching him, he exclaimed, "Into thy hands, O Lord, I commend my spirit!" and repeated often, "Lord receive my spirit!" Mr. Latimer, too, ceased not to say, "O Father of heaven receive my soul!" Embracing the flame, he bathed his hands in it, and soon died, apparently with little pain; but Dr. Ridley, by the ill-adjustment of the fagots, which were green, and placed too high above the furze was burnt much downwards. At this time, piteously entreating for more fire to come to him, his brother-in-law imprudently heaped the fagots up over him, which caused the fire more fiercely to burn his limbs, whence he literally leaped up and down under the fagots, exclaiming that he could not burn; indeed, his dreadful extremity was but too plain, for after his legs were quite consumed, he showed his body and shirt unsinged by the flame. Crying upon God for mercy, a man with a bill pulled the fagots down, and when the flames arose, then he bent himself towards that side; at length the gunpowder was ignited, and then he ceased to move, burning on the other side, and falling down at Mr. Latimer's feet over the chain that had hitherto supported him.

Every eye shed tears at the afflicting sight of these sufferers, who were among the most distinguished persons of their time in dignity, piety, and public estimation. They suffered October 16, 1555.

In the following month died Stephen Gardiner, bishop of Winchester and Lord Chancellor of England. This papistical monster was born at Bury, in Suffolk, and partly educated at Cambridge. Ambitious, cruel, and bigoted, he served any cause; he first espoused the king's part in the affair of Anne Boleyn: upon the establishment of the Reformation, he declared the supremacy of the Pope an execrable tenet; and when queen Mary came to the crown, he entered into all her papistical bigoted views, and became a second time bishop of Winchester. It is conjectured it was his intention to have moved the sacrifice of Lady Elizabeth, but when he arrived at this point, it pleased God to remove him.

It was on the afternoon of the day when those faithful soldiers of Christ, Ridley and Latimer, perished, that Gardiner sat down with a joyful heart to dinner. Scarcely had he taken a few mouthfuls, when he was seized with illness, and carried to his bed, where he lingered fifteen days in great torment, unable in any wise to evacuate, and burnt with a devouring fever, that terminated in death. Execrated by all good Christians, we pray the Father of Mercies, that he may receive that mercy above he never imparted below.

↑ Suggestions for Reading and Writing

1. Specify Foxe's means of slanting his material. Do his final two paragraphs (on Stephen Gardiner) enhance or weaken his narrative?
2. Regardless of your faith—or lack of one—what historical and human lessons can you draw from Foxe's account? What modern practices match the mob lust indicated here?
3. The social historian G. M. Trevelyan ranked Foxe with Richard Hakluyt as a prime influence on the thought and the imagination of Shakespeare's age. Document this statement. (For background on Foxe, see J. F. Mozley's *John Foxe and His Book* [1940].)
4. For a fuller modern view enabling you to check and discuss Foxe's use of history, see J. C. Ryle's *Bishops Latimer and Ridley* (1925).
5. Compare this selection by Foxe with *Life of St. Antony* (fourth century) by Athanasius, a work which helped establish the saint's life as a literary form. Note especially the tone and attitude toward subject expressed in each work. See also Iris Origo's "Biography, True and False" (p. 368) for comments on the place of the saint's life in the history of biography.

THE
DIFFICULT
ART OF
BIOGRAPHY

W. S. Lewis

Clubman, littérateur, author, lecturer, and peripatetic scholar, W. S. Lewis (1895–   ) probably would consider Yale University the focal point of his illustrious career. He not only graduated from Yale but has worked for its university press, engaged in research in the Sterling Library, served as fellow of the Yale University Corporation, and been a trustee of the Library Associates.

Dr. Lewis has devoted his scholarship to editing, bibliography, and biography—with much of his work centering on Horace Walpole, the eighteenth-century English politician, novelist, publisher, and inveterate letter writer. Lewis' works include the twenty-six volumes of Horace Walpole's Correspondence (1937–1961), Private Charity in England, 1747–1757 (1938), Three Tours Through London in the Years 1748, 1776, 1797 (1941), The Yale Collections (1946), Collector's Progress (1951), Horace Walpole's Library (1958), and Horace Walpole (1961). These scholarly endeavors have won Lewis many honorary degrees; and he is a fellow of the American Philosophical Society, the Academy of Arts and Sciences, and the Royal Society of Literature.

Few, then, are better prepared than he to write on "The Difficult Art of Biography," and even fewer could do so with equal clarity and seeming ease.

Just about everyone likes biography. The reason for this is not hard to find. It is the pleasure we get in identifying ourselves with real people who have attained eminence of some sort. By the magic of biography we are transported out of ourselves into kings and queens, generals, poets, lovers, and bankers; we become Eleanor of Aquitaine or George Washington or Babe Ruth. Such being the power of biography, it is remarkable that of all the forms of the literary art it has had the fewest successes: there has been composed in our language only one life that everybody agrees is a masterpiece.

Writing on biography recently Sir Harold Nicolson gave the "Oxford English Dictionary's" definition of it: "the history of the lives of individual men, as a branch of literature." "This excellent definition," he goes on, "contains within itself three principles that any serious biographer should observe. A biography must be 'history,' in the sense that it must be accurate and depict a person in relation to his times. It must describe an 'individual,' with all the gradations of human character, and not merely present a type of virtue or of vice. And it must be composed as 'a branch of literature,' in that it must be written in grammatical English and with an adequate feeling for style."

In a full-dress biography the history begins before the birth of the principal figure; it reaches back into his family, to father, mother, and grandparents, and picks out in the further past any ancestors who have escaped oblivion. The hero then appears, and the story of his life is unfolded to the best of the biographer's abilities as a scholar, as a person, and as a writer.

In collecting his materials the author who is writing the life of a contemporary has certain obvious advantages: he can interview his man and his family, friends, and enemies. He can get answers that a biographer writing in the future will perhaps have to search many books to find, and which he may not find in the end. The contemporary has the additional advantage of knowing how his subject dressed and walked and ate; above all, how he spoke. "In the intervals of articulating," Boswell tells us, Johnson "made various sounds with his mouth, sometimes as if ruminating, or what is called chewing the cud, sometimes giving a half whistle, sometimes making his tongue play backwards from the roof of his mouth, as if clucking like a hen, and sometimes protruding it against his upper gums in front, as if pronouncing quickly under his breath, *too, too, too;* all this accompanied sometimes with a thoughtful look, but more frequently with a smile." These "minute singularities" noted by an eyewitness who was also a genius make the great man live. The notes of some such eyewitness of the first emperors supplied Suetonius a century

Yale Review, XLIV, No. 1 (Autumn 1954), 33–40. Copyright Yale University Press. Reprinted by permission of the *Yale Review*.

after their deaths with his most telling touches: Caesar on a litter carried home from the Capitol "with one arm hanging down"; Augustus "wrapped in four tunics and a heavy toga, besides an undershirt, a woolen chest-protector and wraps for his thighs and shins," rolling dice with little boys. The contemporary biographer will perhaps have the gift the blind have, the ability to sense the state of his man's mind and spirit and to know when he is troubled or serene. If the biographer has this insight it will be his supreme advantage; if he lacks it his work will not reach the first rank.

The contemporary biographer has a still further advantage which is so obvious that it might be overlooked: the advantage of living in the same time as his subject. Were Mr. Aneurin Bevan to write the life of Sir Winston Churchill he would come to his task with grave handicaps, but he would have one advantage that Sir Winston's biographers in future centuries will lack. This is that both were born in a horse-drawn age. Mr. Bevan would have a further advantage in writing his biography, that of being a generation younger than his subject, the same advantage that Boswell and Lockhart had. This advantage is illustrated by the stereoscope, whose slightly divergent photographs give a third dimension to the Taj Mahal or Niagara Falls. You might almost be there, you feel, as you place the frame upon your nose with a gasp of delight. The slightly different point of view of a younger contemporary gives to the subject he is examining the same sense of a third dimension.

It may take much study and thought to discover the details of the setting in which the subject of the biography moved. Mr. Bevan in his life of Churchill will not think of England as it is today when he writes of Sir Winston's part in the Boer War, nor will he present Sir Winston in the First World War in the uniform of the Boer War. In the dozen years that intervened between those wars England and the world had changed. The automobile had appeared, for one thing; suffragettes for another; Blériot had flown the Channel; strange and alarming things had happened in the arts: just as the man in the street was getting used to Monet and Whistler he was called upon to admire the "Nude Descending the Staircase" and ladies with both eyes on the same side of their noses—or did *they* come later? Mr. Bevan will perhaps have to look that point up. Although he will be writing inside the time and so will be more likely to avoid anachronisms than would a later biographer, he, too, must verify his references and allusions. Since Mr. Bevan will have to do so, think what Churchill's biographers of the 24th century will have to do! They will acquire the reputation of being learned men when they discover that television was invented after the bicycle and that ladies began smoking cigarettes at about the same time that they gave up wearing black stockings into the sea. Even well-educated men and women in the year

2300 will not have realized that ladies did wear black stockings into the sea—to say nothing of corsets, and what, by the way, *were* corsets? The historians of the 24th century will have to discriminate, one by one, the differences in thought, speech, customs, and manners that evolved during Churchill's lifetime. Many of these changes will leap to the eye; many, the tacit assumptions of our day, will have to be recovered when the age is, so to say, off its guard.

Such a moment came when Horace Walpole went to hear the Cock Lane Ghost. "We set out from the Opera," Walpole wrote, "changed our clothes at Northumberland House, the Duke of York, Lady Northumberland, Lady Mary Coke, Lord Hertford, and I, all in one hackney coach, and drove to the spot; it rained torrents; yet the lane was full of mob, and the house so full we could not get in—at last they discovered it was the Duke of York, and the company squeezed themselves into one another's pockets to make room for us." There are three tacit assumptions in this passage: that this richly dressed group changed into their ordinary day dress before going into the slums, that they gave up their carriages for the 18th-century equivalent of a taxi, and that "the mob" respected the Duke of York, the King's uncle, enough to make way for him and his party. These three facts were taken for granted by Walpole and his correspondent. He did not write, "You know that if we had gone to Cock Lane in our fine clothes and carriages we might have been pelted with filth and abuse." This glimpse of unmusical people escaping from the opera to go to a more amusing show makes us feel close to 1762. We share their curiosity about the ghost, we understand why they changed their clothes, and why "the mob" was polite to them and not hostile. In these recognitions we find the familiar amid the strange. Were we to return to London in 1762 the strange amid the familiar would shock, sicken, and edify us. The waning survivals of still earlier centuries would confront us on every hand, survivals of ancient manners, customs, and attitudes of mind, such things as visiting madhouses to laugh at the inmates or seeing two women, stripped to the waist, fighting each other with broken bottles, or a party of pleasure on the Thames singing, as they rowed along, to the accompaniment of oboes, bassoons, and violins.

Being in tune with a remote period is like listening to a radio station while motoring. As you approach the limit of its range the program begins to fade. You turn up the volume higher and higher, and when you can turn it no higher you strain to hear. At last you go around a bend in the road or down a long hill and there is silence. So it is as we travel away from our own time into the past. We who were born in the last century can tune in on the 18th century (we, too, were born in a horse-drawn age), but it will be very hard for those born after 1930 to do so: too much has happened in the past fifty years.

The best biographers burst through the time barrier. In spite of all the handicaps of differing speech and customs, they are able to convey to us the essence of the people that they are writing about. They do this by reporting incidents and occasions, many of which appear to be trivial, but which reveal character. Such revelations occur on almost every page of Boswell, as you will find if you will open his book at random. Take that evening when Johnson dined at General Paoli's and had a tiff with Sir Joshua Reynolds on the subject of drinking wine. Boswell tells us about it in dialogue: "JOHNSON (who from drinking only water, supposed everybody who drank wine to be elevated), 'I won't argue any more with you, Sir. You are too far gone.' SIR JOSHUA, 'I should have thought so indeed, Sir, had I made such a speech as you have now done.' JOHNSON (drawing himself in, and, I really thought blushing) 'Nay, don't be angry. I did not mean to offend you.' "

Or, to go back many centuries, take that moment at the well outside the city of Nahor when Abraham's servant had offered Isaac in marriage to Rebekah and had given her a golden earring and two bracelets of ten shekels weight of gold. Rebekah put them on and ran to show them off to her brother Laban. Or, that other time when "the mother of Sisera looked out at a window, and cried through the lattice, 'Why is his chariot so long in coming? Why tarry the wheels of his chariot?' " not knowing what we know, that the stars in their courses have fought against Sisera. The recorders of these moments have reached across the centuries to speak to you and to me and to the men and women of this planet as long as it lasts.

And what advantage has the noncontemporary biographer? The first, I think, is perspective. The hero's career has been studied, his work has been appraised, a sounder judgment of his significance has been reached. The dust storm of opinion and emotion that swirled about him and made dispassionate contemporary appraisal impossible has blown away. "New" material has come to light that has brought him and his age into focus: private letters and diaries and memoirs in which facts and opinions and interviews have been revealed that the subject may have known nothing about, or have forgotten if he ever did know them.

A second advantage that the later biographer has is that he is free to say what he likes without regard to the feelings of living persons or their immediate families, an easiness that increases with the years. The man who writes about Caligula is not constrained by the thought of Caligula's family, but the biographer of a great poet who died only fifty years ago must bear in mind not only what is in good taste, but what is legally perilous in the event that the great poet has a grandson in the hardware business in Weehawken who may consult his lawyer if the biographer reveals that the ethereal Helen of his grandfather's sonnets was something more substantial than a disembodied spirit.

All biographers, those writing of contemporaries and those writing of figures of the past, share certain dangers and disadvantages. The chief danger, I think, is that the biographer will identify himself with his subject. This danger is present whether the central figure is a good man or a bad man, alive or dead, but it is a danger that is particularly strong when the subject is dead. When the subject is alive the author may meet him and see and feel his weaknesses. When the subject is dead the author does not have this salutary corrective. As his study deepens he discovers engaging qualities in the great man that he had not realized were there, hints and signs of humanity and humility that had gone unnoticed by earlier biographers, amiable qualities that place the subject in a new light and show him innocent of many—of most, of all—the charges brought against him. At this point the hero has become a pattern for schoolboys and the biographer a crusader determined to right the injustice done him. To do this the base and ignorant persons who have traduced the hero must be dragged forward to receive their due from an awakened and angry public. In carrying out this agreeable duty the biographer becomes one with his subject: the great man's loves and hates are his loves and hates; criticism of the great man is criticism of the biographer, whose book has now ceased to be the life that the subject lived and has turned into a polemical apology for the author himself.

The chief disadvantage that all biographers share, I think, is ignorance, ignorance of what actually took place in the hero's life. We read of his modest and afflicted beginning; everything seems to be against him, and then—presto! he has arrived. It is never quite clear how; the trick remains a mystery. To be sure, there was that man who gave him a dollar, or published his first verses, or told him to go west, but there must have been much more to it than that. Some of the jars and accidents of the hero's daily life we may know, but what about the inspirations and sudden insights that enabled him to rise above them? The subject himself can seldom recall the answers to these questions in later life because time blots out and twists recollections of what actually took place.

Furthermore, the course of our lives is continually being determined by matters of which we have no knowledge whatever. A man may be chosen—or turned down—for a job that means success or failure in the world's eyes and never learn why he was chosen or rejected. Such decisions are often made as a result of small incidents; the deciding vote may be cast by a man who thinks of the candidate at one observed moment when he appeared admirable—or foolish: a chance remark, a gesture, a smile at the right or wrong time, may change the course of a man's life. How much do we know—does the subject himself ever know—of these critical moments? And of the strength of a man's good and evil components, the struggle in him of ambition and selflessness, or retaliation and charity, the spiritual causes of his illnesses and recoveries—all biographers, no matter how skilful in research they may be, are ultimately left to grope in that region of their subject's souls that Plutarch likens to the unknown portions on old maps where "all beyond is nothing but monsters and tragic fictions." Boswell had the advantage of holding countless conversations with Johnson, of reading his prayers and meditations, and of recovering hundreds of his private letters; yet even Boswell does not tell us why Johnson had to touch lampposts and count his steps. We can guess, but we cannot know.

The first two principles of biography, you recall, are the accurate history of the individual related to his time and the gradations of his character. We now come to the third principle, the principle that biography is "a branch of literature." Few today have the leisure or the will to pursue the art of writing as that art used to be practiced, and few know the works that have formed the best literary styles in English. Lack of familiarity with the Greek and Latin classics and the Authorized Version of the English Bible is not made up for by weaker substitutes, especially when they are presented in the new dialect evolved by the academic profession. Fortunately, in every respectable school and college and university there are diehards who refuse to speak and write this patois. These resolute conservatives are keeping the English language alive in our country, and they are not doing it in secret: this resistance movement does not hide in cellars. Its members are audible, and if only the biographers of the future will listen to them they may yet produce lives that will belong to "a branch of literature."

All biographers hope that they will turn out to be Pygmalions, and that the figure upon which they have spent so much time and affection will come to life. If this miracle is to take place, Pygmalion must do more than execute his work with the utmost skill. He must give his figure those other touches that belong to it and to none other, but he must do still more than that; he must quicken it with those touches that the reader will find in himself, revelations of duplicity inspired by the deepest instincts as well as nobility brought out by suffering: Rebekah showing Jacob how to trick Isaac into getting his father's blessing in Esau's stead, and David crying "Absalom, my son! my son!" In such passages the miracle does occur.

Biography demands much of its practitioners: study, accuracy, insight, and artistry. Its power and responsibility are immense. The subject's life, his many thousand hours, may be set aside by posterity if his biographer is careless or frivolous, idolatrous, or unjust. Immortality on earth is the gift the biographer has to confer. If in the verdict of the best judges in his own and succeeding ages he has made the gift, he will have won, as his reward, immortality for himself.

✦ Suggestions for Reading and Writing

1. Like several other essayists represented here, Lewis makes much of the contemporary biographer's advantages over those who come later. Can you write a cogent rejoinder to this view? Where is his argument strongest? Weakest?
2. Do you find convincing Lewis' view that the "chief danger" for every biographer is that he "will identify himself with his subject"? Can you point to a biographer (here or elsewhere) who has done this? Can you think of one who has reacted in opposite fashion and made a target of his subject?
3. Judging by personal experience, do you believe "a chance remark, a gesture, a smile at the right or wrong time, may change the course of a man's life"? If you do, cite the incident and explain its effects.
4. If the first two principles of biography are "the accurate history of the individual related to his time" and "the gradations of his character," is the third—centering on *style*—very important?
5. Is there an implication in Lewis' final two paragraphs that the creative literary stylist may make a subject important beyond his merits?
6. An interesting paper should result from a discussion of the problems history imposes upon the biographer. (For background, see such essays as Wallace Notestein, "History and the Biographer," *Yale Review*, XXII [March 1933], 549–558; Allan Nevins, "Biography and History," *The Gateway to History* [1938], pp. 318–341; and Oscar Handlin, "History in Men's Lives," *Virginia Quarterly*, XXX [Summer 1954], 534–541. These will lead to other essays on the subject.)

SHAKESPEARE
SUCKLING
DAVENANT

John Aubrey

By conventional standards John Aubrey (1626–1697) was a
failure. He squandered his inheritance, never married, and failed
to reduce his writings to a semblance of order. But had he been
different he would not have produced his memorable biographical sketches, Brief Lives (1698).

A lover of antiquity, anecdotes, folklore, the old astrology,
and the new science, Aubrey filled his daily life with the
sensations and impressions of the life about him. He spent his
time amusing himself in coffeehouses and taverns, buying new
books, exploring Oxford, encountering new foods, drinking
copiously, spending money, and exchanging gossip and scandal.
He liked best of all meeting new people and noting their
appearance, behavior, and gestures. His eye missed no detail,
and he seems to have known something of almost everyone of
prominence in his age. A suggestion from a fellow biographer,
Anthony à Wood, author of the Athenae Oxonienses (1691–
92), started Aubrey on his Brief Lives.

Aubrey had little concern for truth and even less for
coherence. He jotted down gossip, scandal, and libel—even at
third hand. He did little research. Every page of his original
manuscript reveals his erasures, blottings, and marginal additions
as he accumulated bits and pieces of information over the years
from 1669 to 1696. His mistakes and vulgarities are numerous;
his sentences often consist of mere phrases. At his death he left
his manuscript still verging on chaos. Wood, who attempted to

put Aubrey's notes in order, declared: "He was a shiftless person, roving and maggoty-headed, and sometimes little better than crazed."

But from Aubrey's haphazard welter of notes a literary monument emerged. His colloquial, racy, "unbuttoned" style somehow caught not only the personalities behind the public images of his subjects but his own rambling vitality and the flavor of the age. His whimsical afterthoughts, prejudices, and reservations punctured pretentiousness and hypocrisy. As the three brief lives that follow indicate, he often conveyed more in a phrase than many a more polished littérateur in a page.

✓   ✓   ✓   ✓   ✓

✓ William Shakespeare

Mr. William Shakespeare was born at Stratford upon Avon in the county of Warwick. His father was a butcher, and I have been told heretofore by some of the neighbours that when he was a boy he exercised his father's trade, but when he killed a calf he would do it in a high style and make a speech. There was at that time another butcher's son in this town that was held not at all inferior to him for a natural wit, his acquaintance and coetanean, but died young.

This William, being inclined naturally to poetry and acting, came to London, I guess, about eighteen, and was an actor at one of the playhouses, and did act exceedingly well (now B. Jonson was never a good actor, but an excellent instructor). He began early to make essays at dramatic poetry, which at that time was very low; and his plays took well. He was a handsome, well-shaped man: very good company, and of a very ready and pleasant smooth wit.

The humour of the constable, in *Midsummer-Night's Dream*, he happened to take at Grendon in Bucks—I think it was Midsummer night that he happened to lie there—which is the road from London to Stratford, and there was living that constable about 1642, when I first came to Oxon: Mr. Josias Howe is of that parish, and knew him. Ben Jonson and he did gather humours of men daily wherever they came. One time as he was at the tavern at Stratford super Avon, one Combes, an old rich usurer, was to be buried, he makes there this extemporary epitaph,

> Ten in the hundred the Devill allowes,
> But Combes will have twelve, he sweares and vowes:
> If any one askes who lies in this tombe,
> 'Hoh!' quoth the Devill, 'Tis my John o Combe.'

He was wont to go to his native country once a year. I think I have been told that he left 2 or 300 *li.* per annum there and thereabout to a sister.

I have heard Sir William Davenant and Mr. Thomas Shadwell (who is counted the best comedian we have now) say that he had a most prodigious wit, and did admire his natural parts beyond all other dramatical writers. He was wont to say (B. Jonson's *Underwoods*) that he 'never blotted out a line in his life'; said Ben Jonson, 'I wish he had blotted out a thousand.'

His comedies will remain wit as long as the English tongue is understood, for that he handles *mores hominum.* Now our present writers reflect so much upon particular persons and coxcombies, that twenty years hence they will not be understood.

Though, as Ben Jonson says of him, that he had but little Latin and less Greek, he understood Latin pretty well, for he had been in his younger years a schoolmaster in the country.

1 Sir John Suckling

Sir John Suckling, knight, was the eldest son of Suckling, of the Green Cloath, *tempore* (I think) *Car. I.* I have heard Mrs. Bond say that Sir John's father was but a dull fellow (her husband, Mr. Thomas Bond, knew him): the wit came by the mother. *Quaere* Dr. Busby if he was not of Westminster school? He might be about his time. I have heard Sir William Davenant say that he went to the university of Cambridge at eleven years of age, where he studied three or four years (I think, four). By eighteen he had well travelled France and Italy, and part of Germany, and (I think also) of Spain. He returned into England an extraordinary accomplished gentleman, grew famous at court for his ready sparkling wit which was envied, and he was (Sir William said) the bull that was baited. He was incomparably ready at repartyng [repartee], and his wit most sparkling when most set upon and provoked.

He was the greatest gallant of his time and the greatest gamester, both for bowling and cards, so that no shopkeeper would trust him for 6*d.*; as today, for instance, he might, by winning, be worth 200 *li.*, the next day he might not be worth half so much, or perhaps be sometimes *minus nihilo.* He was one of the best bowlers of his time in England. He played at cards rarely well, and did use to practice by himself abed, and there studied how the best way of managing the cards could be. His sisters coming to the Peccadillo bowling green crying for the fear he should lose all [their] portions. Sir William (who was his intimate friend and loved him entirely) would say that Sir John, when he was at his lowest ebb in gaming, I mean when unfortunate, then would make himself most glorious in apparel, and said that it exalted his spirits, and that he had then best luck when he was most gallant, and his spirits were highest.

Sir William would say that he did not much care for a lord's converse, for they were in those days damnably proud and arrogant, and the French would say that '*My lord d'Angleterre, comme un mastif-dog*'; but now the age is more refined, and much by the example of his gracious majesty, who is the pattern of courtesy.

There happened, unluckily, a difference between Sir John Suckling and Sir John Digby (brother to Sir Kenelm) about a mistress or gaming, I have now forgot. Sir John was but a slight timbered man, and of middling stature; Sir John Digby a proper person of great strength and courage answerable, and yielded to be the best swordman of his time. Sir John, with some two or three of his party assaults Sir John Digby, going into a playhouse; Sir J. D. had only his lackey with him, but he flew on them like a tiger, and made them run. 'Twas pity that this accident brought the blemish of cowardice to such an ingenious young spark. Sir J. D. was such a hero that there were very few but he would have served in the like manner.

When the expedition was into Scotland, Sir John Suckling, at his own charge, raised a troop of 100 very handsome young proper men, whom he clad in white doublets and scarlet breeches, and scarlet coats, hats, and feathers, well horsed, and armed. They say 'twas one of the finest sights in those days. But Sir John Menis made a lampoon of it:

> The ladies opened the windows to see
> So fine and goodly a sight-a, &c.

I think the lampoon says he made an inglorious charge against the Scots.

To which Sir John Suckling replied in another ballad:—

> I prithee, fool, who ere thou bee,
> That madest this fine sing-song of mee,
> . . . a sot
> . . . or els some rebill Scott.

He went into France, where after some time being come to the bottom of his fund that was left, reflecting on the miserable and despicable condition he should be reduced to, having nothing left to maintain him, he (having a convenience for that purpose, lying at an apothecary's house, in Paris) took poison, which killed him miserably with vomiting. He was buried in the Protestants' churchyard. This was (to the best of my remembrance) 1646. His picture, which is like him, before his *Poems*, says that he was but twenty-eight years old when he died.

He was of middle stature and slight strength, brisk round eye, reddish faced and red nose (ill liver), his head not very big, his hair a kind of sand colour; his beard turned-up naturally, so that he had brisk and graceful look. He died a bachelor.

He made a magnificent entertainment in London for a great number of ladies of quality, all beauties and young, which cost him hundreds of pounds, where were all the rarities that this part of the world could afford; and the last service of all was silk stockings and garters, and I think also gloves.

Anno Domini 1637 Sir John Suckling, William Davenant, poet laureate (not then knighted), and Jack Young came to the Bath. Sir John came like a young prince for all manner of equipage and convenience, and Sir W. Davenant told me that he had a cartload of books carried down; and 'twas there, at Bath, that he writ the little tract in his book about Socinianism. 'Twas as pleasant a journey as ever men had; in the height of a long peace and luxury, and in the venison season. The second night they lay at Marlborough, and walking on the delicate fine downs at the backside of the town, whilst supper was making ready, the maids were drying of clothes on the bushes. Jack Young had espied a very pretty young girl and had got her consent for an assignation, which was about midnight, which they happened to overhear on the other side of the hedge, and were resolved to frustrate his design. They were wont every night to play at cards after supper a good while; but Jack Young pretended weariness, etc. and must needs go to bed, not to be persuaded by any means to the contrary. They had their landlady at supper with them; said they to her, 'Observe this poor gentleman how he yawns, now is his mad fit coming upon him. We beseech you that you make fast his doors and get somebody to watch and look to him, for about midnight he will fall to be most outrageous; get the hostler, or some strong fellow, to stay up, and we will well content him, for he is our worthy friend, and a very honest gentleman, only, perhaps, twice in a year he falls into these fits.' Jack Young slept not, but was ready to go out as the clock struck to the hour of appointment, and then going to open the door he was disappointed, knocks, bounces, stamps, calls, 'Tapster! Chamberlain! Hostler!' swears and curses dreadfully; nobody would come to him. Sir John and W. Davenant were expectant all this time, and ready to die with laughter. I know not how he happened to get open the door and was coming downstairs. The hostler, a huge lusty fellow, fell upon him, and held him, and cried, 'Good sir, take God in your mind, you shall not go out to destroy yourself.' J. Young struggled and strived, insomuch that at last he was quite spent and dispirited, and fain to go to bed to rest himself. In the morning the landlady of the house came to see how he did and brought him a caudle. 'Oh sir,' said she, 'you had a heavy fit last

night, pray, sir, be pleased to take some of this to comfort your heart.'
Jack Young thought the woman had been mad and, being exceedingly
vexed, flirted the porrenger of caudle in her face. The next day his
comrades told him all the plot, how they cross bit him. That night they
went to Bronham House, Sir Edward Baynton's (then a noble seat, since
burnt in the civil wars), where they were nobly entertained several days.
From thence, they went to West Kington, to Parson Davenant, Sir
William's eldest brother, where they stayed a week—mirth, wit, and
good cheer flowing. From thence to Bath, six or seven miles.

Parson Robert Davenant has told me that that tract about Socinianism was writ on the table in the parlour of the parsonage at West
Kington.

My lady Southcot, whose husband hanged himself, was Sir John
Suckling's sister, to whom he writes a consolatory letter, *viz.* the first. She
afterwards married Corbet, D.D., of Merton Coll. Oxon. At her house in
Bishop's Gate Street, London, is an original of her brother, Sir John, of
Sir Anthony Van Dyck, all at length, leaning against a rock, with a
playbook, contemplating. It is a piece of great value. There is also
another rare picture, *viz.* of that pretty creature Mrs. Jane Shore, an
original.

When his *Aglaura* was [acted], he bought all the clothes himself,
which were very rich; no tinsel, all the lace pure gold and silver, which
cost him, I have now forgot. He had some scenes to it, which in those
days were only used at masques.

Mr. Snowdon tells me, that after Sir John's unlucky rencounter, or
quarrel, with Sir John Digby, wherein he was baffled, 'twas strange to see
the envy and ill nature of people to trample, and scoff àt, and deject one
in disgrace: inhumane as well as unchristian. The lady Moray had made
an entertainment for several persons of quality at Ashley (in Surrey, near
Chertsey), whereat Mr. Snowdon then was. There was the Countess of
Middlesex, whom Sir John had highly courted, and had spent on her,
and in treating her, some thousand of pounds. At this entertainment she
could not forbear, but was so severe and ingrate as to upbraid Sir John of
his late received baffle; and some other ladies had their flirts. The lady
Moray (who invited them) seeing Sir John out of countenance, for
whose worth she always had a respect: 'Well,' said she, 'I am a merry
wench and will never forsake an old friend in disgrace, so come sit down
by me, Sir John' (said she), and seated him on her right hand, and
countenanced him. This raised Sir John's dejected spirits that he threw
his repartees about the table with so much sparklingness and gentleness
of wit, to the admiration of them all.

Sir John Suckling invented the game of cribbage. He sent his cards
to all gaming places in the country, which were marked with private

marks of his: he got 20,000 *li.* by this way. Sir Francis Cornwallis made *Aglaura,* except the end.

✓ Sir William Davenant

Sir William Davenant, knight, poet laureate, was born about the end of February, 1605/6, in the city of Oxford at the Crown Tavern. His father was John Davenant, a vintner there, a very grave and discreet citizen; his mother was a very beautiful woman, and of a very good wit, and of conversation extremely agreeable.

Mr. William Shakespeare was wont to go into Warwickshire once a year, and did commonly in his journey lie at this house in Oxon, where he was exceedingly respected. I have heard Parson Robert [Davenant] say that Mr. W. Shakespeare has given him a hundred kisses. Now Sir William would sometimes, when he was pleasant over a glass of wine with his most intimate friends—*e.g.* Sam. Butler (author of *Hudibras*), etc.—say, that it seemed to him that he writ with the very spirit that Shakespeare, and seemed contented enough to be thought his son. He would tell them the story as above, in which way his mother had a very light report.

He went to school at Oxon to Mr. Sylvester, but I fear he was drawn from school before he was ripe enough. He was preferred to the first Duchess of Richmond to wait on her as a page. I remember he told me she sent him to a famous apothecary for some unicorn's horn, which he was resolved to try with a spider which he encircled in it, but without the expected success; the spider would go over, and through and through, unconcerned.

He was next a servant (as I remember, a page also) to Sir Fulke Greville, Lord Brooke, with whom he lived to his death, which was that a servant of his (that had long waited on him and his lordship had often told him that he would do something for him, but did not but still put him off with delays) as he was trussing up his lord's points coming from stool (for then their breeches were fastened to the doublets with points—then came in hooks and eyes—which not to have fastened was in my boyhood a great crime) stabbed him. This was at the same time that the Duke of Buckingham was stabbed by Felton, and the great noise and report of the duke's, Sir William told me, quite drowned this of his lord's, that 'twas scarce taken notice of. This Sir Fulke G. was a good wit and had been a good poet in his youth. He wrote a poem in folio which he printed not till he was old, and then (as Sir W. said) with too much judgment and refining, spoiled it, which was at first a delicate thing.

He writ a play or plays, and verses, which he did with so much sweetness and grace, that by it he got the love and friendship of his two

Maecenases, Mr. Endymion Porter and Mr. Henry Jermyn (since Earl of St. Albans), to whom he has dedicated his poem called *Madagascar*. Sir John Suckling also was his great and intimate friend. After the death of Ben Jonson he was made in his place poet laureate.

He got a terrible clap of a black handsome wench that lay in Axe Yard, Westminster, whom he thought on when he speaks of Dalga in *Gondibert*, which cost him his nose, with which unlucky mischance many wits were too cruelly bold: *e.g.* Sir John Menis, Sir John Denham, etc.

In 1641, when the troubles began, he was fain to fly into France, and at Canterbury he was seized on by the major—*vide* Sir John Menis' verses:

> For Will had in his face the flawes
> And markes recieved in countrey's cause:
> They flew on him like lyons passant,
> And tore his nose as much as was on't,
> And call'd him superstitious groome,
> And Popish Dog, and Cur of Rome.
> . . . . . 'Twas surely the first time
> That Will's religion was a crime.

In the civil wars in England he was in the army of William, Marquess of Newcastle (since duke), where he was general of the ordinance. I have heard his brother Robert say, for that service there was owing to him by King Charles the First 10,000 *li*. During that war, 'twas his hap to have two aldermen of York his prisoners, who were something stubborn and would not give the ransom ordered by the council of war. Sir William used them civilly, and treated them in his tent, and sat them at the upper end of his table *à la mode de France*, and having done so a good while to his charge, told them (privately and friendly) that he was not able to keep so chargeable guests, and bade them take an opportunity to escape, which they did; but having been gone a little way they considered with themselves that in gratitude they ought to go back and give Sir William their thanks, which they did, but it was like to have been to their great danger of being taken by the soldiers; but they happened to get safe to York.

The King's party being overcome, Sir William Davenant (who received the honour of knighthood from the Duke of Newcastle by commission) went into France; resided chiefly in Paris where the Prince of Wales then was. He then began to write his romance in verse, called *Gondibert*, and had not writ above the first book, but being very fond of it, prints it (before a quarter finished), with an epistle of his to Mr. Thomas Hobbes and Mr. Hobbes' excellent epistle to him printed before it. The courtiers with the Prince of Wales could never be at quiet about this piece, which was the occasion of a very witty but satirical little book of verses in octavo about four sheets, writ by George, Duke of Bucks, Sir John Denham, etc.:

> That thou forsak'st thy sleepe, thy diet,
> And which is more than that, *our quiet.*

This last word Mr. Hobbes told me was the occasion of their writing.

Here he laid an ingenious design to carry a considerable number of artificers (chiefly weavers) from hence to Virginia; and by Mary the Queen Mother's means, he got favour from the king of France to go into the prisons and pick and choose. So when the poor damned wretches understood what the design was, they cried *uno ore*—'*Tout tisseran!*' *i.e.,* *We are all weavers!* Will. [took] 36, as I remember, if not more, and shipped them; and as he was in his voyage towards Virginia, he and his *tisseran* were all taken by the ships then belonging to the Parliament of England. The slaves I suppose they sold, but Sir William was brought prisoner to England. Whither he was first a prisoner at Caresbroke Castle in the Isle of Wight or at the Tower of London, I have forgot: he was a prisoner at both. His *Gondibert* was finished at Caresbroke Castle. He expected no mercy from the Parliament and had no hopes of escaping his life. It pleased God that the two aldermen of York aforesaid hearing that he was taken and brought to London to be tried for his life, which they understood was in extreme danger, they were touched with so much generosity and goodness, as, upon their own accounts and mere motion, to try what they could to save Sir William's life, who had been so civil to them and a means to save theirs, to come to London: and acquainting the Parliament with it, upon their petition, etc., Sir William's life was saved. ('Twas Harry Martyn that saved Sir William Davenant's life in the House. When they were talking of sacrificing one, then said Henry that 'in sacrifices they always offered pure and without blemish: now ye talk of making a sacrifice of an old rotten rascal.' *Vide* H. Martyn's *Life,* where by *this very jest,* then forgot, the lord Falkland saved H. Martyn's life.)

Being freed from imprisonment (because plays, *scil.* tragedies and comedies, were in those Presbyterian times scandalous), he contrives to set up an opera *stylo recitativo,* wherein Sergeant Maynard and several citizens were engagers. It began at Rutland House, in Charterhouse yard; next, at the Cockpit in Drury Lane, where were acted very well *stylo recitativo, Sir Francis Drake's* and *The Siege of Rhodes.* It did affect the eye and ear extremely. This first brought scenes in fashion in England; before, at plays, was only a hanging.

Anno Domini 1660 was the happy restoration of his majesty Charles

II. The tennis court in Little Lincoln's Inn Field was turn'd into a playhouse for the Duke of York's players, where Sir William had lodgings, and where he died. (It is now a tennis court again, upon the building of the duke's house in Dorset Garden.)

I was at his funeral. He had a coffin of walnut tree; Sir John Denham said 'twas the finest coffin that ever he saw. His body was carried in a hearse from the playhouse to Westminster Abbey, where, at the great west door, he was received by the singing men and choristers, who sang the service of the church ('I am the Resurrection, etc.') to his grave, which is in the south cross aisle, on which, on a paving stone of marble, is writ, in imitation of that on Ben Jonson, 'O rare Sir Will. Davenant.'

His first lady was a physician's daughter, by whom he had a very beautiful and ingenious son that died above twenty years since. By his second lady he had several children. I saw some very young ones at the funeral. His eldest is Charles Davenant, LL.Dr., who inherits his father's beauty and fancy. He practises at Doctors' Commons. He writ a play called *Circe*, which has taken very well.

His private opinion was that religion at last,—*e.g.* a hundred years hence—would come to settlement, and that in a kind of ingenious Quakerism.

That sweet swan of Isis, Sir William Davenant, died the seventh day of April last, and lies buried amongst the poets in Westminster Abbey, by his antagonist, Mr. Thomas May, whose inscription of whose marble was taken away by order since the king came in. Sir William was poet laureate; and Mr. John Dryden hath his place. But me thought it had been proper that a laurel should have been set on his coffin—which was not done. He hath writ above 20 plays; besides his *Gondibert* and *Madagascar*.

↑ Suggestions for Reading and Writing

1. Aubrey emphasizes Shakespeare's "pleasant smooth wit." Why? What were the seventeenth-century connotations of "wit"?
2. Biographers have been little daunted by the sparse details of Shakespeare's life. Many have fused fact, speculation, and imagination to produce controversial portraits. After examining such varied studies as Tucker Brooke's *Shakespeare of Stratford* (1926), G. B. Harrison's *Shakespeare Under Elizabeth* (1933), Leslie Hotson's *I, William Shakespeare* (1938), Ivor Brown's *Shakespeare* (1949), and A. L. Rowse's *William Shakespeare* (1964), compile what seems a solid array of facts for a portrait of Shakespeare.
3. Does Aubrey treat Suckling's shortcomings too lightly? Which of

Suckling's qualities does he find most admirable? Do you share his admiration?

4. Do you find any consistency in Aubrey's sketch of Davenant? What does he most admire in him? Are these admirable qualities equally evident in the Davenant of Alfred Harbage's *Sir William Davenant, Poet Venturer* (1935) or Arthur H. Nethercot's *Sir William D'Avenant, Poet-Laureate and Playwright-Manager* (1938)?

5. Aubrey refers in passing to such literary contemporaries as Ben Jonson, Fulke Greville, Thomas Shadwell, Samuel Butler, Thomas Hobbes, and John Dryden. Select one as subject for a critical essay.

6. John Aubrey's own life is of considerable interest. After reading Lytton Strachey's "John Aubrey," *Portraits in Miniature* (1931), and Anthony Powell's *John Aubrey and His Friends* (1948), try your hand at a character sketch of this witty observer of men and manners.

7. The short biography became extremely popular in seventeenth-century England. Prepare a detailed outline of its general approach and structure after reading any two of the following books: Izaac Walton's lives of John Donne (1640), Richard Hooker (1665), and George Herbert (1670); Bishop Thomas Sprat's *Life of Abraham Cowley* (1668); or John Dryden's *Life of Plutarch* (1683). (For background, see Waldo H. Dunn's *English Biography* [1916] and Donald A. Stauffer's *English Biography Before 1700* [1930].)

from

GRACE
ABOUNDING

John Bunyan

John Bunyan (1628–1688) ranks as one of the most surprising narrative geniuses who have written in the English language. The son of an impoverished Bedfordshire tinker, he was trained in his father's trade and received little formal education. He spent two teen-age years in Cromwell's Parliamentary army, then worked as a tinker, married at about twenty, and experienced several years of intense soul-searching and spiritual conflict. He later lamented that he had soiled his youth with lying, swearing, cursing, dancing, ringing the church bell, and playing tip-cat on Sunday. Such heinous misdeeds worked on his vivid imagination and sensitive conscience to produce visions, fears, and doubts.

His first wife's dowry consisted of two books of piety, The Plain Man's Pathway to Heaven and The Practice of Piety; these volumes strongly influenced his thinking—as did his constant reading of Scripture. He was, as he put it, "never out of the Bible either by reading or meditation." In 1653 Bunyan joined a Baptist church in Bedford; and after his wife's death, in about 1656, he became an itinerant "mechanick" preacher.

He married again, in 1659, and following the Restoration, he was thrown into prison for being an unlicensed preacher. There he spent most of the ensuing twelve years because of his religious views and preachings. He put his prison time to good use, reading and re-reading the Bible, Foxe's "Book of Martyrs," and other religious works. But above all he wrote; most of his sixty-odd books and tracts were written in prison. In his later years he preached in the vicinity of London, dying in 1688 of a cold contracted on a journey undertaken to reconcile an estranged father and son.

Bunyan's works have placed his name on the honor roll of significant English writers. His natural story-telling, allegorical, and satirical talents are revealed in religious narratives such as The Holy City (1665), The Pilgrim's Progress (Part I, 1678; Part II, 1684), The Life and Death of Mr. Badman (1680), and The Holy War (1682). These narratives also reveal Bunyan's Hogarthian flair for describing the life of his time.

Most of these qualities are discernible in his spiritual autobiography, Grace Abounding to the Chief of Sinners (1666). In it Bunyan recorded his traumatic struggle against error and described his conversion and call to minister to others. The opening section follows.

* * * * *

In this my relation of the merciful working of God upon my soul, it will not be amiss, if in the first place, I do, in a few words, give you a hint of my pedigree and manner of bringing up; that thereby the goodness and bounty of God towards me may be the more advanced and magnified before the sons of men.

For my descent then, it was, as is well known by many, of a low and inconsiderable generation; my father's house being of that rank that is meanest, and most despised of all the families in the land. Wherefore I have not here, as others, to boast of noble blood, or of a high-born state, according to the flesh; though, all things considered, I magnify the Heavenly Majesty, for that by this door he brought me into this world, to partake of the grace and life that is in Christ by the Gospel.

But yet, notwithstanding the meanness and inconsiderableness of my parents, it pleased God to put it into their hearts to put me to school, to learn both to read and write; the which I also attained, according to the rate of other poor men's children, though to my shame I confess, I did soon lose that little I learned, even almost utterly, and that long before the Lord did work his gracious work of conversion upon my soul.

As for my own natural life, for the time that I was without God in the world, it was indeed 'according to the course of this world, and the spirit that now worketh in the children of disobedience' (Eph. 2. 2, 3). It was my delight to be 'taken captive by the Devil at his will' (2 Tim. 2. 26), being filled with all unrighteousness; the which did also so strongly work and put forth itself, both in my heart and life, and that from a child, that I had but few equals (especially considering my years, which were tender, being few), both for cursing, swearing, lying and blaspheming the holy name of God.

Yea, so settled and rooted was I in these things that they became as a second nature to me; the which, as I also have with soberness considered since, did so offend the Lord that even in my childhood he did scare and affright me with fearful dreams and did terrify me with dreadful visions. For often, after I had spent this and the other day in sin, I have in my bed been greatly afflicted, while asleep, with the apprehensions of devils and wicked spirits, who still, as I then thought, laboured to draw me away with them; of which I could never be rid.

Also I should at these years be greatly afflicted and troubled with the thoughts of the Day of Judgment, and that both night and day, and should tremble at the thoughts of the fearful torments of hell-fire; still fearing that it would be my lot to be found at last amongst those devils and hellish fiends who are there bound down with the chains and bonds of eternal darkness.

These things, I say, when I was but a child, about nine or ten years old, did so distress my soul, that then, in the midst of my many sports and childish vanities, amidst my vain companions, I was often much cast down and afflicted in my mind therewith, yet could I not let go my sins: yea, I was so overcome with despair of life and heaven, that then I should often wish, either that there had been no hell, or that I had been a devil; supposing they were only tormentors; that if it must needs be, that I indeed went thither, I might be rather a tormentor, than tormented myself.

A while after, these terrible dreams did leave me, which also I soon forgot; for my pleasures did quickly cut off the remembrance of them, as if they had never been. Wherefore, with more greediness, according to the strength of nature, I did still let loose the reins to my lusts, and delighted in all transgression against the law of God: so that until I came to the state of marriage, I was the very ringleader of all the youth that kept me company, into all manner of vice and ungodliness.

Yea, such prevalency had the lusts and fruits of the flesh in this poor soul of mine that, had not a miracle of precious grace prevented, I had not only perished by the stroke of eternal justice, but had also laid myself open, even to the stroke of those laws which bring some to disgrace and open shame before the face of the world.

In these days, the thoughts of religion was very grievous to me; I could neither endure it myself, nor that any other should; so that when I have but seen some read in those books that concerned Christian piety, it would be as it were a prison to me. Then I said unto God, 'Depart from me, for I desire not the knowledge of thy ways' (Job 21. 14, 15). I was now void of all good consideration; heaven and hell were both out of sight and mind; and as for saving and damning, they were least in my thoughts. 'O Lord, thou knowest my life, and my ways were not hid from thee.'

Yet this I well remember, that though I could myself sin with the greatest delight and ease, and also take pleasure in the vileness of my companions; yet even then, if I have at any time seen wicked things by those who professed goodness, it would make my spirit tremble. As once above all the rest, when I was in my heighth of vanity, yet hearing one to swear that was reckoned for a religious man, it had so great a stroke upon my spirit, as it made my heart to ache.

But God did not utterly leave me, but followed me still, not now with convictions, but judgements, yet such as were mixed with mercy. For once I fell into a crick of the sea, and hardly escaped drowning. Another time I fell out of a boat into Bedford River, but mercy yet preserved me alive. Besides, another time being in the field with one of my companions, it chanced that an adder passed over the highway, so I having a stick in mine hand, struck her over the back; and having stounded her, I forced open her mouth with my stick, and plucked her sting out with my fingers, by which act had not God been merciful to me, I might by my desperateness have brought myself to mine end.

This also have I taken notice of with thanksgiving. When I was a soldier, I with others were drawn out to go to such a place to besiege it;

but when I was just ready to go, one of the company desired to go in my room, to which, when I had consented, he took my place; and coming to the siege, as he stood sentinel, he was shot into the head with a musket bullet and died.

Here, as I said, were judgements and mercy, but neither of them did awaken my soul to righteousness, wherefore I sinned still, and grew more and more rebellious against God, and careless of mine own salvation.

Presently after this, I changed my condition into a married state, and my mercy was to light upon a wife whose father was counted godly. This woman and I, though we came together as poor as poor might be (not having so much household stuff as a dish or spoon betwixt us both), yet this she had for her part, *The Plain Man's Pathway to Heaven* and *The Practice of Piety*, which her father had left her when he died. In these two books I should sometimes read with her, wherein I also found some things that were somewhat pleasing to me (but all this while I met with no conviction). She also would be often telling of me what a godly man her father was, and how he would reprove and correct vice, both in his house and amongst his neighbours; what a strict and holy life he lived in his day, both in word and deed.

Wherefore these books, with this relation, though they did not reach my heart to awaken it about my sad and sinful state, yet they did beget within me some desires to religion: so that, because I knew no better, I fell in very eagerly with the religion of the times, to wit, to go to church twice a day, and that too with the foremost, and there should very devoutly both say and sing as others did, yet retaining my wicked life. But withal, I was so overrun with the spirit of superstition that I adored, and that with great devotion, even all things (both the high place, priest, clerk, vestments, service, and what else) belonging to the church; counting all things holy that were therein contained; and especially the priest and clerk most happy, and without doubt greatly blessed, because they were the servants, as I then thought, of God, and were principal in the holy temple, to do his work therein.

This conceit grew so strong in little time upon my spirit that had I but seen a priest (though never so sordid and debauched in his life), I should find my spirit fall under him, reverence him, and knit unto him; yea, I thought for the love I did bear unto them (supposing they were the ministers of God), I could have lain down at their feet and have been trampled upon by them; their name, their garb, and work did so intoxicate and bewitch me.

After I had been thus for some considerable time, another thought came into my mind, and that was, whether we were of the Israelites or no? For finding in the Scriptures that they were once the peculiar people of God, thought I, if I were one of this race, my soul must needs be happy. Now again I found within me a great longing to be resolved about this question, but could not tell how I should. At last I asked my father of it, who told me, no, we were not. Wherefore then I fell in my spirit as to the hopes of that and so remained.

But all this while, I was not sensible of the danger and evil of sin; I was kept from considering that sin would damn me, what religion soever I followed, unless I was found in Christ. Nay, I never thought of him, nor whether there was one or no. 'Thus man, while blind, doth wander, but wearieth himself with vanity: for he knoweth not the way to the City of God' (Eccles. 10. 15).

But one day (amongst all the sermons our parson made) his subject was, to treat of the Sabbath day, and of the evil of breaking that, either with labour, sports, or otherwise (now I was, notwithstanding my religion, one that took much delight in all manner of vice, and especially that was the day that I did solace myself therewith). Wherefore I fell in my conscience under his sermon, thinking and believing that he made that sermon on purpose to shew me my evil-doing; and at that time I felt what guilt was, though never before, that I can remember; but then I was for the present greatly loaden therewith, and so went home when the sermon was ended, with a great burden upon my spirit.

This, for that instant, did benumb the sinews of my best delights, and did imbitter my former pleasures to me. But behold, it lasted not; for before I had well dined, the trouble began to go off my mind, and my heart returned to its old course: but oh how glad was I, that this trouble was gone from me, and that the fire was put out, that I might sin again without control! Wherefore, when I had satisfied nature with my food, I shook the sermon out of my mind, and to my old custom of sports and gaming I returned with great delight.

But the same day, as I was in the midst of a game at cat, and having struck it one blow from the hole, just as I was about to strike it the second time, a voice did suddenly dart from heaven into my soul, which said, 'Wilt thou leave thy sins, and go to heaven? Or have thy sins, and go to hell?' At this I was put to an exceeding maze; wherefore, leaving my cat upon the ground, I looked up to heaven, and was as if I had, with the eyes of my understanding, seen the Lord Jesus looking down upon me, as being very hotly displeased with me, and as if he did severely threaten me with some grievous punishment for these and other my ungodly practices.

I had no sooner thus conceived in my mind, but suddenly this conclusion was fastened on my spirit (for the former hint did set my sins again before my face), that I had been a great and grievous sinner, and that it was now too late for me to look after heaven; for Christ would not forgive me, nor pardon my transgressions. Then I fell to musing upon this also; and while I was thinking on it, and fearing lest it should be so, I felt my heart sink in despair, concluding it was too late; and therefore I resolved in my mind I would go on in sin. For thought I, if the case be thus, my state is surely miserable; miserable if I leave my sins, and but miserable if I follow them. I can but be damned; and if I must be so, I had as good be damned for many sins, as be damned for few.

Thus I stood in the midst of my play, before all that then were present; but yet I told them nothing. But, I say, I having made this conclusion, I returned desperately to my sport again; and I well remember that presently this kind of despair did so possess my soul that I was persuaded I could never attain to other comfort than what I should get in sin; for heaven was gone already, so that on that I must not think. Wherefore I found within me a great desire to take my fill of sin, still studying what sin was set to be committed, that I might taste the sweetness of it; and I made as much haste as I could to fill my belly with its delicates, lest I should die before I had my desire; for that I feared greatly. In these things, I protest before God, I lie not, neither do I feign this sort of speech: these were really, strongly, and with all my heart, my desires. The good Lord, whose mercy is unsearchable, forgive me my transgressions!

And I am very confident that this temptation of the devil is more than usual amongst poor creatures than many are aware of, even to overrun their spirits with a scurfy and seared frame of heart, and benumbing of conscience; which frame, he stilly and slyly supplieth with such despair that though not much guilt attendeth the soul, yet they continually have a secret conclusion within them, that there is no hopes for them; 'for they have loved sins, therefore after them they will go' (Jer. 2. 25 & 18. 12).

Now therefore I went on in sin with great greediness of mind, still grudging that I could not be so satisfied with it as I would: this did continue with me about a month, or more. But one day, as I was standing at a neighbour's shop-window, and there cursing and swearing, and playing the madman, after my wonted manner, there sat within the woman of the house, and heard me; who, though she was a very loose and ungodly wretch, yet protested that I swore and cursed at that most fearful rate, that she was made to tremble to hear me; and told me further that I was the ungodliest fellow for swearing that ever she heard in all her life; and that I, by thus doing, was able to spoil all the youth in a whole town, if they came but in my company.

At this reproof I was silenced, and put to secret shame; and that too, as I thought, before the God of heaven. Wherefore, while I stood there, and hanging down my head, I wished with all my heart that I might be a little child again, that my father might learn me to speak without this wicked way of swearing; for, thought I, I am so accustomed to it, that it is but in vain for me to think of a reformation, for I thought it could never be.

But, how it came to pass I know not, I did from this time forward so leave my swearing that it was a great wonder to myself to observe it; and whereas before I knew not how to speak unless I put an oath before, and another behind, to make my words have authority, now, I could, without it, speak better, and with more pleasantness than ever I could before. All this while I knew not Jesus Christ, neither did I leave my sports and play.

But quickly after this, I fell in company with one poor man that made profession of religion; who, as I then thought, did talk pleasantly of the Scriptures, and of the matters of religion: wherefore falling into some love and liking to what he said, I betook me to my Bible, and began to take great pleasure in reading, but especially with the historical part thereof. For, as for Paul's Epistles, and Scriptures of that nature, I could not away with them, being as yet but ignorant either of the corruptions of my nature, or of the want and worth of Jesus Christ to save me.

Wherefore I fell to some outward reformation, both in my words and life, and did set the commandments before me for my way to heaven: which commandments I also did strive to keep, and, as I thought, did keep them pretty well sometimes, and then I should have comfort; yet now and then should break one, and so afflict my conscience; but then I should repent, and say I was sorry for it, and promise God to do better next time, and there get help again, for then I thought I pleased God as well as any man in England.

Thus I continued about a year, all which time our neighbours did take me to be a very godly man, a new and religious man, and did marvel much to see such a great and famous alteration in my life and manners; and indeed so it was, though yet I knew not Christ, nor grace, nor faith, nor hope. And, truly, as I have well seen since, had I then died, my state had been most fearful. Well, this I say, continued about a twelve-month, or more.

But, I say, my neighbours were amazed at this my great conversion, from prodigious profaneness to something like a moral life. And, truly, so they well might; for this my conversion was as great, as for Tom of Bethlem to become a sober man. Now, therefore, they began to praise, to commend, and to speak well of me, both to my face, and behind my back. Now I was, as they said, become godly; now I was become a right honest man. But oh! when I understood that these were their words and opinions of me, it pleased me mighty well. For though, as yet, I was nothing but a poor painted hypocrite, yet I loved to be talked of as one that was truly godly. I was proud of my godliness, and I did all I did either to be seen of, or to be well spoken of, by men; well, this I say, continued for about a twelve-month or more.

Now you must know that before this I had taken much delight in ringing, but my conscience beginning to be tender, I thought that such a practice was but vain, and therefore forced myself to leave it, yet my mind hankered. Wherefore I should go to the steeple house and look on, though I durst not ring. But I thought this did not become religion neither, yet I forced myself and would look on still; but quickly after, I began to think, how if one of the bells should fall? Then I chose to stand under a main beam that lay over thwart the steeple from side to side, thinking there I might stand sure. But then I should think again, should the bell fall with a swing, it might first hit the wall, and then rebounding upon me, might kill me for all this beam; this made me stand in the steeple door, and now thought I, I am safe enough, for if a bell should then fall, I can slip out behind these thick walls, and so be preserved notwithstanding.

So after this, I would yet go to see them ring, but would not go further than the steeple door; but then it came into my head, how if the steeple itself should fall, and this thought (it may fall for aught I know) would when I stood and looked on, continually so shake my mind, that I durst not stand at the steeple door any longer, but was forced to fly, for fear it should fall upon my head.

Another thing was my dancing. I was a full year before I could quite leave it; but all this while, when I thought I kept this or that commandment, or did by word or deed anything that I thought were good, I had great peace in my conscience, and should think with myself, God cannot choose but be now pleased with me. Yea, to relate it in mine own way, I thought no man in England could please God better than I.

But poor wretch as I was, I was all this while ignorant of Jesus Christ, and going about to establish my own righteousness, had perished therein, had not God in mercy shewed me more of my state by nature.

But upon a day, the good providence of God did cast me to Bedford, to work on my calling, and in one of the streets of that town, I came where there was three or four poor women sitting at a door in the sun, and talking about the things of God; and being now willing to hear them discourse, I drew near to hear what they said, for I was now a brisk talker also myself in the matters of religion. But now I may say, 'I heard, but I understood not'; for they were far above out of my reach, for their talk was about a new birth, the work of God on their hearts, also how they were convinced of their miserable state by nature. They talked how God had visited their souls with his love in the Lord Jesus, and with what words and promises they had been refreshed, comforted, and supported against the temptations of the Devil; moreover, they reasoned of the suggestions and temptations of Satan in particular, and told to each other by which they had been afflicted, and how they were borne up under his assaults. They also discoursed of their own wretchedness of heart, of their unbelief, and did contemn, slight, and abhor their own righteousness, as filthy and insufficient to do them any good.

And methought they spake as if joy did make them speak: they spake with such pleasantness of Scripture language, and with such appearance of grace in all they said, that they were to me as if they had found a new world, as if they were 'people that dwelt alone, and were not to be reckoned among their neighbours' (Num. 23.9).

At this I felt my own heart began to shake, as mistrusting my condition to be naught; for I saw that in all my thoughts about religion and salvation, the new birth did never enter into my mind, neither knew I the comfort of the word and promise, nor the deceitfulness and treachery of my own wicked heart. As for secret thoughts, I took no notice of them; neither did I understand what Satan's temptations were, nor how they were to be withstood and resisted, etc.

Thus, therefore, when I had heard and considered what they said, I left them, and went about my employment again, but their talk and discourse went with me; also my heart would tarry with them, for I was greatly affected with their words, both because by them I was convinced that I wanted the true tokens of a truly godly man and also because by them I was convinced of the happy and blessed condition of him that was such a one.

Therefore I should often make it my business to be going again and again into the company of these poor people; for I could not stay away. And the more I went amongst them, the more I did question my condition; and as still I do remember, presently I found two things within me, at which I did sometimes marvel (especially concerning what a blind, ignorant, sordid, and ungodly wretch but just before I was): the one was a very great softness and tenderness of heart, which caused me to fall under the conviction of what by Scripture they asserted; and the other was a great bending in my mind to a continual meditating on them, and on all other good things which at any time I heard or read of.

· · · · ·

✓ Suggestions for Reading and Writing

1. Does Bunyan's confession that he led his youthful companions "into all manner of vice and ungodliness" seem convincing—or merely the traditional lament of the ultra-pious?
2. Does his transition from sinner to saint bear any characteristics of the stereotyped conversion?

3. *Grace Abounding*'s humble expression of faith, hope, and humility has caused it to be viewed as the nearest Protestant equivalent of Saint Augustine's *Confessions*. After reading extensively in both, point out their most significant similarities and differences.

4. In *A Confession of My Faith and A Reason of My Practice* (1672), Bunyan continues the spiritual odyssey begun in *Grace Abounding*. Read both and then write a portrait of the spirit of this highly strung, religiously torn, semi-literate genius. (For background, see such standard studies as G. B. Harrison's *John Bunyan: A Study in Personality* [1928], William Y. Tindall's *John Bunyan, Mechanick Preacher* [1934], Henri A. Talon's *John Bunyan, The Man and His Works* [1951], and Ola E. Winslow's *John Bunyan* [1961].)

5. Of all books in English, *The Pilgrim's Progress* comes closest to rivaling the Bible in popularity. Translated into about 108 languages and dialects, it has gone through innumerable editions. Read it and then try to explain its appeal.

6. An interesting paper on contrasting literary modes, styles, and imagery should result from a comparison of *The Pilgrim's Progress* with such other religious allegories as Dante's *Divine Comedy* (c. 1321) or Edmund Spenser's *The Faerie Queene* (1590).

from
DIARY

Samuel Pepys

There were two Samuel Pepyses—public servant and private person. The latter has proved easily the more fascinating. Son of a poor London tailor, Pepys (1633–1703) attended (with the help of his kinsman and patron Sir Edward Montagu) St. Paul's School and Magdalene College, Cambridge. His Puritan upbringing failed to dampen a natural taste for drink, fellowship,

and a pretty face. At twenty-two, he married fifteen-year-old
Elizabeth St. Michel, with whom he spent an affectionate but
turbulent forty years.

Pepys launched his career as secretary to Montagu (whom
he refers to throughout his Diary as "my lord"). Montagu was
a keen weathercock: one of Oliver Cromwell's naval officers,
he was a leader in the restoration of Charles II and became
Admiral of the Fleet. He had Pepys appointed Clerk of the Acts
for the Navy Office. A helpful start was all Pepys needed.
Devoting his professional life to the British navy, Pepys determined to replace bureaucratic corruption and inefficiency with
discipline, order, and thoroughness.

Events conspired to bring Pepys to the fore. The plague
(1665), the London fire (1666), and the Dutch destruction of
the drydocked English fleet (1667) caused a troubled government to rely increasingly upon him. In 1673 he became Secretary
of the Admiralty and set about placing naval finances and
discipline upon the sound bases that were to insure the navy's
greatness. If Pepys managed in the process to accumulate a
sizable personal fortune, he still saved the government vast
sums. In 1679 he served in Parliament; he also was falsely
accused of treason, forced to resign from the Navy Office, and
even briefly imprisoned. Reinstated in 1684, he was in the same
year elected president of the Royal Society. The Glorious
Revolution of 1688 brought William and Mary to the throne
and sent Pepys into retirement.

Pepys's last years proved quiet but fruitful. In 1690 he
published his Memoirs Relating to the State of the Royal Navy,
for which he had long collected materials. Among the books,
prints, ballads, and broadsides he bequeathed to Magdalene
College was a three-thousand-page manuscript diary, in six
leather-bound volumes. Written in a seventeenth-century shorthand, it covered the decade from January 1, 1660, to May 31,
1669—when his failing eyesight forced Pepys to discontinue.
The manuscript gathered dust for more than a century; then, in
1825, it was deciphered, transcribed, and published in part.

The Diary is a fascinating human document. Pepys's
original purpose in keeping it is uncertain: he simply may have
wanted a record of personal activities during a memorable period
or an alibi in the event of political difficulties. More certain is
his Puritan satisfaction in recording virtually every thought and
deed. He describes, with equal zest, official and family affairs;
his own or friends' habits, vanities, amours, jealousies; Restor-

ation London's theaters, operas, and other entertainments; and such public catastrophes as the plague, the fire, and the Dutch War.

A few glib generalities cannot capture so complex and paradoxical a personality. Pepys reveals himself a selfish, egotistic materialist continually totaling his assets; at the same time, he appears a generous, amiable, kind, and loyal friend. More consistent is his deep love of music, keen eye for art and architecture, and flair for literary expression. His prose is casual but concise; vital and brimming with unconscious art, humor, and curiosity, it expresses Pepys's conscious delight in the savagery, charms, and comforts of urban life. Few have given to posterity so vividly the color and the movement of their age.

✓ ✓ ✓ ✓ ✓

[March 8, 1659/60] . . . This noon I met at the Dog Tavern Captain Philip Holland, with whom I advised how to make some advantage of my lord's going to sea, which he told me might be by having of five or six servants entered on board, and I to give them what wages I pleased, and so their pay to be mine; he was also very urgent to have me take the secretary's place that my lord did proffer me. . . .

[April 8, 1660] (Lord's day). Very calm again, and I pretty well, but my head ached all day. About noon set sail; in our way I see many vessels and masts, which are now the greatest guides for ships. We had a brave wind all the afternoon and overtook two good merchantmen that overtook us yesterday, going to the East Indies. The lieutenant and I lay out of his window with his glass, looking at the women that were on board them, being pretty handsome. . . .

[June 23, 1660] . . . So to my lord's lodgings, where Tom Guy came to me, and there stayed to see the King touch people for the king's evil. But he did not come at all, it rained so; and the poor people were forced to stand all the morning in the rain in the garden. Afterward he touched them in the banqueting house. . . .

[September 25, 1660] To the Office, where Sir W. Batten, Colonel Slingsby, and I sat awhile, and Sir R. Ford coming to us about business, we talked together of the interest of this kingdom to have a peace with Spain and a war with France and Holland; where Sir R. Ford talked like a man of great reason and experience. And afterwards I did send for a cup of tea (a China drink), of which I never had drank before, and went away. . . .

[October 7, 1660] (Lord's day). To Whitehall on foot, calling at my father's to change my long black cloak for a short one (long cloaks being now quite out); but he being gone to church, I could not get one, and therefore I proceeded on and came to my lord before he went to chapel and so went with him, where I heard Dr. Spurstow preach before the King a poor dry sermon; but a very good anthem of Captn. Cooke's afterwards. Going out of chapel I met with Jack Cole, my old friend (whom I had not seen a great while before), and have promised to renew acquaintance in London together. To my lord's and dined with him; he all dinner time talking French to me, and telling me the story how the Duke of York hath got my Lord Chancellor's daughter with child, and that she do lay it to him, and that for certain he did promise her marriage, and had signed it with his blood, but that he by stealth had got the paper out of her cabinet. And that the King would have him to marry her, but that he will not. . . .

[October 13, 1660] . . . I went out to Charing Cross, to see Major General Harrison hanged, drawn, and quartered; which was done there, he looking as cheerful as any man could do in that condition. He was presently cut down, and his head and heart shown to the people, at which there was great shouts of joy. It is said that he said that he was sure to come shortly at the right hand of Christ to judge them that now had judged him; and that his wife do expect his coming again. Thus it was my chance to see the King beheaded at Whitehall and to see the first blood shed in revenge for the blood of the King at Charing Cross. From thence to my lord's, and took Captain Cuttance and Mr. Sheply to the Sun Tavern, and did give them some oysters. After that I went by water home, where I was angry with my wife for her things lying about, and in my passion kicked the little fine basket, which I bought her in Holland, and broke it, which troubled me after I had done it. Within all the afternoon setting up shelves in my study. At night to bed.

[October 20, 1660] . . . To my lord's by land, calling at several places about business, where I dined with my lord and lady; when he was very merry, and did talk very high how he would have a French cook, and a master of his horse, and his lady and child to wear black patches; which methought was strange, but he is become a perfect courtier; and, among other things, my lady saying that she could get a good merchant for her daughter Jem., he answered that he would rather see her with a pedlar's pack at her back, so she married a gentleman, than she should marry a citizen. This afternoon, going through London, and calling at Crowe's, the upholsterer's, in Saint Bartholomew's, I saw the limbs of some of our new traitors set upon Aldersgate, which was a sad sight to see; and a bloody week this and the last have been, there being ten hanged, drawn, and quartered. Home, and after writing a letter to my uncle by the post, I went to bed.

[November 12, 1660] . . . My father and I took occasion to go

forth, and went and drank at Mr. Standing's, and there discoursed
seriously about my sister's coming to live with me, which I have much
mind for her good to have, and yet I am much afeared of her ill nature.
Coming home again, he and I, and my wife, my mother and Pall, went
all together into the little room, and there I told her plainly what my
mind was, to have her come not as a sister in any respect, but as a servant,
which she promised me that she would, and with many thanks did weep
for joy, which did give me and my wife some content and satisfaction. . . .

[November 22, 1660] . . . Mr. Fox came in presently and did
receive us with a great deal of respect; and then did take my wife and I to
the Queen's presence-chamber, where he got my wife placed behind the
Queen's chair, and I got into the crowd, and by and by the queen and
the two Princesses came to dinner. The Queen, a very little plain old
woman, and nothing more in her presence in any respect nor garb than
any ordinary woman. The Princess of Orange I had often seen before.
The Princess Henrietta is very pretty, but much below my expectation;
and her dressing of herself with her hair frizzed short up to her ears did
make her seem so much the less to me. But my wife standing near her
with two or three black patches on, and well dressed, did seem to me
much handsomer than she. . . .

[December 4, 1660] . . . This day the Parliament voted that the
bodies of Oliver, Ireton, Bradshaw, etc., should be taken up out of their
graves in the Abbey and drawn to the gallows, and there hanged and
buried under it: which (methinks) do trouble me that a man of so great
courage as he was should have that dishonour, though otherwise he
might deserve it enough.

[January 28, 1660/61] . . . I went to Mr. Crew's and thence to the
theatre, where I saw again *The Lost Lady*, which do now please me
better than before; and here I sitting behind in a dark place, a lady spit
backward upon me by a mistake, not seeing me, but after seeing her to be
a very pretty lady, I was not troubled at it at all. . . .

[March 25, 1660/61] . . . Then to my father's, and there stayed
talking with my mother and him late about my dinner tomorrow. So
homewards and took up a boy that had a lanthorn, that was picking up of
rags, and got him to light me home, and had great discourse with him
how he could get sometimes three or four bushels of rags in a day, and
got 3*d.* a bushel for them, and many other discourses, what and how
many ways there are for poor children to get their livings hon-
estly. . . .

[April 10, 1661] . . . Here we had, for my sake, two fiddles, the one
a base viol, on which he that played, played well some lyre lessons, but
both together made the worst music that ever I heard. We had a fine

collation, but I took little pleasure in that, for the illness of the music and for the intentness of my mind upon Mrs. Rebecca Allen. After we had done eating, the ladies went to dance, and among the men we had, I was forced to dance too; and did make an ugly shift. Mrs. R. Allen danced very well, and seems the best humoured woman that ever I saw. About nine o'clock Sir William and my lady went home, and we continued dancing an hour or two, and so broke up very pleasant and merry, and so walked home, I leading Mrs. Rebecca, who seemed, I know not why, in that and other things, to be desirous of my favours and would in all things show me respects. Going home, she would needs have me sing, and I did pretty well and was highly esteemed by them. So to Captain Allen's (where we were last night and heard him play on the harpsichord, and I find him to be a perfect good musician) and there, having no mind to leave Mrs. Rebecca, what with talk and singing (her father and I), Mrs. Turner and I stayed there till two o'clock in the morning and was most exceeding merry, and I had the opportunity of kissing Mrs. Rebecca very often. . . .

[April 11, 1661] At two o'clock, with very great mirth, we went to our lodging and to bed, and lay till seven, and then called up by Sir W. Batten, so I arose and we did some business, and then came Captn. Allen, and he and I withdrew and sang a song or two, and among others took pleasure in 'Go and be hanged, that's good-bye.' The young ladies come too, and so I did again please myself with Mrs. Rebecca, and about nine o'clock, after we had breakfasted, we set forth for London, and indeed I was a little troubled to part with Mrs. Rebecca, for which God forgive me. Thus we went away through Rochester, calling and taking leave of Mr. Alcock at the door, Captn. Cuttance going with us. We baited at Dartford, and thence to London, but of all the journeys that ever I made this was the merriest, and I was in a strange mood for mirth. Among other things, I got my lady to let her maid, Mrs. Anne, to ride all the way on horseback, and she rides exceeding well; and so I called her my clerk, that she went to wait upon me. I met two little schoolboys going with pitchers of ale to their schoolmaster to break up against Easter, and I did drink of some of one of them and give him twopence. By and by we come to two little girls keeping cows, and I saw one of them very pretty, so I had a mind to make her ask my blessing, and telling her that I was her godfather, she asked me innocently whether I was not Ned Wooding, and I said that I was, so she kneeled down and very simply called, 'Pray, godfather, pray to God to bless me,' which made us very merry, and I gave her twopence. In several places, I asked women whether they would sell me their children, but they denied me all, but said they would give me one to keep for them, if I would. Mrs. Anne and I rode under the man that hangs upon Shooter's Hill, and a filthy sight it was to see how his flesh is shrunk to his bones. So home and I found all well, and a deal of work done since I went. I sent to see how my wife do, who is well, and my brother John come from Cambridge. To Sir W. Batten's and there supped, and very merry with the young ladies. So to bed very sleepy for last night's work, concluding that it is the pleasantest journey in all respects that ever I had in my life.

[April 23, 1661] About four I rose and got to the Abbey, where I followed Sir J. Denham, the surveyor, with some company that he was leading in. And with much ado, by the favour of Mr. Cooper, his man, did get up into a great scaffold across the north end of the Abbey, where with a great deal of patience I sat from past four till eleven before the King came in. And a great pleasure it was to see the Abbey raised in the middle, all covered with red, and a throne (that is a chair) and footstool on the top of it; and all the officers of all kinds, so much as the very fiddlers, in red vests. At last comes in the Dean and prebends of Westminster, with the bishops (many of them in cloth of gold copes), and after them the nobility, all in their Parliament robes, which was a most magnificent sight. Then the Duke, and the King with a scepter (carried by my Lord Sandwich) and sword and mond before him, and the crown too. The King in his robes, bare-headed, which was very fine. And after all had placed themselves, there was a sermon and the service; and then in the quire at the high altar, the King passed through all the ceremonies of the coronation which to my great grief I and most in the Abbey could not see. The crown being put upon his head, a great shout begun, and he came forth to the throne, and there passed more ceremonies: as taking the oath, and having things read to him by the Bishop; and his lords (who put on their caps as soon as the King put on his crown) and bishops come, and kneeled before him. And three times the King at Arms went to the three open places on the scaffold and proclaimed that if anyone could show any reason why Charles Stuart should not be King of England, that now he should come and speak. And a general pardon also was read by the Lord Chancellor, and medals flung up and down by my Lord Cornwallis, of silver, but I could not come by any. But so great a noise that I could make but little of the music; and indeed, it was lost to everybody. But I had so great a lust to . . . that I went out a little while before the King had done all his ceremonies, and went round the Abbey to Westminster Hall, all the way within rails, and 10,000 people, with the ground covered with blue cloth; and scaffolds all the way. Into the Hall I got, where it was very fine with hangings and scaffolds one upon another full of brave ladies; and my wife in one little one, on the right hand. Here I stayed walking up and down, and at last upon one of the side stalls I stood and saw the King come in with all the persons (but the soldiers) that were yesterday in the cavalcade; and a most pleasant sight it was to see them in their several robes. And the King came in with his crown on, and his sceptre in his hand, under a canopy borne up by six silver staves, carried by Barons of the Cinque Ports, and little bells at every end. And after a long time, he got up to the farther end, and all set themselves down at their several tables; and that was also a brave sight; and the King's first course carried up by the Knights of the Bath. And many fine ceremonies there was of the heralds leading up people before him, and bowing; and my Lord of Albemarle's going to the kitchen and eat a bit of the first dish that was to go to the King's table. But, above all, was these three lords, Northumberland and Suffolk and the Duke of Ormond, coming before the courses on horseback, and staying so all dinner-time, and at last to bring up [Dymock] the King's champion, all in armour on horseback, with his spear and target carried before him. And a herald proclaims 'That if any dare deny Charles Stuart to be lawful King of England, here was a champion that would fight with him'; and with these words, the champion flings down his gauntlet, and all this he do three times in his going up towards the King's table. At last when he is come, the King drinks to him, and then sends him the cup which is of gold, and he drinks it off, and then rides back again with the cup in his hand. I went from table to table to see the bishops and all others at their dinner, and was infinitely pleased with it. And at the lords' table, I met with William Howe, and he spoke to my lord for me, and he did give me four rabbits and a pullet, and so I got it and Mr. Creed and I got Mr. Michell to give us some bread, and so we at a stall eat it, as everybody else did what they could get. I took a great deal of pleasure to go up and down, and look upon the ladies, and to hear the music of all sorts, but above all, the 24 violins. About six at night they had dined, and I went up to my wife, and there met with a pretty lady (Mrs. Frankleyn, a doctor's wife, a friend of Mr. Bowyer's), and kissed them both, and by and by took them down to Mr. Bowyer's. And strange it is to think, that these two days have held up fair till now that all is done, and the King gone out of the Hall; and then it fell a-raining and thundering and lightning as I have not seen it do for some years: which people did take great notice of; God's blessing of the work of these two days, which is a foolery to take too much notice of such things. I observed little disorder in all this, but only the King's footmen had got hold of the canopy, and would keep it from the Barons of the Cinque Ports, which they endeavoured to force from them again, but could not do it till my Lord Duke of Albemarle caused it to be put into Sir R. Pye's hand till tomorrow to be decided. At Mr. Bowyer's; a great deal of company, some I knew, others I did not. Here we stayed upon the leads and below till it was late, expecting to see the fireworks, but they were not performed tonight: only the city had a light like a glory round about it with bonfires. At last I went to King Street, and there sent Crockford to my father's and my house, to tell them I could not come home tonight, because of the dirt, and a coach could not be had. And so after drinking a pot of ale alone at Mrs. Harper's I returned to Mr. Bowyer's, and after a little stay more I took my wife and Mrs. Frankleyn (who I proffered the civility of lying with my wife at Mrs. Hunt's tonight) to Axeyard, in which at the further end there were three great bonfires, and a great many great gallants, men and women; and they laid hold of us, and would have us drink the King's health upon our knees, kneeling upon a faggot, which we all did, they drinking to us one after another. Which we thought a strange frolic; but these gallants continued thus a great while, and I wondered to see how the ladies did tipple. At last I sent my wife and her bedfellow to bed, and Mr. Hunt and I went in with Mr. Thornbury (who did give the company all their wine, he being yeoman of the wine cellar to the King) to his house; and there, with his wife and two of his sisters, and some gallant sparks that were there, we drank the King's health, and nothing else, till one of the gentlemen fell down stark drunk and there lay spewing; and I went to my lord's pretty well. But no sooner a-bed with Mr. Shepley but my head began to hum, and I to vomit, and if ever I was foxed it was now, which I cannot say yet, because I fell asleep and slept till morning. Only when I waked I found myself wet with my spewing. Thus did the day end with joy everywhere; and blessed be God, I have not heard of any mischance to anybody through it all, but only to Sergeant Glynne, whose horse fell upon him yesterday, and is like to kill him, which people do please themselves to see how just God is to punish the rogue at such a time as this; he being now one of the King's sergeants, and rode in the cavalcade with Maynard, to whom people wish the same fortune. There was also this night in King Street, [a woman] had her eye put out by a boy's flinging a firebrand into the coach. Now, after all this, I can say that, besides the pleasure of the sight of these glorious things, I may now shut my eyes against any other objects, nor for the future trouble myself to see things of state and show, as being sure never to see the like again in this world.

[April 24, 1661] Waked in the morning with my head in a sad taking through the last night's drink, which I am very sorry for; so rose and went out with Mr. Creed to drink our morning draft, which he did give me in chocolate to settle my stomach. . . .

[June 5, 1661] This morning did give my wife £4 to lay out upon lace and other things for herself. I to Wardrobe and so to Whitehall and Westminster, where I dined with my lord and Ned Pickering alone at his lodgings. After dinner to the office, where we sat and did business, and Sir W. Penn and I went home with Sir R. Slingsby to bowls in his alley, and there had good sport, and afterwards went in and drank and talked. So home Sir William and I, and it being very hot weather I took my flageolette and played upon the leads in the garden, where Sir W. Penn came out in his shirt into his leads, and there we stayed talking and singing and drinking great drafts of claret, and eating botargo and bread and butter till twelve at night, it being moonshine; and so to bed, very near fuddled.

[July 2, 1661] To Westminster Hall and there walked up and down, it being term time. Spoke with several, among others my cousin Roger Pepys, who was going up to the Parliament House, and inquired whether I had heard from my father since he went to Brampton, which I had done yesterday, who writes that my uncle is by fits stupid, and like a man that is drunk, and sometimes speechless. Home, and after my singing master had done, took coach and went to Sir William Davenant's opera; this being the fourth day that it hath begun and the first that I have seen it. Today was acted the second part of *The Siege of Rhodes.*We stayed a very great while for the king and the queen of Bohemia. And by the breaking of a board over our heads, we had a great deal of dust fell into the ladies' necks and the men's hair, which made good sport. The king being come, the scene opened; which indeed is very fine and magnificent, and well acted, all but the eunuch, who was so much out that he was hissed off the stage. . . .

[July 6, 1661] Waked this morning with news, brought me by a messenger on purpose, that my uncle Robert is dead, and died yesterday; so I rose sorry in some respect, glad in my expectations in another respect. So I made myself ready, went and told my uncle Wight, my lady, and some others thereof, and bought me a pair of boots in St. Martin's, and got myself ready, and then to the Post House and set out about eleven and twelve o'clock, taking the messenger with me that came to me, and so we rode and got well by nine o'clock to Brampton, where I found my father well. My uncle's corpse in a coffin standing upon joint-stools in the chimney in the hall; but it begun to smell, and so I caused it to be set forth in the yard all night, and watched by two men. My aunt I found in bed in a most nasty ugly pickle, made me sick to see it. My father and I lay together tonight, I greedy to see the will, but did not ask to see it till tomorrow.

[July 8–13, 1661] I fell to work, and my father to look over my uncle's papers and clothes, and continued all this week upon that business, much troubled with my aunt's base, ugly humours. We had news of Tom Trice's putting in a caveat against us, in behalf of his mother, to whom my uncle hath not given anything, and for good reason therein expressed, which troubled us also. But above all, our trouble is to find that his estate appears nothing as we expected, and all the world believes; nor his papers so well sorted as I would have had them, but all in confusion, that break my brains to understand them. . . .

[August 24, 1661] . . . called to Sir W. Batten's to see the strange creature that Captain Holmes hath brought with him from Guinea; it is a great baboon, but so much like a man in most things, that though they say there is a species of them, yet I cannot believe but that it is a monster got of a man and she-baboon. I do believe that it already understands much English, and I am of the mind it might be taught to speak or make signs. . . .

[September 7, 1661] . . . to the theatre, where we seated ourselves close by the King and Duke of York and Madame Palmer, which was great content; and, indeed, I can never enough admire her beauty. And here was *Bartholomew Fair*, with the puppet show, acted today, which had not been these forty years (it being so satirical against Puritanism, they durst not till now, which is strange they should already dare to do it, and the King to countenance it), but I do never a whit like it the better for the puppets, but rather the worse. . . .

[December 9, 1661] . . . At noon to dinner to the Wardrobe; where my Lady Wright was, who did talk much upon the worth and the desert of gallantry; and that there was none fit to be courtiers, but such as have been abroad and know fashions. Which I endeavoured to oppose; and was troubled to hear her talk so, though she be a very wise and discreet lady in other things. . . .

[December 31, 1661] My wife and I this morning to the painter's, and there she sat the last time, and I stood by and did tell him some little things to do, that now her picture I think will please me very well; and after her, her little black dog sat in her lap, and was drawn, which made us very merry; so home to dinner, and so to the office; and there late finishing our estimate of the debts of the Navy to this day; and it come to near £374,000. So home, and after supper and my barber had trimmed me, I sat down to end my journal for this year, and my condition at this time, by God's blessing, is thus: my health (only upon catching cold, which brings great pain in my back . . . as it used to be when I had the stone) is very good, and so my wife's in all respects. My servants, W. Hewer, Sarah, Nell, and Wayneman; my house at the Navy Office. I suppose myself to be worth about £500 clear in the world, and my goods of my house my own, and what is coming to me from Brampton, when my father dies, which God defer. . . . I am also upon writing a little treatise to present to the Duke, about our privilege in the seas, as to other nations striking their flags to us. But my greatest trouble is that I have for this last half year been a very great spendthrift in all manner of respects, that I am afeard to cast up my accounts, though I hope I am worth what I say above. But I will cast them up very shortly. I have newly taken a

solemn oath about abstaining from plays and wine, which I am resolved
to keep according to the letter of the oath which I keep by me. . . .

[March 1, 1661/62] . . . Thence my wife and I by coach, first to
see my little picture that is a drawing, and thence to the opera, and there
saw *Romeo and Juliet*, the first time it was ever acted; but it is a play of
itself the worst that ever I heard in my life, and the worst acted that ever
I saw these people do, and I am resolved to go no more to see the first
time of acting, for they were all of them out more or less. Thence home,
and after supper and wrote by the post, I settled to what I had long
intended, to cast up my accounts with myself, and after much pains to do
it and great fear, I do find that I am £500 in money beforehand in the
world, which I was afraid I was not, but I find that I had spent above
£250 this last half year, which troubles me much. . . .

[August 23, 1662] . . . Anon come the King and Queen in a barge
under a canopy with 10,000 barges and boats, I think, for we could see no
water for them, nor discern the King nor Queen. And so they landed at
Whitehall Bridge, and the great guns on the other side went off. But that
which pleased me best was that my Lady Castlemaine stood over against
us upon a piece of Whitehall, where I glutted myself with looking on
her. But methought it was strange to see her lord and her upon the same
place walking up and down without taking notice one of another, only at
first entry he put off his hat, and she made him a very civil salute, but
afterwards took no notice one of another; but both of them now and
then would take their child, which the nurse held in her arms, and
dandle it. One thing more; there happened a scaffold below to fall, and
we feared some hurt, but there was none, but she of all the great ladies
only run down among the common rabble to see what hurt was done,
and did take care of a child that received some little hurt, which
methought was so noble. Anon there came one there booted and spurred
that she talked long with. And by and by, she being in her hair, she put
on his hat, which was but an ordinary one, to keep the wind off. But
methinks it became her mightily, as everything else do. . . .

[September 29, 1662] . . . then to the King's theatre, where we saw
Midsummer's Night's Dream, which I had never seen before, nor shall
ever again, for it is the most insipid ridiculous play that ever I saw in my
life. I saw, I confess, some good dancing and some handsome women,
which was all my pleasure. . . .

[January 13, 1662/63] So my poor wife rose by five o'clock in the
morning, before day, and went to market and bought fowls and many
other things for dinner, with which I was highly pleased, and the chine of
beef was down also before six o'clock, and my own jack, of which I was
doubtful, do carry it very well. Things being put in order, and the cook
come, I went to the office, where we sat till noon and then broke up, and

I home, whither by and by comes Dr. Clarke and his lady, his sister, and a she-cousin, and Mr. Pierce and his wife, which was all my guests. I had for them, after oysters, at first course, a hash of rabbits, a lamb, and a rare chine of beef. Next a great dish of roasted fowl, cost me about 30s., and a tart, and then fruit and cheese. My dinner was noble and enough. I had my house mighty clean and neat; my room below with a good fire in it; my dining room above, and my chamber being made a withdrawing chamber; and my wife's a good fire also. I find my new table very proper, and will hold nine or ten people well, but eight with great room. After dinner the women to cards in my wife's chamber, and the Dr. and Mr. Pierce in mine, because the dining room smokes unless I keep a good charcoal fire, which I was not then provided with. At night to supper, had a good sack posset and cold meat, and sent my guests away about ten o'clock at night, both them and myself highly pleased with our management of this day; and indeed their company was very fine, and Mrs. Clarke a very witty, fine lady, though a little conceited and proud. So weary, so to bed. I believe this day's feast will cost me near £5.

[January 14, 1662/63] . . . So to the office till ten at night upon business, and numbering and examining part of my sea-manuscript with great pleasure, my wife sitting working by me. . . .

[April 19, 1663] (Easter day). Up and this day put on my close-kneed coloured suit, which, with new stockings of the colour, with belt, and new gilt-handled sword, is very handsome. To church alone, and so to dinner, where my father and brother Tom dined with us, and after dinner to church again, my father sitting below in the chancel. After church done, where the young Scotchman preaching I slept all the while, my father and I to see my uncle and aunt Wight, and after a stay of an hour there my father to my brother's and I home to supper, and after supper fell in discourse of dancing, and I find that Ashwell hath a very fine carriage, which makes my wife almost ashamed of herself to see herself so outdone, but tomorrow she begins to learn to dance for a month or two. . . .

[September 9, 1663] . . . and so to Westminster Hall, God forgive me, thinking to meet Mrs. Lane, but she was not there, but here I met with Ned Pickering, with whom I walked three or four hours till evening, he telling me the whole business of my lord's folly with this Mrs. Becke, at Chelsea, of all which I am ashamed to see my lord so grossly play the beast and fool, to the flinging off of all honour, friends, servants, and everything and person that is good, . . . with his carrying her abroad and playing on his lute under her window, and forty other poor sordid things, which I am grieved to hear; but believe it to no purpose for me to meddle with it, but let him go on till God Almighty and his own conscience and thoughts of his lady and family do it. . . .

[September 17, 1663] . . . I begun a journey with them, and with much ado, through the fens, along dikes, where sometimes we were ready to have our horses sink to the belly, we got by night, with great deal of stir and hard riding, to Parson's Drove, a heathen place, where I found my uncle and aunt Perkins and their daughters, poor wretches! in a sad, poor thatched cottage, like a poor barn, or stable, peeling of hemp, in which I did give myself good content to see their manner of preparing of hemp; and in a poor condition of habit took them to our miserable inn, and there, after long stay, and hearing of Frank, their son, the miller, play upon his treble, as he calls it, with which he earns part of his living, and singing of a country bawdy song, we sat down to supper; the whole crew, and Frank's wife and child, a sad company, of which I was ashamed, supped with us. . . . By and by news is brought to us that one of our horses is stole out of the stable, which proves my uncle's, at which I am inwardly glad—I mean, that it was not mine; and at this we were at a great loss; and they doubting a person that lay at next door, a Londoner, some lawyer's clerk, we caused him to be secured in his bed, and other care to be taken to seize the horse; and so about twelve at night or more, to bed in a sad, cold, nasty chamber, only the maid was indifferent handsome, and so I had a kiss or two of her, and I to bed, and a little after I was asleep they waked me to tell me that the horse was found, which was good news, and so to sleep till the morning, but was bit cruelly, and nobody else of our company, which I wonder at, by the gnats.

[October 31, 1663] . . . The Queen continues light-headed, but in hopes to recover. The plague is much in Amsterdam, and we in fears of it here, which God defend. The Turk goes on mightily in the Emperor's dominions, and the princes cannot agree among themselves how to go against him. . . .

[November 3, 1663] . . . By and by comes Chapman, the periwigmaker, and upon my liking it, without more ado I went up, and there he cut off my hair, which went a little to my heart at present to part with it; but, it being over, and my periwig on, I paid him £3 for it; and away went he with my own hair to make up another of, and I by and by, after I had caused all my maids to look upon it; and they conclude it do become me; though Jane was mightily troubled for my parting of my own hair, and so was Bess, I went abroad to the coffeehouse, and coming back went to Sir W. Penn and there sat with him and Captain Cocke till late at night, Cocke talking of some of the Roman history very well, he having a good memory. Sir W. Penn observed mightily and discoursed much upon my cutting off my hair, as he do of everything that concerns me, but it is over, and so I perceive after a day or two it will be no great matter.

[December 21, 1663] . . . being directed by sight of bills upon the walls, I did go to Shoe Lane to see a cock-fighting at a new pit there, a sport I was never at in my life; but, Lord! to see the strange variety of people, from Parliament man (by name Wildes, that was Deputy Governor of the Tower when Robinson was Lord Mayor) to the poorest 'prentices, bakers, brewers, butchers, draymen, and what not; and all these fellows one with another in swearing, cursing, and betting. I soon had enough of it, and yet I would not but have seen it once. . . . One thing more, it is strange to see how people of this poor rank, that look as if they had not bread to put in their mouths, shall bet three or four pounds at one bet, and lose it, and yet bet as much the next battle.

[February 3, 1663/64] . . . In Covent Garden tonight, going to fetch home my wife, I stopped at the great coffeehouse there, where I never was before; where Dryden, the poet (I knew at Cambridge), and all the wits of the town, and Harris, the player, and Mr. Hoole of our college. And had I had time then, or could at other times, it will be good coming thither, for there, I perceive, is very witty and pleasant discourse. But I could not tarry, and as it was late, they were all ready to go away.

[June 13, 1664] . . . Thence walked with Mr. Coventry to St. James's, and there spent by his desire the whole morning reading of some old navy books given him of old Sir John Cooke's by the Archbishop of Canterbury that now is; wherein the order that was observed in the navy then, above what it is now, is very observable, and fine things we did observe in our reading. . . . We did also talk of a history of the navy of England, how fit it were to be writ; and he did say that it hath been in his mind to propose to me the writing of the history of the late Dutch war, which I am glad to hear, it being a thing I much desire, and sorts mightily with my genius; and, if well done, may recommend me much. So he says he will get me an order for making of searches to all records, etc., in order thereto, and I shall take great delight in doing of it. . . .

[September 6, 1664] . . . So home, having called upon Doll, our pretty 'Change woman, for a pair of gloves trimmed with yellow ribbon, to [match the] petticoat my wife bought yesterday, which cost me 20s.; but she is so pretty, that, God forgive me! I could not think it too much—which is a strange slavery that I stand in to beauty, that I value nothing near it. So going home, and my coach stopping in Newgate Market over against a poulterer's shop, I took occasion to buy a rabbit, but it proved a deadly old one when I came to eat it. . . .

[September 10, 1664] Up and to the office, where we sat all the morning, and I much troubled to think what the end of our great sluggishness will be, for we do nothing in this office like people able to carry on a war. We must be put out, or other people put in. Dined at home, and then my wife and I and Mercer to the Duke's house, and there saw *The Rivals*, which is no excellent play, but good acting in it. . . . Thence home and late writing letters, and this night I received, by Will, £105, the first fruits of my endeavours in the late contract for victualling of Tangier, for which God be praised! for I can with a safe conscience say that I have therein saved the King £5,000 per annum, and yet got myself a hope of £300 per annum without the least wrong to the King. So to supper and to bed.

[September 16, 1664] . . . At noon to the 'Change, where by appointment I met Sir W. Warren, and afterwards to the Sun Tavern, where he brought to me, being all alone, a £100 in a bag, which I offered him to give him my receipt for, but he told me, no, it was my own, which he had a little while since promised me and was glad that (as I had told him two days since) it would now do me courtesy, and so most kindly he did give it me, and I as joyfully, even out of myself, carried it home in a coach, he himself expressly taking care that nobody might see this business done, though I was willing enough to have carried a servant with me to have received it, but he advised me to do it myself. . . .

[November 13, 1664] (Lord's day). This morning to church, where mighty sport, to hear our clerk sing out of tune, though his master sits by him that begins and keeps the tune aloud for the parish. Dined at home very well, and spent all the afternoon with my wife within doors, and getting a speech out of *Hamlet*, 'To be or not to be,' without book. In the evening to sing psalms. . . .

[January 9, 1664/65] Up and walked to Whitehall, it being still a brave frost, and I in perfect good health, blessed be God! In my way saw a woman that broke her thigh, in her heels slipping up upon the frosty street. To the Duke, and there did our usual work. Here I saw the Royal Society bring their new book, wherein is nobly writ their charter and laws, and comes to be signed by the Duke as a fellow; and all the fellows' hands are to be entered there, and lie as a monument; and the King hath put his with the word Founder. . . . Holmes was this day sent to the Tower, but I perceive it is made matter of jest only; but if the Dutch should be our masters, it may come to be of earnest to him, to be given over to them for a sacrifice, as Sir W. Raleigh was. . . .

[March 1, 1664/65] . . . At noon I to dinner at Trinity House, and thence to Gresham College, where Mr. Hooke read a second very curious lecture about the late comet; among other things proving very probably that this is the very same comet that appeared before in the year 1618, and that in such a time probably it will appear again, which is a very new opinion; but all will be in print. Then to the meeting, where Sir G. Carteret's two sons, his own and Sir N. Slaning, were admitted of the society; and this day I did pay my admission money, 40s., to the society. Here was very fine discourses and experiments, but I do lack philosophy enough to understand them, and so cannot remember them. Among others, a very particular account of the making of the several sorts of bread in France, which is accounted the best place for bread in the world. . . .

[May 5, 1665] . . . After dinner to Mr. Evelyn's; he being abroad, we walked in his garden, and a lovely noble ground he hath indeed. And among other rarities, a hive of bees, so as being hived in glass, you may see the bees making their honey and combs mighty pleasantly. . . . This day, after I had suffered my own hair to grow long, in order to wearing it, I find the convenience of periwigs is so great that I have cut off all short again and will keep to periwigs.

[June 7, 1665] . . . This day, much against my will, I did in Drury Lane see two or three houses marked with a red cross upon the doors and 'Lord have mercy upon us' writ there; which was a sad sight to me, being the first of the kind that, to my remembrance, I ever saw. It put me into an ill conception of myself and my smell, so that I was forced to buy some roll-tobacco to smell to and chaw, which took away the apprehension.

[June 8, 1665] This day they engaged, the Dutch neglecting greatly the opportunity of the wind they had of us, by which they lost the benefit of their fire-ships. The Earl of Falmouth, Muskerry, and Mr. Richard Boyle killed on board the Duke's ship, the Royal Charles, with one shot, their blood and brains flying in the Duke's face; and the head of Mr. Boyle striking down the Duke, as some say. Earl of Marlborough, Portland, Rear Admiral Sansum (to Prince Rupert), killed, and Capt. Kirby and Ableson. Sir John Lawson wounded on the knee; hath had some bones taken out, and is likely to be well again. Upon receiving the hurt, he sent to the Duke for another to command the Royal Oak. The Duke sent Jordan out of the St. George, who did brave things in her. Capt. Jer. Smith of the Mary was second to the Duke, and stepped between him and Captain Seaton of the Urania (76 guns and 400 men), who had sworn to board the Duke; killed him, 200 men, and took the ship; himself losing 99 men, and never an officer saved but himself and lieutenant. His master indeed is saved, with his leg cut off. Admiral Opdam blown up, Trump killed, and said by Holmes; all the rest of their admirals, as they say, but Everson (whom they dare not trust for his affection to the Prince of Orange) are killed: we having taken and sunk, as is believed, about 24 of their best ships; killed and taken near 8 or 10,000 men, and lost, we think, not above 700. A great[er] victory never known in the world. They are all fled, some 43 got into the Texel, and others elsewhere, and we in pursuit of the rest. Thence, with my heart full of joy, home, and to my office a little; then to my Lady Penn's, where they are all joyed and not a little puffed up at the good success of their father; and good service indeed is said to have been done by him. Had a great bonfire at the gate; and I with my Lady Penn's people and others to Mrs. Turner's great room, and then down into the street. I did give the boys 4s. among them, and mighty merry. So home to bed, with my heart at great rest and quiet, saving that the consideration of the victory is too great for me presently to comprehend.

[August 12, 1665] . . . The people die so that now it seems they are fain to carry the dead to be buried by daylight, the nights not sufficing to do it in. And my Lord Mayor commands people to be within at nine at night all, as they say, that the sick may have liberty to go abroad for air. There is one also dead out of one of our ships at Deptford, which troubles us mightily; the Providence fire-ship, which was just fitted to go to sea. But they tell me today no more sick on board. . . .

[August 31, 1665] Up; and, after putting several things in order to my removal, to Woolwich; the plague having a great increase this week, beyond all expectation, of almost 2,000, making the general bill 7,000, odd 100; and the plague above 6,000. . . . Thus this month ends with great sadness upon the public, through the greatness of the plague everywhere through the kingdom almost. Every day sadder and sadder news of its increase. In the City died this week 7,496, and of them 6,102 of the plague. But it is feared that the true number of the dead this week is near 10,000; partly from the poor that cannot be taken notice of, through the greatness of the number, and partly from the Quakers and others that will not have any bell ring for them. . . .

[October 5, 1665] . . . to Mr. Evelyn's to discourse of our confounded business of prisoners, and sick and wounded seamen, wherein he and we are so much put of out of order. And here he showed me his gardens, which are for variety of evergreens and hedge of holly, the finest things I ever saw in my life. Thence in his coach to Greenwich, and there to my office, all the way having fine discourse of trees and the nature of vegetables. . . .

[November 5, 1665] . . . by water to Deptford, and there made a visit to Mr. Evelyn, who, among other things, showed me most excellent painting in little; in distemper, Indian ink, water colours, graving, and, above all, the whole secret of mezzo-tinto, and the manner of it, which is very pretty, and good things done with it. He read to me very much also of his discourse, he hath been many years and now is about, about gardenage; which will be a most noble and pleasant piece. He read me part of a play or two of his making, very good, but not as he conceits them, I think, to be. He showed me his *Hortus Hyemalis*; leaves laid up in a book of several plants kept dry, which preserve colour, however, and look very finely, better than any herbal. In fine, a most excellent person he is, and must be allowed a little for a little conceitedness; but he may well be so, being a man so much above others. He read me, though with

too much gusto, some little poems of his own, that were not transcendent, yet one or two very pretty epigrams; among others, of a lady
looking in at a grate, and being pecked at by an eagle that was there.
Here comes in, in the middle of our discourse, Captain Cocke, as drunk
as a dog, but could stand, and talk and laugh. . . .

[December 6, 1665] . . . Here the best company for music I ever
was in, in my life, and wish I could live and die in it, both for music and
the face of Mrs. Pierce, and my wife and Knipp, who is pretty enough,
but the most excellent, mad-humoured thing, and sings the noblest
that ever I heard in my life, and Rolt with her, some things together most
excellently. I spent the night in ecstasy almost; and, having invited them
to my house a day or two hence, we broke up. . . .

[December 25, 1665] (Christmas-day). To church in the morning,
and there saw a wedding in the church, which I have not seen many a
day; and the young people so merry one with another, and strange to see
what delight we married people have to see these poor fools decoyed into
our condition, every man and woman gazing and smiling at
them. . . .

[January 3, 1665/66] . . . So home, and find all my good company I had bespoke, as Coleman and his wife, and Lanier, Knipp and
her surly husband; and good music we had, and, among other things,
Mrs. Coleman sang my words I set of 'Beauty retire,' and I think it is a
good song, and they praise it mightily. Then to dancing and supper, and
mighty merry till Mr. Rolt come in, whose pain of the toothache made
him no company, and spoilt ours; so he away, and then my wife's teeth
full of aching, and she to bed. So forced to break up all with a good song,
and so to bed.

[January 6, 1665/66] . . . to Greenwich by water to a great dinner
and much company; Mr. Cottle and his lady and others and I went,
hoping to get Mrs. Knipp to us, having wrote a letter to her in the
morning, calling myself 'Dapper Dicky,' in answer to hers of 'Barbary
Allen,' but could not, and am told by the boy that carried my letter that
he found her crying; but I fear she lives a sad life with that ill-natured
fellow her husband. So we had a great, but I a melancholy dinner, having
not her there, as I hoped. After dinner to cards, and then comes notice
that my wife is come unexpectedly to me to town. So I to her. It is only
to see what I do and why I come not home; and she is in the right that I
would have a little more of Mrs. Knipp's company before I go
away. . . .

[January 28, 1665/66] . . . And the King come to me of himself,
and told me, 'Mr. Pepys,' says he, 'I do give you thanks for your good
service all this year, and I assure you I am very sensible of it.' And the
Duke of York did tell me with pleasure that he had read over my dis-

course about pursers and would have it ordered in my way, and so fell
from one discourse to another. . . .

[March 10, 1665/66] . . . I find at home Mrs. Pierce and Knipp
come to dine with me. We were mighty merry; and, after dinner, I
carried them and my wife out by coach to the New Exchange, and there
I did give my valentine, Mrs. Pierce, a dozen pair of gloves, and a pair of
silk stockings, and Knipp for company's sake, though my wife had, by my
consent, laid out 20s. upon her the other day, six pair of gloves. . . . The
truth is, I do indulge myself a little the more in pleasure, knowing that
this is the proper age of my life to do it; and out of my observation that
most men that do thrive in the world do forget to take pleasure during
the time that they are getting their estate, but reserve that till they have
got one, and then it is too late for them to enjoy it with any pleasure.

[September 2, 1666] (Lord's day). Some of our maids sitting up
late last night to get things ready against our feast today, Jane called us
up about three in the morning, to tell us of a great fire they saw in the
City. So I rose and slipped on my nightgown, and went to her window,
and thought it to be on the back-side of Mark Lane at the farthest; but,
being unused to such fires as followed, I thought it far enough off; and so
went to bed again and to sleep. About seven rose again to dress myself,
and there looked out at the window and saw the fire not so much as it
was and further off. So to my closet to set things to rights after yesterday's cleaning. By and by Jane comes and tells me that she hears that
above 300 houses have been burned down tonight by the fire we saw and
that it is now burning down all Fish Street, by London Bridge. So I
made myself ready presently, and walked to the Tower, and there got up
upon one of the high places, Sir J. Robinson's little son going up with
me; and there I did see the houses at that end of the bridge all on fire
and an infinite great fire on this and the other side the end of the bridge;
which, among other people, did trouble me for poor little Michell and
our Sarah on the bridge. So down, with my heart full of trouble, to the
Lieutenant of the Tower, who tells me that it begun this morning in the
King's baker's house in Pudding Lane, and that it hath burned St. Mag-
nus's Church and most part of Fish Street already. So I down to the
waterside, and there got a boat, and through bridge, and there saw a lamentable fire. Poor Michell's house, as far as the Old Swan, already
burned that way, and the fire running further, that in a very little time it
got as far as the Steelyard, while I was there. Everybody endeavouring to
remove their goods, and flinging into the river or bringing them into
lighters that lay off; poor people staying in their houses as long as till the
very fire touched them, and then running into boats, or clambering from
one pair of stairs by the waterside to another. And among other things,
the poor pigeons, I perceive, were loth to leave their houses, but hovered

about the windows and balconies till they were some of them burned, their wings, and fell down. Having stayed and in an hour's time seen the fire rage every way, and nobody, to my sight, endeavouring to quench it, but to remove their goods and leave all to the fire, and having seen it get as far as the Steelyard, and the wind mighty high and driving it into the City; and everything, after so long a drought, proving combustible, even the very stones of churches, and among other things the poor steeple by which pretty Mrs. —— lives, and whereof my old schoolfellow Elborough is parson, taken fire in the very top, and there burned till it fell down: I to Whitehall (with a gentleman with me who desired to go off from the Tower, to see the fire, in my boat), to Whitehall, and there up to the King's closet in the chapel, where people come about me, and I did give them an account dismayed them all, and word was carried in to the King. So I was called for, and did tell the King and Duke of York what I saw, and that unless his Majesty did command houses to be pulled down nothing could stop the fire. They seemed much troubled, and the King commanded me to go to my Lord Mayor from him, and command him to spare no houses, but to pull down before the fire every way. The Duke of York bid me tell him that if he would have any more soldiers he shall; and so did my Lord Arlington afterwards, as a great secret. Here meeting with Captain Cocke, I in his coach, which he lent me, and Creed with me to Paul's, and there walked along Watling Street, as well as I could, every creature coming away loaden with goods to save, and here and there sick people carried away in beds. Extraordinary good goods carried in carts and on backs. At last met my Lord Mayor in Canning Street, like a man spent, with a handkercher about his neck. To the King's message he cried, like a fainting woman, 'Lord! what can I do? I am spent! people will not obey me. I have been pulling down houses; but the fire overtakes us faster than we can do it.' That he needed no more soldiers; and that, for himself, he must go and refresh himself, having been up all night. So he left me, and I him, and walked home, seeing people all almost distracted, and no manner of means used to quench the fire. The houses, too, so very thick thereabouts, and full of matter for burning, as pitch and tar, in Thames Street; and warehouses of oil and wines and brandy and other things. . . . Met with the King and Duke of York in their barge, and with them to Queenhithe, and there called Sir Richard Browne to them. Their order was only to pull down houses apace, and so below bridge at the waterside; but little was or could be done, the fire coming upon them so fast. Good hopes there was of stopping it at the Three Cranes above, and at Buttolph's Wharf below bridge, if care be used; but the wind carries it into the City, so as we know not by the waterside what it do there. River full of lighters and boats taking in goods, and good goods swimming in the water, and only I observed that hardly one

lighter or boat in three that had the goods of a house in, but there was a
pair of virginals in it. Having seen as much as I could now, I away to
Whitehall by appointment, and there walked to St. James's Park, and
there met my wife and Creed and Wood and his wife, and walked to my
boat; and there upon the water again, and to the fire up and down, it still
increasing, and the wind great. So near the fire as we could for smoke;
and all over the Thames, with one's face in the wind, you were almost
burned with a shower of fire-drops. This is very true; so as houses were
burned by these drops and flakes of fire, three or four, nay, five or six
houses, one from another. When we could endure no more upon the
water, we to a little alehouse on the Bankside, over against the Three
Cranes, and there stayed till it was dark almost, and saw the fire grow;
and, as it grew darker, churches and houses, as far as we could see up the
hill of the City, in a most horrid malicious bloody flame, not like the fine
flame of an ordinary fire. Barbary and her husband away before us. We
stayed till, it being darkish, we saw the fire as only one entire arch of fire
from this to the other side the bridge, and in a bow up the hill for an arch
of above a mile long; it made me weep to see it. The churches, houses,
and all on fire and flaming at once; and a horrid noise the flames made,
and the cracking of houses at their ruin. So home with a sad heart, and
there find everybody discoursing and lamenting the fire; and poor Tom
Hater come with some few of his goods saved out of his house, which is
burned upon Fish Street Hill. I invited him to lie at my house, and did
receive his goods, but was deceived in his lying there, the news coming
every moment of the growth of the fire; so as we were forced to begin to
pack up our own goods, and prepare for their removal; and did by
moonshine (it being brave dry, and moonshine, and warm weather)
carry much of my goods into the garden, and Mr. Hater and I did remove
my money and iron chests into my cellar, as thinking that the safest
place. And got my bags of gold into my office, ready to carry away, and
my chief papers of accounts also there, and my tallies into a box by
themselves. So great was our fear, as Sir W. Batten hath carts come out
of the country to fetch away his goods this night. We did put Mr. Hater,
poor man, to bed a little; but he got but very little rest, so much noise
being in my house, taking down of goods.

[September 4, 1666] . . . Sir W. Batten not knowing how to
remove his wine, did dig a pit in the garden, and laid it in there; and I
took the opportunity of laying all the papers of my office that I could not
otherwise dispose of. And in the evening Sir W. Penn and I did dig
another, and put our wine in it; and I my parmesan cheese, as well as my
wine and some other things. The Duke of York was at the office this day,
at Sir W. Penn's; but I happened not to be within. This afternoon,
sitting melancholy with Sir W. Penn in our garden, and thinking of the

certain burning of this office, without extraordinary means, I did propose for the sending up of all our workmen from Woolwich and Deptford yards (none whereof yet appeared) and to write to Sir W. Coventry to have the Duke of York's permission to pull down houses, rather than lose this office, which would much hinder the King's business. So Sir W. Penn he went down this night, in order to the sending them up tomorrow morning; and I wrote to Sir W. Coventry about the business, but received no answer. This night Mrs. Turner (who, poor woman, was removing her goods all this day, good goods into the garden, and knows not how to dispose of them), and her husband supped with my wife and I at night, in the office, upon a shoulder of mutton from the cook's, without any napkin or anything, in a sad manner, but were merry. Only now and then walking into the garden, and saw how horribly the sky looks, all on a fire in the night, was enough to put us out of our wits; and, indeed, it was extremely dreadful, for it looks just as if it was at us, and the whole heaven on fire. I after supper walked in the dark down to Tower Street, and there saw it all on fire, at the Trinity House on that side, and the Dolphin Tavern on this side, which was very near us; and the fire with extraordinary vehemence. Now begins the practice of blowing up of houses in Tower Street, those next the Tower, which at first did frighten people more than anything; but it stopped the fire where it was done, it bringing down the houses to the ground in the same places they stood, and then it was easy to quench what little fire was in it, though it kindled nothing almost. W. Hewer this day went to see how his mother did, and comes late home, telling us how he hath been forced to remove her to Islington, her house in Pye Corner being burned; so that the fire is got so far that way, and all the Old Bailey, and was running down to Fleet Street; and Paul's is burned, and all Cheapside. I wrote to my father this night, but the post-house being burned, the letter could not go.

[September 5, 1666] I lay down in the office again upon W. Hewer's quilt, being mighty weary, and sore in my feet with going till I was hardly able to stand. About two in the morning my wife calls me up and tells me of new cries of fire, it being come to Barking Church, which is the bottom of our lane. I up, and finding it so, resolved presently to take her away, and did, and took my gold, which was about £2,350, W. Hewer, and Jane down by Proundy's boat to Woolwich; but, Lord! what a sad sight it was by moonlight to see the whole City almost on fire, that you might see it plain at Woolwich as if you were by it. There, when I come, I find the gates shut, but no guard kept at all, which troubled me, because of discourse now begun that there is plot in it and that the French had done it. I got the gates open, and to Mr. Shelden's, where I locked up my gold and charged my wife and W. Hewer never to leave the room without one of them in it, night or day. So back again, by the way seeing my goods well in the lighters at Deptford and watched well by people. Home, and whereas I expected to have seen our house on fire, it being now about seven o'clock, it was not. But to the fire, and there find greater hopes than I expected; for my confidence of finding our office on fire was such that I durst not ask anybody how it was with us till I come and saw it not burned. But going to the fire, I find by the blowing up of houses and the great help given by the workmen out of the King's yards, sent up by Sir W. Penn, there is a good stop given to it, as well as at Mark Lane end as ours; it having only burned the dial of Barking Church and part of the porch, and was there quenched. I up to the top of Barking steeple, and there saw the saddest sight of desolation that I ever saw; everywhere great fires, oil-cellars, and brimstone, and other things burning. I became afeard to stay there long, and therefore down again as fast as I could, the fire being spread as far as I could see it; and to Sir W. Penn's, and there eat a piece of cold meat, having eaten nothing since Sunday, but the remains of Sunday's dinner. Here I met with Mr. Young and Whistler; and having removed all my things and received good hopes that the fire at our end is stopped, they and I walked into the town, and find Fenchurch Street, Gracious Street, and Lombard Street all in dust. The Exchange a sad sight, nothing standing there, of all the statues or pillars, but Sir Thomas Gresham's picture in the corner. Walked into Moorfields (our feet ready to burn, walking through the town among the hot coals), and find that full of people, and poor wretches carrying their goods there, and everybody keeping his goods together by themselves (and a great blessing it is to them that it is fair weather for them to keep abroad night and day); drank there, and paid twopence for a plain penny loaf. Thence homeward, having passed through Cheapside and Newgate Market, all burned, and seen Anthony Joyce's house in fire. And took up (which I keep by me) a piece of glass of Mercers' Chapel in the street, where much more was, so melted and buckled with the heat of the fire like parchment. I also did see a poor cat taken out of a hole in the chimney, joining to the wall of the Exchange, with the hair all burned off the body, and yet alive. So home at night, and find there good hopes of saving our office; but great endeavours of watching all night, and having men ready; and so we lodged them in the office, and had drink and bread and cheese for them. And I lay down and slept a good night about midnight, though when I rose I heard that there had been a great alarm of French and Dutch being risen, which proved nothing. But it is a strange thing to see how long this time did look since Sunday, having been always full of variety of actions and little sleep, that it looked like a week or more, and I had forgot almost the day of the week.

[December 25, 1666] (Christmas day). Lay pretty long in bed, and then rose, leaving my wife desirous to sleep, having sat up till four this morning seeing her maids make mince pies. I to church, where our parson Mills made a good sermon. Then home, and dined well on some good ribs of beef roasted and mince pies; only my wife, brother, and Barker, and plenty of good wine of my own, and my heart full of true joy; and thanks to God Almighty for the goodness of my condition at this day. . . .

[December 31, 1666] . . . Blessed be God! and I pray God make me thankful for it, I do find myself worth in money, all good, above £6,200; which is above £1,800 more than I was the last year. This, I trust in God, will make me thankful for what I have and careful to make up by care next year what by my negligence and prodigality I have lost and spent this year. The doing of this and entering of it fair, with the sorting of all my expenses, to see how and in what points I have exceeded, did make it late work, till my eyes become very sore and ill, and then did give over, and supper, and to bed. Thus ends this year of public wonder and mischief to this nation and, therefore, generally wished by all people to have an end. Myself and family well, having four maids and one clerk, Tom, in my house and my brother, now with me to spend time in order to his preferment. Our healths all well, only my eyes with overworking them are sore as candlelight comes to them, and not else; public matters in a most sad condition; seamen discouraged for want of pay and are become not to be governed; nor, as matters are now, can any fleet go out next year. Our enemies, French and Dutch, great, and grow more by our poverty. The Parliament backward in raising, because jealous of the spending of the money; the City less and less likely to be built again, everybody settling elsewhere, and nobody encouraged to trade. A sad, vicious, negligent court, and all sober men there fearful of the ruin of the whole kingdom this next year; from which, good God deliver us! One thing I reckon remarkable in my own condition is that I am come to abound in good plate, so as at all entertainments to be served wholly with silver plates, having two dozen and a half.

[January 7, 1666/67] . . . to the Duke's house, and saw *Macbeth*, which, though I saw it lately, yet appears a most excellent play in all respects, but especially in divertisement, though it be a deep tragedy; which is a strange perfection in a tragedy, it being most proper here, and suitable. . . .

[February 2, 1666/67] . . . This night comes home my new silver snuff dish, which I do give myself for my closet, which is all I purpose to bestow in plate of myself or shall need, many a day, if I can keep what I have. So to bed. I am very well pleased this night with reading a poem I brought home with me last night from Westminster Hall, of Dryden's, upon the present war; a very good poem.

[June 12, 1667] . . . By and by, after dinner, my wife out by coach to see her mother; and I in another, being afraid, at this busy time, to be seen with a woman in a coach, as if I were idle . . . and so home, where all our hearts do now ache; for the news is true that the Dutch have broken the chain and burned our ships, and particularly the Royal Charles; other particulars I know not, but most sad to be sure. And, the truth is, I do fear so much that the whole kingdom is undone that I do this night resolve to study with my father and wife what to do with the little that I have in money by me, for I give [up] all the rest that I have in the King's hands, for Tangier, for lost. So God help us! and God knows what disorders we may fall into, and whether any violence on this office, or perhaps some severity on our persons, as being reckoned by the silly people, or perhaps may, by policy of state, be thought fit to be condemned by the King and Duke of York, and so put to trouble; though, God knows! I have, in my own person, done my full duty, I am sure. So having with much ado finished my business at the office, I home to consider with my father and wife of things, and then to supper and to bed with a heavy heart. . . .

[August 18, 1667] . . . being wearied, turned into St. Dunstan's Church, where I heard an able sermon of the minister of the place; and stood by a pretty, modest maid, whom I did labour to take by the hand and the body; but she would not, but got further and further from me; and, at last, I could perceive her to take pins out of her pocket to prick me if I should touch her again—which seeing I did forbear, and was glad I did spy her design. And then I fell to gaze upon another pretty maid in a pew close to me, and she on me; and I did go about to take her by the hand, which she suffered a little and then withdrew. So the sermon ended, and the church broke up, and my amours ended also, and so took coach and home, and there took up my wife, and to Islington with her. . . .

[October 5, 1667] . . . to the King's house, and there, going in, met with Knipp, and she took us up into the tiring-rooms and to the women's shift, where Nell was dressing herself and was all unready, and is very pretty, prettier than I thought. And so walked all up and down the house above, and then below into the scene-room, and there sat down, and she gave us fruit; and here I read the questions to Knipp, while she answered me, through all her part of *Flora's Figarys*, which was acted today. But, Lord! to see how they were both painted would make a man mad, and did make me loath them; and what base company of men comes among them, and how lewdly they talk! and how poor the men are in clothes, are yet what a show they make on the stage by candlelight is very observable. But to see how Nell cursed, for having so few people in the pit, was pretty; the other house carrying away all the people at the new play, and is said, nowadays, to have generally most company, as being better players. By and by into the pit, and there saw the play, which is pretty good, but my belly was full of what I had seen in the house, and so, after the play done, away home, and there to the writing my letters, and so home to supper and to bed.

[November 2, 1667] . . . to the King's playhouse, and there saw *Henry the Fourth*, and contrary to expectation, was pleased in nothing more than in Cartwright's speaking of Falstaff's speech about 'What is honour?' The house full of Parliament men, it being holiday with them; and it was observable how a gentleman of good habit, sitting just before us, eating of some fruit in the midst of the play, did drop down as dead, being choked; but with much ado Orange Moll did thrust her finger down his throat and brought him to life again. . . .

[March 5, 1667/68] With these thoughts I lay troubling myself till six o'clock, restless, and at last getting my wife to talk to me to comfort me, which she at last did, and made me resolve to quit my hands of this office and endure the trouble of it no longer than till I can clear myself of it. . . . But I full of thoughts and trouble touching the issue of this day; and, to comfort myself did go to the Dog and drink half a pint of mulled sack, and in the Hall [Westminster] did drink a dram of brandy at Mrs. Hewlett's; and with the warmth of this did find myself in better order as to courage, truly. So we all up to the lobby; and between eleven and twelve o'clock, were called in, with the mace before us, into the House, where a mighty full house; and we stood at the bar, namely, Brouncker, Sir J. Minnes, Sir T. Harvey, and myself, W. Penn being in the House as a member. I perceive the whole House was full, and full of expectation of our defence what it would be, and with great prejudice. After the Speaker had told us the dissatisfaction of the House and read the report of the committee, I began our defence most acceptably and smoothly, and continued at it without any hesitation or loss, but with full scope, and all my reason free about me, as if it had been at my own table, from that time till past three in the afternoon; and so ended, without any interruption from the Speaker; but we withdrew. And there all my fellow officers, and all the world that was within hearing, did congratulate me, and cry up my speech as the best thing they ever heard; and my fellow officers overjoyed in it . . . it is plain we have got great ground; and everybody says I have got the most honour that any could have had opportunity of getting; and so with our hearts mightily overjoyed at this success, we all to dinner to Lord Brouncker's. . . .

[June 19, 1668] . . . my wife fell into her blubbering again, and at length had a request to make to me, which was, that she might go into France, and live there, out of trouble; and then all come out, that I loved pleasure and denied her any, and a deal of do; and I find that there have been great fallings out between my father and her, whom, forever hereafter, I must keep asunder, for they cannot possibly agree. And I said nothing, but, with very mild words and few, suffered her humour to spend, till we begun to be very quiet, and I think all will be over, and friends, and so I to the office, where all the morning doing business. . . .

[December 21, 1668] . . . went into Holborn, and there saw the woman that is to be seen with a beard. She is a little plain woman, a Dane: her name, Ursula Dyan; about forty years old; her voice like a little girl's; with a beard as much as any man I ever saw, black almost, and grizzly; they offered to shew my wife further satisfaction if she desired it, refusing it to men that desired it there, but there is no doubt but by her voice she is a woman; it begun to grow at about seven years old, and was shaved not above seven months ago, and is now so big as any man's almost that ever I saw; I say, bushy and thick. It was a strange sight to me, I confess, and what pleased me mightily. Thence to the Duke's playhouse, and saw *Macbeth*. . . . The King and Duke of York minded me, and smiled upon me. . . .

[January 12, 1668/69] . . . This evening I observed my wife mighty dull, and I myself was not mighty fond, because of some hard words she did give me at noon, out of a jealousy at my being abroad this morning, which, God knows, it was upon the business of the office unexpectedly; but I to bed, not thinking but she would come after me. But waking by and by out of a slumber, which I usually fall into presently after my coming into the bed, I found she did not prepare to come to bed, but got fresh candles and more wood for her fire, it being mighty cold, too. At this being troubled, I after a while prayed her to come to bed, all my people being gone to bed; so, after an hour or two, she silent, and I now and then praying her to come to bed, she fell out into a fury, that I was a rogue and false to her. But yet I did perceive that she was to seek what to say, only she invented, I believe, a business that I was seen in a hackney coach with the glasses up with Deb., but could not tell the time, nor was sure I was he. I did, as I might truly, deny it, and was mightily troubled, but all would not serve. At last, about one o'clock, she come to my side of the bed, and drew my curtain open, and with the tongs red hot at the ends, made as if she did design to pinch me with them, at which, in dismay, I rose up, and with a few words she laid them down; and did by little and little, very sillily, let all the discourse fall. . . .

[February 12, 1668/69] . . . and so home, and there Pelling hath got me W. Penn's book against the Trinity. I got my wife to read it to me; and I find it so well writ as, I think, it is too good for him ever to have writ it; and it is a serious sort of book, and not fit for everybody to read. . . .

[May 31, 1669] . . . And thus ends all that I doubt I shall ever be able to do with my own eyes in the keeping of my journal, I being not able to do it any longer, having done now so long as to undo my eyes almost every time that I take a pen in my hand; and, therefore, whatever comes of it, I must forbear. And, therefore, resolve, from this time forward, to have it kept by my people in longhand, and must therefore be contented to set down no more than is fit for them and all the world to know; or, if there be anything, which cannot be much, now my amours to Deb. are past, and my eyes hindering me in almost all other pleasures, I must endeavour to keep a margin in my book open to add, here and there, a note in shorthand with my own hand.

And so I betake myself to that course, which is almost as much as to see myself go into my grave; for which, and all the discomforts that will accompany my being blind, the good God prepare me!

S. P.

✔ Suggestions for Reading and Writing

1. Even this limited selection from his *Diary* reveals the many-sided Pepys character. What one trait, however, seems predominant? What personal incident included here makes the deepest impression? Why? Do you find yourself attracted to or repelled by him?
2. Has Pepys left his mark on history because he was unique? Or is he remembered today because he had too much of all of us in his make-up?
3. After the publication of the *Diary*, Samuel Taylor Coleridge referred to Pepys as a "pollard" or stunted man, whereas James Russell Lowell saw him as Philistine, naive, and humorless. Do you agree with either, neither, or both? (For added perspective, see such modern studies as Arthur Bryant's lengthy *Samuel Pepys* [1933–38], Percival Hunt's *Samuel Pepys in the Diary* [1958], John H. Wilson's *The Private Life of Mr. Pepys* [1959], and Cecil S. Emden's *Pepys Himself* [1963].)
4. Would Pepys's *Diary* have proved equally or less fascinating if the author had lived during a less eventful period? Explain. (For informative accounts of Pepys's age, see G. M. Trevelyan's *England Under the Stuarts* [1904], David Ogg's *England in the Reign of Charles II* [1934], Hilaire Belloc's *Charles II: The Last Rally* [1939], and Christopher Hill's *The Century of Revolution 1603–1714* [1961].)
5. Read in the *Diary* (1818) of Pepys's friend John Evelyn (1620–1706) those sections dealing with the years covered here. Then compare not only the two men's prose styles and social attitudes, but their characters. (Clara Marburg's *Mr. Pepys and Mr. Evelyn* [1935] should be of some help.)
6. After reading in Pepys and Evelyn (and in any other diaries and journals that may interest you), discuss the apparent advantages and disadvantages of the diary as a form of autobiography. (For diaries, see

the introductions in Arthur Ponsonby's *English Diaries* [1922] and *More English Diaries* [1927] and Kate O'Brien's *English Diaries and Journals* [1947]; for autobiographies, see Anna R. Burr's *The Autobiography: A Critical and Comparative Study* [1909], Arthur M. Clark's *Autobiography: Its Genesis and Phases* [1935], E. Stuart Bates's *Inside Out: An Introduction to Autobiography* [1937], Wayne Shumaker's *English Autobiography: Its Emergence, Materials, Form* [1954], and Roy Pascal's *Design and Truth in Autobiography* [1960].)

[THE SUBJECT MATTER OF BIOGRAPHY]

Leon Edel

Born in Pittsburgh and raised in Canada, Leon Edel (1907–) received his M.A. at McGill University, Montreal (1928), and Litt.D. from the University of Paris (1932). A professor of English at New York University since 1955, he has taught also at Harvard, Princeton, and the Universities of Indiana and Hawaii. Among his awards is a grant from the National Institute of Arts and Letters (1959) for "creative writing in literature."

Edel has written or edited about two dozen books during the past twenty years. These include James Joyce: The Last Journey (1947), Willa Cather: A Critical Biography (1953), and Literary Biography (1957). He is best known, however, as a Henry James specialist, having edited James's tales, essays, plays, and letters. He is now at work on a massive four-volume biography of James, of which the first three volumes have been published: Henry James: The Untried Years (1953), Henry James: The Conquest of London (1962), and Henry James: The Middle Years (1962). These last two volumes won for Professor Edel the 1963 National Book Award for nonfiction.

As a veteran and highly acclaimed practitioner, Leon Edel can speak with special authority on many facets of biography. The following essay is a slightly abridged version of the opening chapter of his Literary Biography.

✓ ✓ ✓ ✓ ✓

I

Lytton Strachey once described biography as "the most delicate and humane of all the branches of the art of writing." Delicate, I suppose, because the biographer seeks to restore the very sense of life to the inert materials that survive an individual's passage on this earth—seeks to recapture some part of what was once tissue and brain, and above all feeling, and to shape a likeness of the vanished figure. Humane, because inevitably the biographical process is a refining, a civilizing—a humanizing—process. And because it is a delicate and humane process, it partakes of all the ambiguities and contradictions of life itself. A biography is a record, in words, of something that is as mercurial and as flowing, as compact of temperament and emotion, as the human spirit itself.

And yet the writer of biography must be neat and orderly and logical in describing this elusive flamelike human spirit which delights in defying order and neatness and logic. The biographer may be as imaginative as he pleases—the more imaginative the better—in the way in which he brings together his materials, *but he must not imagine the materials*. He must read himself into the past; but he must also read that past into the present. He must judge the facts, but he must not sit in judgment. He must respect the dead—but he must tell the truth. James Anthony Froude sought to tell the truth about the Carlyles and succeeded in bringing down upon his writing table all the hornets of literary London—and of Edinburgh to boot. And yet while he was doing this, other Victorians were being commemorated in large, heavy tomes; they were made to seem not men, but angels, clothed in all the innocence of Adam before the Fall. The biographers who offered the public such gilded statues were considered honorable and truthful men; but candor such as Froude's provoked largely indignation and indeed fright. We deal here in large anomalies.

· · · · ·

II

It is not my intention to venture into the history of biography. It would take us too far afield. There is much to say about the deeply human biographical method of the Gospels and their exalted subject; or about the vivid biographical paragraphs in the Old Testament, so evocative in their brevity, devoted to Ruth and David and Joseph; or about Plutarch, who was concerned with the writing of great lives for the valued ethical generalizations they might yield him. It would be tempting to deal also with the hagiographers, who in their lives of the saints made little claim to science and often even less to veracity, but freely transposed, on occasion, episodes from the life of one saint to another. What was important for them was the example of the saintly life, not the facts of the life itself. My concern here is not with history or with biographies remote in time from us, and so rich a part of our religious and secular heritage. The problem I wish to discuss is the very concrete one of how, in modern times, when we have whole libraries of documents, when tape recorders and films bring to us the voice and the image of the biographical subject—how, in these modern times, biography should be written and by what light of theory we are to work.

The interest in the personal and the private life, the life of the inner man, dates in English letters, we might say, from the eighteenth century: certainly it was a harbinger of romanticism. First came the poet, and very much later curiosity about the life of the poet. Had biographical curiosity, or awareness, existed earlier, we would not today be trying to piece together Chaucer's life from those paltry records of his pension and the pitchers of wine bestowed upon him by the royal household. Who would think of writing the life of a modern poet from the record of his check stubs? We write what we pretend is a "life" of Shakespeare from a series of facts which can be set down in a very large hand on a rather small sheet of paper. The Elizabethans had a limited biographical sense; they kept no record of the luminous mind in their midst; but so great is our curiosity that, failing an adequate biography of Shakespeare, certain individuals give him a wholly new life and call him Bacon or the Earl of Oxford.

Modern biography is as modern as the novel; indeed it came to birth almost at the same time. In recent decades there has been a close definition of the craft of fiction, but there has been a singular lack of definition of the craft of biography—and of literary biography in particular. This is not difficult to explain. In the writing of the novel the artist is free to use all the resources of his imagination; in the writing of biography the material is predetermined: the imagination functions only as it plays over this material and shapes it. The art lies in the telling; and the telling must be of such a nature as to leave the material unaltered. The biographer, like the historian, is a slave of his documents. Fewer generalizations are therefore possible. Readers of novels are interested in the problems of storytelling and in theories of fiction; readers of biography take for granted the facts given to them; they are not generally concerned to know how the biographer arrived at them. For these reasons, Percy Lubbock's *The Craft of Fiction* and E. M. Forster's *Aspects of the Novel* continue to be read, while Sir Harold Nicolson's *The Development of English Biography* (I do not speak here of Donald Stauffer's more specialized works) and André Maurois's *Aspects of Biography* tend to be neglected. Yet both Nicolson and Maurois, writing under the fertilizing influence of Lytton Strachey, offered us during the 1920's the liveliest discussion of biography we have had in our half century. The discussion went on around them as well, and we can, if we listen, hear the voices of Strachey himself and of his friend Virginia Woolf, and the group of younger men who learned from them—among them Lord David Cecil and Philip Guedalla. Nicolson reluctantly saw biography as doomed to become a work of science; Maurois argued it could be only an art and should accept itself as such; and Virginia Woolf said it was neither art nor science but a kind of superior *craft*.

Nicolson's survey, which tended to be rather superficial as history, was in reality an essay in definition. He saw biography as "the history of the lives of individual men as a branch of literature" but gloomily predicted that it would eventually become a branch of science. He was writing under the influence of the first popularizations of psychoanalysis a quarter of a century ago and such ephemeral fads as the transplanting of monkey glands. He believed that biographies would tend increasingly to become case histories rather than lives related in literary form. He wrote:

> I would suggest that the scientific interest in biography is hostile to, and will in the end prove destructive of, the literary interest. The former will insist not only on the facts, but on all the facts; the latter demands a partial or artificial representation of facts. The scientific interest, as it develops, will become insatiable; no synthetic power, no genius for representation, will be able to keep pace. I foresee, therefore, a divergence between the two interests. Scientific biography will become specialised and technical. There will be biographies in which psychological development will be traced in

all its intricacy and in a manner comprehensible only to the experts; there will be biographies examining the influence of heredity— biographies founded on Galton, on Lombroso, on Havelock Ellis, on Freud; there will be medical biographies—studies of the influence on character of the endocrine glands, studies of internal secretions; there will be sociological biographies, economic biographies, aesthetic biographies, philosophical biographies. These will doubtless be interesting and instructive, but the emphasis which will be thrown on the analytical or scientific aspect will inevitably lessen the literary effort applied to their composition. The more that biography becomes a branch of science the less will it become a branch of literature.

Now that we have lived a bit into this future, we can see that Sir Harold's forebodings, for the time being at least, have been groundless. There have been some specialized biographies of the sort he envisaged; their public is limited and they certainly have not supplanted traditional biography. Biographers have continued to write fully aware, as M. Maurois insisted in his book, that man is a volatile creature, that so long as the brain and nerves and the human consciousness defy mechanization, biography cannot be wholly scientific. Virginia Woolf, as I said, took a position rather betwixt and between. The biographer was a craftsman, and on this "lower level," as she put it, he helped to relieve the tension of the world of the imagination: thanks to him sober fact is allowed to intrude upon it.

From our mid-century perspective, I would say that the discussion need not be whether biography is a science or an art or even a craft capable of being learned by any serious, intelligent person. It is a process: scientific when it asks the sciences to elucidate whatever they can about the human being and his personality; an art when it uses language to capture human experience; and requiring all the craftsmanship an individual can command in mastering and disciplining himself to deal with material as rich and varied and mercurial as the mind of man. These are tolerably obvious matters. If you press me, however, I will say that much more art than science is involved in the process, since biography deals with emotions as well as with the intellect, and literary biography with those emotions which give the impulse to literary creation. These, I suspect, we shall never be able to place in a test tube.

III

The biographer is called upon to take the base metals that are his disparate facts and turn them into the gold of the human personality, and no chemical process has yet been discovered by which this change can be accomplished. It is a kind of alchemy of the spirit; to succeed the biographer must perform the unusual—and the well-nigh impossible—act of incorporating into himself the experience of another, or shall we say, becoming for a while that other person, even while remaining himself. This does not mean that he must be an actor. The actor gets into the skin of a character and remains that character on stage, wholly dissimulating his real self. The biographer also is required to get into the skin of his subject; he removes himself sometimes to another age; sometimes he even changes his sex; he takes on another's career, the very wink of his eye or shrug of his shoulder: yet all the while he retains his own mind, his own sense of balance and his own appraising eye. He must be warm, yet aloof, involved, yet uninvolved. To be cold as ice in appraisal, yet warm and human and understanding, this is the biographer's dilemma.

Between the biographer and his subject there is established from the outset a significant relationship—ghostly though it may seem. It is a relationship deeply intimate and highly subjective. I speak of the biographer who selects his own subject as distinct from the one who is writing an official or commemorative biography and who may or may not become emotionally involved with the subject. As a rule the subjective relationship dates from the moment the biographer begins to think about writing a given life. On the surface he has been attracted to this or to that figure for reasons which seem clear enough: he likes the writer's work, or he finds it curious; he may discover some little dramatic fact which serves to kindle the fire, or finds what he knows of the writer's personality pleasing. M. Maurois, in his Clark Lectures, told us much about himself when he described how he came to write the life of Shelley. In effect he said that he found in the poet a mirror for his own youthful emotions, and "it seemed to me indeed," he wrote, "that to tell the story of this life would be a way of liberating me from myself." This is an illuminating confession. I am sure that if someone were to attempt to study the psychology of biographers, he would discover that they are usually impelled by deeply personal reasons to the writing of a given life—reasons not always conducive to objectivity and to truth. Sigmund Freud, in his probing of the subterranean motivations of man, offered what seems to me a profound warning in his essay on Leonardo da Vinci—a warning to the biographer who ceases wholly to be himself and proceeds not to write but to *rewrite* the life of his subject. As Freud puts it (in the quaint language of his American translator), these biographers became "fixated on their heroes in a very peculiar manner." And he goes on:

> They frequently select the hero as the object of study because,
> for personal reasons of their own emotional life, they have a special

affection for him from the very outset. They then devote themselves to a work of idealization, which strives to enroll the great man among their infantile models, and to revive through him, as it were, their infantile conception of the father. For the sake of this wish they wipe out the individual features in his physiognomy, they rub out the traces of his life's struggle with inner and outer resistances, and do not tolerate in him anything savoring of human weakness or imperfection; they then give us a cold, strange, ideal form instead of a man to whom we could feel distantly related. It is to be regretted that they do this, for they thereby sacrifice the truth to an illusion, and for the sake of their infantile phantasies they let slip the opportunity to penetrate into the most attractive secrets of human nature.

Freud might equally well have described the opposite of this hero-worshipping kind of biography—the kind in which the biographer selects a subject upon whom he will vent his spleen, not because of any genuine hatred, but because of buried hostilities and unhappy memories which may be fitted to the person selected for vilification.

I think Lytton Strachey had these dangers in mind when he spoke of the biographer's need to maintain his "own freedom of spirit." Another way of putting it might be to say that the biographer must try to know himself before he seeks to know the life of another: and this leads us into a very pretty impasse, since there seems to be considerable evidence that he is seeking to know the life of another in order better to understand himself. The biographer's dilemma thus becomes double: he must appraise the life of another by becoming that other person; and he must be scrupulously careful that in the process the other person is not refashioned in his own image. This, in reality, is the subtle process involved.

But biographers, like their subjects, are human. They do not possess that omniscience which would enable them to see to the very bottom of their own hearts and minds while unraveling the riddle of the heart and mind of another. The best we can hope for, it would seem, is that the biographer should, as Lytton Strachey said, "lay bare the facts of the case, *as he understands them.*" This is obvious enough and yet it is our best—indeed, our sole—answer to the problem of omniscience. Surely a biographer can set forth the data he has gathered and studied only in the light of his own understanding; and his understanding is inevitably a variable, greater or less, depending upon his capacities as well as upon his data. We come round the circle to the basic fact that the biographer can work only by the light of his own intelligence and his own resources. The greater his grasp of reality, the more real his portrait will be. He has taken into his consciousness a great many documents about another's life. And the book that will emerge will be *his* vision, *his* arrangement, *his* picture.

Let us image the great table of biography, for biographers need larger tables or desks than most writers. It is piled high with books and papers: certificates of birth and death, genealogies, photostats of deeds, letters—letters filled with rationalizations and subterfuges, exaggerations, wishful thinking, deliberate falsehoods, elaborate politenesses— and then, testimonials, photographs, manuscripts, diaries, notebooks, bank checks, newspaper clippings, as if we had poured out the contents of desk drawers or of old boxes in an attic: a great chaotic mass of materials, not to forget volumes of memoirs by the contemporaries—how they abound in some cases!—and the diaries and notebooks of these contemporaries, and often biographies of the subject written by other hands. All this material, assembled out of the years, will make its way into the mind—and the heart—of the man who has gathered it. The death of the owner of many of these documents has tended to level them into a relative uniformity. We can no longer determine whether this particular letter, breathing sweetness and affection, was really written in love, or in pretense of love. The voice that gave it its original inflection is gone; the recipient of the letter is perhaps no longer available to furnish a gloss or to testify what it meant to receive it. Things impalpable surround these palpable objects. The diaries and notes reflecting moods ranging from vexation and anger to transcendent joy, bitter animosity to boundless Christian charity, all had a particular meaning when the author was alive. But once he is dead the meaning becomes more general and uninflected. And the biographer can only absorb these documents into his living consciousness: it becomes, for the time, surrogate for the consciousness that has been extinguished. In other words, the living, associating, remembering biographer's mind seeks to restore a time sense to the mass of data that has become timeless. All biography is, in effect, a reprojection into words, into a literary or a kind of semiscientific and historical form, of the inert materials, reassembled, so to speak, through the mind of the historian or the biographer. His becomes the informing mind. He can only lay bare the facts as he has understood them.

IV

Henry James set down some very eloquent words on this subject—of the change that takes place between the moment when a man is alive, holding the thousands of connecting threads that bind him to the world and his fellow men, and the moment when the threads are suddenly snapped, for all time. "After a man's long work is over and the sound of his voice is still," wrote James, "those in whose regard he has held a high place find his image strangely simplified and summarized. The hand of death, in passing over it, has smoothed the folds, made it more typical and general. The figure retained by memory is compressed and intensified; accidents have dropped away from it and shades have ceased to count; it stands, sharply, for a few estimated and cherished things, rather than, nebulously, for a swarm of possibilities." There is indeed an extraordinary simplification, and the life that was so rich, so full of countless moments of experience and emotion, now is rather disconnected and fragmentary. Let us place Henry James's words in their proper context. The novelist was writing of his lately dead friend, James Russell Lowell. When he set down these words it was with the image of Lowell in his mind, as he had known him during more than three decades. The beautiful commemorative essay which he wrote gives us a vision of many Lowells—the Lowell to whom James had listened when he was a young man at Harvard, listened during late winter afternoons when lamps were lit in the classroom and they illuminated the bearded face, giving to it a haunted poetic quality; the vigorous American Lowell in Paris during the 1870's with whom James supped at a little hotel on the Left Bank before crossing the Seine, illumined by gaslight which gave to the water the effect of a varnished surface, to go to the Théâtre Français; the Lowell of the earlier time who set down noble lines in memory of the dead, the young dead, of the American Civil War; and the later Lowell, the man of letters as diplomat, carrying the responsibilities of his ministerial post to the Court of St. James's and into the great houses of Victorian England, the Lowell who lectured the English on the growth of democracy in America. The "estimated and cherished things" were those estimated and cherished by James at the time of Lowell's death in 1891. Yet we, from our distance, more than half a century later, and many years after James's death, find that time has further summarized Lowell and made him more remote. A certain staleness pervades his writings—they seem bookish and derivative; he has stepped into a greater shadow; at moments he seems to us, in our twentieth-century sophistication, a figure naïve and parochial; he *lives* for us vividly only in some of his essays and lectures and largely when a writer, like James, succeeds in making him vivid for us. What James wrote, in turn, has become one more document—a very beautiful document—one more bit of eloquent testimony to be placed upon the already burdened table of Lowell's biography. The figure of James, along with other of Lowell's contemporaries, has moved into the records of Lowell's life; and the biographer, his task more complex than ever, must himself move among these shadows and documents and "points of view," called upon to sift, to evaluate, to re-create. His task grows in magnitude when he encounters, and places upon his worktable, biographies of his subject written by his predecessors. Here we find we must make still further distinctions—distinctions not often made—between the biographer who writes solely from documents and the one who writes, frequently from a commemorative emotion, having known the dead man. This, very properly, brings us to the name and the example of James Boswell.

v

When Boswell began his preparations to write the life of Dr. Johnson, that great ponderous figure still walked at large, and London still seemed to echo to his conversations and opinions. Boswell found himself in a position of high advantage. For one thing, Johnson believed that "nobody can write the life of a man but those who have eat and drunk and lived in social intercourse with him." What biographer, in Johnson's company, would discourage so genial an opinion? Certainly not Boswell, who therefore had easy and sociable access to his subject. He could listen. He could take notes. He could ask questions.

He could do much more. He could at moments become a kind of organizer and sceneshifter in the life of Dr. Johnson: he could create occasions, incidents, encounters for the life he would ultimately write. This is not to say that he actually arranged Johnson's life for him. The learned doctor was, intellectually, the least passive of men. There were moments, however, when Boswell could, by quiet manipulation, place his subject in a better position for the biographical camera, improve a little on the accidents of life; he could carefully plan—shall we say?—"spontaneous" occasions for the unaware object of his biographical urge. What is disarming in the life he finally wrote, is the candor and innocence with which Boswell describes his own maneuvers and clevernesses. There comes to mind the little episode of the visit to the home of the late Reverend Edward Young, the celebrated author of *Night Thoughts on Life, Death and Immortality.* Johnson was traveling with Boswell and they had stopped at Welwyn, where Young had been rector for more than a quarter of a century. The celebrity-loving, pilgrimage-seeking Boswell wanted to visit the Young house, where the poet's son now lived; and he wanted to do it *with* Dr. Johnson. He feared, however, that Johnson might refuse. Let us see how he goes about his little project:

> We stopped at Welwyn, where I wished much to see, in company with Dr. Johnson, the residence of the authour of *Night Thoughts*, which was then possessed by his son, Mr. Young. Here some address was requisite, for I was not acquainted with Mr. Young, and had I proposed to Dr. Johnson that we should send to him, he would have checked my wish, and perhaps been offended. I therefore concerted with Mr. Dilly [their companion on the journey] that I could steal away from Dr. Johnson and him, and

try what reception I could procure from Mr. Young; if unfavourable, nothing was to be said; but if agreeable, I should return and
notify it to them. I hastened to Mr. Young's, found he was at
home, sent in word that a gentleman desired to wait upon him, and
was shewn into a parlour, where he and a young lady, his daughter,
were sitting. He appeared to be a plain, civil, country gentleman;
and when I begged pardon for presuming to trouble him, but that
I wished much to see his place, if he would give me leave; he
behaved very courteously, and answered, "By all means, Sir; we are
just going to drink tea; will you sit down?" I thanked him, but
said, that Dr. Johnson had come with me from London, and I must
return to the inn and drink tea with him; that my name was
Boswell, I had travelled with him in the Hebrides. "Sir, (said he,)
I should think it a great honour to see Dr. Johnson here. Will you
allow me to send for him?" Availing myself of this opening, I said
that "I would go myself and bring him, when he had drunk tea; he
knew nothing of my calling here." Having been thus successful, I
hastened back to the inn, and informed Dr. Johnson that "Mr.
Young, son of Dr. Young, the authour of *Night Thoughts*, whom I
had just left, desired to have the honour of seeing him at the
house where his father lived." Dr. Johnson luckily made no inquiry
how this invitation had arisen, but agreed to go, and when we
entered Mr. Young's parlour, he addressed him with a very polite
bow, "Sir, I had a curiosity to come and see this place. I had the
honour to know that great man, your father." We went into the
garden, where we found a gravel walk, on each side of which was
a row of trees, planted by Dr. Young, which formed a handsome
Gothick arch. Dr. Johnson called it a fine grove. I beheld it with
reverence.

The scene has been set, the visit arranged. Boswell now can listen to
Johnson discourse upon the subject of Dr. Young. The insatiably curious
Bozzy has, for the occasion at least, satisfied his curiosity and succeeded
in his stratagem. The learned doctor seems to enjoy himself; the
deception has been harmless enough. And the episode illustrates for us
the striking advantages an energetic biographer can enjoy when he is
master not only of documents but of living situations, and when his
subject is within easy and friendly reach.

But Boswell not only set his living scenes; he often gave direction to
the conversation within them. He was free, indeed, to discuss even the
subject of biography with his biographical subject.

Talking of biography, I said, writing a life, a man's peculiarities should be mentioned, because they mark his character.
Johnson. "Sir, there is no doubt as to peculiarities: the question is,
whether a man's vices should be mentioned; for instance, whether
it should be mentioned that Addison and Parnell drank too freely:

for people will probably more easily indulge in drinking from knowing this; so that more ill may be done by the example, than good by telling the whole truth."

And Boswell goes on to attempt to reconcile this view with an opposite view expressed by Johnson on another occasion.

> Here was an instance of his varying from himself in talk; for when Lord Hailes and he sat one morning calmly conversing in my house at Edinburgh, I well remember that Dr. Johnson maintained that "If a man is to write A *Panegyrick,* he must keep vices out of sight; but if he professes to write A *Life,* he must represent it really as it was:" and when I objected to the danger of telling that Parnell drank to excess, he said, that "it would produce an instructive caution to avoid drinking, when it was seen, that even the learning and genius of Parnell could be debased by it." And in the Herbides he maintained, as appears from my *Journal,* that a man's intimate friend should mention his faults, if he writes his life.

I cannot take seriously Johnson's "varying from himself in talk"—Boswell's graceful euphemism for contradicting himself—to which the biographer makes allusion. It gives an impression of the play, back and forth, of an active mind, and perhaps even of tongue in cheek. We cannot know, inevitably, when Johnson used a tone of irony; we can no longer catch the precise inflection of his voice; and I am not at all certain that Boswell, ingenious and clever though he was, was always capable of catching *tone.* But we do know that whatever he may have said in his conversations, Johnson insisted emphatically in his writings upon truth and upon psychological insight in the handling of biography. "There are many," he wrote in the *Idler* of 24 November 1759, "who think it an act of piety to hide the faults and failings of their friends, even when they can no longer suffer by detection. We therefore see whole ranks of characters adorned with uniform panegyric, and not to be known from one another but by extrinsic and casual circumstances." And he added that "If we owe regard to the memory of the dead, there is yet more respect to be laid to knowledge, to virtue and to truth." Johnson followed his own counsel in his *Lives of the Poets,* perhaps with an excess of idiosyncrasy and sometimes a want of critical judgment. But it is easy to forgive him, for he strikes a blow for biographical truth and he himself was aware that idiosyncrasy is a part of character, and character makes for individuality in biography. "A blade of grass is always a blade of grass," Johnson told Mrs. Thrale; "men and women are *my* subjects of inquiry."

Boswell set scenes; he sometimes set the course of the conversation; and he boasted openly and truthfully that he made the life of his man of letters more lively, and therefore ultimately more readable:

> In the evening we had a large company in the drawing-room,
> several ladies, the Bishop of Killaloe, Dr. Percy, Mr. Chamberlayne,
> of the Treasury, &c. &c. Somebody said the life of a mere literary
> man could not be very entertaining. *Johnson.* "But it certainly
> may. This is a remark which has been made, and repeated, without
> justice; why should the life of a literary man be less entertaining
> than the life of any other man? Are there not as interesting
> varieties in such a life? As *a literary life* it may be very entertain-
> ing." *Boswell.* "But it must be better surely, when it is diversified
> with a little active variety—such as his having gone to Jamaica; or
> —his having gone to the Hebrides."

"Johnson," adds Boswell after this flattering—and self-flattering—allusion to the tour of which *he* was the chief architect, "was not displeased
at this."

And so we can see how Boswell helped to *live* the biography he was
ultimately to write; it was he who, on occasion, introduced that "little
active variety" into the career of the literary man he had chosen as his
subject—or as the mirror to his own prodigious vanity? For we might ask,
as we read on, where, in this amazing work, does biography begin and
autobiography end? We have seen how Boswell managed to be both
behind the scenes and within the talk, genially and busily intrusive,
ubiquitous friend, ubiquitous biographer. Perhaps intrusive does not
sufficiently describe his Johnsonian activities, for we know that on one
occasion, when he was cross-examining a third person about
Johnson—and in Johnson's company—the doctor became under-
standably impatient. "You have but two subjects," he thundered at
Boswell, "yourself and me. I am sick of both."

There was, for instance, their little journey undertaken early in 1776.
On page after page Boswell gives us those fine everyday details which
make Johnson come alive for us at every turn. Yet there are moments,
such as when Boswell suddenly begins to have anxieties about his family
in London, which, strictly speaking, have nothing to do with the life of
Johnson. Boswell tells us: "I enjoyed the luxury of our approach to
London, the metropolis which we both loved so much, for the high and
varied intellectual pleasure which it furnishes"—and the inimitable
Bozzy here makes us pause. We wonder: is Boswell traveling with
Johnson or Johnson with Boswell? He adds: "I experienced immediate
happiness while whirled along with such a companion." We do not,
indeed, begrudge Boswell his happiness so long as he keeps his companion in sight; and we are happy enough to be in the presence of his own
extraordinary self. But the biographer, coming upon the scene more than
a century later, finds that he must ride in the coach not only with the
subject but with the former biographer! Indeed, the former biographer,

in more instances than can be counted, manages to step squarely in front of his subject.

When death finally ended the busy life of Dr. Johnson, his disciple, friend, companion, admirer set down his monumental record from a vast long-gathered archive, documentary and reminiscential. Boswell wrote out of close observation; he wrote also from records, as we have seen, sometimes deliberately created—mirrors deliberately held up to catch the reflection of the living Johnson. Singlehanded, in this fashion, he created the first great modern biography. Sir Harold Nicolson has very happily contrasted biography before and after Boswell as the difference between a series of studio portraits (or a succession of lantern slides) and the cinema. "Boswell," said Sir Harold, "invented actuality; he discovered and perfected a biographical formula in which the narrative could be fused with the pictorial, in which the pictorial in its turn could be rendered in a series of photographs so vividly, and above all so rapidly, projected as to convey an impression of continuity, of progression—in a word of life." But we must observe that Boswell was aided in his invention of actuality in biography because Dr. Johnson was *actual* to him. For the fact remains that he did know his subject for twenty-one of his seventy-five years; and while it has been estimated that during these twenty-one years, representing one third of the adult life, he was in Johnson's company on two hundred and seventy-six days, or less than one year, he nevertheless knew a palpable Dr. Johnson; and he knew other persons who knew a palpable Dr. Johnson. He had access not only to his subject but to the subject's wide circle of friends. If he invented actuality, he in some ways invented, or "created," Dr. Johnson as well; or if that be too extreme a way of putting it, let us say that he created lively stage sets and adroit stage directions for the drama he was to write. His book speaks for his power and his assertiveness as a biographer; at the same time he has committed his successors to shifting from point of view to point of view, not only coping with the subject, but puzzling out a large series of mirror images, some with as many distortions as the mirrors in a fun house at a fair.

VI

The biographer who works from life, as Boswell did, has an extraordinary advantage over the biographer who works from the document, whether he plays sceneshifter or not. He has seen his man in the flesh, he has been aware of a three-dimensional being, drawing breath and sitting in the midst of an age they both share. In his mind he retains a sharp image of his subject. He has heard the voice and seen the gesture (and even in our age no recording, no cinema picture can provide a substitute for that). The latecoming biographer hears only the rustle of

the pages amid the silence of the tomb. This is explanation enough for
the fact that the greatest biographies in our literature have been those
which were written by men who knew their subjects and who painted
them as the painter paints his picture—within a room, a street, a
landscape, with a background and a context rich with its million points
of contemporaneous attachment. Boswell, Froude, Lockhart, Forster,
repose upon our shelves with vividness and mass and authority which
later biographers cannot possess.

But the later biographers have quite an opposite advantage, that of
greater objectivity gained from wider perspective, their time distance
which Sir Max Beerbohm so comfortably described in his lecture on
Lytton Strachey: "the past is a work of art, free from irrelevancies and
loose ends . . . the dullards have all disappeared. . . . Everything is
settled. There's nothing to be done about it—nothing but to contemplate it and blandly form theories about this or that aspect of it." The
biographers who knew their subjects in life began with a certain picture
of the man they had known; they had a conception of his personality and
an image to which documents might be fitted. The documents might, in
some cases, alter the image for them, but this does not change the fact
that in re-creating it they shuttled from life to the document and then
from the document to life. The biographer of the long-dead subject
shuttles from one document to another: he begins and he ends with his
documents. He is obliged to spend much of his time in trying to form, in
his mind, that image which his predecessor possessed, so to speak, "ready-
made." He labors to visualize its aspect, its style, its manners. Not having
the testimony of his own eyes, he finds he must use the testimony of
others; and then he discovers that the testimony is often contradictory
and invariably colored by individual points of view. But again, precisely
this awareness of contradictions may give the distant biographer a
marked advantage in his search for the truest picture.

There is then always this peculiar relationship between any biographer and his subject. The biographer undertakes to capture—or to
recapture—mirror images, and he must be careful not to reflect a subject
in a mirror which is too much himself. Long before he will have to
indulge in this dual analysis of subject and self, he must discover the
materials out of which his biography will be written. They must be
gathered in a strange and often compulsive quest upon which every
biographer embarks with a single-mindedness which makes him look into
every book index for the mention of his subject and keeps him browsing
endlessly in libraries. He enters a labyrinth, the exit of which he cannot
know. At the beginning his great worktable is comparatively bare. Long
before he has emerged from the maze it will be cluttered with more

material than he can ever use; or it may remain so bare that he has virtually no story to tell—save a tale of general bafflement. . . .

＊ Suggestions for Reading and Writing

1. Read her "The Art of Biography" to determine whether Virginia Woolf would accept or reject Edel's statement that "the biographer may be as imaginative as he pleases . . . *but he must not imagine the materials.*" Explain your answer.
2. Discuss a selection from this anthology in which the biographer adheres to Edel's admonition that "he must judge the facts, but he must not sit in judgment." Compare the selection you have chosen with one in which the biographer does just the opposite.
3. Write a concise summary of the biographer-subject relationship outlined in Edel's essay. Keep in mind his view that "all biography is . . . a reprojection into words . . . of the inert materials reassembled . . . through the mind of the historian or the biographer."
4. After reading the selection from Boswell's *Life of Johnson,* discuss the validity of Edel's doubt that "Boswell, ingenious and clever though he was, was always capable of catching *tone.*"
5. Is there something akin to the unethical in Boswell's attempts to make his subject's life "more lively, and therefore ultimately more readable"? Could he be compared to a reporter attempting to create a story? If not, why not?
6. Does the life of Gray bear out Edel's view that Johnson "strikes a blow for biographical truth" in his awareness "that idiosyncrasy is a part of character, and character makes for individuality in biography." Cite specific incidents in the life of Gray that support your answer.
7. Edel poses a question that perhaps should be delayed until you have read most of this anthology. He raises the issue (as does W. S. Lewis in his essay "The Difficult Art of Biography") of where the greater advantage rests—with "the biographer who works from life" or with "the biographer who works from the document."

GRAY

Samuel Johnson

The son of a poor Lichfield bookseller, Samuel Johnson (1709–1784) rose through determination, taste, and intelligence from the meanest hackwriting to become the most influential English critic, lexicographer, essayist, and biographer of his century. Ugly, melancholic, irritable—he was difficult to approach, even harder to fool. Conservative in thinking and expression, he detested dishonesty, sham, or hypocrisy.

A poet of merit, though not of the first rank, Johnson established his early reputation with two bitterly satiric poems, London (1738) and The Vanity of Human Wishes (1749). In 1749, the actor David Garrick, who had been one of Johnson's private-school pupils, produced the latter's classical tragedy, Irene. Then, during the following decade, Johnson gained a reputation as an important essayist and lexicographer. Literary historians have made much of his indolence; still Johnson published over three hundred periodical essays in three series: The Rambler (1750–52), The Adventurer (1753), and The Idler (1758–60). In 1755, after eight years of hard work, he produced his monumental Dictionary of the English Language; despite its many faults, it provided, in scope and structure, a model for later dictionaries. Johnson closed the decade with Rasselas (1759), an episodic prose narrative in which he satirized man's attempts to attain perfect earthly happiness.

His remaining quarter century was the happiest period in Johnson's life. Receiving a royal pension, he could indulge his favorite indoor sport: talking. A cultivated, pungent, and even humorous conversationalist, he was the center of a group calling itself the "Club"; it included the most noted minds and wits of the period. Johnson had found his natural element; and his penetrating comments on religion, politics, and literature influenced markedly London's intellectual life.

But Johnson's literary labors were far from over. In 1765, he published his perceptive edition of Shakespeare's plays, with a brilliant critical preface. Later, when well along in his sixties, he wrote fifty-two biographical and critical prefaces to a multi-volumed edition of the English poets: his Lives of the English Poets (1779–81). Illuminating and generous when dealing with writers of whom he approved—Addison, Dryden, Pope—he could be blindly unkind to those not suiting his tastes, notably the new Romantics. But in each study he managed to say a good deal about the man and his work.

If critical controversy has raged over these biographies—especially over the life of Gray—Johnson himself harbored no doubts about this phase of his writing. "The biographical part of literature," he informed Boswell, "is what I love most."

In 1775, Oxford, the university Johnson had left reluctantly because of poverty, bestowed upon him the degree of Doctor of Laws.

* * * * *

Thomas Gray, the son of Mr. Philip Gray, a scrivener of London, was born in Cornhill, November 26, 1716. His grammatical education he received at Eton under the care of Mr. Antrobus, his mother's brother, then assistant to Dr. George, and when he left school, in 1734, entered a pensioner at Peterhouse in Cambridge.

The transition from the school to the college is, to most young scholars, the time from which they date their years of manhood, liberty, and happiness; but Gray seems to have been very little delighted with academical gratifications: he liked at Cambridge neither the mode of life nor the fashion of study, and lived sullenly on to the time when his attendance on lectures was no longer required. As he intended to profess the Common Law he took no degree.

When he had been at Cambridge about five years, Mr. Horace Walpole, whose friendship he had gained at Eton, invited him to travel with him as his companion. They wandered through France into Italy, and Gray's letters contain a very pleasing account of many parts of their journey. But unequal friendships are easily dissolved: at Florence they quarrelled and parted, and Mr. Walpole is now content to have it told that it was by his fault. If we look, however, without prejudice on the world, we shall find that men whose consciousness of their own merit sets them above the compliances of servility are apt enough in their association with superiors to watch their own dignity with troublesome and punctilious jealousy, and in the fervour of independence to exact that attention which they refuse to pay. Part they did, whatever was the quarrel, and the rest of their travels was doubtless more unpleasant to them both. Gray continued his journey in a manner suitable to his own little fortune, with only an occasional servant.

He returned to England in September, 1741, and in about two months afterwards buried his father, who had, by an injudicious waste of money upon a new house, so much lessened his fortune that Gray thought himself too poor to study the law. He therefore retired to Cambridge, where he soon after became Bachelor of Civil Law, and where, without liking the place or its inhabitants, or professing to like them, he passed, except a short residence at London, the rest of his life.

About this time he was deprived of Mr. West, the son of a chancellor of Ireland, a friend on whom he appears to have set a high value, and who deserved his esteem by the powers which he shews in his letters, and in the 'Ode to May,' which Mr. Mason has preserved, as well as by the sincerity with which, when Gray sent him part of *Agrippina*, a tragedy that he had just begun, he gave an opinion which probably intercepted the progress of the work, and which the judgement of every reader will confirm. It was certainly no loss to the English stage that *Agrippina* was never finished.

In this year (1742) Gray seems first to have applied himself seriously to poetry, for in this year were produced the 'Ode to Spring,' his 'Prospect of Eton,' and his 'Ode to Adversity.' He began likewise a Latin poem, *'De Principiis Cogitandi.'*

It may be collected from the narrative of Mr. Mason that his first ambition was to have excelled in Latin poetry: perhaps it were reasonable to wish that he had prosecuted his design; for though there is at present some embarrassment in his phrase and some harshness in his lyric numbers, his copiousness of language is such as very few possess, and his lines, even when imperfect, discover a writer whom practice would quickly have made skilful.

He now lived on at Peterhouse, very little solicitous what others did or thought, and cultivated his mind and enlarged his views without any other purpose than of improving and amusing himself; when Mr. Mason, being elected fellow of Pembroke Hall, brought him a companion who was afterwards to be his editor, and whose fondness and fidelity has kindled in him a zeal of admiration, which cannot be reasonably expected from the neutrality of a stranger and the coldness of a critic.

In this retirement he wrote (1747) an ode on 'The Death of Mr. Walpole's Cat,' and the year afterwards attempted a poem of more importance, on 'Government and Education,' of which the fragments which remain have many excellent lines.

His next production (1750) was his far-famed 'Elegy in the Churchyard,' which, finding its way into a magazine, first, I believe, made him known to the public.

An invitation from Lady Cobham about this time gave occasion to an odd composition called 'A Long Story,' which adds little to Gray's character.

Several of his pieces were published (1753), with designs, by Mr. Bentley, and, that they might in some form or other make a book, only one side of each leaf was printed. I believe the poems and the plates recommended each other so well that the whole impression was soon bought. This year he lost his mother.

Some time afterwards (1756) some young men of the college, whose chambers were near his, diverted themselves with disturbing him by frequent and troublesome noises, and, as is said, by pranks yet more offensive and contemptuous. This insolence, having endured it a while, he represented to the governors of the society, among whom perhaps he had no friends, and, finding his complaint little regarded, removed himself to Pembroke Hall.

In 1757 he published 'The Progress of Poetry' and 'The Bard,' two compositions at which the readers of poetry were at first content to gaze in mute amazement. Some that tried them confessed their inability to understand them, though Warburton said that they were understood as well as the works of Milton and Shakespeare, which it is the fashion to admire. Garrick wrote a few lines in their praise. Some hardy champions undertook to rescue them from neglect, and in a short time many were content to be shewn beauties which they could not see.

Gray's reputation was now so high that, after the death of Cibber, he had the honour of refusing the laurel, which was then bestowed on Mr. Whitehead.

His curiosity not long after drew him away from Cambridge to a lodging near the Museum, where he resided near three years, reading and transcribing; and, so far as can be discovered, very little affected by two odes on 'Oblivion' and 'Obscurity,' in which his lyric performances were ridiculed with much contempt and much ingenuity.

When the Professor of Modern History at Cambridge died he was, as he says, 'cockered and spirited up,' till he asked it of Lord Bute, who sent him a civil refusal; and the place was given to Mr. Brocket, the tutor of Sir James Lowther.

His constitution was weak, and believing that his health was promoted by exercise and change of place he undertook (1765) a journey into Scotland, of which his account, so far as it extends, is very curious and elegant; for as his comprehension was ample his curiosity extended to all the works of art, all the appearances of nature, and all the monuments of past events. He naturally contracted a friendship with Dr. Beattie, whom he found a poet, a philosopher, and a good man. The Mareschal College at Aberdeen offered him the degree of Doctor of Laws, which, having omitted to take it at Cambridge, he thought it decent to refuse.

What he had formerly solicited in vain was at last given him without solicitation. The Professorship of History became again vacant, and he received (1768) an offer of it from the Duke of Grafton. He accepted, and retained it to his death; always designing lectures, but never reading them; uneasy at his neglect of duty, and appeasing his uneasiness with designs of reformation, and with a resolution which he believed himself to have made of resigning the office, if he found himself unable to discharge it.

Ill health made another journey necessary, and he visited (1769) Westmoreland and Cumberland. He that reads his epistolary narration wishes that to travel, and to tell his travels, had been more of his employment; but it is by studying at home that we must obtain the ability of travelling with intelligence and improvement.

His travels and his studies were now near their end. The gout, of which he had sustained many weak attacks, fell upon his stomach, and, yielding to no medicines, produced strong convulsions, which (July 30, 1771) terminated in death.

His character I am willing to adopt, as Mr. Mason has done, from a letter written to my friend Mr. Boswell, by the Rev. Mr. Temple, rector of St. Gluvias in Cornwall; and am as willing as his warmest well-wisher to believe it true.

> Perhaps he was the most learned man in Europe. He was equally acquainted with the elegant and profound parts of science, and that not superficially but thoroughly. He knew every branch of history, both natural and civil; had read all the original historians of England, France, and Italy; and was a great antiquarian. Criticism, metaphysics, morals, politics made a principal part of his study; voyages and travels of all sorts were his favourite amusements; and he had a fine taste in painting, prints, architecture, and gardening. With such a fund of knowledge, his conversation must have been equally instructing and entertaining; but he was also a good man, a man of virtue and humanity. There is no character without some speck, some imperfection; and I think the greatest defect in his was an affectation in delicacy, or rather effeminacy, and a visible fastidiousness, or contempt and disdain of his inferiors in science. He also had, in some degree, that weakness which disgusted Voltaire so much in Mr. Congreve: though he seemed to value

others chiefly according to the progress they had made in knowledge, yet he could not bear to be considered himself merely as a man of letters; and though without birth, or fortune, or station, his desire was to be looked upon as a private independent gentleman, who read for his amusement. Perhaps it may be said, What signifies so much knowledge, when it produced so little. Is it worth taking so much pains to leave no memorial but a few poems? But let it be considered that Mr. Gray was, to others, at least innocently employed; to himself, certainly beneficially. His time passed agreeably; he was every day making some new acquisition in science; his mind was enlarged, his heart softened, his virtue strengthened; the world and mankind were shewn to him without a mask; and he was taught to consider everything as trifling, and unworthy of the attention of a wise man, except the pursuit of knowledge and practice of virtue, in that state wherein God hath placed us.

To this character Mr. Mason has added a more particular account of Gray's skill in zoology. He has remarked that Gray's effeminacy was affected most 'before those whom he did not wish to please'; and that he is unjustly charged with making knowledge his sole reason of preference, as he paid his esteem to none whom he did not likewise believe to be good.

What has occurred to me, from the slight inspection of his letters in which my undertaking has engaged me, is that his mind had a large grasp; that his curiosity was unlimited, and his judgement cultivated; that he was a man likely to love much where he loved at all, but that he was fastidious and hard to please. His contempt, however, is often employed, where I hope it will be approved, upon scepticism and infidelity. His short account of Shaftesbury I will insert.

> You say you cannot conceive how Lord Shaftesbury came to be a philosopher in vogue; I will tell you: first, he was a lord; secondly, he was as vain as any of his readers; thirdly, men are very prone to believe what they do not understand; fourthly, they will believe anything at all, provided they are under no obligation to believe it; fifthly, they love to take a new road, even when that road leads nowhere; sixthly, he was reckoned a fine writer, and seems [seemed] always to mean more than he said. Would you have any more reasons? An interval of above forty years has pretty well destroyed the charm. A dead lord ranks [but] with commoners: vanity is no longer interested in the matter; for a new road is [has] become an old one.

Mr. Mason has added from his own knowledge that though Gray was poor, he was not eager of money, and that out of the little that he had, he was very willing to help the necessitous.

As a writer he had this peculiarity, that he did not write his pieces first rudely, and then correct them, but laboured every line as it arose in the train of composition, and he had a notion not very peculiar, that he could not write but at certain times, or at happy moments; a fantastic foppery, to which my kindness for a man of learning and of virtue wishes him to have been superior.

Gray's poetry is now to be considered, and I hope not to be looked on as an enemy to his name if I confess that I contemplate it with less pleasure than his life.

His 'Ode on Spring' has something poetical, both in the language and the thought; but the language is too luxuriant, and the thoughts have nothing new. There has of late arisen a practice of giving to adjectives, derived from substantives, the termination of participles, such as the *cultured* plain, the *daisied* bank; but I was sorry to see, in the lines of a scholar like Gray, 'the *honied* Spring.' The morality is natural, but too stale; the conclusion is pretty.

The poem on the cat was doubtless by its author considered as a trifle, but it is not a happy trifle. In the first stanza 'the azure flowers that blow' shew resolutely a rhyme is sometimes made when it cannot easily be found. Selima, the cat, is called a nymph, with some violence both to language and sense; but there is good use made of it when it is done; for of the two lines,

> What female heart can gold despise?
> What cat's averse to fish?

the first relates merely to the nymph, and the second only to the cat. The sixth stanza contains a melancholy truth, that a 'favourite has no friend,' but the last ends in a pointed sentence of no relation to the purpose; if what glistered had been 'gold,' the cat would not have gone into the water; and, if she had, would not less have been drowned.

The 'Prospect of Eton College' suggests nothing to Gray which every beholder does not equally think and feel. His supplication to father Thames, to tell him who drives the hoop or tosses the ball, is useless and puerile. Father Thames has no better means of knowing than himself. His epithet 'buxom health' is not elegant; he seems not to understand the word. Gray thought his language more poetical as it was more remote from common use: finding in Dryden 'honey redolent of Spring,' an expression that reaches the utmost limits of our language, Gray drove it a little more beyond common apprehension, by making 'gales' to be 'redolent of joy and youth.'

Of the 'Ode on Adversity' the hint was at first taken from '*O Diva, gratum quæ regis Antium*'; but Gray has excelled his original by the variety of his sentiments and by their moral application. Of this piece, at once poetical and rational, I will not by slight objections violate the dignity.

My process has now brought me to the 'Wonderful Wonder of Wonders,' the two Sister Odes; by which, though either vulgar ignorance or commonsense at first universally rejected them, many have been since persuaded to think themselves delighted. I am one of those that are willing to be pleased, and therefore would gladly find the meaning of the first stanza of 'The Progress of Poetry.'

Gray seems in his rapture to confound the images of 'spreading sound' and 'running water.' A 'stream of music' may be allowed; but where does music, however 'smooth and strong,' after having visited the 'verdant vales,' 'rowl down the steep amain,' so as that 'rocks and nodding groves rebellow to the roar'? If this be said of music, it is nonsense; if it be said of water, it is nothing to the purpose.

The second stanza, exhibiting Mars's car and Jove's eagle, is unworthy of further notice. Criticism disdains to chase a schoolboy to his commonplaces.

To the third it may likewise be objected that it is drawn from mythology, though such as may be more easily assimilated to real life. 'Idalia's velvet-green' has something of cant. An epithet or metaphor drawn from nature ennobles art; an epithet or metaphor drawn from art degrades nature. Gray is too fond of words arbitrarily compounded. 'Many-twinkling' was formerly censured as not analogical; we may say *many-spotted*, but scarcely *many-spotting*. This stanza, however, has something pleasing.

Of the second ternary of stanzas, the first endeavours to tell something, and would have told it had it not been crossed by Hyperion; the second describes well enough the universal prevalence of poetry, but I am afraid that the conclusion will not rise from the premises. The caverns of the North and the plains of Chili are not the residences of 'Glory' and 'generous Shame.' But that poetry and virtue go always together is an opinion so pleasing that I can forgive him who resolves to think it true.

The third stanza sounds big with 'Delphi,' and 'Egean,' and 'Ilissus,' and 'Meander,' and 'hallowed fountain' and 'solemn sound'; but in all Gray's odes there is a kind of cumbrous splendour which we wish away. His position is at last false: in the time of Dante and Petrarch, from whom he derives our first school of poetry, Italy was overrun by 'tyrant power' and 'coward vice'; nor was our state much better when we first borrowed the Italian arts.

Of the third ternary, the first gives a mythological birth of Shakespeare. What is said of that mighty genius is true; but it is not said happily: the real effects of this poetical power are put out of sight by the pomp of machinery. Where truth is sufficient to fill the mind, fiction is worse than useless; the counterfeit debases the genuine.

His account of Milton's blindness, if we suppose it caused by study in the formation of his poem, a supposition surely allowable, is poetically true, and happily imagined. But the 'car' of Dryden, with his 'two coursers,' has nothing in it peculiar; it is a car in which any other rider may be placed.

'The Bard' appears at the first view to be, as Algarotti and others have remarked, an imitation of the prophecy of Nereus. Algarotti thinks it superior to its original, and, if preference depends only on the imagery and animation of the two poems, his judgement is right. There is in 'The Bard' more force, more thought, and more variety. But to copy is less than to invent, and the copy has been unhappily produced at a wrong time. The fiction of Horace was to the Romans credible; but its revival disgusts us with apparent and unconquerable falsehood. *Incredulus odi.*

To select a singular event, and swell it to a giant's bulk by fabulous appendages of spectres and predictions, has little difficulty, for he that forsakes the probable may always find the marvellous. And it has little use: we are affected only as we believe; we are improved only as we find something to be imitated or declined. I do not see that 'The Bard' promotes any truth, moral or political.

His stanzas are too long, especially his epodes; the ode is finished before the ear has learned its measures, and consequently before it can receive pleasure from their consonance and recurrence.

Of the first stanza the abrupt beginning has been celebrated; but technical beauties can give praise only to the inventor. It is in the power of any man to rush abruptly upon his subject, that has read the ballad of 'Johnny Armstrong,'

Is there ever a man in all Scotland—

The initial resemblances, or alliterations, 'ruin,' 'ruthless,' 'helm nor hauberk,' are below the grandeur of a poem that endeavours at sublimity.

In the second stanza the bard is well described; but in the third we have the puerilities of obsolete mythology. When we are told that Cadwallo 'hush'd the stormy main,' and that Modred 'made huge Plinlimmon bow his cloud-top'd head,' attention recoils from the repetition of a tale that, even when it was first heard, was heard with scorn.

The 'weaving' of the 'winding sheet' he borrowed, as he owns, from the northern bards; but their texture, however, was very properly the work of female powers, as the art of spinning the thread of life in another mythology. Theft is always dangerous; Gray has made weavers of his slaughtered bards by a fiction outrageous and incongruous. They are then called upon to 'Weave the warp, and weave the woof,' perhaps with no great propriety; for it is by crossing the woof with the warp that men weave the web or piece; and the first line was dearly bought by the admission of its wretched correspondent, 'Give ample room and verge enough.' He has, however, no other line as bad.

The third stanza of the second ternary is commended, I think, beyond its merit. The personification is indistinct. Thirst and hunger are not alike, and their features, to make the imagery perfect, should have been discriminated. We are told, in the same stanza, how 'towers' are 'fed.' But I will no longer look for particular faults; yet let it be observed that the ode might have been concluded with an action of better example: but suicide is always to be had without expense of thought.

These odes are marked by glittering accumulations of ungraceful ornaments: they strike, rather than please; the images are magnified by affectation; the language is laboured into harshness. The mind of the writer seems to work with unnatural violence. 'Double, double, toil and trouble.' He has a kind of strutting dignity, and is tall by walking on tiptoe. His art and his struggle are too visible, and there is too little appearance of ease and nature.

To say that he has no beauties would be unjust: a man like him, of great learning and great industry, could not but produce something valuable. When he pleases least, it can only be said that a good design was ill directed.

His translations of Northern and Welsh poetry deserve praise: the imagery is preserved, perhaps often improved; but the language is unlike the language of other poets.

In the character of his 'Elegy' I rejoice to concur with the common reader; for by the common sense of readers uncorrupted with literary prejudices, after all the refinements of subtlety and the dogmatism of learning, must be finally decided all claim to poetical honours. The 'Churchyard' abounds with images which find a mirrour in every mind, and with sentiments to which every bosom returns an echo. The four stanzas beginning 'Yet even these bones' are to me original: I have never seen the notions in any other place; yet he that reads them here persuades himself that he has always felt them. Had Gray written often thus it had been vain to blame, and useless to praise him.

↑ Suggestions for Reading and Writing

1. To what personal qualities does Johnson attribute Gray's quarrel with Walpole? Does he relate these qualities to his general estimate of Gray's character? Explain. (For more recent views of Gray, see R. W. Ketton

Cremer's *Thomas Gray* [1935] and William P. Jones's *Thomas Gray, Scholar* [1937].)

2. Comment on Johnson's statement that "it is by studying at home that we must obtain the ability of travelling with intelligence and improvement." Is he merely saying that the more we have read about a place, the more we derive from visiting it?

3. What do his comments about Gray's habits of composition tell us about Johnson's own writing habits?

4. Are you impressed by Johnson's narrative technique here? What do you wish he had done differently? Compare *Gray* with his *The Life of Savage* (1744) and point out general similarities and differences in approach. (For background, see Bergen Evans' "Dr. Johnson's Theory of Biography," *Review of English Studies* [1934], 301–310. See also Mark Longaker's *English Biography in the Eighteenth Century* [1931] and Donald A. Stauffer's *The Art of Biography in Eighteenth Century England* [1941].)

5. After reading the poems discussed here, evaluate Johnson's estimate of Gray as poet. Be specific. (For a discussion of Johnson as critic, see Joseph Epes Brown's *The Critical Opinions of Samuel Johnson* [1926] and Jean H. Hagstrum's *Samuel Johnson's Literary Criticism* [1952].)

6. Do you agree completely with Johnson's dictum that "Where truth is sufficient to fill the mind, fiction is worse than useless"? Explain.

7. In discussing Gray's "The Bard," Johnson indicates a poem's value derives from its promotion of "any truth, moral or political." Do you agree? Would you apply this criterion to a short story? To a novel?

8. For a sampling of the famed Johnson wit, dip into the *Dictionary* for the much-quoted definitions of "lexicographer," "network," "oats," "patriotism," "patron," "pension," "Tory," "Whig." What do these—and other definitions you may run across—reveal of Johnson's social and political views?

from

LIFE
OF
JOHNSON

James Boswell

Today James Boswell (1740–1795) is viewed as the most significant biographer between Plutarch and Strachey. Few who knew him, however, would have predicted that this emotional, ambitious, amoral little man would attain lasting literary eminence as author of the greatest biography ever written.

The son of a Scottish landowner and judge, Boswell was born in Edinburgh and attended the universities of Edinburgh, Glasgow, and Utrecht. His father wanted him to study law; however, Boswell had quite different goals: to live a soldier's exciting life and to live it in London. But failing to secure a commission in the Guards, he reluctantly took up the law, married, and began a family.

Boswell had met Dr. Johnson in 1763, but not until a decade later was he able to spend prolonged periods in the great man's company. In 1773 Boswell, despite opposition, was elected to the "Club"—as the intellectual group clustered about Johnson then was called. The same year he and Johnson journeyed to the Hebrides, and in 1776 they again traveled together. Historians calculate Boswell saw Johnson a total of 276 days. Having decided to write a biography of Johnson, Boswell utilized their every moment together—observing and recording almost stenographically the conversation, the incidents, and the experiences they shared.

To most acquaintances Boswell was merely a pushy parasite trying to fashion a literary reputation from his friendship with the great Dr. Johnson. "Who would purchase fame as an author, or in any other way," declared one contemporary, "on such terms as this creature, Boswell?" This view was repeated and expanded by nineteenth-century commentators. Time has proved it grossly unfair. Boswell had traveled much and had been writing since the age of twenty: he had published pamphlets; essays; letters; a political allegory, Dorando (1767); and a travel journal, An Account of Corsica (1768). While these were minor, he was writing also his now famous Malahide diaries. About these his contemporaries knew nothing; they have come to light only in recent years. Illuminating both Boswell and eighteenth-century life, the diaries, or journals, have enhanced his stature as a personality and man of letters.

Johnson himself approved of Boswell's biographical purpose, while the latter let nothing deter his mission; venerating his subject, he nevertheless showed Johnson's occasional bad temper, rudeness, and unreasonableness. After Johnson's death, Boswell published his The Journal of a Tour to the Hebrides with Samuel Johnson, LL.D. (1785). It was a tremendous success. So Boswell assembled his notes and gathered other pertinent materials for the biography. The Life of Johnson appeared in 1791 and ensured immortality for subject and biographer. For in it Boswell had revealed Johnson's great talent: conversation. To catch Johnson at his conversational best, Boswell had been not only observer and recorder but participant, social arranger, and interviewer. In short, he had helped create the matter of his study.

Boswell lived life at a furious pace and died at fifty-four.

1   1   1   1   1

. . . . .

Mr. Thomas Davies, the actor, who then kept a bookseller's shop in Russel Street, Covent Garden, told me that Johnson was very much his friend, and came frequently to his house, where he more than once invited me to meet him; but by some unlucky accident or other he was prevented from coming to us.

Mr. Thomas Davies was a man of good understanding and talents, with the advantage of a liberal education. Though somewhat pompous, he was an entertaining companion; and his literary performances have no inconsiderable share of merit. He was a friendly and very hospitable man.

Both he and his wife (who has been celebrated for her beauty), though upon the stage for many years, maintained an uniform decency of character; and Johnson esteemed them and lived in as easy an intimacy with them as with any family which he used to visit. Mr. Davies recollected several of Johnson's remarkable sayings and was one of the best of the many imitators of his voice and manner while relating them. He increased my impatience more and more to see the extraordinary man whose works I highly valued and whose conversation was reported to be so peculiarly excellent.

At last, on Monday the 16th of May, when I was sitting in Mr. Davies's back-parlour, after having drunk tea with him and Mrs. Davies, Johnson unexpectedly came into the shop; and Mr. Davies having perceived him through the glass door in the room in which we were sitting, advancing towards us,—he announced his awful approach to me, somewhat in the manner of an actor in the part of Horatio, when he addresses Hamlet on the appearance of his father's ghost, 'Look, my lord, it comes.' I found that I had a very perfect idea of Johnson's figure, from the portrait of him painted by Sir Joshua Reynolds soon after he had published his *Dictionary*, in the attitude of sitting in his easy chair in deep meditation, which was the first picture his friend did for him, which Sir Joshua very kindly presented to me, and from which an engraving has been made for this work. Mr. Davies mentioned my name and respectfully introduced me to him. I was much agitated; and recollecting his prejudice against the Scotch, of which I had heard much, I said to Davies, 'Don't tell where I come from.'—'From Scotland,' cried Davies, roguishly. 'Mr. Johnson,' said I, 'I do indeed come from Scotland, but I cannot help it.' I am willing to flatter myself that I meant this as light pleasantry to sooth and conciliate him, and not as an humiliating abasement at the expense of my country. But however that might be, this speech was somewhat unlucky; for with that quickness of wit for which he was so remarkable, he seized the expression 'Come from Scotland,' which I used in the sense of being of that country; and, as if I had said that I had come away from it, or left it, retorted, 'That, sir, I find, is what a very great many of your countrymen cannot help.' This stroke stunned me a good deal; and when we had sat down, I felt myself not a little embarrassed, and apprehensive of what might come next. He then addressed himself to Davies: 'What do you think of Garrick? He has refused me an order for the play for Miss Williams, because he knows the house will be full and that an order would be worth three shillings.' Eager to take any opening to get into conversation with him, I ventured to say, 'O, sir, I cannot think Mr. Garrick would grudge such a trifle to you.' 'Sir,' said he, with a stern look, 'I have known David Garrick longer than you have done, and I know no right you have to talk to me on the subject.' Perhaps I deserved this check; for it was rather presumptuous in me, an entire stranger, to express any doubt of the justice of his animadversion upon his old acquaintance and pupil. I now felt myself much mortified and began to think that the hope which I had long indulged of obtaining his acquaintance was blasted. And, in truth, had not my ardour been uncommonly strong and my resolution uncommonly persevering, so rough a reception might have deterred me forever from making any further attempts. Fortunately, however, I remained upon the field not wholly discomfited; and was soon rewarded by hearing some of his conversation, of which I preserved the following short minute, without marking the questions and observations by which it was produced.

'People (he remarked) may be taken in once, who imagine that an author is greater in private life than other men. Uncommon parts require uncommon opportunities for their exertion.

'In barbarous society, superiority of parts is of real consequence. Great strength or great wisdom is of much value to an individual. But in more polished times there are people to do everything for money; and then there are a number of other superiorities, such as those of birth and fortune, and rank, that dissipate men's attention, and leave no extraordinary share of respect for personal and intellectual superiority. This is wisely ordered by Providence, to preserve some equality among mankind.'

'Sir, this book (*The Elements of Criticism*, which he had taken up) is a pretty essay and deserves to be held in some estimation, though much of it is chimerical.'

Speaking of one who with more than ordinary boldness attacked public measures and the royal family, he said,

'I think he is safe from the law, but he is an abusive scoundrel; and instead of applying to my Lord Chief Justice to punish him, I would send half a dozen footmen and have him well ducked.'

'The notion of liberty amuses the people of England, and helps to keep off the *tædium vitæ*. When a butcher tells you that *his heart bleeds for his country*, he has, in fact, no uneasy feeling.'

'Sheridan will not succeed at Bath with his oratory. Ridicule has gone down before him, and, I doubt, Derrick is his enemy.'

'Derrick may do very well, as long as he can outrun his character; but the moment his character gets up with him, it is all over.'

It is, however, but just to record that some years afterwards, when I reminded him of this sarcasm, he said, 'Well, but Derrick has now got a character that he need not run away from.'

I was highly pleased with the extraordinary vigour of his conversation and regretted that I was drawn away from it by an engagement at another place. I had, for a part of the evening, been left alone with him and had ventured to make an observation now and then, which he received very civilly; so that I was satisfied that though there was a roughness in his manner, there was no ill nature in his disposition. Davies followed me to the door, and when I complained to him a little of the hard blows which the great man had given me, he kindly took upon him to console me by saying, 'Don't be uneasy. I can see he likes you very well.'

A few days afterwards I called on Davies and asked him if he thought I might take the liberty of waiting on Mr. Johnson at his chambers in the Temple. He said I certainly might and that Mr. Johnson would take it as a compliment. So upon Tuesday, the 24th of May, after having been enlivened by the witty sallies of Messieurs Thornton, Wilkes, Churchill and Lloyd, with whom I had passed the morning, I boldly repaired to Johnson. His chambers were on the first floor of No. 1, Inner Temple Lane, and I entered them with an impression given me by the Reverend Dr. Blair of Edinburgh, who had been introduced to him not long before, and described his having 'found the Giant in his den'; an expression, which, when I came to be pretty well acquainted with Johnson, I repeated to him, and he was diverted at this picturesque account of himself. Dr. Blair had been presented to him by Dr. James Fordyce. At this time the controversy concerning the pieces published by Mr. James Macpherson, as translations of Ossian, was at its height. Johnson had all along denied their authenticity; and, what was still more provoking to their admirers, maintained that they had no merit. The subject having been introduced by Dr. Fordyce, Dr. Blair, relying on the internal evidence of their antiquity, asked Dr. Johnson whether he thought any man of a modern age could have written such poems? Johnson replied, 'Yes, sir, many men, many women, and many children.' Johnson, at this time, did not know that Dr. Blair had just published a dissertation, not only defending their authenticity, but seriously ranking them with the poems of Homer and Virgil; and when he was afterwards informed of this circumstance, he expressed some displeasure at Dr. Fordyce's having suggested the topic and said, 'I am not sorry that they got thus much for their pains. Sir, it was like leading one to talk of a book, when the author is concealed behind the door.'

He received me very courteously; but, it must be confessed, that his apartment, and furniture, and morning dress were sufficiently uncouth. His brown suit of clothes looked very rusty; he had on a little old shrivelled unpowdered wig, which was too small for his head; his shirt-neck and knees of his breeches were loose; his black worsted stockings ill drawn up; and he had a pair of unbuckled shoes by way of slippers. But all these slovenly particularities were forgotten the moment that he began to talk. Some gentlemen, whom I do not recollect, were sitting with him; and when they went away, I also rose; but he said to me, 'Nay, don't go.'—'Sir,' said I, 'I am afraid that I intrude upon you. It is benevolent to allow me to sit and hear you.' He seemed pleased with this compliment, which I sincerely paid him, and answered, 'Sir, I am obliged to any man who visits me.'—I have preserved the following short minute of what passed this day.

'Madness frequently discovers itself merely by unnecessary deviation from the usual modes of the world. My poor friend Smart shewed the disturbance of his mind by falling upon his knees and saying his prayers in the street, or in any other unusual place. Now although, rationally speaking, it is greater madness not to pray at all, than to pray as Smart did, I am afraid there are so many who do not pray, that their understanding is not called in question.'

Concerning this unfortunate poet, Christopher Smart, who was confined in a madhouse, he had, at another time, the following conversation with Dr. Burney.—BURNEY. 'How does poor Smart do, sir; is he likely to recover?' JOHNSON. 'It seems as if his mind had ceased to struggle with the disease; for he grows fat upon it.' BURNEY. 'Perhaps, sir, that may be from want of exercise.' JOHNSON. 'No, sir; he has partly as much exercise as he used to have, for he digs in the garden. Indeed, before his confinement, he used for exercise to walk to the alehouse; but he was *carried* back again. I did not think he ought to be shut up. His infirmities were not noxious to society. He insisted on people praying with him; and I'd as lief pray with Kit Smart as anyone else. Another charge was that he did not love clean linen; and I have no passion for it.'

Johnson continued. 'Mankind have a great aversion to intellectual labour; but even supposing knowledge to be easily attainable, more people would be content to be ignorant than would take even a little trouble to acquire it.'

'The morality of an action depends on the motive from which we act. If I fling half a crown to a beggar with intention to break his head and he picks it up and buys victuals with it, the physical effect is good; but, with respect to me, the action is very wrong. So, religious exercises, if not performed with an intention to please God, avail us nothing. As our Saviour says of those who perform them from other motives, "Verily they have their reward." '

'The Christian religion has very strong evidences. It, indeed, appears in some degree strange to reason; but in history we have undoubted facts, against which, in reasoning *à priori*, we have more arguments than we have for them; but then, testimony has great weight, and casts the balance. I would recommend to every man whose faith is yet unsettled, Grotius,—Dr. Pearson,—and Dr. Clarke.'

Talking of Garrick, he said, 'He is the first man in the world for sprightly conversation.'

When I rose a second time he again pressed me to stay, which I did.

He told me that he generally went abroad at four in the afternoon and seldom came home till two in the morning. I took the liberty to ask if he did not think it wrong to live thus, and not make more use of his great talents. He owned it was a bad habit. On reviewing, at the distance of many years, my journal of this period, I wonder how, at my first visit, I ventured to talk to him so freely, and that he bore it with so much indulgence.

Before we parted, he was so good as to promise to favour me with his company one evening at my lodgings; and, as I took my leave, shook me cordially by the hand. It is almost needless to add that I felt no little elation at having now so happily established an acquaintance of which I had been so long ambitious.

My readers will, I trust, excuse me for being thus minutely circumstantial, when it is considered that the acquaintance of Dr. Johnson was to me a most valuable acquisition, and laid the foundation of whatever instruction and entertainment they may receive from my collections concerning the great subject of the work which they are now perusing.

I did not visit him again till Monday, June 13, at which time I recollect no part of his conversation, except that when I told him I had been to see Johnson ride upon three horses, he said, 'Such a man, sir, should be encouraged; for his performances shew the extent of the human powers in one instance and thus tend to raise our opinion of the faculties of man. He shews what may be attained by persevering application; so that every man may hope that by giving as much application, although perhaps he may never ride three horses at a time or dance upon a wire, yet he may be equally expert in whatever profession he has chosen to pursue.'

He again shook me by the hand at parting and asked me why I did not come oftener to him. Trusting that I was now in his good graces, I answered that he had not given me much encouragement and reminded him of the check I had received from him at our first interview. 'Poh, poh!' said he, with a complacent smile, 'never mind these things. Come to me as often as you can. I shall be glad to see you.'

I had learnt that his place of frequent resort was the Mitre Tavern in Fleet Street, where he loved to sit up late, and I begged I might be allowed to pass an evening with him there soon, which he promised I should. A few days afterwards I met him near Temple Bar, about one o'clock in the morning, and asked if he would then go to the Mitre. 'Sir,' said he, 'it is too late; they won't let us in. But I'll go with you another night with all my heart.'

A revolution of some importance in my plan of life had just taken place; for instead of procuring a commission in the footguards, which was my own inclination, I had, in compliance with my father's wishes, agreed to study the law, and was soon to set out for Utrecht, to hear the lectures of an excellent civilian in that university, and then to proceed on my travels. Though very desirous of obtaining Dr. Johnson's advice and instructions on the mode of pursuing my studies, I was at this time so occupied, shall I call it? or so dissipated, by the amusements of London, that our next meeting was not till Saturday, June 25, when happening to dine at Clifton's eating-house, in Butcher Row, I was surprised to perceive Johnson come in and take his seat at another table. The mode of dining, or rather being fed, at such houses in London, is well known to many to be particularly unsocial, as there is no ordinary, or united company, but each person has his own mess, and is under no obligation to hold any intercourse with any one. A liberal and full-minded man, however, who loves to talk, will break through this churlish and unsocial restraint. Johnson and an Irish gentleman got into a dispute concerning the cause of some part of mankind being black. 'Why, sir,' said Johnson, 'it has been accounted for in three ways: either by supposing that they are the posterity of Ham, who was cursed; or that God at first created two kinds of men, one black and another white; or that by the heat of the sun the skin is scorched, and so acquires a sooty hue. This matter has been much canvassed among naturalists, but has never been brought to any certain issue.' What the Irishman said is totally obliterated from my mind; but I remember that he became very warm and intemperate in his expressions; upon which Johnson rose, and quietly walked away. When he had retired, his antagonist took his revenge, as he thought, by saying, 'He has a most ungainly figure, and an affectation of pomposity, unworthy of a man of genius.'

Johnson had not observed that I was in the room. I followed him, however, and he agreed to meet me in the evening at the Mitre. I called on him, and we went thither at nine. We had a good supper, and port wine, of which he then sometimes drank a bottle. The orthodox high-church sound of the Mitre,—the figure and manner of the celebrated Samuel Johnson,—the extraordinary power and precision of his conversation, and the pride arising from finding myself admitted as his companion, produced a variety of sensations, and a pleasing elevation of mind beyond what I had ever before experienced. I find in my journal the following minute of our conversation, which, though it will give but a very faint notion of what passed, is, in some degree, a valuable record;

and it will be curious in this view, as shewing how habitual to his mind were some opinions which appear in his works.

'Colley Cibber, sir, was by no means a blockhead; but by arrogating to himself too much, he was in danger of losing that degree of estimation to which he was entitled. His friends gave out that he *intended* his birthday odes should be bad: but that was not the case, sir; for he kept them many months by him, and a few years before he died he shewed me one of them, with great solicitude to render it as perfect as might be, and I made some corrections, to which he was not very willing to submit. I remember the following couplet in allusion to the King and himself:

> Perched on the eagle's soaring wing,
> The lowly linnet loves to sing.

Sir, he had heard something of the fabulous tale of the wren sitting upon the eagle's wing, and he had applied it to a linnet. Cibber's familiar style, however, was better than that which Whitehead has assumed. *Grand* nonsense is insupportable. Whitehead is but a little man to inscribe verses to players.'

I did not presume to controvert this censure, which was tinctured with his prejudice against players; but I could not help thinking that a dramatic poet might with propriety pay a compliment to an eminent performer, as Whitehead has very happily done in his verses to Mr. Garrick.

'Sir, I do not think Gray a first-rate poet. He has not a bold imagination, nor much command of words. The obscurity in which he has involved himself will not persuade us that he is sublime. His 'Elegy in a Churchyard' has a happy selection of images, but I don't like what are called his great things. His ode which begins

> Ruin seize thee, ruthless King,
> Confusion on thy banners wait!

has been celebrated for its abruptness, and plunging into the subject all at once. But such arts as these have no merit, unless when they are original. We admire them only once; and this abruptness has nothing new in it. We have had it often before. Nay, we have it in the old song of 'Johnny Armstrong':

> Is there ever a man in all Scotland
> From the highest estate to the lowest degree, etc.

And then, sir,

> Yes, there is a man in Westmoreland,
> And Johnny Armstrong they do him call.

there, now, you plunge at once into the subject. You have no previous narration to lead you to it.—The two next lines in that ode are, I think, very good:

> Though fann'd by conquest's crimson wing,
> They mock the air with idle state.'

Here let it be observed that although his opinion of Gray's poetry was widely different from mine, and I believe from that of most men of taste, by whom it is with justice highly admired, there is certainly much absurdity in the clamour which has been raised, as if he had been culpably injurious to the merit of that bard and had been actuated by envy. Alas! ye little shortsighted critics, could Johnson be envious of the talents of any of his contemporaries? That his opinion on this subject was what in private and in public he uniformly expressed, regardless of what others might think, we may wonder, and perhaps regret; but it is shallow and unjust to charge him with expressing what he did not think.

Finding him in a placid humour and wishing to avail myself of the opportunity which I fortunately had of consulting a sage, to hear whose wisdom, I conceived in the ardour of youthful imagination, that men filled with a noble enthusiasm for intellectual improvement would gladly have resorted from distant lands;—I opened my mind to him ingenuously, and gave him a little sketch of my life, to which he was pleased to listen with great attention.

I acknowledged that, though educated very strictly in the principles of religion, I had for some time been misled into a certain degree of infidelity; but that I was come now to a better way of thinking and was fully satisfied of the truth of the Christian revelation, though I was not clear as to every point considered to be orthodox. Being at all times a curious examiner of the human mind, and pleased with an undisguised display of what had passed in it, he called to me with warmth, 'Give me your hand; I have taken a liking to you.' He then began to descant upon the force of testimony and the little we could know of final causes; so that the objections of why was it so? or why was it not so? ought not to disturb us: adding, that he himself had at one period been guilty of a temporary neglect of religion, but that it was not the result of argument, but mere absence of thought.

After having given credit to reports of his bigotry, I was agreeably surprised when he expressed the following very liberal sentiment, which has the additional value of obviating an objection to our holy religion, founded upon the discordant tenets of Christians themselves: 'For my part, sir, I think all Christians, whether Papists or Protestants, agree in the essential articles, and that their differences are trivial, and rather political than religious.'

We talked of belief in ghosts. He said, 'Sir, I make a distinction between what a man may experience by the mere strength of his imagination and what imagination cannot possibly produce. Thus, suppose I should think that I saw a form and heard a voice cry "Johnson, you are a very wicked fellow, and unless you repent you will certainly be punished"; my own unworthiness is so deeply impressed upon my mind that I might *imagine* I thus saw and heard, and therefore I should not believe that an external communication had been made to me. But if a form should appear, and a voice should tell me that a particular man had died at a particular place, and a particular hour, a fact which I had no apprehension of, nor any means of knowing, and this fact, with all its circumstances, should afterwards be unquestionably proved, I should, in that case, be persuaded that I had supernatural intelligence imparted to me.'

Here it is proper, once for all, to give a true and fair statement of Johnson's way of thinking upon the question whether departed spirits are ever permitted to appear in this world, or in any way to operate upon human life. He has been ignorantly misrepresented as weakly credulous upon that subject; and, therefore, though I feel an inclination to disdain and treat with silent contempt so foolish a notion concerning my illustrious friend, yet as I find it has gained ground, it is necessary to refute it. The real fact then is that Johnson had a very philosophical mind, and such a rational respect for testimony as to make him submit his understanding to what was authentically proved, though he could not comprehend why it was so. Being thus disposed, he was willing to inquire into the truth of any relation of supernatural agency, a general belief of which has prevailed in all nations and ages. But so far was he from being the dupe of implicit faith that he examined the matter with a jealous attention, and no man was more ready to refute its falsehood when he had discovered it. Churchill, in his poem entitled 'The Ghost,' availed himself of the absurd credulity imputed to Johnson and drew a caricature of him under the name of 'Pomposo,' representing him as one of the believers of the story of a ghost in Cock Lane, which, in the year 1762, had gained very general credit in London. Many of my readers, I am convinced, are to this hour under an impression that Johnson was thus foolishly deceived. It will therefore surprise them a good deal when they are informed upon undoubted authority that Johnson was one of those by whom the imposture was detected. The story had become so popular that he thought it should be investigated; and in this research he was assisted by the Reverend Dr. Douglas, now Bishop of Salisbury, the great detector of impostures; who informs me, that after the gentlemen who went and examined into the evidence were satisfied of its falsity, Johnson wrote in their presence an account of it which was published in the newspapers and *Gentleman's Magazine*, and undeceived the world.

Our conversation proceeded. 'Sir,' said he, 'I am a friend to subordination, as most conducive to the happiness of society. There is a reciprocal pleasure in governing and being governed.'

'Dr. Goldsmith is one of the first men we now have as an author, and he is a very worthy man too. He has been loose in his principles, but he is coming right.'

I mentioned Mallet's tragedy of *Elvira*, which had been acted the preceding winter at Drury Lane, and that the Honourable Andrew Erskine, Mr. Dempster, and myself had joined in writing a pamphlet entitled *Critical Strictures* against it. That the mildness of Dempster's disposition had, however, relented; and he had candidly said, 'We have hardly a right to abuse this tragedy; for bad as it is, how vain should either of us be to write one not near so good.' JOHNSON. 'Why no, sir; this is not just reasoning. You *may* abuse a tragedy, though you cannot write one. You may scold a carpenter who has made you a bad table, though you cannot make a table. It is not your trade to make tables.'

When I talked to him of the paternal estate to which I was heir, he said, 'Sir, let me tell you, that to be a Scotch landlord, where you have a number of families dependent upon you and attached to you, is, perhaps, as high a situation as humanity can arrive at. A merchant upon the 'Change of London, with a hundred thousand pounds, is nothing: an English duke, with an immense fortune, is nothing: he has no tenants who consider themselves as under his patriarchal care and who will follow him to the field upon any emergency.'

His notion of the dignity of a Scotch landlord had been formed upon what he had heard of the Highland chiefs; for it is long since a lowland landlord has been so curtailed in his feudal authority that he has little more influence over his tenants than an English landlord; and of late years most of the Highland chiefs have destroyed, by means too well known, the princely power which they once enjoyed.

He proceeded: 'Your going abroad, sir, and breaking off idle habits, may be of great importance to you. I would go where there are courts and learned men. There is a good deal of Spain that has not been perambulated. I would have you go thither. A man of inferiour talents to yours may furnish us with useful observations upon that country.' His supposing me, at that period of life, capable of writing an account of my travels that would deserve to be read, elated me not a little.

I appeal to every impartial reader whether this faithful detail of his frankness, complacency, and kindness to a young man, a stranger and a

Scotchman, does not refute the unjust opinion of the harshness of his general demeanour. His occasional reproofs of folly, impudence, or impiety, and even the sudden sallies of his constitutional irritability of temper, which have been preserved for the poignancy of their wit, have produced that opinion among those who have not considered that such instances, though collected by Mrs. Piozzi into a small volume, and read over in a few hours, were, in fact, scattered through a long series of years; years, in which his time was chiefly spent in instructing and delighting mankind by his writings and conversation, in acts of piety to God, and good will to men.

I complained to him that I had not yet acquired much knowledge, and asked his advice as to my studies. He said, 'Don't talk of study now. I will give you a plan; but it will require some time to consider of it.' 'It is very good in you,' I replied, 'to allow me to be with you thus. Had it been foretold to me some years ago that I should pass an evening with the author of the *Rambler*, how should I have exulted!' What I then expressed was sincerely from the heart. He was satisfied that it was, and cordially answered, 'Sir, I am glad we have met. I hope we shall pass many evenings and mornings too, together.' We finished a couple of bottles of port, and sat till between one and two in the morning.

. . . . .

My desire of being acquainted with celebrated men of every description had made me, much about the same time, obtain an introduction to Dr. Samuel Johnson and to John Wilkes, Esq. Two men more different could perhaps not be selected out of all mankind. They had even attacked one another with some asperity in their writings; yet I lived in habits of friendship with both. I could fully relish the excellence of each; for I have ever delighted in that intellectual chemistry which can separate good qualities from evil in the same person.

Sir John Pringle, 'mine own friend and my Father's friend,' between whom and Dr. Johnson I in vain wished to establish an acquaintance, as I respected and lived in intimacy with both of them, observed to me once, very ingeniously, 'It is not in friendship as in mathematics, where two things, each equal to a third, are equal between themselves. You agree with Johnson as a middle quality, and you agree with me as a middle quality; but Johnson and I should not agree.' Sir John was not sufficiently flexible; so I desisted; knowing, indeed, that the repulsion was equally strong on the part of Johnson; who, I know not from what cause, unless his being a Scotchman, had formed a very erroneous opinion of Sir John. But I conceived an irresistible wish, if possible, to bring Dr. Johnson and Mr. Wilkes together. How to manage it was a nice and difficult matter.

My worthy booksellers and friends, Messieurs Dilly in the Poultry,

at whose hospitable and well-covered table I have seen a greater number
of literary men than at any other, except that of Sir Joshua Reynolds, had
invited me to meet Mr. Wilkes and some more gentlemen on Wednesday, May 15. 'Pray,' said I, 'let us have Dr. Johnson.'—'What, with Mr.
Wilkes? Not for the world,' said Mr. Edward Dilly: 'Dr. Johnson would
never forgive me.'—'Come,' said I, 'if you'll let me negotiate for you, I
will be answerable that all shall go well.' DILLY. 'Nay, if you will take it
upon you, I am sure I shall be very happy to see them both here.'

Notwithstanding the high veneration which I entertained for Dr.
Johnson, I was sensible that he was sometimes a little actuated by the
spirit of contradiction, and by means of that I hoped I should gain my
point. I was persuaded that if I had come upon him with a direct
proposal, 'Sir, will you dine in company with Jack Wilkes?' he would
have flown into a passion and would probably have answered, 'Dine with
Jack Wilkes, sir! I'd as soon dine with Jack Ketch.' I therefore, while we
were sitting quietly by ourselves at his house in an evening, took occasion
to open my plan thus:—'Mr. Dilly, sir, sends his respectful compliments
to you, and would be happy if you would do him the honour to dine with
him on Wednesday next along with me, as I must soon go to Scotland.'
JOHNSON. 'Sir, I am obliged to Mr. Dilly. I will wait upon him—'
BOSWELL. 'Provided, sir, I suppose, that the company which he is to have
is agreeable to you.' JOHNSON. 'What do you mean, sir? What do you take
me for? Do you think I am so ignorant of the world, as to imagine that I
am to prescribe to a gentleman what company he is to have at his table?'
BOSWELL. 'I beg your pardon, sir, for wishing to prevent you from
meeting people whom you might not like. Perhaps he may have some of
what he calls his patriotic friends with him.' JOHNSON. 'Well, sir, and
what then? What care I for his *patriotic friends*? Poh!' BOSWELL. 'I
should not be surprised to find Jack Wilkes there.' JOHNSON. 'And if Jack
Wilkes *should* be there, what is that to *me*, sir? My dear friend, let us
have no more of this. I am sorry to be angry with you; but really it is
treating me strangely to talk to me as if I could not meet any company
whatever, occasionally.' BOSWELL. 'Pray forgive me, sir: I meant well.
But you shall meet whoever comes, for me.' Thus I secured him, and
told Dilly that he would find him very well pleased to be one of his
guests on the day appointed.

Upon the much-expected Wednesday, I called on him about half an
hour before dinner, as I often did when we were to dine out together, to
see that he was ready in time, and to accompany him. I found him
buffeting his books, as upon a former occasion, covered with dust, and
making no preparation for going abroad. 'How is this, sir?' said I. 'Don't
you recollect that you are to dine at Mr. Dilly's?' JOHNSON. 'Sir, I did not
think of going to Dilly's: it went out of my head. I have ordered dinner at

home with Mrs. Williams.' BOSWELL. 'But, my dear sir, you know you were engaged to Mr. Dilly, and I told him so. He will expect you and will be much disappointed if you don't come.' JOHNSON. 'You must talk to Mrs. Williams about this.'

Here was a sad dilemma. I feared that what I was so confident I had secured would yet be frustrated. He had accustomed himself to shew Mrs. Williams such a degree of humane attention, as frequently imposed some restraint upon him; and I knew that if she should be obstinate, he would not stir. I hastened downstairs to the blind lady's room and told her I was in great uneasiness, for Dr. Johnson had engaged to me to dine this day at Mr. Dilly's, but that he had told me he had forgotten his engagement, and had ordered dinner at home. 'Yes, sir,' said she, pretty peevishly, 'Dr. Johnson is to dine at home.'—'Madam,' said I, 'his respect for you is such that I know he will not leave you unless you absolutely desire it. But as you have so much of his company, I hope you will be good enough to forego it for a day; as Mr. Dilly is a very worthy man, has frequently had agreeable parties at his house for Dr. Johnson, and will be vexed if the Doctor neglects him today. And then, madam, be pleased to consider my situation; I carried the message, and I assured Mr. Dilly that Dr. Johnson was to come, and no doubt he has made a dinner, and invited a company, and boasted of the honour he expected to have. I shall be quite disgraced if the Doctor is not there.' She gradually softened to my solicitations, which were certainly as earnest as most entreaties to ladies upon any occasion, and was graciously pleased to empower me to tell Dr. Johnson, 'That all things considered, she thought he should certainly go.' I flew back to him still in dust and careless of what should be the event, 'indifferent in his choice to go or stay;' but as soon as I had announced to him Mrs. Williams's consent, he roared, 'Frank, a clean shirt,' and was very soon dressed. When I had him fairly seated in a hackney-coach with me, I exulted as much as a fortune hunter who has got an heiress into a post chaise with him to set out for Gretna-Green.

When we entered Mr. Dilly's drawing room, he found himself in the midst of a company he did not know. I kept myself snug and silent, watching how he would conduct himself. I observed him whispering to Mr. Dilly, 'Who is that gentleman, sir?'—'Mr. Arthur Lee.'—JOHNSON. 'Too, too, too' (under his breath), which was one of his habitual mutterings. Mr. Arthur Lee could not but be very obnoxious to Johnson, for he was not only a *patriot* but an *American*. He was afterwards minister from the United States at the court of Madrid. 'And who is the gentleman in lace?'—'Mr. Wilkes, sir.' This information confounded him still more; he had some difficulty to restrain himself, and taking up a book, sat down upon a window seat and read, or at least kept his eye upon it intently for some time, till he composed himself. His feelings, I dare say, were awkward enough. But he no doubt recollected his having rated me for supposing that he could be at all disconcerted by any company, and he, therefore, resolutely set himself to behave quite as an easy man of the world, who could adapt himself at once to the disposition and manners of those whom he might chance to meet.

The cheering sound of 'Dinner is upon the table,' dissolved his reverie, and we *all* sat down without any symptom of ill humour. There were present, besides Mr. Wilkes and Mr. Arthur Lee, who was an old companion of mine when he studied physic at Edinburgh, Mr. (now Sir John) Miller, Dr. Lettsom, and Mr. Slater, the druggist. Mr. Wilkes placed himself next to Dr. Johnson and behaved to him with so much attention and politeness, that he gained upon him insensibly. No man eat more heartily than Johnson, or loved better what was nice and delicate. Mr. Wilkes was very assiduous in helping him to some fine veal. 'Pray give me leave, sir:—It is better here—A little of the brown—Some fat, sir—A little of the stuffing—Some gravy—Let me have the pleasure of giving you some butter—Allow me to recommend a squeeze of this orange;—or the lemon, perhaps, may have more zest.' —'Sir, sir, I am obliged to you, sir,' cried Johnson, bowing, and turning his head to him with a look for some time of 'surly virtue,' but, in a short while, of complacency.

Foote being mentioned, Johnson said, 'He is not a good mimic.' One of the company added, 'A merry Andrew, a buffoon.' JOHNSON. 'But he has wit too, and is not deficient in ideas, or in fertility and variety of imagery, and not empty of reading; he has knowledge enough to fill up his part. One species of wit he has in an eminent degree, that of escape. You drive him into a corner with both hands; but he's gone, sir, when you think you have got him—like an animal that jumps over your head. Then he has a great range for his wit; he never lets truth stand between him and a jest, and he is sometimes mighty coarse. Garrick is under many restraints from which Foote is free.' WILKES. 'Garrick's wit is more like Lord Chesterfield's.' JOHNSON. 'The first time I was in company with Foote was at Fitzherbert's. Having no good opinion of the fellow, I was resolved not to be pleased; and it is very difficult to please a man against his will. I went on eating my dinner pretty sullenly, affecting not to mind him. But the dog was so very comical, that I was obliged to lay down my knife and fork, throw myself back upon my chair, and fairly laugh it out. No, sir, he was irresistible. He upon one occasion experienced, in an extraordinary degree, the efficacy of his powers of entertaining. Amongst the many and various modes which he tried of getting money, he became a partner with a small-beer brewer, and he was to have a share of the profits for procuring customers amongst his numerous acquaintance. Fitzherbert was one who took his small-beer; but it was so bad that the servants resolved not to drink it. They were at some loss how to notify their resolution, being afraid of offending their master, who they knew liked Foote much as a companion. At last they fixed upon a little black boy, who was rather a favourite, to be their deputy, and deliver their remonstrance; and having invested him with the whole authority of the kitchen, he was to inform Mr. Fitzherbert, in all their names, upon a certain day, that they would drink Foote's small-beer no longer. On that day Foote happened to dine at Fitzherbert's, and this boy served at table; he was so delighted with Foote's stories, and merriment, and grimace, that when he went downstairs, he told them, "This is the finest man I have ever seen. I will not deliver your message. I will drink his small-beer." '

Somebody observed that Garrick could not have done this. WILKES. 'Garrick would have made the small-beer still smaller. He is now leaving the stage; but he will play Scrub all his life.' I knew that Johnson would let nobody attack Garrick but himself, as Garrick once said to me, and I had heard him praise his liberality; so to bring out his commendation of his celebrated pupil, I said, loudly, 'I have heard Garrick is liberal.' JOHNSON. 'Yes, sir, I know that Garrick has given away more money than any man in England that I am acquainted with, and that not from ostentatious views. Garrick was very poor when he began life; so when he came to have money, he probably was very unskilful in giving away, and saved when he should not. But Garrick began to be liberal as soon as he could; and I am of opinion, the reputation of avarice which he has had has been very lucky for him and prevented his having many enemies. You despise a man for avarice, but do not hate him. Garrick might have been much better attacked for living with more splendour than is suitable to a player: if they had had the wit to have assaulted him in that quarter, they might have galled him more. But they have kept clamouring about his avarice, which has rescued him from much obloquy and envy.'

Talking of the great difficulty of obtaining authentic information for biography, Johnson told us, 'When I was a young fellow I wanted to write the life of Dryden, and in order to get materials, I applied to the only two persons then alive who had seen him; these were old Swinney and old Cibber. Swinney's information was no more than this, "That at Will's coffeehouse Dryden had a particular chair for himself, which was set by the fire in winter, and was then called his winter-chair; and that it was carried out for him to the balcony in summer, and was then called his summer-chair." Cibber could tell no more but "That he remembered him a decent old man, arbiter of critical disputes at Will's." You are to consider that Cibber was then at a great distance from Dryden, had perhaps one leg only in the room, and durst not draw in the other.' BOSWELL. 'Yet Cibber was a man of observation?' JOHNSON. 'I think not.'

Boswell. 'You will allow his *Apology* to be well done.' Johnson. 'Very well done, to be sure, sir. That book is a striking proof of the justice of Pope's remark:

> Each might his several province well command,
> Would all but stoop to what they understand.'

Boswell. 'And his plays are good.' Johnson. 'Yes; but that was his trade; *l'esprit du corps*; he had been all his life among players and play-writers. I wondered that he had so little to say in conversation, for he had kept the best company, and learnt all that can be got by the ear. He abused Pindar to me, and then shewed me an ode of his own, with an absurd couplet, making a linnet soar on an eagle's wing. I told him that when the ancients made a simile, they always made it like something real.'

Mr. Wilkes remarked that 'among all the bold flights of Shakespeare's imagination, the boldest was making Birnamwood march to Dunsinane; creating a wood where there never was a shrub; a wood in Scotland! ha! ha! ha!' And he also observed, that 'the clannish slavery of the Highlands of Scotland was the single exception to Milton's remark of "The Mountain Nymph, sweet Liberty," being worshipped in all hilly countries.'—'When I was at Inverary,' said he, 'on a visit to my old friend Archibald, Duke of Argyle, his dependents congratulated me on being such a favourite of his grace. I said, "It is then, gentlemen, truly lucky for me; for if I had displeased the duke, and he had wished it, there is not a Campbell among you but would have been ready to bring John Wilkes's head to him in a charger. It would have been only

> Off with his head! So much for Aylesbury.

I was then member for Aylesbury.'

Dr. Johnson and Mr. Wilkes talked of the contested passage in Horace's *Art of Poetry*, '*Difficile est propriè communia dicere.*' Mr. Wilkes, according to my note, gave the interpretation thus: 'It is difficult to speak with propriety of common things; as, if a poet had to speak of Queen Caroline drinking tea, he must endeavour to avoid the vulgarity of cups and saucers.' But upon reading my note, he tells me that he meant to say, that 'the word *communia*, being a Roman law term, signifies here things *communis juris*, that is to say, what have never yet been treated by anybody; and this appears clearly from what followed,

> ——*Tuque*
> *Rectiùs Iliacum carmen deducis in actus*
> *Quàm si proferres ignota indictaque primus.*

You will easier make a tragedy out of the *Iliad* than on any subject not handled before.' Johnson. 'He means that it is difficult to appropriate to particular persons qualities which are common to all mankind, as Homer has done.'

WILKES. 'We have no City-Poet now: that is an office which has gone into disuse. The last was Elkanah Settle. There is something in *names* which one cannot help feeling. Now *Elkanah Settle* sounds so *queer*, who can expect much from that name? We should have no hesitation to give it for John Dryden, in preference to Elkanah Settle, from the names only, without knowing their different merits.' JOHNSON. I suppose, sir, Settle did as well for aldermen in his time, as John Home could do now. Where did Beckford and Trecothick learn English?'

Mr. Arthur Lee mentioned some Scotch who had taken possession of a barren part of America and wondered why they should choose it. JOHNSON. 'Why, sir, all barrenness is comparative. The *Scotch* would not know it to be barren.' BOSWELL. 'Come, come, he is flattering the English. You have now been in Scotland, sir, and say if you did not see meat and drink enough there.' JOHNSON. 'Why yes, sir; meat and drink enough to give the inhabitants sufficient strength to run away from home.' All these quick and lively sallies were said sportively, quite in jest, and with a smile, which showed that he meant only wit. Upon this topic he and Mr. Wilkes could perfectly assimilate; here was a bond of union between them, and I was conscious that as both of them had visited Caledonia, both were fully satisfied of the strange narrow ignorance of those who imagine that it is a land of famine. But they amused themselves with persevering in the old jokes. When I claimed a superiority for Scotland over England in one respect, that no man can be arrested there for a debt merely because another swears it against him; but there must first be the judgement of a court of law ascertaining its justice; and that a seizure of the person, before judgement is obtained, can take place only if his creditor should swear that he is about to fly from the country or, as it is technically expressed, is *in meditatione fugæ*. WILKES. 'That, I should think, may be safely sworn of all the Scotch nation.' JOHNSON. (to Mr. Wilkes) 'You must know, sir, I lately took my friend Boswell and shewed him genuine civilised life in an English provincial town. I turned him loose at Lichfield, my native city, that he might see for once real civility: for you know he lives among savages in Scotland, and among rakes in London.' WILKES. 'Except when he is with grave, sober, decent people like you and me.' JOHNSON. (smiling) 'And we ashamed of him.'

They were quite frank and easy. Johnson told the story of his asking Mrs. Macaulay to allow her footman to sit down with them, to prove the ridiculousness of the argument for the equality of mankind; and he said to me afterwards, with a nod of satisfaction, 'You saw Mr. Wilkes acquiesced.' Wilkes talked with all imaginable freedom of the ludicrous title given to the Attorney General, *Diabolus Regis*; adding, 'I have reason to know something about that officer, for I was prosecuted for a libel.' Johnson, who many people would have supposed must have been furiously angry at hearing this talked of so lightly, said not a word. He was now, *indeed,* 'a good-humoured fellow.'

After dinner we had an accession of Mrs. Knowles, the Quaker lady, well known for her various talents, and of Mr. Alderman Lee. Amidst some patriotic groans, somebody (I think the alderman) said, 'Poor Old England is lost.' JOHNSON. 'Sir, it is not so much to be lamented that Old England is lost, as that the Scotch have found it.' WILKES. 'Had Lord Bute governed Scotland only, I should not have taken the trouble to write his eulogy, and dedicate *Mortimer* to him.'

Mr. Wilkes held a candle to shew a fine print of a beautiful female figure which hung in the room and pointed out the elegant contour of the bosom with the finger of an arch connoisseur. He afterwards, in a conversation with me, waggishly insisted that all the time Johnson shewed visible signs of a fervent admiration of the corresponding charms of the fair Quaker.

This record, though by no means so perfect as I could wish, will serve to give a notion of a very curious interview, which was not only pleasing at the time, but had the agreeable and benignant effect of reconciling any animosity and sweetening any acidity which, in the various bustle of political contest, had been produced in the minds of two men, who though widely different, had so many things in common—classical learning, modern literature, wit, and humour, and ready repartee—that it would have been much to be regretted if they had been forever at a distance from each other.

Mr. Burke gave me much credit for this successful *negociation*; and pleasantly said, that 'there was nothing to equal it in the whole history of the *Corps Diplomatique.*'

I attended Dr. Johnson home, and had the satisfaction to hear him tell Mrs. Williams how much he had been pleased with Mr. Wilkes's company, and what an agreeable day he had passed.

· · · · ·

⌐ Suggestions for Reading and Writing

1. What qualities of Johnson's personality and character (as here presented) do you find most striking? Why?
2. Do you feel that Boswell, in bringing Johnson and Wilkes together, had motives other than those he mentions? Explain.
3. Do you find the self-portrait revealed here by Boswell rather a surprising one? Describe him as he presents himself. Then fill out this partial

portrait with further reading in the *Life of Johnson* and in Boswell's recently published journals: *Boswell's London Journal* (1950), *Boswell in Holland* (1952), *Boswell on the Grand Tour* (1955), *Boswell for the Defense* (1959), and *Boswell: The Ominous Years* (1963). Secondary portraits are to be found in Chauncey B. Tinker's *Young Boswell* (1922); Lytton Strachey's "James Boswell," *Portraits in Miniature* (1931); Wyndham Lewis' *The Hooded Hawk: Or, the Case of Mr. Boswell* (1946); Philip A. Collins' *James Boswell* (1956); and Hesketh Pearson's *Johnson and Boswell* (1958).

4. Boswell was much criticized by his contemporaries for his fondness for petty personal detail and for revealing not only his subject's virtues but his flaws and foibles. Do you agree that Boswell thus violated discretion and good taste?

5. The portrait of Johnson in the *Life* should be supplemented not only by the one in Boswell's *The Journal of a Tour to the Hebrides* (1785) but also by those in such other contemporary accounts as Hester Thrale Piozzi's *Anecdotes of the Late Samuel Johnson* (1786) and Sir John Hawkins' *Life of Samuel Johnson* (1787). You might then compare the contemporary view of Johnson with that to be found in such twentieth-century studies as Joseph Wood Krutch's *Samuel Johnson* (1944), Robert Lynd's *Dr. Johnson and Company* (1946), James L. Clifford's *Young Sam Johnson* (1955), and Robert Voitle's *Samuel Johnson, the Moralist* (1961).

6. After reading extensively in the *Life of Johnson,* comment on the view that the work would have benefited from drastic abridgement. Which parts would you leave out? Why? If none, explain why also.

7. Like Aubrey, Boswell comments in passing upon a number of colorful literary figures. Richard Sheridan, James Macpherson, Christopher Smart, Colley Cibber, Charles Churchill, and Oliver Goldsmith are but a few of those mentioned and re-mentioned. Select one as subject for a critical essay.

THE
ART
OF
BIOGRAPHY

Virginia Woolf

A major modern writer in her own right, Virginia Woolf
(1882–1941) was the daughter of the political historian Leslie
Stephen and the wife of the political essayist and journalist
Leonard Woolf. She enjoyed the rich heritage of being related
to a half-dozen famous literary families. She, her husband, and
her sister moved, during the twenties and thirties, in a select
group of artists and writers responsible for influencing sharply
the patterns of British culture and intellectual life.

Mrs. Woolf was novelist, biographer, critic, and reviewer of
the first rank. She pioneered, along with James Joyce and
Dorothy Richardson, in what has come to be called stream-of-
consciousness fiction. Her experiments in narrative technique are
evident in such novels as Mrs. Dalloway (1925), To the
Lighthouse (1927), Orlando (1929), and The Waves (1931).
Never a popular writer, she won—and has retained—a solid
following on both sides of the Atlantic; these readers were
attracted by her refinement, beautiful imagery, and delicate
style. She focused on the solitary individual and his supreme
moments, on time, and on the fleeting and the fragile.

Mrs. Woolf's nonfiction also has lasted; perhaps her best
critical essays are those collected in The Common Reader
(1925) and The Second Common Reader (1932). Always the
experimenter, she published Flush (1933), a rather whimsical

biography of Robert and Elizabeth Barrett Browning—from the point of view of Mrs. Browning's dog!

The following essay, summarizing clearly Mrs. Woolf's ideas on biography as an art, appeared first in The Atlantic Monthly (April 1939).

*   *   *   *   *

I

The art of biography, we say—but at once go on to ask, Is biography an art? The question is foolish perhaps, and ungenerous certainly, considering the keen pleasure that biographers have given us. But the question asks itself so often that there must be something behind it. There it is, whenever a new biography is opened, casting its shadow on the page; and there would seem to be something deadly in that shadow, for after all, of the multitude of lives that are written, how few survive!

But the reason for this high death rate, the biographer might argue, is that biography, compared with the arts of poetry and fiction, is a young art. Interest in ourselves and in other people's selves is a late development of the human mind. Not until the eighteenth century in England did that curiosity express itself in writing the lives of private people. Only in the nineteenth century was biography fully grown and hugely prolific. If it is true that there have been only three great biographers,—Johnson, Boswell, and Lockhart,—the reason, he argues, is that the time was short; and his plea, that the art of biography has had but little time to establish itself and develop itself, is certainly borne out by the textbooks. Tempting as it is to explore the reason,—why, that is, the self that writes a book of prose came into being so many centuries after the self that writes a poem, why Chaucer preceded Henry James,—it is better to leave that insoluble question unasked, and so pass to his next reason for the lack of masterpieces. It is that the art of biography is the most restricted of all the arts. He has his proof ready to hand. Here it is in the preface in which Smith, who has written the life of Jones, takes this opportunity of thanking old friends who have lent letters, and 'last but not least' Mrs. Jones, the widow, for that help 'without which,' as he puts it, 'this biography could not have been written.' Now the novelist, he points out, simply says in his foreword, 'Every character in this book is fictitious.' The novelist is free; the biographer is tied.

There, perhaps, we come within hailing distance of that very difficult, again perhaps insoluble, question: What do we mean by calling a book a work of art? At any rate, here is a distinction between biography and fiction—a proof that they differ in the very stuff of which they are made. One is made with the help of friends, or facts; the other is created without any restrictions save those that the artist, for reasons that seem good to him, chooses to obey. That is a distinction; and there is good reason to think that in the past biographers have found it not only a distinction but a very cruel distinction.

The widow and the friends were hard taskmasters. Suppose, for example, that the man of genius was immoral, ill-tempered, and threw the boots at the maid's head. The widow would say, 'Still I loved him—he was the father of my children; and the public, who love his books, must on no account be disillusioned. Cover up; omit.' The biographer obeyed. And thus the majority of Victorian biographies are like the wax figures now preserved in Westminster Abbey that were carried in funeral processions through the street—effigies that have only a smooth superficial likeness to the body in the coffin.

Then, towards the end of the nineteenth century, there was a change. Again for reasons not easy to discover, widows became broader-minded, the public keener-sighted; the effigy no longer carried conviction or satisfied curiosity. The biographer certainly won a measure of freedom. At least he could hint that there were scars and furrows on the dead man's face. Froude's Carlyle is by no means a wax mask painted rosy red. And following Froude there was Sir Edmund Gosse, who dared to say that his own father was a fallible human being. And following Edmund Gosse in the early years of the present century came Lytton Strachey.

II

The figure of Lytton Strachey is so important a figure in the history of biography that it compels a pause. For his three famous books, *Eminent Victorians*, *Queen Victoria*, and *Elizabeth and Essex*, are of a stature to show both what biography can do and what biography cannot do. Thus they suggest many possible answers to the question whether biography is an art, and if not why it fails.

Lytton Strachey came to birth as an author at a lucky moment. In 1918, when he made his first attempt, biography, with its new liberties, was a form that offered great attractions. To a writer like himself, who had wished to write poetry or plays but was doubtful of his creative power, biography seemed to offer a promising alternative. For at last it was possible to tell the truth about the dead; and the Victorian age was rich in remarkable figures many of whom had been grossly deformed by the effigies that had been plastered over them. To recreate them, to show them as they really were, was a task that called for gifts analogous to the poet's or the novelist's, yet did not ask that inventive power in which he found himself lacking.

It was well worth trying. And the anger and the interest that his short studies of Eminent Victorians aroused showed that he was able to make Manning, Florence Nightingale, Gordon, and the rest live as they had not lived since they were actually in the flesh. Once more they were the centre of a buzz of discussion. Did Gordon really drink, or was that an invention? Had Florence Nightingale received the Order of Merit in her bedroom or in her sitting room? He stirred the public, even though a European war was raging, to an astonishing interest in such minute matters. Anger and laughter mixed; and editions multiplied.

But these were short studies with something of the overemphasis and the foreshortening of caricatures. In the lives of the two great Queens, Elizabeth and Victoria, he attempted a far more ambitious task. Biography had never had a fairer chance of showing what it could do. For it was now being put to the test by a writer who was capable of making use of all the liberties that biography had won: he was fearless; he had proved his brilliance; and he had learned his job. The result throws great light upon the nature of biography. For who can doubt after reading the two books again, one after the other, that the *Victoria* is a triumphant success, and that the *Elizabeth* by comparison is a failure? But it seems too, as we compare them, that it was not Lytton Strachey who failed; it was the art of biography. In the *Victoria* he treated biography as a craft; he submitted to its limitations. In the *Elizabeth* he treated biography as an art; he flouted its limitations.

But we must go on to ask how we have come to this conclusion and what reasons support it. In the first place it is clear that the two Queens present very different problems to their biographer. About Queen Victoria everything was known. Everything she did, almost everything she thought, was a matter of common knowledge. No one has ever been more closely verified and exactly authenticated than Queen Victoria. The biographer could not invent her, because at every moment some document was at hand to check his invention. And, in writing of Victoria, Lytton Strachey submitted to the conditions. He used to the full the biographer's power of selection and relation, but he kept strictly within the world of fact. Every statement was verified; every fact was authenticated. And the result is a life which, very possibly, will do for the old Queen what Boswell did for the old dictionary maker. In time to come Lytton Strachey's Queen Victoria will be Queen Victoria, just as Boswell's Johnson is now Dr. Johnson. The other versions will fade and disappear. It was a prodigious feat, and no doubt, having accomplished it, the author was anxious to press further. There was Queen Victoria, solid, real, palpable. But undoubtedly she was limited. Could not biography produce something of the intensity of poetry, something of the excitement of drama, and yet keep also the peculiar virtue that belongs to fact—its suggestive reality, its own proper creativeness?

Queen Elizabeth seemed to lend herself perfectly to the experiment. Very little was known about her. The society in which she lived was so remote that the habits, the motives, and even the actions of the people of that age were full of strangeness and obscurity. 'By what art are we to worm our way into those strange spirits? those even stranger bodies? The more clearly we perceive it, the more remote that singular universe becomes,' Lytton Strachey remarked on one of the first pages. Yet there was evidently a 'tragic history' lying dormant, half revealed, half concealed, in the story of the Queen and Essex. Everything seemed to lend itself to the making of a book that combined the advantages of both worlds, that gave the artist freedom to invent, but helped his invention with the support of facts—a book that was not only a biography but also a work of art.

Nevertheless, the combination proved unworkable; fact and fiction refused to mix. Elizabeth never became real in the sense that Queen Victoria had been real, yet she never became fictitious in the sense that Cleopatra or Falstaff is fictitious. The reason would seem to be that very little was known—he was urged to invent; yet something was known—his invention was checked. The Queen thus moves in an ambiguous world, between fact and fiction, neither embodied nor disembodied. There is a sense of vacancy and effort, of a tragedy that has no crisis, of characters that meet but do not clash.

If this diagnosis is true we are forced to say that the trouble lies with biography itself. It imposes conditions, and those conditions are that it must be based upon fact. And by fact in biography we mean facts that can be verified by other people besides the artist. If he invents facts as an artist invents them—facts that no one else can verify—and tries to combine them with facts of the other sort, they destroy each other.

Lytton Strachey himself seems in the *Queen Victoria* to have realized the necessity of this condition, and to have yielded to it instinctively. 'The first forty-two years of the Queen's life,' he wrote, 'are illuminated by a great and varied quantity of authentic information. With Albert's death a veil descends.' And when with Albert's death the veil descended and authentic information failed, he knew that the biographer must follow suit. 'We must be content with a brief and summary relation,' he wrote; and the last years are briefly disposed of. But the whole of Elizabeth's life was lived behind a far thicker veil than the last years of Victoria. And yet, ignoring his own admission, he went on to write, not a brief and summary relation, but a whole book about those strange spirits and even stranger bodies of whom authentic information was lacking. On his own showing, the attempt was doomed to failure.

III

It seems, then, that when the biographer complained that he was tied by friends, letters, and documents he was laying his finger upon a necessary element in biography; and that it is also a necessary limitation. For the invented character lives in a free world where the facts are verified by one person only—the artist himself. Their authenticity lies in the truth of his own vision. The world created by that vision is rarer, intenser, and more wholly of a piece than the world that is largely made of authentic information supplied by other people. And because of this difference the two kinds of fact will not mix; if they touch they destroy each other. No one, the conclusion seems to be, can make the best of both worlds; you must choose, and you must abide by your choice.

But though the failure of *Elizabeth and Essex* leads to this conclusion, that failure, because it was the result of a daring experiment carried out with magnificent skill, leads the way to further discoveries. Had he lived, Lytton Strachey would no doubt himself have explored the vein that he had opened. As it is, he has shown us the way in which others may advance. The biographer is bound by facts—that is so; but, if it is so, he has the right to all the facts that are available. If Jones threw boots at the maid's head, had a mistress at Islington, or was found drunk in a ditch after a night's debauch, he must be free to say so—so far at least as the law of libel and human sentiment allow.

But these facts are not like the facts of science—once they are discovered, always the same. They are subject to changes of opinion; opinions change as the times change. What was thought a sin is now known, by the light of facts won for us by the psychologists, to be perhaps a misfortune; perhaps a curiosity; perhaps neither one nor the other, but a trifling foible of no great importance one way or the other. The accent on sex has changed within living memory. This leads to the destruction of a great deal of dead matter still obscuring the true features of the human face. Many of the old chapter headings—life at college, marriage, career—are shown to be very arbitrary and artificial distinctions. The real current of the hero's existence took, very likely, a different course.

Thus the biographer must go ahead of the rest of us, like the miner's canary, testing the atmosphere, detecting falsity, unreality, and the presence of obsolete conventions. His sense of truth must be alive and on tiptoe. Then again, since we live in an age when a thousand cameras are pointed, by newspapers, letters, and diaries, at every character from every angle, he must be prepared to admit contradictory versions of the same face. Biography will enlarge its scope by hanging up looking glasses at odd corners. And yet from all this diversity it will bring out, not a riot of confusion, but a richer unity. And again, since so much is known that used to be unknown, the question now inevitably asks itself, whether the lives of great men only should be recorded. Is not anyone who has lived a life, and left a record of that life, worthy of biography—the failures as well as the successes, the humble as well as the illustrious? And what is greatness? And what smallness? He must revise our standards of merit and set up new heroes for our admiration.

I V

Biography thus is only at the beginning of its career; it has a long and active life before it, we may be sure—a life full of difficulty, danger, and hard work. Nevertheless, we can also be sure that it is a different life from the life of poetry and fiction—a life lived at a lower degree of tension. And for that reason its creations are not destined for the immortality which the artist now and then achieves for his creations.

There would seem to be certain proof of that already. Even Dr. Johnson as created by Boswell will not live as long as Falstaff as created by Shakespeare. Micawber and Miss Bates we may be certain will survive Lockhart's Sir Walter Scott and Lytton Strachey's Queen Victoria. For they are made of more enduring matter. The artist's imagination at its most intense fires out what is perishable in fact; he builds with what is durable; but the biographer must accept the perishable, build with it, imbed it in the very fabric of his work. Much will perish; little will live. And thus we come to the conclusion that he is a craftsman, not an artist; and his work is not a work of art, but something betwixt and between.

Yet on that lower level the work of the biographer is invaluable; we cannot thank him sufficiently for what he does for us. For we are incapable of living wholly in the intense world of the imagination. The imagination is a faculty that soon tires and needs rest and refreshment. But for a tired imagination the proper food is not inferior poetry or minor fiction,—indeed they blunt and debauch it,—but sober fact, that 'authentic information' from which, as Lytton Strachey has shown us, good biography is made. When and where did the real man live; how did he look; did he wear laced boots or elastic-sided; who were his aunts, and his friends; how did he blow his nose; whom did he love, and how; and when he came to die did he die in his bed like a Christian, or . . .

By telling us the true facts, by sifting the little from the big, and shaping the whole so that we perceive the outline, the biographer does more to stimulate the imagination than any poet or novelist save the very greatest. For few poets and novelists are capable of that high degree of tension which gives us reality. But almost any biographer, if he respects facts, can give us much more than another fact to add to our collection. He can give us the creative fact; the fertile fact; the fact that suggests and engenders. Of this, too, there is certain proof. For how often, when a biography is read and tossed aside, some scene remains bright, some figure lives on in the depths of the mind, and causes us, when we read a poem or a novel, to feel a start of recognition, as if we remembered something that we had known before.

↗ Suggestions for Reading and Writing

1. Mrs. Woolf seems to agree with the popular view that England has had but three great biographers: Johnson, Boswell, and Lockhart. From their selections in this volume, what literary qualities do these three writers have in common—if any?

2. Pinpoint and elaborate upon Mrs. Woolf's distinctions between biography as a craft and as an art. Is there included in this volume a biography which disproves her contention that fact and fiction do not mix?

3. After reading *Elizabeth and Essex* (1928), substantiate or disprove Mrs. Woolf's claim that it is a failure because in it Strachey treats biography as an art rather than a craft.

4. Do you agree that the biographer "has the right to all the facts that are available"? Or are some lurid—perhaps even harmful—details better left unsaid? Document your view by references to specific works and events.

5. David Daiches (1942), E. M. Forster (1942), and Joan Bennett (1945) have written books entitled *Virginia Woolf*. Select one and evaluate it in terms of Mr. Woolf's essay.

6. Letters and journals (little touched on in this volume) belong at least on the fringe of autobiography. An interesting paper and rewarding human insights should result from digging into the private journals of three such challenging literary women as Virginia Woolf, Katherine Mansfield, and Dorothy Wordsworth.

7. All students of the novel should read Mrs. Woolf's brief essay "Mr. Bennett and Mrs. Brown" (1924). It not only whacks the Edwardians, but it provides the manifesto for modern psychological fiction. Apply its tenets to one of Mrs. Woolf's own novels.

from

LIFE OF
SIR
WALTER
SCOTT

John Gibson Lockhart

His savage literary reviews for Blackwood's Edinburgh Magazine earned John Gibson Lockhart (1794–1854), early in his career, the nickname of "the Scorpion." He later moved on to edit the Quarterly Review and to write original verse, translations, and novels. His literary reputation, however, rests on his seven-volume biography of his father-in-law, the famed Sir Walter Scott (1771–1832).

Indeed, Lockhart's Life of Sir Walter Scott (1836–38) has been called one of the triumphs of English biography and been more often compared to Boswell's Life of Johnson than has any other such work. Using letters, diaries, journals, and prefaces along with his own intimate recollections, Lockhart fashioned a rambling but revealing portrait of the poet, novelist, antiquarian, lawyer, and landed-aristocrat who was Walter Scott.

Many were quick to complain of Lockhart's verbosity and overpraise of his subject. Yet no subsequent biography of Scott has altered significantly Lockhart's depiction. Despite his obvious bias and tact, Lockhart also was attacked for revealing faults some held should have been buried with Scott. His most eloquent defender was Scottish historian-biographer Thomas Carlyle, who crushed most of the critics by declaring: "How

delicate, decent, is English biography, bless its mealy mouth!"
The following compilation of scattered passages from the
Life of Sir Walter Scott attempts to catch and convey Lockhart's
style, approach, and view of his hero. Lockhart's footnotes have
been omitted.

✓   ✓   ✓   ✓   ✓

. . . . .

In his German studies, Scott acquired, about this time, another
assistant in Mr. Skene of Rubislaw—a gentleman considerably his junior,
who had just returned to Scotland from a residence of several years in
Saxony. Their fondness for the same literature, with Scott's eagerness to
profit by his new acquaintance's superior attainment in it, opened an
intercourse which general similarity of tastes, and I venture to add, in
many of the most important features of character, soon ripened into the
familiarity of a tender friendship—'An intimacy,' Mr. Skene says, in a
paper before me, 'of which I shall ever think with so much pride—a
friendship so pure and cordial as to have been able to withstand all the
vicissitudes of nearly forty years, without ever having sustained even a
casual chill from unkind thought or word.' Mr. Skene adds—'During the
whole progress of his varied life, to that eminent station which he could
not but feel he at length held in the estimation, not of his countrymen
alone, but of the whole world, I never could perceive the slightest shade
of variance from that simplicity of character with which he impressed me
on the first hour of our meeting.'

Among the common tastes which served to knit these friends
together was their love of horsemanship, in which, as in all other manly
exercises, Skene highly excelled; and the fears of a French invasion
becoming every day more serious, their thoughts were turned with
corresponding zeal to the project of mounted volunteers. 'The London
Light-horse had set the example,' says Mr. Skene; 'but in truth it was to
Scott's ardour that this force in the North owed its origin. Unable, by
reason of his lameness, to serve amongst his friends on foot, he had
nothing for it but to rouse the spirit of the moss-trooper, with which he
readily inspired all who possessed the means of substituting the sabre for
the musket.' On the 14th February 1797, these friends and many more
met and drew up an offer to serve as a body of volunteer cavalry in
Scotland, which was accepted by Government. The organisation of the
corps proceeded rapidly; they extended their offer to serve in any part of
the island in case of invasion; and this also being accepted, the whole
arrangement was shortly completed; when Charles Maitland of Rankeil-
lor was elected Major-Commandant; William Rae of St. Catharine's,

Captain; William Forbes of Pitsligo and James Skene of Rubislaw, Cornets; Walter Scott, Paymaster, Quartermaster, and Secretary. But the treble duties thus devolved on Scott were found to interfere too severely with his other avocations, and Colin Mackenzie of Portmore relieved him from those of paymaster.

'The part of quartermaster,' says Mr. Skene, 'was purposely selected for him, that he might be spared the rough usage of the ranks; but, notwithstanding his infirmity, he had a remarkably firm seat on horseback, and in all situations a fearless one: no fatigue ever seemed too much for him, and his zeal and animation served to sustain the enthusiasm of the whole corps, while his ready "mot à rire" kept up, in all, a degree of good-humour and relish for the service, without which the toil and privations of long *daily* drills would not easily have been submitted to by such a body of gentlemen. At every interval of exercise, the order, *sit at ease*, was the signal for the quartermaster to lead the squadron to merriment; every eye was intuitively turned on "Earl Walter," as he was familiarly called by his associates of that date, and his ready joke seldom failed to raise the ready laugh. He took his full share in all the labours and duties of the corps, had the highest pride in its progress and proficiency, and was such a trooper himself, as only a very powerful frame of body and the warmest zeal in the cause could have enabled anyone to be. But his habitual good-humour was the great charm, and at the daily mess (for we all dined together when in quarters) that reigned supreme.' Earl Walter's first charger, by the way, was a tall and powerful animal named Lenore. These daily drills appear to have been persisted in during the spring and summer of 1797; the corps spending moreover some weeks in quarters at Musselburgh. The majority of the troop having professional duties to attend to, the ordinary hour for drill was five in the morning; and when we reflect that after some hours of hard work in this way, Scott had to produce himself regularly in the Parliament House with gown and wig, for the space of four or five hours at least, while his chamber practice, though still humble, was on the increase—and that he had found a plentiful source of new social engagements in his troop connexions—it certainly could have excited no surprise had his literary studies been found suffering total intermission during this busy period. That such was not the case, however, his correspondence and notebooks afford ample evidence. . . . He had no turn, at this time of his life, for early rising; so that the regular attendance at the morning drills was of itself a strong evidence of his military zeal; but he must have, in spite of them, and of all other circumstances, persisted in what was the usual custom of all his earlier life, namely, the devotion of the best hours of the night to solitary study. In general, both as a young man, and in more advanced age, his constitution required a good allowance of sleep, and he, on principle, indulged in it, saying, 'he was but half a man if he had not full seven hours of utter unconsciousness;' but his whole mind and temperament were, at this period, in a state of most fervent exaltation, and spirit triumphed over matter.

. . . . .

'At this early period, Scott was more like the portrait by Saxon, engraved for *The Lady of the Lake*, than to any subsequent picture. He retained in features and form an impress of that elasticity and youthful vivacity which he used to complain wore off after he was forty, and by *his own* account was exchanged for the plodding heaviness of an operose student. He had now, indeed, somewhat of a boyish gaiety of look, and in person was tall, slim, and extremely active.' He and Erskine were about to start on a walk to Roslin, and Mr. Gillies accompanied them. In the course of their walk, Scott's foot slipped, as he was scrambling towards a cave on the edge of a precipitous bank, and 'had there been no trees in the way,' says this writer, 'he must have been killed; but midway he was stopped by a large root of hazel, when, instead of struggling, which would have made matters greatly worse, he seemed perfectly resigned to his fate, and slipped through the tangled thicket till he lay flat on the river's brink. He rose in an instant from his recumbent attitude, and with a hearty laugh called out—"Now, let me see who else will do the like." He scrambled up the cliff with alacrity, and entered the cave, where we had a long dialogue.' Even after he was an old and hoary man, he continually encountered such risks with the same recklessness. The extraordinary strength of his hands and arms was his great reliance in all such difficulties, and if he could see anything to lay hold of, he was afraid of no leap, or rather hop, that came in his way.

. . . . .

It was in that autumn that Scott first saw Wordsworth. Their common acquaintance, Stoddart, had so often talked of them to each other that they met as if they had not been strangers; and they parted friends.

Mr. and Miss Wordsworth had just completed their tour in the Highlands, of which so many incidents have since been immortalised, both in the poet's verse and in the hardly less poetical prose of his sister's diary. On the morning of the 17th of September, having left their carriage at Roslin, they walked down the valley to Lasswade and arrived there before Mr. and Mrs. Scott had risen. 'We were received,' Mr. Wordsworth has told me, 'with that frank cordiality which, under whatever circumstances I afterwards met him, always marked his manners; and, indeed, I found him then in every respect—except, perhaps, that his animal spirits were somewhat higher—precisely the same man that you knew him in later life; the same lively, entertaining conversation, full of anecdote, and averse from disquisition; the same unaffected modesty about himself; the same cheerful and benevolent and hopeful views of man and the world. He partly read and partly recited, sometimes in an enthusiastic style of chant, the first four cantos of *The Lay of the Last Minstrel*; and the novelty of the manners, the clear picturesque descriptions, and the easy glowing energy of much of the verse, greatly delighted me.'

After this he walked with the tourists to Roslin and promised to meet them in two days at Melrose. The night before they reached Melrose they slept at the little quiet inn of Clovenford, where, on mentioning his name, they were received with all sorts of attention and kindness,—the landlady observing that Mr. Scott, 'who was a very clever gentleman,' was an old friend of the house, and usually spent a good deal of time there during the fishing season; but, indeed, says Mr. Wordsworth, 'wherever we named him, we found the word acted as an *open sesamum*; and I believe that, in the character of the *Sheriff's* friends, we might have counted on a hearty welcome under any roof in the border country.'

He met them at Melrose on the 19th, and escorted them through the Abbey, pouring out his rich stores of history and tradition. They then dined together at the inn; but Miss Wordsworth observed that there was some difficulty about arranging matters for the night, 'the landlady refusing to settle anything until she had ascertained from *the Sheriff himself* that he had no objection to sleep in the same room with *William.*' Scott was thus far on his way to the Circuit Court at Jedburgh, in his capacity of Sheriff, and there his new friends again joined him; but he begged that they would not enter the court, 'for,' said he, 'I really would not like you to see the sort of figure I cut there.' They did see him casually, however, in his cocked hat and sword, marching in the Judge's procession to the sound of one cracked trumpet, and were then not surprised that he should have been a little ashamed of the whole ceremonial.

. . . . .

I have already said something of the beginning of Scott's acquaintance with 'the Ettrick Shepherd.' Shortly after their first meeting, Hogg, coming into Edinburgh with a flock of sheep, was seized with a sudden ambition of seeing himself in type, and he wrote out that same night a few ballads, already famous in the Forest, which some obscure bookseller gratified him by printing accordingly; but they appear to have attracted no notice beyond their original sphere. Hogg then made an excursion into the Highlands, in quest of employment as overseer of some extensive sheep-farm; but, though Scott had furnished him with strong recommendations to various friends, he returned without success. He printed an account of his travels, however, in a set of letters in the *Scots Magazine*, which, though exceedingly rugged and uncouth, had abundant traces of the native shrewdness and genuine poetical feeling of this remarkable man. These also failed to excite attention; but, undeterred by such disappointments, the Shepherd no sooner read the third volume of the *Minstrelsy* than he made up his mind that the editor's 'Imitations of the Ancients' were by no means what they should have been. 'Immediately,' he says, in one of his many memoirs of himself, 'I chose a number of traditional facts, and set about imitating the manner of the ancients myself.' These imitations he transmitted to Scott, who warmly praised the many striking beauties scattered over their rough surface. The next time that business carried him to Edinburgh, Scott invited him to dinner, in company with Laidlaw, who happened also to be in town, and some other admirers of the rustic genius. When Hogg entered the drawing-room, Mrs. Scott, being at the time in a delicate state of health, was reclining on a sofa. The Shepherd, after being presented, and making his best bow, took possession of another sofa placed opposite to hers, and stretched himself thereupon at all his length; for, as he said afterwards, 'I thought I could never do wrong to copy the lady of the house.' As his dress at this period was precisely that in which any ordinary herdsman attends cattle to the market, and his hands, moreover, bore most legible marks of a recent sheep-smearing, the lady of the house did not observe with perfect equanimity the novel usage to which her chintz was exposed. The Shepherd, however, remarked nothing of all this—dined heartily and drank freely, and, by jest, anecdote, and song, afforded plentiful merriment. As the liquor operated, his familiarity increased; from Mr. Scott, he advanced to 'Sherra,' and thence to 'Scott,' 'Walter,' and 'Wattie,'—until, at supper, he fairly convulsed the whole party by addressing Mrs. Scott as 'Charlotte.'

The collection entitled 'The Mountain Bard' was eventually published by Constable, in consequence of Scott's recommendation, and this work did at last afford Hogg no slender share of the reputation for which he had so long thirsted. It is not my business, however, to pursue the details of his story.

. . . . .

. . . Previously it had been his custom, whenever professional business or social engagements occupied the middle part of his day, to seize some hours for study after he was supposed to have retired to bed. His physician suggested that this was very likely to aggravate his nervous headaches, the only malady he was subject to in the prime of his manhood; and, contemplating with steady eye a course not only of unremitting but of increasing industry, he resolved to reverse his plan. In short he had now adopted the habits in which, with slender variation, he ever after persevered when in the country. He rose by five o'clock, lit his own fire when the season required one, and shaved and dressed with great deliberation—for he was a very martinet as to all but the mere coxcombries of the toilet, not abhorring effeminate dandyism itself so cordially as the slightest approach to personal slovenliness, or even those 'bed-gown and slipper tricks,' as he called them, in which literary men are so apt to indulge. Clad in his shooting-jacket, or whatever dress he meant to use till dinner time, he was seated at his desk by six o'clock, all his papers arranged before him in the most accurate order, and his books of reference marshalled around him on the floor, while at least one favourite dog lay watching his eye, just beyond the line of circumvalla-tion. Thus, by the time the family assembled for breakfast between nine and ten, he had done enough (in his own language) '*to break the neck of the day's work*.' After breakfast, a couple of hours more were given to his solitary tasks, and by noon he was, as he used to say, 'his own man.' When the weather was bad, he would labour incessantly all the morning; but the general rule was to be out and on horseback by one o'clock at the latest; while, if any more distant excursion had been proposed overnight, he was ready to start on it by ten; his occasional rainy days of uninter-mitted study forming, as he said, a fund in his favour, out of which he was entitled to draw for accommodation whenever the sun shone with special brightness.

It was another rule, that every letter he received should be answered that same day. Nothing else could have enabled him to keep abreast with the flood of communications that in the sequel put his good nature to the severest test—but already the demands on him in this way also were numerous; and he included attention to them among the necessary business which must be despatched before he had a right to close his writing-box, or as he phrased it, 'to say, *out damned spot*, and be a gentleman.' In turning over his enormous mass of correspondence, I have almost invariably found some indication that, when a letter had re-mained more than a day or two unanswered, it was because he found occasion for inquiry.

. . . . .

Conversing with Scott, towards the end of his toils, about the tumult of engagements in which he was thus involved, he said, 'Aye—it was enough to tear me to pieces—but there was a wonderful exhilaration about it all: my blood was kept at fever-pitch—I felt as if I could have grappled with anything and everything; then there was hardly one of all my schemes that did not afford me the means of serving some poor devil of a brother author. There were always huge piles of materials to be arranged, sifted, and indexed—volumes of extracts to be transcribed

—journeys to be made hither and thither, for ascertaining little facts and dates,—in short, I could commonly keep half-a-dozen of the ragged regiment of Parnassus in tolerable case.' I said he must have felt something like what a locomotive engine on a railway might be supposed to do, when a score of coal waggons are seen linking themselves to it the moment it gets the steam up, and it rushes on its course regardless of the burden. 'Yes,' said he, laughing, and making a crashing cut with his axe (for we were felling larches), 'but there was a cursed lot of dung carts too.' He was seldom, in fact, without some of these appendages, and I admired nothing more in him than the patient courtesy, the unwearied gentle kindness with which he always treated them, in spite of their delays and blunders, to say nothing of the almost incredible vanity and presumption which more than one of them often exhibited in the midst of their fawning; and, I believe, with all their faults, the worst and weakest of them repaid him by a canine fidelity of affection. This part of Scott's character recalls by far the most pleasing trait in that of his last predecessor in the plenitude of literary authority—Dr. Johnson. There was perhaps nothing (except the one great blunder) that had a worse effect on the course of his pecuniary fortunes, than the readiness with which he exerted his interest with the booksellers on behalf of inferior writers. Even from the commencement of his connexion with Constable in particular, I can trace a continual series of such applications. They stimulated the already too sanguine publisher to numberless risks; and when these failed, the result was, in one shape or another, some corresponding deduction from the fair profits of his own literary labour. 'I like well,' Constable was often heard to say in the sequel, 'I like well Scott's *ain bairns*—but heaven preserve me from those of his fathering!'

Every now and then, however, he had the rich compensation of finding that his interference had really promoted the interests of some meritorious obscure. None more meritorious could be named than John Struthers, a shoemaker of Glasgow, whose very striking poem, 'The Poor Man's Sabbath,' being seen in MS. by Miss Joanna Baillie when on a visit to her native district, was by her recommended to Scott, and by him to Constable, who published it in 1808. Mr. Struthers made a pilgrimage of gratitude to Ashestiel, where he was received with hearty kindness; and it is pleasing to add, that he ended his life in a very respectable position—as keeper of Stirling's Library, an old endowment in Glasgow.

.   .   .   .   .   .

. . . I ought to say a few words on Scott's method of treating his children in their early days. He had now two boys and two girls;—and he never had more. He was not one of those who take much delight in a mere infant; but no father ever devoted more time and tender care to his offspring than he did to each of his, as they reached the age when they could listen to him and understand his talk. Like their playmates, Camp and the greyhounds, they had at all times free access to his study; he never considered their prattle as any disturbance; they went and came as pleased their fancy; he was always ready to answer their questions; and when they, unconscious how he was engaged, entreated him to lay down his pen and tell them a story, he would take them on his knee, repeat a ballad or a legend, kiss them, and set them down again to their marbles or ninepins, and resume his labour, as if refreshed by the interruption. From a very early age he made them dine at table, and 'to sit up to supper' was the great reward when they had been 'very good bairns.' In short, he considered it as the highest duty as well as the sweetest pleasure of a parent to be the companion of his children; he partook all their little joys and sorrows, and made his kind unformal instructions to blend so easily and playfully with the current of their own sayings and doings that so far from regarding him with any distant awe, it was never thought that any sport or diversion could go on in the right way, unless *papa* were of the party, or that the rainiest day could be dull, so he were at home.

Of the irregularity of his own education he speaks with regret, in the autobiographical fragment written this year at Ashestiel; yet his practice does not look as if that feeling had been strongly rooted in his mind;—for he never did shew much concern about regulating systematically what is usually called *education* in the case of his children. It seemed, on the contrary, as if he attached little importance to anything else, so he could perceive that the young curiosity was excited—the intellect, by whatever springs of interest, set in motion. He detested and despised the whole generation of modern children's books, in which the attempt is made to convey accurate notions of scientific minutiæ: delighting cordially, on the other hand, in those of the preceding age, which, addressing themselves chiefly to the imagination, obtain through it, as he believed, the best chance of stirring our graver faculties also. He exercised the memory by selecting for tasks of recitation passages of popular verse the most likely to catch the fancy of children; and gradually familiarised them with the ancient history of their own country, by arresting attention, in the course of his own oral narrations, on incidents and characters of a similar description. Nor did he neglect to use the same means of quickening curiosity as to the events of sacred history. On Sunday he never rode—at least not until his growing infirmity made his pony almost necessary to him—for it was his principle that all domestic animals have a full right to their Sabbath of rest; but after he had read the prayers and lessons of the day, he usually walked with his whole family, dogs included, to some favourite spot at a considerable distance from the house—most frequently the ruined tower of Elibank—and there dined with them in the open air on a basket of cold provisions, mixing his wine with the water of the brook beside which they all were grouped around him on the turf; and here, or at home, if the weather kept them from their ramble, his Sunday talk was just such a series of biblical lessons as that which we have preserved for the permanent use of rising generations, in his *Tales of a Grandfather* on the early history of Scotland. . . . He had his Bible, the Old Testament especially, by heart; and on these days inwove the simple pathos or sublime enthusiasm of Scripture, in whatever story he was telling, with the same picturesque richness as in his weekday tales the quaint Scotch of Pitscottie, or some rude romantic old rhyme from Barbour's *Bruce* or Blind Harry's *Wallace*.

By many external accomplishments, either in girl or boy, he set little store. He delighted to hear his daughters sing an old ditty, or one of his own framing; but, so the singer appeared to feel the spirit of her ballad, he was not at all critical of the technical execution. There was one thing, however, on which he fixed his heart hardly less than the ancient Persians of the *Cyropædia*: like them, next to love of truth, he held love of horsemanship for the prime point of education. As soon as his eldest girl could sit a pony, she was made the regular attendant of his mountain rides; and they all, as they attained sufficient strength, had the like advancement. He taught them to think nothing of tumbles, and habituated them to his own reckless delight in perilous fords and flooded streams; and they all imbibed in great perfection his passion for horses—as well, I may venture to add, as his deep reverence for the more important article of that Persian training. 'Without courage,' he said, 'there cannot be truth; and without truth there can be no other virtue.'

He had a horror of boarding schools; never allowed his girls to learn anything out of his own house; and chose their governess—Miss Miller—who about this time was domesticated with them, and never left them while they needed one,—with far greater regard to her kind good temper and excellent moral and religious principles than to the measure of her attainments in what are called fashionable accomplishments. The admirable system of education for boys in Scotland combines all the advantages of public and private instruction; his carried their satchels to the High School, when the family was in Edinburgh, just as he had done before them, and shared of course the evening society of their happy home. But he rarely, if ever, left them in town, when he could himself be in the country; and at Ashestiel he was, for better or for worse, his eldest boy's daily tutor, after he began Latin.

. . . . .

I must, however, open the year 1814 with a melancholy story. Mention has been made in connection with an unlucky edition of

Beaumont and Fletcher, of Henry Weber, a German scholar, who, escaping to this country in 1804, from misfortunes in his own, excited Scott's compassion, and was thenceforth furnished, through his means, with literary employment of various sorts. Weber was a man of considerable learning; but Scott, as was his custom, appears to have formed an exaggerated notion of his capacity, and certainly countenanced him, to his own severe cost, in several most unhappy undertakings. When not engaged on things of a more ambitious character, he had acted for ten years as his protector's amanuensis, and when the family were in Edinburgh, he very often dined with them. There was something very interesting in his appearance and manners: he had a fair, open countenance, in which the honesty and the enthusiasm of his nation were alike visible; his demeanour was gentle and modest; and he had not only a stock of curious antiquarian knowledge, but the reminiscences, which he detailed with amusing simplicity, of an early life chequered with many strange-enough adventures. He was, in short, much a favourite with Scott and all the household; and was invited to dine with them so frequently, chiefly because his friend was aware that he had an unhappy propensity to drinking, and was anxious to keep him away from places where he might have been more likely to indulge it. This vice had been growing on him; and of late Scott had found it necessary to make some rather severe remonstrances about habits which were at once injuring his health and interrupting his literary industry. They had, however, parted kindly when Scott left Edinburgh at Christmas; and the day after his return, Weber attended him as usual in his library—being employed in transcribing extracts during several hours, while his friend, seated over against him, continued working at the *Life of Swift*. The light beginning to fail, Scott threw himself back in his chair and was about to ring for candles, when he observed the German's eyes fixed upon him with an unusual solemnity of expression. 'Weber,' said he, 'what's the matter with you?' 'Mr. Scott,' said Weber, rising, 'you have long insulted me, and I can bear it no longer. I have brought a pair of pistols with me, and must insist on your taking one of them instantly;' and with that he produced the weapons, which had been deposited under his chair, and laid one of them on Scott's manuscript. 'You are mistaken, I think,' said Scott, 'in your way of setting about this affair—but no matter. It can, however, be no part of your object to annoy Mrs. Scott and the children; therefore, if you please, we will put the pistols into the drawer till after dinner, and then arrange to go out together like gentlemen.' Weber answered with equal coolness, 'I believe that will be better,' and laid the second pistol also on the table. Scott locked them both in his desk, and said, 'I am glad you have felt the propriety of what I suggested—let me only request farther that nothing may occur while we are at dinner to give my wife any suspicion of what has been passing.' Weber again assented, and Scott withdrew to his dressing-room, from which he despatched a message to one of Weber's companions,—and then dinner was served, and Weber joined the circle as usual. He conducted himself with composure, and everything seemed to go on in the ordinary way until, whisky and hot water being produced, Scott, instead of inviting his guest to help himself, mixed two moderate tumblers of toddy and handed one of them to Weber, who, upon that, started up with a furious countenance, but instantly sat down again, and when Mrs. Scott expressed her fear that he was ill, answered placidly that he was liable to spasms, but that the pain was gone. He then took the glass, eagerly gulped down its contents, and pushed it back to Scott. At this moment the friend who had been sent for made his appearance; and Weber, on seeing him enter the room, rushed past him and out of the house, without stopping to put on his hat. The friend, who pursued instantly, came up with him at the end of the street, and did all he could to soothe his agitation, but in vain. The same evening he was obliged to be put into a strait-waistcoat; and though in a few days he exhibited such symptoms of recovery that he was allowed to go by himself to pay a visit in the North of England, he there soon relapsed, and continued ever afterwards a hopeless lunatic, being supported to the end of his life, in June 1818, at Scott's expense, in an asylum at York.

. . . . .

I never thought it lawful to keep a journal of what passes in private society, so that no one need expect from the sequel of this narrative any detailed record of Scott's familiar talk. What fragments of it have happened to adhere to a tolerably retentive memory and may be put into black and white without wounding any feelings which my friend, were he alive, would have wished to spare, I shall introduce as the occasion suggests or serves. But I disclaim on the threshold anything more than this; and I also wish to enter a protest once for all against the general fidelity of several literary gentlemen who have kindly forwarded to me private lucubrations of theirs, designed to Boswellise Scott, and which they may probably publish hereafter. To report conversations fairly, it is a necessary prerequisite that we should be completely familiar with all the interlocutors, and understand thoroughly all their minutest relations, and points of common knowledge and common feeling, with each other. He who does not, must be perpetually in danger of misinterpreting sportive allusions into serious statement; and the man who was only recalling, by some jocular phrase or half-phrase, to an old companion, some trivial reminiscence of their boyhood or youth, may be represented as expressing, upon some person or incident casually tabled, an opinion which he had never framed, or if he had, would never have given words to in any mixed assemblage—not even among what the world calls *friends* at his own board. In proportion as a man is witty and humorous, there will always be about him and his a widening maze and wilderness of cues and catchwords, which the uninitiated will, if they are bold enough to try interpretation, construe, ever and anon, egregiously amiss—not seldom into arrant falsity. For this one reason, to say nothing of many others, I consider no man justified in journalising what he sees and hears in a domestic circle where he is not thoroughly at home; and I think there are still higher and better reasons why he should not do so where he is.

. . . . .

. . . Even while the weather was most unpropitious, nothing could induce him to remain in the carriage when we approached any ruined or celebrated edifice. If he had never seen it before, his curiosity was like that of an eager stripling: if he had examined it fifty times, he must renew his familiarity and gratify the tenderness of youthful reminiscences. While on the road, his conversation never flagged—story suggested story, and ballad came upon ballad in endless succession. But what struck me most was the apparently omniverous grasp of his memory. That he should recollect every stanza of any ancient ditty of chivalry or romance that had once excited his imagination could no longer surprise me: but it seemed as if he remembered everything without exception, so it were in anything like the shape of verse, that he had ever read. For example, the morning after we left Allanton, we went across the country to breakfast with his friend Cranstoun (Lord Corehouse), who accompanied us in the same carriage; and his Lordship happening to repeat a phrase, remarkable only for its absurdity, from a magazine poem of the very silliest feebleness, which they had laughed at when at college together, Scott immediately began at the beginning, and gave it us to the end, with apparently no more effort than if he himself had composed it the day before. I could after this easily believe a story often told by Hogg, to the effect that, lamenting in Scott's presence his having lost his only copy of a long ballad composed by him in his early days, and of which he then could recall merely the subject, and one or two fragments, Sir Walter forthwith said, with a smile,—'Take your pencil, Jamie, and I'll dictate your ballad to you, word for word;'—which was done accordingly.

As this was among the first times that I ever travelled for a few days in company with Scott, I may as well add the surprise with which his literary diligence, when away from home and his books, could not fail to be observed. Wherever we slept, whether in the noble mansion or in the shabbiest of country inns, and whether the work was done after retiring at night or before an early start in the morning, he *very rarely* mounted the carriage again without having a packet of the well-known aspect, ready sealed and corded, and addressed to his printer in Edinburgh.

．　．　．　．　．

About this time, being again a traveller, I lost the opportunity of witnessing his reception of several eminent persons;—among others . . . Mr. Thomas Moore. This last fortunately found Sir Walter in an interval of repose—no one with him at Abbotsford but Lady and Miss Scott—and no company at dinner except the Fergussons and Laidlaw. The two poets had thus the opportunity of a great deal of quiet conversation; and from the hour they met, they seem to have treated each other with a full confidence, the record of which, however touchingly honourable to both, could hardly be made public *in extenso* while one of them survives. The first day they were alone after dinner, and the talk turned chiefly on the recent death of Byron—from which Scott passed unaffectedly to his own literary history. Mr. Moore listened with great interest to details, now no longer new, about the early days of Mat Lewis, the *Minstrelsy*, and the poems; and 'at last,' says he, 'to my no small surprise, as well as pleasure, he mentioned the novels, without any reserve, as his own. He gave me an account of the original progress of those extraordinary works, the hints supplied for them, the conjectures and mystification to which they had given rise, etc., etc.:' he concluded with saying, 'they have been a mine of wealth to me—but I find I fail in them now—I can no longer make them so good as at first.' This frankness was met as it should have been by the brother poet; and when he entered Scott's room next morning, 'he laid his hand,' says Mr. Moore, 'with a sort of cordial earnestness on my breast, and said—"Now, my dear Moore, we are friends for life." ' They sallied out for a walk through the plantations, and among other things, the commonness of the poetic talent in these days was alluded to. 'Hardly a magazine is now published,' said Moore, 'that does not contain verses which some thirty years ago would have made a reputation.' —Scott turned with his look of shrewd humour, as if chuckling over his own success, and said, 'Ecod, we were in the luck of it to come before these fellows;' but he added, playfully flourishing his stick as he spoke, 'we have, like Bobadil, taught them to beat us with our own weapons.' —'In complete novelty,' says Moore, 'he seemed to think, lay the only chance for a man ambitious of high literary reputation in these days.'

Moore says—'I parted from Scott with the feeling that all the world might admire him in his works, but that those only could learn to love him as he deserved who had seen him at Abbotsford. I give you *carte blanche* to say what you please of my sense of his cordial kindness and gentleness; perhaps a not very dignified phrase would express my feeling better than any fine one—it was that he was a *thorough good fellow*.'

What Scott thought of his guest appears from this entry in a private notebook:—'Tom Moore's is the most exquisite warbling I ever heard. . . . There is a manly frankness, with perfect ease and good-breeding, about him, which is delightful. Not the least touch of the poet or the pedant. A little—very little man—less, I think, than Lewis, and something like him in person; God knows, not in conversation, for Mat, though a clever fellow, was a bore of the first description. Moreover, he looked always like a schoolboy. Now Moore has none of this insignificance. His countenance is plain, but the expression so very animated, especially in speaking or singing, that it is far more interesting than the finest features could have rendered it. I was aware that Byron had often spoken of Moore and myself in the same breath, and with the same sort of regard; so I was curious to see what there could be in common betwixt us, Moore having lived so much in the gay world, I in the country, and with people of business, and sometimes with politicians; Moore a scholar, I none; he a musician and artist, I without knowledge of a note; he a democrat, I an aristocrat—with many other points of difference; besides his being an Irishman, I a Scotchman, and both tolerably national. Yet there is a point of resemblance, and a strong one. We are both good-humoured fellows, who rather seek to enjoy what is going forward than to maintain our dignity as lions; and we have both seen the world too widely and too well not to contemn in our souls the imaginary consequence of literary people, who walk with their noses in the air, and remind me always of the fellow whom Johnson met in an alehouse, and who called himself *"the great Twalmly—inventor of the flood-gate iron for smoothing linen."* He also enjoys the *mot pour rire,* and so do I.'

. . . . .

Since I have been led to touch on what many always considered as the weak part of his character—his over-respect for worldly things in general,—I must say one word as to the matter of rank, which undoubtedly had far more effect on him than money. In the first place, he was all along courted by the great world—not it by him; and, secondly, pleased as he was with its attentions, he derived infinitely greater pleasure from the trusting and hearty affection of his old equals and the inferiors whose welfare he so unweariedly promoted. But, thirdly, he made acute discriminations among the many different orders of claimants who jostle each other for pre-eminence in the curiously complicated system of modern British society. His imagination had been constantly exercised in recalling and embellishing whatever features of the past it was possible to connect with any pleasing ideas, and a historical name was a charm that literally stirred his blood. But not so a mere title. He reverenced the Duke of Buccleuch—but it was not as a duke, but as the head of his clan,

the representative of the old knights of Branxholm. In the Duke of
Hamilton he saw not the premier peer of Scotland, but the lineal heir of
the heroic old Douglasses; and he had profounder respect for the chief of
a Highland clan, without any title whatever, and with an ill-paid rental
of two or three thousand a year, than for the haughtiest magnate in a
blue ribbon, whose name did not call up any grand historical reminiscence. I remember once when he had some young Englishmen of high
fashion in his house, there arrived a Scotch gentleman of no distinguished appearance, whom he received with a sort of eagerness and
empressement of reverential courtesy that struck the strangers as quite
out of common. His name was that of a Scotch earl, however, and no
doubt he was that nobleman's son. 'Well,' said one of the Southrons to
me,—'I had never heard that the Earl of —— was one of your very
greatest lords in this country; even a second son of his, booby though he
be, seems to be of wonderful consideration.' The young English lord
heard with some surprise that the visitor in question was a poor
lieutenant on half-pay, heir to a tower about as crazy as Don Quixote's,
and noways related (at least according to English notions of relationship) to the Earl of ——. 'What, then,' he cried, 'what *can* Sir Walter
mean?' 'Why,' said I, 'his meaning is very clear. This gentleman is the
male representative (which the Earl of —— may possibly be in the female line) of a knight who is celebrated by our old poet Blind Harry as
having signalised himself by the side of Sir William Wallace, and from
whom every Scotchman that bears the name of —— has at least the ambition of being supposed to descend.'—Sir Walter's own title came un-
sought; and that he accepted it, not in the foolish fancy that such a title,
or any title, could increase his own personal consequence, but because
he thought it fair to embrace the opportunity of securing a certain external distinction to his heirs at Abbotsford, was proved pretty clearly by his
subsequently declining the greatly higher, but intransmissible rank of a
Privy-Councillor. At the same time, I daresay his ear liked the knightly
sound; and undoubtedly he was much pleased with the pleasure his wife
took, and gaily acknowledged she took, in being my lady.

The circumstances of the King's visit in 1822, and others already
noted, leave no doubt that imagination enlarged and glorified for him
many objects to which it is very difficult for ordinary men in our
generation to attach much importance; and perhaps he was more apt to
attach importance to such things, during the prosperous course of his
own fortunes, than even a liberal consideration of circumstances can
altogether excuse. To myself it seems to have been so; yet I do not think
the severe critics on this part of his story have kept quite sufficiently in
mind how easy it is for us all to undervalue any species of temptation to
which we have not happened to be exposed. I am aware, too, that there

are examples of men of genius, situated to a certain extent like him, who have resisted and repelled the fascinations against which he was not entirely proof; but I have sometimes thought that they did so at the expense of parts of their character nearer the marrow of humanity than those which his weakness in this way tended to endamage; that they mingled, in short, in their virtuous self-denial, some grains of sacrifice at the shrine of a cold, unsocial, even sulky species of self-conceit. But this digression has already turned out much longer than I intended.

. . . . . .

↗ Suggestions for Reading and Writing

1. Write a character sketch of the Walter Scott that emerges here. Do you find him too good to be true? Or does he reveal the characteristics you would expect of the author of *The Heart of Midlothian, Ivanhoe,* and *Quentin Durward?* Explain.
2. The life of Scott presents both contrasts and similarities to that of Lord Byron, his English contemporary. After reading a standard study of each, write an essay pointing up their shared and differing characteristics. (Representative studies are André Maurois' *Byron* [1930], John Drinkwater's *The Pilgrim of Eternity: Byron—A Conflict* [1925], John Buchan's *Sir Walter Scott* [1932], and David Cecil's *Sir Walter Scott* [1933].)
3. Evaluate Lockhart's criticism of those biographers who make use of private conversation. Refer, as he does, to Boswell. Do you feel Lockhart's view may result (in part, at least) from his being Scott's son-in-law? (For background on Lockhart, see H. J. C. Grierson's *Lang, Lockhart, and Biography* [1934].)
4. Is Lockhart's defense of Scott against the charge of snobbery convincing? Explain. H. J. C. Grierson, in his *Walter Scott, Bart.* (1938), attempts to supplement and correct Lockhart. How well does he succeed?
5. Write a brief summary of the Scott-Lockhart relationship as outlined in Donald Carswell's *Scott and His Circle* (1930); see especially pp. 216–270.

Biography Present

from

THE
NEW
BIOGRAPHY

Edward Hayes O'Neill

An avid bibliographer, editor, and literary historian, Edward Hayes O'Neill (1898–1963) was for many years a professor of English at the University of Pennsylvania. He taught also at Villanova University. During and after World War II he was an editor for the Philco Corporation, the John C. Winston Company, and the Radio Corporation of America.

O'Neill's special interest was American biography, and his publications included A History of American Biography, 1800–1935 (1935) and Biography by Americans 1658–1936: A Subject Bibliography (1939). He also edited The Cowled Lover & Other Plays by Robert Montgomery Bird (1941), Pennsylvania Historical Survey (1941), and The Complete Poems and Stories of Edgar Allan Poe (1946).

A History of American Biography was the first detailed study of this special field. Covering the years from 1800 to the year of publication, it traced the development of life-writing in this country from memoir, eulogy, and reference work to a literary genre as clearly defined as the novel or essay.

"The New Biography" introduced the book's final section. O'Neill's footnotes and fewer than a dozen lines of the selection have been omitted here.

The World War, which has been held responsible for much that is good and bad in our modern civilization, has had some effect on modern biography. Since the war most of us have looked at life and men from a point of view much different from that of previous generations. We have questioned everything, from God to government, and we have tried to see men and things as they are and were, not as we should like to have them. Our scepticism has not been irreverent; we have not been iconoclasts; we have been and are trying to seek the truth about the world and the people in it. It is no longer the fashion to accept authority; we must investigate for ourselves. Our fiction has gone beyond realism into naturalism and plain reporting; our poetry has taken on new and strange forms, some good and some bad; our drama has become the medium for examining and generally satirizing our social customs and habits; our biography has become creative or re-creative and sometimes, unfortunately, imaginative.

There are other reasons for our present interest in biography. The world has grown larger, and the machine age has made man much smaller than he was fifty years ago. Circumstances have made the average man stationary; he has neither the time nor the money to travel and meet different kinds of people. At the same time education, the press, the "movies" have aroused in him a desire to know the great men and women of the past. Modern life has made it impossible for the great majority to come in contact with many people; most of us live and die in a small groove of life. The fact that we may meet many people will give us little or no idea of who and what they are. It is doubtful if anyone knew Napoleon in his own day as we know him, for we can read at least six great biographies of the man. Man and woman can come to know each other only by living together. We turn to biography because we can live with a hundred men in a year, if we can read rapidly, and we get to know those men intimately.

Modern man is more conscious of himself than was the man of a century ago. He tries to find reflections of himself in the lives of great men and to act as they acted. That is why many men and women read biography. We may find that we are a combination of Leonardo da Vinci, Casanova, and George Washington. If we read sufficient biographies, we may be able to analyze and help ourselves, or find that we are great men, denied the opportunity to prove our greatness. These are only a few of the reasons for the present popularity of biography.

Biography has made more definite progress in the last fifteen years than has any other form of literature. Every branch of literature has been the subject of experiment; some of the experiments have succeeded,

From *The History of American Biography, 1800–1935,* by Edward O'Neill. Reprinted by permission of the University of Pennsylvania Press.

more have failed. Modern fiction, modern poetry, and modern drama are in various experimental stages, but biography has emerged and has taken on, not a new form, but a form that is the logical development of the various methods that have been tried since 1918. We have seen the rise of the psychological, psychopathic, and pathological methods in life-writing. We have seen the two or three volumes of life and letters reduced to a sketch, an analysis, or a psychograph. We have seen the biography of an earlier day rewritten in modern slang and scientific jargon. We have seen facts sacrificed to effect, biography made into fiction or plain falsehood. We have seen the "debunking" school pulling figures from pedestals and then breaking the pedestals. Some of the exhibitions were painful to many of us, but the operations eventually saved the patient. The journalist who imbibed enough psychology to use some of the terms showed us that biography cannot be written that way; the psychologist or psychiatrist who tried to intensify his subject with the method of the journalist showed that biography cannot be written that way. The more serious writer who started with a preconceived idea of his subject and used only that source material which would prove his case showed us that biography cannot be written that way. The critic, turned biographer and always judging the individual in terms of his art, showed us that biography cannot be written that way. . . .

The period between 1919 and 1935 was the most prolific in the history of biographical writing in America. At times, the demand seemed to exceed the supply. People became interested in the lives of soldiers, statesmen, scientists, novelists, poets, ecclesiastics, suffragists, reformers, prize fighters, not as soldiers, statesmen, scientists, and so forth, but as men and women. It is only when we are interested in people as individuals rather than as folk-heroes that we can write or read about them intelligently.

Apparently, interest in the great men and women of the past was not the only reason for the popularity of modern biography. The methods used had a great influence on the popularity, and these methods had their beginnings, at least, abroad. The year 1919 has been chosen as the beginning of modern biography because the greatest influences were published in that year and in 1918.

In 1918, Lytton Strachey published *Eminent Victorians*, a volume of biographical studies of Cardinal Manning, Florence Nightingale, General Gordon, and Arnold of Rugby. This was not Strachey's first book, *Landmarks in French Literature* having been published before the war, but it was the first book in which his particular biographical genius was noticed. It became a best seller here and in England, and he became the literary lion of the hour. The appearance of *Queen Victoria* in 1921 seemed to justify all the praise that had been heaped on *Eminent*

Victorians. In *Books and Characters* (1922) Strachey published bio-graphical studies, ranging from Voltaire and Sir Thomas Browne to Lady Hester Stanhope, that represent some of his best work in this field. *Elizabeth and Essex* (1928) merely enhanced his reputation as a biographer and stylist. *Portraits in Miniature* (1931) added nothing to Strachey's position, though the portraits are extremely interesting in themselves. Mr. Strachey's death in 1932 brought to a close a career that had really just begun, for he was only fifty-two years old when he died.

Strachey's methods are outside the province of this study of Ameri-can biography, but some explanation of his influence must be given. While Strachey never set forth his theory of life-writing as completely as did Maurois or Ludwig, the preface to *Eminent Victorians* tells us as much as we need to know. The following passage seems to me to illustrate his purpose and his method:

> The art of biography seems to have fallen on evil times in England. We have had, it is true, a few masterpieces, but we have never had, like the French, a great biographical tradition. . . . With us, the most delicate and humane of all the branches of the art of writing has been relegated to the journeymen of letters; we do not reflect that it is perhaps as difficult to write a good life as to live one. Those two fat volumes, with which it is our custom to commemo-rate the dead—who does not know them, with their ill-digested masses of material, their slip-shod style, their tone of tedious panegyric, their lamentable lack of selection, of detachment of design? They are as familiar as the *cortege* of the undertaker, and wear the same air of slow, funereal barbarism. One is tempted to suppose, of some of them, that they were composed by that functionary, as the final item of his job. The studies in this book are indebted, in more ways than one, to such works—works which certainly deserve the name of Standard Biographies. For they have provided me not only with much indispensable information, but with something even more precious—an example. How many lessons are to be learned from them! But it is hardly necessary to particularize. To preserve, for instance, a becoming brevity—a brevity which excludes everything that is redundant and nothing that is significant—that, surely, is the first duty of the biographer. The second, no less surely, is to maintain his own freedom of spirit. It is not his business to be complimentary, it is his business to lay bare the facts of the case as he understands them. That is what I have aimed at in this book—to lay bare the facts of some cases, as I understand them, dispassionately, impartially, and with-out ulterior intentions.

There is no question that Strachey's first books sounded the death knell of the two-volume panegyric, but that he wrote with no other intention than to lay bare the facts as he understood them is open to argument. It is sufficient to state here that *Eminent Victorians* and *Queen Victoria* gave him his position as the father of modern biography.

Lytton Strachey revolutionized biographical writing, for he approached biography from a new angle. He was not concerned with his subject's life as a whole, but rather those aspects of it that brought out the individual characteristics. Even in *Queen Victoria*, his only full-length biography, there are great gaps in the chronology because those years provided nothing new in characterization. Her birth, her accession, her marriage, and the length of her rule were the principal events of her life, the events which made the Victoria who gave her name to an age.

The subjects in *Eminent Victorians* are less fully treated, and *Elizabeth and Essex* primarily concerns Elizabeth in her middle years. Nevertheless we know Manning, Gordon, Florence Nightingale, Arnold, and Queen Elizabeth when we have finished these books, but we do not know them completely, and that is one of the faults in Strachey's method. He is inclined to show us only one side of the picture, the ironical side. As a portrayer of character, Strachey is unexcelled in modern times; as a true biographer he has limitations, but they were imposed by himself. He succeeded admirably in accomplishing the purpose he had in mind.

Strachey's art was developed through the choice of his subjects. In every instance he took an unusual individual, saturated himself with knowledge and then produced the essence of the material. Strachey chose his material as carefully as a novelist chooses his, for the commonplace, everyday life of an individual meant nothing to him. He arranged his material as a dramatist sets his stage, and achieved the same effects. When you have carefully chosen facts arranged with dramatic effect and handled by a master of the method who has a style as original as the method, you will have a work of art. When you have this method used by men who have not or cannot choose such facts, who have not the ability to dramatize as the master does, and who have not acquired a distinctive style, you will have something less than art.

Lytton Strachey was a man of wide and profound knowledge of history, psychology, and human nature. He knew what people wanted to know about the great and the famous, and he knew how to write. These requisites are lacking in many of his disciples and that is why their work falls so far below his. Strachey had a genius for irony, together with the ability to keep his ironic tone; most of his followers, in trying to imitate his ironic tone, descended to satire or invective, neither of which is successful in biography. Strachey seemed to take pleasure in trying to lay bare the inmost thoughts of his subjects, and always succeeded in showing their littleness even though they also had something of the great in their characters. His imitators, unable to probe into character and mind, sometimes became vulgar and more often untruthful. The trouble with Strachey's method is that it looks so easy and in reality is so difficult. Knowledge, culture, genius, and a peculiar mentality were combined in Strachey as they have been in no biographer who has tried to imitate him.

I have tried to explain Strachey's method and the reasons for his success because he has been more widely followed in America than any other modern biographer. Many writers have learned much from him without succumbing to frank imitation; others have followed him slavishly and have failed for the reasons given. Many more have been inspired by his method and success to work out methods of their own, and these have generally succeeded. It is his influence rather than his method itself that has helped to raise biography to the position of an art.

Emil Ludwig has had a different influence on our biographical writing from that exercised by Strachey. Ludwig's purpose seems to be dramatic representation of life. There is more movement, more analysis of motivation, more desire to get at the whole man in Ludwig than in Strachey. Strachey, of course, had the dramatic instinct (we have only to read the famous last paragraphs of "Cardinal Manning" and *Queen Victoria* to realize this), but Strachey uses drama only for effect while Ludwig bases his entire method on dramatic principles. Strachey had developed his method by the time he came to write *Eminent Victorians*; if we follow Ludwig from his first long biography, *Goethe* (1919), through *Bismarck* (1924), to *Napoleon* (1925) we will see a steady development that reached its climax in the last-named life. Ludwig's reputation has suffered in England and America because *Napoleon* was translated before either *Bismarck* or *Goethe*. He has published a number of biographies which were written after Napoleon, but they do not show any improvement in technique. As a matter of fact, his popularity has led him to write too much.

It seems that Ludwig's work more nearly approaches the biographical ideal than Strachey's. Ludwig's biographies are full and complete; they carry us along with Goethe, Napoleon, and Bismarck; and we see these men in their successes and failures, in their periods of depression and exaltation. We see their characters develop, and we are able to judge whether that development is good or bad. We see the man as he was to himself and to others. And always there is life in terms of drama, and it is that dramatic method that makes Ludwig's books so interesting. They have not the distinction of style, the brevity, the irony that characterize Strachey's writings, but they have a fullness, a rapidity of movement, a reality that make for great life-writing. Ludwig's influence has not extended over so long a period as has Strachey's, but it seems to have had a marked effect on American biography, a more wholesome effect than the sometimes cruel irony of Strachey.

André Maurois is the third European who has influenced modern biography. Like Strachey and Ludwig he has contributed something new to life-writing. Strachey desired to reform biography; Ludwig has dramatized and vivified it; Maurois has made it, according to his own statement, a means of self-expression. Maurois has written extensively on the subject; his book *Aspects of Biography*, in which he states his ideas and beliefs in regard to biography as an art, should be read by everyone interested in life-writing.

Maurois' three important biographies are *Ariel, the Life of Shelley* (1923), *Disraeli* (1927), and *Byron* (1930). The first one exemplifies his fundamental principle that biography should be a means of self-expression for the author as well as an explanation and interpretation of the subject. The average person, knowing nothing of Maurois or his method, might consider *Ariel* a historical romance rather than a biography, and he would not be far wrong. It has all the appearances of a novel based on fact. It is not a complete record of Shelley's life nor is it an interpretation of Shelley's character. The method is too novel to be successful. *Ariel* was very successful in this country, but it had a very bad effect in that it tempted writers of biography to use conversation to heighten interest; and very frequently that conversation had no basis in fact. I believe that *Ariel* is largely responsible for the fictional biography with which we are plagued and which is totally untrue. Fictional biography differs from biographical fiction in that the latter is fiction based on fact while the former purports to be fact when, in reality, it is the product of the writer's imagination.

In his second biography, *Disraeli*, Maurois changed his method somewhat, adhering more closely to the conventional form, and the third, *Byron*, is completely conventional in form. As biography, *Byron* is infinitely superior to *Ariel*.

Maurois' method is very much the same as that of Strachey and Ludwig. He stresses character and personality rather than day-by-day events, which is as it should be. There is no reason to believe that Maurois' method is not his own, although he must have been influenced by the writings of the other men. His books are as interesting as Strachey's, as complete as Ludwig's, if we except *Ariel*, and they have the further charm of an excellent and individual style. I know of no better way of judging the comparative merits of these three biographers than to read *Queen Victoria, Napoleon,* and *Disraeli*.

There are other names prominent in the new biography such as

Philip Guedalla, Harold Nicolson, and the American, Gamaliel Bradford. Each has contributed to the development of modern biography;
Bradford has given us what may be called a new form. Of the other two,
Guedalla has produced in the *Third Empire, Palmerston,* and *Wellington,* biographies which will have permanent places in our literature. This
is particularly true of *Wellington.* In addition to these long biographies
Guedalla has written a number of volumes of excellent biographical
essays.

✦ Suggestions for Reading and Writing

1. Discuss O'Neill's comment: "If we read sufficient biographies, we
   may . . . find that we are great men, denied the opportunity to prove
   our greatness."
2. O'Neill's essay was published in 1935. Have our views of the world and
   of great men changed since then in ways that seriously affect biographical
   writing?
3. Do you agree with Strachey's quoted statement "that it is perhaps as
   difficult to write a good life as to live one"? How would you interpret
   "good life" in each instance?
4. After reading Strachey's "Dr. Arnold" or "General Gordon" (in
   Eminent Victorians [1918]), discuss whether Strachey tends to lay
   "bare the facts . . . dispassionately, impartially, and without ulterior
   intentions." How evident is his "genius for irony"?
5. Follow O'Neill's suggestion and compare Strachey's *Queen Victoria*
   (1921), Emil Ludwig's *Napoleon* (1925), and André Maurois' *Disraeli*
   (1927). How strong is Strachey's influence upon the other two? Is it
   (in a literary sense) a positive or a negative influence?
6. What specific contributions to modern biography can be traced to
   Philip Guedalla, Gamaliel Bradford, and Harold Nicolson? (For background, see Edgar Johnson's *One Mighty Torrent* [1937], George
   Carver's *Alms for Oblivion* [1946], and John Garraty's *The Nature of
   Biography* [1957].)

from

AUTOBIOGRAPHIES

William Butler Yeats

The Dublin-born son of an Irish-Protestant painter, William Butler Yeats (1865–1939) fashioned one of the most noteworthy and productive careers in modern English letters. He published over a hundred volumes of his own poems, dramas, folklore, and prose, as well as editions and anthologies of others' writings. Restless, curious, and self-probing, he lived for extended periods in London and Paris and on the Italian Riviera. But he returned repeatedly to his native Ireland for intellectual and spiritual inspiration.

Fascinated not only by Ireland's history but by its lore and legends, Yeats absorbed, preserved, and commented on his country's Gaelic tales and Celtic myths in a number of literary works. No mere dreamer, he became involved in the Young Ireland society, helped found the Irish National Theater Society (1899) and the Abbey Theater (1910), and led the Irish Literary Revival. He wanted a national poetry that could be written in clear, simple English but would remain spiritually Irish; thus he used folk materials in a number of prose and verse dramas—of which Cathleen ni Houlihan (1902) and Deirdre (1907) are early examples.

Yeats was first and last a poet. Such early volumes of verse as The Wanderings of Oisin (1889), A Book of Irish Verse (1895), and The Wind Among the Reeds (1899) were essentially romantic in theme and treatment; centering upon love, Irish fairy tales, and Celtic myths, they tended to be sensuous, fanciful, and sentimental. But the modern currents of the new century altered his poetic views and his verse. His

subsequent poems (as collected, for instance, in Collected
Poems, Definitive Edition [1956], and The Variorum Edition
of the Poems of W. B. Yeats [1957], edited by Peter Alt and
Russell K. Alspach) revealed increasingly the ideas of Ezra
Pound and the Imagists. Yeats reflected especially their emphasis upon clarity of image, concreteness, verbal economy,
conversational tone, and freedom of subject matter. These
later poems contributed notably to Yeats's winning the 1924
Nobel Prize for literature. He continued writing poems with no
diminishing of intellectual powers until his death, at seventy-
three.

In later life Yeats became increasingly interested in
astrology, theosophy, clairvoyance, and oriental speculation. Yet
these interests are not evident in his two-part account of his
early life, Reveries Over Childhood and Youth (1915; from
which the following passages are taken) and The Trembling of
the Veil (1922). Later the two books were published together
as Autobiographies (1926).

✦ ✦ ✦ ✦ ✦

I

My first memories are fragmentary and isolated and contemporaneous, as though one remembered some first moments of the Seven
Days. It seems as if time had not yet been created, for all thoughts
connected with emotion and place are without sequence.

I remember sitting upon somebody's knee, looking out of an Irish
window at a wall covered with cracked and falling plaster, but what wall
I do not remember, and being told that some relation once lived there. I
am looking out of a window in London. It is at Fitzroy Road. Some boys
are playing in the road and among them a boy in uniform, a telegraph
boy perhaps. When I ask who the boy is, a servant tells me that he is
going to blow the town up, and I go to sleep in terror.

After that come memories of Sligo, where I live with my grandparents. I am sitting on the ground looking at a mastless toy boat with the
paint rubbed and scratched, and I say to myself in great melancholy, "It
is further away than it used to be", and while I am saying it I am looking
at a long scratch in the stern, for it is especially the scratch which is
further away. Then one day at dinner my great-uncle William Middleton says, "We should not make light of the troubles of children. They

are worse than ours, because we can see the end of our trouble and they can never see any end," and I feel grateful for I know that I am very unhappy and have often said to myself, "When you grow up, never talk as grown-up people do of the happiness of childhood." I may have already had the night of misery when, having prayed for several days that I might die, I began to be afraid that I was dying and prayed that I might live. There was no reason for my unhappiness. Nobody was unkind, and my grandmother has still after so many years my gratitude and my reverence. The house was so big that there was always a room to hide in, and I had a red pony and a garden where I could wander, and there were two dogs to follow at my heels, one white with some black spots on his head and the other with long black hair all over him. I used to think about God and fancy that I was very wicked, and one day when I threw a stone and hit a duck in the yard by mischance and broke its wing, I was full of wonder when I was told that the duck would be cooked for dinner and that I should not be punished.

Some of my misery was loneliness and some of it fear of old William Pollexfen my grandfather. He was never unkind, and I cannot remember that he ever spoke harshly to me, but it was the custom to fear and admire him. He had won the freedom of some Spanish city, for saving life perhaps, but was so silent that his wife never knew it till he was near eighty, and then from the chance visit of some old sailor. She asked him if it was true and he said it was true, but she knew him too well to question and his old shipmate had left the town. She too had the habit of fear. We knew that he had been in many parts of the world, for there was a great scar on his hand made by a whaling-hook, and in the dining-room was a cabinet with bits of coral in it and a jar of water from the Jordan for the baptizing of his children and Chinese pictures upon rice-paper and an ivory walking-stick from India that came to me after his death. He had great physical strength and had the reputation of never ordering a man to do anything he would not do himself. He owned many sailing ships and once, when a captain just come to anchor at Rosses Point reported something wrong with the rudder, had sent a messenger to say "Send a man down to find out what's wrong." "The crew all refuse" was the answer, and to that my grandfather answered, "Go down yourself," and not being obeyed, he dived from the main deck, all the neighbourhood lined along the pebbles of the shore. He came up with his skin torn but well informed about the rudder. He had a violent temper and kept a hatchet at his bedside for burglars and would knock a man down instead of going to law, and I once saw him hunt a party of men with a horsewhip. He had no relation for he was an only child and, being solitary and silent, he had few friends. He corresponded with Campbell of Islay who had befriended him and his crew after a shipwreck, and

Captain Webb, the first man who had swum the Channel and who was drowned swimming the Niagara Rapids, had been a mate in his employ and a close friend. That is all the friends I can remember and yet he was so looked up to and admired that when he returned from taking the waters at Bath his men would light bonfires along the railway line for miles; while his partner William Middleton whose father after the great famine had attended the sick for weeks, and taken cholera from a man he carried in his arms into his own house and died of it, and was himself civil to everybody and a cleverer man than my grandfather, came and went without notice. I think I confused my grandfather with God, for I remember in one of my attacks of melancholy praying that he might punish me for my sins, and I was shocked and astonished when a daring little girl—a cousin I think—having waited under a group of trees in the avenue, where she knew he would pass near four o'clock on the way to his dinner, said to him, "If I were you and you were a little girl, I would give you a doll."

Yet for all my admiration and alarm, neither I nor any one else thought it wrong to outwit his violence or his rigour; and his lack of suspicion and something helpless about him made that easy while it stirred our affection. When I must have been still a very little boy, seven or eight years old perhaps, an uncle called me out of bed one night, to ride the five or six miles to Rosses Point to borrow a railway-pass from a cousin. My grandfather had one, but thought it dishonest to let another use it, but the cousin was not so particular. I was let out through a gate that opened upon a little lane beside the garden away from ear-shot of the house, and rode delighted through the moonlight, and awoke my cousin in the small hours by tapping on his window with a whip. I was home again by two or three in the morning and found the coachman waiting in the little lane. My grandfather would not have thought such an adventure possible, for every night at eight he believed that the stable-yard was locked, and he knew that he was brought the key. Some servant had once got into trouble at night and so he had arranged that they should all be locked in. He never knew, what everybody else in the house knew, that for all the ceremonious bringing of the key the gate was never locked.

Even to-day when I read *King Lear* his image is always before me and I often wonder if the delight in passionate men in my plays and in my poetry is more than his memory. He must have been ignorant, though I could not judge him in my childhood, for he had run away to sea when a boy, "gone to sea through the hawse-hole" as he phrased it, and I can but remember him with two books—his Bible and Falconer's *Shipwreck*, a little green-covered book that lay always upon his table; he belonged to some younger branch of an old Cornish family. His father had been in the Army, had retired to become an owner of sailing ships, and an engraving of some old family place my grandfather thought should have been his hung next a painted coat of arms in the little back parlour. His mother had been a Wexford woman, and there was a tradition that his family had been linked with Ireland for generations and once had their share in the old Spanish trade with Galway. He had a good deal of pride and disliked his neighbours, whereas his wife, a Middleton, was gentle and patient and did many charities in the little back parlour among frieze coats and shawled heads, and every night when she saw him asleep went the round of the house alone with a candle to make certain there was no burglar in danger of the hatchet. She was a true lover of her garden, and before the care of her house had grown upon her, would choose some favourite among her flowers and copy it upon rice-paper. I saw some of her handiwork the other day and I wondered at the delicacy of form and colour and at a handling that may have needed a magnifying-glass it was so minute. I can remember no other pictures but the Chinese paintings, and some coloured prints of battles in the Crimea upon the wall of a passage, and the painting of a ship at the passage end darkened by time.

. . . . . .

The only lessons I had ever learned were those my father taught me, for he terrified me by descriptions of my moral degradation and he humiliated me by my likeness to disagreeable people; but presently I was sent to school at Hammersmith. It was a Gothic building of yellow brick: a large hall full of desks, some small class-rooms and a separate house for boarders, all built perhaps in 1860 or 1870. I thought it an ancient building and that it had belonged to the founder of the school, Lord Godolphin, who was romantic to me because there was a novel about him. I never read the novel, but I thought only romantic people were put in books. On one side, there was a piano factory of yellow brick, upon two sides half-finished rows of little shops and villas all yellow brick, and on the fourth side, outside the wall of our playing field, a brick-field of cinders and piles of half-burned yellow bricks. All the names and faces of my school-fellows have faded from me except one name without a face and the face and name of one friend, mainly no doubt because it was all so long ago, but partly because I only seem to remember things dramatic in themselves or that are somehow associated with unforgettable places.

For some days as I walked homeward along the Hammersmith Road, I told myself that whatever I most cared for had been taken away. I had found a small, green-covered book given to my father by a Dublin man of science; it gave an account of the strange sea creatures the man of science had discovered among the rocks at Howth or dredged out of

Dublin Bay. It had long been my favourite book; and when I read it I believed that I was growing very wise, but now I should have no time for it nor for my own thoughts. Every moment would be taken up learning or saying lessons, or in walking between school and home four times a day for I came home in the middle of the day for dinner. But presently I forgot my trouble, absorbed in two things I had never known, companionship and enmity. After my first day's lesson, a circle of boys had got around me in a playing field and asked me questions, "Who's your father?" "What does he do?" "How much money has he?" Presently a boy said something insulting. I had never struck anybody or been struck, and now all in a minute, without any intention upon my side, but as if I had been a doll moved by a string, I was hitting at the boys within reach and being hit. After that I was called names for being Irish, and had many fights and never, for years, got the better in any one of them; for I was delicate and had no muscles. Sometimes, however, I found means of retaliation, even of aggression. There was a boy with a big stride, much feared by little boys, and finding him alone in the playing field, I went up to him and said, "Rise upon Sugaun and sink upon Gad." "What does that mean?" he said. "Rise upon hay-leg and sink upon straw," I answered and told him that in Ireland the sergeant tied straw and hay to the ankles of a stupid recruit to show him the difference between his legs. My ears were boxed, and when I complained to my friends, they said I had brought it upon myself, and that I deserved all I got. I probably dared myself to other feats of a like sort, for I did not think English people intelligent or well-behaved unless they were artists. Every one I knew well in Sligo despised Nationalists and Catholics, but all disliked England with a prejudice that had come down perhaps from the days of the Irish Parliament. I knew stories to the discredit of England, and took them all seriously. My mother had met some English woman who did not like Dublin because the legs of the men were too straight, and at Sligo, as everybody knew, an Englishman had once said to a car-driver, "If you people were not so lazy, you would pull down the mountain and spread it out over the sand and that would give you acres of good fields." At Sligo there is a wide river mouth and at ebb tide most of it is dry sand, but all Sligo knew that in some way I cannot remember it was the spreading of the tide over the sand that left the narrow channel fit for shipping. At any rate the carman had gone chuckling all over Sligo with his tale. People would tell it to prove that Englishmen were always grumbling. "They grumble about their dinners and everything—there was an Englishman who wanted to pull down Knock-na-Rea" and so on. My mother had shown them to me kissing at railway stations, and taught me to feel disgust at their lack of reserve, and my father told how my grandfather, William Yeats, who had died before I was born, when he came home to his Rectory in County Down from an English visit, spoke of some man he had met on a coach road who "Englishman-like" told him all his affairs. My father explained that an Englishman generally believed that his private affairs did him credit, while an Irishman, being poor and probably in debt, had no such confidence. I, however, did not believe in this explanation. My Sligo nurses, who had in all likelihood the Irish Catholic political hatred, had never spoken well of any Englishman. Once when walking in the town of Sligo I had turned to look after an English man and woman whose clothes attracted me. The man I remember had grey clothes and knee-breeches and the woman a grey dress, and my nurse had said contemptuously, "Tow-rows"—perhaps before my time, there had been some English song with the burden "tow row row"—and everybody had told me that English people ate skates and even dog-fish, and I myself had only just arrived in England when I saw an old man put marmalade in his porridge.

I was divided from all those boys, not merely by the anecdotes that are everywhere perhaps a chief expression of the distrust of races, but because our mental images were different. I read their boys' books and they excited me, but if I read of some English victory, I did not believe that I read of my own people. They thought of Cressy and Agincourt and the Union Jack and were all very patriotic, and I, without those memories of Limerick and the Yellow Ford that would have strengthened an Irish Catholic, thought of mountain and lake, of my grandfather and of ships. Anti-Irish feeling was running high, for the Land League had been founded and landlords had been shot, and I, who had no politics, was yet full of pride, for it is romantic to live in a dangerous country.

I daresay I thought the rough manners of a cheap school, as my grandfather Yeats had those of a chance companion, typical of all England. At any rate I had a harassed life and got many a black eye and had many outbursts of grief and rage. Once a boy, the son of a great Bohemian glass-maker, who was older than the rest of us, and had been sent out of his country because of a love affair, beat a boy for me because we were "both foreigners". And a boy, who grew to be the school athlete and my chief friend, beat a great many. His are the face and name that I remember—his name was of Huguenot origin and his face like his gaunt and lithe body had something of the American Indian in colour and lineament.

I was very much afraid of the other boys, and that made me doubt myself for the first time. When I had gathered pieces of wood in the corner for my great ship, I was confident that I could keep calm among the storms and die fighting when the great battle came. But now I was ashamed of my lack of courage; for I wanted to be like my grandfather who thought so little of danger that he had jumped overboard in the Bay of Biscay after an old hat. I was very much afraid of physical pain, and one day when I had made some noise in class, my friend the athlete was accused and I allowed him to get two strokes of the cane before I gave myself up. He had held out his hands without flinching and had not rubbed them on his sides afterwards. I was not caned, but was made to stand up for the rest of the lesson. I suffered very much afterwards when the thought came to me, but he did not reproach me.

I had been some years at school before I had my last fight. My friend, the athlete, had given me many months of peace, but at last refused to beat any more and said I must learn to box, and not go near the other boys till I knew how. I went home with him every day and boxed in his room, and the bouts had always the same ending. My excitability gave me an advantage at first and I would drive him across the room, and then he would drive me across and it would end very commonly with my nose bleeding. One day his father, an elderly banker, brought us out into the garden and tried to make us box in a cold-blooded, courteous way, but it was no use. At last he said I might go near the boys again and I was no sooner inside the gate of the playing field than a boy flung a handful of mud and cried out, "Mad Irishman". I hit him several times on the face without being hit, till the boys round said we should make friends. I held out my hand in fear; for I knew if we went on I should be beaten, and he took it sullenly. I had so poor a reputation as a fighter that it was a great disgrace to him, and even the masters made fun of his swollen face; and though some little boys came in a deputation to ask me to lick a boy they named, I had never another fight with a school-fellow.

. . . . .

⌐ Suggestions for Reading and Writing

1. Yeats recalls his early childhood as being full of misery and loneliness. Does this strike a responsive chord, or are your own early recollections different?
2. Does William Pollexfen here attain heroic stature? Or does he seem a rather ordinary figure inflated by an imaginative grandson's romanticizings?
3. What comment does Yeats make, in effect, on his own youthful prejudices against the English?
4. A less self-conscious self-portrait than *Autobiographies* but an equally rich mine of biographic information is the posthumously published *Letters on Poetry from W. B. Yeats to Dorothy Wellesley* (1940). After dipping into the letters, write a character sketch of Yeats. Check your findings against such standard studies as Joseph Hone's *W. B. Yeats*

(1943), Richard Ellmann's *Yeats: The Man and the Masks* (1948), and Monk Gibbon's *The Masterpiece and the Man: Yeats As I Knew Him* (1959).

5. After reading his two Byzantium poems, "A Dialogue of Self and Soul," the eight "Crazy Jane" poems, "Lapis Lazuli," and "Long-legged Fly," you should be able to summarize Yeats's later views of man, civilization, and the life-death cycle. (The best studies of his work are in Edmund Wilson's *Axel's Castle* [1931], Stephen Spender's *The Destructive Element* [1935], David Daiches' *Poetry and the Modern World* [1940], and Louis MacNeice's *The Poetry of W. B. Yeats* [1941]. See also James Hall and Martin Steinmann, eds., *The Permanence of Yeats: Selected Criticism* [1950].)

6. Yeats's mystic phase has been much discussed by literary critics. After reading his *A Vision* (1956; reissued with the author's final revisions), summarize the basic concepts presented there. (Consult the biographical and the critical studies already mentioned for any help you may need.)

7. Compare the contrasting dramatic treatments of Irish heroic saga in Yeats's *Deirdre* (1907) and in *Deirdre of the Sorrows* (1910), by his great fellow playwright John Millington Synge. (For Yeats's ideas on poetry, the theater, and life in general, read one of his volumes of essays, such as *Ideas of Good and Evil* [1903], *Discoveries* [1907], *The Cutting of an Agate* [1912], or *Dramatis Personae* [1936].)

FLORENCE NIGHTINGALE

Lytton Strachey

Twentieth-century biography bears the strong imprint of Giles Lytton Strachey (1880–1932), who reshaped life-writing into an imaginative literary form. Like Virginia Woolf, Strachey enjoyed a rich cultural heritage. The son of an army general and government official, he was educated in France and at Trinity

College, Cambridge. He moved naturally into the Bloomsbury Group, which included John Maynard Keynes, Desmond McCarthy, the Woolfs, Clive Bell, and E. M. Forster. Sensitive, awkward, and frail, he was destined by fate and inclination to be more life observer than participant.

Strachey revealed early his literary gifts. At Trinity College he won the Chancellor's medal for English verse and already was writing essays and reviews revealing that lucid, concise prose and flair for "swift, indelible portraiture" soon to establish his reputation. At thirty-two he published his judicious and balanced Landmarks of French Literature (1912) and stamped himself an author of merit.

But Strachey's heart was not in literary history. In addition, the new century and the war were changing the intellectual climate. A spreading scientific attitude—shaped primarily by Freud and other depth-psychologists—was demolishing Victorian biography's polite reticence. War-fed disenchantment and cynicism were replacing the traditional reverence for the famous and successful. In America, by the end of the war, Gamaliel Bradford had published his Lee the American (1912) and three other volumes of short "psychographs" utilizing the new psychology and objectivity.

Strachey harnessed these scientific and cynical attitudes and in Eminent Victorians (1918) raised them to new levels of art and irony. In his preface he states that it is not the biographer's "business to be complimentary; it is his business to lay bare the facts of the case as he understands them." Thus he set himself to "de-pedestalizing" the lives of Cardinal Manning, Florence Nightingale, Dr. Thomas Arnold, and General Gordon. Each life exemplifies Strachey's dominant characteristics: brevity, irony, lucidity, wit, and an irreverent fusion of fact and conjecture.

Strachey himself felt that his approach was as valid as that of such predecessors as Plutarch and Samuel Johnson. But to many he was a mere opportunistic iconoclast robbing four venerated figures of their halos. His superb comic sense and disdain for conventional biographic modes evoked the epithet "Satanic." But he captured the imagination of a war-weary generation eager to reject all that smacked of Victorianism. In his next book, Queen Victoria (1921), Strachey blended art and fact so effectively that even his detractors realized the "life and times" school of life-writing was dead. Books and Characters (1922), Pope (1925), and Elizabeth and Essex (1928) followed,

but not until Portraits in Miniature (1931) did he again
approach the level of Eminent Victorians and Queen Victoria.

A host of imitators followed, most of whom lacked
Strachey's taste, discipline, or craftsmanship. These practitioners
of the New Biography debased his innovations and exploited his
weak points: they exposed, debunked, homogenized fact and
myth; filled gaps by intuition; and omitted inconvenient data.
Having showed the way, Strachey must bear partial blame for
their cheap, shoddy exposés. His own reputation, however, seems
established; he produced a new approach, pushed back
boundaries, and made ponderous research readable. Above all,
he restored English prose style to the status of art.

ı ı ı ı ı

I

Everyone knows the popular conception of Florence Nightingale.
The saintly, self-sacrificing woman, the delicate maiden of high degree
who threw aside the pleasures of a life of ease to succour the afflicted, the
Lady with the Lamp, gliding through the horrors of the hospital at
Scutari, and consecrating with the radiance of her goodness the dying
soldier's couch—the vision is familiar to all. But the truth was different.
The Miss Nightingale of fact was not as facile fancy painted her. She
worked in another fashion, and towards another end; she moved under
the stress of an impetus which finds no place in the popular imagination.
A Demon possessed her. Now demons, whatever else they may be, are
full of interest. And so it happens that in the real Miss Nightingale there
was more that was interesting than in the legendary one; there was also
less that was agreeable.

Her family was extremely well-to-do, and connected by marriage
with a spreading circle of other well-to-do families. There was a large
country house in Derbyshire; there was another in the New Forest; there
were Mayfair rooms for the London season and all its finest parties; there
were tours on the Continent with even more than the usual number of
Italian operas and of glimpses at the celebrities of Paris. Brought up
among such advantages, it was only natural to suppose that Florence
would show a proper appreciation of them by doing her duty in that state
of life unto which it had pleased God to call her—in other words, by
marrying, after a fitting number of dances and dinner-parties, an eligible
gentleman, and living happily ever afterwards. Her sister, her cousins, all

From *Eminent Victorians*, by Lytton Strachey. Reprinted by permission of Harcourt,
Brace & World, Inc., James Strachey, and Chatto & Windus Ltd.

the young ladies of her acquaintance, were either getting ready to do this or had already done it. It was inconceivable that Florence should dream of anything else; yet dream she did. Ah! To do her duty in that state of life unto which it had pleased God to call her! Assuredly she would not be behindhand in doing her duty; but unto what state of life *had* it pleased God to call her? That was the question. God's calls are many, and they are strange. Unto what state of life had it pleased Him to call Charlotte Corday, or Elizabeth of Hungary? What was that secret voice in her ear, if it was not a call? Why had she felt, from her earliest years, those mysterious promptings towards . . . she hardly knew what but certainly towards something very different from anything around her? Why, as a child in the nursery, when her sister had shown a healthy pleasure in tearing her dolls to pieces, had *she* shown an almost morbid one in sewing them up again? Why was she driven now to minister to the poor in their cottages, to watch by sick-beds, to put her dog's wounded paw into elaborate splints as if it was a human being? Why was her head filled with queer imaginations of the country house at Embley turned, by some enchantment, into a hospital, with herself as matron moving about among the beds? Why was even her vision of heaven itself filled with suffering patients to whom she was being useful? So she dreamed and wondered, and, taking out her diary, she poured into it the agitations of her soul. And then the bell rang, and it was time to go and dress for dinner.

As the years passed, a restlessness began to grow upon her. She was unhappy, and at last she knew it. Mrs. Nightingale, too, began to notice that there was something wrong. It was very odd; what could be the matter with dear Flo? Mr. Nightingale suggested that a husband might be advisable; but the curious thing was that she seemed to take no interest in husbands. And with her attractions, and her accomplishments, too! There was nothing in the world to prevent her making a really brilliant match. But no! She would think of nothing but how to satisfy that singular craving of hers to be *doing* something. As if there was not plenty to do in any case, in the ordinary way, at home. There was the china to look after, and there was her father to be read to after dinner. Mrs. Nightingale could not understand it; and then one day her perplexity was changed to consternation and alarm. Florence announced an extreme desire to go to Salisbury Hospital for several months as a nurse; and she confessed to some visionary plan of eventually setting up in a house of her own in a neighbouring village, and there founding "something like a Protestant Sisterhood, without vows, for women of educated feelings." The whole scheme was summarily brushed aside as preposterous; and Mrs. Nightingale, after the first shock of terror, was able to settle down again more or less comfortably to her embroidery.

But Florence, who was now twenty-five and felt that the dream of her life had been shattered, came near to desperation.

And, indeed, the difficulties in her path were great. For not only was it an almost unimaginable thing in those days for a woman of means to make her own way in the world and to live in independence, but the particular profession for which Florence was clearly marked out both by her instincts and her capacities was at that time a peculiarly disreputable one. A "nurse" meant then a coarse old woman, always ignorant, usually dirty, often brutal, a Mrs. Gamp, in bunched-up sordid garments, tippling at the brandy-bottle or indulging in worse irregularities. The nurses in the hospitals were especially notorious for immoral conduct; sobriety almost unknown among them; and they could hardly be trusted to carry out the simplest medical duties. Certainly, things have changed since those days; and that they *have* changed is due, far more than to any other human being, to Miss Nightingale herself. It is not to be wondered at that her parents should have shuddered at the notion of their daughter devoting her life to such an occupation. "It was as if," she herself said afterwards, "I had wanted to be a kitchen-maid." Yet the want, absurd, impracticable as it was, not only remained fixed immovably in her heart, but grew in intensity day by day. Her wretchedness deepened into a morbid melancholy. Everything about her was vile, and she herself, it was clear, to have deserved such misery, was even viler than her surroundings. Yes, she had sinned—"standing before God's judgment seat." "No one," she declared, "has so grieved the Holy Spirit"; of that she was quite certain. It was in vain that she prayed to be delivered from vanity and hypocrisy, and she could not bear to smile or to be gay, "because she hated God to hear her laugh, as if she had not repented of her sin."

A weaker spirit would have been overwhelmed by the load of such distresses—would have yielded or snapped. But this extraordinary young woman held firm, and fought her way to victory. With an amazing persistency, during the eight years that followed her rebuff over Salisbury Hospital, she struggled and worked and planned. While superficially she was carrying on the life of a brilliant girl in high society, while internally she was a prey to the tortures of regret and of remorse, she yet possessed the energy to collect the knowledge and to undergo the experience which alone could enable her to do what she had determined she would do in the end. In secret she devoured the reports of medical commissions, the pamphlets of sanitary authorities, the histories of hospitals and homes. She spent the intervals of the London season in ragged schools and workhouses. When she went abroad with her family, she used her spare time so well that there was hardly a great hospital in Europe with which she was not acquainted, hardly a great city whose slums she had not passed through. She managed to spend some days in a convent school in Rome, and some weeks as a "Sœur de Charité" in Paris. Then, while her mother and sister were taking the waters at Carlsbad, she succeeded in slipping off to a nursing institution at Kaiserswerth, where she remained for more than three months. This was the critical event of her life. The experience which she gained as a nurse at Kaiserswerth formed the foundation of all her future action and finally fixed her in her career.

But one other trial awaited her. The allurements of the world she had brushed aside with disdain and loathing; she had resisted the subtler temptation which, in her weariness, had sometimes come upon her, of devoting her baffled energies to art or literature; the last ordeal appeared in the shape of a desirable young man. Hitherto, her lovers had been nothing to her but an added burden and a mockery; but now—. For a moment, she wavered. A new feeling swept over her—a feeling which she had never known before, which she was never to know again. The most powerful and the profoundest of all the instincts of humanity laid claim upon her. But it rose before her, that instinct, arrayed—how could it be otherwise?—in the inevitable habiliments of a Victorian marriage; and she had the strength to stamp it underfoot.

> I have an intellectual nature which requires satisfaction [she noted], and that would find it in him. I have a passional nature which requires satisfaction, and that would find it in him. I have a moral, an active nature which requires satisfaction, and that would not find it in his life. Sometimes I think that I will satisfy my passional nature at all events. . . .

But no, she knew in her heart that it could not be. "To be nailed to a continuation and exaggeration of my present life . . . to put it out of my power ever to be able to seize the chance of forming for myself a true and rich life"—that would be a suicide. She made her choice, and refused what was at least a certain happiness for a visionary good which might never come to her at all. And so she returned to her old life of waiting and bitterness.

> The thoughts and feelings that I have now [she wrote] I can remember since I was six years old. A profession, a trade, a necessary occupation, something to fill and employ all my faculties, I have always felt essential to me, I have always longed for. The first thought I can remember, and the last, was nursing work; and in the absence of this, education work, but more the education of the bad than of the young. . . . Everything has been tried, foreign travel, kind friends, everything. My God! What is to become of me?

A desirable young man? Dust and ashes! What was there desirable in such a thing as that? "In my thirty-first year," she noted in her diary, "I see nothing desirable but death."

Three more years passed, and then at last the pressure of time told; her family seemed to realise that she was old enough and strong enough to have her way; and she became the superintendent of a charitable nursing home in Harley Street. She had gained her independence, though it was in a meagre sphere enough; and her mother was still not quite resigned: surely Florence might at least spend the summer in the country. At times, indeed, among her intimates, Mrs. Nightingale almost wept. "We are ducks," she said with tears in her eyes, "who have hatched a wild swan." But the poor lady was wrong; it was not a swan that they had hatched; it was an eagle.

I I

Miss Nightingale had been a year in her nursing-home in Harley Street, when Fate knocked at the door. The Crimean War broke out; the battle of the Alma was fought; and the terrible condition of our military hospitals at Scutari began to be known in England. It sometimes happens that the plans of Providence are a little difficult to follow, but on this occasion all was plain; there was a perfect co-ordination of events. For years Miss Nightingale had been getting ready; at last she was prepared—experienced, free, mature, yet still young—she was thirty-four—desirous to serve, accustomed to command: at that precise moment the desperate need of a great nation came, and she was there to satisfy it. If the war had fallen a few years earlier, she would have lacked the knowledge, perhaps even the power, for such a work; a few years later and she would, no doubt, have been fixed in the routine of some absorbing task, and moreover, she would have been growing old. Nor was it only the coincidence of Time that was remarkable. It so fell out that Sidney Herbert was at the War Office and in the Cabinet; and Sidney Herbert was an intimate friend of Miss Nightingale's, convinced, from personal experience in charitable work, of her supreme capacity. After such premises, it seems hardly more than a matter of course that her letter, in which she offered her services for the East, and Sidney Herbert's letter, in which he asked for them, should actually have crossed in the post. Thus it all happened, without a hitch. The appointment was made, and even Mrs. Nightingale, overawed by the magnitude of the venture, could only approve. A pair of faithful friends offered themselves as personal attendants; thirty-eight nurses were collected; and within a week of the crossing of the letters Miss Nightingale, amid a great burst of popular enthusiasm, left for Constantinople.

Among the numerous letters which she received on her departure was one from Dr. Manning, who at that time was working in comparative obscurity as a Catholic priest in Bayswater. "God will keep you," he wrote, "and my prayer for you will be that your one object of Worship, Pattern of Imitation, and source of consolation and strength may be the Sacred Heart of our Divine Lord."

To what extent Dr. Manning's prayer was answered must remain a matter of doubt; but this much is certain, that, if ever a prayer was needed, it was needed then for Florence Nightingale. For dark as had been the picture of the state of affairs at Scutari, revealed to the English public in the despatches of the *Times* correspondent and in a multitude of private letters, yet the reality turned out to be darker still. What had occurred was, in brief, the complete break-down of our medical arrangements at the seat of war. The origins of this awful failure were complex and manifold; they stretched back through long years of peace and carelessness in England; they could be traced through endless ramifications of administrative incapacity—from the inherent faults of confused systems to the petty bunglings of minor officials, from the inevitable ignorance of Cabinet Ministers to the fatal exactitudes of narrow routine. In the inquiries which followed it was clearly shown that the evil was in reality that worst of all evils—one which has been caused by nothing in particular and for which no one in particular is to blame. The whole organisation of the war machine was incompetent and out of date. The old Duke had sat for a generation at the Horse Guards repressing innovations with an iron hand. There was an extraordinary overlapping of authorities, an almost incredible shifting of responsibilities to and fro. As for such a notion as the creation and the maintenance of a really adequate medical service for the army—in that atmosphere of aged chaos, how could it have entered anybody's head? Before the war, the easy-going officials at Westminster were naturally persuaded that all was well—or at least as well as could be expected; when someone, for instance, actually had the temerity to suggest the formation of a corps of army nurses, he was at once laughed out of court. When the war had begun, the gallant British officers in control of affairs had other things to think about than the petty details of medical organisation. Who had bothered with such trifles in the Peninsula? And surely, on that occasion, we had done pretty well. Thus the most obvious precautions were neglected, the most necessary preparations put off from day to day. The principal medical officer of the army, Dr. Hall, was summoned from India at a moment's notice, and was unable to visit England before taking up his duties at the front. And it was not until after the battle of the Alma, when we had been at war for many months, that we acquired hospital accommodation at Scutari for more than a thousand men.

Errors, follies, and vices on the part of individuals there doubtless were; but, in the general reckoning, they were of small account—insignificant symptoms of the deep disease of the body politic—the enormous calamity of administrative collapse.

Miss Nightingale arrived at Scutari—a suburb of Constantinople, on the Asiatic side of the Bosphorus—on November 4th, 1854; it was ten days after the battle of Balaclava, and the day before the battle of Inkerman. The organisation of the hospitals, which had already given way under the stress of the battle of the Alma, was now to be subjected to the further pressure which these two desperate and bloody engagements implied. Great detachments of wounded were already beginning to pour in. The men, after receiving such summary treatment as could be given them at the smaller hospitals in the Crimea itself, were forthwith shipped in batches of two hundred across the Black Sea to Scutari. This voyage was in normal times one of four days and a half; but the times were no longer normal, and now the transit often lasted for a fortnight or three weeks. It received, not without reason, the name of "the middle passage." Between, and sometimes on the decks, the wounded, the sick, and the dying were crowded—men who had just undergone the amputation of limbs, men in the clutches of fever or of frostbite, men in the last stages of dysentery and cholera—without beds, sometimes without blankets, often hardly clothed. The one or two surgeons on board did what they could; but medical stores were lacking, and the only form of nursing available was that provided by a handful of invalid soldiers, who were usually themselves prostrate by the end of the voyage. There was no other food beside the ordinary salt rations of ship diet; and even the water was sometimes so stored that it was out of reach of the weak. For many months, the average of deaths during these voyages was seventy-four in the thousand; the corpses were shot out into the waters; and who shall say that they were the most unfortunate? At Scutari, the landing-stage, constructed with all the perverseness of Oriental ingenuity, could only be approached with great difficulty, and, in rough weather, not at all. When it was reached, what remained of the men in the ships had first to be disembarked, and then conveyed up a steep slope of a quarter of a mile to the nearest of the hospitals. The most serious cases might be put upon stretchers—for there were far too few for all; the rest were carried or dragged up the hill by such convalescent soldiers as could be got together, who were not too obviously infirm for the work. At last the journey was accomplished; slowly, one by one, living or dying, the wounded were carried up into the hospital. And in the hospital what did they find?

Lasciate ogni speranza, voi ch'entrate: the delusive doors bore no such inscription; and yet behind them Hell yawned. Want, neglect, confusion, misery—in every shape and in every degree of intensity—filled the endless corridors and the vast apartments of the gigantic barrack-house, which, without forethought or preparation, had been hurriedly set aside as the chief shelter for the victims of the war. The very building itself was radically defective. Huge sewers underlay it, and cess-pools loaded with filth wafted their poison into the upper rooms. The floors were in so rotten a condition that many of them could not be scrubbed; the walls were thick with dirt; incredible multitudes of vermin swarmed everywhere. And, enormous as the building was, it was yet too small. It contained four miles of beds, crushed together so close that there was but just room to pass between them. Under such conditions, the most elaborate system of ventilation might well have been at fault; but here there was no ventilation. The stench was indescribable. "I have been well acquainted," said Miss Nightingale, "with the dwellings of the worst parts of most of the great cities in Europe, but have never been in any atmosphere which I could compare with that of the Barrack Hospital at night." The structural defects were equalled by the deficiencies in the commonest objects of hospital use. There were not enough bedsteads; the sheets were of canvas, and so coarse that the wounded men recoiled from them, begging to be left in their blankets; there was no bedroom furniture of any kind, and empty beer-bottles were used for candlesticks. There were no basins, no towels, no soap, no brooms, no mops, no trays, no plates; there were neither slippers nor scissors, neither shoebrushes nor blacking; there were no knives or forks or spoons. The supply of fuel was constantly deficient. The cooking arrangements were preposterously inadequate, and the laundry was a farce. As for purely medical materials, the tale was no better. Stretchers, splints, bandages—all were lacking; and so were the most ordinary drugs.

To replace such wants, to struggle against such difficulties, there was a handful of men overburdened by the strain of ceaseless work, bound down by the traditions of official routine, and enfeebled either by old age or inexperience or sheer incompetence. They had proved utterly unequal to their task. The principal doctor was lost in the imbecilities of a senile optimism. The wretched official whose business it was to provide for the wants of the hospital was tied fast hand and foot by red tape. A few of the younger doctors struggled valiantly, but what could they do? Unprepared, disorganised, with such help only as they could find among the miserable band of convalescent soldiers drafted off to tend their sick comrades, they were faced with disease, mutilation, and death in all their most appalling forms, crowded multitudinously about them in an ever increasing mass. They were like men in a shipwreck, fighting, not for safety, but for the next moment's bare existence—to gain, by yet another frenzied effort, some brief respite from the waters of destruction.

In these surroundings, those who had been long inured to scenes of human suffering—surgeons with a world-wide knowledge of agonies, soldiers familiar with fields of carnage, missionaries with remembrances of famine and of plague—yet found a depth of horror which they had never known before. There were moments, there were places, in the Barrack Hospital at Scutari, where the strongest hand was struck with trembling, and the boldest eye would turn away its gaze.

Miss Nightingale came, and she, at any rate, in that Inferno, did not abandon hope. For one thing, she brought material succour. Before she left London she had consulted Dr. Andrew Smith, the head of the Army Medical Board, as to whether it would be useful to take out stores of any kind to Scutari; and Dr. Andrew Smith had told her that "nothing was needed." Even Sidney Herbert had given her similar assurances; possibly, owing to an oversight, there might have been some delay in the delivery of the medical stores, which, he said, had been sent out from England "in profusion," but "four days would have remedied this." She preferred to trust her own instincts, and at Marseilles purchased a large quantity of miscellaneous provisions, which were of the utmost use at Scutari. She came, too, amply provided with money—in all, during her stay in the East, about £7000 reached her from private sources; and, in addition, she was able to avail herself of another valuable means of help. At the same time as herself, Mr. Macdonald, of the *Times*, had arrived at Scutari, charged with the duty of administering the large sums of money collected through the agency of that newspaper in aid of the sick and wounded; and Mr. Macdonald had the sense to see that the best use he could make of the *Times* Fund was to put it at the disposal of Miss Nightingale.

> I cannot conceive [wrote an eye-witness], as I now calmly look back on the first three weeks after the arrival of the wounded from Inkerman, how it could have been possible to have avoided a state of things too disastrous to contemplate, had not Miss Nightingale been there, with the means placed at her disposal by Mr. Macdonald.

But the official view was different. What! Was the public service to admit, by accepting outside charity, that it was unable to discharge its own duties without the assistance of private and irregular benevolence? Never! And accordingly when Lord Stratford de Redcliffe, our Ambassador at Constantinople, was asked by Mr. Macdonald to indicate how the *Times* Fund could best be employed, he answered that there was indeed one object to which it might very well be devoted—the building of an English Protestant Church at Pera.

Mr. Macdonald did not waste further time with Lord Stratford, and immediately joined forces with Miss Nightingale. But, with such a frame of mind in the highest quarters, it is easy to imagine the kind of disgust and alarm with which the sudden intrusion of a band of amateurs and females must have filled the minds of the ordinary officer and the ordinary military surgeon. They could not understand it; what had women to do with war? Honest Colonels relieved their spleen by the cracking of heavy jokes about "the Bird"; while poor Dr. Hall, a rough terrier of a man, who had worried his way to the top of his profession, was struck speechless with astonishment, and at last observed that Miss Nightingale's appointment was extremely droll.

Her position was, indeed, an official one, but it was hardly the easier for that. In the hospitals it was her duty to provide the services of herself and her nurses when they were asked for by the doctors, and not until then. At first some of the surgeons would have nothing to say to her, and, though she was welcomed by others, the majority were hostile and suspicious. But gradually she gained ground. Her good will could not be denied, and her capacity could not be disregarded. With consummate tact, with all the gentleness of supreme strength, she managed at last to impose her personality upon the susceptible, overwrought, discouraged, and helpless group of men in authority who surrounded her. She stood firm; she was a rock in the angry ocean; with her alone was safety, comfort, life. And so it was that hope dawned at Scutari. The reign of chaos and old night began to dwindle; order came upon the scene, and common sense, and forethought, and decision, radiating out from the little room off the great gallery in the Barrack Hospital where day and night, the Lady Superintendent was at her task. Progress might be slow, but it was sure. The first sign of a great change came with the appearance of some of those necessary objects with which the hospitals had been unprovided for months. The sick men began to enjoy the use of towels and soap, knives and forks, combs and tooth-brushes. Dr. Hall might snort when he heard of it, asking, with a growl, what a soldier wanted with a tooth-brush; but the good work went on. Eventually the whole business of purveying to the hospitals was, in effect, carried out by Miss Nightingale. She alone, it seemed, whatever the contingency, knew where to lay her hands on what was wanted; she alone could dispense her stores with readiness; above all she alone possessed the art of circumventing the pernicious influences of official etiquette. This was her greatest enemy, and sometimes even she was baffled by it. On one occasion 27,000 shirts sent out at her instance by the Home Government, arrived, were landed, and were only waiting to be unpacked. But the official "Purveyor" intervened; "he could not unpack them," he said, "without a Board." Miss Nightingale pleaded in vain; the sick and wounded lay half-naked shivering for want of clothing; and three weeks elapsed before the

Board released the shirts. A little later, however, on a similar occasion, Miss Nightingale felt that she could assert her own authority. She ordered a Government consignment to be forcibly opened, while the miserable "Purveyor" stood by, wringing his hands in departmental agony.

Vast quantities of valuable stores sent from England lay, she found, engulfed in the bottomless abyss of the Turkish Customs House. Other ship-loads, buried beneath munitions of war destined for Balaclava, passed Scutari without a sign, and thus hospital materials were sometimes carried to and fro three times over the Black Sea, before they reached their destination. The whole system was clearly at fault, and Miss Nightingale suggested to the home authorities that a Government Store House should be instituted at Scutari for the reception and distribution of the consignments. Six months after her arrival this was done.

In the meantime she had reorganised the kitchens and the laundries in the hospitals. The ill-cooked hunks of meat, vilely served at irregular intervals, which had hitherto been the only diet for the sick men were replaced by punctual meals, well-prepared and appetising, while strengthening extra foods—soups and wines, and jellies ("preposterous luxuries," snarled Dr. Hall)—were distributed to those who needed them. One thing, however, she could not effect. The separation of the bones from the meat was no part of official cookery: the rule was that the food must be divided into equal portions, and if some of the portions were all bone—well, every man must take his chance. The rule, perhaps, was not a very good one; but there it was. "It would require a new Regulation of the Service," she was told, "to bone the meat." As for the washing arrangements, they were revolutionised. Up to the time of Miss Nightingale's arrival the number of shirts which the authorities had succeeded in washing was seven. The hospital bedding, she found, was "washed" in cold water. She took a Turkish house, had boilers installed, and employed soldiers' wives to do the laundry work. The expenses were defrayed from her own funds and that of the *Times*; and henceforward the sick and wounded had the comfort of clean linen.

Then she turned her attention to their clothing. Owing to military exigencies the greater number of the men had abandoned their kit; their knapsacks were lost for ever; they possessed nothing but what was on their persons, and that was usually only fit for speedy destruction. The "Purveyor," of course, pointed out that, according to the regulations, all soldiers should bring with them into hospital an adequate supply of clothing, and he declared that it was no business of his to make good their deficiencies. Apparently, it was the business of Miss Nightingale. She procured socks, boots, and shirts in enormous quantities; she had trousers made, she rigged up dressing-gowns. "The fact is," she told Sidney Herbert, "I am now clothing the British Army."

All at once, word came from the Crimea that a great new contingent of sick and wounded might shortly be expected. Where were they to go? Every available inch in the wards was occupied; the affair was serious and pressing, and the authorities stood aghast. There were some dilapidated rooms in the Barrack Hospital, unfit for human habitation, but Miss Nightingale believed that if measures were promptly taken they might be made capable of accommodating several hundred beds. One of the doctors agreed with her; the rest of the officials were irresolute: it would be a very expensive job, they said; it would involve building; and who could take the responsibility? The proper course was that a representation should be made to the Director-General of the Army Medical Department in London; then the Director-General would apply to the Horse Guards, the Horse Guards would move the Ordnance, the Ordnance would lay the matter before the Treasury, and, if the Treasury gave its consent, the work might be correctly carried through, several months after the necessity for it had disappeared. Miss Nightingale, however, had made up her mind, and she persuaded Lord Stratford—or thought she had persuaded him—to give his sanction to the required expenditure. A hundred and twenty-five workmen were immediately engaged, and the work was begun. The workmen struck; whereupon Lord Stratford washed his hands of the whole business. Miss Nightingale engaged two hundred other workmen on her own authority, and paid the bill out of her own resources. The wards were ready by the required date; five hundred sick men were received in them; and all the utensils, including knives, forks, spoons, cans and towels, were supplied by Miss Nightingale.

This remarkable woman was in truth performing the function of an administrative chief. How had this come about? Was she not in reality merely a nurse? Was it not her duty simply to tend to the sick? And indeed, was it not as a ministering angel, a gentle "lady with a lamp" that she actually impressed the minds of her contemporaries? No doubt that was so; and yet it is no less certain that, as she herself said, the specific business of nursing was "the least important of the functions into which she had been forced." It was clear that in the state of disorganisation into which the hospitals at Scutari had fallen the most pressing, the really vital, need was for something more than nursing; it was for the necessary elements of civilised life—the commonest material objects, the most ordinary cleanliness, the rudimentary habits of order and authority. "Oh, dear Miss Nightingale," said one of her party as they were approaching Constantinople, "when we land, let there be no delays, let us get straight to nursing the poor fellows!" "The strongest will be wanted at the wash-tub," was Miss Nightingale's answer. And it was upon the wash-tub, and all that the wash-tub stood for, that she expended her greatest energies. Yet to say that is perhaps to say too much. For to those who watched her at work among the sick, moving day and night from bed to bed, with that unflinching courage, with that indefatigable vigilance, it seemed as if the concentrated force of an undivided and unparalleled devotion could hardly suffice for that portion of her task alone. Wherever, in those vast wards, suffering was at its worst and the need for help was greatest, there, as if by magic, was Miss Nightingale. Her superhuman equanimity would, at the moment of some ghastly operation, nerve the victim to endure and almost to hope. Her sympathy would assuage the pangs of dying and bring back to those still living something of the forgotten charm of life. Over and over again her untiring efforts rescued those whom the surgeons had abandoned as beyond the possibility of cure. Her mere presence brought with it a strange influence. A passionate idolatry spread among the men: they kissed her shadow as it passed. They did more. "Before she came," said a soldier, "there was cussin' and swearin', but after that it was as 'oly as a church." The most cherished privilege of the fighting man was abandoned for the sake of Miss Nightingale. In those "lowest sinks of human misery," as she herself put it, she never heard the use of one expression "which could distress a gentlewoman."

She was heroic; and these were the humble tributes paid by those of grosser mould to that high quality. Certainly, she was heroic. Yet her heroism was not of that simple sort so dear to the readers of novels and the compilers of hagiologies—the romantic sentimental heroism with which mankind loves to invest its chosen darlings: it was made of sterner stuff. To the wounded soldier on his couch of agony she might well appear in the guise of a gracious angel of mercy; but the military surgeons, and the orderlies, and her own nurses, and the "Purveyor," and Dr. Hall, and even Lord Stratford himself could tell a different story. It was not by gentle sweetness and womanly self-abnegation that she had brought order out of chaos in the Scutari Hospitals, that, from her own resources, she had clothed the British Army, that she had spread her dominion over the serried and reluctant powers of the official world; it was by strict method, by stern discipline, by rigid attention to detail, by ceaseless labour, by the fixed determination of an indomitable will. Beneath her cool and calm demeanour lurked fierce and passionate fires. As she passed through the wards in her plain dress, so quiet, so unassuming, she struck the casual observer simply as the pattern of a perfect lady; but the keener eye perceived something more than that— the serenity of high deliberation in the scope of the capacious brow, the sign of power in the dominating curve of the thin nose, and the traces of a harsh and dangerous temper—something peevish, something mocking, and yet something precise—in the small and delicate mouth. There was humour in the face; but the curious watcher might wonder whether it was humour of a very pleasant kind; might ask himself, even as he heard the laughter and marked the jokes with which she cheered the spirits of her patients, what sort of sardonic merriment this same lady might not give vent to, in the privacy of her chamber. As for her voice, it was true of it, even more than of her countenance, that it "had that in it one must fain call master." Those clear tones were in no need of emphasis: "I never heard her raise her voice," said one of her companions. Only, when she had spoken, it seemed as if nothing could follow but obedience. Once, when she had given some direction, a doctor ventured to remark that the thing could not be done. "But it must be done," said Miss Nightingale. A chance bystander, who heard the words, never forgot through all his life the irresistible authority of them. And they were spoken quietly—very quietly indeed.

Late at night, when the long miles of beds lay wrapped in darkness, Miss Nightingale would sit at work in her little room, over her correspondence. It was one of the most formidable of all her duties. There were hundreds of letters to be written to the friends and relations of soldiers; there was the enormous mass of official documents to be dealt with; there were her own private letters to be answered; and, most important of all, there was the composition of her long and confidential reports to Sidney Herbert. These were by no means official communications. Her soul, pent up all day in the restraint and reserve of a vast responsibility, now at last poured itself out in these letters with all its natural vehemence, like a swollen torrent through an open sluice. Here, at least, she did not mince matters. Here she painted in her darkest colours the hideous scenes which surrounded her; here she tore away remorselessly the last veils still shrouding the abominable truth. Then she would fill pages with recommendations and suggestions, with criticisms of the minutest details of organisation, with elaborate calculations of contingencies, with exhaustive analyses and statistical statements piled up in breathless eagerness one on the top of the other. And then her pen, in the virulence of its volubility, would rush on to the discussion of individuals, to the denunciation of an incompetent surgeon or the ridicule of a self-sufficient nurse. Her sarcasm searched the ranks of the officials with the deadly and unsparing precision of a machine-gun. Her nicknames were terrible. She respected no one: Lord Stratford, Lord Raglan, Lady Stratford, Dr. Andrew Smith, Dr. Hall, the Commissary-General, the Purveyor—she fulminated against them all. The intolerable futility of mankind obsessed her like a nightmare, and she gnashed her teeth against it. "I do well to be angry," was the burden of her cry. How many just men were there at Scutari? How many who cared at all for the sick, or had done anything for their relief? Were there ten? Were there five? Was there even one? She could not be sure.

At one time, during several weeks, her vituperations descended upon the head of Sidney Herbert himself. He had misinterpreted her wishes, he had traversed her positive instructions, and it was not until he had admitted his error and apologised in abject terms that he was allowed again into favour. While this misunderstanding was at its height an aristocratic young gentleman arrived at Scutari with a recommendation from the Minister. He had come out from England filled with a romantic desire to render homage to the angelic heroine of his dreams. He had, he said, cast aside his life of ease and luxury; he would devote his days and nights to the service of that gentle lady; he would perform the most menial offices, he would "fag" for her, he would be her footman—and feel requited by a single smile. A single smile, indeed, he had, but it was of an unexpected kind. Miss Nightingale at first refused to see him, and then, when she consented, believing that he was an emissary sent by Sidney Herbert to put her in the wrong over their dispute, she took notes of her conversation with him, and insisted on his signing them at the end of it. The young gentleman returned to England by the next ship.

This quarrel with Sidney Herbert was, however, an exceptional incident. Alike by him, and by Lord Panmure, his successor at the War Office, she was firmly supported; and the fact that during the whole of her stay at Scutari she had the Home Government at her back, was her trump card in her dealings with the hospital authorities. Nor was it only the Government that was behind her: public opinion in England early recognised the high importance of her mission, and its enthusiastic appreciation of her work soon reached an extraordinary height. The Queen herself was deeply moved. She made repeated inquiries as to the welfare of Miss Nightingale; she asked to see her accounts of the wounded, and made her the intermediary between the throne and the troops.

> Let Mrs. Herbert know [she wrote to the War Minister] that I wish Miss Nightingale and the ladies would tell these poor noble, wounded, and sick men that *no one* takes a warmer interest or feels *more* for their sufferings or admires their courage and heroism *more* than their Queen. Day and night she thinks of her beloved troops. So does the Prince. Beg Mrs. Herbert to communicate these my words to those ladies, as I know that *our* sympathy is much valued by these noble fellows.

The letter was read aloud in the wards by the Chaplain. "It is a very feeling letter," said the men.

And so the months passed, and that fell winter which had begun with Inkerman and had dragged itself out through the long agony of the investment of Sebastopol, at last was over. In May, 1855, after six months of labour, Miss Nightingale could look with something like satisfaction at the condition of the Scutari hospitals. Had they done nothing more than survive the terrible strain which had been put upon them, it would have been a matter for congratulation; but they had done much more than that; they had marvellously improved. The confusion and the pressure in the wards had come to an end; order reigned in them, and cleanliness; the supplies were bountiful and prompt; important sanitary works had been carried out. One simple comparison of figures was enough to reveal the extraordinary change: the rate of mortality among the cases treated had fallen from 42 per cent. to 22 per thousand. But still the indefatigable lady was not satisfied. The main problem had been solved—the physical needs of the men had been provided for; their mental and spiritual needs remained. She set up and furnished reading-rooms and recreation-rooms. She started classes and lectures. Officers were amazed to see her treating their men as if they were human beings, and assured her that she would only end by "spoiling the brutes." But that was not Miss Nightingale's opinion, and she was justified. The private soldier began to drink less, and even—though that seemed impossible—to save his pay. Miss Nightingale became a banker for the army, receiving and sending home large sums of money every month. At last, reluctantly, the Government followed suit, and established machinery of its own for the remission of money. Lord Panmure, however, remained sceptical; "it will do no good," he pronounced; "the British soldier is not a remitting animal." But, in fact, during the next six months, £71,000 was sent home.

Amid all these activities, Miss Nightingale took up the further task of inspecting the hospitals in the Crimea itself. The labour was extreme, and the conditions of life were almost intolerable. She spent whole days in the saddle, or was driven over those bleak and rocky heights in a baggage cart. Sometimes she stood for hours in the heavily falling snow, and would only reach her hut at dead of night after walking for miles through perilous ravines. Her powers of resistance seemed incredible, but at last they were exhausted. She was attacked by fever, and for a moment came very near to death. Yet she worked on; if she could not move, she could at least write; and write she did until her mind had left her; and after it had left her, in what seemed the delirious trance of death itself, she still wrote. When, after many weeks, she was strong enough to travel, she was to return to England, but she utterly refused. She would not go back, she said, before the last of the soldiers had left Scutari.

This happy moment had almost arrived, when suddenly the smouldering hostilities of the medical authorities burst out into a flame.

Dr. Hall's labours had been rewarded by a K.C.B.—letters which, as Miss Nightingale told Sidney Herbert, she could only suppose to mean "Knight of the Crimean Burial-grounds"—and the honour had turned his head. He was Sir John, and he would be thwarted no longer. Disputes had lately arisen between Miss Nightingale and some of the nurses in the Crimean hospitals. The situation had been embittered by rumours of religious dissensions, for, while the Crimean nurses were Roman Catholics, many of those at Scutari were suspected of a regrettable propensity towards the tenets of Dr. Pusey. Miss Nightingale was by no means disturbed by these sectarian differences, but any suggestion that her supreme authority over all the nurses with the Army was in doubt was enough to rouse her to fury; and it appeared that Mrs. Bridgeman, the Reverend Mother in the Crimea, had ventured to call that authority in question. Sir John Hall thought that his opportunity had come, and strongly supported Mrs. Bridgeman—or, as Miss Nightingale preferred to call her, the "Reverend Brickbat." There was a violent struggle; Miss Nightingale's rage was terrible. Dr. Hall, she declared, was doing his best to "root her out of the Crimea." She would bear it no longer; the War Office was playing her false; there was only one thing to be done—Sidney Herbert must move for the production of papers in the House of Commons, so that the public might be able to judge between her and her enemies. Sidney Herbert with great difficulty calmed her down. Orders were immediately dispatched putting her supremacy beyond doubt, and the Reverend Brickbat withdrew from the scene. Sir John, however, was more tenacious. A few weeks later, Miss Nightingale and her nurses visited the Crimea for the last time, and the brilliant idea occurred to him that he could crush her by a very simple expedient—he would starve her into submission; and he actually ordered that no rations of any kind should be supplied to her. He had already tried this plan with great effect upon an unfortunate medical man whose presence in the Crimea he had considered an intrusion; but he was now to learn that such tricks were thrown away upon Miss Nightingale. With extraordinary foresight, she had brought with her a great supply of food; she succeeded in obtaining more at her own expense and by her own exertions; and thus for ten days, in that inhospitable country, she was able to feed herself and twenty-four nurses. Eventually the military authorities intervened in her favour, and Sir John had to confess that he was beaten.

It was not until July, 1856—four months after the Declaration of Peace—that Miss Nightingale left Scutari for England. Her reputation was now enormous, and the enthusiasm of the public was unbounded. The Royal approbation was expressed by the gift of a brooch, accompanied by a private letter.

> You are, I know, well aware [wrote Her Majesty] of the high
> sense I entertain of the Christian devotion which you have displayed
> during this great and bloody war, and I need hardly repeat to you
> how warm my admiration is for your services, which are fully equal
> to those of my dear and brave soldiers, whose sufferings you have
> had the *privilege* of alleviating in so merciful a manner. I am,
> however, anxious of marking my feelings in a manner which I
> trust will be agreeable to you, and therefore send you with this
> letter a brooch, the form and emblems of which commemorate
> your great and blessed work, and which I hope you will wear as a
> mark of the high approbation of your Sovereign!

"It will be a very great satisfaction to me," Her Majesty added, "to make the acquaintance of one who has set so bright an example to our sex."

The brooch, which was designed by the Prince Consort, bore a St. George's cross in red enamel, and the Royal cypher surmounted by diamonds. The whole was encircled by the inscription, "Blessed are the Merciful."

III

The name of Florence Nightingale lives in the memory of the world by virtue of the lurid and heroic adventure of the Crimea. Had she died—as she nearly did—upon her return to England, her reputation would hardly have been different; her legend would have come down to us almost as we know it to-day—that gentle vision of female virtue which first took shape before the adoring eyes of the sick soldiers at Scutari. Yet, as a matter of fact, she lived for more than half a century after the Crimean War; and during the greater part of that long period all the energy and all the devotion of her extraordinary nature were working at their highest pitch. What she accomplished in those years of unknown labour could, indeed, hardly have been more glorious than her Crimean triumphs; but it was certainly more important. The true history was far stranger even than the myth. In Miss Nightingale's own eyes the adventure of the Crimea was a mere incident—scarcely more than a useful stepping-stone in her career. It was the fulcrum with which she hoped to move the world; but it was only the fulcrum. For more than a generation she was to sit in secret, working her lever: and her real life began at the very moment when, in the popular imagination, it had ended.

She arrived in England in a shattered state of health. The hardships and the ceaseless effort of the last two years had undermined her nervous system; her heart was pronounced to be affected; she suffered constantly from fainting-fits and terrible attacks of utter physical prostration. The doctors declared that one thing alone would save her—a complete and prolonged rest. But that was also the one thing with which she would have nothing to do. She had never been in the habit of resting; why should she begin now? Now, when her opportunity had come at last; now, when the iron was hot, and it was time to strike? No; she had work to do; and, come what might, she would do it. The doctors protested in vain; in vain her family lamented and entreated, in vain her friends pointed out to her the madness of such a course. Madness? Mad—possessed—perhaps she was. A demoniac frenzy had seized upon her. As she lay upon her sofa, gasping, she devoured blue-books, dictated letters, and, in the intervals of her palpitations, cracked her febrile jokes. For months at a stretch she never left her bed. For years she was in daily expectation of Death. But she would not rest. At this rate, the doctors assured her, even if she did not die, she would become an invalid for life. She could not help that; there was the work to be done; and, as for rest, very likely she might rest . . . when she had done it.

Wherever she went, in London or in the country, in the hills of Derbyshire, or among the rhododendrons at Embley, she was haunted by a ghost. It was the spectre of Scutari—the hideous vision of the organisation of a military hospital. She would lay that phantom, or she would perish. The whole system of the Army Medical Department, the education of the Medical Officer, the regulations of hospital procedure . . . *rest?* How could she rest while these things were as they were, while, if the like necessity were to arise again, the like results would follow? And, even in peace and at home, what was the sanitary condition of the Army? The mortality in the barracks was, she found, nearly double the mortality in civil life. "You might as well take 1100 men every year out upon Salisbury Plain and shoot them," she said. After inspecting the hospitals at Chatham, she smiled grimly. "Yes, this is one more symptom of the system which, in the Crimea, put to death 16,000 men." Scutari had given her knowledge; and it had given her power too: her enormous reputation was at her back—an incalculable force. Other work, other duties, might lie before her; but the most urgent, the most obvious of all was to look to the health of the Army.

One of her very first steps was to take advantage of the invitation which Queen Victoria had sent her to the Crimea, together with the commemorative brooch. Within a few weeks of her return, she visited Balmoral, and had several interviews both with the Queen and the Prince Consort. "She put before us," wrote the Prince in his diary, "all the defects of our present military hospital system and the reforms that are needed." She related the whole story of her experiences in the East; and, in addition, she managed to have some long and confidential talks with His Royal Highness on metaphysics and religion. The impression which she created was excellent. "Sie gefällt uns sehr," noted the Prince, "ist sehr bescheiden." Her Majesty's comment was different—"Such a *head!* I wish we had her at the War Office."

But Miss Nightingale was not at the War Office, and for a very simple reason: she was a woman. Lord Panmure, however, *was* (though indeed the reason for that was not quite so simple); and it was upon Lord Panmure that the issue of Miss Nightingale's efforts for reform must primarily depend. That burly Scottish nobleman had not, in spite of his most earnest endeavours, had a very easy time of it as Secretary of State for War. He had come into office in the middle of the Sebastopol campaign, and had felt himself very well fitted for the position, since he had acquired in former days an inside knowledge of the Army—as a Captain of Hussars. It was this inside knowledge which had enabled him to inform Miss Nightingale with such authority that "the British soldier is not a remitting animal." And perhaps it was this same consciousness of a command of his subject which had impelled him to write a dispatch to Lord Raglan, blandly informing the Commander-in-Chief in the Field just how he was neglecting his duties, and pointing out to him that if he would only try he really might do a little better next time. Lord Raglan's reply, calculated as it was to make its recipient sink into the earth, did not quite have that effect upon Lord Panmure, who, whatever might have been his faults, had never been accused of being super-sensitive. However, he allowed the matter to drop; and a little later Lord Raglan died—worn out, some people said, by work and anxiety. He was succeeded by an excellent red-nosed old gentleman, General Simpson, whom nobody has ever heard of, and who took Sebastopol. But Lord Panmure's relations with him were hardly more satisfactory than his relations with Lord Raglan; for, while Lord Raglan had been too independent, poor General Simpson erred in the opposite direction, perpetually asked advice, suffered from lumbago, doubted, his nose growing daily redder and redder, whether he was fit for his post, and, by alternate mails, sent in and withdrew his resignation. Then, too, both the General and the Minister suffered acutely from that distressingly useful new invention, the electric telegraph. On one occasion General Simpson felt obliged actually to expostulate.

> I think, my Lord [he wrote], that some telegraphic messages reach us that cannot be sent under due authority, and are perhaps unknown to you, although under the protection of your Lordship's name. For instance, I was called up last night, a dragoon having come express with a telegraphic message in these words, "Lord Panmure to General Simpson—Captain Jarvis has been bitten by a centipede. How is he now?"

General Simpson might have put up with this, though to be sure it did seem "rather too trifling an affair to call for a dragoon to ride a couple of miles in the dark that he may knock up the Commander of the Army out of the very small allowance of sleep permitted him"; but what was really more than he could bear was to find "upon sending in the morning another mounted dragoon to inquire after Captain Jarvis, four miles off, that he never has been bitten at all, but has had a boil, from which he is fast recovering." But Lord Panmure had troubles of his own. His favourite nephew, Captain Dowbiggin, was at the front, and to one of his telegrams to the Commander-in-Chief the Minister had taken occasion to append the following carefully qualified sentence—"I recommend Dowbiggin to your notice, should you have a vacancy, and if he is fit." Unfortunately, in those early days, it was left to the discretion of the telegraphist to compress the messages which passed through his hands; so that the result was that Lord Panmure's delicate appeal reached its destination in the laconic form of "Look after Dowb." The Headquarters Staff were at first extremely puzzled; they were at last extremely amused. The story spread; and "Look after Dowb" remained for many years the familiar formula for describing official hints in favour of deserving nephews.

And now that all this was over, now that Sebastopol had been, somehow or another, taken, now that peace was, somehow or another, made, now that the troubles of office might surely be expected to be at an end at last—here was Miss Nightingale breaking in upon the scene, with her talk about the state of the hospitals and the necessity for sanitary reform. It was most irksome; and Lord Panmure almost began to wish that he was engaged upon some more congenial occupation—discussing, perhaps, the constitution of the Free Church of Scotland—a question in which he was profoundly interested. But no; duty was paramount; and he set himself, with a sigh of resignation, to the task of doing as little of it as he possibly could.

"The Bison" his friends called him; and the name fitted both his physical demeanour and his habit of mind. That large low head seemed to have been created for butting rather than for anything else. There he stood, four-square and menacing, in the doorway of reform; and it remained to be seen whether the bulky mass, upon whose solid hide even the barbed arrows of Lord Raglan's scorn had made no mark, would prove amenable to the pressure of Miss Nightingale. Nor was he alone in the doorway. There loomed behind him the whole phalanx of professional conservatism, the stubborn supporters of the out-of-date, the worshippers and the victims of War Office routine. Among these it was only natural that Dr. Andrew Smith, the head of the Army Medical

Department, should have been pre-eminent—Dr. Andrew Smith, who had assured Miss Nightingale before she left England that "nothing was wanted at Scutari." Such were her opponents; but she too was not without allies. She had gained the ear of Royalty—which was something; at any moment that she pleased she could gain the ear of the public—which was a great deal. She had a host of admirers and friends; and—to say nothing of her personal qualities—her knowledge, her tenacity, her tact—she possessed, too, one advantage which then, far more even than now, carried an immense weight—she belonged to the highest circle of society. She moved naturally among Peers and Cabinet Ministers—she was one of their own set; and in those days their set was a very narrow one. What kind of attention would such persons have paid to some middle-class woman with whom they were not acquainted, who possessed great experience of army nursing and had decided views upon hospital reform? They would have politely ignored her; but it was impossible to ignore Flo Nightingale. When she spoke, they were obliged to listen; and, when they had once begun to do that—what might not follow? She knew her power, and she used it. She supported her weightiest minutes with familiar witty little notes. The Bison began to look grave. It might be difficult—it might be damned difficult—to put down one's head against the white hand of a lady.

Of Miss Nightingale's friends, the most important was Sidney Herbert. He was a man upon whom the good fairies seemed to have showered, as he lay in his cradle, all their most enviable gifts. Well born, handsome, rich, the master of Wilton—one of those great country-houses, clothed with the glamour of a historic past, which are the peculiar glory of England—he possessed, besides all these advantages, so charming, so lively, so gentle a disposition that no one who had once come near him could ever be his enemy. He was, in fact, a man of whom it was difficult not to say that he was a perfect English gentleman. For his virtues were equal even to his good fortune. He was religious—deeply religious: "I am more and more convinced every day," he wrote, when he had been for some years a Cabinet Minister, "that in politics, as in everything else, nothing can be right which is not in accordance with the spirit of the Gospel." No one was more unselfish; he was charitable and benevolent to a remarkable degree; and he devoted the whole of his life with an unwavering conscientiousness to the public service. With such a character, with such opportunities, what high hopes must have danced before him, what radiant visions of accomplished duties, of ever-increasing usefulness, of beneficent power, of the consciousness of disinterested success! Some of those hopes and visions were, indeed, realised; but, in the end, the career of Sidney Herbert seemed to show that, with all their generosity, there was some gift or other—what was it? some essential gift which the good fairies had withheld, and that even the qualities of a perfect English gentleman may be no safeguard against anguish, humiliation, and defeat.

That career would certainly have been very different if he had never known Miss Nightingale. The alliance between them, which had begun with her appointment to Scutari, which had grown closer and closer while the war lasted, developed, after her return, into one of the most extraordinary of friendships. It was the friendship of a man and a woman intimately bound together by their devotion to a public cause; mutual affection, of course, played a part in it, but it was an incidental part; the whole soul of the relationship was a community of work. Perhaps out of England such an intimacy could hardly have existed—an intimacy so utterly untinctured not only by passion itself but by the suspicion of it. For years Sidney Herbert saw Miss Nightingale almost daily, for long hours together, corresponding with her incessantly when they were apart; and the tongue of scandal was silent; and one of the most devoted of her admirers was his wife. But what made the connection still more remarkable was the way in which the parts that were played in it were divided between the two. The man who acts, decides, and achieves; the woman who encourages, applauds, and—from a distance—inspires:—the combination is common enough; but Miss Nightingale was neither an Aspasia nor an Egeria. In her case it is almost true to say that the rôles were reversed; the qualities of pliancy and sympathy fell to the man, those of command and initiative to the woman. There was one thing only which Miss Nightingale lacked in her equipment for public life; she had not—she never could have—the public power and authority which belong to the successful politician. That power and authority Sidney Herbert possessed; the fact was obvious, and the conclusion no less so: it was through the man that the woman must work her will. She took hold of him, taught him, shaped him, absorbed him, dominated him through and through. He did not resist—he did not wish to resist; his natural inclination lay along the same path as hers; only that terrific personality swept him forward at her own fierce pace and with her own relentless stride. Swept him—where to? Ah! Why had he ever known Miss Nightingale? If Lord Panmure was a bison, Sidney Herbert, no doubt, was a stag—a comely, gallant creature springing through the forest; but the forest is a dangerous place. One has the image of those wide eyes fascinated suddenly by something feline, something strong; there is a pause; and then the tigress has her claws in the quivering haunches; and then——!

Besides Sidney Herbert, she had other friends who, in a more restricted sphere, were hardly less essential to her. If, in her condition of bodily collapse, she were to accomplish what she was determined that she should accomplish, the attentions and the services of others would be absolutely indispensable. Helpers and servers she must have; and accordingly there was soon formed about her a little group of devoted disciples upon whose affections and energies she could implicitly rely. Devoted, indeed, these disciples were, in no ordinary sense of the term; for certainly she was no light task-mistress, and he who set out to be of use to Miss Nightingale was apt to find, before he had gone very far, that he was in truth being made use of in good earnest—to the very limit of his endurance and his capacity. Perhaps, even beyond those limits; why not? Was she asking of others more than she was giving herself? Let them look at her lying there pale and breathless on the couch; could it be said that she spared herself? Why, then, should she spare others? And it was not for her own sake that she made these claims. For her own sake, indeed! No! They all knew it! it was for the sake of the work. And so the little band, bound body and soul in that strange servitude, laboured on ungrudgingly. Among the most faithful was her "Aunt Mai," her father's sister, who from the earliest days had stood beside her, who had helped her to escape from the thraldom of family life, who had been with her at Scutari, and who now acted almost the part of a mother to her, watching over her with infinite care in all the movements and uncertainties which her state of health involved. Another constant attendant was her brother-in-law, Sir Harry Verney, whom she found particularly valuable in parliamentary affairs. Arthur Clough, the poet, also a connection by marriage, she used in other ways. Ever since he had lost his faith at the time of the Oxford Movement, Clough had passed his life in a condition of considerable uneasiness, which was increased rather than diminished by the practice of poetry. Unable to decide upon the purpose of an existence whose savour had fled together with his belief in the Resurrection, his spirits lowered still further by ill-health, and his income not all that it should be, he had determined to seek the solution of his difficulties in the United States of America. But, even there, the solution was not forthcoming; and when, a little later, he was offered a post in a government department at home, he accepted it, came to live in London, and immediately fell under the influence of Miss Nightingale. Though the purpose of existence might be still uncertain and its nature still unsavoury, here, at any rate, under the eye of this inspired woman, was something real, something earnest: his only doubt was—could he be of any use? Certainly he could. There were a great number of miscellaneous little jobs which there was nobody handy to do. For instance, when Miss Nightingale was travelling, there were the railway-tickets to be taken; and there were proof-sheets to be corrected; and then there were parcels to be done up in brown paper, and carried to the post. Certainly he could be useful. And so, upon such occupations as these, Arthur Clough was set to work. "This that I see, is not all," he comforted himself by reflecting, "and this that I do is but little; nevertheless it is good, though there is better than it."

As time went on, her "Cabinet," as she called it, grew larger. Officials with whom her work brought her into touch and who sympathised with her objects, were pressed into her service; and old friends of the Crimean days gathered round her when they returned to England. Among these the most indefatigable was Dr. Sutherland, a sanitary expert, who for more than thirty years acted as her confidential private secretary, and surrendered to her purposes literally the whole of his life. Thus sustained and assisted, thus slaved for and adored, she prepared to beard the Bison.

Two facts soon emerged, and all that followed turned upon them. It became clear, in the first place, that that imposing mass was not immovable, and, in the second, that its movement, when it did move, would be exceeding slow. The Bison was no match for the Lady. It was in vain that he put down his head and planted his feet in the earth; he could not withstand her; the white hand forced him back. But the process was an extraordinarily gradual one. Dr. Andrew Smith and all his War Office phalanx stood behind, blocking the way; the poor Bison groaned inwardly, and cast a wistful eye towards the happy pastures of the Free Church of Scotland; then slowly, with infinite reluctance, step by step, he retreated, disputing every inch of the ground.

The first great measure, which, supported as it was by the Queen, the Cabinet, and the united opinion of the country, it was impossible to resist, was the appointment of a Royal Commission to report upon the health of the Army. The question of the composition of the Commission then immediately arose; and it was over this matter that the first hand-to-hand encounter between Lord Panmure and Miss Nightingale took place. They met, and Miss Nightingale was victorious; Sidney Herbert was appointed Chairman; and, in the end the only member of the commission opposed to her views was Dr. Andrew Smith. During the interview, Miss Nightingale made an important discovery: she found that "the Bison was bullyable"—the hide was the hide of a Mexican buffalo, but the spirit was the spirit of an Alderney calf. And there was one thing above all others which the huge creature dreaded—an appeal to public opinion. The faintest hint of such a terrible eventuality made his heart dissolve within him; he would agree to anything—he would cut short his grouse-shooting—he would make a speech in the House of Lords—he would even overrule Dr. Andrew Smith—rather than that. Miss Nightingale held the fearful threat in reserve—she would speak out what she knew; she would publish the truth to the whole world, and let the whole world judge between them. With supreme skill, she kept this sword of Damocles poised above the Bison's head, and more than once she was actually on the point of really dropping it. For his recalcitrancy grew and grew. The *personnel* of the Commission once determined upon, there was a struggle, which lasted for six months, over the nature of its powers. Was it to be an efficient body, armed with the right of full inquiry and wide examination, or was it to be a polite official contrivance for exonerating Dr. Andrew Smith? The War Office phalanx closed its ranks, and fought tooth and nail; but it was defeated: the Bison was bullyable.

> Three months from this day [Miss Nightingale had written at last] I publish my experience of the Crimean Campaign, and my suggestions for improvement, unless there has been a fair and tangible pledge by that time for reform.

Who could face that?

And, if the need came, she meant to be as good as her word. For she had now determined, whatever might be the fate of the Commission, to draw up her own report upon the questions at issue. The labour involved was enormous; her health was almost desperate; but she did not flinch, and after six months of incredible industry she had put together and written with her own hand her "Notes affecting the Health, Efficiency, and Hospital Administration of the British Army." This extraordinary composition, filling more than eight hundred closely printed pages, laying down vast principles of far-reaching reform, discussing the minutest details of a multitude of controversial subjects, containing an enormous mass of information of the most varied kinds—military, statistical, sanitary, architectural—was never given to the public, for the need never came; but it formed the basis of the Report of the Royal Commission; and it remains to this day the leading authority on the medical administration of armies.

Before it had been completed the struggle over the powers of the Commission had been brought to a victorious close. Lord Panmure had given way once more; he had immediately hurried to the Queen to obtain her consent; and only then, when her Majesty's initials had been irrevocably affixed to the fatal document, did he dare to tell Dr. Andrew Smith what he had done. The Commission met, and another immense load fell upon Miss Nightingale's shoulders. To-day she would, of course, have been one of the Commission herself; but at that time the idea of a woman appearing in such a capacity was unheard of; and no one even suggested the possibility of Miss Nightingale's doing so. The result was that she was obliged to remain behind the scenes throughout, to coach Sidney Herbert in private at every important juncture, and to convey to him and to her other friends upon the Commission the vast funds of her expert knowledge—so essential in the examination of witnesses—by means of innumerable consultations, letters, and memoranda. It was even doubtful whether the proprieties would admit of her giving evidence; and at last, as a compromise, her modesty only allowed her to do so in the form of written answers to written questions. At length the grand affair was finished. The Commission's Report, embodying almost word for word the suggestions of Miss Nightingale, was drawn up by Sidney Herbert. Only one question remained to be answered—would anything, after all, be done? Or would the Royal Commission, like so many other Royal Commissions before and since, turn out to have achieved nothing but the concoction of a very fat blue-book on a very high shelf?

And so the last and the deadliest struggle with the Bison began. Six months had been spent in coercing him into granting the Commission effective powers; six more months were occupied by the work of the Commission; and now yet another six were to pass in extorting from him the means whereby the recommendations of the Commission might be actually carried out. But, in the end, the thing was done. Miss Nightingale seemed indeed, during these months, to be upon the very brink of death. Accompanied by the faithful Aunt Mai, she moved from place to place—to Hampstead, to Highgate, to Derbyshire, to Malvern—in what appeared to be a last desperate effort to find health somewhere; but she carried that with her which made health impossible. Her desire for work could now scarcely be distinguished from mania. At one moment she was writing a "last letter" to Sidney Herbert; at the next she was offering to go out to India to nurse the sufferers in the Mutiny. When Dr. Sutherland wrote, imploring her to take a holiday, she raved. Rest—

> I am lying without my head,. without my claws, and you all peck at me. It is *de rigueur, d'obligation*, like the saying something to one's hat, when one goes into church, to say to me all that has been said to me 110 times a day during the last three months. It is the *obbligato* on the violin, and the twelve violins all practise it together, like the clocks striking 12 o'clock at night all over London, till I say like Xavier de Maistre, *Assez, je le sais, je ne le sais que trop*. I am not a penitent; but you are like the R. C. confessor, who says what is *de rigueur*. . . .

Her wits began to turn, and there was no holding her. She worked like a slave in a mine. She began to believe, as she had begun to believe at Scutari, that none of her fellow-workers had their hearts in the business; if they had, why did they not work as she did? She could only see slackness and stupidity around her. Dr. Sutherland, of course, was grotesquely muddle-headed; and Arthur Clough incurably lazy. Even Sidney Herbert . . . oh yes, he had simplicity and candour and quickness of perception, no doubt; but he was an eclectic; and what could one hope for from a man who went away to fish in Ireland just when the Bison most needed bullying? As for the Bison himself he had fled to Scotland, where he remained buried for many months. The fate of the vital recommendation in the Commission's Report—the appointment of four Sub-Commissions charged with the duty of determining upon the details of the proposed reforms and of putting them into execution—still hung in the balance. The Bison consented to everything; and then, on a flying visit to London, withdrew his consent and hastily returned to Scotland. Then for many weeks all business was suspended; he had gout—gout in the hands, so that he could not write. "His gout was always handy," remarked Miss Nightingale. But eventually it was clear even to the Bison that the game was up, and the inevitable surrender came.

There was, however, one point in which he triumphed over Miss Nightingale. The building of Netley Hospital had been begun, under his orders, before her return to England. Soon after her arrival she examined the plans, and found that they reproduced all the worst faults of an out-of-date and mischievous system of hospital construction. She therefore urged that the matter should be reconsidered, and in the meantime building stopped. But the Bison was obdurate; it then would be very expensive, and in any case it was too late. Unable to make any impression on him, and convinced of the extreme importance of the question, she determined to appeal to a higher authority. Lord Palmerston was Prime Minister; she had known him from her childhood; he was a near neighbour of her father's in the New Forest. She went down to the New Forest, armed with the plans of the proposed hospital and all the relevant information, stayed the night at Lord Palmerston's house, and convinced him of the necessity of rebuilding Netley.

> It seems to me [Lord Palmerston wrote to Lord Panmure] that at Netley all consideration of what would best tend to the comfort and recovery of the patients has been sacrificed to the vanity of the architect, whose sole object has been to make a building which should cut a dash when looked at from the Southampton river. . . . Pray, therefore, stop all further progress in the work until the matter can be duly considered.

But the Bison was not to be moved by one peremptory letter, even if it was from the Prime Minister. He put forth all his powers of procrastination, Lord Palmerston lost interest in the subject, and so the chief military hospital in England was triumphantly completed on unsanitary principles, with unventilated rooms, and with all the patients' windows facing northeast.

But now the time had come when the Bison was to trouble and to be troubled no more. A vote in the House of Commons brought about the fall of Lord Palmerston's Government, and Lord Panmure found himself at liberty to devote the rest of his life to the Free Church of Scotland. After a brief interval, Sidney Herbert became Secretary of State for War. Great was the jubilation in the Nightingale Cabinet; the day of achievement had dawned at last. The next two and a half years (1859–61) saw the introduction of the whole system of reforms for which Miss Nightingale had been struggling so fiercely—reforms which make Sidney Herbert's tenure of power at the War Office an important epoch in the history of the British Army. The four Sub-Commissions, firmly established under the immediate control of the Minister, and urged forward by the relentless perseverance of Miss Nightingale, set to work with a will. The barracks and the hospitals were remodelled; they were properly ventilated and warmed and lighted for the first time; they were given a water supply which actually supplied water, and kitchens where, strange to say, it was possible to cook. Then the great question of the Purveyor—that portentous functionary whose powers and whose lack of powers had weighed like a nightmare upon Scutari—was taken in hand, and new regulations were laid down, accurately defining his responsibilities and his duties. One Sub-Commission reorganised the medical statistics of the Army. Another established—in spite of the last convulsive efforts of the Department—an Army Medical School. Finally the Army Medical Department itself was completely reorganised; an administrative code was drawn up; and the great and novel principle was established that it was as much a part of the duty of the authorities to look after the soldier's health as to look after his sickness. Besides this, it was at last officially admitted that he had a moral and intellectual side. Coffee-rooms and reading-rooms, gymnasiums and workshops were instituted. A new era did in truth appear to have begun. Already by 1861 the mortality in the Army had decreased by one half since the days of the Crimea. It was no wonder that even vaster possibilities began now to open out before Miss Nightingale. One thing was still needed to complete and to assure her triumphs. The Army Medical Department was indeed reorganised; but the great central machine was still untouched. The War Office itself—!—If she could remould *that* nearer to her heart's desire—there indeed would be a victory! And until that final act was accomplished, how could she be certain that all the rest of her achievements might not, by some capricious turn of Fortune's wheel—a change of Ministry, perhaps, replacing Sidney Herbert by some puppet of the permanent official gang—be swept to limbo in a moment?

Meanwhile, still ravenous for more and yet more work, her activities had branched out into new directions. The army in India claimed her attention. A Sanitary Commission, appointed at her suggestion, and

working under her auspices, did for our troops there what the four Sub-
Commissions were doing for those at home. At the same time, these very
years which saw her laying the foundations of the whole modern system
of medical work in the army, saw her also beginning to bring her
knowledge, her influence, and her activity into the service of the country
at large. Her *Notes on Hospitals* (1859) revolutionised the theory of
hospital construction and hospital management. She was immediately
recognised as the leading expert upon all the questions involved; her
advice flowed unceasingly and in all directions, so that there is no great
hospital today which does not bear upon it the impress of her mind. Nor
was this all. With the opening of the Nightingale Training School for
Nurses at St. Thomas's Hospital (1860), she became the founder of
modern nursing.

But a terrible crisis was now fast approaching. Sidney Herbert had
consented to undertake the root and branch reform of the War Office.
He had sallied forth into that tropical jungle of festooned obstructive-
ness, of intertwisted irresponsibilities, of crouching prejudices, of abuses
grown stiff and rigid with antiquity, which for so many years to come was
destined to lure reforming ministers to their doom.

> The War Office [said Miss Nightingale] is a very slow office, an
> enormously expensive office, and one in which the Minister's in-
> tentions can be entirely negatived by all his sub-departments, and
> those of each of the sub-departments by every other.

It was true; and, of course, at the first rumour of a change, the old
phalanx of reaction was bristling with its accustomed spears. At its head
stood no longer Dr. Andrew Smith, who, some time since, had followed
the Bison into outer darkness, but a yet more formidable figure, the
permanent Under-Secretary himself, Sir Benjamin Hawes—Ben Hawes
the Nightingale Cabinet irreverently dubbed him—a man remarkable
even among civil servants for adroitness in baffling inconvenient inquiries, resource in raising false issues, and, in short, a consummate command
of all the arts of officially sticking in the mud. "Our scheme will probably
result in Ben Hawes's resignation," Miss Nightingale said; "and that is
another of its advantages." Ben Hawes himself, however, did not quite
see it in that light. He set himself to resist the wishes of the Minister by
every means in his power. The struggle was long and desperate; and, as it
proceeded, it gradually became evident to Miss Nightingale that something was the matter with Sidney Herbert. What was it? His health,
never very strong, was, he said, in danger of collapsing under the strain of
his work. But, after all, what is illness, when there is a War Office to be
reorganised? Then he began to talk of retiring altogether from public life.
The doctors were consulted, and declared that, above all things, what

was necessary was rest. Rest! She grew seriously alarmed. Was it possible that, at the last moment, the crowning wreath of victory was to be snatched from her grasp? She was not to be put aside by doctors; they were talking nonsense; the necessary thing was not rest but the reform of the War Office; and, besides, she knew very well from her own case what one could do even when one was on the point of death. She expostulated vehemently, passionately: the goal was so near, so very near; he could not turn back now! At any rate, he could not resist Miss Nightingale. A compromise was arranged. Very reluctantly, he exchanged the turmoil of the House of Commons for the dignity of the House of Lords, and he remained at the War Office. She was delighted. "One fight more, the best and the last," she said.

For several more months the fight did indeed go on. But the strain upon him was greater even than she perhaps could realise. Besides the intestine war in his office, he had to face a constant battle in the Cabinet with Mr. Gladstone—a more redoubtable antagonist even than Ben Hawes—over the estimates. His health grew worse and worse. He was attacked by fainting-fits; and there were some days when he could only just keep himself going by gulps of brandy. Miss Nightingale spurred him forward with her encouragements and her admonitions, her zeal and her example. But at last his spirit began to sink as well as his body. He could no longer hope; he could no longer desire; it was useless, all useless; it was utterly impossible. He had failed. The dreadful moment came when the truth was forced upon him: he would never be able to reform the War Office. But a yet more dreadful moment lay behind; he must go to Miss Nightingale and tell her that he was a failure, a beaten man.

Blessed are the merciful! What strange ironic prescience had led Prince Albert, in the simplicity of his heart, to choose that motto for the Crimean brooch? The words hold a double lesson; and, alas! when she brought herself to realise at length what was indeed the fact and what there was no helping, it was not in mercy that she turned upon her old friend.

> Beaten! [she exclaimed]. Can't you see that you've simply thrown away the game? And with all the winning cards in your hands! And so noble a game! Sidney Herbert beaten! And beaten by Ben Hawes! It is a worse disgrace. . . . [her full rage burst out at last] . . . a worse disgrace than the hospitals at Scutari.

He dragged himself away from her, dragged himself to Spa, hoping vainly for a return of health, and then, despairing, back again to England, to Wilton, to the majestic house standing there resplendent in the summer sunshine, among the great cedars which had lent their shade to Sir Philip Sidney, and all those familiar, darling haunts of beauty which he loved, each one of them, "as if they were persons"; and at Wilton he died. After having received the Eucharist he had become perfectly calm; then, almost unconscious, his lips were seen to be moving. Those about him bent down. "Poor Florence! Poor Florence!" they just caught. ". . . Our joint work . . . unfinished . . . tried to do . . ." and they could hear no more.

When the onward rush of a powerful spirit sweeps a weaker one to its destruction, the commonplaces of the moral judgment are better left unmade. If Miss Nightingale had been less ruthless, Sidney Herbert would not have perished; but then, she would not have been Miss Nightingale. The force that created was the force that destroyed. It was her Demon that was responsible. When the fatal news reached her, she was overcome by agony. In the revulsion of her feelings, she made a worship of the dead man's memory; and the facile instrument which had broken in her hand she spoke of for ever after as her "Master." Then, almost at the same moment, another blow fell upon her. Arthur Clough, worn out by labours very different from those of Sidney Herbert, died too: never more would he tie up her parcels. And yet a third disaster followed. The faithful Aunt Mai did not, to be sure, die; no, she did something almost worse: she left Miss Nightingale. She was growing old, and she felt that she had closer and more imperative duties with her own family. Her niece could hardly forgive her. She poured out, in one of her enormous letters, a passionate diatribe upon the faithlessness, the lack of sympathy, the stupidity, the ineptitude of women. Her doctrines had taken no hold among them; she had never known one who had *appris à apprendre*; she could not even get a woman secretary; "they don't know the names of the Cabinet Ministers—they don't know which of the Churches has Bishops and which not." As for the spirit of self-sacrifice, well—Sidney Herbert and Arthur Clough were men, and they indeed had shown their devotion; but women—! She would mount three widow's caps "for a sign." The first two would be for Clough and for her Master; but the third, "the biggest widow's cap of all"—would be for Aunt Mai. She did well to be angry; she was deserted in her hour of need; and, after all, could she be sure that even the male sex was so impeccable? There was Dr. Sutherland, bungling as usual. Perhaps even he intended to go off, one of these days, too? She gave him a look, and he shivered in his shoes. No!—she grinned sardonically; she would always have Dr. Sutherland. And then she reflected that there was one thing more that she would always have—her work.

IV

Sidney Herbert's death finally put an end to Miss Nightingale's dream of a reformed War Office. For a moment, indeed, in the first agony of her disappointment, she had wildly clutched at a straw; she had written to Mr. Gladstone to beg him to take up the burden of Sidney Herbert's work. And Mr. Gladstone had replied with a sympathetic account of the funeral.

Succeeding Secretaries of State managed between them to undo a good deal of what had been accomplished, but they could not undo it all; and for ten years more (1862–72) Miss Nightingale remained a potent influence at the War Office. After that, her direct connection with the army came to an end, and her energies began to turn more and more completely towards more general objects. Her work upon hospital reform assumed enormous proportions; she was able to improve the conditions in infirmaries and workhouses; and one of her most remarkable papers forestalls the recommendations of the Poor Law Commission of 1909. Her training school for nurses, with all that it involved in initiative, control, responsibility, and combat, would have been enough in itself to have absorbed the whole efforts of at least two lives of ordinary vigour. And at the same time her work in connection with India, which had begun with the Sanitary Commission on the Indian Army, spread and ramified in a multitude of directions. Her tentacles reached the India Office and succeeded in establishing a hold even upon those slippery high places. For many years it was *de rigueur* for the newly appointed Viceroy, before he left England, to pay a visit to Miss Nightingale.

After much hesitation, she had settled down in a small house in South Street, where she remained for the rest of her life. That life was a very long one; the dying woman reached her ninety-first year. Her ill-health gradually diminished; the crises of extreme danger became less frequent, and at last, altogether ceased; she remained an invalid, but an invalid of a curious character—an invalid who was too weak to walk downstairs and who worked far harder than most Cabinet Ministers. Her illness, whatever it may have been, was certainly not inconvenient. It involved seclusion; and an extraordinary, an unparalleled seclusion was, it might almost have been said, the mainspring of Miss Nightingale's life. Lying on her sofa in the little upper room in South Street, she combined the intense vitality of a dominating woman of the world with the mysterious and romantic quality of a myth. She was a legend in her lifetime, and she knew it. She tasted the joys of power, like those Eastern Emperors whose autocratic rule was based upon invisibility, with the mingled satisfactions of obscurity and fame. And she found the machinery of illness hardly less effective as a barrier against the eyes of men than the ceremonial of a palace. Great statesmen and renowned generals were obliged to beg for audiences; admiring princesses from foreign countries found that they must see her at her own time, or not at all; and the ordinary mortal had no hope of ever getting beyond the downstairs sitting-room and Dr. Sutherland. For that indefatigable disciple did, indeed, never desert her. He might be impatient, he might be restless, but he remained. His "incurable looseness of thought," for so she termed it, continued at her service to the end. Once, it is true, he had actually ventured to take a holiday; but he was recalled, and he did not repeat the experiment. He was wanted downstairs. There he sat, transacting business, answering correspondence, interviewing callers, and exchanging innumerable notes with the unseen power above. Sometimes word came down that Miss Nightingale was just well enough to see one of her visitors. The fortunate man was led up, was ushered, trembling, into the shaded chamber, and, of course, could never afterwards forget the interview. Very rarely, indeed, once or twice a year, perhaps, but nobody could be quite certain, in deadly secrecy, Miss Nightingale went out for a drive in the Park. Unrecognised, the living legend flitted for a moment before the common gaze. And the precaution was necessary; for there were times when, at some public function, the rumour of her presence was spread abroad; and ladies, mistaken by the crowd for Miss Nightingale, were followed, pressed upon, and vehemently supplicated—"Let me touch your shawl,"—"Let me stroke your arm"; such was the strange adoration in the hearts of the people. The vast reserve of force lay there behind her; she could use it, if she would. But she preferred never to use it. On occasions, she might hint or threaten; she might balance the sword of Damocles over the head of the Bison; she might, by a word, by a glance, remind some refractory minister, some unpersuadable viceroy, sitting in audience with her in the little upper room, that she was something more than a mere sick woman, that she had only, so to speak, to go to the window and wave her handkerchief, for . . . dreadful things to follow. But that was enough; they understood; the myth was there—obvious, portentous, impalpable; and so it remained to the last.

With statesmen and governors at her beck and call, with her hands on a hundred strings, with mighty provinces at her feet, with foreign governments agog for her counsel, building hospitals, training nurses—she still felt that she had not enough to do. She sighed for more worlds to conquer—more, and yet more. She looked about her—what was there left? Of course! Philosophy! After the world of action, the world of thought. Having set right the health of the British Army, she would now do the same good service for the religious convictions of mankind. She had long noticed—with regret—the growing tendency towards free-thinking among artisans. With regret, but not altogether with surprise: the current teaching of Christianity was sadly to seek; nay, Christianity itself was not without its defects. She would rectify these errors. She would correct the mistakes of the Churches; she would point out just where Christianity was wrong; and she would explain to the artisans what the facts of the case really were. Before her departure for the Crimea, she had begun this work; and now, in the intervals of her other labours, she completed it. Her "Suggestions for Thought to the Searchers after Truth among the Artisans of England" (1860), unravels, in the course of three portly volumes, the difficulties—hitherto, curiously enough, unsolved—connected with such matters as Belief in God, the Plan of Creation, the Origin of Evil, the Future Life, Necessity and Free Will, Law, and the Nature of Morality. The Origin of Evil, in particular, held no perplexities for Miss Nightingale. "We cannot conceive," she remarks, "that Omnipotent Righteousness would find satisfaction in *solitary existence.*" This being so, the only question remaining to be asked is, "What beings should we then conceive that God would create?" Now, He cannot create perfect beings, "since, essentially, perfection is one"; if He did so, He would only be adding to Himself. Thus the conclusion is obvious: He *must* create *im*perfect ones. Omnipotent Righteousness, faced by the intolerable *impasse* of a solitary existence, finds itself bound, by the very nature of the case, to create the hospitals at Scutari. Whether this argument would have satisfied the artisans, was never discovered, for only a very few copies of the book were printed for private circulation. One copy was sent to Mr. Mill, who acknowledged it in an extremely polite letter. He felt himself obliged, however, to confess that he had not been altogether convinced by Miss Nightingale's proof of the existence of God. Miss Nightingale was surprised and mortified; she had thought better of Mr. Mill; for surely her proof of the existence of God could hardly be improved upon. "A law," she had pointed out, "implies a lawgiver." Now the Universe is full of laws—the law of gravitation, the law of the excluded middle, and many others; hence it follows that the Universe has a lawgiver—and what would Mr. Mill be satisfied with, if he was not satisfied with that?

Perhaps Mr. Mill might have asked why the argument had not been pushed to its logical conclusion. Clearly, if we are to trust the analogy of human institutions, we must remember that laws are, as a matter of fact, not dispensed by lawgivers, but passed by Act of Parliament. Miss Nightingale, however, with all her experience of public life, never stopped to consider the question whether God might not be a Limited Monarchy.

Yet her conception of God was certainly not orthodox. She felt towards Him as she might have felt towards a glorified sanitary engineer; and in some of her speculations she seems hardly to distinguish between the Deity and the Drains. As one turns over these singular pages, one has the impression that Miss Nightingale has got the Almighty too into her clutches, and that, if He is not careful, she will kill Him with overwork.

Then, suddenly, in the very midst of the ramifying generalities of her metaphysical disquisitions there is an unexpected turn, and the reader is plunged all at once into something particular, something personal, something impregnated with intense experience—a virulent invective upon the position of women in the upper ranks of society. Forgetful alike of her high argument and of the artisans, the bitter creature rails through a hundred pages of close print at the falsities of family life, the ineptitudes of marriage, the emptinesses of convention, in the spirit of an Ibsen or a Samuel Butler. Her fierce pen, shaking with intimate anger, depicts in biting sentences the fearful fate of an unmarried girl in a wealthy household. It is a *cri du cœur:* and then, as suddenly, she returns once more to instruct the artisans upon the nature of Omnipotent Righteousness.

Her mind was, indeed, better qualified to dissect the concrete and distasteful fruits of actual life than to construct a coherent system of abstract philosophy. In spite of her respect for Law, she was never at home with a generalisation. Thus, though the great achievement of her life lay in the immense impetus which she gave to the scientific treatment of sickness, a true comprehension of the scientific method itself was alien to her spirit. Like most great men of action—perhaps like all—she was simply an empiricist. She believed in what she saw, and she acted accordingly; beyond that she would not go. She had found in Scutari that fresh air and light played an effective part in the prevention of the maladies with which she had to deal; and that was enough for her; she would not inquire further; what were the general principles underlying that fact—or even whether there were any—she refused to consider. Years after the discoveries of Pasteur and Lister, she laughed at what she called the "germ-fetish." There was no such thing as "infection"; she had never seen it, therefore it did not exist. But she *had* seen the good effects of fresh air; therefore there could be no doubt about them; and therefore it was essential that the bedrooms of patients should be well ventilated. Such was her doctrine; and in those days of hermetically sealed windows it was a very valuable one. But it was a purely empirical doctrine, and thus it led to some unfortunate results. When, for instance, her influence in India was at its height, she issued orders that all hospital windows should be invariably kept open. The authorities, who knew what an open window in the hot weather meant, protested, but in vain; Miss Nightingale was incredulous. She knew nothing of the hot weather, but she did know the value of fresh air—from personal experience; the authorities were talking nonsense and the windows must be kept open all the year round. There was a great outcry from all the doctors in India, but she was firm; and for a moment it seemed possible that her terrible commands would have to be put into execution. Lord Lawrence, however, was Viceroy, and he was able to intimate to Miss Nightingale, with sufficient authority, that he himself had decided upon the question, and that his decision must stand, even against her own. Upon that, she gave way, but reluctantly and quite unconvinced; she was only puzzled by the unexpected weakness of Lord Lawrence. No doubt, if she had lived to-day, and if her experience had lain, not among cholera cases at Scutari but among yellow-fever cases in Panama, she would have declared fresh air a fetish, and would have maintained to her dying day that the only really effective way of dealing with disease was by the destruction of mosquitoes.

Yet her mind, so positive, so realistic, so ultra-practical, had its singular revulsions, its mysterious moods of mysticism and of doubt. At times, lying sleepless in the early hours, she fell into long strange agonised meditations, and then, seizing a pencil, she would commit to paper the confessions of her soul. The morbid longings of her pre-Crimean days came over her once more; she filled page after page with self-examination, self-criticism, self-surrender. "O Father," she wrote, "I submit, I resign myself, I accept with all my heart this stretching out of Thy hand to save me. . . . O how vain it is, the vanity of vanities, to live in men's thoughts instead of God's!" She was lonely, she was miserable. "Thou knowest that through all these horrible twenty years, I have been supported by the belief that I was working with Thee who wert bringing everyone, even our poor nurses, to perfection,"—and yet, after all, what was the result? Had not even she been an unprofitable servant? One night, waking suddenly, she saw, in the dim light of the night-lamp, tenebrous shapes upon the wall. The past rushed back upon her. "Am I she who once stood on that Crimean height?" she wildly asked—" 'The Lady with a lamp shall stand. . . .' The lamp shows me only my utter shipwreck."

She sought consolation in the writings of the Mystics and in a correspondence with Mr. Jowett. For many years the Master of Balliol acted as her spiritual adviser. He discussed with her in a series of enormous letters the problems of religion and philosophy; he criticised her writings on those subjects with the tactful sympathy of a cleric who was also a man of the world; and he even ventured to attempt at times to instil into her rebellious nature some of his own peculiar suavity. "I sometimes think," he told her, "that you ought seriously to consider how your work may be carried on, not with less energy, but in a calmer spirit. I am not blaming the past. . . . But I want the peace of God to settle on the future." He recommended her to spend her time no longer in "conflicts with Government offices," and to take up some literary work. He urged her to "work out her notion of Divine Perfection," in a series of essays for *Frazer's Magazine*. She did so; and the result was submitted to

Mr. Froude, who pronounced the second essay to be "even more pregnant than the first. I cannot tell," he said, "how sanitary, with disordered intellects, the effects of such papers will be." Mr. Carlyle, indeed, used different language, and some remarks of his about a lost lamb bleating on the mountains having been unfortunately repeated to Miss Nightingale, all Mr. Jowett's suavity was required to keep the peace. In a letter of fourteen sheets, he turned her attention from this painful topic towards a discussion of Quietism. "I don't see why," said the Master of Balliol, "active life might not become a sort of passive life too." And then, he added, "I sometimes fancy there are possibilities of human character much greater than have been realised." She found such sentiments helpful, underlining them in blue pencil; and, in return, she assisted her friend with a long series of elaborate comments upon the Dialogues of Plato, most of which he embodied in the second edition of his translation. Gradually her interest became more personal; she told him never to work again after midnight, and he obeyed her. Then she helped him to draw up a special form of daily service for the College Chapel, with selections from the Psalms, under the heads of "God the Lord, God the Judge, God the Father, and God the Friend,"—though, indeed, this project was never realised; for the Bishop of Oxford disallowed the alterations, exercising his legal powers, on the advice of Sir Travers Twiss.

Their relations became intimate. "The spirit of the twenty-third psalm and the spirit of the nineteenth psalm should be united in our lives," Mr. Jowett said. Eventually, she asked him to do her a singular favour. Would he, knowing what he did of her religious views, come to London and administer to her the Holy Sacrament? He did not hesitate, and afterwards declared that he would always regard the occasion as a solemn event in his life. He was devoted to her; though the precise nature of his feelings towards her never quite transpired. Her feelings towards him were more mixed. At first, he was "that great and good man,"—"that true saint, Mr. Jowett"; but, as time went on, some gall was mingled with the balm; the acrimony of her nature asserted itself. She felt that she gave more sympathy than she received; she was exhausted, she was annoyed, by his conversation. Her tongue, one day, could not refrain from shooting out at him. "He comes to me, and he talks to me," she said, "as if I were someone else."

v

At one time she had almost decided to end her life in retirement, as a patient at St. Thomas's Hospital. But partly owing to the persuasions of Mr. Jowett, she changed her mind; for forty-five years she remained in South Street; and in South Street she died. As old age approached, though her influence with the official world gradually diminished, her activities seemed to remain as intense and widespread as before. When hospitals were to be built, when schemes of sanitary reform were in agitation, when wars broke out, she was still the adviser of all Europe. Still, with a characteristic self-assurance, she watched from her Mayfair bedroom over the welfare of India. Still, with an indefatigable enthusiasm, she pushed forward the work, which, perhaps, was nearer to her heart, more completely her own, than all the rest—the training of nurses. In her moments of deepest depression, when her greatest achievements seemed to lose their lustre, she thought of her nurses, and was comforted. The ways of God, she found, were strange indeed. "How inefficient I was in the Crimea," she noted. "Yet He has raised up from it trained nursing."

At other times she was better satisfied. Looking back, she was amazed by the enormous change which, since her early days, had come over the whole treatment of illness, the whole conception of public and domestic health—a change in which, she knew, she had played her part. One of her Indian admirers, the Aga Khan, came to visit her. She expatiated on the marvellous advances she had lived to see in the management of hospitals, in drainage, in ventilation, in sanitary work of every kind. There was a pause; and then, "Do you think you are improving?" asked the Aga Khan. She was a little taken aback, and said, "What do you mean by 'improving'?" He replied, "Believing more in God." She saw that he had a view of God which was different from hers. "A most interesting man," she noted after the interview; "but you could never teach him sanitation."

When old age actually came, something curious happened. Destiny, having waited very patiently, played a queer trick on Miss Nightingale. The benevolence and public spirit of that long life had only been equalled by its acerbity. Her virtue had dwelt in hardness, and she had poured forth her unstinted usefulness with a bitter smile upon her lips. And now the sarcastic years brought the proud woman her punishment. She was not to die as she had lived. The sting was to be taken out of her: she was to be made soft; she was to be reduced to compliance and complacency. The change came gradually, but at last it was unmistakable. The terrible commander who had driven Sidney Herbert to his death, to whom Mr. Jowett had applied the words of Homer, ἄμοτον μεμαυῖα—raging insatiably—now accepted small compliments with gratitude, and indulged in sentimental friendships with young girls. The author of "Notes on Nursing"—that classical compendium of the besetting sins of the sisterhood, drawn up with the detailed acrimony, the vindictive relish, of a Swift—now spent long hours in composing sympathetic Addresses to Probationers, whom she petted and wept over in turn. And, at the same time there appeared a corresponding alteration in her physical mould. The thin, angular woman, with her haughty eye and her acrid mouth had vanished; and in her place was the rounded bulky form of a fat old lady, smiling all day long. Then something else became visible. The brain which had been steeled at Scutari was indeed, literally, growing soft. Senility—an ever more and more amiable senility—descended. Towards the end, consciousness itself grew lost in a roseate haze, and melted into nothingness. It was just then, three years before her death, when she was eighty-seven years old (1907), that those in authority bethought them that the opportune moment had come for bestowing a public honour on Florence Nightingale. She was offered the Order of Merit. That Order, whose roll contains, among other distinguished names, those of Sir Laurence Alma Tadema and Sir Edward Elgar, is remarkable chiefly for the fact that, as its title indicates, it is bestowed because its recipient deserves it, and for no other reason. Miss Nightingale's representatives accepted the honour, and her name, after a lapse of many years, once more appeared in the Press. Congratulations from all sides came pouring in. There was a universal burst of enthusiasm—a final revivification of the ancient myth. Among her other admirers, the German Emperor took this opportunity of expressing his feelings towards her. "His Majesty," wrote the German Ambassador, "having just brought to a close a most enjoyable stay in the beautiful neighbourhood of your old home near Romsey, has commanded me to present you with some flowers as a token of his esteem." Then, by Royal command, the Order of Merit was brought to South Street, and there was a little ceremony of presentation. Sir Douglas Dawson, after a short speech, stepped forward, and handed the insignia of the Order to Miss Nightingale. Propped up by pillows, she dimly recognised that some compliment was being paid her. "Too kind—too kind," she murmured; and she was not ironical.

✦ Suggestions for Reading and Writing

1. Strachey's prose style has been much discussed. Analyze his use of diction, imagery, and sentence structure. How do these elements create the pervasive tone of irony? (You may find Charles R. Sanders' *Lytton Strachey: His Mind and Art* [1957] of some interest.)
2. Discuss Strachey's manner of underscoring the differences between Florence Nightingale's external and internal worlds—that is, between her fashionable background and "her instincts and her capacities."
3. How do present social attitudes toward the nurse differ from those of Miss Nightingale's day? How does today's public image of the nurse differ from that of the doctor?
4. How much importance does Strachey ascribe to fate, coincidence, and

circumstance as forces shaping his heroine's life? Does he seem to make too much of them, or not enough?

5. Does Strachey's depiction of Florence Nightingale seem essentially realistic or romantic? Does he gloss over her strengths to exaggerate her weaknesses—or are good and bad carefully balanced? Is there a shift in tone in the last two chapters?

6. Compare Strachey's Florence Nightingale with Cecil Woodham-Smith's in her *Lonely Crusader: The Life of Florence Nightingale* (1951). After reading both studies, write your own profile of this famed "lady with the lamp." Then trace each author's indebtedness to Sir Edward Cook's *The Life of Florence Nightingale* (1913). (For a poetic version of the Nightingale legend, see Henry Wadsworth Longfellow's "Santa Filomena" [1857].)

7. To determine for yourself whether Strachey is more deserving of praise than of censure, compare his *Queen Victoria* (1921) with such contemporary studies as Gamaliel Bradford's "James McNeill Whistler," *American Portraits 1925–1900* (1922); Sir Sidney Lee's *Life of King Edward VII* (1925–27); and Philip Guedalla's *Palmerston* (1926). (The literature on Strachey is large—as witness the references to him in the essays included in this volume. But other interesting points are made in Mark Longaker's *Contemporary Biography* [1934], Edgar Johnson's *One Mighty Torrent* [1937], Cyril Clements' *Lytton Strachey* [1942], and Max Beerbohm's published lecture *Lytton Strachey* [1943].)

8. The changes wrought by 250 years of English life-writing should become evident (at least in part) from a comparison of Strachey's "Cardinal Manning," in *Eminent Victorians*, and George Cavendish's *Life of Cardinal Wolsey* (1667). Summarize their principal differences—and similarities—in style, technique, and attitude toward their respective subjects.

from

DISRAELI

André Maurois

André Maurois (1885–   ) is a noted French critic, novelist, historian, and biographer with a cosmopolitan outlook. His more than thirty books deal with English, American, and French history, culture, and persons. Forty years ago Maurois launched his literary career with popular biographies of three famous Englishmen: Ariel: The Life of Shelley (1923), Disraeli (1927), and Byron (1930).

Viewing biography as the "story of the evolution of the human soul," and influenced by Lytton Strachey's deftly ironic portraits, Maurois rejected scientific research for art and imagination. In these early biographies he blended history and fiction to introduce a new school of romantic biography. Short, readable, fast moving, they promised the reader both pleasure and profit; they seemed as much novels as history.

Disraeli has proved the most durable of the three. Maurois catches the colorful, complex Benjamin Disraeli (1804–1881), political novelist-turned-statesman, in his most vivid and characteristic poses. If Maurois often treats Disraeli, "this great artist in living," as a fictional hero, such romanticism seems singularly apt. Disraeli's life appeared to him to have all the characteristics of a tale of The Thousand and One Nights. For, as Maurois puts it, in the end "self-confidence and audacity triumph . . . nor is the good fairy, Queen Victoria, wanting. . . . Yes, I think with Disraeli Scheherazade would have survived."

The following selection, translated by Hamish Miles, comprises chapters four and five of Disraeli. One footnote has been omitted.

"The Chief"—it was thus that the Conservatives henceforward styled Disraeli, and the word betokened a great change. The adventurer, his genius tolerated by some, his authority contested by others, referred to as "Dizzy" with a familiarity sometimes affectionate, sometimes scornful, had now become an object of respect. Age had helped him in this; in all countries old age is a virtue in a public man, but especially in England. No people are more sensitive than the English to the beauty wherewith time can adorn an object; they love old statesmen, worn and polished by the struggle, as they love old leather and old wood. The Conservatives had not always understood the politics of their Chief, but he had led them to the most astounding victory the party had ever achieved. The fact must be faced: his spells might not be intelligible, but they were potent.

Apart from a few old men, almost the whole body of the party now had always known him as at their head, first as Lord Derby's colleague, and then by himself. There were many who still associated with his name some confused notion of Oriental mystery, but not so as to take fright. Just as a beautiful Moorish doorway, brought back stone by stone by some colonist returned home, reconstructed on a trimly mown lawn, and gradually overgrown by ivy and climbing roses, will slowly acquire a grace that is altogether English and blend discreetly with the green harmony of its setting, so too the old Disraeli, laden with British virtues, British whims, British prejudices, had become a natural ornament of Parliament and Society. True, a close observer might occasionally detect beneath the dark foliage the rather startling curve of an arch or the exotic line of an arabesque, but the slight discord would only heighten the beauty of this noble ruin with a barely perceptible touch of poetry and power.

From this time too there was mingled with the respect of the party, a manifest affection. Avowed enemies had become few and far between. The loyalty and good will of the Chief was admitted by nearly all. Even amongst his adversaries it was realized that, while he could deal stern blows to an enemy worthy of his steel, he always spared a weaker swordsman in debate. The examples of Peel and of Gladstone had proved that he never struck a man who was down. During his short tenure of power in 1868 he granted a pension to the children of John Leech, the *Punch* draughtsman, who had mercilessly attacked him for thirty years. Now, in 1874, his first action was to offer the highest distinction within his power to Thomas Carlyle, who had formerly asked how much longer John Bull would suffer this absurd monkey to dance on his chest. When a partisan of a more vindictive turn expressed astonish-

"The Chief" and from "Action" (Chapters IV and V), *Disraeli: A Picture of the Victorian Age*, by André Maurois, by permission of Appleton-Century.

ment at his meekness, he replied: "I never trouble to be avenged. When a man injures me, I put his name on a slip of paper and lock it up in a drawer. It is marvellous to see how the men I have thus labelled have the knack of disappearing."

With a strong majority to lean upon, and the support of the Queen, who welcomed his return with unconcealed delight, he at last had in his hands what all his life he had longed for: Power. The memory of youthful wounds was effaced. To Lady Dorothy Nevill, formerly the confidante of his trials, he said: "All goes well now. I feel my position assured." The security of victory brought a kind of relaxation. Never had the man been so completely natural. At last he knew that he would be accepted for what he was. He loosened his grip on himself. His wit was less harsh, less sarcastic. He spoke with less reserve of the sorrows of his young days. He freely delivered up a past which now had been redeemed. Walking with Lady Derby among his beech-woods, and pointing out Bradenham, he suddenly said to her:

"It was there that I spent my miserable youth."

"Why 'miserable'? Surely you were happy here."

"Not in those days. I was devoured by irresistible ambition, and had no means of satisfying it."

Social ambition had no further object. When a Duke tried to intimidate him, he exclaimed, "Dukes! I don't care for Dukes!" And it was true. Far indeed were the days when Isaac D'Israeli would ask, "Dukes? What does Ben know of Dukes?" A princess of the blood was merely a young woman, and one for whom he refused to put himself out in the morning. The Queen was a familiar figure, an old friend, a little difficult, but well liked. Yes, this time he was indeed at the summit. No longer did he feel within him that restless need of climbing ever higher, of domination. At last he ought to be happy.

But to a friend's congratulations he replied: "For me, it is twenty years too late. Give me your age and your health!" And he was heard to murmur, "Power! It has come to me too late. There were days when, on waking, I felt I could move dynasties and governments; but that has passed away." He had always been so great an admirer of youth, and his own had been frittered away because his starting-point was set too low; he had needed forty years to reach the level from which a Peel, a Gladstone, a Manners, had started off. A misfortune of birth—the hardest maybe of all, because the most unjust. Now it had come "too late." Hardly was he in power before his aged body broke down in various ways; the gout attacked him, and he had to attend Parliament in slippers; he had asthma, and to speak meant exhaustion. No one was at his side to tend him, save the faithful Montagu Corry. Fame is worthless, except as an offering of homage to those whom one loves. What could he do with this importunate fame of his? "Perhaps, and probably, I ought to be pleased. I can only tell you the truth. . . . I am wearied to extinction and profoundly unhappy. . . . I do not think there is really any person much unhappier than I am, and not fantastically so. Fortune, fashion, fame, even power, may increase, and do heighten happiness, but they cannot create it. Happiness can only spring from the affections. I am alone, with nothing to sustain me, but, occasionally, a little sympathy on paper, and that grudgingly. It is a terrible lot, almost intolerable."

What possible pleasures can power bestow? One at least: the press of business which allows one to forget oneself. But what vexations also: railway journeys when every station brings its crowd of enthusiasts shouting, "Here he is!" small boys running after one and standing open-mouthed before the compartment; young ladies begging for autographs; town bands at the door of the hotel. Ah, how little suited Disraeli was for these popular familiarities! One day he was waiting for a train at Swindon, slowly pacing up and down the platform, when a bagman, a hearty, downright fellow, approached him. "I have always voted for you, Mr. Disraeli, for twenty years now . . . and I should like to shake you by the hand." Disraeli raised his tired eyes and shook his head. "I don't know you," he said, and resumed his pacing to and fro. Mr. Gladstone, on a similar encounter, would have given both hands to the man and noted the fact in his journal. But Mr. Gladstone had the enthusiasm of a vigorous woodman; and this old man was worn out. His *mots* were still repeated, but their tone was altered. Hardly did a faint savour of irony keep afloat still on this ocean of melancholy. "Are you quite well, Mr. Disraeli?"—"Nobody is quite well. . . ." And if the lady of a house asked him what should be done for his diversion, "Ah!" he would answer, "let me exist."

One passion survived in this beaten body, and that was the taste for the fantastic. When he was alone, forced by his sufferings into silence and immobility, unable even to read, he would reflect with all an artist's pleasure on his marvellous adventures. Was there any tale of the Thousand and One Nights, any story of a cobbler made sultan, that could match the picturesqueness of his own life? Had he not realized, even in detail, the dreams of that small boy who lay stretched under the trees in the Italian garden, listening to his grandpapa's mandoline? "At last I have made my dream real." He had kept his preference for the tales and manners of chivalry. In this old heart Young England lived on. Amid "all his grandmothers," in the Russian Ambassador's mocking phrase, he believed himself at the tribunal of the Queen of Beauty. He gathered his feminine acquaintance into an order, and gave to each newly-elected lady a brooch fashioned like a Bee. True enough, the order was mainly composed of grandmothers—Lady Chesterfield, Lady

Bradford—but there were a few young women too, such as the Princess Beatrice, with the permission of the Queen. And no doubt its Grand-Mistress was the Queen herself, whom he styled no longer the Queen, but the Faery.

Osborne. The green shades were restful to the eye after the fervent glare of the voyage. From the house one could see the blue bay studded with white sails. Hardly had the old visitor time to sit down for a moment in his room, before the august mistress of the place was asking for him. Downstairs he would come, and she would receive him with such delight that for an instant he thought she was going to embrace him. So full of smiles was she that she looked younger, and almost pretty. She twittered and glided about the room like a bird. She was happy. She had recovered her Minister, the only Minister who gave her confidence in herself. For the Queen had had a difficult life. She had been unpopular, very unpopular. She had seen people in London turn their backs on her carriage in the streets. First it was because of Lord Melbourne; and then it had been poor Albert, whom the public would not pardon for being a German; and then the Queen had been reproached for her mourning, and not one of her Ministers had defended her. All those Whigs were jealous of the Throne. But Mr. Disraeli had the same ideas on the Monarchy as the Queen herself. Doubtless he did not desire the Queen ever to oppose the will of Parliament, but he believed that the wisdom and experience of a constant and impartial witness provided a valuable ballast for the ship of Empire. Mr. Disraeli gave such fine expression to those ideas which had always been in the Queen's mind! "To think of you having the gout all the time! How you must have suffered! And you ought not to stand now. You shall have a chair!"

Mr. Disraeli was overcome by this unprecedented favour. No one had ever been seated during an audience with the Queen. Lord Derby had once told him, in token of her great kindness, how the Queen, seeing him one day when he was very ill, had said, "I am very sorry that etiquette does not allow me to ask you to be seated." Mr. Disraeli remembered the incident, and sighed with contentment; but he declined. He could very well remain standing. The Queen was kinder and kinder; she opened her heart to him on all subjects; and as she knew his curiosity, she showed him her most secret correspondence. She talked, she talked without stopping. She talked like Mary Anne, talked as women can talk. But she had risen greatly in Mr. Disraeli's intellectual esteem. She really had good sense, and was a sound judge of character. For instance, she saw through Gladstone. How lucky it was for Disraeli that England had a Queen and not a King! At dinner the conversation was lively and pleasant. Mr. Disraeli had never felt less constrained. He said all he had to say, in the most surprising terms, and the Queen

thought she had never seen any one so amusing. She was enchanted by
the bold simplicity with which he asked her over the table: "Madame,
did Lord Melbourne ever tell your Majesty that you were not to do this
or that?" Sometimes when they were alone, the Minister's compliments
became flowery and almost direct. But the Queen excused him when she
recalled that he had Eastern blood. The Queen loved the East. She
delighted to have an Indian servant standing behind her chair, and at the
head of her Realms this ingenious and sentimental Grand Vizier.

She invited him everywhere. She asked him to come and see her at
Balmoral, where life was simpler and more free. Unfortunately, the guest
was often ill. The long journeys fatigued him. The Queen sent her
physician, the famous Sir William Jenner, to Mr. Disraeli's sick-room.
Sir William insisted on the Premier keeping his bed. In the morning the
Queen came to see him. "What do you think," he wrote to Lady
Chesterfield, "of receiving your Sovereign in slippers and a dressing-
gown?" Seeing him so weak, she became maternal. Their relations
became entirely human. She talked to him of Albert; he told her of Mary
Anne. Minister and Sovereign had both found happiness in marriage, in
the past, and here was one more bond between them. When he returned
to London, he received a box of flowers. "Mr. Disraeli, with his humble
duty to your Majesty. Yesterday eve, there appeared in Whitehall
Gardens, a delicate-looking case, with a royal superscription, which,
when he opened, he thought, at first, that your Majesty had graciously
bestowed upon him the stars of your Majesty's principal orders. And,
indeed, he was so much impressed with this graceful illusion, that,
having a banquet, where there were many stars and ribbons, he could not
resist the temptation, by placing some snowdrops on his breast, of
showing that he, too, was decorated by a gracious Sovereign.

"Then, in the middle of the night, it occurred to him, that it might
all be enchantment, and that, perhaps, it was a Faery gift and came from
another monarch: Queen Titania, gathering flowers, with her Court, in a
soft and sea-girt isle, and sending magic blossoms, which, they say, turn
the heads of those who receive them."

. . . . .

In a strongly organized country, of an ancient and untouched
civilization, man does not so much take power, as he is taken by power. A
Bonaparte, after a revolution, may find a clean sweep made, and can
impose the mould of his mind on a nation for a century. A Disraeli,
Prime Minister of England, can only move within circumscribed limits.
Events impose daily acts, and acts not always desired. Day after day goes
by in repairing the blunders of a fool, or battling against the obstinacy of
a friend. To have any immense plan would be useless, and the man had
lived too long not to know it.

From the first days of his Ministry, the Queen and the Bishops obliged him to push forward a Bill designed to put a stop to Ritualism, that is, Romanist practices within the Anglican Church. Clergymen were to be prosecuted if their sacerdotal vestments or the splendour of their altars were offensive to Protestant eyes. Disraeli had a profound dread of ecclesiastical legislation, knowing only too well what violent passions might be roused. Even in the parish of Hughenden, small as it was, a civil war raged between partisans of the offertory made in a plate, and those who would only admit of a closed almsbox. "My friend the vicar will take what I call a collection and he calls an offertory, and it will be placed on what he calls an altar or on what his parishioners call a table."

But the Bishops were resolute. The Queen intervened: "Her *earnest* wish is that Mr. Disraeli should *go as far as he can without embarrassment* to the Government, in *satisfying* the *Protestant* feeling of the country in relation to this matter." And the Prime Minister had to spend the first weeks of his reign in amending, and then defending, a measure which he considered inopportune. However, the measures of which he disapproved actually increased his popularity for a time. Life is a topsy-turvy business.

But indeed it was not with laws of repression that he wished his name to be linked. On the contrary, he was anxious that the Conservative party's advent to power should be marked by a policy of generosity. Now was the moment to put into action the ideas of *Coningsby* and *Sybil*. Law after law was passed: equality of obligations between employers and employed; enlargement of the rights of Trade Unions; reduction of the hours of work to fifty-six in the week; half-holidays on Saturday; and numerous sanitary laws. The party's watchword, said Disraeli, should be *"Sanitas sanitatum et omnia sanitas."* A plumber's policy, said his enemies.

Another idea cherished by the Prime Minister from his youth upwards and now installed in power with him, was the idea of the Empire, the idea that England nowadays could not be considered apart from the Colonies. Twenty years earlier, he had proposed to Derby to grant representation to the Colonies and to create an Imperial Parliament. Forty years earlier, he had sung in poesy of Federal Power as the Spirit of the Future. Every time that a utilitarian had risen in Parliament to prove that the Colonies, and India in particular, were over-costly jewels of the Crown, and that it was desirable to renounce them, Disraeli had risen to insist that England is nothing if not the metropolis of a vast colonial Empire, and that the anti-colonists, in looking only at financial balance-sheets, were neglecting the political considerations which alone make a nation's greatness. For the organization of this Empire he had a programme: colonial autonomy, accompanied by an Imperial customs tariff, a Crown right over unoccupied territory, a military *entente*, and, lastly, the creation of an Imperial Parliament in London. So new and so bold did this policy seem, that he could not yet apply it, but he seized every opportunity of a striking display of his sentiments, and the importance he attached to Imperial communications.

On November 15th, 1875, Frederick Greenwood, the editor of the *Pall Mall Gazette*, called upon Lord Derby at the Foreign Office. He had dined on the previous evening with a financier well versed in Egyptian affairs, and had learned that the Khedive, being short of money, was desirous of pledging his 177,000 shares in the Suez Canal. There were in all 400,000 Suez shares, the majority in the hands of French capitalists. Greenwood considered that it was in England's interest to acquire the Khedive's holding, as the Canal was the highway to India. Derby showed no great enthusiasm; he had a horror of large projects. But Disraeli's imagination was fired. He telegraphed to the British Agent in Egypt and learned that the Khedive had given an option to a French syndicate for £3,680,000 up to the following Tuesday. The Khedive was glad enough to deal with England, but he required money at once. Parliament was not in session, and four millions was not a sum which could be taken on to the Budget without a vote of credit. "Scarcely breathing time! But the thing must be done," wrote Disraeli to the Queen. The French Government offered no obstacles; on the contrary, the Duc Decazes was very anxious for Disraeli's support against Bismarck, and discouraged the French banks, who renounced their option. But £4,000,000 had to be found. On the day of the Cabinet's deliberation, Montagu Corry was posted in the anteroom. The Chief put his head round the half-opened door, and said one word: "Yes." Ten minutes later Corry was in New Court at Rothschild's, whom he found at table. He told him that Disraeli needed four millions on the following day. Rothschild was eating grapes. He took one, spat out the skin, and said: "What is your security?"

"The British Government."

"You shall have it."

"Mr. Disraeli, with his humble duty to your Majesty:

"It is just settled. You have it, Madam. . . . Four millions sterling! and almost immediately. There was only one firm that could do it—Rothschild's. They behaved admirably; advanced the money at a low rate, and the entire interest of the Khedive is now yours, Madam."

The Queen was overjoyed. Never had Disraeli seen her so smiling; she kept him to dinner, "nothing but smiles and infinite *agaceries*."

What particularly delighted the Faery was the thought of Bismarck's fury, for only shortly before he had insolently declared that England had ceased to be a political force.

Under Gladstone, with England abstaining and France crushed by the war, the German Chancellor had acquired a habit of playing the master of Europe. With Disraeli, England once more had a foreign policy and desires which she meant to have respected. In 1875, when Bismarck menaced Belgium and then threatened France, Disraeli wrote to Lady Chesterfield that Bismarck was really another old Bonaparte, and had to be bridled. He spoke of it to the Queen, who approved and offered to write to the Emperor of Russia. England and Russia acted simultaneously at Berlin, and Bismarck beat a retreat. England's return into European politics had been triumphant, and the Queen was in ecstasies. How strong she felt, Disraeli being Consul!

All of a sudden she demanded the title of Empress of India. There had been some question of this in 1858, at the time when India, after the Mutiny, had been brought under the Crown, and Disraeli had supported it in principle. But in 1875 the moment was unfavourable. Disraeli knew that this rather un-English idea would be attributed to the Prime Minister's taste for Oriental tinsel. He made endless attempts to obtain a few years of patience from Her Majesty. But in vain. She was obstinate, and a Bill had to be brought forward.

The public outcry was great. The English do not like changes. The Queen had always been the Queen: why should she not continue so? "The title of Emperor," said the puritans, "evokes the images of conquest, of persecution, and even of debauchery." Pamphlets were published: "How Little Ben, the innkeeper, changed the Sign of the Queen's Inn to the Empress Hotel Limited and what was the Result," or "Dizzi-ben-Dizzi, the Orphan of Bagdad." The embassies found it a comical story. "It is the freak of an artist and a king-maker in Dizzy," wrote the French *chargé d'affaires*. "In the Queen, the freak of an upstart; she imagines that her standing will be raised and that her children find a better place for themselves in life with this Imperial title. It is my impression that it is a grave mistake thus to raise the veil which ought to cover the origins of Crowns; these things ought not to be played with. One is born emperor and king, but it is very dangerous to become one."

Dizzy was to reassure everybody. As regards the evil associations of the name of Emperor, he pointed out that the golden age of humanity had been the era of the Antonines. As for the title of Queen, that would be maintained in England, and in all documents related to Europe; only in acts concerning India and in the commissions of officers (who might be called upon to serve in India), the title of "Empress of India" would follow that of "Defender of the Faith." The Queen was much grieved by the opposition showed to *her* law, and especially by the personal attacks which her wishes had loosed against her dear Mr. Disraeli, but she was all the more closely drawn to him. When at last she had her title, she wrote him a letter of thanks, signing it "Victoria, Regina et Imperatrix," with a childlike delight. Then the new Empress gave a dinner, at which she appeared, contrary to all her customs, covered with Oriental jewels presented to her by the Indian princes. At the end of the repast, Disraeli rose, in conscious violation of etiquette, and proposed the health of the Empress of India in a short speech as crowded with imagery as a Persian poem, and the Queen, far from being scandalized, responded with a smiling bow that was almost a curtsey.

Thus the political vessel, tossed on the waves of fortune and climate, of the favour of the House and the humour of the Sovereign, rode the seas pretty well. But the skipper was very ill. So poor did his health become that more than once he told the Queen that he wanted to leave political life. This was a prospect which she would not have at any price, and she suggested that it would be easy to elevate the Prime Minister to the House of Lords, "where the fatigue would be *far less* and where he would be able to *direct* everything." This time he accepted. He took the name which he had had bestowed on Mary Anne, that of Beaconsfield, but whereas she had been only a Viscountess, he became the Earl of Beaconsfield and Viscount Hughenden of Hughenden. "Earl!" said Gladstone ironically, when he learned of this new avatar of the Evil One, "I cannot forgive him for not having himself made a Duke."

To avoid a farewell scene, affecting but unwelcome to his taste, he spoke for the last time in the Commons on the eve before the decision was announced. The secret had been well kept, and members were far from supposing that they would never again hear their leader. When the House rose, he walked slowly down the floor, right to the end, at the bar of the House. There he turned, and for a moment or two looked round the long room, at its benches and galleries, at the seat from which he had made his first speech, the Treasury Bench where he had seen the massive figure and the fine features of Peel, at the Opposition bench which he himself had occupied for so long a time. Then he came back, passed in front of the Speaker's chair, and, wrapped in his long white overcoat, leaning on the arm of his secretary, went out. A young man who was passing noticed that there were tears in his eyes, but could not tell why.

When members learned the news at the meeting of the House next day, they gathered in groups, deeply moved. Voices were lowered on the benches, as if there were a coffin in the chamber. A supporter, Sir

William Hart Dyke, said: "All the real chivalry and delight of party politics seem to have departed; nothing remains but routine." And that was the feeling of the whole House. The interest taken by this old man in the game of life had in the end communicated itself to all those about him. With him one never knew what the morrow might not bring, but one could be certain that at least it would be nothing dull. "He corrected an immense platitude." The presence of this great artist in living had succeeded in making debates into works of art. "He was not only brilliant in himself, but he made others brilliant." Since his conquest of a position of authority, he had used it to impose a universal courtesy and respect for forms. An interruption from one of his own followers would make him turn round and cast a displeased look in his direction. In a discussion on finance he contrived to see a veritable tournament, and he made others see the same. "Your departure," wrote Manners, "terminates for me all personal interest in House of Commons life"; and Sir William Harcourt, an opponent, wrote: "Henceforth the game will be like a chessboard when the queen is gone—a petty struggle of pawns." And he quoted in conclusion the words of Metternich on the death of Napoleon: "You will perhaps think that when I heard of his death I felt a satisfaction at the removal of the great adversary of my country and my policy. It was just the reverse. I experienced only a sense of regret at the thought that I should never again have converse with that great intelligence." "Alas! alas!" wrote another, "we shall never see your like again. The days of the giants are over. Ichabod! Ichabod!"

When shortly afterwards the Queen opened the session of Parliament, a strange, motionless figure was seen standing by her side, draped in scarlet and ermine. It was the new Lord Beaconsfield. The fairest peeresses had come to see him take his seat. Derby and Bradford were his sponsors. With perfect composure he came forward and bowed, shook hands, raised his hat, as the ritual demanded, and then, having become Leader of the House of Lords on the very day of his entering it, he had to speak at its very first sitting. At twenty-five he had written in *The Young Duke:* "One thing is quite clear—that a man may speak very well in the House of Commons, and fail very completely in the House of Lords. There are two distinct styles requisite: I intend, in the course of my career, to give a specimen of both. In the Lower House, *Don Juan* may perhaps be our model; in the Upper House, *Paradise Lost.*" In both cases he had been mistaken, but even if it had taken him some time in the House of Commons to abjure his Byronic manner, he never in the House of Lords adopted the Miltonic style. A shade of difference there was, but it was subtle, and more indefinable than his youthfulness had foreseen. He noted it with perfect artistry. "I am dead," he said on coming out from his first sitting, "dead, but in the Elysian Fields."

↟ **Suggestions for Reading and Writing**

1. Do you agree with Disraeli that "Fortune, fashion, fame, even power
   . . . heighten happiness, but they cannot create it. Happiness can only
   spring from the affections"?
2. Maurois remarks that Victoria and Disraeli had the same ideas on the
   monarchy. Read Lytton Strachey's *Queen Victoria* to see if you can
   write a concise summary of these ideas.
3. Investigate the labor laws passed during Disraeli's tenure as prime
   minister. How do they compare with today's practices in England and
   in America?
4. Do Disraeli's ideas of Empire seem hopelessly outmoded in terms of
   England's present political role? Were Winston Churchill's ideas (when
   he was prime minister) on the subject generally similar to Disraeli's,
   or in strong contrast?
5. Disraeli helped make the novel a vehicle for political, social, and religious ideas in *Coningsby* (1844), *Sybil* (1845), *Tancred* (1847), and
   Endymion (1880). Select one for a study of Disraeli as political novelist. (Refer, if necessary, to F. T. Russell's *Satire in the Victorian
   Novel* [1920] or Monroe E. Speare's *The Political Novel* [1924]; for
   general background, see Irving Howe's *Politics and the Novel* [1957].)
6. In what ways does Maurois' handling of the Suez episode reveal his
   approach to history and biography? Is his approach in keeping with the
   views expressed in his *Aspects of Biography* (1929)? (For more on the
   Rothschilds, see Cecil Roth's *The Magnificent Rothschilds* [1939] and
   Frederic Morton's *The Rothschilds: A Family Portrait* [1962].)

from

EXPERIMENT
IN
AUTOBIOGRAPHY

H. G. Wells

H. G. Wells (1866–1946) was, with John Galsworthy and Arnold Bennett, one of the Edwardians, Britain's major pre-World War One novelists. Of this trio he was easily the most prolific and versatile, writing more than eighty books of fiction, history, sociology, politics, economics, religion, science, and science fiction.

Essentially a journalist, propagandist, and social reformer, Wells viewed fiction as a means of disseminating social criticism and utopian concepts. Trained early in biology, he believed science would lead men to a perfect civilization. With this belief in mind—and influenced by Jules Verne's books—he wrote a series of early scientific fantasies; of these, The Time Machine (1895), The Invisible Man (1897), and The War of the Worlds (1898) are best remembered. Indeed, The Time Machine is now viewed as the prototype for modern science fiction in English.

In the new century Wells moved on to humorous treatments of middle-class life, and then to a lengthy series of utopian novels—ranging from In the Days of the Comet (1906) to The Autocracy of Mr. Parham (1930). Here, as in his other fiction, he surpassed even the Victorian sociological novelists in allowing ideas to overshadow character and thesis to obscure plot. His polemical approach to fiction is especially obvious when he exposes unethical business practices in Tono-Bungay (1909) and political shenanigans in The New Machiavelli (1911), or in such an unabashed piece of war propaganda as Mr. Britling Sees It Through (1916). He was much more in his element with nonfiction, be it straight history, as in The Outline of History (1920), or in a political treatise such as The Shape of Things to Come (1933).

Today Wells's writings, as a whole, are of more interest to the historian of the Victorian-Edwardian eras than to the literary student. In fact, his Experiment in Autobiography (1934) proved both a biographical landmark and shocker; it set off a wave of true confessions, notably among fellow writers like Arnold Bennett and Noel Coward, who then hastened to publish their own memoirs.

Wells describes his autobiography as the "history and adventures of a brain," and in the following section he focuses on the educational forces that from 1890 to 1893 helped to shape this brain.

↟ ↟ ↟ ↟ ↟

During 1889 my efforts to "write," so far as I can remember or trace them now, died down to hardly anything at all. My hope of an income from that source had faded, and it seemed to me that such prospects in life as remained open to me, lay in school teaching. They were not brilliant prospects anyhow, because I was quite obstinately resolved not to profess Christianity, but my self-conceit was in a phase of unwholesome deflation and a mediocre rôle seemed a good enough objective for my abilities. Milne had interested me in teaching method, and I decided that if I secured a teaching diploma and took up my degree in the London University, I might, in spite of my religious handicap, get a sufficiently good position to marry upon. I wanted to marry; I had indeed a gnawing desire to marry, and my life in close proximity to my cousin was distressing and humiliating me in a manner she could not possibly comprehend. I was keen and eager and she was tepid and rational. Plain risks dismayed her. It seemed the most obvious thing in the world to her that I should first win my way to a fairly safe place and the status of a householder before my devotion was rewarded. In pursuance of this intensely personal objective, I took my Intermediate Science Examination in July '89 with only second-class honours in zoology, and I got the

From "The University Correspondence College (1890–1893)," *Experiment in Autobiography*, by H. G. Wells. Reprinted by permission of the Executors of the Estate of H. G. Wells.

diploma of licentiate of the College of Preceptors at the end of the year.

I have already said a word or two about this College of Preceptors in my account of Morley's Academy. Its requirements were not very exacting, and its diplomas were sought chiefly by teachers without university degrees. It offered papers in a number of subjects, and it allowed candidates to pass in one subject at one time and another later on, so that the grade of competing examinee was a lowly one. I took the whole range of subjects at a swoop, got what was called honours—80 per cent of the maximum marks—in most of the subjects and secured the three prizes for the theory and practice of education (£10), mathematics (£5) and natural science (£5). That itself was a useful accession of money, but the greater benefit of this raid upon the college was that I was obliged to read something of the history and practice of education, some elementary psychology, (a mere rudiment of a science at that date) and logic. I was greatly interested in these subjects and, superficial though the standard was, they cleared up my mind upon various issues and started some valuable trains of thought. I planned to go on with mental and moral science and to take that, with zoology and geology, for my degree examination in London University in 1890, but I did not do so because I found that botany would be a more immediately marketable commodity and so I went back to botany.

Armed with this L.C.P. diploma and my second class intermediate honours, I became exacting with J. V. Milne. He raised my salary £10 a year and agreed to cut down the hours I had to spend at Henley House. I looked about for supplementary employment and presently found myself in correspondence with a certain William Briggs, M.A., the organizer of a University Correspondence College at Cambridge, an institution which I still think one of the queerest outgrowths of the disorderly educational fermentations of that time. It flourishes still. Briggs was able not only to offer me just the additional work I wanted to keep me going until I took my degree of B.Sc., but his peculiar requirements enabled him to set a premium upon my taking honours in that examination. I went down to Cambridge to see him; we fixed up an immediate arrangement for me to earn at least £2 a week by doing his correspondence tuition in biology which was in urgent need of attention, and we further agreed that if I took my degree in October, I should leave Henley House School and have a permanent appointment with him in a Tutorial College he was developing in London, at a rate of pay to be determined by my class in honours. He was to give me at least thirty hours' work a week all over the year at 2s. 2d., 2s. 4d. or 2s. 6d. an hour, according to whether I obtained third-, second- or first-class honours. Honours were very important to him from the prospectus point of view.

His list of tutors displayed an almost unbroken front of Cambridge, Oxford and London "firsts." High honours men in biology were rare in those days, and it was characteristic of Briggs that he should decide to make one out of me for himself.

I left Henley House at the end of the summer term, I took my degree with first-class honours in zoology and second-class honours in geology. I had already been working for some months in my surplus time with Briggs, and I carried on first with classes in a small room above a bookshop in that now vanished thoroughfare Booksellers Row, and afterwards in a spacious well-lit establishment in Red Lion Square. There I had a reasonably well furnished teaching laboratory, with one side all blackboards and big billiard-room lamps for night teaching. Briggs gave me enough work to make an average of nearly fifty hours a week, on a system of piecework that enabled me at times to compress a number of nominal half-crown hours into a normal one and so, by the middle of 1891, I found myself in a position to satisfy my cousin's requirements, take a small house, 28 Haldon Road in East Putney, and release her from her daily journey to that Regent Street workroom. She intended, however, to retouch at home and to take pupils.

. . . . . .

We were married very soberly in Wandsworth Parish Church on October 31st, 1891. My cousin was grave and content but rather anxious about the possibility of children, my aunt was very happy and my elder brother Frank, who had come up for the ceremony, was moved by a confusion of his affections and wept suddenly in the vestry.

But I will tell what matters about my domestic life later. What is of much more general interest, is the peculiar organization of that University Correspondence College of which I had now become a tutor. Briggs in his way was as accidental and marvellous as Northcliffe, and as illustrative of the planless casualness of our contemporary world.

. . . . . .

Nowhere yet was there a really comprehensive apprehension of what was happening. The gist of my individual story is the growth of that apprehension, belatedly, in one fairly quick-witted but not very powerful brain. But a partial and reluctant disposition to adaptation became more and more operative in the nineteenth century and produced a structure of universal elementary education throughout Europe, a great multiplication of technical and secondary schools, a growth in the numbers upon existing university rolls and the foundation of a great number of new universities. This adaptation was more quantitative than qualitative. The need for more and more widely extended education was realized long before the need for a new sort of education. Schools and universities were multiplied but not modernized. The spirit of the old educational order was instructive and not constructive; it was a system of conservation, and to this day it remains rather a resistance than a help to the growing creative will in man.

So to the multitudinous demand of the advancing new generations for light upon what they were, upon what was happening to them and whither they were going, the pedagogues and professors replied in just as antiquated and unhelpful forms as possible. They remained not only out of touch themselves with new knowledge and new ideas, but they actually intercepted the approach to new knowledge and new ideas, by purveying the stalest of knowledge and the tritest, most exhausted ideas to these hungry swarms of a new age groping blindly for imperfectly conceived mental food. It is illuminatingly symbolical that everywhere the new universities dressed themselves up in caps and gowns and Gothic buildings and applied the degrees of the mediaeval curricula, bachelor, master, doctor, to the students of a new time. I have already pointed out the oddity—seeing that I had little Latin and no Greek—of my calling my early plan of study at Midhurst a "schema" and my first draft of the *Time Machine*, the "Chronic Argonauts." But this snobbish deference to the pomps, dignities and dialects of a vanishing age, ran through the whole world of education. There was no possibility of teaching (profitably and successfully), or indeed of practising any profession, without a university degree embodying great chunks of that privileged old learning. And when by means of clamour from without, such subjects as physical science and biology were thrust into the curricula, they underwent a curious standardization and sterilization in the process.

Now the urge to spread new knowledge of the modern type widely through the community, was so imperative, and the resistance of the established respectable educational organization, the old universities and the schools with prestige and influence, to any change and any adequate growth, was so tough, that a vast amount of educational jerry-building went on, precisely analogous to that jerry-built housing of London in the nineteenth century on which I have already expatiated. London was jerry-built because the ground landlords were in possession: English national education was jerry-built because Oxford and Cambridge were in possession. The British elementary teacher was an extremely hasty improvisation and I have already given a glimpse of Horace Byatt, Esq., M.A. (Dublin) earning grants for teaching me "advanced" sciences of which he knew practically nothing. Equally jerry-built and provisional were the first efforts to create an urgently needed supply of teachers and university graduates beyond the expensive limits of Oxford and Cambridge. New degree-giving universities were brought into existence with only the most sketchy and loosely connected colleges and laboratories, or with evening classes or with no definite teaching arrangements at all.

Most typical of these was our London University. This at first was essentially an examining board. It aimed primarily at graduating the students in the great miscellany of schools and classes that was growing up in London, but its examinations and degrees were open to all comers from every part of the world. I for instance was examined by my own professors in the South Kensington Science Schools, but the examinations I passed to take my degree in London University, were entirely independent of these college tests.

And this is where the great work of Mr. (afterwards Dr.) William Briggs comes in. It was at once preposterous and necessary. The practice of general examination boards is almost bound to be narrow and rigidly stereotyped. They must never do the unexpected because that might be unfair. The outside student working without direction or working under teachers who had no regard for the requirements of an examining board, was all too apt to wander into fields of interest that were not covered by the syllabus or to fail to get up prescribed topics because his attention had not been drawn to them. His tendency was to be as variable as the examining board was invariable. All the more to the credit of the intelligent student, you will say, but that is beside the present explanation. The ambitious new outsider had to be standardized—because for a time there was no other way of dealing with him. At that early stage in the popularization of education and the enlargement of the educational field, it is hard to see how the stimulus and rough direction of these far flung Education Department, school certificate and London University examinations could have been dispensed with. It was the only way of getting any rapid diffusion of learning at all. Quality had to come later. It was a phase of great improvisations in the face of much prejudice and resistance.

Waste and absurdity stalk mankind relentlessly, and it is impossible to ignore the triumphs of waste and absurdity occurring in that early struggle to produce an entirely educated community. It was the most natural thing for the human mind to transfer importance from the actual learning of things, a deep, dark, intricate process, to the passing of examinations, and to believe that a man who had a certificate in his hand had a subject in his head. With only the facilities for teaching at the utmost a few thousand men to experience chemical fact and know chemical science, there were produced hundreds of thousands with certificates in chemistry. When I matriculated in London University my certificate witnessed that I had passed in Latin, German and French and nevertheless I was quite unable to read, write or speak any of these tongues. About a small and quite insufficient band of men who knew and wanted to teach, seethed everywhere an earnest multitude of examinees. Briggs began life as an examinee. He was a man of great simplicity and honesty. To the end of his days I do not think he realized that there was any possible knowledge but certified knowledge. He became almost a king among examinees. All his life he was adding letters to the honourable cluster at the end of his name; LL.D., D.C.L., M.A., B.Sc., and so forth and so on. He was a thick-set, shortish, dark, round-faced earnest-mannered man with a tendency to plumpness. I never knew him laugh. He was exactly five years older than myself, to a day. Having passed some sort of teachers' examinations—I believe in Yorkshire—he coached a few other candidates for the same distinction. But unlike most coaches he was modest about his abilities and honest in delivering the goods, and for some of the subjects he called in help. He employed assistant tutors. He had organizing power. Presently he turned from little teachers' qualifying examinations, to the widely sought after London University Matriculation. His pupils multiplied and he engaged more tutors. No doubt, like Northcliffe, he began with the ambition of making a few hundred pounds and like Northcliffe he was blown up to real opulence and influence. When I went down to Cambridge to interview him about his biological work, he already had a tutorial staff with over forty first-class honours men upon it, and he was dealing with hundreds of students and thousands of pounds.

The Briggs tutorial method was broadly simple. It rested upon the real absence of any philosophy or psychology in the educational methods of the time. The ordinary professor knew hardly anything of teaching except by rule of thumb and nothing whatever of the persistent wickedness of the human heart and, when this poor specialized innocent became an examiner in the university, almost his first impulse was to look over the papers of questions set in preceding years. These questions he parodied or if they had not turned up for some years he revived them. Rarely did he ever look at the syllabus of his subject before setting a paper, and still more rarely did he attempt any novelties in his exploration of the way in which that syllabus had been followed. Accordingly in almost every subject the paper set repeated various combinations and permutations of a very finite number of questions. Meditating upon these phenomena, Briggs was struck by the idea that if his pupils were made to write out a hundred or so model answers and look over these exercises freshly before entering the examination room, they would certainly be fully prepared and trained to answer the six or seven that would be put to them.

Accordingly he procured honours-men already acquainted with the examination to be attacked, and induced them to divide the proper textbook into thirty equal pieces of reading and further to divide up a sample collection of questions previously set, so as to control the reading done. The pupil after reading each of his thirty lessons sat down and answered the questions assigned to that lesson in a special copy-book supplied for the purpose and sent it in to the tutor, who read, marked, criticized and advised in red ink. "You must read § 35 again" he wrote or "You have missed the v.i. (vitally important) footnote on p. 11." Or "the matter you have introduced here is not required for a pass." This was a systemization of the note-book style of teaching I have already described as a success at the Midhurst Grammar School, and as, under circumstances of wider opportunity, a mental torture in Professor Judd's geological work. A few University Correspondence students, I believe, became insane, but none who pursued the thirty lessons to the end, failed to pass the examination for which they had been prepared. It was merely their thirty-first paper and different from its predecessors merely by containing no novel questions.

Now "elementary biology" had long been regarded as a difficult subject. It was required for the Intermediate examination of all Bachelors of Science and for the Preliminary Scientific examination for the medical degrees, and it stood like a barrier in the way of a multitude of aspirants to the London B.Sc., M.B. and M.D. There were no textbooks that precisely covered the peculiar mental habits of the university examiners, and the careless student ran very grave risks of learning things outside the established requirements and becoming an intellectual nomad. Moreover there was a practical examination which proved an effectual "stumper" to men who had merely crammed from books. I set to work under Briggs to devise the necessary disciplines and economies of effort for making both the written and the practical examinations in biology safe for candidates.

That was an absolutely different thing from teaching biological science. I took over and revised a course of thirty correspondence instruction papers and later on expanded them into a small *Textbook of Biology* (my first published book for which I arranged to charge Briggs four or five hundred hours, I forget which), and I developed an efficient drilling in the practical work to cover about forty hours or so of intensive laboratory work. These forty odd hours could be spread over a session of twenty or more evening classes of two hours each, or compressed, for the convenience of students coming to London for the vacation or a last revision, into a furious grind of five or six hours a day for a fortnight. We met the demand for biological tutoring as it had never been met before and if it was a strange sort of biology we taught, that was the fault of the university examinations.

My classes varied in numbers from half a dozen to our maximum capacity of about thirty-two. For the bigger classes I had an assistant, who was my understudy in case of a breakdown. My students sat with their rabbits, frogs, dogfish, crayfish or other material before them and I stood at the black-board, showed swiftly and clearly what had to be done and then went round to see that it was done. I had to organize the supply and preparation of material and meet all sorts of practical difficulties. For instance it was impossible in those days to buy a student's microscope in London for less than five pounds; this was a prohibitive price for many of our people until we discovered and imported a quite practicable German model at half the price, and arranged for its resale at second-hand after it had done its work for its first owner. I carried the books of answers of my correspondence students in buses and trains to and from the Red Lion Square laboratories and marked them in any odd time, with a red-filled fountain pen. Each book was a nominal twenty minutes' work for me, but I became very swift and expert with them, swifter indeed than expert. My notes and comments were sometimes more blottesque than edifying, but on the whole they did their work.

I must confess that for a time I found this rapid development of an examiner defeating mechanism very exciting and amusing, and it was only later on that I began to consider its larger aspects. Briggs had a bookshop in Booksellers Row, which also dealt with those microscopes, his Tutorial College in Red Lion Square and a little colony of small villas for his resident tutors and students, and postal distribution in Cambridge. Later, I think, in the order of things was his printing plant at Foxton and the workers' cottages and gardens. I liked the persistent vigour with which he expanded his organization. My exploit with the L.C.P. diploma and my success in honours for the B.Sc. had made me an amateur examinee of some distinction and won his sympathetic respect. At the end of 1891 I raided the College of Preceptors again, took its highest diploma of Fellow and carried off a Doreck scholarship of £20.

Briggs hailed my marriage with warm approval. He liked his tutors to marry young and settle down to his work. I cannot estimate how much the early marriage of university honours men made his constellation of first-classes possible, but it was indisputably a factor of some importance. These prize boys, these climbers of the scholarship ladder, trained to lives of decorum, found themselves in the course of nature, as I found myself, the prey to a secret but uncontrollable urge towards early marriage. Emerging at last as the certified triumphs of the university process, missing immediate promotion to orthodox academic posts and finding no other employment open to them except teaching at schools, in which they were at a great disadvantage because of their feebly developed skill at games, the offer from Briggs of a secure three or four hundred pounds a year and probably more, seemed like the opening of the gates of Paradise with Eve just inside. Hastily selecting wives and suitable furniture for a villa, they entered the University Correspondence organization, and found it extremely difficult thereafter to return to legitimate academic courses. For there can be no denying that at the outset both the University Correspondence College and the Tutorial College had an extremely piratical air and awakened the perplexed suspicion and hostility of more respectably constituted educational organizations to a very grave extent. I was never under any illusion that my classes would open up a way of return for me to genuine scientific work and my spirit resounded richly to this piratical note.

The success of these classes of ours in satisfying the biological requirements of the examiners in London University without incurring any serious knowledge of biology, was great and rapid. We drew away a swarm of medical students from the rather otiose hospital teaching in biology, we got a number of ambitious teachers, engineering and technical students who wanted the B.Sc. degree, and so forth, and in the school holidays we packed our long black-boarded room with the cream of the elementary teachers up from the country, already B.A.'s, and taking an intensive course in order to add B.Sc. to their caudal adornments and their qualifications for a headmastership. We passed them neatly and surely. In one year, the entire first class in Preliminary Scientific consisted of my men; we had so raised the examinee standard, that all the papers from other competing institutions were pushed into the second class. Harley Street is still dotted with men who found us useful in helping them over an unreasonable obstacle, and I am continually meeting with the victim-beneficiaries of my smudgy uncomplimentary corrections and my sleight of hand demonstrations. Lord Horder was one, the late Rt. Hon. E. S. Montagu, the Secretary of State for India (1917–22) another. We put all sorts of competing coaches out of business. One of those for whom we made life harder was Dr. Aveling, the son-in-law of old Karl Marx, at Highgate, and I suppose I contributed, unaware of what I was doing, to the difficulties my old friend A. V. Jennings encountered in his efforts to establish a private laboratory of his own.

At various times I have thought of making a large rambling novel out of William Briggs and his creations; *Mr. Miggs and the Mind of the World,* or some such title. There were many technical difficulties in the way, but the more serious one lay in the uniqueness of his effort. It would have needed to be recognizably him and his staff because there was nothing else in the world like them. And, quite apart from the probability of blundering into libel, there was the impossibility of varying the personalities and relationships sufficiently to alleviate a touch of personal cruelty to the tutors and so forth in the foreground. These of course could be invented, but whatever one invented, that type of reader who insists upon reading between the lines would say "that is old X" or "that is Mrs. Y. Now we know about her." Which is enormously regrettable, because the whole Briggs adventure from start to finish, done on a big canvas and with an ample background of education ministries and immensely dignified university personages and authorities, is fraught with comedy of the finest sort. Apart from the endless quaintness of the detail there is the absurdity of the whole thing. That general absurdity, at least, we can glance at here.

At one pole of the business, you have the remote persons and wills and forces which are presumably seeking or tending to produce a soundly educated community. That, if you will, is the spirit in things which makes for the modern world-state, that is the something not ourselves that makes for righteousness, or—the dawning commonsense of mankind. At that pole it is realized that in the new activities of biological science there is illumination and inspiration of a very high order. Thence comes a real drive and effort to bring this powerful new knowledge into effective relation to as much of the general mind as can be reached by formal teaching.

But this drive towards biological education has to work not only against passive resistances, but also against a great multitude of common desires, impulses and activities, that are not so much plainly antagonistic as running counter to the creative power. First the new subject has to establish its claim to a leading place in education. It is claiming space in a curriculum already occupied. Everyone in authority who as yet knows nothing about it, and everyone teaching a subject already established and already suffering from the progressive overloading of curricula, will resist its claims. When they cannot exclude it altogether they will try compromises, they will try to cut down the share of time and equipment conceded to it, to a minimum.

They will accuse the new subject of being "revolutionary" and they will do so with perfect justice. Every new subject involves a change in the general attitude. Biology was and is a particularly aggressive and revolutionary subject, and that is why so many of us are urgent to make it a basal and primary subject in a new education. But in order to attain their ends many of the advocates of the innovation, minimize its revolutionary quality. To minimize that is to minimize its value. So they are led to consent to an emasculated syllabus from which all "controversial matters" are excluded by agreement. In our biological syllabus for instance there was not a word about evolution or the ecological interplay of species and varieties. Biology had indeed been introduced to the London University examination, rather like a ram brought into a flock of sheep to improve the breed, but under protest and only on the strictest understanding and with the most drastic precautions that there should be no breach of chastity.

The fact that biology as we examination-ruled teachers knew it, was a severely *blinkered* subject, might not in itself have prevented our introducing scientific habits of interrogation and verification to our students, if we had had any sort of linkage with, or intelligent backing from, the men who were directly carrying on the living science and who were also the university examiners. But we were thrust out of touch with them. We never got to them, though we certainly got at them.

It is not always the professors, experts and researchers in a field of human interest who are the best and most trustworthy teachers of that subject to the common man. This is a point excessively ignored by men of science. They do not realize their specialized limitations. They think that writing and teaching come by nature. They do not understand that science is something far greater than the community of scientific men. It is a culture and not a club. The Royal Society resists the admission that there is any science of public education or social psychology whatever, and contemporary economists assembled at the British Association are still reluctant to admit the possibility of a scientific planning of public affairs.

Of all that I may write later. But here it has to be recorded that biology, having got its foot into the door of the university education, was wedged at that. It was represented only by a syllabus which presented a sort of sterilized abbreviation of the first half year of the exemplary biological course of Professor Huxley at Kensington. It began and ended with the comparative anatomy of a few chosen animal and vegetable types. It was linked with no other subject. Such reflection as it threw upon the problems of life was by implication. The illuminating structural identities and contrasts between the vertebrated types, were the most suggestive points to seek, and such real teaching of biological generalizations as was possible in my classes, was done in casual conversation while I and my assistant went round the dissections. In spite of such moments, the fact remains that when we had done with the majority of our students and sent them up for their inevitable passes, they knew indeed how to dissect out the ovary of an earthworm, the pedal ganglion of a mussel or the recurrent laryngeal nerve of a rabbit, and how to draw a passable diagram of the alimentary canal of a frog or the bones of its pelvic girdle or the homologies of the angiosperm oophore, but beyond these simple tricks they knew nothing whatever of biology.

My realization of what I was doing during my three years with Briggs was gradual. The requirements for the diplomas of L.C.P. and F.C.P. were not very exacting, but they involved a certain amount of reading in educational theory and history; I had to prepare a short thesis on Froebel for the former and on Comenius for the latter; and I presently added to my income by writing, in conjunction with a colleague on Briggs' staff, Walter Low, who was, until his untimely death in 1895, my very close friend, most of a monthly publication called the *Educational Times*. For the *Educational Times* I reviewed practically every work upon education that was being published at that time. Educational theory was forced upon me. This naturally set me asking over again, what I had already asked myself rather ineffectively during my time at Henley House School: "What on earth am I really up to here? Why am I giving these particular lessons in this particular way? If human society is anything more than a fit of collective insanity in the animal kingdom, what *is* teaching for?"

At intervals, but persistently, I have been working out the answer to that all my life, and it will play an increasing rôle in the story to follow.

Later on, having perhaps that early *Textbook of Biology*, already alluded to, on my conscience, I exerted myself to create a real textbook of biology for the reading and use of intelligent people. I got Julian Huxley and my eldest son Gip, both very sound and aggressive teachers of biology, to combine with me in setting down as plainly and clearly as we could everything that an educated man—to be an educated man—ought to know about biological science. This is the *Science of Life* (1929). It really does cover the ground of the subject, and I believe that to have it read properly, to control its reading by test writing and examination, and to substantiate it by a certain amount of museum work and demonstrations, would come much nearer to the effective teaching in general biology which is necessary for any intelligent approach to the world, than anything of the sort that is so far being done by any university. Other interests would arrange themselves in relation to it. . . .

But I am moving ahead of my story. The main moral I would draw from this brief account of these two remarkable growths upon the London University, the University Correspondence College and the Tutorial College, is this: that the progressive spirit must not only ask for education but see that he gets it. And seeing that you get it is the real job. We did not so much exploit London University as expose it. The unsoundness was already there. We were its *reductio ad absurdum*. The new expanded educational system was not yet giving a real education at all, and Briggs' widely advertised and ever growing lists of graduated examinees merely stripped the state of affairs down to its fundamental bareness.

Could the organization of this correspondence and extra-collegiate teaching have been made, could it even yet be made, of real educational use to the community? I believe it could. It was the dream of Briggs' later years to be formally incorporated in the English university system. I believe the defects of our tuition were and are not so much in the tuition itself as in the indolence and slovenly incompetence of the University examiners and in the lack of full and able direction in the university syllabuses. There is nothing inherently undesirable in the direction and testing of reading by correspondence, and nothing harmful in intelligent examining. But, as it was, we were, with the greatest energy and gravity, just missing the goal. We went beside the mark. The only results we produced were examination results which merely looked like the real thing. In the true spirit of an age of individualistic competition, we were selling wooden nutmegs or umbrellas that wouldn't open, or brass sovereigns or a patent food without any nourishment in it, or whatever other image you like for an unsound delivery of goods. And our circumstances almost insisted upon that unsound delivery. We could not have existed except as teachers who did not teach, but pass.

⟁ Suggestions for Reading and Writing

1. Does Wells's picture of late nineteenth-century England's "disorderly educational fermentations" sound strange today? Or can you point out parallels in present American higher education?
2. Were he writing today would Wells feel there is still much confusion between the actual learning of things and the passing of examinations? Explain. Can you suggest any remedies for what he calls the "note-book style of teaching"?
3. Comment upon Wells's statement that "the professors, experts and researchers in a field" are not always "the best and most trustworthy teachers . . . to the common man." Who should teach in their place?
4. After reading the *Experiment* entire, move on to a standard study of Wells as preparation for a critical essay. Norman Nicholson (1950), Vincent Brome (1951), and Montgomery Belgion (1953) have studies entitled *H. G. Wells* that should be of help.
5. In *The Contemporary Novel* (1912), Wells stated bluntly that in the future "the subterfuge of fiction" would be replaced by the truth of "more searching and outspoken biography and autobiography." He may have been rationalizing the strongly autobiographical flavor of his novel *The New Machiavelli* (1911). Read this novel to find another view of the author and to observe his blending of fact and fiction.
6. Dipping into Arnold Bennett's *Things That Have Interested Me* (1906–25) and *Journals* (1932–33) will broaden your view of post-Victorian England. After a representative sampling here and in the *Experiment*, compare the two contrasting views of time and place.
7. Kingsley Amis, in his study of science fiction, *New Maps of Hell* (1960), discusses Wells's contribution to this newly respectable literary subgenre. You might use Amis' discussion as basis for a comparison of *The Time Machine* and a current science-fiction novel. To extend the scope of such a study, examine Bernard Bergonzi's *The Early H. G. Wells: A Study of the Early Scientific Romances* (1961) and George Orwell's "Wells, Hitler, and the World State," *Dickens, Dali, and Others: Studies In Popular Culture* (1946).

THE
SKEPTICAL
BIOGRAPHER

Bernard De Voto

Born in Utah and educated at Harvard, Bernard De Voto
(1897–1955) managed during his life span to be historian,
biographer, teacher, novelist, essayist, short-story writer, critic,
and editor. From 1922 to 1936 he taught at Northwestern and
Harvard. He edited from 1936 to 1938 the Saturday Review of
Literature, and for the two decades from 1935 until his death
he wrote the "Easy Chair" column in Harper's.

A prolific commentator on politics, society, and literature,
De Voto published three significant studies of Mark Twain,
four volumes on American thought, and at least five serious
novels. He also found time to write magazine fiction under the
pseudonym "John August." De Voto will be best remembered,
however, for his trilogy on the impact of the West upon American history and ideas: The Year of Decision: 1846 (1943),
Across the Wide Missouri (1947; Pulitzer Prize in history), and
The Course of Empire (1952).

No matter what the subject, De Voto expressed himself
freely and pungently, inviting rather than avoiding controversy.
This was especially true—as the following essay indicates—
when he was dealing with something as close to his heart as
biography. A single footnote has been omitted from the text,
which is otherwise complete.

Harper's Magazine, CLXVI (January 1933), 181–192. Reprinted by permission of
Mrs. Bernard De Voto.

Some years ago a new biography of a famous American was published. Most of the subject's life, including behavior of public importance, was explained as the result of the subject's impotence, here for the first time diagnosed. The biographer offered no evidence for his discovery but made the diagnosis by psychoanalyzing what the dead man had written and may be supposed to have said. Evidence exists, but was not mentioned by the biographer, that on two different occasions women were forced to defend themselves against sexual assault by the subject of the biography. There is also in existence an autograph letter written by his wife, whose virtue there is no reason to suspect, in which she tells her mother that she has just had a miscarriage. . . . Another recent biography also diagnoses impotence. Acknowledged and proved descendants of this impotent man are alive to-day. The biographer had neglected to investigate his subject's relations with his slaves. . . . The personality and entire career of an American woman have been explained as the result of a frustrated love affair. Three biographers have identified three different men as her lover. Two of them must necessarily be wrong, but it happens that all three are. She had no love affair. . . . Several studies of Walt Whitman present him as a homosexual. Another study finds that he was "a-sexual," that he was incapable of feeling sexual love. The same evidence is open to all biographers of Whitman.

Classify the foregoing specimens as simple ignorance. What happens in biography when simple ignorance is ornamented by guessing? Well, there is "Ethan Brand," a moral fable by Nathaniel Hawthorne. It has played an important part in two recent biographies, one of Hawthorne, the other of Melville. The lesson of the story is that a search for the unattainable leads to disaster. According to both biographies, Hawthorne wrote it to rebuke if not to repel his friend Melville. He made Melville the hero of "Ethan Brand" in order to discourage Melville's demands for perfect friendship, to indicate to him the folly of metaphysical absolutes, and to assert the boundaries of propriety. This, you will understand, was all very regrettable. It illustrates the Puritanical inhibitions of Hawthorne's nature, and they imply the Philistinism of American life and show that America is hostile to artists. Also, the publication of "Ethan Brand" deeply wounded Melville and helped to bring on the (supposed) despair that kept him silent for a good many years. But "Ethan Brand" was published several months before Hawthorne and Melville met for the first time—before there was any friendship between them, before the famous letters were written. Furthermore, it was written several years before it was published, and had existed in Hawthorne's notebooks for some time before it was written. A little work in a library would have revealed the facts of publication to either biographer, and it would seem fair to require both to be familiar with Hawthorne's notebooks. But, in a condition of ignorance, the guess that the hero of the story must be Melville was too attractive to be resisted.

What, then, about the lighthearted omission of evidence? In a life of General Grant the biographer tells a story which he says is significant, one which was first told by a member of Grant's staff. While a great battle was raging, while hundreds of men were being killed, Grant saw a teamster flogging a horse. He was horrified, and violently rebuked the teamster. And what, for the purposes of the biographer's thesis, does this tale establish? Why, that Grant was insensitive to human suffering but could be horribly upset by the infliction of pain on a horse. He was, says the biographer, a "zoöphile." Perhaps. But a member of General Robert E. Lee's staff tells an exactly similar story about Marse Robert. Was Lee also a "zoöphile"? If he was, just what does the word mean? The biographer must have read the Confederate version. (If he hasn't he has read less about the Civil War than a man should read before he writes a life of Grant.) If the behavior is significant enough to diagnose zoöphily, wasn't he under an implicit obligation to tell us that Lee behaved in exactly the same way? Or was he?

The next step takes us to the distortion of evidence for special effects, to "creative" biography. The term, in our time, has meant the work of Mr. Lytton Strachey, with Maurois and Ludwig following his plow, and after them some seven thousand inconsiderables diluting Strachey to the hundredth attenuation. Mr. Strachey had an enormous reading knowledge of history and literature, a knowledge which tended toward pedantry and preciosity. He possessed also a talent for irony and a prose style of great distinction. For a while he wrote literary criticism, an activity in which uncontrolled speculation is virtuous and responsibility is almost impossible. Then, turning biographer, he published *Eminent Victorians*, and from that moment the minds of dead men have yielded up their secrets to anyone who cared to reach for a pen.

A Strachey biography is an adult form of art, and anyone who happens to know something about its subject may derive from it an intense æsthetic pleasure. But God help the man who comes to Strachey ignorant and desirous of learning the truth. Mr. Strachey was not in the truth business. In his last book, to be sure, he was content to be guided by fact—the facts about Elizabeth and Essex were sufficiently sardonic and perfumed and paradoxical for his purposes—but it was not his last book that inspired the seven thousand. His Queen Victoria has very little in common with the actual maiden and wife and widow of Windsor. His Chinese Gordon could never have worn a uniform; his Florence Nightingale is only a series of epigrams about a nurse, and not even that much links his Doctor Arnold with the master of Rugby. These portraits are enormously entertaining. Strachey's pyrotechnic method overwhelms the reader, and his flashes of insight are hardly to be equalled outside of great poetry. But if they are brilliant portraits, they are also studies in deliberate deception. One reason for reading biography may be the desire to know the truth about its subject. Is it a valid reason? Has it any bearing on the conduct of a biographer?

Finally, an inquiry into motives may be made—the motives, that is, not of the subject but of the biographer. It was Mr. Woodward, I believe, who suggested that certain historical personages should be "debunked." So the seven thousand promptly took his tip, and if he had overthrown Parson Weems, he had only set up the *Daily Graphic* in his place. For some years biography in America seemed to be no more than a high-spirited game of yanking out shirt-tails and setting fire to them. In *The Life and Times of* anyone, you might be sure before you began to read that the life would prove to be ridiculous, the time barbarous, and both corrupt. Genius was mere disease (though few biographers had read widely enough to quote Nordau). Reputation was just publicity. Sexual aberration or incontinence was to be taken for granted, and with it cowardice and venality in public life, cowardice and hypocrisy in private life. Our ancestors were far more vigorous than we, it developed, for they could play the villain's role, whereas we are only victims of circumstance. And always the clothes they wore and the way they decorated their houses were, to us emancipated, simply preposterous. The debunker has never lost his astonishment at those silly clothes. . . . But the man who starts out to write a debunking biography has notified us that he is either a special pleader or a charlatan. He has something to prove. His purpose is not to find out and report the facts of history; it is to argue *ex parte*. He is not a judge. At best he is a prosecuting attorney; at a lower level, he is a kept detective; at the lowest level—one fairly common in recent years—he is the man who designs "composographs" for a scandal sheet. His art may solace his own needs, it may pay him pleasant royalties, it may even entertain intelligent people in moments which they would otherwise waste listening to tenors. But it has nothing to do with fact or integrity, and so it is not biography.

A historian was discussing Mr. Lewisohn's *Expression in America* with a prominent literary editor. He took exception to one of Mr. Lewisohn's chapters on the ground that it rested on statements of fact which he, having recently investigated them, knew to be altogether wrong. (That Mr. Lewisohn, a critic, had taken them in good faith from a recent biography establishes one of the obligations of a biographer.) The editor listened courteously but shook her head. The facts didn't matter, she said, for "It's a very interesting interpretation." The historian was obstinate. It didn't matter how interesting the interpretation might be, he asserted—the facts were wrong, and since they were wrong, the interpretation was wrong also. But no. The lady kept on shaking her head. Not only was the interpretation interesting; she would commit herself to calling it brilliant. . . .

Has a biographer this privilege? Should he refrain from making statements of fact until he has found out what the facts are? Or may he be ignorant of his subject so long as he makes an interesting interpretation?

Asking the lady's forbearance, I think he may not be. Biography differs from imaginative literature in that readers come to it primarily in search of information. The man who reads *The Life and Times* wants to learn something about the life and times. He wants to know how this particular person was entangled with the world, what the conditions of his life were, what they did to him, how he dealt with destiny, what he overcame, what overcame him. He desires this knowledge not only because of the curiosity that is our simian heritage but because he too is entangled and hopes for wisdom. Conceivably, something of his knowledge and wisdom will depend on what he learns from this biography. It is a jigsaw piece to be fitted into his picture of the world. Some of his decisions, some of his behavior, will in part depend on what the book tells him. Multiply him by a sufficient exponent and you have the next generation—part of whose knowledge of the world will be derived from biography.

It seems both precarious and absurd for a biographer to add unnecessarily to the ignorance and misinformation with which they will have to deal.

II

Literary people should not be permitted to write biography. The literary mind may be adequately described as the mind least adapted to the utilization of fact. It is, to begin with, much too simple. The novelist, the dramatist, the poet, or the critic selects vivid phases of experience and coördinates them in such a manner that they give us an illusion of the whole. The significance, the ultimate value, of the process resides in its omissions. But biography cannot simplify and must not omit. The experience with which it deals is not simple. A novelist may invent a motive or a situation of magnificent simplicity; but that is fiction, and the motives and situations of fact are not simple but complex. The novelist deals with social organization only so far as he sees fit; but the subject of a biography was part of a web so intricate that only an objectification beyond the reach of fiction can comprehend it. The mathematics of a complex variable are forbidden to the literary mind.

That mind is also habitually, even professionally, inaccurate. Accuracy is not a criterion of fiction, drama, or poetry; to ask for it would be as absurd as to appraise music by its weight or painting by its smell. Hence the literary person is horribly inept at the practice of biography, whose first condition is absolute, unvarying, unremitted accuracy. He is subject to credulity—a reliance on intuition, on appearance, on rumor and conjecture and sheer imaginative creation. He is sometimes unable to read accurately and is nearly always unable to report what he has read. Some years ago a literary critic, writing the life of a novelist, demonstrated that he could not even read his subject's books. He ascribed words and actions of characters in them to other characters; he erred in summarizing the plots of books; he asserted that events happened in them which did not happen, which were even specifically denied; in general, he appeared unable to report either the geography or the events in them as they really exist. This form of illiteracy is buttressed by another defect in accuracy, unwillingness to turn a page. One grows weary of seeing passages quoted from letters, journals, and notebooks in support of ideas or sentiments which the next manuscript page, usually the same entry, categorically denies.

The literary mind, furthermore, is naïve. That is its charm. From this unspoiled freshness, this eager willingness to believe, this awe and wonder, the world's poems and romances are woven. But it disqualifies its possessor for biography, which requires an all-inclusive skepticism and a cynicism that are best cultivated in human intercourse. The artist is usually a simple, home-loving person, given to nerves or paternity or the cultivation of some bourgeois hobby. He has little experience of the great world and none at all of the world of action. He knows nothing about the conditions of practical life, the way in which members of trades and professions and businesses must conduct themselves. He is ignorant even of rudimentary organization, business, military, political, diplomatic, economic, or religious. He could not conduct a horse trade, a sales drive, a senatorial campaign, an order of battle, or a revival, and usually has never observed one. Yet when he essays a biography of Napoleon, St. Francis, Roscoe Conkling, or Jay Gould he must not only master these mechanisms but must also understand their laws. In a novel or a play the problem is simple: he may brood about Napoleon till his own special talents invent something that will give us an illusion. But it is not illusion that biography demands—it is fact. The literary mind can imagine a world for St. Francis but it cannot deal with the actual, the factual, world of St. Francis. It succumbs to fantasy, which is its proper medium. It is effective when it is evolving a world out of its own inner necessities, when it is creating its own material and data. But that is why the literary mind has worked so much stupidity in biography. We do not want illusion there, however convincing—we want reality. We do not want invented facts, created motives, phantasmally generated problems solved by intuition. We do not want anything whatever that imagination, intuition, or creation can give us. We want facts; and the literary mind is incapable of finding them, understanding them, and presenting them.

That is why the literary biographer has been victimized by preposterous methods. Unfitted to understand the nature of fact and bountifully endowed with credulity, he has relied on preposterous instruments for the ascertainment of fact. Most notably, in the last decade, on psycho-analysis.

Psycho-analysis has no value whatever as a method of arriving at facts in biography. No psycho-analytical biography yet written can be taken seriously—as fact. The assertion holds for the work of the master himself, whose study of Leonardo is absolute bilge uncontaminated by the slightest perceptible filtrate of reality, and for other biographies by professional analysts. But if the professional's rare excursions into biography are worthless, why has the method so gratified the literary?

The answer is that an acquaintance with the terminology of psycho-analysis gives the literary a means of transcending their limitations. It shifts the field of biography from the empirical world where the subject mingled with his fellows, lived, worked, struggled, and, it may be, loved. In that world there are all sorts of dark places, mysterious bare spots about which nothing can be found, lacunæ, ellipses, conflicts of testimony and narrative, contradictions in evidence, insoluble problems, and sheer chaos. The lay biographer, denied the resources of Freud, must deal with these as best he may—by the swink of a never-ending labor which terrifies his slumber with the dread that he may have missed something, and which enables him in the end to say only "*a* is more probable than *b*." Labor and nightmare are spared the amateur psycho-analyst. He needs only the subject's letters and diaries, his books and speeches if he wrote any, the more intimate letters of his friends, and an earlier biography. Not all of these items are indispensable: much brilliant work has been done on the basis of the last alone. The external world is to be disregarded; the amateur Freud will devote himself to a far richer field, his subject's mind. He has, for the exploration of that field, an infallible instrument. It is the celestial virtue of psycho-analysis that it can make no mistakes. The amateur will never stub his toe on the discouragement of the biographer—he will never find that no evidence exists on a question he is trying to answer, or that the evidence which exists is insufficient. All of his subject's mind is of one piece and all his life is a unity, and so anything that is desired can be recovered from anything else. And if he finds a conflict of evidence, that too is simple. The principle of ambivalence tells him that all evidence means the same thing.

The amateur begins with a set of necessities to which his subject must be fitted. The science he has acquired from a month's reading—more often from a couple of popular outlines—gives him a number of patterns and a series of keys. He knows before he begins that Diogenes, Brutus, or Cleopatra must have had this complex, or, if not, then that one. He knows in advance that inhibition must have been responsible for something, under-sublimation for something else, over-sublimation for still more. He knows that one kind of behavior indicates a form of sublimated anal erotic interest, another kind, oral eroticism. The indices of sadism are given on page 114 of Tridon, those of masochism in the third chapter of Hinkle. The Œdipus complex (Freud's modernization of original sin) may be expected to show itself in one of certain catalogued ways. It will produce such other universals as the castration complex. These in turn will work out, sometimes through other complexes, in behavior whose meaning and symbolism have been carefully charted. There remain such beautiful and versatile instruments as the death-wish to explain any chance fragment that might seem incommensurable with the rest. Or if something is still left over, the biographer has the blithe freedom of dropping Freud and picking up one of Freud's murderously incompatible opponents. Perhaps the uninterpreted residue of Cæsar's unconscious had better be treated in the light of Jung's types, which are beautifully systematic and have recently been doubled for American use. Few biographers, however orthodox in their use of Freud, have been able to refuse the help of Adler's *Minderwertigkeit*—fewer still have used it to mean what Adler means. It is a reasonable expectation that few will hesitate to marry the death-wish to the birth-trauma when an adequate exposition of the former works into the outlines.

The rabbit, perceive, has been hidden in the hat. There remains only to pull it out with a smile of reassuring omniscience. It is obvious how unnecessary are the researches and verifications of the biographer. Conversations which no one ever recorded can be reproduced and explained. Interviews which no one ever witnessed can be described. Documents long since vanished from the earth can be recreated and interpreted. The method cannot make mistakes: it is, in literary hands, infallible. You have what the dead man wrote, what it is said he said, and what some people have said about him. Your method dissolves all doubts, settles all contradictions, and projects the known or guessed into absolute certainty about the unknowable. You wonder, perhaps, what Diogenes said at the grave of Keats or where Apollonius was and what he did on a certain fourth of July? If you are a historian you examine all possible sources of information and if you find no information, you report "I don't know." But if you are an amateur analyst, to hell with uncertainty. You have discovered that Diogenes possessed a mother fixation as the result of jealousy before his second birthday (evidence of what was in the mind of a child twenty centuries ago does not exist, but no matter), that he had a mania for overripe plums as the result of an incestuous admiration of his sister, and that his Id and Ego were abnormally at peace with each other. What, therefore, must Diogenes have said on the specific occasion? Where, therefore, must Apollonius have been? Obviously, where he must have been is where he was.

That *must* is the mechanism of psycho-analytical biography. It is the invention of the biographer, his deduction from an *a priori* principle. It has no relation to the subject of *The Life and Times*. It does not tell what did happen. It tells us instead what must have happened. Biography proper is not concerned with the *must* but only with the *did*. Between them is a sheer gulf which no theory can possibly bridge. Psycho-analysis cannot come into effective relationship, into any relationship, with a dead man.

Professionally, it does not try. The physician to diseased minds is engaged in a process whose aim is therapeutic—empirical. He practices an art whose entire condition is the mutual association of living minds. His technic requires a constant interplay of a myriad variables, a constant shift and adaptation, a constant accommodation and reexamination and reinterpretation—all of which are impossible to biography. Psycho-analysis is dynamic or it is nothing. The professional must deal with phenomena which his trade-jargon calls Displacement, Conversion, Resistance, Transference, and with similar psychic energies which perish when the patient dies. These phenomena never engage the attention of a biographer: no dead man exhibits them. The amateur does not hesitate to dispense with them. He has his pattern, his clues, his guidebooks, and they are enough. As the result of his skill, they create his patient for him.

The result may be, as our literary editor insisted, an interpretation in the highest degree entertaining. It may be a brilliant exposition of its author's sentiments or his talent for denunciation or his exhortatory power. When produced by an intelligent man it may approximate the art of the detective story, whose clues are also invented and whose deductions are also made to fit. But it exists always on the left side of a fixed line. On the right side of that line are the materials of biography. The findings of psycho-analysis, any findings whatever, belong forever on the left side, with guesses, improvisations, fairy stories, and mere lies. The obligation of a biographer is to find facts. When he employs psycho-

analysis he cannot arrive at facts but only at "interpretations," which is
to say theory, which is to say nonsense.

III

Honesty in biography is a gradation. In a way, the most dishonest is
the most honest, for its nature is most easily perceived. The late Senator
Lodge's life of Alexander Hamilton, for instance, is clearly an item in
Mr. Lodge's lifelong effort to prove that the Republican party was the
heir of both Federalism and God. It may be described as political pro-
bunking biography. Most biographies by recent converts to Marxism are
easily recognizable as products of generous emotion, tracts, acts of faith,
studies in the propagation of a religion. The words of convertites, out of
whom much matter is to be seen and learned, have always a legitimate
use. More difficult are the products of prejudice, which also make a
gradation. Least offensive are those like Henry Adams's life of John
Randolph. One knows what an Adams had to do with a Southerner who
had expressed his dissent from the Adams conviction that the family
beliefs were indistinguishable from God's will. Not many advocacies are
so easily corrected—notably the recent swarm of lives of Civil War
notables, most of which are really passionate attacks on or defenses of
political, economic, or sociological theses. The iridescent rhetoric that
played round these same notables two generations ago was, effectively,
more honest.

In every biography ever written certain passages are printed in
invisible italics, the involuntary emphasis of the biographer which
springs from his emotional, intellectual, religious, economic, political,
social, and racial prejudices. The reader has a problem in moving points.
A conscientious biographer will have faced the same problem and made
what adjustments he could. There would be no occasion to state here the
bald platitude that a biographer must have integrity if fashion had not
permitted it to be ignored. A reader may accurately estimate a biographer's integrity by the force of his refusal to depart from verifiable fact.
The disciplined biographer will say, in effect, "Here are the facts I have
found. Anyone who is interested in testing them may consult sources *a*,
b, *c*, etc." If for any reason he cares to enlarge on his facts, he will give
unmistakable notice that the discussion is shifting to a different plane.
He will say, in effect, "I infer from *a* . . . ," or "*b* leads me to guess," or
"my hunch is," or "it may be but I can't establish it." He will supply
actual italics.

There remains the biographer whose dishonesty is deliberate—or
who, to designate him more charitably, practices a flexible art. So many
recent biographers have been novelists turned rancid, so much success
has rewarded fiction mislabeled biography, that the technical devices of

novel-writing have usurped the place of factual instruments. There is, for instance, "incorporation," a method now almost universally employed in lives of writers, orators, and others who committed anything to paper. The biographer selects something from the subject's written works, his essays or his novels or his diary, and without quotation marks sets it down as part of the subject's thoughts on a given occasion. The ideas, the emotions, and the phraseology of the diary thus become the content of the subject's mind. Passages written years later than the time indicated, or years before it, have been used to illustrate states of mind widely different from those indicated by the context. Passages widely separated in time have been combined. Highly important phrases or sentences have been left out, so that the meaning of the passage has been vitally changed. Such misrepresentation of the defenseless dead is dishonesty of the rankest kind, but the device is dishonest no matter how carefully employed or how rigorously controlled. It is not accountable. Between what a man thinks or feels and what he writes about it, especially what he writes creatively or polemically or for purposes of self-analysis, there is a difference that no skill or selection or representation can reconcile.

The device, however, enables the biographer to assert something about his subject's mind, as psycho-analysis also enables him to do. For the same reason a different kind of biographer employs another method of fiction. He enters his subject's mind and reports what he finds there. This is a novelist's instrument, whether it reports merely "Diogenes thought . . ." or extends farther toward the "interior soliloquy" or "stream of consciousness" of the post-war novel. From Queen Victoria to Lord Byron, from Herman Melville to Boss Croker, how many dead people have confided to us thoughts they could never have set down in a private journal? They have been presented to us with an accuracy of reporting that catches the minutest syllable of their minds. The reason why this method of fiction is illegitimate in biography is, however obvious, worth noting at length.

A character in fiction is invented—made to order. The requirements of fiction are served if his creator succeeds in making us believe in him, in giving us an illusion that he really exists. When the thoughts of Tristram Shandy or Molly Bloom are reported to us, we receive the thoughts of phantoms and the only necessity is that they shall seem to be real thoughts. The interior soliloquy of Molly Bloom is not the actual content of a mind, for Molly Bloom never lived. It is the possible content of an imagined mind. It is only one of many possible sequences of thought, any other of which would conceivably give us as convincing an illusion. It succeeds when that illusion is created.

But Molly Bloom is one kind of person and Queen Victoria is

another kind. Swann and Charlus, Clara Middleton and Carol Kenni-cott are imaginary persons, whereas Nathaniel Hawthorne, Julius Cæsar, and Catherine the Great really lived. The biographer who tries to tell us what they were thinking at any given moment must work in the domain of historical fact. At that moment Hawthorne was thinking one thought or one group of thoughts and no other. With all the resources of art and science, research, imaginative sympathy, and sheer good luck on his side, no biographer can recover it. Have you ever stood at the bedside of a dying person and wondered what images were flickering across that fading mind? You stared into a mystery which no biographer could ever penetrate. He can guess, he can "interpret," he can invent. He can build a beautiful and convincing illusion for us, but it is only a possible, an unconditioned mind that he gives us, not the actual mind of a person who lived in the world. If he presents it as "interpretation" he is a novelist. If he presents it as fact he is a charlatan.

But, I am told, the biographer has the testimony of his material. He has a letter or an entry in a journal. His subject has actually written, "I was greatly moved. I thought that . . ." and so on. For the most part "interpretative" biography derives its stream of consciousness from the biographer's own mind, but even when it uses intimate personal docu-ments it remains invention. No man can recover the past of his own mind. He can say "I was grief-stricken" or "I was overjoyed." He can describe his thoughts and emotions with general nouns—anger, delight, ecstasy, melancholy, discouragement, despair. Sometimes he can recall images, metaphors, or curious perceptions of the exterior world, but even here he is almost certain to be victimized by creative reminiscence. The biographer may write "Cæsar wrote to Pompey that he thought . . ." or "Margaret Fuller wrote in her diary that she felt . . . ," or even "Melville believed that he had thought . . ." Such statements may be statements of fact. But such a statement as "Cæsar thought . . ." or "Margaret felt . . ." is just guesswork, just theory, just nonsense.

Still, the rebuttal runs, a biographer is entitled to "interpret" his subject. The point of view of the literary editor already quoted sanctions him to transcend the limitations of fact. That transcendence being sanctioned, he is free to recreate his subject's mind. Excuse me: he is not. The interior of his subject's mind is forbidden him by the nature of reality. He may tell us what the subject has said or written about his mind, but he may not on his own authority make any statement whatever about the immediate content of that mind. He cannot know what is there, he can only guess. Any guess whatever is a clear warning to his reader. When he makes it, he departs from fact and enters theory. We will not dispute about words: you need not follow me in calling a guess dishonest. But certainly it is theoretical—and if theoretical, then contingent, inexistent, and mystical. And, therefore, improper to biography.

I V

And the moral? The moral is: Back to Lockhart, back to Froude, back to Morley. Back, in short, to Victorian biography. For the great Victorians, however timorous in refusing to call fornication by a ruder name, had as biographers an invincible integrity. They acted upon an implied contract, they accepted obligations to the reader. They assumed that the reader's interest was in the subject and not in the biographer; wherefore they resolutely submerged their own personalities. They assumed that biography dealt with fact; so they refrained from guessing. They assumed that fact-finding requires accuracy; so they checked their dates and titles, verified their quotations, and abstained from reporting what they had never seen or heard or read. They assumed that recreation of their sitter's thoughts was impossible; and they sacrificed the God's-eye view. So one may read their biographies in the assurance that he is not being deceived, whether through ignorance, guesswork, special pleading, or deliberate fraud. Such confidence would have its value, these gloomy days.

It would imply, I am afraid, the disappearance of the literary from biography and the occupation of the field by historians, students, and analytical searchers after fact. We should lose a great deal of beautiful writing; for most historians and most scholars appear to write with something between a bath sponge and an axe. But we could accept that loss in gratitude for the loss of beautiful thinking as well. There would be no more "restitutions"—the journalist's discovery that Andrew Johnson had his points twenty-five years after the historians had done him justice would be spared us. There would be no debunking of great men about whom no one acquainted with history had ever believed any bunk. We could pick up the life of a Civil War leader confident that the colonels would not be called generals, that armies five hundred miles apart would not fight battles of which history has no record, that Chattanooga would not be fought in 1864 or Vicksburg surrendered on the wrong side of the river. In that Era of Accuracy the Shenandoah Valley will not be a prairie; they will not mine gold on the Comstock; Jesse James will not ride to the attack on Lawrence at the age of nine; Robert Burns will not die when Washington Irving is three; Mrs. Hale will not write to Rufus Griswold thirteen months after his death; Rouen will not contain rival cathedrals; John Keats will not read a translation of "Oberon" that Southey did not write. Biographers will know who was President of the

United States in any given year. When they describe the appearance of Charles Dickens during his 1842 visit to America they will not take their data from the reports of people who saw him on his second visit a quarter-century later. There is hope that they will master the fashions of the past and refuse to seat Edgar Allan Poe on an antimacassar. There is hope that they will quote the titles of books as they were written, even that they will learn to find out when they were published. A vision now wholly chimerical may be fulfilled: American biographers may become acquainted with the more salient facts of European history and literature. Still, if a contemporary American historian can misdate the Regency by forty-six years, it would be romantic to ask the merely literary to know who wrote *I Promessi Sposi*, to understand the difference between an abbé and an abbot, or to identify the author of "The Wanderings of Cain."

But accuracy will be only a lesser glory of that great dawn. When we read about Uncle Billy Sherman we shall not be told of an infantile fixation which the biographer has deduced from the letters to Joe Johnston before Atlanta. John Greenleaf Whittier's dislike of slavery will not spring from a sense of guilt acquired in his fourth year, which intense brooding in the night watches has revealed to the author of the life and times. Jay Gould's manipulation of Erie will not be symbolic of his erotic reveries and, though we search wonderingly, we shall not read an interior soliloquy which Andrew Jackson aimed at the twentieth century on the eve of New Orleans. Psycho-analysis will retreat from biography to the consulting room, where it belongs, and to the literary speakeasy, where thereafter it will have to compete with the Revolution. With it will go all the other instruments of amateur psychology—they are worthless in biography. They have been eloquent helps in the production of absurdity. They have given the half-educated a feeling of profundity. They have comforted a good many wishful, believing minds and softened a harsh world for the tender. All this is probably a social service, an accessory to the public welfare; but let it go.

We should forfeit much amusement if these things disappeared, but the loss would be compensated. The republic of letters would gain in dignity. Something of its vulgarity springs from our permitting gentlemen in the service of causes to lie ignorantly about dead men. In an honest world the Rosicrucian, the Humanist, the Marxist, the Fascist, the politician, the economist, the regionalist, the evangelist—in short, the doctrinaire—would be required to conduct his propaganda in the open. In such a world the lecturer to adolescent girls would be required to report accurately on what he reads, and told that a generous spirit is not in itself enough for the perception of facts. He and all the hopeful minds of which he is symbolic would be, in a tradition of integrity, forbidden to misrepresent the past, no matter how beautiful their motives.

What about the "interpretation"? Well, it has a valid place as the most intelligent of literary guessing games, and something more. Given an alert mind and some horse sense, a "psychographer" may contrive a stimulating essay. It must remain an interpretation of the unknowable in terms of the author's personality, but if the author is a distinguished person it may be a fine art. It may be a vehicle for wit and malice and good writing, of which the world can never hold enough, and an expression of literary talents which find no other form well adapted to them. Mr. Gamaliel Bradford wrote the "psychograph" in its most legitimate form. He was too disciplined to offer the pompous fiction of a Maurois or a Ludwig as history. He had too much Victorian integrity to plead a cause, and he refrained from the delicate distortion of plain truth that constitutes the art of Strachey. The same integrity made him notify his reader on nearly every page: this is what I think or suspect or infer. But his interest and his field can be observed in the word which worked into so many of his titles, the soul. It is an honest interest, a legitimate field. But just what is it? Biography knows nothing about the soul.

Biography is the wrong field for the mystical, and for the wishful, the tender minded, the hopeful, and the passionate. It enforces an unremitting skepticism—toward its material, toward the subject, most of all toward the biographer. He cannot permit himself one guess or one moment of credulity, no matter how brilliantly it may illuminate the darkness he deals with or how it may solace his ignorance. He must doubt everything. He must subject his conclusions and all the steps that lead to them to a corrosive examination, analysis, and verification—a process which he must hope will reveal flaws, for if it does he has added one more item of certainty to his small store. He has, apart from such negatives, very little certainty. His job is not dramatic: it is only to discover evidence and to analyze it. And all the evidence he can find is the least satisfactory kind, documentary evidence, which is among the most treacherous phenomena in a malevolent world. With luck, he will be certain of the dates of his subject's birth and marriage and death, the names of his wife and children, a limited number of things he did and offices he held and trades he practiced and places he visited and manuscript pages he wrote, people he praised or attacked, and some remarks made about him. Beyond that, not even luck can make certainty possible. The rest is merely printed matter, and a harassed man who sweats his life out in libraries, courthouses, record offices, vaults, newspaper morgues, and family attics. A harassed man who knows that he cannot find everything and is willing to believe that, forever concealed from him, exists something which, if found, would prove that what he thinks are facts are only appearances.

From this quicksand and mirage he will derive facts. Only a few of them are unmixed fact, free of misunderstanding, misinformation, and plain ignorance. The rest he will grade in a hierarchy, and arrange them as their nature, value, and validity make necessary—not as some wish or religion of his own would like them arranged. In the end he can say, "A did this, and I think he did that, and for the rest I am ignorant and refuse to guess." This is the act of judgment, and it contains three different stages, each one of them serviceable to his reader—who will use them, according to their degree, in his acquisition of knowledge. When he has said this much, the biographer has done his job. He will say, "A did this," but he will not try to say why. For that is speculative, the gate that lets the motive in, and with the motive enter all the guessing, hoping, and chicanery that have debauched his profession.

His result lacks brilliance. It is without the certainty of the ignorant and the psychological—the certainty that is the unmistakable hallmark of the theorist's cocksureness. It is without the ingenious nonsense of the interpreter. It is without the invective of the debunker, without the contrived, humanitarian unity of the hopeful, without the passion of the generous. It is without teaching, without preaching, without hope for a better world: altruistic desire does not come into it. It will not make life seem easier to optimists and has no bearing on reform or revolution. It is only an intelligent man's efforts to deal with facts. It is a faulty, imperfect picture, a blurred image, an uncompleted map. But such as it is, it is trustworthy: it looks toward reality. It establishes part of a pattern, makes out some lines of the obscured page, recovers something from the past. Like other controlled and tested knowledge, it is usable. It is an accounting, the settling of a stewardship. Momentarily, mists have partly blown away and the North Star, though blurred, has been visible. It is an effort in the direction of truth. Such an effort has a value that no ignorance, however brilliant, and no wishfulness, however kind, can offer in competition with it.

⌁ Suggestions for Reading and Writing

1. After reading Strachey's *Florence Nightingale*, do you agree with De Voto that it "is only a series of epigrams about a nurse"?
2. De Voto sees the debunking biographer as "either a special pleader or a charlatan." Evaluate this charge after reading Edmund Pearson, "Plutarch *et Fils*," *Outlook*, CXLVI (1927), 54–56; C. M. Fuess, "Debunkery and Biography," *Atlantic Monthly*, CLI (1933), 347–356; and, especially, Frank Klement, "Debunking the Debunkers," *Social Studies*, XXXVIII (1947), 366–369.

3. How valid is De Voto's charge that the literary mind is too simple, inaccurate, and naive to produce biography based soundly upon fact, skepticism, and cynicism? Can you cite a biography that substantiates his charge? One that refutes it?

4. Summarize and discuss De Voto's arguments against psychoanalysis as a biographical tool. The literature on psychological biography is vast. For counterbalancing articles on the subject, see J. A. Garraty, "The Interrelationship of Psychology and Biography," *Psychological Bulletin*, LI (1954), 569–582 and Franz Alexander, "Psychology and the Interpretation of History," *The Cultural Approach to History*, ed. C. F. Ware (1940), pp. 48–57. On the other side are Charles Whibley, "The Indiscretions of Biography," *English Review*, XXXIX (1924), 769–772 and W. C. Abbot, "Some 'New' History and Historians," *Massachusetts Historical Society Proceedings*, LXIV (1931), 286–293.

5. Apply De Voto's comments in part three of his essay to the excerpt included here from Maurois' *Disraeli*. In what ways does Maurois "transcend the limitations of fact"?

6. De Voto refers favorably to Lockhart as biographer. Read the selection included here from the latter's life of Scott to see if De Voto might also have had Lockhart in mind when declaring that most historians "write with something between a bath sponge and an axe."

7. For a recent and rounded characterization of De Voto himself, see *Four Portraits and One Subject: Bernard De Voto* (1963), with an introduction by Wallace Stegner.

THE
SILVER
HORN

Thomas Sancton

Thomas Sancton (1915–   ) is an editor, novelist, and
teacher who comes from New Orleans and who broke into
journalism as a reporter on the Times-Picayune. In this personal
memoir, "The Silver Horn," he aimed at and attained a "simple evocation of summer and youth and the past." He wrote
it in 1944, for Harper's, after adding free-lance writing to his
journalistic activities. It proved immediately popular and has
been much anthologized during the past two decades.

Sancton, since then, has taught at Tulane University and
been an editor or feature writer for the New Republic, the
Nation, and the Associated Press. His two novels—Count
Roller Skates (1956) and By Starlight (1960)—were well re-
ceived; he is now at work on a book tentatively titled New
Orleans Is My Town.

✓   ✓   ✓   ✓   ✓

The scene is a Boy Scout summer camp, thickly grown with pines
and cypress. There is a row of green clapboard cabins, with clean floors
and neat double-decker bunks; there is an open field and a flag hanging
still in the heavy air; and at the field's edge the land drops down a little to
the dark water of a bayou. I spent five summers here, from the time I was

Harper's Magazine, CLXXXVIII (February 1944), 264–270. Copyright © 1944 by
Harper & Brothers. Reprinted by permission of Russell & Volkening, Inc.

twelve until I entered college. I did my first real living and my first real thinking in this camp.

And I think of it now. Like some reader of a long novel who turns back through the pages to find a forgotten part of the plot, and who comes with a flash of recognition across old scenes and dialogues, and characters who have gone out of the narrative but whose personalities and substance once filled pages and pages, I have gone turning back through the pages of my life. When was it and where was it—I have been asking—that I first began to believe what I now believe about the Southern world I left not many years ago, about Negroes, about democracy, about America, about life and death, about men and all their curious fates? This search has been long and turning. Often it has led me back to the years of my early teens and to the summers I spent in the camp.

I was born to the sidewalks and asphalt of the largest city and the widest street in the South. In New Orleans, broad Canal Street was never empty of speeding automobiles and streetcars, even late at night, and of people walking by, their footsteps echoing on the sidewalk. But here on the bayou another world existed. In the morning it was the strange, thin call of a bugle that broke into our sleep. Almost before we were awake we could smell the wet exercise field and the forest. Birds popped from tree to tree, plump and colorful, bluejays, mockingbirds, cardinals, flickers—Audubon had painted in these woods. Rabbits ran into the bushes. Snakes we had no fear of, long thick blue racers and speckled king snakes, slid through the weeds at our approach.

Standing in the wet grass, still yawning and sleepy, we took the morning exercises. Night chill was in the air, but behind our backs the sun was rising, and its warmth crept onto our shoulders. After the exercises we raced along a wagon road to the swimming pool, and as we ran up, shouting and excited, two or three startled frogs made tremendous leaps and plumped beneath the glassy surface of the water. After the swim we dried our skinny sunburned bodies and ran to the mess hall.

Most of us in the camp were poor boys, or boys who were almost poor. It was not a welfare camp, but the fees were low, less than a dollar a day for a camper. As a consequence it was filled with boys from modest New Orleans neighborhoods and also from the tough ones. There was always a smattering of the democratic rich: the son of the traction company president came every summer. So did his cousin from Texas, a wild, hard towhead with plenty of money and the soul of a true picaroon. He fascinated and dominated the rest of us. He was the first colorful outlaw I ever knew. But most of the well-to-do families sent their boys to camps in the Maine woods or the North Carolina mountains. Our camp was only forty miles from the city. Department store clerks, streetcar motormen, little grocers could afford the fees.

We had no saddle horses, no golf course, and only a weed-grown tennis court which no one used. For diversion we fell back on nature. In the morning we performed a work detail, cutting a patch of weeds or hauling dirt in wheelbarrows to mend a road. After this we were free to swim, to paddle on the bayou in slender little Louisiana boats called pirogues, to fish for the boisterous black bass and yellow perch and fat blue catfish, and to work for our Boy Scout medals and merit badges, tracking through the grassy cut-over pine lands, cooking dough and bacon on sweet-gum spits, bandaging one another with first-aid splints.

These little medals and bits of colored ribbon meant a great deal to us. We wrote home enthusiastic letters about our progress, describing in detail how we had passed the tests, forwarding the comments of some eighteen-year-old camp officer as though it really mattered. Our parents, most of whom did not have very big events happening in their own lives, were just as eager and simple-hearted about these things, and one or two of the fathers were foolishly ambitious to have their sons win the highest number of merit badges in the area.

Little things that happened during these years seemed of great importance. I remember that in my first year at camp I wore an ill-fitting Boy Scout hat. One of the councillors, a boy five years my senior who seemed to me to belong already to the grown-up world of brilliance and authority, began, in a pleasant way, to tease me about the hat. Every morning for a week he led us to the abandoned logging road and clocked us as we walked and trotted a measured mile. My hat was anchored down by a heavy chin strap; it flopped and sailed about my head as I ran to the finish line. The boy began to laugh at me. He waved his arms and called out, "Come on, you rookie!" The other kids took it up and Rookie became my first nickname. I loved it. I tingled when someone called it out. I painted it on my belt, carved it in my packing case, inked it into my hatband, and began to sign it to my letters home. Years later when we were grown I knew this camp officer again. The gap between our ages had vanished and in real life now he seemed to me a rather colorless young lawyer. He did not remember about the hat.

At mealtime we ate ravenously in the mess hall. There were steaming platters of pork and beans and cabbage and stew. As we walked to the long clapboard building with our hair freshly combed and water glistening on our faces, which we washed at the flowing pipe of a big artesian well, we existed in a transport of driving hunger. In the steamy fragrance of the mess hall we set up a clatter of knives and forks and china, and afterward we went to our cabins and flopped on the bunks in a state of drowsy satisfaction. Somehow, fat never formed on our skinny frames. We ran too much. We paddled in the boats. We swam. We cut firewood and played softball after supper. When there was nothing else to do we climbed in the rafters of our cabins, trying to invent complicated monkey swings that no one else could do. Every year some campers broke their arms.

II

A giant Negro named Joe did the camp's heavy work. He cut and trimmed the big trees, dug the deep post holes, mixed the cement, cleaned out the underbrush. His strength was a never-ending fascination for the rest of us. Joe was a light-eyed Negro, with a tan cast of skin and a huge bald dome of a head. One of his grandparents must certainly have been a white man. He lived half a mile down the bayou with his large and hazily defined family, in an old "plantation house."

Actually it was not, and never had been, a pretentious place, and I do not know what kind of plantation could have been there. The ground round it was alternately sandy and swampy and there are no plantations where pine trees grow. Pines mean sandy land. In slave days the Negroes had boiled Southern history down to a couplet:

> Cain't make a living on sandy lan'—
> Ruther be a nigger den a po' white man.

Joe's place stood on a cleared bend in the bayou. The weatherboards and shingles were green with age. The house rested on high slender pillars and there were patches of bright red brick where the covering mortar had fallen away. The yard was shaded by two enormous water oaks, hung with gray Spanish moss, and an iron kettle stood beneath the trees where women did the washing. At the bank of the bayou five or six towering cypress trees leaned heavily toward the water, for the slow currents of a century had washed their roots completely bare of soil. To get a new anchorage on the land the trees had sent out a forest of gnarled roots and stubby knees along the shoreline. The house seemed beautiful and somber in these surroundings as we paddled past it on our expeditions down the bayou to the lake.

Obviously a white man had built this place long ago, and if he had not been a plantation owner, he had at least been a man of substance. Perhaps this had been the summer home for some wealthy old New Orleans Frenchman in years gone by. Sometimes the camp officers spoke of Joe as "caretaker" on the place. But that was hardly possible. He and his family inhabited every room; chickens roamed freely, and washing hung on lines stretched across the wide porch. It was clear to us that the Negro giant was no caretaker here. He possessed this place, to have and to hold. How he got it and why we never asked him; and his presence there did not seem a very curious thing to us. Already a dark, subjective understanding of Louisiana's history was in our blood and bones.

Joe smoked strong cigarettes and chewed tobacco. His teeth were rotted stumps. We delighted in bringing him supplies of smokes from the nearby town on Saturdays to win his quick and genuine appreciation. There were two or three measures of a Cajun French ditty he used to sing, dancing and stomping the ground, waving his hat and swaying his heavy shoulders with real grace. The words and the stomping finished together, with two hard accents. He would do this every time in exchange for a gift. Yet he did it in such a way that we knew always that this was nothing more than a grown-up man doing monkey-shines for children. He enjoyed making us laugh. There was nothing servile about it.

He got to be one of the people I liked best of all—not only in the camp but in my whole circumscribed world. I liked Joe very simply because he was a nice man. He recognized me every year when I returned to the camp, and after the second or third year I could tell that he considered me a real friend and was glad to have me back. We talked together often, equally and easily, and when I was sixteen and seventeen and by then a councillor in the camp, Joe would do me the honor of becoming quite serious with me and of placing our whole friendship on a mature plane. I do not remember many of the things we talked about, but I do remember that a conversation with him was a reassurance and a satisfaction; that it was always good to find him walking on the road and to fall in with him.

I saw a brief notice in the paper, some years after I had stopped going to the camp, that Joe had died of blood poisoning in the New Orleans Charity Hospital. I thought of those stumps of teeth, and of the many years they had been seeping infection into his system. I thought also of the tall trees I had seen him fell, and that now Joe too had come toppling to the earth. And, though I felt a quiet sorrow, I felt no anguish. Life grew rank and lush along the bayou. His old house was teeming with the spawn of his years. The sun would beat upon the water forever, the trout would break the surface, the rushes would grow thick and green. Joe had done his share of hauling and of digging. Now he could lie down in the warm and sun-drenched earth and sleep.

III

During those summers in camp a love grew up in me for the rhythms of nature, for tropical rains that came sweeping through the pines and oaks, for the fiery midday sun, for long evenings, and the deep black nights. Great campfires were lit beside the bayou and a rushing column of luminous smoke and sparks ascended to the cypress trees. Fire gleamed in the water where bass were sleeping in the stumps. Campers wandered toward the meeting place, their flashlights swinging in the woods. We sat about the fire, singing, beating deep rumbling tom-toms made of hollowed oak logs, performing an ageless repertoire of skits and mimicry. And after these sessions one leader took the Protestant boys and another the Catholics and, standing in the open fields, in our separate groups, we prayed aloud.

My heart had strayed already from the formal, repetitious praying. A towering pine tree at the field's edge made a silhouette in the starry sky. I knew the constellations, the Giant, the Dipper, the Bear. I looked for the two inseparable stars, Misar and Alcar, horse and rider, and sensed the fact that Arabs named these stars a thousand years before me, and even in my boy's ignorance I felt aware of man's long and varied time upon the earth. I knew this night-filled wilderness had stretched beneath these stars for endless ages before Frenchmen had come in boats to build New Orleans. I thought of the Indians who had fished and hunted here, whose bones and broken pottery we sometimes found in grassy mounds. I felt worshipful of the earth, the pine tree, the night itself.

Sometimes we packed provisions and tents and mosquito bars and paddled down the bayou to the lake, ten miles away. The lake was a great inland finger of the Gulf of Mexico, twenty miles long, ten wide. Twenty miles below us, in prehistoric times, the mouth of the Mississippi river had built up new land, and these watery prairies had pinched off the small inland gulf and made a lake of it, but it connected still through a series of passes with the Mexican Gulf. The lake teemed with croakers, catfish, shrimp, and big blue-clawed crabs. At the northern end, where we camped, a network of tributary bayous emptied into the lake. For the last mile or so of their crooked lengths, where the brackish water of the lake crept into the slow-moving bayous, fish and small life were abundant, bass fed in the rushes, and muskrats built their cities of the plains.

There was a relatively high, sandy point near the mouth of the bayou, where we camped. The sun went down red into the lake and left a long, clear twilight. A few stars came out. A salty wind blew in from the Mexican Gulf; it came out of the south every night. The breeze swept over the rushes and made small waves break on the sandy, grassy shore. There was a red beacon light on weather-beaten piles out in the lake and its long reflection shimmered in the water. We sprayed our mosquito netting with citronella and built up a driftwood fire and lay down on canvas bedrolls spread upon the thin, tough grass and sand. The trade wind blew through our tents throughout the night. We listened to the waves. We could smell the vast salt marshes far below us. A yellow moon

came out of the gulf. Far down the lake we could see the lights of a
railroad bridge. We felt the beauty of this wilderness like a hunger.

After two days of fishing and swimming in the lake, our shoulders
and faces darker from the sun, we paddled back up the winding bayou.

IV

One summer when I was sixteen a party of us, paddling upstream to
buy some candy at a crossroads store, came upon three young girls who
were bathing in a sandy cove. There were four of us in the long pirogue,
all of an age. For a long moment we were speechless. At last we said
hello, and they answered in warm gay voices. We drifted the boat into
the cove and began to speak to them. Two of the girls were sisters. The
three of them had come to visit a relative who kept a fine summer lodge
in the woods across the bayou from the camp. One of the sisters was
fifteen and the others were seventeen. They were aglow with fresh and
slender beauty, and their bathing suits were bright flags of color. Their
impact upon us was overwhelming. We grew silly, tongue-tied, said
foolish things we did not mean to say, shoved one another about in the
boat, and finally overturned it. The loreleis laughed musical little laughs.
They seemed unbearably beautiful. We had no idea what to do about
it.

The girls had been at the lodge for a week. They missed their beaux
in New Orleans, they missed the dating and the dancing and the music.
It was a gay town in the summertime. The older girls looked upon us as
children; but still—they must have reflected—we were not such children
at that. The younger sister, a slender child with thick brown hair and
heavily crimsoned lips, sat on the bank and regarded us with a happy
open face.

At last we took courage and asked if we could call on them that
night.

"Oh, yes!" they cried eagerly. Life at that moment was dazzling.

Making this rendezvous was an impulsive thing to do, for it was
midweek and we should have to steal away after taps and walk down a
path without flashlights through a snake-infested lowland and—because
the boats were counted and chained at nightfall—swim across the bayou,
holding our clothes above our heads.

We crept from our cabins at ten o'clock that night and met in the
pine woods. One of us intoned a counting-out rhyme; the loser had to
walk first down the path through the snake hole. He cut a long gum
sapling and rattled it down the path ahead of us. We walked bunched
tightly together, tense with fear, giggling at our own unbelievable
audacity, trembling in our eagerness. At the bayou's edge we slipped out

of our shorts and shirts and sneakers and, holding them above our heads with one hand, we felt our way round the knees and along the sunken roots of a cypress tree, and pushed off into the bayou and began to swim.

The moon had not yet risen. We had only the silhouettes of trees to guide us. We swam closely together, cautioning one another to silence, bursting into convulsive squeals as water lilies brushed against our bodies or when a fish broke the surface near us. We swam upstream from the camp, past two bends, and waded from the water in the cove where we had met the girls. Now we were laughing with relief and excitement, and popping one another on the backsides. We scraped the glistening water from our bodies, dressed, and combed our wet hair and hurried off down the wagon path into the woods. Long ago the cove had been a landing stage for small schooners which came to load pine firewood for New Orleans.

The girls were waiting for us, dressed in bright print cotton dresses and wearing hair ribbons. The soft light gave age and mystery to their youthful shoulders, to their slender bodies; and, like nameless night-blooming vines in the woods about us, they bore a splendid fragrance all their own, a fragrance of youth and cleanliness and fresh cosmetics. They were playing a phonograph on the wide porch of the lodge. This was the summer of Maurice Chevalier's great success in American movies. The little sister sang his song, rolling her eyes, turning out her soft pink lip:

> If ze night-ting gail
> Cood zing lak you . . .

And she sang another:

> . . . you make me feel so grand
> I want to hand the world to you.
> You seem to understand
> Each foolish little dream I'm dreaming, scheme I'm scheming . . .

I was so in love with her I could hardly catch my breath. I was in love with the other sister too, and with their friend. All of the boys were in love with all of the girls; the girls—so they said—had crushes on each of us. Our hearts were afire.

We walked hand in hand down the wagon trail to the cove and built a bonfire. We stretched out on blankets, laughing, singing. We sang the songs that people always sing by rivers and campfires, "There's a Long, Long Trail A-winding," "The Sweetheart of Sigma Chi," all the rest. We kissed the girls and they held fast to us. Before this night we had been only boys, holding hands with girls in movies, not quite sure why we pursued them and acted silly. Now, lying beneath the open sky, for the first time we understood the poignance and the beauty of the human heritage.

Every night for two weeks we came to see them. And when they told us good-by the last kiss was as much a discovery as the first, and we knew that love was a thing that could never grow old. After they had gone we would steal from our cabins to sit on the back porch of the camp hospital, on a hill, where we could see the bayou and the cove and the woods where we had found them; and we sat there talking late into the night, like daemon lovers in the ballads of old. I never passed the cove again, even years later when I would paddle down the bayou fishing, without remembering our meetings with a suddenly racing heart. First love is unforgettable.

V

I had no lessons to do in those summer months of camp life. There was plenty of time to think. I was living a communal life with other boys. Among us were embryonic bullies, scoundrels, cheats, promoters, Babbitts, Christers, and stuffed shirts; and there were also the boys of good heart, the unselfish, the humorous, the courageous, boys who were the salt of the earth, but who, often in their later lives, would be misled and preyed upon and set against one another by the sharp ones. One and all we lived together, ate together, slept together. Our personalities clashed, fermented, or formed amalgams. Sitting together at night in the lamplit cabins, with darkness and towering woods closing in upon us, we had our first grave talks about religion, about death, about sex. The future stretching before us was wide and fathomless. And all about us, in the grass, in the underbrush, in towering summer skies, we beheld the face of nature and the earth's wide harmonies as they had never been revealed in our city lives. At night we could stretch out upon the field, observe the stars, and grasp for the first time the fact that some were vastly deeper in space than others. In our star-study courses we heard phrases like "light years." It began to seep into the consciousness of many of us that a hundred years or the life of an individual had little meaning in the total universe; and from this point some of us began our first gropings after moral philosophy, gropings for a belief that could give the total universe a meaning in our own lives.

There was a bugler in our camp who was the first consummate expert, in any field, that I had known. He had no other talent but his music. He was a good-natured, chubby, curly-headed Italian boy, rather lazy, and when he was not back in the woods practicing his cornet he walked round with a dreamy look, as though our own handicrafts could not possibly be of interest to him.

Paolo had a silver trumpet and he preferred it to the bugle. He wanted to be a great musician. He would take his horn and music back into a pine clearing a quarter of a mile from the camp and all day long we could hear him practicing the runs. He blew the trumpet with a clear, sweet tone. We had supreme confidence as we stood at attention on the parade grounds and the flag came down the creaking flagpole pulley in the late afternoon sunlight, and Paolo stood alone, with everyone watching, and bugled. We were proud of him when visitors came. He had that ability of experts to create a sense of possessiveness in others.

It was at bedtime that Paolo gathered up into his clear, thin music all the ineffable hungering of our awakening lives. At ten o'clock he climbed a high ladder to a life-guard platform we had nailed into the branches of a tall cypress tree beside the bayou. Paolo lived for this moment and, with the whole camp silent and listening below him in the darkness, he blew taps with a soft and ghostly beauty all his own. Somehow the music spoke for us, uttered the thing we knew but had no words for, set up a wailing in the pine trees of the brevity and splendor of human life. Lying in our bunks in the darkness of the cabin, some of us fell into sleep; but some lay in silence thinking longer, alive to the night, and I was of these.

One night some ten years later I entered a smoke-filled tavern in another city where Paolo was playing in a band. By this time he had made a small reputation as a boy with a hot trumpet. I watched his now older face as he tore through the hot routines. He was tired. The silver horn made noise but, though I knew little about it, I could see that he was not a great jazz musician.

I did not go to see him any more. I wanted to remember Paolo before he had lost something, before any of us had lost it, a kind of innocence. I wanted to remember him in the land of our first discoveries, when he had climbed into a cypress tree to blow his horn, and there was a kind of Gothic night-drench in our lives.

⟋ Suggestions for Reading and Writing

1. You may have had camp experiences which helped shape your adolescence. Fashioning them into a readable memoir should contribute to self-knowledge. Try it.
2. Does Sancton's disenchantment with the former teen-age camp counselor and with Paolo the trumpet player sound familiar? Is such a loss of innocence inevitable? (For a fictional treatment of the same theme, see Stephen Vincent Benét's "Too Early Spring.")
3. Sancton devotes just seven paragraphs to his friend Joe. How does he engrave Joe upon the reader's memory in such little space?
4. Sancton allows even less space to describing himself directly. Yet the sensitive reader should be able to write an interesting—and recognizable—character sketch of him.

5. As accomplished men of letters, Thomas Sancton and Alfred Kazin now undoubtedly would find much to talk about. Would this have been true when they were teen-agers? Would either have found the young Dylan Thomas a compatible companion?
6. "The Silver Horn" was first anthologized in William H. Davenport and Paul Bowerman, eds., *Modern Exposition* (1946). It has since appeared in at least fifteen different collections. Can you account for its popularity?
7. If you enjoyed this brief recollection of what it was like to come to maturity during the first decades of this century, you might sample Lincoln Steffen's *Autobiography* (1931), Louis Adamic's *Laughing in the Jungle* (1932), Bliss Perry's *And Gladly Teach* (1935), and William A. Percy's *Lanterns on the Levee* (1941). Each provides materials for an interesting character sketch of the author.

from

PORTRAIT
OF THE
ARTIST
AS A
YOUNG DOG

Dylan Thomas

Dylan Thomas (1914–1953) was born in Swansea, Wales, and educated at the local grammar school. He turned early to journalism, substituting newspaper reporting and radio broadcasting for further formal education. He lived with his wife and three children in the village of Laugharne on the Welsh coast.

Thomas published his first volume of poems at twenty. Several other volumes followed rapidly. Many of his unfettered early poems and eleven short stories were published in The World I Breathe (1939). Complex, brilliant, often obscure to the point of surrealism, his verses reveal rich, sensitive borrowings from Welsh bardic lore, romantic mysticism, and the Bible. "Dylan" means "wave," and the sea's ebb and flow underlie, color, and shape his sexual symbols, themes of dark violence, and images of pain and death. A lyric poet of great power, he created lulling rhythms and cadences that overflow common syntax.

Thomas literally burst on a postwar literary scene dominated by metaphysical intellectuality. Blessed with a beautifully resonant voice and a remarkable gift for oral delivery, he was at his best reading his own poetry. He made three extensive reading tours of the United States. On these tours he drew criticism for his open fondness for the bottle, an addiction which carried him off one night in a Greenwich Village tavern. His Collected Poems appeared in the same year, 1953. Moral judgments aside, few who have heard Thomas in person or on record, or have read his evocative, pulsating lyrics, will soon forget his emotional impact. (The lecture tours were dramatized by playwright Sidney Michaels in his play Dylan, with Alec Guinness as the poet in the Broadway production.)

As difficult and involved as much of his poetry might be, Thomas' prose tends to be simple, direct, humorous, moving. Certainly such terms describe the language of his autobiography, Portrait of the Artist as a Young Dog (1940); in it, Thomas tried hard to grasp those qualities basic to his time, his nation, his progenitors, and himself.

↟ ↟ ↟ ↟ ↟

One afternoon, in a particularly bright and glowing August, some years before I knew I was happy, George Hooping, whom we called Little Cough, Sidney Evans, Dan Davies, and I sat on the roof of a lorry travelling to the end of the Peninsula. It was a tall, six-wheeled lorry, from which we could spit on the roofs of the passing cars and throw our applestumps at women on the pavement. One stump caught a man on a bicycle in the middle of the back, he swerved across the road, for a moment we sat quiet and George Hooping's face grew pale. And if the lorry runs over him, I thought calmly as the man on the bicycle swayed towards the hedge, he'll get killed and I'll be sick on my trousers and perhaps on Sidney's too, and we'll all be arrested and hanged, except George Hooping who didn't have an apple.

But the lorry swept past; behind us, the bicycle drove into the hedge, the man stood up and waved his fist, and I waved my cap back at him.

'You shouldn't have waved your cap,' said Sidney Evans, 'he'll know what school we're in.' He was clever, dark, and careful, and had a purse and a wallet.

'We're not in school now.'

'Nobody can expel me,' said Dan Davies. He was leaving next term to serve in his father's fruit shop for a salary.

We all wore haversacks, except George Hooping whose mother had given him a brown-paper parcel that kept coming undone, and carried a suitcase each. I had placed a coat over my suitcase because the initials on it were 'N.T.' and everybody would know that it belonged to my sister. Inside the lorry were two tents, a box of food, a packing-case of kettles and saucepans and knives and forks, an oil-lamp, a primus stove, ground sheets and blankets, a gramophone with three records, and a table cloth from George Hooping's mother.

We were going to camp for a fortnight in Rhossilli, in a field above the sweeping five-miles beach. Sidney and Dan had stayed there last year, coming back brown and swearing, full of stories of campers' dances round the fires at midnight, and elderly girls from the training college who sunbathed naked on ledges of rocks surrounded by laughing boys, and singing in bed that lasted until dawn. But George had never left home for more than a night; and then, he told me one half-holiday when it was raining and there was nothing to do but to stay in the washhouse racing his guinea-pigs giddily along the benches, it was only to stay in St. Thomas, three miles from his house, with an aunt who could see through the walls and who knew what a Mrs. Hoskin was doing in the kitchen.

'How much further?' asked George Hooping, clinging to his split parcel, trying in secret to push back socks and suspenders, enviously watching the solid green fields skim by as though the roof were a raft on an ocean with a motor in it. Anything upset his stomach, even liquorice and sherbet, but I alone knew that he wore long combinations in the summer with his name stitched in red on them.

'Miles and miles,' Dan said.

'Thousands of miles,' I said. 'It's Rhossilli, U.S.A. We're going to camp on a bit of rock that wobbles in the wind.'

'And we have to tie the rock on to a tree.'

'Cough can use his suspenders,' Sidney said.

The lorry roared round a corner—'Upsy-daisy! Did you feel it then, Cough? It was on one wheel'—and below us, beyond fields and farms, the sea, with a steamer puffing on its far edge, shimmered.

'Do you see the sea down there, it's shimmering, Dan,' I said.

George Hooping pretended to forget the lurch of the slippery roof and, from that height, the frightening smallness of the sea. Gripping the rail of the roof, he said: 'My father saw a killer whale.' The conviction in his voice died quickly as he began. He beat against the wind with his cracked, treble voice, trying to make us believe. I knew he wanted to find a boast so big it would make our hair stand up and stop the wild lorry.

'Your father's a herbalist.' But the smoke on the horizon was the white, curling fountain the whale blew through his nose, and its black nose was the bow of the poking ship.

'Where did he keep it, Cough, in the washhouse?'

'He saw it in Madagascar. It had tusks as long as from here to, from here to . . .'

'From here to Madagascar.'

All at once the threat of a steep hill disturbed him. No longer bothered about the adventures of his father, a small, dusty, skull-capped and alpaca-coated man standing and mumbling all day in a shop full of herbs and curtained holes in the wall, where old men with backache and young girls in trouble waited for consultations in the half-dark, he stared at the hill swooping up and clung to Dan and me.

'She's doing fifty!'

'The brakes have gone, Cough!'

He twisted away from us, caught hard with both hands on the rail, pulled and trembled, pressed on a case behind him with his foot, and steered the lorry to safety round a stone-walled corner and up a gentler hill to the gate of a battered farm-house.

Leading down from the gate, there was a lane to the first beach. It was high-tide, and we heard the sea dashing. Four boys on a roof—one tall, dark, regular-featured, precise of speech, in a good suit, a boy of the world; one squat, ungainly, red-haired, his red wrists fighting out of short, frayed sleeves; one heavily spectacled, small-paunched, with indoor shoulders and feet in always unlaced boots wanting to go different ways; one small, thin, indecisively active, quick to get dirty, curly—saw their field in front of them, a fortnight's new home that had thick, pricking hedges for walls, the sea for a front garden, a green gutter for a lavatory, and a wind-struck tree in the very middle.

I helped Dan unload the lorry while Sidney tipped the driver and George struggled with the farm-yard gate and looked at the ducks inside. The lorry drove away.

'Let's build our tents by the tree in the middle,' said George.

'Pitch!' Sidney said, unlatching the gate for him.

We pitched our tents in a corner, out of the wind.

'One of us must light the primus,' Sidney said, and, after George had burned his hand, we sat in a circle outside the sleeping-tent talking about motor cars, content to be in the country, lazily easy in each other's company, thinking to ourselves as we talked, knowing always that the sea dashed on the rocks not far below us and rolled out into the world, and that to-morrow we would bathe and throw a ball on the sands and stone a bottle on a rock and perhaps meet three girls. The oldest would be for Sidney, the plainest for Dan, and the youngest for me. George broke his spectacles when he spoke to girls; he had to walk off, blind as a bat, and the next morning he would say: 'I'm sorry I had to leave you, but I remembered a message.'

It was past five o'clock. My father and mother would have finished tea; the plates with famous castles on them were cleared from the table; father with a newspaper, mother with socks, were far away in the blue haze to the left, up a hill, in a villa, hearing from the park the faint cries of children drift over the public tennis court, and wondering where I was and what I was doing. I was alone with my friends in a field, with a blade of grass in my mouth, saying, 'Dempsey would hit him cold,' and thinking of the great whale that George's father never saw thrashing on the top of the sea, or plunging underneath, like a mountain.

'Bet you I can beat you to the end of the field.'

Dan and I raced among the cowpads, George thumping at our heels.

'Let's go down to the beach.'

Sidney led the way, running straight as a soldier in his khaki shorts, over a stile, down fields to another, into a wooded valley, up through heather on to a clearing near the edge of the cliff, where two broad boys were wrestling outside a tent. I saw one bite the other in the leg, they both struck expertly and savagely at the face, one struggled clear, and, with a leap, the other had him face to the ground. They were Brazell and Skully.

'Hullo, Brazell and Skully!' said Dan.

Skully had Brazell's arm in a policeman's grip; he gave it two quick twists and stood up, smiling.

'Hullo, boys! Hullo, Little Cough! How's your father?'

'He's very well, thank you.'

Brazell, on the grass, felt for broken bones. 'Hullo, boys! How are your fathers?'

They were the worst and biggest boys in school. Every day for a term they caught me before class began and wedged me in the waste-paper-basket and then put the basket on the master's desk. Sometimes I could get out and sometimes not. Brazell was lean, Skully was fat.

'We're camping in Button's field,' said Sidney.

'We're taking a rest cure here,' said Brazell. 'And how is Little Cough these days? Father given him a pill?'

We wanted to run down to the beach, Dan and Sidney and George and I, to be alone together, to walk and shout by the sea in the country, throw stones at the waves, remember adventures and make more to remember.

'We'll come down to the beach with you,' said Skully.

He linked arms with Brazell, and they strolled behind us, imitating George's wayward walk and slashing the grass with switches.

Dan said hopefully: 'Are you camping here for long, Brazell and Skully?'

'For a whole nice fortnight, Davies and Thomas and Evans and Hooping.'

When we reached Mewslade beach and flung ourselves down, as I scooped up sand and let it trickle grain by grain through my fingers, as George peered at the sea through his double lenses and Sidney and Dan heaped sand over his legs, Brazell and Skully sat behind us like two warders.

'We thought of going to Nice for a fortnight,' said Brazell—he rhymed it with ice, dug Skully in the ribs—'but the air's nicer here for the complexion.'

'It's as good as a herb,' said Skully.

They shared an enormous joke, cuffing and biting and wrestling again, scattering sand in the eyes, until they fell back with laughter, and Brazell wiped the blood from his nose with a piece of picnic paper. George lay covered to the waist in sand. I watched the sea slipping out, with birds quarrelling over it, and the sun beginning to go down patiently.

'Look at Little Cough,' said Brazell. 'Isn't he extraordinary? He's growing out of the sand. Little Cough hasn't got any legs.'

'Poor Little Cough,' said Skully, 'he's the most extraordinary boy in the world.'

'Extraordinary Little Cough,' they said together, 'extraordinary, extraordinary, extraordinary.' They made a song out of it, and both conducted with their switches.

'He can't swim.'

'He can't run.'

'He can't learn.'

'He can't bowl.'

'He can't bat.'

'And I bet he can't make water.'

George kicked the sand from his legs. 'Yes, I can!'

'Can you swim?'

'Can you run?'

'Can you bowl?'

'Leave him alone,' Dan said.

They shuffled nearer to us. The sea was racing out now. Brazell said in a serious voice, wagging his finger: 'Now, quite truthfully, Cough, aren't you extraordinary? Very extraordinary? Say "Yes" or "No." '

'Categorically, "Yes" or "No," ' said Skully.

'No,' George said. 'I can swim and I can run and I can play cricket. I'm not frightened of anybody.'

I said: 'He was second in the form last term.'

'Now isn't that extraordinary? If he can be second he can be first. But no, that's too ordinary. Little Cough must be second.'

'The question is answered,' said Skully. 'Little Cough is extraordinary.' They began to sing again.

'He's a very good runner,' Dan said.

'Well, let him prove it. Skully and I ran the whole length of Rhossilli sands this morning, didn't we, Skull?'

'Every inch.'

'Can Little Cough do it?'

'Yes,' said George.

'Do it, then.'

'I don't want to.'

'Extraordinary Little Cough can't run,' they sang, 'can't run, can't run.'

Three girls, all fair, came down the cliff-side arm in arm, dressed in short, white trousers. Their arms and legs and throats were brown as berries; I could see when they laughed that their teeth were very white; they stepped on to the beach, and Brazell and Skully stopped singing. Sidney smoothed his hair back, rose casually, put his hands in his pockets, and walked towards the girls, who now stood close together, gold and brown, admiring the sunset with little attention, patting their scarves, turning smiles on each other. He stood in front of them, grinned, and saluted: 'Hullo, Gwyneth! do you remember me?'

'La-di-da!' whispered Dan at my side, and made a mock salute to George still peering at the retreating sea.

'Well, if this isn't a surprise!' said the tallest girl. With little studied movements of her hands, as though she were distributing flowers, she introduced Peggy and Jean.

Fat Peggy, I thought, too jolly for me, with hockey legs and tomboy crop, was the girl for Dan; Sidney's Gwyneth was a distinguished piece and quite sixteen, as immaculate and unapproachable as a girl in Ben Evan's stores; but Jean, shy and curly, with butter-coloured hair, was mine. Dan and I walked slowly to the girls.

I made up two remarks: 'Fair's fair, Sidney, no bigamy abroad,' and 'Sorry we couldn't arrange to have the sea in when you came.'

Jean smiled, wriggling her heel in the sand, and I raised my cap.

'Hullo!'

The cap dropped at her feet.

As I bent down, three lumps of sugar fell from my blazer pocket. 'I've been feeding a horse,' I said, and began to blush guiltily when all the girls laughed.

I could have swept the ground with my cap, kissed my hand gaily, called them señoritas, and made them smile without tolerance. Or I could have stayed at a distance, and this would have been better still, my hair blown in the wind, though there was no wind at all that evening, wrapped in mystery and staring at the sun, too aloof to speak to girls; but I knew that all the time my ears would have been burning, my stomach would have been as hollow and as full of voices as a shell. 'Speak to them quickly, before they go away!' a voice would have said insistently over the dramatic silence, as I stood like Valentino on the edge of the bright, invisible bull-ring of the sands. 'Isn't it lovely here!' I said.

I spoke to Jean alone; and this is love, I thought, as she nodded her head and swung her curls and said: 'It's nicer than Porthcawl.'

Brazell and Skully were two big bullies in a nightmare; I forgot them when Jean and I walked up the cliff, and, looking back to see if they were baiting George again or wrestling together, I saw that George had disappeared around the corner of the rocks and that they were talking at the foot of the cliff with Sidney and the two girls.

'What's your name?'

I told her.

'That's Welsh,' she said.

'You've got a beautiful name.'

'Oh! it's just ordinary.'

'Shall I see you again?'

'If you want to.'

'I want to alright! We can go and bathe in the morning. And we can try to get an eagle's egg. Did you know that there were eagles here?'

'No,' she said. 'Who was that handsome boy on the beach, the tall one with dirty trousers?'

'He's not handsome, that's Brazell. He never washes or combs his hair or anything. And he's a bully and he cheats.'

'I think he's handsome.'

We walked into Button's field, and I showed her inside the tents and gave her one of George's apples. 'I'd like a cigarette,' she said.

It was nearly dark when the others came. Brazell and Skully were with Gwyneth, one each side of her holding her arms. Sidney was with Peggy, and Dan walked, whistling, behind with his hands in his pockets.

'There's a pair,' said Brazell, 'they've been here all alone and they aren't even holding hands. You want a pill,' he said to me.

'Build Britain's babies,' said Skully.

'Go on!' Gwyneth said. She pushed him away from her, but she was laughing, and she said nothing when he put his arm around her waist.

'What about a bit of fire?' said Brazell.

Jean clapped her hands like an actress. Although I knew I loved her, I didn't like anything she said or did.

'Who's going to make it?'

'He's the best, I'm sure,' she said, pointing to me.

Dan and I collected sticks, and by the time it was quite dark there was a fire crackling. Inside the sleeping-tent, Brazell and Jean sat close together; her golden head was on his shoulder; Skully, near them, whispered to Gwyneth; Sidney unhappily held Peggy's hand.

'Did you ever see such a sloppy lot?' I said, watching Jean smile in the fiery dark.

'Kiss me, Charley!' said Dan.

We sat by the fire in the corner of the field. The sea, far out, was still making a noise. We heard a few nightbirds—' "To-whit! to-whoo!" Listen! I don't like owls,' Dan said, 'they scratch your eyes out!'—and tried not to listen to the soft voices in the tent. Gwyneth's laughter floated out over the suddenly moonlit field, but Jean, with the beast, was smiling and silent in the covered warmth; I knew her little hand was in Brazell's hand.

'Women,' I said.

Dan spat in the fire.

We were old and alone, sitting beyond desire in the middle of the night, when George appeared, like a ghost, in the firelight and stood there, trembling, until I said: 'Where've you been? You've been gone hours. Why are you trembling like that?'

Brazell and Skully poked their heads out.

'Hullo, Cough my boy! How's your father? What have you been up to to-night?'

George Hooping could hardly stand. I put my hand on his shoulder to steady him, but he pushed it away.

'I've been running on Rhossilli sands! I ran every bit of it! You said I couldn't, and I did! I've been running and running!'

Someone inside the tent put a record on the gramophone. It was a selection from *No, No, Nannette*.

'You've been running all the time in the dark, Little Cough?'

'And I bet I ran it quicker than you did, too!' George said.

'I bet you did,' said Brazell.

'Do you think we'd run five miles?' said Skully.

Now the tune was *Tea for Two*.

'Did you ever hear anything so extraordinary? I told you Cough was extraordinary. Little Cough's been running all night.'

'Extraordinary, extraordinary, extraordinary Little Cough,' they said.

Laughing from the shelter of the tent into the darkness, they looked like a boy with two heads. And when I stared round at George again he was lying on his back fast asleep in the deep grass and his hair was touching the flames.

✦ Suggestions for Reading and Writing

1. Does Thomas convince you that all this is the way it happened—or merely the way he later remembered it?
2. The selections by Thomas and Sancton seem to indicate that certain adolescent experiences are universal. Point out the similarities and discuss them.
3. After reading the *Portrait* entire, select a somewhat comparable American work—perhaps James Thurber's *My Life and Hard Times* (1933). Then write an essay on Welsh and American humor, with special reference to the use of irony and understatement.
4. Compare the narrator of the *Portrait* with the hero of John Malcolm Brinnin's biased but dramatic *Dylan Thomas in America* (1955).
5. Thomas' skill at verbal portraiture is revealed in his *Under Milk Wood: A Play for Voices* (1957). Following the recordings with the written text should enable an entire class to find material for fascinating character sketches.
6. Read Henry Treece's *Dylan Thomas* (1949) or Elder Olson's *The Poetry of Dylan Thomas* (1954) and in Thomas' *Collected Poems*; then try to explain Herbert Read's comment that Thomas' was "the most absolute poetry." (Listening to the poet's recordings, on the Caedmon label, will help you make your explanation.)

from

A WALKER
IN THE
CITY

Alfred Kazin

A leading literary critic, Alfred Kazin (1915–   ) is a native New Yorker with a B.S. from City College and an M.A. from Columbia. He has been an editor for the New Republic and Fortune, has received two Guggenheim Fellowships and a literature award from the National Institute of Arts and Letters (1949), and has gone on cultural missions for the State Department.

Dividing his time between teaching and writing, Kazin has lectured at, among other places, Harvard, Columbia, the New School, Smith, and Amherst. Besides editing or co-editing volumes on Blake, Fitzgerald, and Dreiser, he has written essays for the nation's best intellectual periodicals; many of these essays have been collected in The Inmost Leaf (1955) and Contemporaries (1962).

Kazin established a critical reputation in his mid-twenties with On Native Grounds: An Interpretation of Modern American Prose Literature (1942). He has also written a second autobiographical work, called Starting Out in the Thirties (1965). It continues the memoir of his Brownsville (east Brooklyn) childhood and youth described in A Walker in the City (1951), from which the following passages are taken.

Every time I go back to Brownsville it is as if I had never been away. From the moment I step off the train at Rockaway Avenue and smell the leak out of the men's room, then the pickles from the stand just below the subway steps, an instant rage comes over me, mixed with dread and some unexpected tenderness. It is over ten years since I left to live in "the city"—everything just out of Brownsville was always "the city." Actually I did not go very far; it was enough that I could leave Brownsville. Yet as I walk those familiarly choked streets at dusk and see the old women sitting in front of the tenements, past and present become each other's faces; I am back where I began.

It is always the old women in their shapeless flowered housedresses and ritual wigs I see first; they give Brownsville back to me. In their soft dumpy bodies and the unbudging way they occupy the tenement stoops, their hands blankly folded in each other as if they had been sitting on these stoops from the beginning of time, I sense again the old foreboding that all my life would be like this. *Urime Yidn. Alfred, what do you want of us poor Jews?*

The early hopelessness burns at my face like fog the minute I get off the subway. I can smell it in the air as soon as I walk down Rockaway Avenue. It hangs over the Negro tenements in the shadows of the El-darkened street, the torn and flapping canvas sign still listing the boys who went to war, the stagnant wells of candy stores and pool parlors, the torches flaring at dusk over the vegetable stands and pushcarts, the neon-blazing fronts of liquor stores, the piles of *Halvah* and chocolate kisses in the windows of the candy stores next to the *News* and *Mirror*, the dusty old drugstores where urns of rose and pink and blue colored water still swing from chains, and where next door Mr. A.'s sign still tells anyone walking down Rockaway Avenue that he has pants to fit any color suit. It is in the faces of the kids, who before they are ten have learned that Brownsville is a nursery of tough guys, and walk with a springy caution, like boxers approaching the center of the ring. Even the Negroes who have moved into the earliest slums deserted by the Jews along Rockaway Avenue have been infected with the damp sadness of the place, and slouch along the railings of their wormy wooden houses like animals in a cage. The Jewish district drains out here, but eddies back again on the next street; *they* have no connection with it. A Gypsy who lives in one of the empty stores is being reproached by a tipsy Negro in a sweater and new pearl-gray fedora who has paid her to tell his fortune. *You promis' me, didnja? Didnja promis', you lousy f . . . ?* His voice fills the street with the empty rattle of a wooden wheel turning over and over.

The smell of damp out of the rotten hallways accompanies me all the way to Blake Avenue. Everything seems so small here now, old, mashed-in, more rundown even than I remember it, but with a heart-breaking familiarity at each door that makes me wonder if I can take in anything new, so strongly do I feel in Brownsville that I am walking in my sleep. I keep bumping awake at harsh intervals, then fall back into my trance again. In the last crazy afternoon light the neons over the delicatessens bathe all their wares in a cosmetic smile, but strip the street of every personal shadow and concealment. The torches over the pushcarts hold in a single breath of yellow flame the acid smell of half-sour pickles and herrings floating in their briny barrels. There is a dry rattle of loose newspaper sheets around the cracked stretched skins of the "chiney" oranges. Through the kitchen windows along every ground floor I can already see the containers of milk, the fresh round poppy-seed evening rolls. Time for supper, time to go home. The sudden uprooting I always feel at dusk cries out in a crash of heavy wooden boxes; a dozen crates of old seltzer bottles come rattling up from the cellar on an iron roller. Seltzer is still the poor Jew's dinner wine, a mild luxury infinitely prized above the water out of the faucets; there can be few families in Brownsville that still do not take a case of it every week. It sparkles, it can be mixed with sweet jellies and syrups; besides, the water in Europe was often unclean.

. . . . .

We were of the city, but somehow not in it. Whenever I went off on my favorite walk to Highland Park in the "American" district to the north, on the border of Queens, and climbed the hill to the old reservoir from which I could look straight across to the skyscrapers of Manhattan, I saw New York as a foreign city. There, brilliant and unreal, the city had its life, as Brownsville was ours. That the two were joined in me I never knew then—not even on those glorious summer nights of my last weeks in high school when, with what an ache, I would come back into Brownsville along Liberty Avenue, and, as soon as I could see blocks ahead of me the Labor Lyceum, the malted milk and Fatima signs over the candy stores, the old women in their housedresses sitting in front of the tenements like priestesses of an ancient cult, knew I was home.

We were the end of the line. We were the children of the immigrants who had camped at the city's back door, in New York's rawest, remotest, cheapest ghetto, enclosed on one side by the Canarsie flats and on the other by the hallowed middle-class districts that showed the way to New York. "New York" was what we put last on our address, but first in thinking of the others around us. *They* were New York, the Gentiles, America; we were Brownsville—*Brunzvil,* as the old folks said—the dust of the earth to all Jews with money, and notoriously a

place that measured all success by our skill in getting away from it. So
that when poor Jews left, *even* Negroes, as we said, found it easy to settle
on the margins of Brownsville, and with the coming of spring, bands of
Gypsies, who would rent empty stores, hang their rugs around them like
a desert tent, and bring a dusty and faintly sinister air of carnival into our
neighborhood.

. . . . .

In Brownsville tenements the kitchen is always the largest room and
the center of the household. As a child I felt that we lived in a kitchen to
which four other rooms were annexed. My mother, a "home" dress-
maker, had her workshop in the kitchen. She told me once that she had
begun dressmaking in Poland at thirteen; as far back as I can remember,
she was always making dresses for the local women. She had an innate
sense of design, a quick eye for all the subtleties in the latest fashions,
even when she despised them, and great boldness. For three or four
dollars she would study the fashion magazines with a customer, go with
the customer to the remnants store on Belmont Avenue to pick out the
material, argue the owner down—all remnants stores, for some reason,
were supposed to be shady, as if the owners dealt in stolen goods—and
then for days would patiently fit and baste and sew and fit again. Our
apartment was always full of women in their housedresses sitting around
the kitchen table waiting for a fitting. My little bedroom next to the
kitchen was the fitting room. The sewing machine, an old nut-brown
Singer with golden scrolls painted along the black arm and engraved
along the two tiers of little drawers massed with needles and thread on
each side of the treadle, stood next to the window and the great coal-
black stove which up to my last year in college was our main source of
heat. By December the two outer bedrooms were closed off, and used to
chill bottles of milk and cream, cold borscht and jellied calves' feet.

The kitchen held our lives together. My mother worked in it all day
long, we ate in it almost all meals except the Passover *seder*, I did my
homework and first writing at the kitchen table, and in winter I often
had a bed made up for me on three kitchen chairs near the stove. On the
wall just over the table hung a long horizontal mirror that sloped to a
ship's prow at each end and was lined in cherry wood. It took up the
whole wall, and drew every object in the kitchen to itself. The walls were
a fiercely stippled whitewash, so often rewhitened by my father in slack
seasons that the paint looked as if it had been squeezed and cracked into
the walls. A large electric bulb hung down the center of the kitchen at
the end of a chain that had been hooked into the ceiling; the old gas ring
and key still jutted out of the wall like antlers. In the corner next to the
toilet was the sink at which we washed, and the square tub in which my
mother did our clothes. Above it, tacked to the shelf on which were

pleasantly ranged square, blue-bordered white sugar and spice jars, hung calendars from the Public National Bank on Pitkin Avenue and the Minsker Progressive Branch of the Workman's Circle; receipts for the payment of insurance premiums, and household bills on a spindle; two little boxes engraved with Hebrew letters. One of these was for the poor, the other to buy back the Land of Israel. Each spring a bearded little man would suddenly appear in our kitchen, salute us with a hurried Hebrew blessing, empty the boxes (sometimes with a sidelong look of disdain if they were not full), hurriedly bless us again for remembering our less fortunate Jewish brothers and sisters, and so take his departure until the next spring, after vainly trying to persuade my mother to take still another box. We did occasionally remember to drop coins in the boxes, but this was usually only on the dreaded morning of "mid-terms" and final examinations, because my mother thought it would bring me luck. She was extremely superstitious, but embarrassed about it, and always laughed at herself whenever, on the morning of an examination, she counseled me to leave the house on my right foot. "I know it's silly," her smile seemed to say, "but what harm can it do? It may calm God down."

The kitchen gave a special character to our lives; my mother's character. All my memories of that kitchen are dominated by the nearness of my mother sitting all day long at her sewing machine, by the clacking of the treadle against the linoleum floor, by the patient twist of her right shoulder as she automatically pushed at the wheel with one hand or lifted the foot to free the needle where it had got stuck in a thick piece of material. The kitchen was her life. Year by year, as I began to take in her fantastic capacity for labor and her anxious zeal, I realized it was ourselves she kept stitched together. I can never remember a time when she was not working. She worked because the law of her life was work, work and anxiety; she worked because she would have found life meaningless without work. She read almost no English; she could read the Yiddish paper, but never felt she had time to. We were always talking of a time when I would teach her how to read, but somehow there was never time. When I awoke in the morning she was already at her machine, or in the great morning crowd of housewives at the grocery getting fresh rolls for breakfast. When I returned from school she was at her machine, or conferring over *McCall's* with some neighborhood woman who had come in pointing hopefully to an illustration—"Mrs. Kazin! Mrs. Kazin! Make me a dress like it shows here in the picture!" When my father came home from work she had somehow mysteriously interrupted herself to make supper for us, and the dishes cleared and washed, was back at her machine. When I went to bed at night, often she was still there, pounding away at the treadle, hunched over the wheel, her hands steering a piece of gauze under the needle with a finesse that always contrasted sharply with her swollen hands and broken nails. Her left hand had been pierced through when as a girl she had worked in the infamous Triangle Shirtwaist Factory on the East Side. A needle had gone straight through the palm, severing a large vein. They had sewn it up for her so clumsily that a tuft of flesh always lay folded over the palm.

The kitchen was the great machine that set our lives running; it whirred down a little only on Saturdays and holy days. From my mother's kitchen I gained my first picture of life as a white, overheated, starkly lit workshop redolent with Jewish cooking, crowded with women in housedresses, strewn with fashion magazines, patterns, dress material, spools of thread—and at whose center, so lashed to her machine that bolts of energy seemed to dance out of her hands and feet as she worked, my mother stamped the treadle hard against the floor, hard, hard, and silently, grimly at war, beat out the first rhythm of the world for me.

Every sound from the street roared and trembled at our windows—a mother feeding her child on the doorstep, the screech of the trolley cars on Rockaway Avenue, the eternal smash of a handball against the wall of our house, the clatter of *"der Italyéner"*'s cart packed with watermelons, the sing-song of the old-clothes men walking Chester Street, the cries *"Árbes! Árbes! Kinder! Kinder! Heyse gute árbes!"* All day long people streamed into our apartment as a matter of course—"customers," upstairs neighbors, downstairs neighbors, women who would stop in for a half-hour's talk, salesmen, relatives, insurance agents. Usually they came in without ringing the bell—everyone knew my mother was always at home. I would hear the front door opening, the wind whistling through our front hall, and then some familiar face would appear in our kitchen with the same bland, matter-of-fact inquiring look: no need to stand on ceremony: my mother and her kitchen were available to everyone all day long.

At night the kitchen contracted around the blaze of light on the cloth, the patterns, the ironing board where the iron had burned a black border around the tear in the muslin cover; the finished dresses looked so frilly as they jostled on their wire hangers after all the work my mother had put into them. And then I would get that strangely ominous smell of tension from the dress fabrics and the burn in the cover of the ironing board—as if each piece of cloth and paper crushed with light under the naked bulb might suddenly go up in flames. Whenever I pass some small tailoring shop still lit up at night and see the owner hunched over his steam press; whenever in some poorer neighborhood of the city I see through a window some small crowded kitchen naked under the harsh light glittering in the ceiling, I still smell that fiery breath, that warning of imminent fire. I was always holding my breath. What I must have felt most about ourselves, I see now, was that we ourselves were like kindling—that all the hard-pressed pieces of ourselves and all the hard-used objects in that kitchen were like so many slivers of wood that might go up in flames if we came too near the white-blazing filaments in that naked bulb. Our tension itself was fire, we ourselves were forever burning—to live, to get down the foreboding in our souls, to make good.

Twice a year, on the anniversaries of her parents' deaths, my mother placed on top of the ice-box an ordinary kitchen glass packed with wax, the *yortsayt*, and lit the candle in it. Sitting at the kitchen table over my homework, I would look across the threshold to that mourning-glass, and sense that for my mother the distance from our kitchen to *der heym*, from life to death, was only a flame's length away. Poor as we were, it was not poverty that drove my mother so hard; it was loneliness—some endless bitter brooding over all those left behind, dead or dying or soon to die; a loneliness locked up in her kitchen that dwelt every day on the hazardousness of life and the nearness of death, but still kept struggling in the lock, trying to get us through by endless labor.

With us, life started up again only on the last shore. There seemed to be no middle ground between despair and the fury of our ambition. Whenever my mother spoke of her hopes for us, it was with such unbelievingness that the likes of us would ever come to anything, such abashed hope and readiness for pain, that I finally came to see in the flame burning on top of the ice-box death itself burning away the bones of poor Jews, burning out in us everything but courage, the blind resolution to live. In the light of that mourning-candle, there were ranged around me how many dead and dying—how many eras of pain, of exile, of dispersion, of cringing before the powers of this world!

It was always at dusk that my mother's loneliness came home most to me. Painfully alert to every shift in the light at her window, she would suddenly confess her fatigue by removing her pince-nez, and then wearily pushing aside the great mound of fabrics on her machine, would stare at the street as if to warm herself in the last of the sun. "How sad it is!" I once heard her say. "It grips me! It grips me!" Twilight was the bottommost part of the day, the chillest and loneliest time for her. Always so near to her moods, I knew she was fighting some deep inner dread, struggling against the returning tide of darkness along the streets that invariably assailed her heart with the same foreboding— Where? Where now? Where is the day taking us now?

Yet one good look at the street would revive her. I see her now, perched against the windowsill, with her face against the glass, her eyes almost asleep in enjoyment, just as she starts up with the guilty cry—"What foolishness is this in me!"—and goes to the stove to prepare supper for us: a moment, only a moment, watching the evening crowd of women gathering at the grocery for fresh bread and milk. But between my mother's pent-up face at the window and the winter sun dying in the fabrics—"Alfred, see how beautiful!"—she has drawn for me one single line of sentience.

. . . . . .

↑ Suggestions for Reading and Writing

1. Write a coherent summary of Kazin's emotional reactions to his youthful surroundings. Do you find his reactions fresh and real? Do you get any sense of a self-conscious literary mind at work?
2. Can you share any of Kazin's memories and experiences? Or was your own childhood so different as to make this impossible?
3. What differences in style and tone are there between Kazin's description of his youth and Dylan Thomas' of his? James Baldwin's of his? Thomas Sancton's of his? Which do you find most memorable? Why?
4. Do you recall your impressions of your neighborhood or town upon returning after a prolonged absence? Could you shape them into an interesting memoir?
5. What are the most memorable impressions of your own childhood? Do you consider them very similar to those of your contemporaries—or highly exceptional? Explain.

[OLIVER WENDELL HOLMES]

Catherine Drinker Bowen

During the past two decades Catherine Drinker Bowen
(1897–   ), born and bred in Pennsylvania, has gained recognition as one of America's most distinguished living biographers. Combining research, an unfailing sense of history,
dramatic flair, and imaginative gap-filling, she captures not only
her characters' unique qualities but the special flavor of their
time and place. Her books have won her book-club selection,
national awards, and several honorary doctorates.

Her professional interests have caused Mrs. Bowen to deal
with subjects as varied as Tchaikovsky, the Rubinsteins, and
John Adams. Her studies of Oliver Wendell Holmes, Edward
Coke, and Francis Bacon illustrate clearly her special liking for
lawyers as subjects. The following selection is from Yankee
from Olympus (1944), her life of Justice Holmes (1841–1935);
this work, which did much to establish Mrs. Bowen's literary
reputation, has also been made into a successful play and
motion picture.

✐ ✐ ✐ ✐ ✐

September, 1864 . . . A young man walks up the steps of Dane
Hall on Harvard Square, up between the white columns, through the

From Yankee from Olympus, by Catherine Drinker Bowen, by permission of Little,
Brown and Co., Atlantic Monthly Press, and Harold Ober Associates Incorporated.
Copyright 1943, 1944 by Catherine Drinker Bowen.

wide doors, and takes his seat in the lecture room of Judge Joel Parker. He is eager, but he is also more than a little confused. He is by no means sure of himself. He has only the stubborn, hazy conviction that the law is what he is going to do next and do with all his might. Within the boundaries of this conviction he is slated for hours, days, years of doubt and bitter uncertainty.

Law student, Holmes had written with a flourish three years ago in his army identification papers. On his return from the war in July of 1864 he would have liked to go over to Cambridge immediately and enroll in the Law School. But he hesitated. It was a serious step. Was the law really his objective in life—not merely the "starting point" he had called it in his class autobiography? There was one other possibility: philosophy, with the eventual goal a professorship at Harvard. Since his undergraduate days and the prize essay on Plato, Holmes's passion for philosophy had grown steadily deeper. Metaphysics, dialectics, formal logic, theories of government and theories of sovereignty: these things fascinated him. And in 1864, these were the things that lay behind the law.

The question was, should such knowledge be pursued with only itself as goal, or was it better to have a focus, a boundary, some clinical application outside the classroom such as a money-making law practice that brought a man up against the world and the living problems of the world? Mr. Robert Morse, who had a very good law practice on Pemberton Square, said Wendell was born for the law.

Wendell received this statement with skepticism. The only thing he felt born for was to use his powers to the full. Even more clearly than when he was in the army, Holmes recognized that his powers were intellectual, that he was an "internal" man, to whom ideas were more interesting than things. For three years, he had lived a life as external as it would be possible to live. He had slept on the ground, had killed men with his own hand, saved men's lives by his own hand. Now he was free, and the life of pure scholarship beckoned. But if he embraced it, if he followed in the footsteps of such a man as Emerson, might he not, at forty, find himself dwelling in a cloud land of pure speculation, his own vital force dilute in this rarefied region?

All his youth he had looked up to Emerson as the wisest man he knew. When you were young you found your hero, never doubting that you could pattern yourself upon him, follow after him. But life changed you. Or at least, the things that happened brought you to yourself. Behind Emerson's highest flights of writing, behind his most magnetic utterances, one could discern always a moral purpose. Not a narrow purpose; of all men Emerson was most tolerant.

But examining himself, Holmes felt no such crusader's impulse.

Merely, he desired to use his brain, drive it to its fullest capacity. He desired to examine and understand the laws of social being, the pattern men followed in their lives. In the law, if one dug far enough, would not one find recorded all the customs of mankind? In Wendell Holmes's day, anthropology did not exist as a science or as a study. Neither did sociology. Political economy existed—but it was a dry subject, filled with statistics. What had Carlyle called it? *The dismal science.*

You heard stories of great men and how they chose their professions. Jeremy Bentham as a young man had examined himself severely to see if he had a *genius* for anything. The answer had come clearly—"a genius for legislation." Bentham had followed that voice and because of it the course of English history had changed and was still changing. But were these stories true, about great men? Did not luck have a lot to do with it? It seemed to Wendell Holmes that success in a chosen profession depended as much upon luck as upon logic.

At home he said nothing of his plans, aware that his father had long ago studied the law and hated it. Dr. Holmes liked philosophy no better, having the scientist's mistrust for abstract speculation. It seemed to him that lawyers went about solving their problems—and what dreary problems!—in a manner both unreal and devious. He had a quotation from Gulliver about lawyers that he loved to air. "*It is a maxim among . . . lawyers, that whatever hath been done before may legally be done again: and therefore . . .*" Recollection of it kept Wendell's lips sealed. He had no wish to be preached at concerning the uselessness of lawyers and philosophers in a hard, practical world.

"What are you going to do?" Dr. Holmes asked continually. "What about science? Science is the coming thing. What about teaching? It's true the professor's chair has an insulating quality that cuts it off from contact with reality. I've said that rather well in the *Autocrat*. But combined with writing or some more practical application, teaching is a very satisfactory way to make a living."

He had talked until his wife cautioned him to be still, let Wendell alone, give him a chance for a rest and a few months' vacation before making his decision. If the war was not over by spring the boy would probably re-enlist whether he was physically fit or not. Let him have a winter free of responsibility. Give him time to look round, get flesh on his bones, heal up his nervous system.

On the first of August, Holmes was mustered out of the Twentieth Regiment in a ceremony on the Common with the other three-year men. He carried the title of Lieutenant Colonel, brevetted for "gallant and meritorious service at the battle of Chancellorsville." Afterward the Regiment marched around Faneuil Hall behind the brass band, ending up at the Apollo Gardens for beer and an excellent supper provided by the Citizens' Committee. Wendell sat by Captain Magnitzky, from Germany, who had enlisted as a private a month after reaching this country and served right through the war. Wendell was immensely fond of him. "Do not look so troubled," Magnitzky told him now. "You have done your part. You were a good soldier, Colonel Holmes. And you were not born for it. In six months, eight months, if we do not beat the Rebels you can perhaps re-enlist. Now it is time for you to forget soldiering and be a scholar. It is time for you to do for a little while the things you were born to do."

A few days later, Holmes went out to Concord to see Emerson. In the warm summer afternoon the two sat under the elms, talking earnestly. Emerson said nothing definite. He never gave advice, having too much respect for a man's freedom. He talked eloquently, passionately, about his beliefs, about the world that lay ahead after this war and the part a young man might take in rebuilding that world. Holmes was stirred. But traveling home by the cars in the summer twilight, he knew that Emerson had not reached him as once he would have reached him. About it all there had been something remote. Wendell's teeth needed a harder bite, something tougher to cut on. "You are a lawyer," Dr. Johnson had said to—somebody or other. "*Lawyers know life practically. A bookish man should always have them to converse with. They have what he wants.*"

Next morning Holmes knocked on the door of his father's study. "I am going to the Law School," he said without preamble.

Dr. Holmes looked up from his desk. "What is the use of that?" he said. "What's the use of that, Wendell? A lawyer can't be a great man."

The remark was instinctive. But if he had tried, Dr. Holmes could not have devised a statement more provocative to his son. *A lawyer can't be a great man.* To Wendell the statement combined a paternal cocksureness concerning the universe and its arrangements with a bland assurance that any son of Dr. Oliver Wendell Holmes could be a great man if he started out right. The words struck home, pointed, steel-shafted. If there had been doubts, they were resolved now. Wendell would go over to Cambridge and sign his name on the rolls at Dane Hall, not for a starting point but as a profession that would last a lifetime. . . .

His father looked at him sharply. Had Wendell heard what Dean Swift had to say about lawyers? Before Wendell could reply, Dr. Holmes reached for a book on his desk. "Here!" he said. "Gulliver is talking to the Houyhnhnms. '*It is a maxim among these lawyers, that whatever hath been done before, may legally be done again: and therefore they take special care to record all the decisions formerly made against common justice, and the general reason of mankind. These, under the name of precedents, they produce as authorities, to justify the most iniquitous opinions; and the judges never fail of directing accordingly.' "*

Highly pleased with the aptness of the allusion, the doctor returned *Gulliver* to its place. Uncle John, he continued, had tried the law and abandoned it. Had Wendell discussed a law career with Uncle John?

Wendell had, but he saw no reason for telling his father about it. Uncle John did not hate the law, he merely laughed at it. "So," Uncle John had said, "you will be nursemaid to the ambulatory will, with all its little codicils running around after it? . . . Wendell, it does not matter what career you choose. If a man is adequate in native force he probably will be happy, no matter what fate has in store for him. I think you have that adequacy. There is no reason why you should not apply it to the law as well as to anything."

Wendell Holmes did not repeat this to his father. Leaving the book-lined study, leaving Gulliver and Dr. Holmes, he went over to Cambridge and signed his name in the rolls. . . . But his father's words went with him. A *lawyer can't be a great man.* When he was ninety, Wendell Holmes would quote that phrase, adding that his father had kicked him upstairs into the law and he supposed he should be grateful.

But what Dr. Holmes had said about the law was not, Wendell knew in all fairness, dictated wholly by the personal prejudice of a man who had tried a profession and failed. There was tradition behind his remark. Not so very long ago, America had despised lawyers. Colonial America had looked upon them as mere tradesmen who earned a questionable living by cleverness and chicanery. Paid attorneys were barred from the courts, rigidly restricted as to fees and procedure. Later, lawyers rose to power simply because America desired to fit the English common law to its own local needs, and lawyers were the only men who could do it. Lawyers drafted the Constitution. John Adams was trained in the law. So were Jefferson, Madison, Monroe, John Quincy Adams. With truth, Burke had remarked in Parliament that the American Union was governed by lawyers.

Even so, the public was slow to separate statesmen from lawyers and continued to mistrust the latter. The American law had had of necessity a slow growth. The grandfather of one of Holmes's classmates—James Kent Stone—became Chancellor of New York in 1814. For the nine years that Chancellor Kent held office, not a single decision or opinion of his American predecessors was cited to him or even suggested. Now in 1864 the traditional English material, worked over for a hundred years, was becoming available in its American form. The Harvard Law School was not yet fifty years old; it had amounted to little until Judge Story had come there in '29, determined that a lawyer should have training beyond the customary apprenticeship in a lawyer's office. Two years of such apprenticeship—unless you were lucky enough to get into the office of a man of genius—usually resulted in nothing more than a good scrivener's handwriting.

But it was hard to alter custom. In 1864, the Harvard Law School was conducted very much like a lawyer's office. The three lecturers had all been practising lawyers; they shared the outlook of their day as to how their various subjects should be taught. They were all elderly men who never heard of teaching law by the case system or indeed by any system other than giving the student a text to read and commenting on it. As the life of the law lies in its application, this system was not only dull but remote. There were no requirements for admission. It was not necessary to be a college graduate or take an examination. The student could enter at any time during the winter, sit down with the others and try to catch up. When Holmes signed the register he paid exactly what a student in a law office paid: one hundred dollars for the year. At the end of eighteen months he would receive, without examination, a certificate called LL.B. which would not, of course, admit him to the bar.

Wendell Holmes had no complaint to make concerning this system. How could he, when nothing existed with which to compare it? He had read a fair amount of social theory: Montesquieu and Plato, Hume, Locke, Hobbes, John Mill, Spencer. Long ago, Thomas Jefferson had advised the law student to make all knowledge his province, to read the natural sciences, history, *belles-lettres*, criticism, rhetoric, oratory—and read from dawn until bedtime. It was a program to appeal to Wendell Holmes. Profession of the law was not a way to make money on Court Street. The law was a door opening into knowledge. It was a window, opening out on all mankind.

Sitting in Judge Parker's lecture room on a bright day of September, Holmes took out his notebook as the Judge began to speak. It was a large class; the war had not caused college enrollments to fall off. The last undergraduate class at Harvard had in fact been much larger than Wendell's own class of '61. George Morison sat just across the aisle, Sedgwick next to him; both Boston men. Peter Olney, Robert Lincoln. Strange to be a student once more—to sit, notebook in hand, waiting for the professor's voice. What an impressive-looking man Judge Parker was! Senior professor of the Law School, he had been Chief Justice of New Hampshire. His black eye shot lightning, his features were strong, he carried himself very straight. When he strode through the room and onto the platform he looked as if he were going to walk right on through the other side. He was sixty-nine; he had lectured at the school for sixteen years. A good fight was meat and drink to Parker. He was much concerned with politics and for the past two years had bitterly condemned Lincoln's use of wartime powers. Everyone knew what Judge Parker had said to the president of Dartmouth. "Sir!" roared Parker. "This modern education is all a humbug!"

President Lord had only sighed. "Judge Parker," he replied, "it is."

There was no other way to converse with Judge Parker. His knowledge of the law was vast. It was also exact, formal, and involved to the point of obscurity. Holmes had been warned not to try to understand Parker's lectures. Just get what he said into a notebook and then learn it by heart. Wendell had been scornful of this. He was no undergraduate trying to skim through college. He was a man of twenty-three who had been to the wars and desired knowledge.

But after the first twenty minutes of Joel Parker, Holmes was not so scornful of his adviser. He could not make sense of one word the Judge was saying. Holmes glanced around. Everyone else had stopped writing too. Morison looked dazed, Sedgwick's eye was glassy. Only Peter Olney leaned forward, intent, frowning. Was this the frown of understanding or the anxious pucker that goes with hopeless incomprehension? Holmes hoped it was the latter. Only last night, Harry James had told him that he had sat through an entire winter of lectures at the Law School without understanding a single word. Then he had joyfully abandoned the law. Father, Uncle John, Harry James . . . not stupid men. . . .

At home that night Wendell Holmes was unusually silent. Next day Professor Parsons lectured. And Professor Parsons, fortunately, was a different matter altogether. At sixty-seven, Parsons seemed years younger than Judge Parker. He was ruddy-cheeked and big. He liked to tell a good story and he was interested in many things outside the law—the *Free Press* which he had edited for years; Swedenborgianism, to which he was almost as ardent a convert as Mr. Henry James the elder. Parsons hated the more technical parts of the law, such as pleading and property, and did not hesitate to say so. His father had been Chief Justice of Massachusetts, his own book on contracts was getting ready its fifth edition and was so much used in the courts that a student was heard to ask if there was a statute making Parsons an authority. Even so he seemed more *litterateur* than lawyer. Holmes was drawn to him immediately.

Parsons always gave his first lecture of the year on the ethics of the profession and it always opened with the same words. The students grinned with anticipation: "*If a young lawyer pays for his sign the first year and his office rent the next, he can tell himself he is doing very well.*". . .

The third professor, Emory Washburn, was a strikingly handsome man in his early sixties. In the early days of the war Holmes had been much impressed by seeing him march up and down, gun on shoulder, guarding Cambridge Arsenal with his students. Like the other two professors, Washburn was descended from a long line of patriots. He himself had been state Senator, Judge, Whig Governor of the Commonwealth. This summer Holmes had twice seen him walking behind soldiers' funerals in the uniform of the Home Guard. The bushy gray eyebrows and side whiskers of the former Governor looked strange under a private's cap, and somehow touching. "Oh, I like to help when I can," Washburn said. He was the best lecturer in the school, he could breathe life even into Coke on Littleton and the dreadful logic of Fearne on Contingent Remainders. When he laughed you could hear him across the Yard, and the students loved him. Holmes said it was Washburn who taught him the meaning of the phrase, *enthusiasm of the lecture room*. Non-law students, seen mounting the steps of Dane Hall, explained that they were going in to hear Washburn talk law for a while.

So far, so good. Under teachers of first-rate minds, strong characters and contagious personalities, Holmes could start off with enthusiasm. He lived at his father's house on Charles Street, going back and forth to Boston in the crowded horsecars over the West Bridge, carrying large brown books to study at home—Spence and Fearne and Austin. Austin's *Jurisprudence* was new. Its second edition, published in London in 1861, had taken sudden fire from discussion of the impending Reform Bill. Austin was a Utilitarian. Lawyers said his book attempted to untangle law from ethics, to separate old theories of political sovereignty from the historical foundations of society. But the book made very unpleasant reading. Later, in London, Frederick Pollock said that Austin "dogmatized overmuch," and with typical Pollockian candor declared the author to be "uncouth and excessive," his literary manner so repulsive that even at his most accurate it was difficult to believe what he said.

Not all the books Holmes studied were British. From the Law School itself came some of the best ones: Story's commentaries, Greenleaf on Evidence, Stearns on Real Actions, Parsons on Contracts. For American jurisprudence Holmes had a book he liked: Walker's *Introduction to American Law*. It was, he said afterward, one of the two books that gave him a glimpse of what he was seeking—the law in its general, historical aspect. The other was the first volume of Spence's *Equitable Jurisdiction*.

Timothy Walker, a student at the Law School under Judge Story, had written his book as a very young man, apologizing in the preface because somebody older and wiser had not written it instead. In it he examined American law from the Bill of Rights to Civil Procedure, discussed the conflict of laws and from state to state quoted case and precedent to support him. The student was advised to shun delights and live laborious days. "Genius without toil," Holmes read on page nineteen, "may, to some extent distinguish a man elsewhere; but here he must labor, or he cannot succeed. No quickness of intuition can supply the place of patient investigation. A clear mind might determine at once what the law ought to be, but actual inspection alone can determine what the law is."

Wendell Holmes did not spurn this investigation. He reveled in it, pursued it mightily. In the students' law club—the Marshall Club, it was called—he argued cases with Olney and Lincoln. At home he continued the argument until his father, rebelling, said if Wendell went on talking law he would get out his fiddle and play against him right here in the library.

> Come you of the law, who can talk, if you please,
> Till the man in the moon will allow it's a cheese.

Did Wendell remember, his father demanded, those very apt lines from his poem written long ago for the Berkshire Jubilee? Wendell laughed. How much pleasanter his father was to get on with, now that the decision was made and he was actually committed to the law! Wendell had not looked forward to living at home. After being a captain in the army, how could he submit even outwardly to his father's authority? Yet he had no choice. He had no money, he was twenty-three. It was his business to get through Law School as cheaply as possible.

Neddy was a sophomore at Harvard, he came home only for holidays. Wendell's sister Amelia was twenty-one—a tiny, brisk creature, very congenial with her father. But Mrs. Holmes's pleasure in having her eldest son once more under her roof was extreme. It touched Dr. Holmes, made him suddenly more tolerant. When Mrs. Holmes heard Wendell's voice she came quickly into the room and sat down, watching him with an expression of such bright pleasure that Wendell turned instinctively, addressing the rest of his remarks to her. Once, while Wendell was speaking, his father got up and, putting an arm over his wife's shoulder, patted her gently, then left the room.

Mrs. Holmes was interested in every detail her son brought home from the Law School. She did not want to talk about the war, she said. She had had enough of war. Wendell had earned the right to use his mind. Let him use it then, while the chance was given him. The Rebels were not beaten; God knew what lay ahead. Mrs. Holmes was especially interested in the Marshall Club debates. Wendell had a talent for speaking, she said. Dr. Holmes did not agree, but for once he kept silence. The law was a bowl of sawdust; Wendell had undertaken to swallow it down. Let him swallow it then. His father wished him well. But what exactly was that phrase? *Sawdust without butter* . . . Some English barrister had said it to a young aspirant. *"If you can eat sawdust without butter, young man, you will be a success in the law."* He must look the phrase up, have it ready for Wendell next time the boy began to orate on the virtues of jurisprudence over against medicine, as a mind trainer.

John Ropes, coming in one evening, found Wendell sparring with his father and was hugely amused. At the end of October he wrote John Gray that Wendell seemed well and happy and had just written a sonnet for the *Transcript*—"really strong and good," Ropes added.

Actually, the sonnet sounds like bad Matthew Arnold. But compared with most of the poems in the papers and magazines of the period, it was sterling work. In the same issue was a poem called "A Sea-Shell." "Cool lips of shell, sing, sea-shell warm and sweet!". . . Even the *Atlantic Monthly* gave space, under the name of poetry, to effusions so sentimental one is astonished to see the famous names appended to them.

Wendell published his sonnet anonymously. He had loved Henry Abbott, it was good to relieve himself of the burden of debt to a comrade-at-arms:—

H. L. A.

Twentieth Massachusetts Volunteers

He steered unquestioning nor turning back,
Into the darkness and the unknown sea;
He vanished in the starless night, and we
Saw but the shining of his luminous wake.
Thou sawest light, but ah, our sky seemed black,
And all too hard the inscrutable decree,
Yet noble heart, full soon we follow thee,
Lit by the deeds that flamed along thy track. . . .

To Holmes, out of the war himself, it seemed particularly terrible to see soldiers' funerals along the streets. Day after day the muffled drums, the slow processions over Beacon Hill. The war news itself was very favorable. Atlanta captured, Jubal Early routed in Virginia. It was a good thing, too, with a Presidential election only a few weeks off. If news from the front had continued bad, Lincoln supporters would have had a hard time putting a stop to the premature peace talk. Faneuil Hall in September had been the scene of a tremendous Democratic rally.

Orators reminded the people that four years of war had failed to save the Union—and that Lincoln started the war.

On the Republican side, George Shattuck was very active. Holmes liked to see him in the public forum, vigorous, confident, with his handsome gray head, his skillful oratory of the trial lawyer. As election day approached, victory looked safe for Lincoln. Higginson was home, honorably discharged from the army, looking white and wobbly, but campaigning passionately for Lincoln. On November 8, a day of rain and wind, it was decided. "Lincoln will walk the course, God bless him!" Professor Asa Gray of Harvard wrote his friend, Charles Darwin. "Homely, ungainly Lincoln is the representative man of the country." By the middle of December, Sherman was within five miles of Savannah. It began to look as though the end were in sight. News from the front was almost pushed off the newspapers by advertisements of new petroleum and coal companies. In the early mornings Wendell saw smartly turned out broughams lining the sidewalks downtown. Ladies in furs, waiting for the brokers' offices to open so they might be first in line.

One evening in December, Mr. Robert Morse stopped in to see Wendell. He had a proposition to make. How would Wendell like to come into his office for the rest of the winter, part time of course, and see a little practical application of all this theory he was reading in Cambridge? Might do him good to handle a real writ, acquire a practical conviction of the difference between assumpsit and trover. After all, lawyers weren't made in libraries. The old apprentice system had had its points.

Wendell did not hesitate. Next Monday afternoon he sat on a high stool behind a desk in Barrister's Hall and copied wills, deeds, trusts, for three hours. He could not pretend it was invigorating work. But as the weeks wore on he was continually surprised at the speed with which Morse moved when a question was brought to him. At law school it had seemed that such questions would require weeks of argument, reference, and cross reference before a decision was reached. It left Wendell open-mouthed, he told the family at supper, to see the swift certainty with which a master of his business turned it off.

Dr. Holmes, helping himself to butter from the dish on the table, paused, knife in hand. "*Sawdust*" he murmured. "*Sawdust without butter.*" He looked up. The old gleam was in his eye. "Wendell, have you heard what the English judge said to the young man who asked how a person could recognize a real vocation for the law?"

Under the table Neddy kicked his brother swiftly. Across the table Amelia watched, her brown eyes quick as a bird's. Mrs. Holmes poured Wendell's tea, handing it to him serenely. Wendell looked at his mother; their eyes met without expression.

"No, Father," Wendell said gravely. "I haven't heard. What did the judge say to the young man who wanted to be a lawyer?"

Wendell Holmes, returning to Boston in September, 1866, expected somehow to find the whole face of nature changed. What had happened to him was important, exciting. Like many a returning traveler he never doubted the excitement would be reflected everywhere.

But it was not reflected. Here at home, things were remarkably the same. Dr. Holmes went off to Grove Street every day to lecture. He had ceased—mercifully—to play the violin, but he was writing a new novel and burned to talk about it. Neddy, a senior at Harvard, came home over the week ends. Amelia was brisk and cheerful, helping her mother with the housekeeping, going to her Sewing Circle and to such festivities as the season afforded.

The supper table listened for a night or two to the elder brother's adventures abroad, then turned eagerly to its own affairs. They had been to Nahant in the summer, in a cottage near Longfellow and Agassiz. Dr. Holmes had suffered his usual Nahant asthma. The Indians had been a real nuisance, coming in swarms for the fishing, pitching their dirty tents right against the Lodges' hedge over on the Point.

Ben Butler down in Washington wanted to impeach the President, Neddy interposed. But of course, Wendell never had been interested in politics. In England, had he continued his absurd habit of not reading the newspapers? . . . "Your grandfather, Judge Jackson, never read the newspapers," Mrs. Holmes said quickly. "At least; during the three years he was reading law I know he never looked at a paper. He told me himself."

Dr. Holmes laughed. Wendell would never lack a champion while his mother lived, he said. . . . But even his esteemed father-in-law, Judge Jackson, had the defects of his qualities. Would the Judge's daughter permit him to recall the contemporary estimate of her father?

"I remember very well," Mrs. Holmes replied serenely. "You have often reminded me. *'Law knowledge, 100 per cent adequate. Political knowledge, 30 per cent. Classical knowledge, 10 per cent. Talent, 80. Integrity, 100. Practice of law, 100 . . .'* " Mrs. Holmes paused, smiling. "*Wit, 0,*" she finished.

Never mind about Grandfather Jackson, Neddy went on. Even if Wendell didn't read newspapers, he would be interested in what was going on in Boston. Laboring men here and all over the country were combining against their employers. The Eight-hour Movement was the talk everywhere. Cousin Wendell Phillips had thrown himself into it, and orated away on platforms about how ten hours of work ruined a man's soul. There had been a printers' strike in Boston during the summer. There seemed to be an actual trend toward Federal socialism. Somebody had even suggested publishing income returns in the newspapers. It would be a sad day when our government ceased to protect the privacy of individuals. But anyway, a boss blacksmith told the commissioners at the State House that a man working only eight hours could be of more value to an employer than one who worked ten. He said when a man got too tired he used tobacco and liquor. Pure nonsense of course. A harness maker had stood up and said he couldn't fail to notice that the men who worked shorter hours were always more intelligent. . . . What did John Mill in London say about the Eight-hour Movement?

Nobody waited for Wendell's reply. Fourteen chapters of his new novel were finished, Dr. Holmes said eagerly. *The Guardian Angel,* he was going to call it. It was a kind of sequel to *Elsie Venner,* on the same theme of heredity. But he was taking a hard crack at the old-fashioned hell-fire type of clergy. Dr. Bellamy Stoker, the villain of the story, had three sermons on hell—his *sweating* sermon, his *fainting* sermon, and his *convulsion-fit* sermon. He hadn't made that up, the doctor added quickly. He had got it from an actual instance in a town in Maine back in his lecture-circuit days. The *Atlantic* probably would publish the novel serially.

"You had better be careful," Wendell told his father. "There was trouble enough about *Elsie* and the *Autocrat.* People will be calling you a Free-thinker all over again."

Dr. Holmes rubbed his small hands delightedly. "In New England they weld iron bands around the sapling elms to keep them within bounds. Your Uncle John and I, Wendell, were banded with iron in our youth. My books help me to get the iron of Calvinism out of my soul."

"Uncle John," Neddy said irrelevantly, "only goes abroad so he can have the extreme pleasure of coming back to Boston. In Venice he used to go every day to some perfectly commonplace spot and stand there. He said it reminded him of the junction of Broadway and Cambridge Streets in Cambridge. . . . Mr. Appleton told me."

Boston people were hopelessly provincial, Dr. Holmes said genially. Had Wendell noticed it, after being abroad? As he had once written Motley, your Boston man carries the Common in his head as a unit of space, the State House as the standard of architecture, and measures off men in Edward Everetts as with a yardstick. He himself had often been accused of provincialism. But he was not at all sure, for a literary man, that it was a weakness.

"They are still trying to name the new hotel," Amelia said, complacently pursuing her own line of conversation. "It is nearly finished and it is enormous. It will have a passenger elevator as big as a room.

They cannot decide between The Hub Hotel and Everett House. Father, if they name it The Hub you will have to be godfather and assist at the christening. Wasn't it you who called Boston the hub of the universe?"

Neddy fixed his sister with a cold eye. Quite a long time ago he had asked his brother a question about the eight-hour day. Was it never possible, he asked, to get an answer from this family before somebody started their irrelevant *chatter?*

Looking around the table, Wendell was amused. He had no slightest intention of telling this supper table what John Mill thought about the Eight-hour Movement. He had already told Fanny Dixwell, before he had been home forty-eight hours, every word Mill had said. Fanny did not interrupt a man to tell stories of her own. She listened attentively, her comments and questions intelligent. This family could not hold its peace for two consecutive moments. Yet, listening now to their talk, Wendell recognized, with the fresh eye of the returned traveler, that his family, while undoubtedly irritating, was very far from dull. This was not the wit of London dinner tables, but whatever it was, it had life. *Provinciality!* There was something good about it, something vigorous and plain.

"Mother!" Wendell said suddenly. His strong voice came out easily above the rest. "Did you hear what Saint Peter said to the Boston man at the pearly gates?" *

Surprisingly, the table was silent, waiting.

On a Monday morning, Holmes went down to Court Street to the office of Chandler, Shattuck and Thayer. Mr. Shattuck greeted him with enormous heartiness. Peleg Chandler, the senior partner, came out. Gray whiskers grew all around under his chin; his wing collar came up to his ears. He shook Wendell's hand. "How is your father?" he said. "No candidate from this office ever failed a Bar examination, my boy." He bowed slightly and disappeared.

George Shattuck winked. It would take a half-wit to fail the Bar examination, he said. If Holmes had sat three years in this office he would be admitted without examination. As it was, he had been to Law School instead, and the Commonwealth took no account of law schools. "Make sure you don't know too much," Shattuck said. "The examiners don't like smart young men from the Law School. I've known them to fail a man because he tried to show off. I've also known them to drive a nice little bargain, promising not to ask the candidate any question he couldn't answer if the candidate would do the same by them."

A client came in. George Shattuck vanished. Holmes stood at a loss,

* Answer: *"You won't like it here."*

looking at the rows of familiar brown books on the shelves. A heavy film of dust lay over most of them. There was dust on the long windows. In the street below, a market dray rumbled past, and from the wharf near by a steamer whistle sounded.

The inner door opened. James Bradley Thayer came out. He was ten years older than Holmes. He had got his LL.B. at Harvard in '56. Rumor said he was aiming for a professorship at the Law School. He wore his fine dark hair rather long, he had the dreamy, gentle eye of the scholar. Shattuck, it appeared, had turned over the student end of the office to Thayer. "Sit down," Thayer said. "Now, what are you after, Holmes? Admission to the Bar or perhaps a trifle more education with it? No thinking will be required at the Court House. Judge Shaw used to make them think, but the rules are changed. Only memory is required. . . . But they can lay it on pretty thick, in spite of what Shattuck says. If you get old Asaph Churchill he is partial to Coke. Wasn't Churchill in college with your father? Do you know the rule in Shelley's Case?"

That autumn, Holmes's card at the Athenaeum listed *Coke on Littleton*, Austin's *Jurisprudence*, Stephens' history of English criminal law, Gibbon, Humboldt, Mill's *Logic* again, Bracton's *Relation to the Roman Law*, Montesquieu's *Spirit of the Laws*. Holmes was fascinated by Montesquieu. Here was a lonely scholar, sitting in a library—yet his book had done as much to remodel the world as any material product of the eighteenth century. Montesquieu was an authority for the writers of the *Federalist*. He was the precursor of Burke, of modern political economy, of Adam Smith and the Mills.

Sitting in the outer room of Chandler, Shattuck and Thayer, the *Esprit des Lois* open on his knee, Holmes was struck anew with the awful power of ideas to change a world. Montesquieu commanded the future more surely from his study than Napoleon from his throne. A valid idea was worth a regiment any day. The man of action has the present, yes—but does not the thinker control the future?

Perhaps a man had to fight in a war to find that out. When you were twenty it was the Henry Abbotts, the Caspar Crowninshields—external men all—who seemed to rule the world.

But this picture Montesquieu drew of the government of England—was it valid? Montesquieu divided it into three distinct parts, the legislative, executive, judicial. Surely that was a fiction, even two centuries ago! Holmes got up, knocked on Thayer's door. . . . "Find out for yourself," Thayer said. "Read Bagehot. How well do you know Stephens on English criminal law? Have you read Reeves?"

An enormous impatience began to possess Wendell Holmes. He could not find what he wanted fast enough. On his card at the

Athenaeum appeared Bagehot on *The English Constitution,* Argyll's *Reign of Law,* Gladstone's *Reform Speeches,* McCosh on *Mill's Philosophy.* Holmes read Lecky, Phillimore's *Principles and Maxims of Jurisprudence,* Forsyth's *History of Trial by Jury,* Reeves's *History of English Law,* Palgrave's *English Commonwealth.* It seemed no more than a drop in the bucket of knowledge. His age had begun to worry him. He was nearly twenty-six. He had lost three years by the war. Men younger than he were well along now in law offices, done years ago with such puerilities as Bar examinations.

"When will you come up for examination?" Dr. Holmes asked just before Christmas. He had asked at least three times in the past month. "In the January term of Court," Wendell replied.

It was, actually, the twenty-seventh of February before George Shattuck wrote the conventional letter of recommendation, testifying to his good moral character. Holmes took it to the courthouse. His petition was filed. Asaph Churchill and Charles W. Huntington were appointed his examiners.

On a Wednesday morning, by appointment, Holmes walked up a flight of dark stairs to Mr. Churchill's office. He felt more curious than apprehensive. "Good morning, Holmes," Churchill said. "How is your father? We were at college together. Afterward, I believe he was not so successful at law as at writing verse. . . . You gentlemen from the Law School have the advantage of us. Huntington, here, and I got our law the hard way, in a lawyer's office."

Behind Churchill, Charles Huntington grinned broadly. He was a much younger man, graduate of Harvard in '54, but he had not been to Law School. Asaph Churchill motioned Holmes to be seated across the big desk. He put on his glasses. His face was serious but Holmes was conscious that Churchill was enjoying himself. "We might as well begin," Churchill said. "Huntington, with your permission . . . Now, Holmes, who owns the land between high and low water mark?"

"In Massachusetts and nowhere else," Holmes replied with equal gravity, "the land belongs to the owner of the adjoining land. . . ."

An hour later, Holmes walked out on Court Street. He felt exhilarated. They had let him off too easily, he thought. After one or two routine questions, the three had simply sat and talked law. But it was not bad fun, being examined for the Bar. He could have got through with a third of his knowledge, a fifth of it. There were six hundred lawyers in Boston. Had they all slipped through so easily?

He turned in at 4 Court Street. George Shattuck whacked him on the shoulder. "Did you know the rule in Shelley's Case, my boy?" he said. "Chandler will take you to court Monday to be sworn in. Like to go myself, but I have a client coming. This will call for celebration. Come to my house Monday evening. Bring Ropes and Gray. I will ask Parkman and Warner and Green. I have a receipt for a new gin toddy. There is nothing better for drinking the healths of newborn counsellors at law."

Monday morning was dark and gusty, with a threat of rain. Peleg Chandler, his ears entirely hidden inside his shirt collar, walked to the courthouse with Holmes. It was barely a block, on the same side of the street. The pillared granite portico was dark and high. Holmes always entered the place with a quick sensation, not so much of excitement as recognition. This courthouse was a part of him, of his background and childhood. Here Judge Loring had sentenced the runaway slaves, Sims and Burns. Manacled to these very benches, they had waited the verdict. Up these wide granite stairs, Higginson had led the mob that tried to rescue Sims. Holmes had been eight years old. He had stood at his bedroom window on Montgomery Place, three blocks away. There had been shouts, feet running on Tremont Street. . . .

Entering the wide doorway with Peleg Chandler, Holmes did not think of these things. Merely, he was conscious of them. They were part of him, and what he was about to do would make these remembered things, this dark high hallway, even more a part of him. . . .

Holmes and Chandler were early. Court sat at nine-thirty. Behind the Judge's Bench the new oaken panels shone yellow in the gaslight. There were five lawyers in court, they sat facing the Bench. Holmes recognized two of them; they nodded to him. Peleg Chandler walked back and took his seat with the spectators.

Judge Lord came in, thrust back his coattails, and sat down, looking toward Holmes, who sat alone on the petitioners' bench. Lord was nearsighted; he raised his bearded chin, his face straining slightly toward Holmes.

". . . and God save the Commonwealth and this Honorable Court," the crier finished.

There was a rustling of papers among the members of the Bar. The Clerk stood up. His voice was loud, monotonous: "The Court will attend to the taking of the oath."

Holmes came forward. It was like graduation, like walking up for your diploma, like the Brevet-Colonelship given him three years ago on the Common. It was absurd to feel so solemn. But Holmes did feel solemn. He liked ceremony. You did your work, and someone in a black gown handed you a piece of paper, bowed to you. . . .

The five lawyers stood up, so did the spectators. The room was silent. Holmes swore true faith and allegiance to the Commonwealth, swore to support the Constitution of Massachusetts and of the United States. Then with his hand on the Bible he took the Attorneys' Oath:—

I solemnly swear that I will do no falsehood nor consent to the doing of any in Court; I will not wittingly or willingly promote or sue any false, groundless or unlawful suit, nor give aid or consent to the same; I will delay no man for lucre or malice; but I will conduct myself in the office of an attorney within the Courts according to the best of my knowledge and discretion, and with all good fidelity as well to the Courts as my clients. So help me God.

Judge Lord smiled, inclined his head. "Come and sign the Bar Book," Peleg Chandler said. It was in the next room, on a high desk against the wall. At the bottom of the page was room for one more name. There were twelve names inscribed in this January term of court. Most of them, Holmes noted, were from the Law School. Horace Graves, Josiah Bellows . . .

Holmes signed his name carefully. There was no flourish to the way he did it. Peleg Chandler peered over his shoulder. "Horace Graves," he read. "Promising fellow, Graves. I knew his father. Well well, Holmes! You can have a sign on your door now. Be sure you bring us in some clients."

For Peleg Chandler, this was unusually facetious. Holmes put down the pen, turned, and followed Shattuck's senior partner to the door. On the portico, rain drove through the pillars, wind blew back the skirts of Chandler's overcoat. Turning up his coat collar, Holmes descended the steps and followed Peleg Chandler down the gray slope of Court Street.

A week later, the secretary of the class of '61, Harvard University, received a small card in the mail:—

OLIVER WENDELL HOLMES, JR. [it read]
Counsellor at Law
4 Court Street, Boston.

↗ Suggestions for Reading and Writing

1. Holmes here views himself as an "internal" person, "to whom ideas were more interesting than things." Is this—or the reverse—true of you? Explain.
2. Defend or attack Holmes's opinion "that success in a chosen profession depended as much upon luck as upon logic."
3. Mrs. Bowen has been accused of writing the father down in order to write the son up. Read and compare her *Yankee from Olympus* and Eleanor Tilton's *Amiable Autocrat: A Biography of Dr. Oliver Wendell Holmes* (1947) and evaluate the charge.

4. An interesting comparative paper in biographical method, style, and effect should result from a joint study of Mrs. Bowen's *John Adams and the American Revolution* (1950) and C. Page Smith's *John Adams* (1962).

5. Mrs. Bowen's dual interest in law and language is evident in a 1951 lecture before the Brandeis Society; it is available as a pamphlet entitled *The Lawyer and the King's English*. Use it as the basis for an analysis of the selection you have just read. You might also use it as a springboard into more specialized studies, such as Alpheus T. Mason's *Brandeis: A Free Man's Life* (1946), Samuel J. Konefsky's *The Legacy of Holmes and Brandeis* (1956), or Mark A. De Wolfe Howe's *Justice Holmes: The Shaping Years* (1957).

6. Mrs. Bowen has presented her professional creed in her book *Adventures of a Biographer* (1959) and in a printed lecture, *The Writing of Biography* (1951). After reading them, discuss how well she applies her theories in her books *The Lion and the Throne* (1956) or *Francis Bacon: The Temper of a Man* (1963).

NOTES
OF A
NATIVE
SON

James Baldwin

Born and raised in Harlem, James Baldwin (1924–   ) has emerged during the past decade as a major novelist and essayist and a spokesman for American Negroes. Indeed, the Negro's social and spiritual role in American life is at the center of most of his writings. Three of his six books are novels: the partially autobiographical Go Tell It on the Mountain (1953), Giovanni's Room (1956), and Another Country (1961). Each attempts to shatter the stereotyped characterizations and themes of the conventional Negro novel.

Baldwin's essays have attracted even more critical and public attention than his fiction. Impassioned, condemnatory, tightly reasoned, and autobiographical, they have been collected in three widely discussed volumes: Notes of a Native Son (1955; from which the following selection is taken), Nobody Knows My Name: More Notes of a Native Son (1961), and The Fire Next Time (1963). Despite being controversial, Baldwin has won literary grants, awards, and fellowships from, among others, the Eugene F. Saxton Memorial Trust (1945), the Guggenheim Foundation (1954), Partisan Review (1956), the National Institute of Arts and Letters (1956), Best American Short Stories (1958 and 1961), and the O. Henry Awards (1959).

After a decade in Paris as an expatriate, Baldwin returned to this country a few years ago to gain new recognition as a lecturer and a playwright. His plays Blues for Mr. Charlie and The Amen Corner were produced in 1964 and praised by the critics.

↑   ↑   ↑   ↑   ↑

I

On the twenty-ninth of July, in 1943, my father died. On the same day, a few hours later, his last child was born. Over a month before this, there had been, in Detroit, one of the bloodiest race riots of the century. A few hours after my father's funeral, a race riot broke out in Harlem. On the morning of August third we drove him to the graveyard through a wilderness of smashed plate glass.

The day of my father's funeral had also been my nineteenth birthday. It seemed to me that God Himself had devised, to mark my father's end, the most sustained and brutally dissonant of codas. And it seemed to me, too, that the violence which rose all about us as my father left the world had been devised as a corrective for the pride of his eldest son. I had inclined to be contemptuous of my father for the conditions of his life, for the conditions of our lives. When his life had ended I began to wonder about that life and also, in a new way, to be apprehensive about my own.

I had not known my father very well. We had got on badly, partly because we shared, in our different fashions, the vice of stubborn pride. When he was dead I realized that I had hardly ever spoken to him. It seems to be typical of life in America, where nothing, as yet, is stratified, and where opportunities, real and fancied, are thicker than anywhere else on the globe, that the second generation has no time to talk to the first. No one, including my father, seems to have known exactly how old he was, but his mother had been born during slavery. He was of the first generation of free men. He, along with thousands of other Negroes, came North after 1919 and I was part of that generation which had never seen the landscape of what Negroes sometimes called the Old Country.

He had been born in New Orleans and had been a young man there during the time that Louis Armstrong, a boy, was running errands for the dives and honky-tonks of what was always presented to me as one of the most wicked of cities. He was, I think, very handsome. Handsome, proud, and ingrown, "like a toenail," somebody said. But he looked to me, as I grew older, like pictures I had seen of African tribal chieftains: he really should have been naked, with warpaint on and barbaric mementos, standing among spears. He could be chilling in the pulpit and indescribably cruel in his personal life and he was certainly the most bitter man I have ever met; yet it must be said that there was something else buried in him, which lent him his tremendous power and, even, a rather crushing charm. It had something to do with his blackness, I think—he was very black—and his beauty, and the fact that he knew that he was black but did not know he was beautiful.

He claimed to be proud of his blackness but it had also been the cause of much humiliation. He was not a young man when we were growing up and he had already suffered many kinds of ruin; in his outrageously demanding and protective way he loved his children, who were black like him and menaced like him; and all these things sometimes showed in his face when he tried, never to my knowledge with any success, to establish contact with any of us.

When he took one of his children on his knee to play with them, they always became fretful and began to cry; when he tried to help one of us with our homework, the absolutely unabating tension which emanated from him caused our minds and our tongues to become paralyzed, so that he, scarcely knowing why, flew into a rage and the child, not knowing why, was punished. If it ever entered his head to bring a surprise home for his children, it was, almost unfailingly, the wrong surprise, and even the big watermelons he often brought home on his back in the summer led to the most appalling scenes.

I do not remember, in all those years, that a single one of his children was ever glad to see him come home. From what I was able to gather of his early life, it seemed that this inability to establish contact with other people had always marked him. There was something in him, therefore, groping and tentative, which was never expressed. One saw it most clearly when he was facing new people and hoping to impress them. But he never did, not for long. We went from church to smaller and more improbable church, he found himself in less and less demand as a minister, and by the time he died none of his friends had come to see him for a long time. He had lived and died in an intolerable bitterness of spirit and it frightened me, as we drove him to the graveyard through those unquiet, ruined streets, to see how powerful and overflowing this bitterness could be and to realize that it now was mine.

When he died I had been away from home for a little over a year. In that year I had had time to become aware of the meaning of all my father's warnings, had discovered the secret of his proudly pursed lips and rigid carriage: I had discovered the weight of white people in the world.

He had been ill a long time—in the mind, as we now realized, reliving instances of his fantastic intransigence in the new light of his affliction and endeavoring to feel a sorrow for him which never, quite, came true. We had not known that he was being eaten up by paranoia, and the discovery that his cruelty, to our bodies and our minds, had been one of the symptoms of his illness was not, then, enough to enable us to forgive him. The younger children felt, quite simply, relief that he would not be coming home any more. My mother's observation that it was he, after all, who had kept them alive all these years meant nothing because the problems of keeping children alive are not real for children. The older children felt, with my father gone, that they could invite their friends to the house without fear of insult.

His illness was beyond all hope of healing before anyone realized that he was ill. He had always been so strange and had lived, like a prophet, in such unimaginably close communion with the Lord that his long silences, punctuated by moans and hallelujahs and snatches of old songs while he sat at the living-room window, never seemed odd to us. It was not until he refused to eat because, he said, his family was trying to poison him that my mother was forced to accept as a fact what had, until then, been only an unwilling suspicion. When he was committed, it was discovered that he had tuberculosis, and the disease of his mind allowed the disease of his body to destroy him. For the doctors could not force him to eat, either, and, though he was fed intravenously, it was clear from the beginning that there was no hope for him.

In my mind's eye I could see him sitting at the window, locked up in his terrors; hating and fearing every living soul, including his children who had betrayed him too, by reaching toward the world which had despised him. There were nine of us. I began to wonder what it could have felt like for such a man to have had nine children whom he could barely feed. He spent great energy keeping us away from the people who surrounded us, people who had all-night rent parties to which we listened when we should have been sleeping, people who cursed and drank and flashed razor blades on Lenox Avenue. He could not understand why, if they had so much energy to spare, they could not use it to make their lives better. He treated almost everybody on our block with a most uncharitable asperity and neither they, nor, of course, their children were slow to reciprocate.

The only white people who came to our house were welfare workers and bill collectors. It was clear that my father felt their very presence in his home to be a violation: this was conveyed by his carriage, almost ludicrously stiff, and by his voice, harsh and vindictively polite. When I was around nine or ten I wrote a play which was directed by a young, white schoolteacher named Orilla Miller, who then took an interest in me, gave me books to read, and decided to take me to see what she somewhat tactlessly referred to as "real" plays. Theater-going was forbidden in our house, but, with the really cruel intuitiveness of a child, I suspected that the color of this woman's skin would carry the day for me. When, at school, she suggested taking me out, I agreed that she should pick me up at my house one evening. I then, very cleverly, left all the rest to my mother, who suggested to my father, as I knew she would, that it would not be very nice to let such a kind woman make the trip for nothing. Also, since it was a schoolteacher, I imagine that my mother countered the idea of sin with the idea of "education," which word, even with my father, carried a kind of bitter weight.

Before the teacher came, my father took me aside to ask *why* she was coming, what *interest* she could possibly have in a boy like me. And I understood that my father was waiting for me to say something—I didn't quite know what; perhaps that I wanted his protection against this teacher and her "education."

I said none of these things and the teacher came and we went out. It was clear, during the brief interview in our living-room, that my father would have refused permission if he had dared. The fact that he did not dare caused me to despise him; I had no way of knowing that he was facing in that living-room, a wholly unprecedented and frightening situation.

Later, when my father had been laid off from his job, this woman went to a great deal of trouble to be of help to us. My mother called her by the highest name she knew; she said she was a "Christian." My father could scarcely disagree but during the four or five years of our relatively close association he never trusted her. In later years, particularly when it began to be clear that this "education" of mine was going to lead me to perdition, he became more explicit and warned me that my white friends in high school were not really my friends and that I would see, when I was older, how white people would do anything to keep a Negro down. Some of them could be nice, he admitted, but none of them were to be trusted. I did not feel this way and I was certain, in my innocence, that I never would.

But the year which preceded my father's death had made a great change in my life. I had been living in New Jersey, working in defense plants, working and living among Southerners, white and black. I knew about the South, of course, and how Southerners treated Negroes and expected them to behave; but it had never entered my mind that anyone would look at me and expect *me* to behave that way. I learned in New Jersey that to be a Negro meant, precisely, that one was never looked at but was simply at the mercy of the reflexes the color of one's skin caused in other people. I acted in New Jersey as I had always acted, that is as though I thought a great deal of myself—I had to *act* that way—with results that were, simply, unbelievable. I had scarcely arrived before I had earned the enmity of all my superiors and nearly all my co-workers. In the beginning, to make matters worse, I simply did not know what was happening, I did not know what I had done, and I shortly began to wonder what *anyone* could possibly do, to bring about such unanimous, active, and unbearably vocal hostility.

I knew about Jim Crow but I had never experienced it. I went to the same self-service restaurant three times and stood with all the Princeton boys before the counter; it was always an extraordinarily long time before anything was set before me; but it was not until the fourth visit that I learned that, in fact, nothing had ever been set before me: I had simply picked something up. Negroes were not served there, I was told, and they had been waiting for me to realize that I was always the only Negro present.

It was the same story all over New Jersey, in bars, bowling alleys, diners, places to live. I very shortly became notorious and children giggled behind me when I passed and their elders whispered or shouted—they really believed that I was mad. And it did begin to work on my mind, of course; I began to be afraid to go anywhere and to compensate for this I went places to which I really should not have gone and where, God knows, I had no desire to be.

My reputation in town naturally enhanced my reputation at work, and my working day became one long series of acrobatics designed to keep me out of trouble. I was fired once and contrived, with the aid of a friend from New York, to get back on the payroll; was fired again, and bounced back again. It took a while to fire me for the third time, but the third time took.

That year in New Jersey lives in my mind as though it were the year during which my veins were, daily, pumped full of poison. Or, as though it were the year in which, having an unsuspected predilection for it, I first contracted some dread, chronic disease, the unfailing symptoms of which are a kind of blind fever, a pounding in the skull, and fire in the bowels. Once this disease is contracted, it can, without an instant's warning, recur at any moment. There is not a Negro alive who does not have this rage in his blood—one has the choice, merely, of living with it consciously or surrendering to it. As for me, this fever has recurred in me, and does, and will until the day I die.

My last night in New Jersey, a white friend took me to the nearest big town, Trenton. Almost every detail of that night stands out very clearly in my memory. I even remember the name of the movie we saw because its title impressed me as being so aptly ironical. It was about the German occupation of France, and it was called "This Land Is Mine." I remember the name of the diner we walked into when the movie ended: the *American Diner*. The counterman asked what we wanted and I remember answering with the casual sharpness which had become my habit: "We want a hamburger and a cup of coffee, what do you think we want?"

I do not know why, after a year of such rebuffs, I completely failed to anticipate his answer, which was, of course, "We don't serve Negroes here." I made some sardonic comment about the name of his diner, and we walked out into the streets.

This was the time of the "brown-out," when the lights in all American cities were very dim. When we re-entered the streets something happened to me which had the force of an optical illusion, or a nightmare. People were moving in every direction but it seemed to me, in that instant, that all of the people I could see, and many more, were moving toward me, against me, and that everyone was white. I remember how their faces gleamed. And I felt, like a physical sensation, a *click* at the nape of my neck as though some interior string connecting my head to my body had been cut. I began to walk. I heard my friend call after me, but I ignored him. Heaven only knows what was going on in his mind, but he had the good sense not to touch me—I don't know what would have happened if he had—and to keep me in sight.

I don't know what was going on in my mind, either—I certainly had no conscious plan. I wanted to do something to crush these white faces, which were crushing me. I walked until I came to an enormous, glittering restaurant in which I knew not even the intercession of the

Virgin would cause me to be served. I pushed through the doors and took the first vacant seat I saw, at a table for two, and waited.

I rather wonder what I could possibly have looked like. Whatever I looked like, I frightened the waitress who shortly appeared, and the moment she appeared all of my fury flowed toward her. I felt that if she found a black man so frightening I would make her fright worthwhile.

She did not ask me what I wanted, but repeated, as though she had learned it somewhere, "We don't serve Negroes here." She did not say it with the blunt, derisive hostility to which I had grown so accustomed, but rather with a note of apology in her voice and fear. This made me colder and more murderous than ever. I felt I had to do something with my hands. I wanted her to come close enough for me to get her neck between my hands.

So I pretended not to have understood her, hoping to draw her closer. And she did step a very short step closer, with her pencil poised incongruously over her pad, and repeated the formula: " . . . don't serve Negroes here."

Somehow, with the repetition of that phrase, I realized that she would never come any closer. There was nothing on the table but an ordinary mug, half full of water, and I picked this up and hurled it at her. She ducked and it shattered against the mirror behind the bar. With that sound, my frozen blood abruptly thawed, I returned from wherever I had been, I *saw*, for the first time, the restaurant, the people, with their mouths open, already, as it seemed to me, rising as one man, and I realized what I had done, and I was frightened. I rose and began running for the door. A round, potbellied man grabbed me by the nape of the neck and began to beat me about the face. I kicked him and got loose and ran into the streets. My friend whispered *"Run!"* and I ran.

My friend stayed outside the restaurant long enough to misdirect my pursuers. I do not know what I said to him when he came to my room that night. I felt, in the oddest, most awful way, that I had somehow betrayed him. I lived it over and over and over again. I could not get over two facts, both equally difficult for the imagination to grasp, and one was that I could have been murdered. But the other was that I had been ready to commit murder. My life, my real life, was in danger, and not from anything other people might do but from the hatred I carried in my own heart.

II

I returned home around the second week in June—in great haste because it seemed that my father's death and my mother's confinement were both but a matter of hours. In the case of my mother, it soon became clear that she had simply made a miscalculation. I don't believe that a single one of us arrived in the world, or has since arrived anywhere else, on time. But none of us dawdled so intolerably about the business of being born as did my baby sister. We sometimes amused ourselves, during those endless stifling weeks, by picturing the baby sitting in the safe, warm dark, bitterly regretting the necessity of becoming a part of our chaos and stubbornly putting it off as long as possible.

Death, however, sat as purposefully at my father's bedside as life stirred within my mother's womb, and it was harder to understand why he so lingered in that long shadow. It seemed that he had bent, and for a long time, too, all of his energies toward dying. Now death was ready for him but my father held back.

All of Harlem, indeed, seemed to be infected by waiting. I had never before known it to be so violently still. Racial tensions throughout this country were exacerbated during the early years of the war, partly because the labor market brought together hundreds of thousands of ill-prepared people and partly because Negro soldiers, regardless of where they were born, received their military training in the South. What happened in defense plants and Army camps had repercussions, naturally, in every Negro ghetto. The Harlem police force had been augmented in March, and the unrest grew. Perhaps the most revealing news item, out of the steady parade of reports of muggings, stabbings, shootings, assaults, gang wars, and accusations of police brutality, was the item about six Negro girls who set upon a white girl in the subway because, as they all too accurately put it, she was stepping on their toes. Indeed she was, all over the nation.

I had never before been so aware of policemen, on foot, on horseback, on corners, everywhere, always two by two. Nor had I ever been so aware of small knots of people. Never, when I passed these groups, did the usual sound of a curse or a laugh ring out. Neither did there seem to be any hum of gossip. There was certainly, on the other hand, occurring between them communication extraordinarily intense.

Another thing that was striking was the unexpected diversity of the people who made up these groups. Usually one would see a group of sharpies standing on the street corner, or a group of older men, usually, for some reason, in the vicinity of a barber shop, discussing baseball scores, or the numbers, or the women they had known. Women, in a general way, tended to be seen less often together—unless they were church women, or very young girls, or prostitutes. But that summer I saw the strangest combinations: large, respectable, churchly matrons standing on the stoops or the corners with their hair tied up, together with a girl in sleazy satin whose face bore the marks of gin and the razor, or heavy-set, abrupt, no-nonsense older men in company with the most disreputable and fanatical "race" men, or these same "race" men with the sharpies, or these sharpies with the churchly women. And on each face these seemed to be the same strange, bitter shadow.

The churchly women and the matter-of-fact no-nonsense men had children in the Army. The sleazy girls they talked to had lovers there; the sharpies and the "race" men had friends and brothers there. It would have demanded an unquestioning patriotism, happily as uncommon in this country as it is undesirable, for these people not to have been disturbed by the letters they received, by the newspaper stories they read. It was only the "race" men, to be sure, who spoke ceaselessly of being revenged—how this vengeance was to be exacted was not clear—for the indignities and dangers suffered by Negro boys in uniform; but everybody felt a directionless, hopeless bitterness, as well as that panic which can scarcely be suppressed when one knows that a human being one loves is beyond one's reach, and in danger. Perhaps the best way to sum all this up is to say that the people I knew felt, mainly, a peculiar kind of relief when they knew that their boys were being shipped out of the South, to do battle overseas. Now, even if death should come, it would come with honor and without the complicity of their countrymen. Such a death would be, in short, a fact with which one could hope to live.

It was on the twenty-eighth of July that I visited my father for the first time during his illness and for the last time in his life. The moment I saw him I knew why I had put off this visit so long. I had told my mother that I did not want to see him because I hated him. But this was not true. It was only that I *had* hated him and I wanted to hold on to this hatred. I did not want to look on him as a ruin; it was not a ruin I had hated. I imagine that one of the reasons people cling to their hates so stubbornly is that they sense, once hate is gone, that they will be forced to deal with pain.

We traveled out to him, his older sister and myself, to what seemed to be the very end of Long Island. It was hot and dusty and we wrangled all the way out over the fact that I had recently begun to smoke and, as my aunt said, to give myself airs. But I knew that she wrangled with me because she could not bear to face the fact of her brother's dying. Neither could I endure the reality of her despair, her unstated bafflement as to what had happened to her brother's life, and her own. From time to time she fell into a heavy reverie. Covertly, I watched her face, which was the face of an old woman; soon she would be dying, too.

In my childhood—it had not been so long ago—I had thought her beautiful. At one time one of my brothers and myself had thought of running away to live with her. Now she made me feel pity and revulsion and fear; it was awful to realize that she no longer caused me to feel affection.

She began to cry the moment we entered the hospital room and she saw him lying there, all shriveled and still, like a little black monkey. The great, gleaming apparatus which fed him and would have compelled him to be still even if he had been able to move brought to mind, not beneficence, but torture; the tubes entering his arm made me think of colored pictures I had seen when a child of Gulliver tied down by the pygmies. My aunt wept and wept, there was a whistling sound in my father's throat; nothing was said; he could not speak.

I wanted to take his hand, to say something. But I do not know what I could have said, even if he could have heard me. He was not really in that room with us, he had at last really embarked on his journey; and though my aunt told me that he said he was going to meet Jesus, I did not hear anything except that whistling in his throat.

In the morning came the telegram saying that he was dead. Then the house became absolutely hideous with relatives, friends, hysteria, and confusion, and I left my mother and the children to the care of those impressive women who, in Negro communities at least, automatically appear at times of bereavement armed with lotions, proverbs, and patience, and an ability to cook. I went downtown. By the time I returned, later the same day, my mother had been carried to the hospital and the baby had been born.

III

For my father's funeral I had nothing black to wear and this posed a nagging problem all day long. It was one of those problems to which the mind insanely clings in order to avoid the mind's real trouble. I spent most of that day at the downtown apartment of a girl I knew, celebrating my birthday with whisky and wondering what to wear that night. This girl had anticipated taking me out for a big dinner and a night club afterward. Sometime during the course of that long day we decided that we would go out anyway, when my father's funeral service was over. I imagine I decided it, since, as the funeral hour approached, it became clearer and clearer to me that I would not know what to do with myself when it was over. The girl found a black shirt for me somewhere and ironed it, and dressed in the darkest pants and jacket I owned, and slightly drunk, I got to my father's funeral.

The chapel was full, but not packed, and very quiet. There were, mainly, my father's relatives, and his children, and here and there I saw faces I had not seen since childhood, the faces of my father's friends. Chief among the mourners was my aunt, who had quarreled with my father all his life. I suppose that she was one of the few people in the world who had loved him, and their incessant quarreling proved, precisely, the strength of the tie that bound them. The only other person in the world, as far as I knew, whose relationship to my father rivaled my aunt's in depth was my mother, who was not there.

It seemed to me that it was a very long funeral. But it was, if anything, a rather shorter funeral than most, nor, since there were no overwhelming, uncontrollable expressions of grief, could it be called—if I dare use the word—successful. The minister who preached my father's funeral sermon was one of the few my father had still been seeing as he neared his end. He presented to us in his sermon a man whom none of us had ever seen—a man thoughtful, patient, and forbearing, a Christian inspiration to all who knew him, and a model for his children. And no doubt the children, in their disturbed and guilty state, were almost ready to believe this: he had been remote enough to be anything.

His sister moaned and this was taken as corroboration. The other faces held a dark, noncommittal thoughtfulness. This was not the man they had known, but they had scarcely expected to be confronted with *him*; this was, in a sense deeper than questions of fact, the man they had not known, and the man they had not known may have been the real one. The real man, whoever he had been, had suffered and now he was dead; this was all that was sure and all that mattered now.

While the preacher talked and I watched the children—years of changing their diapers, scrubbing them, slapping them, taking them to school, and scolding them had had the perhaps inevitable result of making me love them, though I am not sure I knew this then—my mind was busily breaking out with a rash of disconnected impressions. Snatches of popular songs, indecent jokes, bits of books I had read, movie sequences, faces, voices, political issues—I thought I was going mad; all these impressions suspended, as it were, in the solution of the faint nausea produced in me by the heat and liquor. For a moment I had the impression that my alcoholic breath, inefficiently disguised with chewing gum, filled the entire chapel. Then someone began singing one of my father's favorite songs and, abruptly, I was with him, sitting on his knee, in the hot, enormous, crowded church which was the first church we attended. It was the Abyssinia Baptist Church on 138th Street. We had not gone there long.

With this image, a host of others came. I had forgotten, in the rage of my growing up, how proud my father had been of me when I was little. Apparently, I had a voice and my father had liked to show me off before the members of the church. I had forgotten what he had looked like when he was pleased but now I remembered that he had always been grinning with pleasure when my solos ended. I even remember certain expressions on his face when he teased my mother—had he loved her? I would never know. And when had it all begun to change? For now it seemed that he had not always been cruel. I remembered being taken for a haircut and scraping my knee on the foot rest of the barber's chair and I remembered my father's face as he soothed my crying and applied the stinging iodine. Then I remembered our fights, fights which had been of the worst possible kind because my own technique had been silence.

I remembered the one time in all our life together when we had ever really spoken to each other.

It was on a Sunday and it must have been shortly before I left home. We were walking, just the two of us, in our usual silence, to or from church. I was in high school and had been doing a lot of writing. But I had also been a Young Minister and had been preaching from the pulpit. Lately, I had been taking fewer engagements and preached as rarely as possible.

My father asked me abruptly, "You'd rather write than preach, wouldn't you?"

I was astonished at his question—because it was a real question. I answered, "Yes."

That was all we said. It was awful to remember that that was all we had *ever* said.

The casket now was opened and the mourners were being led up the aisle to look for the last time on the deceased. The assumption was that the family was too overcome with grief to make this journey alone. I disapproved of forcing the children to look on their dead father, considering that the shock of his death, or, more truthfully, the shock of death as a reality, was already a little more than a child could bear, but my judgment in this matter had been overruled and there they were, bewildered and frightened and very small, being led, one by one, to the casket. But there is also something very gallant about children at such moments. It has something to do with their silence and gravity and with the fact that one cannot help them. Their legs, somehow, seem *exposed*, so that it is at once incredible and terribly clear that their legs are all they have to hold them up.

I had not wanted to go to the casket myself and I certainly had not wished to be led there, but there was no way of avoiding either of these forms. One of the deacons led me up and I looked on my father's face. I cannot say that it looked like him at all. His blackness had been equivocated by powder and there was no suggestion in that casket of what his power had, or could have been. He was simply a corpse, and it was hard to believe that he had ever given anyone either joy or pain. Yet his life filled that room. Further up the avenue his wife was holding his new-born child. Life and death so close together, and love and hatred, and right and wrong, said something to me which I did not want to hear concerning man, concerning the life of man.

After the funeral, while I was downtown, desperately celebrating my birthday, a Negro soldier in the lobby of the Hotel Braddock got into a fight with a white policeman over a Negro girl. This was certainly not the first time such an incident had occurred. It was destined, however, to receive an unprecedented publicity, for it ended with the shooting of the soldier. Rumor, flowing immediately to the streets outside, stated that the soldier had been shot in the back, and that he had died protecting a Negro woman. The facts were somewhat different—the soldier had not been shot in the back, and was not dead—but no one was interested in the facts. They preferred the invention because it expressed and corroborated their hates and fears so perfectly. It is just as well to remember that people are always doing this. Perhaps many of those legends, including Christianity, to which the world clings, began their conquest of the world with just some such concerted surrender to distortion. The effect, in Harlem, of this particular legend was like the effect of a lit match in a tin of gasoline. The mob gathered before the doors of the Hotel Braddock simply began to swell and to spread in every direction, and Harlem exploded.

The mob did not cross the ghetto lines. It seems to have been mainly interested in something more potent and real than the white face, that is, in white power, and the principal damage was to white business establishments in Harlem. It might have been a far bloodier story, of course, if, at the hour the riot began, these establishments had still been open. Bars, stores, pawnshops, restaurants, even little luncheonettes were smashed open and looted—looted, it might be added, with more haste than efficiency. Cans of beans and soup and dog food, along with toilet paper, corn flakes, sardines, and milk, tumbled every which way, and abandoned cash registers and cases of beer leaned crazily out of the splintered windows and were strewn along the avenues. Sheets, blankets, and clothing of every description formed a kind of path, as though people had dropped them while running. I truly had not realized that Harlem *had* so many stores until I saw them all smashed open; the first time the word *wealth* ever entered my mind in relation to Harlem was when I saw it scattered in the streets. But one's first, incongruous impression of plenty was countered immediately by an impression of waste. It would have been better to have left the plate glass as it had been and the goods lying in the stores.

It would have been better, but it would also have been intolerable, for Harlem had needed something to smash. To smash something is the ghetto's chronic need—most of the time it is the members of the ghetto who smash each other, and themselves. But as long as the ghetto walls are standing there will always come a moment when these outlets do not work. If ever, indeed, the violence which fills Harlem's churches, pool-halls, and bars erupts outward in a more direct fashion, Harlem and its citizens are likely to vanish in an apocalyptic flood.

That this is not likely to happen is due to a great many reasons, most hidden and powerful among them the Negro's real relation to the white American. This relation prohibits, simply, anything as uncomplicated and satisfactory as pure hatred. In order really to hate white people, one has to blot so much out of the mind—and the heart—that this hatred itself becomes an exhausting and self-destructive pose. But this does not mean that love comes easily; the white world is too powerful, too complacent, too ready with gratuitous humiliation, and, above all, too ignorant and too innocent for that. One is absolutely forced to make perpetual qualifications and one's own reactions are always canceling each other out. It is this, really, which has driven so many people mad, both white and black. One is always in the position of having to decide between amputation and gangrene. Amputation is swift but time may prove that the amputation was not necessary—or one may delay the amputation too long. Gangrene is slow, but it is impossible to be sure that one is reading one's symptoms right. The idea of going through life as a cripple is more than one can bear, and equally unbearable is the risk of swelling up slowly, in agony, with poison. And the trouble, finally, is that the risks are real even if the choices do not exist.

But "As for me and my house," my father had said, "we will serve the Lord." I wondered, as we drove him to his resting place, what this line had meant for him. I had heard him preach it many times. I had preached it once myself, proudly giving it an interpretation different from my father's. Now the whole thing came back to me, as though my father and I were on our way to Sunday school and I were memorizing the golden text: *And if it seem evil unto you to serve the Lord, choose you this day whom you will serve: whether the gods which your fathers served that were on the other side of the flood, or the gods of the Amorites, in whose land ye dwell: but as for me and my house, we will serve the Lord.*

I suspected in these familiar lines a meaning which had never been there for me before. All of his texts and songs, which I had decided were meaningless, were arranged before me at his death like empty bottles, waiting to hold the meaning which life would give them for me. This was his legacy: nothing is ever escaped. That bleakly memorable morning I hated the unbelievable streets and the Negroes and whites who had, equally, made them that way. But I knew that it was folly, as my father would have said, this bitterness was folly. It was necessary to hold on to

the things that mattered. The dead man mattered, the new life mattered; blackness and whiteness did not matter; to believe that they
did was to acquiesce in one's own destruction.

It began to seem that one would have to hold in the mind forever
two ideas which seemed to be in opposition. The first idea was acceptance, the acceptance of life as it is, and men as they are: in the light of
this idea, it goes without saying that injustice is a commonplace. But this
did not mean that one could be complacent, for the second idea was of
equal power: that one must never, in one's own life, accept these
injustices as commonplace but must fight them with all one's strength.
This fight begins, however, in the heart, and it now had been laid to my
charge to keep my own heart free of hatred and despair. This intimation
made my heart heavy and, now that he was irrecoverable, I wished that
my father had been beside me so that I could have searched his face for
the answers which only the future would give me now.

↗ Suggestions for Reading and Writing

1. Do you agree with Baldwin that "It seems to be typical of life in America
   . . . that the second generation has no time to talk to the first"? Explain.
2. Baldwin's feelings toward his father (as he here describes them) are
   extremely ambivalent. Summarize them in your own words.
3. How would you characterize Baldwin's self-image? Note his comment:
   "My life, my real life, was in danger, and not from anything other people
   might do but from the hatred I carried in my own heart."
4. Discuss Baldwin's use here of public events to heighten and illuminate
   personal experience.
5. Do you accept Baldwin's view that people cling stubbornly to their
   hatreds because "once hate is gone . . . they will be forced to deal with
   pain"? Are hatred and pain inevitable alternatives?
6. A partial meaning derived by Baldwin from his father's life and death
   was that "bitterness was folly." After reading one of his novels, discuss
   whether it was written by a man who has cleansed himself of bitterness.
   Do the same with a volume of his essays.
7. Read *Notes of a Native Son* entire and compare the author's social
   attitude with that found either in the poet James Weldon Johnson's
   autobiography, *Along This Way* (1933), or the novelist Richard
   Wright's autobiography, *Black Boy* (1945). Should you decide to use
   Black Boy, be sure to read "Alas, Poor Richard" (Baldwin's account of
   his friendship with Wright) in *Nobody Knows My Name*.

from

A C T

O N E

Moss Hart

Moss Hart (1904–1961) was born and raised in the Bronx. A stagestruck youth, he developed his theatrical talents along New York's Borscht Circuit and won Broadway fame first as playwright and librettist and later as director and producer.

Hart's early successes were gained in collaboration with the veteran playwright George S. Kaufman. Together they wrote Once in a Lifetime (1930), You Can't Take It With You (1936; Pulitzer Prize for 1937), I'd Rather Be Right (1937), The Man Who Came to Dinner (1939), and George Washington Slept Here (1940). Hart also wrote the librettos for such musical productions as Face the Music (1932), As Thousands Cheer (1933), and Lady in the Dark (1941). During the war he wrote a drama for the Air Force, Winged Victory (1943), which toured widely with a military cast.

In postwar years Hart turned increasingly to directing and producing. He directed the extremely successful My Fair Lady (1957) and was busy producing and directing Camelot (1961) when he died. Hart and his actress-wife, Kitty Carlisle, had two children. He was for seven years president of the Dramatists Guild, as well as president of the Authors League of America, when his autobiography, Act One (1959), appeared.

Hart's death at the peak of his career was, among other things, cause for regret that he didn't live to write Act Two and Act Three. For Act One has proved the most highly acclaimed of America's many show-business autobiographies. (A motion

*picture based on it was produced by Dore Schary, who figures
prominently in the narrative.)*
The final chapter of the autobiography follows.

⁊   ⁊   ⁊   ⁊   ⁊

. . . . .

The proceedings which take place backstage on an opening night,
immediately following the fall of the curtain, follow a set pattern and are
almost a law unto themselves. At least half of the audience hurries
through the stage door to jam the stairways, throng the dressing rooms
and overflow onto the stage itself. A kind of formalized bedlam ensues in
which the same words echo up and down the halls and float out the open
doors of every dressing room. No one is expected to believe the words
which are being spoken or the emotional kisses and embraces which
usually precede them; they are always the same and are used for both
failure or success. Not to come backstage and speak them, however, is
considered a remission of friendship or downright cowardice. Both sides
know exactly what is expected of them, and the performance backstage
sometimes equals or betters the one which has just taken place in front of
the footlights. With an obvious failure, or what seems to be an obvious
failure, the embraces and kisses are of necessity a little more flamboyant,
the words a little more belligerent, and the recurring phrase, "Well, I
loved it," uttered with great vehemence, is to be heard on all sides. No
one is actually lying, for short of a blatant or outright fiasco, everyone is
aware of the complete untrustworthiness of critics. Everyone knows that
it is just as likely for the certain failure to be greeted the following
morning with glowing and triumphant notices as it is for the apparent
success to receive its death sentence.

There are some opening nights, however, when a play seems
destined for success in spite of critical perfidy, and on these nights the
backstage throng assumes the proportions of a hysterical and unruly
mob. On these occasions a backstage appearance is no longer an
unpleasant duty, but a vital necessity—it seems to contain some basic
need of human beings to identify themselves or to be identified with
success. On such nights the dressing rooms and stairways are a solid mass
of humanity crushed one against the other into every available inch of
space. *Once in a Lifetime* must have had all the earmarks of such an
evening, for I could hardly fight my way through the stage door. I
struggled up the stairway to reach Mr. Kaufman's dressing room, but
there was a great horde of people clustered in front of it waiting for the

crowd within to come out. Beatrice Kaufman caught sight of me, blew me a kiss and waved to me to make my way in, but I shook my head. What I wanted to say to him could not be said in front of strangers. I shouted back, "Tell him I was here," and pushed my way down the stairs again.

Each dressing room and every landing was jammed—swarms of people surged in and out of the densely packed rooms, all talking at once. I caught a glimpse of Jean Dixon and Hugh O'Connell over the tops of heads and started toward them, but the congestion was too great, and as I reached the stage I heard Sam Harris' soft laughter rise from the crowd that surrounded him; but I made no attempt to go toward him.

I felt unaccountably disconnected from the uproar that was taking place all around me; none of it seemed to have any connection with what had made the evening possible—with hotel rooms, a typewriter and curtains drawn against the light; with pacing up and down in the dark; with actors in bathrobes standing on a stage after a performance, the pilot light etching the exhaustion on each face under the make-up—none of this seemed to have anything to do with any of the people who had been part of all that had gone before. Those people were disappearing under my eyes, had vanished already in fact, and suddenly I knew what was vanishing along with them: that tight little cabal against the world—the conspiracy that had begun with the first day's rehearsal and had been pledged in stale sandwiches and cold coffee in cardboard containers, the unspoken compact of long days on dim stages and dirty out-of-town dressing rooms, the common bond of the same shared hopes and fears—that sustaining conspiracy was over and the world had moved in. That old secret world removed and remote from everything but the play and ourselves had ended.

I walked across the stage to where my family and friends stood waiting, a little knot of alien corn in the mass of black ties and jewels and evening gowns that swirled all around them. I felt as alien as they looked. We stood uncomfortably together, not quite knowing what to do. After I had kissed my mother and father and listened to the congratulations of Dore and Lester and Eddie and the others, I stood helplessly rooted to the spot. I felt my face freeze into an apelike grin and tried to unleash my tongue, but I could not; nor could I think of what to do next. I had lived for this moment for so long that it was difficult to accept it as reality—even now it still seemed frozen in fantasy. I have always understood the unbelieving look in the eyes of those whom success touches early—it is a look half fearful, as though the dream were still in the process of being dreamed and to move or to speak would shatter it.

It was Joe Hyman, not I, who finally shepherded all of us toward the stage door and took everyone to a restaurant to wait for the notices.

Somewhere or other along the line of that long wait I began to believe that a play of mine had opened on Broadway and that the notices I was waiting to read might transform that lifelong fantasy into a reality that would change my life from this moment onward. Someone gave me a drink and I began to shake so that it was impossible to lift the second drink to my lips—a fortunate moment of panic, I believe, for two drinks under the circumstances might easily have made me quite drunk and would have robbed me of the pleasure of being able to hear the notices read aloud. That fateful moment is not one to be missed. Whatever the state of one's nerves, it is wise at all costs to remain clear-headed on the gambler's chance that the notices will be good, for good notices read aloud are a joy not to be cheated out of. In that first reading, each word is glorious, and no words of praise afterward will ever shine with the same splendor.

The notices of *Once in a Lifetime* as I listened to them were a blaze of glory—each word incrusted with a special luster of its own, and I made the sound decision never to look at them again. They could not possibly be as brilliant, as peerless, as superlative or as downright wonderful as I now thought them to be, and I paid them the honor of letting them remain an imperishable memory. When the last notice had been read, I took that second drink, for I knew now that my life was indeed changed forever—and I drank a silent toast to the new one.

Is success in any other profession as dazzling, as deeply satisfying, as it is in the theatre? I cannot pretend to know, but I doubt it. There are other professions where the rewards are as great or greater than those the theatre offers, there are professions where the fruits of success are as immediate, and still others where the pursuit of a more admirable goal undoubtedly brings a nobler sense of fulfillment. But I wonder if success in any of them tastes as sweet. Again, I am inclined to doubt it. There is an intensity, an extravagance, an abundant and unequivocal gratification to the vanity and the ego that can be satisfied more richly and more fully by success in the theatre than in any other calling. Like everything else about the theatre, its success is emphatic and immoderate. Perhaps what makes it so marvelously satisfying is that it is a success that is anything but lonely—everyone seems to share in it, friends and strangers alike—and a first success in the theatre is the most intoxicating and beguiling time imaginable. No success afterward surpasses it. It roars and thumps and thunders through the blood the way that second drink seemed to be coursing through my veins right now, so that it seemed hardly bearable to have to wait until tomorrow to start savoring it.

I asked someone what time it was and blinked my surprise when I was told it was four thirty in the morning. It seemed but a few short

minutes since we had waited impatiently for two thirty to come to be able
to read the first notice in the *Times*. The morning editions appeared very
much later in those days, and it was the custom to go directly to each
newspaper in turn and wait for the first copies to roll off the presses.
Everyone in the theatre knew what time each paper would appear and
where to go for them. The *Times* appeared first at about two thirty, the
Tribune about three, and the *Daily News* last at four o'clock in the
morning. The *World* was far downtown on Park Row and would have to
wait until tomorrow, but with three ecstatic notices under my arm, the
World, in more ways than just the name of a newspaper, could wait.

    We were all standing outside the News Building, where the last
notice had been read—or, rather, acted out brilliantly by Dore
Schary—and just as it seemed to me but a few moments ago that he had
read aloud those exalted words in the *Times*, so it seemed now to be
some years ago and not just yesterday that I had watched another dawn
lighten the sky, as it was about to do once more. It seemed impossible
that it could have been only yesterday that I had sat listening to Sam
Harris tell me the story of *Once in a Lifetime*—it seemed to have been
someone other than I who walked out of the Music Box with him to see
that other dawn beginning. That other I now seemed someone infinitely
different from my present self—a fearful, inept, wretchedly uncertain
fellow. He was someone I knew and remembered very well, but it was a
memory already growing shadowy and dim.

    Can success change the human mechanism so completely between
one dawn and another? Can it make one feel taller, more alive,
handsomer, uncommonly gifted and indomitably secure with the certainty that this is the way life will always be? It can and it does! Only
one aspect of that other self remained to spill over into the new. I was
once again wolfishly, overpoweringly hungry. It would take at least two
more successes to make me lose my appetite, and it is only fair to point
out that success can and does accomplish this, too. Everyone but me,
however, had eaten during the long wait for the notices, and only that
bitter-ender, Joe Hyman, was not too exhausted by this time to declare
himself ready to sit though a full meal with me. The others were visibly
wilting and I did not press them to stay. My family had long since gone
home on the strength of that first glowing notice in the *Times*—indeed,
their own glow must have sped the train halfway to Brooklyn with no
help from the subway system at all.

    I protested a little during the good-byes, but I was secretly relieved
that the others were going now, too, for a childish reason of my own. It
satisfied my sense of drama to complete the full circle of *Once in a
Lifetime* alone with Joe Hyman—the circle that had begun with a dinner
alone with him before the opening in Atlantic City and would end with

this dinner alone with him now after the opening in New York. It is a childish game I have always played and have never been able to resist—a game of arranging life, whenever possible, in a series of scenes that make perfect first-act or third-act curtains. When it works, and it often does, it lends an extra zest and a keener sense of enjoyment to whatever the occasion may be where my thirst for drama has contrived to make life imitate a good third act. It worked beautifully now.

I cannot recall one word that was exchanged between us, but it must have taken a fairly long time to satisfy my sense of the dramatic entities, for when we came out of the restaurant it was six o'clock in the morning and broad daylight. For the second dawn in a row I peered down the streets of a sleeping city, searching for a taxi. This dawn, however, was going to usher in an historic moment. My last subway ride was behind me. Never again would I descend those dingy steps or hear those turnstiles click off another somber day behind me.

Joe Hyman asked, "Got enough money to get to Brooklyn?"

I nodded. That fifteen dollars was still intact—there could not be a better way to spend it than to keep that long-ago promise to myself, and a taxi ride to Brooklyn was keeping it with a vengeance.

A cab pulled up beside us and Joe Hyman and I silently shook hands. The driver eyed me warily when I gave him a Brooklyn address, and I was conscious, looking at Joe Hyman, of how disreputable I too must look. I looked at him again and burst into laughter. His eyes were red-rimmed with excitement and weariness, his face grimy with a full day-and-night's growth of beard, and his suit looked as though he had slept in it. The driver obviously and quite rightly was wondering if there was enough money between us to pay for that long ride, or if we had not already spent every cent in some speakeasy. I took a ten-dollar bill out of my pocket and waved it at him and climbed into the cab. I waved at Joe Hyman through the rear window until the cab turned the corner, and then settled back in the seat, determined that I would not fall asleep. I had no intention of dozing through the first ride to Brooklyn above ground—I intended to enjoy every visible moment of it and I very shortly reaped the reward for staying awake.

No one has ever seen the skyline of the city from Brooklyn Bridge as I saw it that morning with three hit notices under my arm. The face of the city is always invested with grandeur, but grandeur can be chilling. The overpowering symmetry of that skyline can crush the spirit and make the city seem forbidding and impenetrable, but today it seemed to emerge from cold anonymity and grant its acknowledgment and accept-ance. There was no sunlight—it was a gray day and the buildings were half shrouded in mist, but it was a city that would know my name today, a city that had not turned me aside, and a city that I loved. Unexpectedly and without warning a great wave of feeling for this proud and beautiful city swept over me. We were off the bridge now and driving through the sprawling, ugly area of tenements that stretch interminably over the approaches to each of its boroughs. They are the first in the city to awake, and the long unending rows of drab, identical houses were already stirring with life. Laundry was being strung out to dry along roof tops and fire escapes, men with lunch boxes were coming out of the houses, and children returning from the corner grocery with bottles of milk and loaves of bread were hurrying up the steps and into the doorways.

I stared through the taxi window at a pinch-faced ten-year-old hurrying down the steps on some morning errand before school, and I thought of myself hurrying down the street on so many gray mornings out of a doorway and a house much the same as this one. My mind jumped backward in time and then whirled forward, like a many-faceted prism—flashing our old neighborhood in front of me, the house, the steps, the candy store—and then shifted to the skyline I had just passed by, the opening last night, and the notices I still hugged tightly under my arm. It was possible in this wonderful city for that nameless little boy—for any of its millions—to have a decent chance to scale the walls and achieve what they wished. Wealth, rank or an imposing name counted for nothing. The only credential the city asked was the boldness to dream. For those who did, it unlocked its gates and its treasures, not caring who they were or where they came from. I watched the boy disappear into a tailor shop and a surge of shamefaced patriotism overwhelmed me. I might have been watching a victory parade on a flag-draped Fifth Avenue instead of the mean streets of a city slum. A feeling of patriotism, however, is not always limited to the feverish emotions called forth by war. It can sometimes be felt as profoundly and perhaps more truly at a moment such as this.

It had suddenly begun to rain very hard and in a few minutes I could no longer see much of anything through the windows. All too quickly I made that swift turnabout from patriotism to enlightened self-interest. I closed my eyes and thought about how I would spend the money that would soon start to pour in. To my surprise, affluence did not seem nearly as easy to settle into as I had always imagined it would be. Try as I would, I could not think of how to begin or in what ways I wanted to spend the large sums that would now be mine to command. I could think of little ways to spend it—new suits, new shirts, new ties, new overcoats—but after that my mind went disappointingly blank. In some ways sudden riches are no easier to live with than poverty. Both demand artistry of a kind, if one or the other is not to leave the mark of a sour and lingering cynicism, and opulence in many ways is harder to manage than penury. It is, however, one of the pleasantest problems with which to drift off to sleep. It is a problem that apparently also induces the deepest and most refreshing kind of sleep. I cheated myself out of the major portion of that first taxi ride by sleeping soundly through the rest of it. The driver had to leave his seat and shake me awake to collect his fare.

I was wide awake again, thoroughly wide awake, and disappointed to find the shades still drawn and the family fast asleep when I unlocked the door and stepped into the apartment. It was, of course, only a little after seven o'clock in the morning, but today was too memorable a day to waste on anything so commonplace as sleep. I was tempted to wake them up at once and show them the other notices, but I went into the kitchen instead and fixed a pot of coffee. I wanted a little more time alone to think about something.

I stood in the doorway of the kitchen while I waited for the water to boil and gazed at the sleeping figure of my brother on the daybed in the dining room, and beyond it at the closed door of the one bedroom where my parents slept. The frayed carpet on the floor was the carpet I had crawled over before I could walk. Each flower in the badly faded and worn design was sharply etched in my mind. Each piece of furniture in the cramped dim room seemed mildewed with a thousand double-edged memories. The ghosts of a thousand leaden meals hovered over the dining-room table. The dust of countless black-hearted days clung to every crevice of the squalid ugly furniture I had known since childhood. To walk out of it forever—not piecemeal, but completely—would give meaning to the wonder of what had happened to me, make success tangible, decisive.

The goal behind the struggle for success is not always one goal, but many—some real, some hidden; some impossible to achieve, even with success piled upon success. The goal differs with each of us in the mysterious and wonderful way each human being is different from any other, in the way each of us is the sum total of the unexpressed longings and desires that strew the seas of childhood and are glimpsed long afterward from a safe distance—a submerged iceberg, only the tip of which is seen.

Whatever dominant force in my nature shaped the blind demands that made it imperative to me to make the theatre my goal, had taken possession of me early and I was still possessed by it. What fulfillment it held I would know only when I walked resolutely out of one world and into another. I poured myself a cup of coffee, and by the time I had finished it, my mind was made up.

It is always best if one is about to embark on a wild or reckless venture not to discuss it with anybody beforehand. Talk will rob the scheme of its fire and make what seemed mettlesome and daring merely foolhardy. It is easier on everyone concerned to present it as an accomplished fact, turn a deaf ear to argument, and go ahead with it.

I awakened my brother by dumping the papers on the bed for him to read and then called through the bedroom door to my mother and father to get up right away. I gave them barely enough time to read the notices and then plunged. "We're moving into New York today—as soon as you have a cup of coffee—and we're not taking anything with us. We're walking out of here with just the clothes on our backs and nothing else. The coffee's on the stove, so hurry up and get dressed."

My mother stared at me and then spoke quietly, as if a raised voice at this moment might send me further out of my senses. "Where are we going?" she asked logically enough.

"To a hotel," I said, "until we find an apartment and furnish it." There was a stunned silence and before anyone else could speak, I spoke again, not impatiently but as if what I was saying was inarguable. "There's nothing to pack; we just walk out of the door. No," I added in answer to my mother's mute startled look around the room, "not a thing. We leave it all here just as it stands, and close the door. We don't take anything—not even a toothbrush, a bathrobe, pajamas or nightgown. We buy it all new in New York. We're walking out of here and starting fresh."

My mother walked to the window and pulled up the shades as though she might hear or understand what I was saying better with more light, and then turned helplessly toward my father.

He was the first to recover his breath and his wits. "We just paid two months' rent in advance," he said, as though that solid fact would help me recover my own.

"That gives us the right to let this stuff sit here and rot, or you can give it to the janitor," I replied. "We're walking out of here with just what clothes you put on and tomorrow we'll get rid of those, too."

This second bit of information created an even more astonished silence than the first. "Don't you understand?" I heard myself shouting. "All I'm asking you to do *now* is—"

"I'm not walking out of here without the pictures," my mother said with great firmness.

It was my turn to be astonished. "What pictures?" I asked.

"*All* the pictures," she replied. "The baby pictures of you and Bernie and the pictures of my father and my sister, and Bernie's diploma and your letters, and all the other pictures and things I've got in the closet in that big box."

I threw my arms around her and kissed her. I had won. It was being accepted as a fact—incomprehensible but settled.

"One suitcase," I ordered, "Put it all into one suitcase, but one suitcase—that's all."

I looked at my brother, who had remained silent through all of this. He handed the papers back to me with a flourish and winked. "Don't you have to give *some* of the money to George Kaufman?" he said.

"Half," I replied. "But my share will be over a thousand dollars a week."

"That'll buy a lot of toothbrushes," he said. "I'm going to get ready." And he climbed out of bed.

My mother and father stared at us as if to make sure we were not indulging in some elaborate joke for their benefit.

"It's true," I said soberly. "It's not a salary. I get a percentage of every dollar that comes into the box office. Don't you understand how it works?"

Obviously, they did not, and I realized somewhat belatedly that it had never occurred to either of them to translate good fortune in the theatre into anything more than what my mother's friends defined as "making a good living." No wonder my proposal had sounded lunatic, but now as the belief came to them that what I had just said might be the literal truth, they were suddenly seized with some of my own excitement. My mother's reaction was a curious one. She burst into a peal of laughter. She had a merry and ringing laugh and it was contagious. My father and I joined in her laughter, though we would have been hard put to tell exactly what we were laughing at. I was reminded of that moment and of her laughter long, long afterward, when I heard someone say, "Nothing makes people laugh like money—the rich get wrinkles from laughing." It was said sardonically, of course, but it is not without an element of truth. Money does generate its own kind of excitement, and its sudden acquisition creates an *ambiance* of gaiety and merriment that it would be nonsense to deny or not to enjoy. It induces, moreover, a momentum of its own. Everything moves with an unaccustomed and almost miraculous speed.

We were all ready to leave in less than an hour, despite the fact that there were more things of heaven and earth in that box in the closet than could be contained in one suitcase. I carried the box, my father and brother each carried a suitcase, and my mother, her victory complete, hugged a brown paper parcel of last-minute treasures that had turned up in an old tin box. We walked out of the door and waited in the lobby while my brother hurried out in the rain to try to get a taxi. The rain was pouring down in a great solid sheet now and gusts of wind were slashing it against the building. I watched it burst savagely against the glass doors of the lobby and was seized by a sudden and irresistible impulse.

"I forgot something," I said shortly. "I'll be right back."

I unlocked the door of the empty apartment and closed and locked it again carefully behind me. I took one quick look around to keep the memory of that room forever verdant and then walked to each window and threw it wide open. The rain whipped in through the windows like a broadside of artillery fire. I watched a large puddle form on the floor and spread darkly over the carpet. The rain streamed across the top and down the legs of the dining-room table and splashed over the sideboard and the china closet. It soaked the armchair and cascaded down the sofa. It peppered the wallpaper with large wet blotches and the wind sent two lamps crashing to the floor. I kicked them out of my way and walked over to the daybed, which was still dry, and pulled it out into the middle of the room, where a fresh onset of wind and rain immediately drenched it. I looked around me with satisfaction, feeling neither guilty nor foolish. More reasonable gestures have seldom succeeded in giving me half the pleasure this meaningless one did. It was the hallmark, the final signature, of defiance and liberation. Short of arson, I could do no more.

I slammed the door behind me without looking back.

To everyone's surprise, including my own, a strange silence fell upon us in the taxi, in spite of the fact that my brother read aloud the glowing notice in the *World*, which he had picked up on his way to get the cab. Instead of heightening our excitement or reinforcing our high spirits, it seemed, curiously enough, to put a damper on them. My brother stared out the window and my mother and father stared straight ahead, silent and solemn. I talked on for a moment or two and then grew silent myself. Perhaps there was in all of us, including myself, a feeling of unreality in what we were doing or a separate awareness in each of us that this great change—this almost too great change in our life—would change us, too, as a family; that the struggle which had welded us so tightly together was over now, and success in some mysterious way might separate us, each from the other.

My mother, still silent, took out her handkerchief and wiped her eyes. They were not, I suspected, tears of joy for my success. They were not tears for the beginning of something, but for the end of something none of us could name. Not until we came within sight of Brooklyn Bridge did anyone speak. Then, as suddenly as it had fallen, the silence lifted. Crossing the bridge, as it had for me earlier that morning, seemed to put an old way of life behind us and make inevitable the new one we were rushing headlong into. We started to talk, all of us at once, almost at the same moment, as if crossing the bridge had cut the ties irrevocably and was a symbol of entry into a world as dazzling as the skyline in front of us.

Suddenly no one seemed to have an unexpressed thought. Everyone talked incessantly, oblivious of what anyone else might be saying.

We were at 34th Street before I thought to glance out the window. I had told the driver to take us to the Edison Hotel on 47th Street, for no other reason except that it was practically around the corner from the Music Box and seemed more of a family hotel than any other I could think of; but as the cab moved into Times Square, I asked the driver to stop first at the Music Box.

Even through the rain-splashed windows of the cab, I could see a long double line of people extending the full length of the lobby from the box office. The line spilled out under the marquee where another line was patiently forming under umbrellas. I got out of the cab and walked into the lobby and stood gaping at all the people. It was not yet half-past nine in the morning. How long I stood there, forgetful of everything else but the wonder of that line, I do not know, but the box-office man, looking up for a moment to glance across the lobby, caught sight of me and smiled. There is no smile as bright as the smile of a box-office man the morning after a hit. It flashes with the iridescence of stage jewelry under spotlights and is as wide as the proscenium itself. His smile did not waver—it grew more brilliant as the telephones jangled behind him and visions of ticket speculators, like sugar plums, danced across his mind. He waved me over to the head of the line and stuck his hand out through the opening in the grille to shake my own.

"A year at least," he said. "It's the hottest ticket in town. What can I do for you?"

"I wanted to draw $500.00," I said quickly. "I'm moving into town."

"Sure, sure—anything you want," he said. He reached for an I.O.U. slip and rapidly filled it in. "How do you want it?" he asked.

"A few fifties," I replied, "the rest in twenties and tens."

I signed the slip as he counted out the money, conscious that the people immediately in back of me were whispering to each other. "It is *not* George Kaufman," I heard a woman's voice say. "It must be the other one."

As nearly as I could, I tried to achieve a look of modesty with the back of my head while I waited for him to finish. He pushed the rather formidable stack of bills toward me and his smile floodlit the box office. "Come around any time," he said, "we'll be here for a long, long time."

I doubled the bills in my fist and walked out and into the taxi. Without a word I went through the pretense of counting the money, thoroughly aware of the awed silence around me.

"When," my brother said quietly, "do they change the name of the theatre to the Money Box?"

It was the first of a perpetual and unremitting series of bad puns that he was to launch and send racketing down the years, and the effect of this historic first one was not only uproarious but explosive. We started to laugh and could not stop. We laughed as though we were out of our wits, uncontrolled and breathless with laughter, and startled because we could not stop laughing, try as we would. My brother's words seemed to have touched off the edge of hysteria our overwrought state had brought us to. The exhaustion and excitement of the last few days and of this morning needed a release, and that atrocious pun had been both a means and a blessing. We laughed as though we might never stop.

The driver, too, started to shake with laughter and turned around apologetically. "I don't know what you're laughing at, folks," he said, "but it must be pretty good to make people laugh that way." No one could answer him; we were all still helpless. He burst into laughter again himself and turned the cab toward Broadway.

My fatal weakness for standing aside from whatever was happening around me and translating it into vignettes of drama overcame me once more. I could hear myself telling the whole story to Sam Harris. Unresisting, I let it assemble and take shape in my mind. The wait for the notices, the first taxi ride home, the decision to walk out and leave everything behind us, the trip back to open the windows and let the rain pour in—I could hear myself telling it all to him, right down to counting the money in the cab, our paroxysm of laughter, and the cab driver turning around to add the final touch. I could see myself some time later this afternoon standing in his office in the Music Box and telling it to him with the proper embellishment, making it all come out a rounded, dramatic entity. I could see his eyes squint with amusement as I told it and hear his soft laughter afterward. I could even, I thought, hear his comment.

"Not bad, kid," he would say. "Not a bad curtain for a first act."

INTERMISSION

↑ Suggestions for Reading and Writing

1. Hart expresses doubt that success in any other profession can be "as dazzling, as deeply satisfying, as it is in the theatre." Do you agree?
2. Does Hart perhaps make too much of the material and egoistic aspects of his success? Or is he being merely inevitably human and unexpectedly candid?
3. Was Hart's letting the rain pour into the apartment "the hallmark, the final signature, of defiance and liberation"—or something else? Explain. Having thought of it, would you have done the same in his position, or would you have repressed the impulse?

4. After reading *Act One* entire, discuss the critic Walter Kerr's references to Hart's "firm way with a memory" and his "almost rigid honesty that prohibits cant."
5. The playwright S. N. Behrman has called *Act One* the best book on show business in the United States in our day. Check this claim against such other first-person theater narratives as Ilka Chase's *Past Imperfect* (1942), George Middleton's *These Things Are Mine* (1947), Lawrence Langner's *The Magic Curtain* (1951), Agnes De Mille's *Dance to the Piper* (1952), and Artie Shaw's *The Trouble with Cinderella* (1952).
6. Hart writes movingly of his collaborator, George S. Kaufman. Augment his reminiscences with James Thurber's in "The Man Who Was Comedy" (collected in *Credos and Curios* [1962]). You then should be able to write a profile in depth of this influential theatrical figure.

BIOGRAPHY,
TRUE
AND
FALSE

Iris Origo

The Marchesa Iris Origo (1902–   ), English by birth, lives with her husband in a villa outside Rome. During the Second World War the Origos served actively with the Italian underground.

A respected biographer and essayist, the Marchesa has written Leopardi: A Biography (1935); a brief study of Byron's daughter, Allegra (1935); a personal narrative, War in Val d'Orcia: A Diary (1947); The Last Attachment: The Story of Byron and Teresa Guiccioli (1949); A Measure of Love (1958); and two biographies of late fourteenth-century Italy: The Merchant of Prato, Francesco di Marco Datini (1957) and The World of San Bernardino (1962). *She wrote the introduction to the final diary of the famed art historian-critic Bernard Berenson, Sunset and Twilight: From the Diaries of 1947–1958 (1963).*

A onetime Harvard lecturer, Iris Origo has written on biography for intellectual and popular journals on both sides of the Atlantic. The following essay was drawn from the Ann Radcliffe lecture she delivered in Cambridge during the autumn of 1958.

✓ ✓ ✓ ✓ ✓

I do not remember who it was who once remarked that every great man has his disciples, but it is always Judas who is the biographer.

Whether or not this is entirely true, there are certainly more ways than one in which a biographer can betray his subject—and not all of them spring from bad intentions. "Whatever you do, do not prettify me!" said Walt Whitman to his friend Horace Traubel, the author of *With Walt Whitman in Camden.* "Include all the hells and damns." But other great men have considered that any biography can hardly fail to be a betrayal, for the very sound reason that no one really knows anything about anyone else. "The world will never know my life," said Carlyle, "if it should write and read a hundred biographies of me. The main facts of it are known, and are likely to be known, to myself alone, of all created men." And these words stand on the first page of the long life written by his closest friend, James Froude.

We would all agree as to which is the most satisfactory biography—most satisfactory owing to the unmistakable, unrelenting veracity of the biographer. Boswell has told us very clearly what he was aiming at: he thought that a life should be "like a flawless print struck off from the engraved plate which is bitten into our memory." Biography, in his view, should not be a selection or a monument or a thesis, but the *duplication* of an image in the mind. Unfortunately, as Geoffrey Scott remarked in his penetrating preface to Boswell's *Notes and Journals,* "This is an aim beyond human reach." But Scott also shrewdly added: "The knowledge that his arrow pointed to that impossible mark, was Boswell's source of confidence. Other biographies might forestall his book; that they could rival it, he never, in his most sombre moments, conceived. Those others did not even know that biography is impossible."

Atlantic Monthly, CCIII (February 1959), 37–42. Reprinted by permission of the author.

Impossible or not, the biography written by a man's daily companion belongs to a genre that has a perennial charm: it gratifies our wish to believe. When a biographer records—with a sharp ear and a selective eye—what a great man actually said to him, he awakens a degree of conviction that no other form of narrative or analysis can achieve. "I wonder why we hate the past so," says Howells ruminatively to Mark Twain, and when Mark Twain replies, "It's so damned humiliating!" we know, without a doubt, that that is precisely what the great man did say. To open such a book is like entering a room—a room, I think, in an old-fashioned English country house—greeted by a mixture of wood smoke, old books, wet dogs, and fresh roses. One enters, and one is at home.

This is, perhaps, why Dr. Johnson himself asserted: "Nobody can write the life of a man, but those who have eaten and drunk and lived in social intercourse with him." Failing personal acquaintance, he maintained that a biographer must at least be able to talk with his subject's friends, though he also admitted that their reports were often highly unsatisfactory. In his own youth, he related, he determined to write a life of Dryden, and applied to two men who knew him, Sweeney and Cibber. 'Sweeney's information," he said, "was no more than this, that at Will's coffee-house Dryden had a particular chair for himself, which was set by the fire in winter and was called his winter chair; and that it was carried out for him to the balcony in summer, and was then called his summer chair."

What, then, is the wretched biographer who is not a contemporary to do, the writer who has no plate bitten into his memory, who must juggle, two or three centuries later, bare facts and documents, and who has, at best, an occasional portrait to look at? The further back we go, the more evident our presumption becomes. From the seventeenth century onwards we have at least some private papers to help us: someone writes a love letter, someone scolds an erring daughter, someone else sets down in a diary his fear of death; but earlier, what is there? A mass of public documents, but a terrible dearth of private ones. How can we dare, from such fragmentary and formal knowledge, to reconstruct a man?

Two methods are open to the biographer: he can try, in the manner of the three-volume Victorian biography and of the exhaustive modern biographies which are again becoming popular, to set down everything he can find out; or he can attempt the selective portrait, the "work of art." The first method, unavoidably, must be that of the official biographer, who writes at the request of the family or of the state, or sometimes, nowadays, is financed by some great foundation. He works with one great advantage—a vast supply of material—and sometimes with a corresponding disadvantage, that part of it must be suppressed.

For him the only solution seems to be the one recommended by William Allen White to a young historian: "Kill the widow!" Sometimes, too, it is the subject himself who has taken a great deal of trouble to cover his own tracks. In an essay on George Sand, Henry James suggested that the artist who fears to become the subject of a biography should take an unlimited degree of trouble to destroy all his private papers, leaving only his considered creation behind him. "Then," he wrote, "the cunning inquiry will exceed in subtlety and ferocity anything we today conceive, and the pale forewarned victim, with every track covered, every paper burnt and every letter unanswered, will, in the tower of art, stand, without a sally, the siege of years."

Most biographers of our own time, however, and certainly those dealing with public men, are more likely to complain of too much material than too little. Even Boswell, according to his own diary, was so overwhelmed by the amount of his material when he started to put it together that he would sit in London coffeehouses with tears pouring down his cheeks; Virginia Woolf was hardly less dismayed by the number of Roger Fry's papers. But what must Franklin Roosevelt's biographer have felt, surveying the forty tons of documents at his disposal?

We live in a historically minded age, and I understand that an American statesman of our time was even in the habit of having his telephone conversations recorded in large diaries. This is, surely, a formidable prospect. Moreover, in addition to the written word, it is now possible to see again our subject's face and gestures in a hundred newsreels, to hear again the very accents of his voice in recorded broadcasts. With such a plethora of material, every biography must to some extent become a selective one. But here problems of a different nature at once arise, problems of choice: is it possible to choose without revealing a bias, to reject and not to falsify? Every biographer is familiar with the seductive tricks of the trade: the slight juggling with dates, the suppression of inconvenient letters or of remarks that are out of character or merely flat, the placing of a telling conversation or document where it is most effective, the smoothing out and the touching up. In the end a portrait is built up: slick, vivid, convincing, and false.

There are also, of course, the mistakes of sheer ignorance. I am thinking at the moment of one of my own, which was kindly pointed out to me in a letter from Rebecca West. I had mentioned, as an example of Mrs. Carlyle's touchiness, the disastrous Christmas party at the Grange, at which Lady Ashburton presented her, from the Christmas tree, with a silk dress, after which Jane retired to her bedroom in tears. I thought she was making a good deal of unnecessary fuss, or rather that she was using this pretext to express a deeper resentment against her hostess. Rebecca

West, however, pointed out my mistake. Her great-aunt Isabella Campbell, who belonged to the Carlyle period, had often spoken of the episode and thought it "a most extraordinary thing for Lady Ashburton to have done, as a silk dress was the recognized present for a housekeeper, and a friend of the family would have felt bewildered at receiving it. To wear a dress which one had not ordered from the start and had fitted according to one's own measures was a sign of social inferiority." Plainly, therefore, on this occasion Jane was right to be offended, and I did not know what I was talking about. I still think, however, that Mrs. Carlyle was glad of so good an excuse to express her irritation with the woman whom her husband described as having "the soul of a princess and a captainess" and whom he considered, which was worse, as witty as herself.

One way of guarding against making too many such mistakes is to write only about those times and places with which one is familiar. Another safeguard is to become acquainted with the whole surrounding scene. I remember, for instance, once reading a translation of Leopardi's "Sabato del Villaggio" in which the *fascio dell' erba*, the bundle of grass, which the girl in the poem is carrying is translated as "a truss of hay." The image brought to mind is one of green hayfields and wagons and pitchforks and buxom country girls—an Austrian scene, or an English. But there are no hayfields near Recanati. There are only steep, dun-colored hills on which olive trees grow, with wheat beneath them and perhaps a few vines, and by the edge of the road there are sometimes tufts of grass, of which town dwellers cut an armful to feed their rabbits. This was the bundle of grass brought home by Leopardi's *donzelletta*. A single misleading sentence—written not because the translator did not know Italian but because he did not know Leopardi's birthplace—conjured up a whole nonexistent world.

Three insidious temptations assail the biographer: to suppress, to invent, and to sit in judgment, and of these the earliest and most frequent is suppression. In the Middle Ages, indeed, it was rendered inevitable by the purpose which biography was intended to fulfill to produce a noble example. The medieval view of history was that of a drama enacted within an established pattern—God's pattern for mankind. The lives of the men who came nearest to conforming with this pattern were related as an example to other, lesser men, and consequently a disproportionate number of medieval biographies are concerned with the lives of saints, while others are about rulers or leaders rather larger than life size.

The first English author who admitted that a biography might also aim at what he calls "lawful delight" was Thomas Fuller, who in the introduction to his *History of the Worthies of England* (in 1662) places this as the fourth and last of his purposes in writing: "First, to gain some glory to God. Secondly, to preserve the manoeuvres of the Devil. Thirdly, to present examples to the Living." And only fourthly, "to Entertain the reader with Delight."

In this respect, the attitude of classical biography was much nearer to our own. It was by the example of Plutarch that writers justified themselves when taste began to turn, in the seventeenth century, from what Dr. Johnson later called "honeysuckle lives" to a more varied, livelier curiosity. Dryden, for instance, admired Plutarch precisely because he had dared to show his heroes in undress. "You may behold," he said, "Scipio and Laelius gathering cockle shells on the shore, Augustus playing at bounding-stones, and Agesilaus riding on a hobbyhorse, among his children. The pageantry of life is taken away: you see the poor reasonable animal as naked as ever nature made him; are acquainted with his follies, and find the demi-god, a man."

Here, surely, is the prelude to modern biography; but with the admission that heroes, too, should be shown as naked and fallible, the problem arose as to whether this true picture was likely to dismay or to corrupt the reader. And if this danger existed, had the biographer the right to speak the truth?

The problem was set by Boswell to Dr. Johnson. Was it right to relate that Addison, having lent a hundred pounds to Steele, recovered his loan by sending an officer to remove his friend's furniture? Dr. Johnson charitably speculated that perhaps Addison had done this with the intention of reforming Steele, but he also declared that, whether this kind of interpretation was true or not, the facts should be told. "Of such speculations," he said, "there is no end; we cannot see into the hearts of men, but their actions are open to observation." And he added that another reason for telling the whole truth was that "if nothing but the bright side of characters should be shown, we should sit in despondency and think it utterly impossible to imitate them in *anything*." He believed, in short, that the whole truth should be told, for a highly characteristic reason: "It keeps mankind from despair."

In the nineteenth century, however, the suppression of unedifying or inconvenient facts came into favor again, partly owing to Victorian reticence and prudery, and partly to the same taste which created the Albert Memorial. "Too long and too idolatrous!" was the comment of Leslie Stephen on one of the great three-volume Victorian lives, and "How delicate," exclaimed Carlyle, "how decent is English biography, bless its mealy mouth!"

There is, however, a still more serious temptation for the biographer than suppression, and that is sheer invention. A good instance is the one quoted by Professor Trevor-Roper in a somewhat merciless attack on Lytton Strachey: the length of Dr. Arnold's legs. Strachey had formed a very clear image of Dr. Arnold in his mind; he saw him as a noble, pompous figure, and—to introduce just the right additional touch of absurdity, of debunking—it was necessary that his legs should have been too short. Unfortunately, however, as Strachey himself once admitted to a friend, there is absolutely no evidence to show that Dr. Arnold's legs were shorter than any other man's.

Now the danger of this kind of invention is that, once discovered, it shakes our capacity to believe anything that its inventor has said. "Suppose we believe one half of what he tells," suggested Lord Mansfield to Boswell, about an acquaintance whose stories, he said, "we unhappily found to be very fabulous." "Yes," Dr. Johnson replied, "but we don't know *which* half to believe. By his lying we lose not only our reverence for him, but all comfort in his conversation."

In Strachey's own opinion a biographer's equipment consists in three points: "a capacity for absorbing facts, a capacity for stating them, and a point of view." The definition is a good one, for without a point of view no history can be written, but there is also a danger that it may not only shape but distort the facts. The biographer who puts his wits above his subject will end by writing about one person only—himself. My personal complaint about *Eminent Victorians* would be not that it is inaccurate, but that it is *thin*, and that its thinness springs from condescension. If you wish to see a person, you must not start by seeing through him. Another instance of this occurs in the first sentence of a very fine biography, Harold Nicholson's *Tennyson*. "We smile today at our Victorians," it begins, "not confidently, as of old, but with a shade of hesitation: a note of perplexity, a note of anger, sometimes a note of wistfulness, has come to mingle with our laughter."

The fatal words are, of course, the first ones, "We smile today." The biographer has started by putting up a barrier—and even if, in the next few words, he suggests that it is beginning to crumble, he is still writing from the other side. He has, in short, succumbed to yet another of the biographer's temptations: the desire to sit in judgment. "To penetrate," wrote the French historian Marc Bloch, "into the unknown being of a man separated from us by a long stretch of generations, one must almost cast off one's own self. To pull him to pieces, one need only remain oneself. The effort is undeniably less strenuous."

Every work of art, of course, implies a previous process of assessment, and it is the writer's implicit view of life that gives style and flavor to his work. Even though the assessment and criticism of manners and morals which were once assumed by the biographer and the novelist have now largely been handed over to the psychologist, the judgment of character still remains the central problem of biography. But insofar as a biographer is also a historian, he should, I think, be very careful not to drown his subject's voice with his own. One peculiar function of biography is to show history as it was to the participant, to observe for a moment *das Gewordene als Werdendes*, what has come to pass, while it is still occurring. Through the man whose life we are describing, we can see history in the course of being lived. In one sense, all organized histories are unsatisfactory, because they are written with the wisdom of the future. But in individual lives we can seize, if nothing else, a vivid sense of actuality; it is a pity to blur it.

Besides, our own judgments are surely not immune from change. We shall not, at the age of fifty, judge a man in the same way as we did at twenty-five. Ten days before his death, Dr. Johnson asserted that he was "ready now to call a man a *good* man, on much easier terms than formerly." With the passing of the years, the muscles of moral indignation sometimes begin to sag and the voice becomes less sharp, and this is true even in the field of abstract thought. I remember asking George Santayana, in his old age—when he was preparing an abridged edition of the great work of his youth, *The Life of Reason*—whether there were many things that he would now like to change. "No," he gently replied, "I feel I have much the same things to say—but I wish to say them in a different tone of voice."

Recently the psychologists have invented some ingenious devices which, they claim, will provide short cuts to assessing a man's character and state of mind. A German called Busemann advises us to count, in a man's letters and journals, the relative number of adjectives and of active verbs, thus obtaining what he calls his A/Q or Action Quotient. A prevalence of adjectives, he says, indicates a state of emotional tension. The process has even been applied to William James's letters, showing that between the ages of forty and fifty his letters to women were more emotional, and after sixty, those to men. Two American psychologists have invented a more complicated device. By counting, in interviews with people suffering from emotional problems, the words expressing some form of discomfort, which they call D, and those expressing relief, which they call R, they obtain what they call a DR Quotient, which, when set down on a graph, accurately reflects their clients' states of mind at the time. They therefore suggest that the same method should be applied by biographers. We might ask ourselves, for instance, what Churchill's Discomfort Relief Quotient was when he offered the British nation blood, sweat, and tears.

I am myself not very good at counting, but even if I were, I do not think that either A/Q or DR/Q is going to take us much further in the complicated task of assessing human personality. They will hardly take the place of those unscientific, uncertain old instruments: intelligence and intuition. Yet how often even these fail us! We can hang mirrors, as Virginia Woolf advised, at every corner; we can look at our subject's face at every angle and in every light. We can discover strange and curious pieces of information: that Aristotle had a hot-water bottle made of leather, filled with hot oil, and that Leopardi, in the winter in Bologna, spent his days in a bag lined with feathers, from which he emerged looking like Papageno. But never, never do we see enough. Beneath the conscious personality, the purposing man, there is in each of us an underworld of discarded characters who have still some life in them. These, too, the biographer must seek. "In every fat man," said Cyril Connolly, "there is a thin man, trying to get out."

To Virginia Woolf the central problem of biography was how to mold "into one seamless whole" the "granite-like solidity" of truth and "the rainbow-like intangibility" of personality. It is, surely, impossible—but few writers have come closer to it than she did. The problem was one that fascinated her, not only in literature but in life. "Go on, this is enthralling," she would say, when her friends brought her an exciting piece of gossip. "I feel as if a buried statue were being dug up, piece by piece."

One of her friends once told me that on a cold November evening, as he was making his way to her house, he came upon Virginia Woolf standing in the fog beside an apple barrow and asking the old apple woman, in her deep, throaty, compelling voice: "Tell me, what does it *feel* like to stand here in the fog on a dark evening, selling apples?" I cannot vouch for the truth of this story, but certainly the question was one she often asked. "What does it feel like," she would say to me, "to wake up in the morning on a Tuscan farm?" And once I heard her say, perhaps not wholly without malice, to a disconcerted young peer: "Tell me, what does it feel like to be a lord?"

Yet when, in later years, she came to write a life of Roger Fry, who had been one of her closest friends, the book was curiously less vivid, more conventional, than the etchings in her essays. She found, indeed, the sheer effort of putting together the material for a full biography almost unbearably tedious. "Donkey work," she recorded in A *Writer's Diary*, "sober drudgery, appalling grind." And when at last the book was finished, there was a most revealing final note: "What a curious relation is mine with Roger at this moment—I who have given him a kind of shape after his death. Was he like that? I feel very much in his presence at the moment, as if I were intimately connected with him: as if we together had given birth to this vision of him; a child born of us. Yet he had no power to alter it. And yet for some years it will represent him."

Is biography, then, worth attempting at all? Where there are so many snares, would we do better to be silent? I think not. Many critics would deny to any biographical portrait the essential reality, the truth that is truer than truth, of the novelist's or dramatist's creations, but I do not think that this need be so. The biographer has, of course, a fixed pattern; he is, as Desmond MacCarthy once said, "an artist upon oath." But the calls upon his imagination and intuition are hardly less exacting than the novelist's. The novelist and dramatist, after all, do not create their characters in a void, but out of experience informed and illuminated by the imagination. And this is the only stuff that all art is made of.

Shakespeare himself invented hardly any of his plots, but, having accepted a ready-made pattern for the actions of his characters, was then free to give his whole attention to bringing them to life. And so surely, too, the biographer's true function—the transmission of personality— may also be, within its own pattern, an act of creation, giving shape, in Virginia Woolf's phrase, to a man after his death and endowing him with what is, when we come to think of it, a very odd form of immortality. For of many great men of the past we know only what their biographers or portrait painters saw. Just as we know no other face for Pope Julius II than Raphael's, no other Federico da Montefeltro than Piero della Francesca's, so Strachey's *Queen Victoria* will probably become for many the only Queen Victoria, and it is Boswell's *Johnson* whom most people call Dr. Johnson. All that the biographer did not see or could not fit conveniently into his picture has faded into mist.

What, however, it is possible to wonder is whether in the near future there will be any demand for biography at all. Reading is a private pleasure, and not only is privacy disappearing from a world of ready-made designs for living, in which men are looking not so much for individuality as for protective coloring, but people's curiosity about other people's lives can now be satisfied in more dramatic ways than any book can offer. The radio and television now enable every man to interpret for himself, without the filter of another man's mind, the character and actions of his contemporaries.

I do not really believe this. The story of public exploits may become, to some extent, the field of the radio and of television, but the slow development of character, the processes of thought of the writer and the artist, and above all the relation of human beings to each other—these are things that cannot be simplified and that will always have to be set down, however imperfectly, in words.

"The true history of the human race," wrote E. M. Forster in a recent article, "is the story of human affections. In comparison with it all other histories—even economic history—are false." He goes on to say that owing to its reticent nature it can never be written down completely, and this of course is true, yet what little we do know of this aspect of history has come to us through biography or autobiography. And as long as human beings go on feeling affection for each other, this material will be renewed—material as complicated and yet simple, intense and yet intermittent, various and yet unchanging, as the human heart. In this sense biography is, or should be, a *completion* of life, giving a shape and a significance to the humblest, most pedestrian existence, seeing in the routine and triviality of common experience the universal pattern which gives it harmony and meaning. Every individual life is also the story of Everyman, and while it is the biographer's business to describe the passions, foibles, and idiosyncrasies which make his subject a person, his work will be very thin if these individual traits are not also seen as part of a universal drama. "A man's life of any worth," said Keats, "is a continual allegory, and very few eyes can see the Mystery."

There is an image in Pasternak's great novel, *Doctor Zhivago*, which has moved me very much—of a candle, which has melted a little patch in the icy crust on a windowpane, through which the candle's light is seen by Yura from the dark street below. "Its light seemed to fall into the street as deliberately as a glance, as if the flame were keeping a watch on the passing carriages, and waiting for someone." Perhaps that is the most that a biographer can ever hope to do: to clear, in the icy crust of each man's incomprehension of other men, a little patch, through which a faint, intermittent light can shine. But at the best, it will always be a very little patch of light, in a great sea of darkness—and it is wiser not to be too solemn about what we are doing, since the life that we are describing, like our own, is brittle and shadowy, and it is surely very arrogant to try to give it a set form. All that needs to be said about this was said by Sir William Temple in his essay on poetry, in a single, perfect sentence: "Human life is, at the greatest and the best, but like a froward child, that must be played with and humored a little to keep it quiet till it falls asleep—and then the care is over."

I do not think of truth as being made of granite, but rather as resembling a note in music, a note which we instantly recognize as the right one as soon as it is struck. Proust, the great master of the art of memory, describes in a famous passage in *Swann's Way* how in later life he was sometimes able to hear again certain sounds which, he wrote, "in reality had never stopped": the sobs which had shaken him at a crucial moment of his childhood. "It is only because life is now growing silent about me," he said, "that I hear them afresh, like convent bells which one might believe were not rung nowadays, because during the day they are drowned by the city hubbub, but which may be heard clearly enough in the stillness of the evening."

The biographer with a similar awareness of the continuity of emotion may realize at certain moments, "when life is silent about him," that he has suddenly become aware of something about his subject for which he could not give chapter and verse but which he now knows to be true. For all genuine emotion leaves behind it an eternal reverberation. Whether it is always possible for the biographer to hear and to reproduce it is another matter, unless indeed he has at his disposal such material as Keats's *Letters*—and even then, even then . . . But certainly even the faintest echo can only be heard by temporarily casting aside one's own self and one's own opinions. For this reason I would say to the young biographer who has upon his desk his first, intriguing file of papers to examine them, if he can, with an almost blank mind: to let them produce their own effect. Later on, the time will come to compare, to sift, and to draw conclusions; but first he should listen without interrupting. Sometimes then, as he deciphers the faded ink, a phrase will stand out which reveals the hand that wrote it. He may see—as suddenly as, at the turn of a passage, one comes upon one's own image in a mirror—a living face. It is then, in this fleeting moment, that he may perhaps have a faint apprehension—as near to the truth as we are ever likely to get—of what another man was like.

⌁ Suggestions for Reading and Writing

1. Can you cite a significant work substantiating the charge that "every great man has his disciples, but it is always Judas who is the biographer"? Can you point to an autobiography that reveals much more than its author intended?

2. Iris Origo says that "to sit in judgment" on a subject is one of the "insidious temptations" assailing the biographer. How well does she herself avoid this temptation in *Allegra* or in *The Last Attachment?*

3. Is she contradicting herself when she subsequently declares that "The judgment of character still remains the central problem of biography"?

4. Do you agree with Dr. Johnson that mankind finds its heroes' weaknesses reassuring? Explain.

5. After reading Strachey's "Florence Nightingale" do you agree with Iris Origo that it is "thin"? If not, what term would you apply to it? Why?

6. Iris Origo seems to have mixed feelings here about the contributions of modern psychology to biography. Summarize her views, noting especially her comment that "beneath the conscious personality . . . there is in each of us an underworld of discarded characters. . . ."

7. Explain her statement that today "men are looking not so much for individuality as for protective coloring."

8. She puts forth, then rejects the idea that television enables "every man to interpret for himself, without the filter of another man's mind, the character and actions of his contemporaries." Do you agree with her rejection of the idea?

[ERNEST HEMINGWAY]

Gertrude Stein

The Autobiography of Alice B. Toklas (1933) is a literary hoax concocted by Gertrude Stein (1874–1946). Using the name of her secretary and long-time companion, Miss Stein presented her own life story as seen through another's eyes. (Miss Toklas recently has written her own bona-fide memoir, What Is Remembered [1963].)

Gertrude Stein was born in Pennsylvania, graduated from Radcliffe, and spent four years in Johns Hopkins Medical School before heading for France, in 1902. There she remained until her death, her Paris apartment becoming a salon for struggling young artists of the twenties. She there fed, advised, and helped many to recognition: Picasso, Matisse, Hemingway, Fitzgerald, and Sherwood Anderson were but a few of her intimates.

In addition to her keen eye for young genius, Gertrude Stein gained fame for having coined the phrase "the lost generation"and for her experimental prose and poetry. Violating the laws of punctuation, grammar, and logic, she created her own linguistic principles. She rejected conventional forms for intuitive bursts, sounds without meaning, and incremental repetition of phrases slightly changed—like movie-film frames moved slowly through a portable viewer. Her more than twenty books include character portraits (Three Lives [1909]), poetry (Tender Buttons [1914]), an opera libretto (Four Saints in Three Acts [1934]), and novels (Ida [1941]), as well as literary and art criticism, children's literature, and social commentary.

Another postwar American generation was discovering
Miss Stein when she died in 1946. The following section from
The Autobiography of Alice B. Toklas reveals her talent both
for character insights and for inside gossip.

† † † † †

The first thing that happened when we were back in Paris was
Hemingway with a letter of introduction from Sherwood Anderson.

I remember very well the impression I had of Hemingway that first
afternoon. He was an extraordinarily good-looking young man, twenty-
three years old. It was not long after that that everybody was twenty-six.
It became the period of being twenty-six. During the next two or three
years all the young men were twenty-six years old. It was the right age
apparently for that time and place. There were one or two under twenty,
for example George Lynes but they did not count as Gertrude Stein
carefully explained to them. If they were young men they were twenty-
six. Later on, much later on they were twenty-one and twenty-two.

So Hemingway was twenty-three, rather foreign looking, with passionately interested, rather than interesting eyes. He sat in front of
Gertrude Stein and listened and looked.

They talked then, and more and more, a great deal together. He
asked her to come and spend an evening in their apartment and look at
his work. Hemingway had then and has always a very good instinct for
finding apartments in strange but pleasing localities and good femmes de
ménage and good food. This his first apartment was just off the Place du
Tertre. We spent the evening there and he and Gertrude Stein went over
all the writing he had done up to that time. He had begun the novel that
it was inevitable he would begin and there were the little poems
afterwards printed by McAlmon in the Contact Edition. Gertrude Stein
rather liked the poems, they were direct, Kiplingesque, but the novel she
found wanting. There is a great deal of description in this, she said, and
not particularly good description. Begin over again and concentrate, she
said.

Hemingway was at this time Paris correspondent for a canadian
newspaper. He was obliged there to express what he called the canadian
viewpoint.

He and Gertrude Stein used to walk together and talk together a
great deal. One day she said to him, look here, you say you and your wife
have a little money between you. Is it enough to live on if you live
quietly. Yes, he said. Well, she said, then do it. If you keep on doing

newspaper work you will never see things, you will only see words and that will not do, that is of course if you intend to be a writer. Hemingway said he undoubtedly intended to be a writer. He and his wife went away on a trip and shortly after Hemingway turned up alone. He came to the house about ten o'clock in the morning and he stayed, he stayed for lunch, he stayed all afternoon, he stayed for dinner and he stayed until about ten o'clock at night and then all of a sudden he announced that his wife was enceinte and then with great bitterness, and I, I am too young to be a father. We consoled him as best we could and sent him on his way.

When they came back Hemingway said that he had made up his mind. They would go back to America and he would work hard for a year and with what he would earn and what they had they would settle down and he would give up newspaper work and make himself a writer. They went away and well within the prescribed year they came back with a new born baby. Newspaper work was over.

The first thing to do when they came back was as they thought to get the baby baptised. They wanted Gertrude Stein and myself to be god-mothers and an english war comrade of Hemingway was to be god-father. We were all born of different religions and most of us were not practising any, so it was rather difficult to know in what church the baby could be baptised. We spent a great deal of time that winter, all of us, discussing the matter. Finally it was decided that it should be baptised episcopalian and episcopalian it was. Just how it was managed with the assortment of god-parents I am sure I do not know, but it was baptised in the episcopalian chapel.

Writer or painter god-parents are notoriously unreliable. That is, there is certain before long to be a cooling of friendship. I know several cases of this, poor Paulot Picasso's god-parents have wandered out of sight and just as naturally it is a long time since any of us have seen or heard of our Hemingway god-child.

However in the beginning we were active god-parents, I particularly. I embroidered a little chair and I knitted a gay coloured garment for the god-child. In the meantime the god-child's father was very earnestly at work making himself a writer.

Gertrude Stein never corrects any detail of anybody's writing, she sticks strictly to general principles, the way of seeing what the writer chooses to see, and the relation between that vision and the way it gets down. When the vision is not complete the words are flat, it is very simple, there can be no mistake about it, so she insists. It was at this time that Hemingway began the short things that afterwards were printed in a volume called In Our Time.

One day Hemingway came in very excited about Ford Madox Ford and the Transatlantic. Ford Madox Ford had started the Transatlantic some months before. A good many years before, indeed before the war, we had met Ford Madox Ford who was at that time Ford Madox Hueffer. He was married to Violet Hunt and Violet Hunt and Gertrude Stein were next to each other at the tea table and talked a great deal together. I was next to Ford Madox Hueffer and I liked him very much and I liked his stories of Mistral and Tarascon and I liked his having been followed about in that land of the french royalist, on account of his resemblance to the Bourbon claimant. I had never seen the Bourbon claimant but Ford at that time undoubtedly might have been a Bourbon.

We had heard that Ford was in Paris, but we had not happened to meet. Gertrude Stein had however seen copies of the Transatlantic and found it interesting but had thought nothing further about it.

Hemingway came in then very excited and said that Ford wanted something of Gertrude Stein's for the next number and he, Hemingway, wanted The Making of Americans to be run in it as a serial and he had to have the first fifty pages at once. Gertrude Stein was of course quite overcome with her excitement at this idea, but there was no copy of the manuscript except the one that we had had bound. That makes no difference, said Hemingway, I will copy it. And he and I between us did copy it and it was printed in the next number of the Transatlantic. So for the first time a piece of the monumental work which was the beginning, really the beginning of modern writing, was printed, and we were very happy. Later on when things were difficult between Gertrude Stein and Hemingway, she always remembered with gratitude that after all it was Hemingway who first caused to be printed a piece of The Making of Americans. She always says, yes sure I have a weakness for Hemingway. After all he was the first of the young men to knock at my door and he did make Ford print the first piece of The Making of Americans.

I myself have not so much confidence that Hemingway did do this. I have never known what the story is but I have always been certain that there was some other story behind it all. That is the way I feel about it.

Gertrude Stein and Sherwood Anderson are very funny on the subject of Hemingway. The last time that Sherwood was in Paris they often talked about him. Hemingway had been formed by the two of them and they were both a little proud and a little ashamed of the work of their minds. Hemingway had at one moment, when he had repudiated Sherwood Anderson and all his works, written him a letter in the name of american literature which he, Hemingway, in company with his contemporaries was about to save, telling Sherwood just what he, Hemingway thought about Sherwood's work, and, that thinking, was in no sense complimentary. When Sherwood came to Paris Hemingway naturally was afraid. Sherwood as naturally was not.

As I say he and Gertrude Stein were endlessly amusing on the subject. They admitted that Hemingway was yellow, he is, Gertrude Stein insisted, just like the flat-boat men on the Mississippi river as described by Mark Twain. But what a book, they both agreed, would be the real story of Hemingway, not those he writes but the confessions of the real Ernest Hemingway. It would be for another audience than the audience Hemingway now has but it would be very wonderful. And then they both agreed that they have a weakness for Hemingway because he is such a good pupil. He is a rotten pupil, I protested. You don't understand, they both said, it is so flattering to have a pupil who does it without understanding it, in other words he takes training and anybody who takes training is a favourite pupil. They both admit it to be a weakness. Gertrude Stein added further, you see he is like Derain. You remember Monsieur de Tuille said, when I did not understand why Derain was having the success he was having that it was because he looks like a modern and he smells of the museums. And that is Hemingway, he looks like a modern and he smells of the museums. But what a story that of the real Hem, and one he should tell himself but alas he never will. After all, as he himself once murmured, there is the career, the career.

But to come back to the events that were happening.

Hemingway did it all. He copied the manuscript and corrected the proof. Correcting proofs is, as I said before, like dusting, you learn the values of the thing as no reading suffices to teach it to you. In correcting these proofs Hemingway learned a great deal and he admired all that he learned. It was at this time that he wrote to Gertrude Stein saying that it was she who had done the work in writing The Making of Americans and he and all his had but to devote their lives to seeing that it was published.

He had hopes of being able to accomplish this. Some one, I think by the name of Sterne, said that he could place it with a publisher. Gertrude Stein and Hemingway believed that he could, but soon Hemingway reported that Sterne had entered into his period of unreliability. That was the end of that.

In the meantime and sometime before this Mina Loy had brought McAlmon to the house and he came from time to time and he brought his wife and brought William Carlos Williams. And finally he wanted to print The Making of Americans in the Contact Edition and finally he did. I will come to that.

In the meantime McAlmon had printed the three poems and ten

stories of Hemingway and William Bird had printed In Our Time and Hemingway was getting to be known. He was coming to know Dos Passos and Fitzgerald and Bromfield and George Antheil and everybody else and Harold Loeb was once more in Paris. Hemingway had become a writer. He was also a shadow-boxer, thanks to Sherwood, and he heard about bull-fighting from me. I have always loved spanish dancing and spanish bull-fighting and I loved to show the photographs of bull-fighters and bull-fighting. I also loved to show the photograph where Gertrude Stein and I were in the front row and had our picture taken there accidentally. In these days Hemingway was teaching some young chap how to box. The boy did not know how, but by accident he knocked Hemingway out. I believe this sometimes happens. At any rate in these days Hemingway although a sportsman was easily tired. He used to get quite worn out walking from his house to ours. But then he had been worn by the war. Even now he is, as Hélène says all men are, fragile. Recently a robust friend of his said to Gertrude Stein, Ernest is very fragile, whenever he does anything sporting something breaks, his arm, his leg, or his head.

In those early days Hemingway liked all his contemporaries except Cummings. He accused Cummings of having copied everything, not from anybody but from somebody. Gertrude Stein who had been much impressed by The Enormous Room said that Cummings did not copy, he was the natural heir of the New England tradition with its aridity and its sterility, but also with its individuality. They disagreed about this. They also disagreed about Sherwood Anderson. Gertrude Stein contended that Sherwood Anderson had a genius for using a sentence to convey a direct emotion, this was in the great american tradition, and that really except Sherwood there was no one in America who could write a clear and passionate sentence. Hemingway did not believe this, he did not like Sherwood's taste. Taste has nothing to do with sentences, contended Gertrude Stein. She also added that Fitzgerald was the only one of the younger writers who wrote naturally in sentences.

Gertrude Stein and Fitzgerald are very peculiar in their relation to each other. Gertrude Stein had been very much impressed by This Side of Paradise. She read it when it came out and before she knew any of the young american writers. She said of it that it was this book that really created for the public the new generation. She has never changed her opinion about this. She thinks this equally true of The Great Gatsby. She thinks Fitzgerald will be read when many of his well known contemporaries are forgotten. Fitzgerald always says that he thinks Gertrude Stein says these things just to annoy him by making him think that she means them, and he adds in his favourite way, and her doing it is the cruellest thing I ever heard. They always however have a very good time when they meet. And the last time they met they had a good time with themselves and Hemingway.

Then there was McAlmon. McAlmon had one quality that appealed to Gertrude Stein, abundance, he could go on writing, but she complained that it was dull.

There was also Glenway Wescott but Glenway Wescott at no time interested Gertrude Stein. He has a certain syrup but it does not pour.

So then Hemingway's career was begun. For a little while we saw less of him and then he began to come again. He used to recount to Gertrude Stein the conversations that he afterwards used in The Sun Also Rises and they talked endlessly about the character of Harold Loeb. At this time Hemingway was preparing his volume of short stories to submit to publishers in America. One evening after we had not seen him for a while he turned up with Shipman. Shipman was an amusing boy who was to inherit a few thousand dollars when he came of age. He was not of age. He was to buy the Transatlantic Review when he came of age, so Hemingway said. He was to support a surrealist review when he came of age, André Masson said. He was to buy a house in the country when he came of age, Josette Gris said. As a matter of fact when he came of age nobody who had known him then seemed to know what he did do with his inheritance. Hemingway brought him with him to the house to talk about buying the Transatlantic and incidentally he brought the manuscript he intended sending to America. He handed it to Gertrude Stein. He had added to his stories a little story of meditations and in these he said that The Enormous Room was the greatest book he had ever read. It was then that Gertrude Stein said, Hemingway, remarks are not literature.

After this we did not see Hemingway for quite a while and then we went to see some one, just after The Making of Americans was printed, and Hemingway who was there came up to Gertrude Stein and began to explain why he would not be able to write a review of the book. Just then a heavy hand fell on his shoulder and Ford Madox Ford said, young man it is I who wish to speak to Gertrude Stein. Ford then said to her, I wish to ask your permission to dedicate my new book to you. May I. Gertrude Stein and I were both awfully pleased and touched.

For some years after this Gertrude Stein and Hemingway did not meet. And then we heard that he was back in Paris and telling a number of people how much he wanted to see her. Don't you come home with Hemingway on your arm, I used to say when she went out for a walk. Sure enough one day she did come back bringing him with her.

They sat and talked a long time. Finally I heard her say, Hemingway, after all you are ninety percent Rotarian. Can't you, he said, make it eighty percent. No, said she regretfully, I can't. After all as she always says, he did, and I may say, he does have moments of disinterestedness.

After that they met quite often. Gertrude Stein always says she likes to see him, he is so wonderful. And if he could only tell his own story. In their last conversation she accused him of having killed a great many of his rivals and put them under the sod. I never, said Hemingway, seriously killed anybody but one man and he was a bad man and, he deserved it, but if I killed anybody else I did it unknowingly, and so I am not responsible.

It was Ford who once said of Hemingway, he comes and sits at my feet and praises me. It makes me nervous. Hemingway also said once, I turn my flame which is a small one down and down and then suddenly there is a big explosion. If there were nothing but explosions my work would be so exciting nobody could bear it.

However, whatever I say, Gertrude Stein always says, yes I know but I have a weakness for Hemingway.

† Suggestions for Reading and Writing

1. Describe the portrait of Gertrude Stein that is revealed here. What is added by the third-person device? Compare this portrait of Miss Stein with that depicted in Miss Toklas' *What Is Remembered.*
2. Is the treatment of Hemingway here essentially nonsympathetic? Is it corroborated by the Canadian writer Morley Callaghan's incisive memoirs of both Hemingway and Fitzgerald in his *That Summer in Paris* (1963)?
3. Compare Miss Stein's Hemingway with the man and writer described in such standard studies as Philip Young's *Ernest Hemingway* (1952), Charles A. Fenton's *The Apprenticeship of Ernest Hemingway* (1954), and Carlos Baker's *Hemingway: The Writer as Artist* (1956).
4. Does the hero of such recent family portraits as Leicester Hemingway's *My Brother, Ernest Hemingway* (1962) and Marcelline Hemingway Sanford's *At the Hemingways* (1962) bear much resemblance to the Papa Hemingway of Lillian Ross's "How Do You Like It Now, Gentlemen?" *New Yorker* (May 13, 1950), p. 36 ff.?
5. Miss Stein here claims to have influenced greatly Hemingway's prose style. Does a reading of her *The Making of Americans* (1925) or *Composition and Explanation* (1926) and the latter's *In Our Time* (1925) or *The Sun Also Rises* (1926) bear this out?
6. How valid is her comment that Hemingway "looks like a modern and he smells of the museums"? Explain.
7. Hemingway's posthumously published *A Moveable Feast* (1964) contains a sketch of Miss Stein. Compare his sketch with this one, and discuss the emotions and the attitudes underlying each.
8. After reading *This Side of Paradise* (1920) or *The Great Gatsby*

(1925), discuss Miss Stein's observation that Scott Fitzgerald "was the only one of the younger writers who wrote naturally in sentences."

9. Gertrude Stein-isms have amused several college generations. "Pigeons on the grass, alas" and "A rose is a rose is a rose" are the best-known examples. Do you see in this use of language any parallels to recent experiments in music or art? (For background, see Donald Sutherland's *Gertrude Stein, A Biography of Her Work* [1951], John Malcolm Brinnin's *The Third Rose: Gertrude Stein and Her World* [1959], or Frederick J. Hoffman's short critical study, *Gertrude Stein* [1961].)

[MORT SAHL]

Robert Rice

The New Yorker magazine has gained international recognition for the cerebral wit, humor, and satire of its contents. The founder and editor, Harold Wallace Ross (1892–1951), said bluntly that his weekly was "not for the old lady in Dubuque" but the "caviar sophisticates." E.B. White, Alexander Woollcott, James Thurber, Ogden Nash, Dorothy Parker, Robert Benchley, and Clifton Fadiman made their reputations in its pages; so did the cartoonists Peter Arno, Charles Addams, Sam Cobean, Syd Hoff, Saul Steinberg, Gluyas Williams, and Thurber.

In its own way the New Yorker's prose is as highly stylized as Time magazine's; some critics see in both the same anonymity of style. Others credit the New Yorker with having helped raise the level of recent American writing. Value judgments aside, the most popular New Yorker features over the years have been its slightly suggestive one-line-caption cartoons; its complex, low-keyed fiction; such departments as "Notes and Comments" and "Talk of the Town"; and its biographical "Profiles."

The New Yorker "Profile" is less a full portrait than a one-angled study-in-depth. It may be satiric or sympathetic, long or short, but it is always witty, urbane, and at least slightly highbrow. Robert Rice's "Profile" of comedian Mort Sahl exemplifies most of these qualities. Since 1938, Rice (1916–) has worked for publications such as the New York Telegraph, PM, and the New Yorker as reporter, critic, editor, and feature writer. He also has written a book, The Business of Crime (1956).

✓ ✓ ✓ ✓ ✓

Mort Sahl, a dark and savage wit who spends most of his working life fulminating through the haze, late at night, from the stage of one night club or another, is almost certainly the most widely acclaimed and best-paid nihilist ever produced by Western civilization. Unlike most men in the upper tax brackets, he is against practically everything. During one recent forty-five-minute night-club monologue, he disparaged, sometimes at length and sometimes merely in passing, the following persons, places, objects, institutions, and ideas, in the following order: Charles de Gaulle; Dwight Eisenhower; segregation; Shelley Berman; trade unions; "Marty;" jazz; New York City; Berkeley, California; Samuel Beckett; newspapers; coffeehouses; sandals; J. D. Salinger; soiled raincoats; natural-shoulder suits; women; filter-tip cigarettes; capital punishment; Zen Buddhism; the Chinese Nationalists; the Chinese Communists; Candlestick Park; atheism; policemen; Chicago; the Moskvich automobile; advertising; the Edsel automobile; "Death of a Salesman;" the Daughters of the American Revolution; the Woman's Christian Temperance Union; movies; the concept of guilt; astronauts; Josephine Baker; the hydrogen bomb; the State Department; Senator George Smathers; Cuba; Israel; Fidel Castro; Richard Nixon; Dave Garroway; John Kennedy; birth control; "On the Beach;" Dick Clark; American youth; schoolteachers; Christmas; German radios; corruption; Charles Van Doren; Adlai Stevenson; the Columbia Broadcasting System; prostitution; drug manufacturers; Elizabeth Arden; cheating on examinations; John Steinbeck; Norman Cousins; the Russians; *Fortune*; Miami; multiple-choice questions; the Federal Bureau of Investigation; the Pacific Gas & Electric Co.; Dave Brubeck; the Taft-Hartley Act; former Governor Earl Long; Disneyland; Arturo Frondizi; the Diners' Club; the foreign-aid bill; Ezra Taft Benson; and the *Saturday Evening Post*. That didn't nearly exhaust the list of his animosities, of course; on the evening

"The Fury," *New Yorker*, XXXVI (July 30, 1960), 31–53. Reprinted by permission; © 1960 The New Yorker Magazine, Inc.

in question he didn't get around to a number of his favorite targets, like Christian Herter, sports cars, Billy Graham, civil defense, California freeways, psychoanalysis, General Motors, Tennessee Williams, the Strategic Air Command, *Playboy*, the American Medical Association, and beards.

Sahl's manner is as uncompromising as his matter. He hurls his words ferociously at his listeners, almost without pausing to breathe. He has big white teeth, which, when he says something destructive enough to amuse even him, suddenly glare from his lean and sardonic face in a wolfish grin, and if he becomes truly transported by the damage he is doing, he erupts into a staccato two-syllable bark of triumph. Though his basic idiom is accurate and cultivated English, he decorates it defiantly with some of the most repellent jargon of hipsters and of Ph.D.s. Sahl's words are meant to be heard, not read, and to get an idea of his style one must remember that passages like the one that follows are delivered at top speed and with passionate earnestness: "You know, chicks dig psychoanalysis the most—much better than guys. That's a generalization, of course. I do generalize a lot without specific knowledge. The head of psychoanalytic research at Mount Sinai Hospital—the same hospital that gave you Oscar Levant, kids—said he liked the way I could focus on a group, like advertising men, and talk about nailed-down collars and thin ties with stickpins through the body and wrought-iron glasses. He said, 'With a minimal distribution of energy, you focus on their mores and level them.' Of course, what he doesn't understand is that I have no specific knowledge of the subject, and that I generalize and use stereotypes, so if I weren't perceptive I could be a bigot." Talk like that can't be what an expense-account hedonist, intent on getting away from it all for an evening, expects to hear when he wanders into one of the night clubs where Sahl performs—the hungry i, in San Francisco, say, or Basin Street East, in New York; Mister Kelly's, in Chicago; the Crescendo, in Los Angeles; the Americana, in Miami Beach; or the Flamingo, in Las Vegas. Still, Sahl has never been hooted off the stage. On the contrary, large numbers of people apparently enjoy having their intellects, their sensibilities, and their beliefs pummelled by him. ("Are there any groups I haven't offended?" is one sentence that he often uses to get offstage. "I congratulate you on your attention span" is another.) They show up in sufficient force at whatever club he is performing in to enable the club to turn over to him from five thousand to seventy-five hundred dollars a week. The secret of his success is by no means mysterious. A lot of the time Sahl is very funny, as only a very serious man can be.

The subject that Sahl is best known for making serious jokes about is politics—perhaps because it is the least esoteric of the matters that he ordinarily deals with. (Actually, he devotes more words to another topic—women. But women as described by Sahl are apt to be so esoteric as to be unrecognizable. " 'What do you see in the moon?' she asks me. Chicks are always using the moon as a kind of a Rorschach," he may say, or "This chick smokes a lot, which is a sign that she's very advanced. She smokes filter-tip mentholated cigarettes through a holder with a filter in it. She wants to change the world, but she doesn't want to get a sore throat.") Sahl's attitude toward politics, like his other attitudes, is entirely negative. "I'm not so much interested in politics as I am in overthrowing the government," he often says, and he also often laments, "I wish I had a cause, because I've got a lot of enthusiasm." While nonpartisan ridicule of the actions and personalities of politicians goes back at least to the birth of the republic, it is doubtful whether anyone has ever practiced it with more zeal than Sahl, who has told his audience, "I don't tell jokes, I give little lectures." Some of the lectures, little as they are, contain as much meat as most orations. "Kennedy is trying to buy the country and Nixon is trying to sell it," Sahl will say. Or "Eisenhower is for integration, but gradually; Stevenson, on the other hand, is for integration, but moderately. It should be possible to compromise between those extremes." Or "For a while, every time the Russians threw an American in jail, the Un-American Activities Committee would retaliate by throwing an American in jail, too." Or " 'On the Beach' is an escapist film; it takes your mind off birth control." Since a reputation for having a sense of humor is considered a political asset in this country, the butts of Sahl's political jokes tend to laugh at them more heartily—if not always more sincerely—than anyone else, and Sahl has become a sort of fixture on the hundred-dollar-a-plate-dinner circuit, where he has publicly convulsed the likes of Harry Truman, Henry Cabot Lodge, Herbert Lehman, Carmine De Sapio, and Jacob Javits. Some politicians have even been impelled to enter into private relations with him. He has discussed what to do about American humor and the State Department backstage at Mister Kelly's with Hubert Humphrey; he has exchanged more or less portentous small talk with John Kennedy at a number of Hollywood parties; and he has maintained fairly brisk communication with Adlai Stevenson, who was one of his first admirers.

Since Sahl talks so much about politics, he has inevitably been compared to Will Rogers, the only other major entertainer in recent history who ventured to trespass on that territory. It is characteristic of Sahl that this annoys him; he feels that he alone has the right to choose the people he is mentioned in the same breath with. Some years ago, he told a reporter for this magazine that he had "a Christlike image" of himself. The remark attracted considerable attention, not all of it favorable, and Sahl presently began telling his night-club audiences, "I won't cop out; I said it. I think if you're going to model yourself on someone, you ought to really come on." (Sahl is as hostile to religion as he is to everything else, and only slightly more reticent about showing it; naturally, he is against agnostics and atheists, too.) In any case, Sahl certainly isn't much like Will Rogers. Whereas Rogers assumed the role of a yokel who questioned the common sense of the educated men managing the government, Sahl is an intellectual who is scornful of the government because he feels that it is managed by yokels whose sense is all too common. Indeed, intellect, which, by long tradition is contraband in the area of show business where Sahl customarily operates, is one of the qualities that have earned him renown. As the first entertainer in years who contrived to smuggle his brains past a velvet rope, he has been a pathfinder for a stimulating new generation of comedians, including Shelley Berman, Mike Nichols and Elaine May, Lenny Bruce, and Bob Newhart, most of whom have little in common with Sahl except that they are bright and therefore suspect. Sahl has also heartened that substantial section of the public that has a normal desire to drink too much, spend too much money, and stay up too late but hesitates to do any of those things if the only available excuse is a chanteuse, a pair of adagio dancers, or Jerry Lewis. Perhaps the most eloquent testimony to the intellectual rigor of Sahl's act has been given, admiringly, by Dave Brubeck, whose quartet appeared with Sahl at the Crescendo a few years ago. The Brubeck group headed the bill and therefore went on after Sahl. It was an arrangement that Brubeck found frustrating. "Mort's impossible to follow," he recently said. "He demands so much of an audience that it hasn't the strength for anyone else."

A second un-Rogerslike quality of Sahl's is his perpetual and comprehensive indignation. A few of the people who know him well— among them his mother and the motion-picture producer Jerry Wald— profess to believe that at heart Sahl is just a wholesome American boy who wants to get ahead in show business, and that what he says is all in fun, like Jack Benny pretending he's stingy. Wald likes to be quoted as saying, "They call Mort an Angry Young Man, but I don't call Mort an Angry Young Man. I call Mort a Funny Young Man." There is little doubt that Sahl wants to get ahead in show business, but there is even less doubt that he means just about every word he says to his audiences. Privately as well as professionally, he is appalled by the world he lives in. "If this were a movie, there would now be a dissolve, but unfortunately my life has no dissolves. I have to live every agonizing moment of it," he has said, in performance after performance. A few weeks ago, a night-club owner who has seen a lot of him on and off the stage said, "Make no mistake, Mort's Hostility City all the way."

If Sahl's intellect has moved intellectuals to admiration, his discontent has provoked enthusiasm among the discontented, a considerably larger group. For a section of the college population, especially, Sahl has been not so much an entertainer as a spokesman. When he began to perform, the era of Joe McCarthy had not yet come to an end; it was a time when indignation, though it doubtless smoldered in many breasts, was seldom expressed with much vehemence in places like night clubs, where it might be overheard. As a matter of fact, Sahl was given his first job, at seventy-five dollars a week, by Enrico Banducci, the proprietor of the hungry i—then an extraordinarily dim cellar in which the San Francisco Fire Department allowed no more than eighty-three beatniks to assemble at any one time—on the strength of a McCarthy joke. "The rest of Mort's audition was terrible, but that joke killed me," says Banducci, whose club is still in a cellar, but a roomy one about which Sahl has nothing more derogatory to say than that it reminds him of the ruins of Frankfurt. (He has never been in Frankfurt.) The McCarthy joke, an elaborate affair, started with a detailed description of an Eisenhower jacket equipped with what Sahl called, in his carefree way, "multi-directional zippers," and ended with a suggestion for an improved model, a McCarthy jacket, with an extra zipper to go across the mouth. The news of such audacity at such a time rapidly reached the campuses in the San Francisco area, and the hungry i's regular clientele soon found itself competing for those eighty-three places with college students, who were delighted not only with Sahl's boldness but with his working costume—a sweater over a shirt with an unbuttoned collar—and with the knowing way he spoke about jazz, psychiatry, sports cars, Christmas-vacation jobs at the post office, and other matters close to their hearts. They recognized him at once as a battle-scarred member of their tribe.

Sahl's scars are evidently many and deep, though the precise nature of the battles in which he won them is not clear. It is only under some duress that he is willing to reminisce at all about the first twenty-three years of his life, from May, 1927, when he was born in Montreal, to June, 1950, when he graduated, as a Bachelor of Science who had specialized in city management, from the School of Public Administration of the University of Southern California. When he is persuaded to dwell briefly on those years, his exposition of the facts is littered with obscure asides, like "Lenin said, 'You have to destroy before you can build,' " or "Society was yelling in my ear, 'You're a cripple because you have ability,' " or, more simply, when he is feeling blander and more lucid than usual, "I wasn't an organization cat." Sahl's father, a New Yorker who is now retired, devoted most of his career to working as a civil servant in various departments of the federal government. Once, however, he took a four-year leave of absence from government, during which he made an unrewarding attempt to operate a tobacco shop in Montreal, the city his wife comes from, and it was at that time that Morton Lyon, the couple's only child, was born. Sahl grew up in a number of cities besides Montreal, among them Washington, Chattanooga, and Honolulu, but if any place on earth can properly be called his home, it is Los Angeles, where the family moved when he was seven, and which remained its base from then on. ("Los Angeles isn't a home town; it's a weather-observation satellite somewhere out in space," a friend of Sahl's remarked a while ago. "No wonder Mort's a displaced person.") As his mother remembers it, he started to talk at the age of seven months. "When he was ten," she says, "he spoke like a man of thirty." It was in his early teens that he began to season his talk heavily with imitations and jokes; "I found people looked better to me when they smiled," he has explained. At the various public schools he attended, he apparently neither had nor took much trouble with his studies. At high school, R.O.T.C. was his chief interest—"I was a martinet as a kid," he has said—and at the end of his sophomore year, when he was fifteen, he persuaded an Army recruiting officer that he was eighteen, and became a soldier. He did have the grace to leave a note behind, so his mother was able to locate him, at Fort MacArthur, near Los Angeles, and retrieve him after a couple of weeks of active duty. "Gee, Mom, why do you have to spoil everything?" he said on that occasion, or so she recalls it. For the next two years, he more or less docilely attended his classes, and then, when he graduated, he enlisted in the Army Air Forces. By this time, he had ceased to be a martinet, and had become an insurrectionist, and he remained a private during his entire period of service—thirty-one months, a good part of them spent at Elmendorf Field, in Anchorage, Alaska. At one point, he says—in what may be one of his characteristic evocations of the mood, rather than the facts, of his life—he was given K.P. duty for eighty-three straight days for publishing various insubordinate remarks about his commanding officer in a paper he was editing, called *Poop from the Group*.

Sahl came out of the Air Force with a strong desire to tell the world what was wrong with it, preferably by writing and performing, but with no notion of how to make the world listen. Consequently, he deferred to his father's wishes and continued his studies, under the G.I. Bill, at Compton Junior College. With his mustering-out pay, he realized a long-cherished dream by buying a car, which he describes as "a Model-A roadster, chopped, with the frame zeed in and a suicide front end." The description seems to convey a vivid picture to his fellow-tribesmen, if to no one else. Even with the suicide front end, Sahl's college years—two at Compton and two at Southern California—were not satisfactory to him.

He tinkered with his car, listened to jazz, dated as many girls as he could, and was careful neither to attend any more classes than he had to nor to take any courses scheduled earlier than eleven in the morning, but he was simply not very happy. Then, one day in the fall of 1950, just after his graduation from U.S.C., he drove up to Berkeley in his latest car—a forty-dollar Chevrolet—to visit a girl who was doing graduate work at the University of California. (Eventually, Sahl married the girl, but after two years they were divorced, and he has not been married since.) The physical beauty of the San Francisco area and the intellectual ferment on the Berkeley campus so invigorated Sahl that he abandoned once and for all any idea of becoming a traffic engineer or a city manager. "I was born in San Francisco," he often says.

During the next three years, he concentrated on writing and performing—activities from which he earned, by his calculation, one hundred and eighteen dollars. Among his arenas were an obscure Hollywood outfit called Theatre X—the initial stood for "experimental," not, as it might well have, for "unknown"—and a magazine published by the Altruistic Artists Foundation, for which he wrote movie reviews, editorials, and an article entitled "Art and Poetry, the Siamese Twins of Beauty." Occasionally, when his finances were particularly desperate, he would settle down for a week or two as a messenger or a used-car salesman in Los Angeles, but he spent as much time as he could lurking on or about the Berkeley campus as a member of a nocturnal, poverty-stricken, exuberant band of poets, Trotskyites, Nietzsche-lovers, and other advanced types. He is often overcome by nostalgia for those days, when he customarily slept on a window seat in the apartment of three girls he knew, and for one period of some weeks subsisted mainly on leftover pies from an all-night hamburger joint where one of the Nietzsche-lovers was a short-order cook. "Things were simple then," he told an audience not long ago. "All there was to worry about was man's destiny." Finally, Banducci gave him the job at the hungry i, and, as a friend noted not long ago, "Right then and there was when Mort became a success; after all, there's a hell of a lot more difference between seventy-five dollars a week and nothing than there is between seventy-five and seventy-five hundred."

Sahl's excellent credentials as a rebellious youth have been strongly reinforced by his convoluted and self-deriding manner of expressing his rebellion. It is a manner that apparently gives accurate expression to the way many of his contemporaries and juniors—or, as he often calls them, "my people"—look at themselves and the world. "After all, if we couldn't laugh about these things, we might do something about them," he sometimes says. If ever a sentence called for exegesis, that one does, so it may be pardonable, if ponderous, to note that it can be taken in the following eight ways, at least:

It is a joke, in classic, surprise-ending form.

It is a piece of sarcasm aimed at the folklore that extolls a sense of humor above all other virtues.

It is an analysis of the origin and function of humor.

It is a general condemnation of society.

It is a denunciation of the audience for being in a night club instead of on the barricades.

It is a plea to the audience that he be given serious attention.

It is a confession that his work is unlikely to change things.

It is a characteristic defensive maneuver designed to disarm his critics in advance.

Sahl feels that intricacies of this sort are the crux of his work. He is fairly sure that audiences in Las Vegas or Miami Beach, say, are not up to coping with them, and therefore he isn't able to give his best shows in such places. He is at his very best, he thinks, when he makes one of his infrequent appearances on a campus, before an audience of his people. Not long ago, in conversation with a friend, he compared his act to an archipelago, completely submerged except for a few mountain peaks—his surefire gags. When he plays a college, he says, the waters recede, the lowlands become visible, and the country lies open to exploration. Those who have explored it—his people—can testify that Sahl country offers them little cover. What surrounds the celebrated gags about Richard Nixon, General Motors, the Strategic Air Command, Chiang Kai-shek, and the rest of his people's favorite enemies is a ceaseless and unsparing attack on his people themselves, or, to put it another way, on Sahl himself. He excoriates their mating habits, their avocations, and their intellectual attitudes. He keeps up a drumfire against almost everything they are attracted to—coffeehouses, earnest young women, sports cars, stereophonic jazz, even "Pogo." ("What kind of civilization are we living in when a possum says something and we all say, 'I wish I'd said that'?") His very language, with its thick overlay of jazz and academic jargon, is a deliberate parody of the way his people talk. Perhaps the most famous of his early routines described the notes passed between a group of college men who were trying to hold up the Fairmont Hotel in San Francisco—what they planned to do with the money was live in the hotel for the rest of their lives—and the hotel cashier, also a college man: "Give us the money and act normal." "First you must define your terms. What do you mean by normal?" "This is not a debating society. Give us the money." And so forth. Sahl's people, naturally, favored Adlai Stevenson for the Presidency, and so, just as naturally, Sahl has made Stevenson the target of some of his most carefully squeezed-off shots. A routine he used a good deal this spring was a rundown of public men in terms of the sort of relatives they appeared to him to resemble. Eisenhower, he said, was not so much a father as a stepfather; Nixon was an uncle; Kennedy was a kid brother; Symington was a very distant relation; and Stevenson was a rich uncle who would keep bringing you presents as long as you got good marks. Just before the Democratic Convention, he went on television with newsreels of the candidates arriving at the Los Angeles airport. He had his own version of what they said as they got off their planes:

> Kennedy: "I am here to accept the nomination."
> Johnson: "I am a candidate, but I can't be here because
>   I have to run the country."
> Stevenson: "I am not a candidate and I am not here."

Because a rolled-up newspaper is an essential part of Sahl's working gear, because he often starts a show by commenting on some of the day's news, and because his talk bristles with references to published matter ranging from Nietzsche epigrams to *Hot Rod*, his supporters assume that he is a voluminous reader. It is true that any quarters he occupies—his home, in Hollywood, or a hotel room on the road—are likely to contain all the local papers, the *Times, Playboy, Fortune, Variety, Newsweek,* The Manchester *Guardian, TV Guide, Down Beat, Life,* and a dozen other magazines, plus an assortment of books, which recently included "Cuba: Island of Paradox," James MacGregor Burns' biography of Kennedy, Adlai Stevenson's "Putting First Things First," Norman Mailer's "Advertisements for Myself," Irwin Shaw's "Two Weeks in Another Town," a volume of Nietzsche, a couple of Henry James novels, and Theodore Reik's "Creation of Woman." Actually, though, Sahl is a voluminous skimmer. His imagination responds so energetically to just about any sentence his eye happens to catch that—for professional purposes, at least—he never needs to finish a paragraph. (The entertainment section is the one part of any daily paper that he does read from beginning to end, to the disillusionment of many new acquaintances, who would not have believed that he would ever choose Winchell over Lippmann. Even when he was living on pies in Berkeley, he managed, most weeks, to find a quarter for *Variety.*) His hotel-robbery routine was suggested by a newspaper headline about an attempt to hold up the Fairmont, to be sure, but the routine had nothing to do with the actual story, which he may not even have read. In a Russian-spy routine that he first used at the Village Vanguard, he used the name of Colonel Rudolf Abel, but except for the name he totally ignored the facts. His Colonel Abel lived in Greenwich Village; the two New York addresses that the real Colonel Abel maintained were a studio on Fulton Street in Brooklyn and a room in a hotel in the East Twenties. The reason Sahl moved Abel to the Village was typically complex. In the routine, F.B.I. men asked the spy's neighbors how it was that they hadn't known what he was up to, and they answered that they had known and had thought of notifying the F.B.I., but then they had figured, "That's the Village." There are endless instances of Sahl's disregard for the facts—as opposed to what he feels is the essence—of the news. Only a few weeks ago, for the sake of a little lecture, he said that Secretary of State Herter was in Geneva, when one of the day's principal stories was about a conference that Herter was attending in Washington. In general, Sahl doesn't so much comment on what the news is as on what he thinks it is. As he says, if he weren't perceptive he'd be a bigot.

Sahl's method of working up his act is as unorthodox as the act itself. None of his material is composed by anyone by himself, none of it is written down, and very little of it is ever repeated word for word. "I'm overcommunicative, as Riesman would say," he remarked recently. (He is forever trying to implicate some more or less innocent bystander—Riesman, Freud, the government, society, civilization—in what he does.) He even says he doesn't utter a word that was not conceived right onstage—a statement that, like so many of the other things he says, is only approximately factual. To many of his acquaintances, it appears that he spends most of the non-working part of every day in a sort of low-pressure rehearsal that consists of flipping through whatever reading matter happens to be around, studying whatever environment he happens to be in, and trying out the ideas he gets from these activities on whoever happens to be handy. It is quite true, though, that he is never sure which of the ideas to keep, which to modify, and which to discard until he is in the process of putting them before an audience. Like any congenital performer, he lives more intensely when he is onstage than at any other time; it is not merely that audience reaction gives him a clue to the worth of his notions but that he himself does not really hear what he says until he says it in public. Quite often he says something that doesn't sound funny to the audience but does to him. On those occasions, he tends to become stubborn and to repeat the remark, with variations, night after night until he either succeeds in making his listeners like it or grudgingly decides that he never will succeed. Each of his regular routines began with a stray, embryonic thought that was well received by both the audience and himself; in successive performances, Sahl would force-feed such a thought until it had developed into a routine—a process that usually takes him two or three weeks. Once a routine has matured fully, Sahl tends to lose interest in it, and though he keeps it in his head as what he calls a "saver" for nights when he and the audience are not getting along well, he uses it less

and less, and seldom to its best effect. Paul Desmond, the saxophonist of
the Brubeck quartet, is one of Sahl's closest friends. (Their relationship
is described by the inscription on a cigarette lighter Sahl once gave
Desmond: "To the sound from the fury.") Now and then over the years,
Desmond has had occasion to see Sahl perform every night for a week or
two at a stretch. "It's like watching a garden in time-lapse photography"
is the way he describes the waxing and waning of a Sahl routine.

Desmond and Brubeck, among other jazz musicians, are fascinated
by Sahl, because they feel that he improvises in much the way they do,
first stating a theme and then letting his mind or his feelings vary it ad
lib. Certainly jazz is part of Sahl's fibre. Ever since his teens, when he
discovered Stan Kenton—to whom he now refers as "a father figure,"
apparently in an attempt to implicate Freud in his fondness for
music—it seems to have provided him with the only reliable escape he
has been able to find from his black musings about his own problems and
the world's. He is undeniably a jazz connoisseur and his memory for
what he has heard is so prodigious that he has no trouble abashing
Desmond, say, by singing, with complete accuracy, a Desmond chorus
from a record Desmond made ten years before and has forgotten about.
Whether or not Sahl consciously uses a jazz technique, his show, like any
worthwhile jazz outfit's, changes so much from night to night, and even
between ten in the evening and two in the morning, and is so vivid a
reflection of his mood of the moment, that some employees and habitués
of the clubs he works at watch every one of his performances obsessively.
Many such adepts look forward to his late, late show on a Friday or
Saturday night, when the audience has drunk itself into semi-
insensibility and Sahl is tired and querulous. "That's when Mort's
entrails really show," one of them said gleefully a few weeks ago, and
went on to recall that during one such performance in May, just before
his thirty-third birthday, Sahl, in the course of discussing the theory that
he had achieved a good deal for a young man, said bitterly, "Look at
Castro. *He's* thirty-two and he has a country. It kills me." Sahl probably
thinks he's entitled to a country, too—a large one, like the United States
of America—but saying so was an indiscretion of the kind he has enough
grace not to commit when he is in full control of his feelings; however
much it delighted the adept, it provoked a titter, rather than a laugh,
from the rest of the audience, and he probably hasn't repeated it. A while
ago, one of his friends, leading an informal symposium on Sahl's
character, said, "What I admire most about Mort is that, angry and
frustrated and sometimes childish as he is, he tries so hard, and usually so
well, not to put anything but the best of himself into his work. And,
believe me, for Mort it *is* hard. It takes real heroism for a multiple schizoid like him to keep so many of his neuroses out of his act."

For a star performer, an ordinary night-club week comprises between thirteen and eighteen shows, each of them lasting forty or fifty minutes; Saturday is always a three-show night, Friday often is, and there are either two or three shows on four other nights, depending on local custom and the fine print in the star's contract. This sort of schedule exhausts even the conventional comedian, each of whose shows is pretty much a verbatim repetition of the one before it, or whose repertory, at best, includes three standard shows, to avoid repeating one on any given night. For Sahl, every night is, in his phrase, a lifetime. Though he clearly has enough nervous energy for a troupe, and must have considerable stamina, too, brawn is not one of his assets. He is neither very tall nor very broad, standing about five feet ten and weighing no more than a hundred and fifty. He is wiry, though; eight or ten years ago, as a result of a program of weight-lifting, he put an inch on his biceps in two weeks—of all his accomplishments, the one of which he is probably vainest. Every couple of years he comes down with mononucleosis, a disease that is generally attributed to fatigue, and it keeps him in bed for several weeks. He doesn't smoke and he doesn't drink ("We're living in a society in which girls drink and I don't," he complained recently, attempting to implicate society in the problems he has when he is out on a date), and he doesn't eat much, either. He drinks coffee in quantities so large that once a week or so he has to switch to tea for a day to get the taste of it out of his mouth. He has a headache most of the time, and after a night's work his legs and back ache, too; it takes him several hours to unwind to the point of being able to sleep. He spends those hours in coffeehouses, or driving a sports car with or without company, or just lying on a couch listening to old Kenton records. Whenever possible, in fact, he has a phonograph or a radio going, preferably loud. If it is a radio, he insists that it be FM; his ear is so sensitive, or he likes to think it is, that he can't endure the inaccuracies of AM broadcasting. Since he spends so much time driving, he regards the perfecting of an FM automobile radio as perhaps the only encouraging development in the recent history of the United States. Finding a place to stay that is either without neighbors or with neighbors who will accept Kenton records at top volume at four in the morning is a recurrent problem in his life.

Next to listening to jazz, the activity that relaxes him most is buying things, and in his view the ability to gratify his eccentric acquisitive impulses is the chief blessing of having as much money as he now has. The objects sold by stationery or hardware or sporting-goods or music stores appeal to him particularly, and his pleasure seems to come rather from the act of buying than from the fact of ownership. (One psychiatrically oriented acquaintance attributes what he calls "Mort's purchase compulsion" to the fact that Sahl grew up in a family that had almost no

possessions—not even furniture or crockery—since, owing to his father's migratory habits, the Sahls usually lived in furnished apartments.)
A friend who knew Sahl on the Berkeley campus recalls that in those
days he could pass an absorbed and contented half hour picking out the
lead pencil he had decided to spend his last nickel on. When he began
making a little money, he started laying in ball-point pens, and as he
became increasingly affluent he branched out into sunglasses, transistor
radios, clocks and watches, binoculars, high-fidelity sets, and, finally,
sports cars. He also likes maps and charts and logs and timetables—
"anything that will guide me through the day," as he puts it. When he is
in New York, he gravitates toward the nearest Hoffritz cutlery store, into
whose window he can gaze raptly for what seems to be an eternity, or
toward the nearest Liberty Music Shop, where he may survey the latest
Japanese issue of transistor radios, or toward the Scandinavian Ski &
Sport Shop, where, on his last visit, he ordered a fancy assortment of
sunglasses. A lot of what he buys he gives away, but he keeps a lot, too,
and there is no telling how many of each of the objects of his
affection—even cars—he has at any moment.

Sahl finds it less easy to enjoy some of the other aspects of his
success. Since the end of April, for example, he has been a corporation
chartered by the State of California, and thus, possibly, the sort of
respectable institution that, by his own canon, ought to be overthrown.
He is quite able to see the joke in a man who is famous for refusing to
wear a jacket or a tie in public yet supports an agent, a press agent, a
personal manager, a business manager, a lawyer, and a tax man. (He
wants to change the world, but he doesn't want to get second billing.)
Perhaps that is the reason he has lately taken to going around town, or
even appearing onstage once in a while, fashionably dressed in a narrow
suit. On the other hand, this sartorial reconditioning, which started
smashingly two years ago when he put on full dress for an appearance
on the Academy Awards television show ("My people will think I've
gone over to the enemy," he said lugubriously), may be part of a larger
strategy. Sahl wants to withdraw as fast as he can afford to from night-
club work and infiltrate television, with, if possible, a regular show,
which he visualizes as "a bright March of Time." Among the numerous
reasons Sahl is eager to have a television show of his own—good money,
easier working conditions, wider recognition—is that he thinks of himself as an apostle, whose mission is to bring his anti-gospel, if that is the
word for bad tidings, to as many people as possible. When he is asked
why he takes dates in places like Miami Beach, Las Vegas, and the
Copacabana in New York, he says, "I can't let those audiences go by
default." He also keeps saying, "History will absolve me."

So far, Sahl's experiences with television have been mainly frustrating, largely because network executives and advertising-agency chiefs, even if they are interested in him, feel that a man who has his mind on being absolved by history instead of by Trendex is too "special" or too "controversial" to appear as a regular performer. In 1954, at the beginning of his career, he was under contract for thirteen weeks to the Columbia Broadcasting System, and never got on the air. In 1956, the National Broadcasting Company signed him for a year and, after letting him work once on something called the "Colgate Comedy Hour," confined him to a scattering of shows late at night or early in the afternoon. He has been the guest (as who hasn't?) of Steve Allen and Jack Paar on a number of occasions, and of Eddie Fisher once. (That show produced a moment that Sahl fans cherish. Fisher gave him an effusive introduction, the burden of which was that Sahl was one of the funniest people alive, and then said, "Say something funny, Mort," whereupon Sahl strode purposefully front and center, stopped, glared at the camera, and said slowly and distinctly, "John Foster Dulles.") And last season he was the central figure in a pair of unspectacular spectaculars. What exasperates him about television more than any of these not especially memorable appearances is that the same network officials who consider him too "special" or "cerebral" frequently beg him to work at staff lunches and dinners. Sahl asserts, with some show of logic, that if N.B.C.'s sales force can understand him, its audience certainly can.

Since Sahl wants so badly to be given the opportunity to compete with "Father Knows Best," "The Untouchables," and professional wrestlers, and has had so much trouble getting it, he has resorted, in his most recent guest appearances on television, to what he has always found the most reliable technique for making himself heard: appealing to the audience over the head of the program director—or, as one of his friends describes the method, "Whatever the smart money says, do the opposite." The smart money thinks Sahl should be bland and jolly and tolerant—qualities that frequently get compressed into the opaque adjective "human"—if he wants to reach and hold a national audience, and therefore Sahl has been even more fierce and censorious than usual. In June, he was on the Steve Allen show for eight minutes, and in that brief period he delivered a number of little lectures that were ferocious even by his standards. Among them was a description of a typically cheerful domestic scene at the Nixons', with Mrs. Nixon sitting in a rocker knitting an American flag, and a discussion of the U-2 episode that concluded with Captain Beach, the commander of the round-the-world nuclear submarine Triton, being decorated at the White House as the one officer whose whereabouts the President always knew. Whether direct assault will work as well for Sahl on television as it has worked in night clubs remains to be seen, but one thing that seems clear is that he is in no danger of becoming mellow. Not long ago, one of John Kennedy's henchmen—presumably without Kennedy's knowledge—suggested privately to Sahl that since he obviously liked Kennedy personally, he might, as a friendly gesture, drop the "Kennedy's trying to buy the country" joke. Sahl became so enraged that in his next show he used every Kennedy joke he had ever thought up. "You don't have to worry that Mort will learn to keep his temper," a man who knows him well said a few weeks ago. "All you've got to do to find out how serene he's feeling is to look up the casualty list of his business associates. He's on his fourth personal manager, I guess, and his second agent and second press agent. I don't see him more than once a year or so, and when I do I look at the entourage he travels with, and, you know, the people are always the same but the faces are different. When he begins getting along with his associates, I'll believe he's gone into a decline, but I'm not going to hold my breath till it happens. If a guy has a persecution complex, he'll keep on feeling persecuted no matter how many pairs of sunglasses he can afford."

As long as there is one other angry person in the world, Sahl, with his overcommunicativeness, will continue to be a spokesman for somebody. His ability to make so many of his listeners feel that he has the same hopes and fears, the same ideas, problems, and tastes, that they have is perhaps the most impressive—and most inexplicable—of his gifts. Of course, he has a line that deals with that situation, too: "People tell me there are a lot of guys like me, which doesn't explain why I'm lonely."

✓ Suggestions for Reading and Writing

1. Most of you are familiar with Mort Sahl's personality as it comes through the TV screen or across the stage. How well does Rice capture it here? Does his essay contain any surprises?
2. What are the implications of Rice's observation that "Sahl's words are meant to be heard, not read"? Do you agree?
3. What seems the basic appeal of Sahl's humor, which is frequently described as "cerebral," "negative," "esoteric," "angry"? Do you, as a college student, consider yourself one of his "people"?
4. Rice presents eight possible interpretations of Sahl's statement that "if we couldn't laugh about these things, we might do something about them." Which interpretations seem most accurate? Why?
5. Having read this essay and observed Sahl on TV, do you agree that if "he weren't perceptive he'd be a bigot"? Would you substitute another word for "perceptive"? Explain.

6. Is Rice's statement that Sahl "wants to change the world, but he doesn't want to get second billing" an indication of the author's subtle hostility toward his subject?

7. There are interesting similarities and differences in personality, material, and style between Sahl and his fellow stand-up comedian Lenny Bruce. Base a comparative essay on a stage performance or recording by Bruce. For added material, see Martin Williams' "The Comedy of Lenny Bruce," *Saturday Review* (November 24, 1962), pp. 60–61; Albert Goldman's "Stand-Up Shaman," *New Leader* (March 4, 1963), p. 31; Benjamin De Mott's "Sicknik Time," *Hells and Benefits* (1962), pp. 13–39. See also Lenny Bruce's six-part "How to Talk Dirty and Influence People: An Autobiography," *Playboy* (October 1963–March 1964).

8. For an analysis of those elements of style and format common to most *New Yorker* "Profiles," read such interesting past examples as those of Helena Rubenstein, Walter Winchell, and Marlon Brando.

[A M Y
L O W E L L]

Louis Untermeyer

Louis Untermeyer (1885–   ) left a successful jewelry-manufacturing business in 1923 to devote his life to literature. During the past four decades he has written and compiled more than thirty volumes of verse, fiction, parodies, translations, and criticism. He is perhaps best known, however, as an anthologist; his Modern American Poetry *(1919) and* Modern British Poetry *(1920), singly and in a combined volume, have gone into many editions and revisions and have been widely used as textbooks. He recently edited* The Letters of Robert Frost to Louis Untermeyer *(1963).*

Mr. Untermeyer has busied himself through the years with teaching, public-lecturing, and editing. He has been poet-in-residence or visiting lecturer at many colleges and universities and has conducted summer courses at Vermont's Bread Loaf Writers' Conference; he also has served as an editor for the Liberator, the Seven Arts, and the American Mercury, and has written for the Encyclopedia Britannica.

Few, then, have been more directly involved in the past half-century with America's writers, critics, and poets. He describes many of his early encounters in his autobiography, From Another World (1939); it contains the following sketch of another famed poet-biographer, Amy Lowell (1874–1925).

* * * * *

That was a strange evening the first time I visited Amy Lowell. It was strange that I should have been there at all. A year or two before this I had reviewed her first book, and reviewed it most unfavorably. It had come to my desk with several other pleasantly competent volumes, from which it differed in no distinguishable way. It seemed the conventional "slender sheaf" full of apostrophes to dead romantic poets, second-rate imitations of Robert Louis Stevenson, and a lengthy tribute to the Boston Athenaeum whose spirit dominated the book; everything about it was familiar except the author's name. Not being a Bostonian, and unaware of any august relationship, I had pictured the author as a young female Laocoön struggling, not too strenuously, in the coils of poetic stereotype. I had resolved to read her a lesson. My review must have been insufferably patronizing—she told me later it was one of the few reviews that had ever made her weep—and I remember that I concluded the offensive paragraph by saying that the only good line in the book was the title, A Dome of Many-Colored Glass, and that was taken from Shelley. Less than two years after I had disposed of the sentimental disciple of Tennyson and Keats, I had to change my tune. Another Amy Lowell had confronted me with Sword Blades and Poppy Seed. It was an experimental and far more belligerent poet who exhibited a new individuality and range, who expressed herself with equal determination in precise cameos of verse and rough-hewn masses of polyphonic prose. I was astonished at the transmogrification, and I said so in print.

And now I was waiting for her to descend the great staircase of the famous house, which, according to rumor, was occupied only by herself, a companion, and a retinue of servants—a house fronted by its own park and backed by a fabulous garden, a house where the mirrors were always draped in black, whose every door-knob was of sterling, and in which the owner lived in a kind of shrouded battlement on the top floor of her castle. I had even heard that, like the legendary princess, she slept on a bed made of eighteen pillows because ordinary sheets were too coarse for her. Like Caesar, she was reputed to keep two secretaries continually at work. She ignored the clock, and her world waited until she woke and the sleeping palace accommodatingly came to life.

I waited. I had been summoned to appear at seven in the evening. I learned later that all new guests, obviously on probation, were put through an ordeal not of fire but of patience. I did not know it then—so I waited. Sometime between thirty minutes and an hour after my arrival Miss Lowell appeared. It was easy for her. Her routine was the opposite of everyone's. A wealthy woman, she could indulge herself not only in her fancies but in her hours. She slept all day and worked all night, claiming that in this way she was free from the telephone, the importunities of friends and tradesmen, and all the countless interruptions of the day. She awoke about three in the afternoon, planned the details for the following day with her housekeeper over a four o'clock breakfast, and came down to dinner, her first real meal of the day, at eight. After dinner there were friends, concerts or other diversions. This lasted until midnight. Then she began to work, to write new poems and revise old ones. At five in the morning she sustained herself with a light lunch, arranged the manuscripts for the secretaries, and so to bed. Nothing could interrupt, no one could intrude upon her. It was a system much to be recommended—for those who could afford it.

Miss Lowell came down the stairs. She waved no plumes and rattled no sabers, but she seemed to be advancing at the head of a victorious army. There was gunfire in the air; I thought I heard bugles. She endeavored to put me, a stranger, at my ease. She offered me a cigarette, pulling out a drawer which seemed to contain the contents of the United Cigar Stores, Incorporated.

"No, thank you," I said, "I do not smoke."

"I hope you don't mind that I do," said she, taking up a rich-looking cigar. "My doctor tells me the paper in cigarettes is injurious. Besides, I prefer tobacco wrapped in its own leaf."

The shock was only for a moment. I had heard of Hungarian duchesses who smoked cigars imperturbably and, years later, I was to know a Viennese grand dame who cherished a meerschaum pipe. But I was unprepared to watch a Lowell, the sister of Harvard University, knocking the ash from a colorado claro. (She had a supply of ten thousand.) The apparition seemed the more grotesque because of Miss Lowell's size. I do not know what she weighed at the time, but, although she was forty, it must have been well over two hundred pounds. To make the effect still more incongruous, she preferred high-collared dresses sprinkled with beads and lavishly trimmed with passementerie. Some glandular defect made the heavy body seem more swollen and the short frame more stunted than it really was. ("Lord," she would say, "I'm a walking side-show.") Yet the rakish cigar and the abnormal stoutness were forgotten five minutes after she had seated herself. One noticed only the marvelous neatness, the fine hands and delicate ankles, the small mobile mouth, the coolly modulated voice, the quick-appraising but not unkind eyes, the fine features and almost transparent skin. One saw a woman who was not only intelligent but—there is no other word for it—pretty. The most implacable adversary, more masculine than most males, she could also be the most charming feminine persuader. I capitulated. I think I apologized for not smoking. Then we went in to dinner.

It was a good, even a grand, dinner. But I was not comfortable. There were six or eight celebrities at the table; but it was not the guests or the service that undid me. It was the dogs. They were English sheep-dogs, immense longhaired creatures, and there seemed to be a ferocious flock of them. They sat around the dining-room in a semicircle, their mouths dribbling with hungry anticipation. As the meal progressed their eyes grew larger and larger, like the magic dogs in Hans Christian Andersen's tale, and I felt more and more like a frightened bone.

Dinner over, the guests, led by Ada Dwyer Russell, who served as Amy Lowell's companion, confessor, wailing wall and buffer state, trailed into the imposing library. I had barely begun to examine the famous collection of volumes with Keats's own annotations when I was motioned to a chair. The other guests were seated; they knew the ritual which was to ensue. We were grouped about a fireplace large enough to roast an ox or a critic. One maid entered with the coffee. Another followed with a huge pile of bath towels.

"Thank you very much," I said, trying to cover my bewilderment with a poor facetiousness, "but I had my bath this morning, and I rarely spill the coffee."

"Don't be absurd," Miss Lowell replied. "It's for the dogs."

"Surely, you're not going to bathe them here?"

"Nonsense." She made a moue. "The darlings don't need a bath, either. But they are so companionable, and their hair is so long, and they *do* dribble after food, and they like to put their heads in your lap."

So there we sat with towels across our knees, while the seven dogs—there seemed to be seventeen—alternately guzzled their food and nuzzled us, and the conversation grew increasingly animated.

But my contretemps with Amy Lowell's pet monsters was nothing compared to the misadventure suffered by another poet. Maxwell Bodenheim was expected to arrive at about seven one evening. Amy sent her huge Pierce Arrow (with tires deflated for luxurious driving) for the more important guests; the others arrived by the blue Chestnut Hill street car. Bodenheim was not one of the favored; he was intransigent and his clothes were shabby. He got off at Heath Street and walked up the curving driveway to the entrance of Sevenels. There was a sign: "Motors be careful not to run over the dogs." Ordinarily the dogs were put in their kennels before strange visitors arrived; but Bodenheim, fearful of being late, arrived much too early. The seven oversize dogs spied him. They wanted to play. Barking, they sprang about—and on—him. Bodenheim misunderstood their motives. He dodged behind a tree.

"Aha!" thought the dogs. "Here is a new diversion. Here is a bone that runs." Immediately a thousand pounds of dog leaped to the chase. Bodenheim zigzagged desperately, trying to throw them off the scent. But they surrounded him, barking all the more furiously. He reached the house, spent and bespattered, guided but not helped by the stone statue of Flora which stood, apathetically, above the doorway. He had just strength enough to ring the bell. A maid, incongruously small, appeared.

"Shoo!" she cried. Bodenheim did not know whether to be grateful or offended. Then he realized she was talking to the dogs.

"Shoo!" she said a second time, stamping her little foot. The monstrous seven, the worst watch-dogs in the world, dropped their tails and fell over each other in an awkward rush to escape.

A similar mishap occurred to Randolph Bourne. Bourne, as I have said in the preceding chapter, was a hunchback, physically weak and easily frightened. He was sure that the dogs had viciously attacked him, and he was so terrified that he could not rise to his hostess's sallies during dinner. Amy, in turn, despised the "weakling." Her repulsion extended even to his writing; in a talk with James Oppenheim and me she insisted that his deformity showed itself in his "tortured style and twisted mentality." Oppenheim told me she returned to the false charge at another session with him.

"Everything he writes," she repeated, "shows he is a cripple."

Intending nothing more than a sententious generality Oppenheim said, "Aren't we all cripples?"

Amy's aggressiveness fell away from her. "Yes," she said, surveying her enormous girth. "Look at me. I'm nothing but a disease."

At the time I knew little about Amy Lowell's militancy. It was not until later that I heard (and saw) how she invaded editorial offices, bore down upon the heads of magazines and publishing offices, treated editors as if they were office boys, and brought every kind of armament into play—wealth, charm, political astuteness, family background, good-fellowship, and dictatorial commands—to forward her powerful offensive. Every new book was a new campaign, and never has there been a more determined general. "I am as bad as Napoleon," she wrote unashamedly to the editor of *The New York Tribune*. "I believe in my star."

I remember one of her sorties into what she considered enemy territory. She descended upon New York, accompanied by the faithful Mrs. Russell, and put up at the Hotel St. Regis, from which she sent out her summonses. I shall never forget that "receiving room." As in her own home, the mirrors were concealed behind black cloths. One table held a dozen pitchers of ice-water; another table was precariously balanced with scores of the latest books; a third table was a litter of clippings, letters, telegrams, memoranda. During dinner, which was served in her rooms, Amy discharged a battery of dicta; gave orders over the telephone to obviously cowed listeners; alternately blandished and bullied the waiters—"Here! put all my vegetables on one plate. I don't want them sitting around in little bird-baths"—and kept her guests in a state of amusement and apprehension. Joyce Kilmer told me she had "made" him interview her on the subject of the new poetry. What is more (such was her power) she got him to send her his manuscript and permitted him to print it in *The New York Times* only after she had approved it.

Later she attempted to bring a weightier influence to bear upon the newspapers. "You advertise so much in the *Times*," she wrote to her publishers, "that you ought to force them into a somewhat less hostile attitude." She believed in controversy, not only for its own sake but for its advertising value. I mocked her once by saying, "Sweet are the uses of publicity," and she did not resent it. She wrote to Ezra Pound, "I consider you an uncommonly fine poet. You ought to have an impresario—your knowledge of how to 'get yourself over,' as we say in this little country, is *nil*."

It was Ezra Pound who told me how Amy had "captured" the Imagist movement. . . .

In London in 1912 Pound and one or two others, chiefly T. E. Hulme, revolted against the current "morbid romantic attitude and outworn false generalities." Seeking, most of all, a cure for the stock allusions and general vagueness, they hit upon the *image* as a clear and definite objective. To express this definiteness Pound and his coadjutors, organizing themselves into a group, drew up a manifesto which declared for "the hard, definite word. Each word," they continued, "must be an image seen, not a counter or cliché. Images in verse are not mere decorations, but the very essence of an intuitive language." Endeavoring to use no word that did not contribute to the presentation of the image, the group was led by Pound to challenge the critics with *Imagisme*. Pound says he invented the term "to avoid vain gabble as to the nature of poetry." He wrote me during the brief period following my Italian sojourn when we seemed to be friends, "I have no objection to the pleasure others have had in exploiting the label and offering cheap imitations, but I regret the loss of critical distinction between poetry which uses no word which does not contribute to the presentation—and verbosity (more or less rhythmic)." Pound attracted and repelled disciples; one of them, Hilda Doolittle, born in Bethlehem, Pennsylvania, began signing her Tanagra-like poems "H. D., Imagiste." While the movement was gaining momentum, Amy Lowell arrived in London with a letter of introduction to Pound. The two, born doctrinaires and dictators, met head on. A few months later Amy returned to America at the head of an Imagist movement of her own. Her group consisted of three Englishmen: D. H. Lawrence, Richard Aldington, and F. S. Flint; and three Americans: H. D., John Gould Fletcher, and herself. Pound's anthology, *Des Imagistes*, was published in 1914; Amy's collections, *Some Imagist Poets*, appeared in 1915, 1916, and 1917. Pound repudiated any connection with the American wing which he always referred to as "the Amygist movement."

Pound made light of the defection when he told me about it as we sat in the *Giardino Pubblico* looking toward Sestri. But there must have been a day when he threatened suit, for, in November, 1914, Amy wrote to him, "So far as I know you have not copyrighted the name 'Imagiste.' I never heard of a school of poetry being copyrighted; I doubt if it could be done. But if you should feel inclined to sue, I should be exceedingly delighted, as then they would put new jackets on the book, which I should greatly prefer. Also, it would be a good advertisement." Imperturbable and magnificent Amy! Anything for "a good advertisement." Lowell or no, she would have made an independent fortune as a promoter of bond issues or the head of a public relations firm.

Never has there been a leadership like Amy's. She used every form of persuasion, every kind of weapon. She fought alone and with badgered recruits; she stormed every battlement of convention. As a determined Imagist she not only laid siege to Poetry, she invaded it. Since much of the work was written in unrhymed lines with "cadence" instead of a regular rhythm. Imagism became (falsely) synonymous with

free verse, that contradiction in terms. The emancipated champions of
vers libre were maliciously ticketed as "vers-libertines." Free verse, more
challengingly than free love, became a fighting phrase, and Amy exulted
in the conflict. "By Jove!" she ended one of her letters to me in the midst
of the controversy. "We are pushing the Philistines to the wall!"

Pound could never have done it; Pound, she wrote in one of the first
letters I received from her, "would have ruined the movement, important
though it was, as he has ruined everything he has touched. You are quite
right in implying that bitterness has upset his brain. The only thing I
object to in your article is your saying that it was under his leadership
'that the Imagists became not only a group, but a fighting protest.' It was
not. The Imagists during the year and a half in which he headed the
movement were unknown and jeered at, when they were not absolutely
ignored. It was not until I entered the arena, and Ezra dropped out, that
Imagism began to be considered seriously. I feel sure that if I had not
done all I did and worked hard to prove the value of the movement, the
thing would never have achieved the recognition it now has. . . . The
name is his; the idea was wide-spread; but changing the whole public
attitude from derision to consideration came from my work." This was
Amy *in excelsis*.

At this time her letters were variations on the theme. She evidently
kept carbon copies of every letter she wrote, for I read excerpts in Foster
Damon's comprehensive biography, quoting from letters whose originals
I must have destroyed. Yet in 1916 alone I find more than twenty
epistles, all on the chaste and businesslike letterhead: "Miss A. Lowell,
Heath Street, Brookline, Mass." Her very first communication was a
reproach for not being sufficiently enthusiastic about the new gospel.
After thanking me for a *causerie* in which I praised her, she wrote, "I
think perhaps you are a little hard on the Imagists. Don't you think you
are reading into them characteristics which perhaps they have not got?
One of the things which they represent to my mind, is the ascendancy of
the purely imaginative impulse. It is this quality of imagination which
has seemed so hard to get America to fitly understand. It frightens them,
worries them, repels them."

It was the form, rather than the imagination itself, which worried
the critics. Amy herself continually violated the Imagist manifesto and
extended her work far beyond its tenets; but she, too, confused the form
with the substance. It was not until much later that she was able to
separate the true "inwardness" of the poem from the outer technique.
She was (at least in the flush of her Imagist triumph) so convinced that
vers libre was the only possible contemporary form that she extended her
prejudice into the past. She intimated that even translations of the
classics should be "cadenced"; in the midst of a highly complimentary

review of my Heine versions she wrote, "Why, O why, has Mr. Untermeyer chosen to follow Heine in his tight little rhythms and mathematically cut stanzas?" At about this time Keith Preston, then writing a lively column in Chicago, sent me a paraphrase of his much-quoted quatrain:

> A toast to Amy Lowell,
> That most incredible She,
> And all the little magazines
> That died to make verse free.

Amy would have relished it. She enjoyed the quick thrust and parry; she did not disdain puns. (Referring to my Michigan lectures at Ann Arbor she hoped I had been pleasantly entertained by the "Ann Arborigines.") It was only in (and about) her work that she lacked a sense of humor. I remember once, when we were discussing the Imagist credo, she insisted that words could render not only the exact nuances of music but record the most minute differences of color. "But," she added, "it takes an unusually trained vision to apprehend and register the shades of difference. For example, you must have noticed how the color of a country road is changed when seen through the spokes of a fast-moving car. What color would you say it was?"

"Well," I hazarded, trying to play the game, "earth-color. Or dull brown. Or dusty tan. Or . . ."

"Cinnamon" she shouted triumphantly. "Use your eyes!"

Although she herself was not precious as a person, she pushed theory into preciosity. She claimed so much for her pet project that she rated Emily Dickinson as a precursor of the Imagists. ("It is an odd story," she wrote, "this history of Imagism, and perhaps the oddest and saddest moment in it is comprised in the struggle of this one brave, fearful, and unflinching woman.") She went further; she insisted that Emily Dickinson would have been a better poet had she written in *vers libre*; "a knowledge of the principles of unitary verse (that is, verse based upon a unit of time instead of a unit of accent) would have liberated Emily Dickinson from the bonds against which she chafed." She pushed her theory so far in this instance that she completely misread and misunderstood the poet to whom she was paying tribute. "She (Emily Dickinson) made use of what I have called elsewhere the 'unrelated' method; that is, the describing of a thing *by its appearance only*." Misapprehension can go no further than the italicized phrase (the italics are mine), for no poet dealt less with "appearance only" than Emily Dickinson. Her descriptions, startlingly vivid and exact though they were, were backgrounds for the play of the restless mind; the outer and inner world surpassed appearance to form "the landscape of the soul."

III

The effect of the new poetry was explosive, and Amy laid much of the dynamite. Although her illness was aggravated by an umbilical hernia that necessitated four operations within three years, she stormed about the country, horrified the pedants, made enemies in order to fight them, and shocked her audiences into feverish debate. She was continually traveling "for the cause," although train trips were a torture to her, for her blood pressure compelled her to sit at open windows no matter how much other passengers complained. Once she broke a glass pane in a sleeping-car to get air. The hotels rarely had the accommodations she required; she was never satisfied with a suite of less than four rooms—a whole floor in the smaller hotels—clocks had to be stopped, mirrors covered, meals served in the middle of the night. The lecture halls were never right; the lecterns had the wrong slant, and the lights were such that she always carried her own reading lamp with her. This led to a curious mishap at the University of Michigan. When her lamp was plugged in, it blew a fuse and the hall was in a dark confusion while chairmen and the heads of various departments fumbled for the janitor who was groping for them. Wherever she went she astounded the naïve and sophisticates alike; a storm center in Brookline and a cyclone on the warpath. She was not merely a lecturer, she was an event, a national phenomenon, a freak of nature, a dynamo on the loose.

In personal relationships she was the kindest of friends and the warmest of defenders. She fought until the experiments of John Gould Fletcher were acknowledged and H. D. was established. Yet her most admiring friends could not help but resent her assumption of power, even when it was exercised in their behalf. Upon my first return from Europe, H. D. wrote me from Switzerland, "Do let me know how Amy is now. I expect you to give her tactful messages from me, for I do wish the best in the world for her. My only objection is: she will NOT leave other people alone." Fletcher had less cause to complain; he realized she was "chiefly responsible for the furor caused in academic circles by the new poetry." But he, too, was indignant at her high-handedness, yet had not the temerity to gainsay her.

· · · · ·

IV

It was Amy's own delight in parody and masquerade that made her publish A *Critical Fable* anonymously. But she did more than that. To insure secrecy she misled almost everyone concerned in the publication. Even if a literary detective had had access to her publisher's files, he would have found that the author was William Williams John—who happened to be the husband of one of her secretaries. The work itself was a heterogeneous picture-gallery of the leading living American poets, somewhat in the manner of her distant dead relative, James Russell Lowell. To increase the confusion Amy subtly and mendaciously spread reports that various poets were responsible. She wrote blandly to John Farrar, then editor of *The Bookman*, "Have you seen *A Critical Fable?* I must say I find it immensely amusing in spite of not particularly enjoying the part about myself. . . . I wonder who wrote it? Louis Untermeyer guessed me, and I guessed him; and then we agreed to cry quits on the strength of each other's denial and find a third person. Sara Teasdale says it is Gamaliel Bradford; Gamaliel Bradford says it is Leonard Bacon; who Leonard Bacon says I do not know. . . ."

From the beginning I was certain that Amy was the author, partly because the critical estimates generally agreed with those she had so often expressed, partly because of the hit-and-miss rhythms and the wretched rhymes. I was not at all complimented when Amy insisted that she recognized my touch throughout. Purist that I was in the matter of rhyme, my teeth were continually set on edge by such awkward pairings as "grand-aren't," "absurdities-acerbities," "Piano-and so," "clearly-really," "Olympus-impasse," "goddess-progress," "parley-finale." Yet I could not help but be flattered by the pleasant pages she devoted to me in the volume, and her letter of disclaimer was as disarming as it was disingenuous. She wrote in part:

> My dear Louis, You are mad if you think I wrote it; I wish to God I had. And permit me to offer my congratulations on your excellent *bluff!* From the first moment I opened the book, I said to myself: Louis is the *only* person who would have been likely to write this book—and now you hastily forestall me by suggesting that I have done it, which is one of the neatest little side-steppings I have ever seen. Oh, Louis, Louis! So you were not going to do that sort of thing again, weren't you. *Heavens* was to be your last skit! And all the time you had this up your sleeve. All I can say is I envy you in the way you have got us all off and the neatness of your versification. [*Sic! L. U.*] Oh, but don't I recognize that neatness: I chuckled again when I read your "Roast Leviathan." How anybody, after reading that poem, can think it was not written by the same man who wrote *A Critical Fable* I do not see. I think it is a bully book, and you have hit the people off wonderfully. If nothing else gave it away, your remarks about my "thunderous" quality would have done it.

By the time I had finished the letter and had received other congratulations (prompted by Amy) I was almost ready to believe that I *had* written the book. I was beginning to see new virtues in it; in another

month I would have convinced myself that the rhymes were as daring as
Emily Dickinson's. However, it never came to that. Amy could never
keep a secret from her public; she enjoyed herself—and her public—too
much.

I will never forget the pleasure she took in one of the most curious
public functions I have ever attended. It was a Civic Forum dinner given
at the Hotel Astor for a group of poets. Ten of us were guests of
honor—three English and seven American poets—and its chief reason
was a hail-and-farewell to John Masefield, who had been in America as
"an ambassador of good will." I was seated at the speaker's table between
Amy and a tall southerner whose name I had not caught.

"But we have met," he said. "Not in the flesh, but in the newspaper
columns—in one of your reviews."

"That's gratifying," I smiled. "I hope I said something more than
ordinarily pleasant."

"On the contrary," he replied without a smile. "You were extraordinarily *un*pleasant. You began your attack with the title of your review
and ended it with a gratuitous insult. You quoted my worst lines,
including the typographical errors, and you turned my most serious
phrases into shoddy flippancies. You ridiculed my tragedies, you—"

"There is only one living poet I ever treated like that," I interrupted,
still trying to hold a smile. "And that was—years ago—Cale Young
Rice."

"I," he echoed grimly, "am Cale Young Rice."

Since, at that time, the Hotel Astor did not offer alcoholic comfort,
I spent the rest of the dinner talking to Amy Lowell. At the end of it she
said, "Louis, I've never heard you talk so much and so badly. I haven't
the faintest idea what you've been saying—and I don't think you have
either."

It was not only my discomfiture she enjoyed, but her eminence.
Each of the guests of honor read, spoke, or mumbled. Next to Masefield,
Amy received the most applause. But she raised her hand and asked
them to stop. "Just to make me feel at home," she said, "please add a
few hisses. I'm not used to speaking without them." Later, when she attacked some of the enshrined poets of the past, the hissing was renewed
—and this time the audience meant it.

(A newspaper cut is before me as I write. There we are: "American
Poets Gathered at Farewell Dinner." Amy is in the center, seated on a
Louis Quinze couch much too frail for her. She is clad in a magnificently
unbecoming dress with half-length sleeves and a yoke calculated to
increase her width, strewn with a maze of gold beadwork. She is
clutching a purse and a program, her head cocked, daring the world to
come to blows. Seated next to her is the only other woman; birdlike,

bright-eyed Josephine Dodge Daskam Bacon, with the smile of a canary that has just swallowed the cat. The rest of us are grouped about Amy. Reading from the traditional left to right, they are Laurence Housman, brother of A. E. Housman, bearded, dark-browed, staring into eternity like a bashful, even a benevolent, Mephistopheles; Witter Bynner, tall, immaculate, and aloof; Percy MacKaye, his arm about Bynner's shoulder, smiling archly at the camera; Edwin Markham, looking like a slightly blurred composite photograph of four Hebrew prophets and all the New England poets; Cale Young Rice, trying to forget he was the husband of Mrs. *Wiggs of the Cabbage Patch*; I, a cross between a frightened rabbit and a complacent anteater; Vachel Lindsay, his head tilted back dangerously as though he were about to explode in a chant; Alfred Noyes, doggedly facing his inquisitors and desperately clutching one of his own books; and John Masefield, quizzical and vague, like a benign but slightly befuddled leprechaun.)

v

In 1920 . . . I was living in Vienna, and Amy was deep in her Keats biography: "Keats is nearly killing me. I have completed six hundred and thirty pages and have three hundred and seventy left to do. I think I shall never want to undertake so long a job again."

The last sentence was prophetic. If Keats was killed by the critics, Amy, by the same exaggeration, was killed by Keats. She had been a sick woman for more than ten years; her first letter to me in 1915 ends: "Do try and get here as early as possible before they have quite minced me to pieces and swept me up in the dustpan." Her labors on the Keats material, of which she owned one of the largest collections in existence, and the almost vituperative English reviews, aggravated her ailment. She was as unaffectedly in love with Keats as Elinor Wylie was with Shelley; and when such presumably friendly critics as J. C. Squire and Robert Lynd questioned her conclusions, they seemed to be suddenly striking at her and exposing a wound so vulnerable as to be vital. For Keats she spent interminable nights puzzling over his manuscripts, tracking down his annotations, and retracing the worn pencil-scrawls; for Keats she suffered uncounted pains in head and groin and ruptured the small blood-vessels of her eyes. Into the dead poet she poured her life-blood, and after the transfusion she died.

Perhaps this is not altogether exact. She also poured her life-blood into her poetry; her vivacity invigorated it, her gusty personality gave it color and warmth. After her death the blood went out of it. The color seemed superficially applied, the warmth simulated; with the exception of some seven or eight poems the verse was suddenly lifeless. Robert Frost once said that she never touched the deep emotions because she did not know where to look for them, and D. H. Lawrence wrote, "If it doesn't come out of your own heart, real Amy Lowell, it is no good, however many colors it may have. . . . How much nicer, finer, bigger you are, intrinsically, than your poetry is."

This much seems apparent: Amy too often wrote to fit a theory, to mold her work in the fashion of the moment; she cast herself in the rôle of public poet. Instead of being urged by the quiet subconscious self, she continually prodded the conscious will. She sacrificed a slow searching for quick brilliance, and exchanged a broad understanding for narrow contemporaneousness. Her amazing range of subject and variety of techniques—the adaptations of Indian folklore, extensions of Peruvian myths, translations from the French, melodramas in New England dialect, verbal imitations of Stravinsky, Japanese lacquer prints, Chinese legends, exotic impressionism, homespun couplets—no longer hide the central poverty. She had energy, enthusiasm, power, skill, "everything," as one poet, paraphrasing Goethe, said of her, "everything except genius." It might be truer to say that she had genius—genius for everything except the thing she wanted most: permanence as a poet. Yet how could she have attained it? She had many pleasures, few ecstasies; she wept because of little griefs, never touched by immedicable woes. "It is hard," Malcolm Cowley wrote, "to write true poems when one is rich, blanketed with four-percent debentures and rocked to sleep in a cradle of sound common stocks."

She died an isolated patrician, antagonistic to radicals, suspicious of liberals, and scornful of "the ignorant proletariat." It sometimes seems a pity she determined to be a poet at all; she would have been so much happier as the Senator from Massachusetts.

Her poems, shrunk to a repeated few, still find their way into the anthologies. But her memorial is the collection she bequeathed to the Widener Library at Harvard. The Poetry Room contains not only her invaluable Keats letters, rare manuscripts, first drafts and first editions, but holograph manuscripts and volumes by almost every modern poet, a record of private influence and public accomplishment. Here is Amy's great mausoleum, a library, once the setting for what seemed the controversial battles of the century.

Several years after her death I stood there, in the Poetry Room of the Harvard College Library, waiting for her ghost. Except for the pale young custodian and myself, the room was empty. It remained unvisited during the time I rummaged about the unresponsive shelves and investigated the sacred vault. Not a sound penetrated, not a specter raised its reminiscent head. After an hour of silent loneliness I thought I detected a murmur. I was not wrong. The murmur grew to a hum, a rumble, a roar. The undergraduates were now underneath the window, loudly returning from the stadium. They went by, and the room was quieter than ever. The shadows did not stir. Even the past refused to speak.

ᛲ Suggestions for Reading and Writing

1. Untermeyer mentions some interesting names: Bodenheim, Bourne, Pound, Hulme, Aldington, and Fletcher, among others. Select, as subject for a critical essay, one of the writers referred to in this sketch.
2. Trace the structural pattern of the sketch. How does Untermeyer introduce, develop, and explain his heroine?
3. Is the author's tone here essentially admiring, sympathetic, patronizing, or ironic? Explain.
4. Untermeyer declares that Amy Lowell "continually violated the Imagist manifesto . . . [and] confused the form with the substance." Evaluate this statement after reading some of her most characteristic poems, such as "Patterns," "Evelyn Ray," "The Taxi," "In Excelsis," "Lilacs," and "The Sisters." (For a detailed bibliography on the Imagist movement, see Glen Hughes's *Imagism and the Imagists* [1941].)
5. Evaluate also Untermeyer's claim that Miss Lowell too often "cast herself in the rôle of public poet." But first read S. Foster Damon's *Amy Lowell: A Chronicle* (1935) or Horace Gregory's *Amy Lowell: Portrait of the Poet in Her Time* (1958).
6. Do you agree with the critic Malcolm Cowley that "It is hard to write true poems when one is rich, blanketed with four-percent debentures and rocked to sleep in a cradle of sound common stocks"?
7. Dip into Miss Lowell's *John Keats* (1925) as preparation for a critique evaluating this memorable lady's abilities as a biographer.

M Y
F R I E N D
McNULTY

James Thurber

No headnote can do justice to James Thurber (1894–1961).
One of America's notable humorists, he was born in Columbus,
Ohio, and there attended Ohio State University. After two
years in the diplomatic service in France, he turned to journal-
ism. He worked on Columbus newspapers and the New York
Herald's Paris edition. In 1926 he joined the New Yorker.

The twenties and the thirties comprised a golden era for
American humor, and Thurber mingled with such wits as
Donald Ogden Stewart, Robert Benchley, and Dorothy Parker.
On the New Yorker staff he formed, with E. B. White, the
wittiest familiar-essay team since Addison and Steele. A steady
stream of sad-eyed dogs, hatchet-faced women, and meek little
men flowed from his pen; from his typewriter came sham-
piercing sketches of people real and fictional, sane and
borderline.

Collected in such books as Is Sex Necessary? (1929; with
E. B. White), The Owl in the Attic and Other Perplexities
(1931), The Middle Aged Man on the Flying Trapeze (1935),
Fables for Our Time, and Famous Poems Illustrated (1940),
Men, Women, and Dogs (1943) and The Thurber Carnival
(1945), and many others—his essays, stories, and drawings brim
with unpredictable insights, wildly revealing word-play, mocking
but gentle laughter, and unnerving sanity. His humor derives
primarily from the spirit-shattering tragi-comedy of modern man
as victim; his bemused nonheroes are repressed, humiliated,

and blocked by malignant chance, overbearing bosses or wives, broken beds, unreliable dams, burglars, or windblown newspapers.

Thurber was also a successful playwright; his The Male Animal (1940; with Elliot Nugent), well received on Broadway and as a movie, has remained a favorite with campus and community theater groups. His own failing eyesight did not keep him from television appearances, starring in a Broadway dramatization of The Thurber Carnival, or creating to the end his wise and discomfiting "fables for our time."

In the sketch of John McNulty, a newspaper friend and associate, Thurber says: "Nothing, however commonplace, that he touched with words remained commonplace." It is a fitting epitaph for Thurber himself.

↟ ↟ ↟ ↟ ↟

The angel that writes names in a book of gold must long ago have put McNulty down as one who delighted in his fellow man. His delight in human beings was warm and deep and, though he deserved to be called a social critic, he was concerned mainly with men, not Man, with persons, not People. McNulty's love of humanity was not expressed at a distance, from a platform, but in pieces that have the lasting pulse of life in every sentence. He moved among men, shoulder to shoulder, from morning till night until the end of his too brief sixty years on earth.

American writing in our time has developed few men with so keen an eye and so sharp an ear. Nothing, however commonplace, that he touched with words remained commonplace, but was magnified and enlivened by his intense and endless fascination with the stranger in the street, the drinker at the bar and the bartender behind it, the horse player, the cab driver, the guy at the ball game, the fellow across the room, the patient in the next hospital bed. John McNulty, city man and newspaperman, self-assigned in his mature years to human-interest stories of the world about him, left not only a body of work that throbs with his love of life but a vast and equally durable legacy of spoken words that remain vivid in the memory of his friends. The only person who could get McNulty down in words was McNulty himself, but those of us who knew and loved him like to sit around at night in Tim and Joe Costello's Bar and Restaurant on Third Avenue and talk about him. This is the only real way to bring McNulty to life. Cold type could never do justice to such a man.

After John McNulty died, I wrote a short piece about him for the crowded pages of *The New Yorker,* and I reproduce it here in part: "Nobody who knew McNulty as man or writer could ever have confused him for a moment with anybody else. His presence in a room—or in a town, for that matter—was as special as the way he put words down on paper. His death darkened the skies for literally countless friends and acquaintances, for he seemed to know everybody. He came back to New York in the early thirties from a long sojourn in the Middle West, and in 1937 he began writing pieces for *The New Yorker.* They were the reports of a true and eager eye and ear that found high excitement in both the unusual and the common phrases and postures of men, and turned them into the sparkle of his unique idiom.

"The days didn't go by for John McNulty; they happened to him. He was up and out at six every morning, wandering the beloved streets and 'avenyas' of his city, stopping to talk and listen to everybody. His week was a seven-day circus that never lost its savor. He was not merely an amusing companion; he was one of the funniest of men. When he told a tale of people or places, it had a color and vitality that faded in the retelling by anyone else. The name McNulty, for us, meant 'Inimitable,' and at the same time something in lower case, familiar and cherished—a kind of synonym for laughter. We grieve that such a man cannot be replaced, in our hearts or on our pages."

The pages of *The New Yorker* sparkled with his pieces from the first one, which appeared on Christmas Day, 1937, until the last one, which was printed on New Year's Eve, 1955.

McNulty and I were reporters together on Columbus, Ohio, newspapers in the early 1920's. He did general assignments for a morning paper while I covered City Hall for an afternoon paper, but our offices were just a few blocks apart, in the center of town, and I bumped into him almost every day, often at the corner of Broad and High streets, the city's main intersection. He was invariably excited about something, the cabin lights of the Shenandoah which he had seen twinkling in the sky the night before, a girl at the James Theatre who sang "Roses Are Shining in Picardy," Donn Byrne's novel *The Changelings,* which he demanded that I begin reading right away, there on that crowded corner, or a song called "Last Night on the Back Porch" which he insisted on playing for me, then and almost there. Actually, he took me around the corner to a music store and began beating out the song on the first piano he came to, to the astonishment of the store's staff. "It's McNulty," I explained to them in a whisper and they all nodded and breathed his name in unison, obviously believing that he was a great pianist, come to play at Memorial Hall, who had suddenly been seized by a rare moment of relaxation and frivolity. He had once played the piano in a movie theatre in the days of silent films and, within his range, there wasn't anything he couldn't make the keys do. While playing "My Gal Sal" he used to recite the succession to the presidency, and it was upon the conclusion of that bravura performance that we left the music shop and its startled and transfigured staff. Once he got me up before breakfast to play on my victrola two records that had entranced him—"Singin' Sam from Alabam'" and a bright arrangement of "Everybody Calls Me Honey," in which piano, trumpet, and banjo alternately took over the solo.

McNulty was a widely experienced newspaperman at twenty-five, when he arrived in Columbus from the East, to work for the *Ohio State Journal* at sixty dollars a week, higher pay than any reporter in town had been getting. I have forgotten, if I ever knew, what whim or compulsion had sent him into the Middle West. It was probably an impulse peculiar to his volatile spirit, such as that which sent him one day, years later, to New Iberia, Louisiana, to visit the tabasco factory there. In Columbus he lingered for a dozen years. Before the first of these had passed he knew more people in the city than I did, although I had been born and brought up there. They included everybody from taxi drivers, cops, prizefighters, and bellboys to the mayor of the city and the governor of the state. He wrote speeches for one successful candidate for governor, and in that, as in everything else, he had the time of his life.

John once explained to me, "Two thirds of the Irish blood is grease paint," and he was a fine offhand actor and raconteur rampant, who would jump from his chair in a living room and theatrically bring to life one of the characters he had so fondly collected during his wanderings. I think he did as much as anyone, with his acting, to ridicule the Ku Klux Klan out of existence in Columbus. He had arranged for me to accost him whenever I saw him at Broad and High in the company of a group of men—he was always surrounded by men—and loudly try to enroll him in the Klan. "We are looking for likely one hundred percent Americans," I would say, "so we can build up in this city the biggest Kleagle in the country."

"Klavern," he would correct me, and while his companions stared at me in disbelief, he would take off his hat, present to me the shining map of Ireland that was his face, and say proudly, "The name is John Aloysius McNulty." At this I would slink away, muttering, while his friends stared after me. "Them guys must be crazy!" I heard a boxer named Sully exclaim after one of these rituals, and the word got around town that the local Klan was made up of imbeciles. It didn't last long.

Trying to describe McNulty is a little like trying to describe Ed Wynn or George M. Cohan. "A small, jaunty man, best described as Irish of face and manner" is the way the *New York Times* went about it in that paper's appreciative obituary. He was small, I guess, measured by physical height and weight, but I have a tendency to look up when I think of him, for to me he was nine feet tall. This was the stature, at any rate, of his unflagging comic spirit. The dictionary has no exact words for the face and voice of the man, or for the shape and color of the moods he put on every morning with his clothes. There was nothing of the literary elf about McNulty, who once said to me, "Only people with Vincent for a middle name write about leprechauns." It is true that the world of John McNulty bordered on Oz and Wonderland, but it consisted mainly of Ireland, New York's Third Avenue, the city rooms of American newspapers, and the race tracks of the world, with many an odd and unexpected nook and corner. From the border states came curious and wondrous figures, attracted to McNulty, not magically, but naturally. This gave his world, and his comments on it, a strange truth, undreamed of in ordinary philosophies. When he said, of 1885, "That was the year the owls were so bad," or when he told a lady trying to think of her hairdresser's name, "Girls named Dolores become hairdressers," or when he tracked down a bookie in a jewelry shop by suddenly remembering "All watch repairers are named Schneider," the listener felt that this was not mere whimsy but McNulty fact. There was always, faint or sharp, in what he said or did a critical comment on our tangled civilization, a sound parody of the ways of men. Walking about the streets of any city with McNulty was to be taken on a guided tour of what William James called, in another context, unexplored experience. Two men would pass by you, one of them saying, "It's the biggest gorilla in the world. They call it Garganetta," or a waiter in a cafe would tell him, "We get stranglers come in here at all hours." Through the ears of many of us such things pass unregistered, but McNulty's sensitized mind recorded everything. "The lady was a Bostonian, they call them" rang like a bell in his consciousness. To a man whose awareness was always on the lookout for the unusual, as well as the typical, the world was a book he was reading with intense concentration. He loved sentiment, being Irish, and he came right out with it. Of a pretty young bride he once wrote about in the *Daily News* he said, "She was as cute as a little red wagon." He once called me long distance to tell me he had just read something lovely which I had to hear. It was the four words of a lover: "My eyes desire you." My phone brought me often, but not often enough, phrases, sentences, or paragraphs from an enthusiastic McNulty who had just stumbled upon them. Sometimes he read me a whole piece.

There were a dozen shops of all kinds on New York's East Side with whose proprietors McNulty, making his daily rounds, kept up some kind of running gag. Once when I lived on East Fifty-seventh Street, a region he knew well, he took me into a small corner store after explaining,

"There's a wonderful guy runs this place." He was a wonderful guy, too, in the McNulty tradition, perfectly suited to their particular running gag, which was managed deadpan, as if the two had never met before. "What can I do for you, sir?" the man said. McNulty consulted the back of an envelope. "Elephant goad," he said finally. An amateur actor of McNulty's stripe, the man began snapping his fingers, humming, and searching his shelves and opening doors underneath the shelves, at length turning around to report, "Sorry, seem to be fresh out of elephant goads. Anything else?" McNulty shook his head sorrowfully and out we went. I found out later, dropping into the shop, some of the other things McNulty had asked for in vain—fetlock cleaners, beagle harness, and noiseless dice. "He says he supplies dice to a couple of fugitives holed up in this house with marble floors," the proprietor said. This is the thinnest ice of comedy and it takes experts to skate on it without falling in. You had to behold such performances yourself to understand the skill of McNulty and his stooges. I have never read a critic who captured the subtle essence of Beatrice Lillie's comic art, and none of them could do justice to McNulty's, either, on flat paper. His timing was perfect, and so were the tricks of his tones of voice. One day a few years ago I phoned him to ask if he remembered the year he had interviewed Donald Ogden Stewart (a great McNulty admirer) for the *Ohio State Journal*. McNulty's answer was prompt, and in the tone of a professional quiz panelist. "It was the year Black Gold win the Derby," he said, and having given me all the help a true horseplayer should need, he hung up. I had to look up in the World Almanac the year Black Gold win the Derby. Checking later with the *Journal* files, I found out, of course, that the answer was correct.

John Augustine McNulty (Aloysius had been invented for effect) was capable of a fine anger that could rise to fury. Like my own temper, his was sometimes as unreasonable as it was quick, but our occasional disagreements, as sudden as summer storms, passed just as quickly. After one loud hour of argument over the play *Shadow and Substance*, about which I think we were both right, we parted like men who would never see each other again. But we had a running-gag manner of making up, during which the cause of the trouble was never mentioned or even hinted at. Spotting him in a bar, I would present myself, politely, as a man just in from Columbus, Ohio, with a letter to him from Sully. "Let me see the letter," he would say, and there ensued a search through all my pockets, in which he helped. "Let me have another go at your coat," he would say grimly, but the letter was never there. "Well, when you find it," he would say, "bring it around. If I'm not here, I'll probably be somewhere else. Meanwhile, let's have a drink to old Sully." His gallery of persons he disliked was not large, but it included the right figures, the phony, or "wax banana," the snob, the show-off, the blowhard, the bigot, the unfriendly, the humorless, and all their cold ilk.

I happened to be in Columbus in 1933 when McNulty decided to return to the New York he hadn't seen for more than a decade, and I came back on the train with him. We hadn't ridden in a taxi more than three blocks from Pennsylvania Station before he began waving at guys he knew. "You're obvious New York born and bred, Mac," the taxi driver told him, adding that he was studying "human psychology." He picked me as a stranger "from the outlands" and said to my companion, "Better look after your friend. You don't know your way around, it's a tough town." In the next few years McNulty worked on the *Mirror*, the *Daily News*, and the *Herald Tribune* under its great city editor Stanley Walker, who once told me, "There is a kind of story that only McNulty could write, and it was a pleasure to have him around." He meant the kind of feature story that calls for the use of the heart as well as the mind.

McNulty was a fast writer, but before he reached his typewriter his alert photographic mind, backed up by an amazing memory, had worked the story out in all but a few details. He was temperamental if the thing didn't come out right, but he discarded his temperament like an overcoat when he set out to explore his fascinating world. His first assignment on *The New Yorker* was a "Reporter at Large" piece and he went out, got the facts, came back, and batted out the story within a couple of hours. "He can't get over writing for a newspaper deadline," said the late Harold Ross, but McNulty learned to slow down. When he left for a stint in Hollywood, Ross was genuinely reluctant to see him go. "Well, God bless you, McNulty, goddam it," said Ross. As John told me later, "Ross has two gods, Upper Case and lower case." Through Ross and the rest of us McNulty met a few people he hadn't known before. I remember his delight, one night in "21," when Marc Connelly told him some of Lloyd Lewis's anecdotes about the Southwest, one of which involved a rancher whose cat had been missing for three weeks. "Then one day I turned over my mattress," said the rancher, "and there, between the mattress and the springs, was Boss, pressed as pretty as a flower." The next day McNulty said to me, "The cat's name wasn't Boss. The cat's name was Pete. All ranchers' cats are named Pete." I'm sure Connelly would have lost money betting against this intuitive bit of McNulty truth.

McNulty was not New York born, for he first saw the enchanting light of his world in Lawrence, Massachusetts, where his mother ran a little store after the death of his father. Her son has done some justice to these early scenes, but not as much as I wish he had, for his mother is one of the vivid memories of my life. I first met her in Columbus when she visited him there, and he and I went to the train together to see her off, both of us, by coincidence, carrying identical boxes of candy. He knew what to do about that. "If you cry," he told her affectionately, "you get the box of candy that's poisoned. If you're good, you get the other one." The leave-taking was as jolly as it could be when two McNultys parted. Years later in New York, Mrs. McNulty was knocked down by a taxi on Park Avenue, and my wife and I went with John to call on her. Before we could tiptoe into the bedroom, where she was supposed to be lying wrapped in bandages from head to foot, we heard a small clatter in the kitchen and her son went to investigate. It was Mama, of course. "And did you think I'd let the Thurbers call on me," she said indignantly, "and not fix them a cup o' tea?" It took more than a New York taxi to finish off a McNulty. John himself, although he never talked about it, and wrote about it only sparingly and obliquely, had gone through some of the toughest battles of the First World War, in the Infantry. He got a leg full of shrapnel at Fère-en-Tardenois, and he was made a sergeant when the company's sergeants were killed in battle. After the war, he spent a year in hospital, and his wounds gave him trouble from then on. He was once a pet patient for three weeks in a hospital in Columbus, but none of us knew for a long time that Fère-en-Tardenois had sent him there. He made lasting friendships, of course, with doctors, nurses, and orderlies.

A few years before he died he gave me his precious copy of Mencken's *The American Language*, saying, "This is the book I love the most." Mencken once spoke to me, in the Algonquin lobby, in praise of McNulty and his handling of the people and the parlance of Third Avenue, and I remember how McNulty's face lighted up when I told him about it. He had a lot of favorite books, including the Oxford English Dictionary, which he read as if it were a novel filled with wonders and suspense. There must be many of us who have books that McNulty once owned. "He couldn't keep a book he loved," Faith McNulty told me once. "He wasn't happy until he had given it to some friend."

In the last ten years of his life, alas, we ran into each other only occasionally, but we talked a lot on the phone and exchanged letters. His letters were invariably carefully thought out single sentences, each relating some highlight of his city adventures. The last one I ever got was different, though, and puzzled me. It began, as always, "Dear Jimmy," and went on to say, "I think that maybe threescore years and ten is subject to change without notice." I searched it for the laugh, and realized there weren't going to be any more laughs. One night shortly afterward my phone rang in the country and I was told that he was dead. I had been planning to write him suggesting that he read certain poems and pieces by Dylan Thomas, particularly the poem that ends: "They shall have stars at elbow and foot . . . and death shall have no dominion. And death shall have no dominion." But I was too late. If Thomas was right about these bright eternal ornaments, John Augustine McNulty has his stars, and never you mind about that.

⟋ Suggestions for Reading and Writing

1. Thurber states that "Cold type could never do justice to such a man" as McNulty. Does he here belie his own words?
2. Check the *New Yorker* files for the years 1937 to 1955 and select three or four pieces by McNulty. Then write a paper on him as life observer and writer.
3. After reading a volume of Thurber's stories and sketches, discuss his statement that "Humor is a kind of emotional chaos told about calmly and quietly in retrospect."
4. Walter Mitty has become a universal folk hero and his name a part of the English language. Read (or, more likely, re-read) Thurber's "The Secret Life of Walter Mitty," *My World—And Welcome To It* (1942), and explain why.
5. An interesting companion-piece to "My Friend McNulty" is Thurber's "E.B.W.," *Credos and Curios* (1962), on his associate E. B. White. This noted wit for many years wrote the *New Yorker*'s "Talk of the Town" feature; White presents a sharp contrast in personality to McNulty. Try to capture their varying characteristics in a short paper.
6. Editor of the *New Yorker* during the Thurber-White era was the colorful Harold Wallace Ross. Thurber has bequeathed to posterity Ross's creative, off-beat, and volatile personality in his full length account, *The Years with Ross* (1959). After reading it, see if you can catch something of this paradoxical figure in a profile of your own.

THE
MONSTER

Deems Taylor

Critic, composer, editor, music commentator, and native New York, Deems Taylor (1885–   ) graduated from New York University to become a war correspondent during the First World War. He combined writing and music in ensuing years, acting as an associate editor of Collier's Weekly and as a music critic on the New York World and filling various editorial chairs for Musical America, Encyclopaedia Britannica, and the Nelson Encyclopedia.

An articulate spokesman for the musical profession, as well as a prolific composer, he served several terms as president of the American Society of Authors, Composers, and Publishers. His works include the tone poem Siren Song, such choral works as The Chambered Nautilus and The Highwayman, and the orchestral suite Through the Looking Glass. He also composed two successful operas, The King's Henchman (with libretto by Edna St. Vincent Millay) and Peter Ibbetson.

Taylor has added to his other talents that of performer. He appeared as commentator in Walt Disney's Fantasia, acted as radio host for "Musical Americana," visited frequently on "Information Please," and narrated both the Metropolitan Opera and New York Philharmonic broadcasts. His radio discussions of diverse music personalities and themes were collected and published in Of Men and Music (1937) and The Well-Tempered Listener (1940). He has also written A Pictorial History of the Movies (1943).

The following character sketch appeared in Of Men and Music.

He was an undersized little man, with a head too big for his body—a sickly little man. His nerves were bad. He had skin trouble. It was agony for him to wear anything next to his skin coarser than silk. And he had delusions of grandeur.

He was a monster of conceit. Never for one minute did he look at the world or at people, except in relation to himself. He was not only the most important person in the world, to himself; in his own eyes he was the only person who existed. He believed himself to be one of the greatest dramatists in the world, one of the greatest thinkers, and one of the greatest composers. To hear him talk, he was Shakespeare, and Beethoven, and Plato, rolled into one. And you would have had no difficulty in hearing him talk. He was one of the most exhausting conversationalists that ever lived. An evening with him was an evening spent in listening to a monologue. Sometimes he was brilliant; sometimes he was maddeningly tiresome. But whether he was being brilliant or dull, he had one sole topic of conversation: himself. What *he* thought and what *he* did.

He had a mania for being in the right. The slightest hint of disagreement, from anyone, on the most trivial point, was enough to set him off on a harangue that might last for hours, in which he proved himself right in so many ways, and with such exhausting volubility, that in the end his hearer, stunned and deafened, would agree with him, for the sake of peace.

It never occurred to him that he and his doing were not of the most intense and fascinating interest to anyone with whom he came in contact. He had theories about almost any subject under the sun, including vegetarianism, the drama, politics, and music; and in support of these theories he wrote pamphlets, letters, books . . . thousands upon thousands of words, hundreds and hundreds of pages. He not only wrote these things, and published them—usually at somebody else's expense—but he would sit and read them aloud, for hours, to his friends and his family.

He wrote operas; and no sooner did he have the synopsis of a story, but he would invite—or rather summon—a crowd of his friends to his house and read it aloud to them. Not for criticism. For applause. When the complete poem was written, the friends had to come again, and hear *that* read aloud. Then he would publish the poem, sometimes years before the music that went with it was written. He played the piano like a composer, in the worst sense of what that implies, and he would sit down at the piano before parties that included some of the finest pianists of his time, and play for them, by the hour, his own music, needless to say. He had a composer's voice. And he would invite eminent vocalists to his house, and sing them his operas, taking all the parts.

He had the emotional stability of a six-year-old child. When he felt out of sorts, he would rave and stamp, or sink into suicidal gloom and talk darkly of going to the East to end his days as a Buddhist monk. Ten minutes later, when something pleased him, he would rush out of doors and run around the garden, or jump up and down on the sofa or stand on his head. He could be grief-stricken over the death of a pet dog, and he could be callous and heartless to a degree that would have made a Roman emperor shudder.

He was almost innocent of any sense of responsibility. Not only did he seem incapable of supporting himself, but it never occurred to him that he was under any obligation to do so. He was convinced that the world owed him a living. In support of this belief, he borrowed money from everybody who was good for a loan—men, women, friends, or strangers. He wrote begging letters by the score, sometimes groveling without shame, at others loftily offering his intended benefactor the privilege of contributing to his support, and being mortally offended if the recipient declined the honor. I have found no record of his ever paying or repaying money to anyone who did not have a legal claim upon it.

What money he could lay his hands on he spent like an Indian rajah. The mere prospect of a performance of one of his operas was enough to set him to running up bills amounting to ten times the amount of his prospective royalties. On an income that would reduce a more scrupulous man to doing his own laundry, he would keep two servants. Without enough money in his pocket to pay his rent, he would have the walls and ceiling of his study lined with pink silk. No one will ever know—certainly he never knew—how much money he owed. We do know that his greatest benefactor gave him $6,000 to pay the most pressing of his debts in one city, and a year later had to give him $16,000 to enable him to live in another city without being thrown into jail for debt.

He was equally unscrupulous in other ways. An endless procession of women marches through his life. His first wife spent twenty years enduring and forgiving his infidelities. His second wife had been the wife of his most devoted friend and admirer, from whom he stole her. And even while he was trying to persuade her to leave her first husband he was writing to a friend to inquire whether he could suggest some wealthy woman—*any* wealthy woman—whom he could marry for her money.

He was completely selfish in his other personal relationships. His liking for his friends was measured solely by the completeness of their devotion to him, or by their usefulness to him, whether financial or artistic. The minute they failed him—even by so much as refusing a dinner invitation—or began to lessen in usefulness, he cast them off without a second thought. At the end of his life he had exactly one friend left whom he had known even in middle age.

He had a genius for making enemies. He would insult a man who disagreed with him about the weather. He would pull endless wires in order to meet some man who admired his work, and was able and anxious to be of use to him—and would proceed to make a mortal enemy of him with some idiotic and wholly uncalled-for exhibition of arrogance and bad manners. A character in one of his operas was a caricature of one of the most powerful music critics of his day. Not content with burlesquing him, he invited the critic to his house and read him the libretto aloud in front of his friends.

The name of this monster was Richard Wagner. Everything that I have said about him you can find on record—in newspapers, in police reports, in the testimony of people who knew him, in his own letters, between the lines of his autobiography. And the curious thing about this record is that it doesn't matter in the least.

Because this undersized, sickly, disagreeable, fascinating little man was right all the time. The joke was on us. He *was* one of the world's great dramatists; he *was* a great thinker; he *was* one of the most stupendous musical geniuses that, up to now, the world has ever seen. The world did owe him a living. People couldn't know those things at the time, I suppose; and yet to us, who know his music, it does seem as though they should have known. What if he did talk about himself all the time? If he had talked about himself for twenty-four hours every day for the span of his life he would not have uttered half the number of words that other men have spoken and written about him since his death.

When you consider what he wrote—thirteen operas and music dramas, eleven of them still holding the stage, eight of them unquestionably worth ranking among the world's great musico-dramatic masterpieces—when you listen to what he wrote, the debts and heartaches that people had to endure from him don't seem much of a price. Eduard Hanslick, the critic whom he caricatured in *Die Meistersinger* and who hated him ever after, now lives only because he was caricatured in *Die Meistersinger*. The women whose hearts he broke are long since dead; and the man who could never love anyone but himself has made them deathless atonement, I think, with *Tristan und Isolde*. Think of the luxury with which for a time, at least, fate rewarded Napoleon, the

man who ruined France and looted Europe; and then perhaps you will
agree that a few thousand dollars' worth of debts were not too heavy a
price to pay for the *Ring* trilogy.

What if he was faithless to his friends and to his wives? He had one
mistress to whom he was faithful to the day of his death: Music. Not for
a single moment did he ever compromise with what he believed, with
what he dreamed. There is not a line of his music that could have been
conceived by a little mind. Even when he is dull, or downright bad, he is
dull in the grand manner. There is greatness about his worst mistakes.
Listening to his music, one does not forgive him for what he may or may
not have been. It is not a matter of forgiveness. It is a matter of being
dumb with wonder that his poor brain and body didn't burst under the
torment of the demon of creative energy that lived inside him, struggling, clawing, scratching to be released; tearing, shrieking at him to
write the music that was in him. The miracle is that what he did in the
little space of seventy years could have been done at all, even by a great
genius. It is any wonder that he had no time to be a man?

✦ Suggestions for Reading and Writing

1. Analyze Taylor's means of catching and focusing the reader's attention.
   Discuss his use of concrete imagery, short sentences, and tightly linked
   paragraphs.
2. Why does Taylor wait so long to identify his subject? Does the delay
   strengthen or weaken the sketch? Did the sudden revelation of identity
   alter your evaluation of the subject's character?
3. Do you agree with Taylor that Wagner's personal record "doesn't matter
   in the least"? Explain.
4. Is Taylor's sudden reversal of judgment convincing? Is his Wagner-
   Napoleon analogy valid? In short, do you accept Taylor's thesis that the
   artist-genius must be judged by a special moral code?
5. Do you feel that this sketch may affect your appreciation of Wagner's
   music? Would you prefer not to have the private lives of your culture
   heroes revealed? Explain.
6. For additional insights into Wagner's character, you might turn to
   Ernest Newman's *Wagner as Man and Artist* (1925) and Jacques
   Barzun's *Darwin, Marx, Wagner* (1957). Unexpectedly revealing is
   Wagner's own *On Conducting* (1940).

MAYOR
WILLIAM J.
GAYNOR

Harry Golden

Publisher, editor, and writer of the Carolina Israelite, Harry
Golden (1902–   ) has drawn extensively upon his youth on
New York's Lower East Side for much of his early writings. He
now lives in Charlotte, North Carolina, from which vantage
point he comments on national, international, and historical
events and on people in numerous articles, a syndicated column,
and his own newspaper, as well as on the lecture platform.

Golden's special brand of journalism embodies elements of
nineteenth-century crusading editors and such eighteenth-
century familiar essayists as Joseph Addison and Richard Steele.
An incisive commentator upon current foibles he also looks
with nostalgia upon those happier days "when mother emptied
the drip pan under the icebox."

His good friend Carl Sandburg has said that "whatever is
human interests Harry Golden. Honest men, crooks, knuckle-
heads, particularly anybody out of the ordinary if even a half-wit,
any of them is in his line. He writes about them." The following
sketch of Mayor Gaynor, from Golden's Only in America
(1958), is of one of his "honest men."

✓ ✓ ✓ ✓ ✓

The first time the name Gaynor began to mean more to me than
that of another politician was when I was a kid on the Lower East Side.

One afternoon I saw a cop beating up a bearded old peddler. I remember the peddler rolling in the gutter, holding his head, and, as the night stick kept crashing down again and again, the policeman was screaming: "Gaynor ain't mayor any more! Gaynor ain't mayor any more!"

Let me tell you about Mayor William J. Gaynor.

He was an irascible old cuss, a bearded Unitarian, who got himself elected mayor by the Catholics, Protestants, and Jews of New York in November, 1909. The reason behind his election followed a general pattern. Whenever Tammany Hall was exposed in some thievery, the sachems picked an "independent"; a man as "unspotted from the world" as it is possible to be in public life. In other words, they were always willing to take a chance on a man who was nominally a Democrat, rather than allow the opposition to beat them. On this occasion they picked a judge of the Appellate Division of the Supreme Court, a man with an international reputation as a jurist.

After he was inaugurated, they wished they had let the Republicans capture City Hall.

Mayor Gaynor fired every Tammany officeholder; tore up every Tammany Hall recommendation; and once sent word that he would arrest any Tammany politician found loitering around City Hall. In the process, however, Gaynor threw overboard any chance he may have had to become Governor of New York, and perhaps President of the United States. When the Democrats were preparing for their 1912 convention (which resulted in the nomination of Woodrow Wilson) the national party leaders kept coming to New York's City Hall to see Gaynor.

Late in the year 1911 Colonel Edward Mandell House of Texas began his career as a political "power behind the throne." In order to achieve this goal you must first go out and get yourself a "throne" to be a power behind—or at least help make someone the President of the United States. The first man to interest Colonel House was the amazing Mayor Gaynor. And so House went to New York and formally invited Gaynor to make a speech before the State Legislature of Texas. A high honor. On the appointed day Gaynor did not show up in Texas. When the frantic House finally reached him, Gaynor said, "Haven't the faintest idea what you're talking about. This is the first I know anything about a visit to Texas."

But House was not ready to give up. He still thought Gaynor would make a wonderful candidate, and so he went to New York again. And it turned out to be one of Gaynor's better weeks. On Monday he made a speech in which he insulted the members of the press. He was talking to the Board of Estimate and made a reference to the Roman Senator, Cato. Gaynor leaned forward to the press table and repeated to the reporters: "Cato— I said, Cato— Has any one of you ever heard of him?" On Tuesday he attacked a bishop of the Roman Catholic Church—said if the priest continued to hang around City Hall he would have the sergeant-at-arms throw him out. On Wednesday Gaynor delivered a blistering attack on Rabbi Stephen S. Wise as a meddler; and that same night in a public address he told an audience that the great publisher William Randolph Hearst was "the most heinous force in American life," and to round out the week, Mayor Gaynor told the Protestant clergyman, Dr. Parkhurst, "You are not pious, you are merely bilious." By this time Colonel House was already swimming across the Hudson River to Governor Woodrow Wilson. He wouldn't even wait for the ferry.

When a group of reformers sent him a list of small hotels in New York where (they alleged) unmarried couples could get accommodations, Gaynor sent the list back with the notation: "Why isn't the Waldorf-Astoria on your list?" When an evangelist applied for a license to preach the gospel in an all-Jewish neighborhood, Mayor Gaynor returned the application with the following remarks: "Please attach a list of the Jews you have already converted, and I'll give your application further consideration. In the meanwhile do not annoy these people."

Nothing escaped Mayor Gaynor. Once he sent a memorandum to his street-cleaning commissioner, Bill Edwards, after the Mayor had seen a group of men shoveling snow while the driver of the truck stood idly by: "Do you want the driver to freeze to death? Give him a shovel."

Mayor Gaynor was so free with advice on any and all matters, trivial or complex, that a popular retort of the day to anyone with a problem was, "Tell it to Gaynor." The opposition *Tribune* wrote, "Nothing that does not concern him is too difficult for his brain."

Today the mayors of our cities hand the "complaint" to a secretary who writes: "Your letter has been turned over to the proper department for study." Individualism is gone. The day when the mayor locked himself in his office and had all visitors screened for whips, guns, knives, and clubs is gone, and that's a pity, too.

In answer to a letter from the National Publicity Bureau asking him for a statement, Gaynor replied, "You ask me to give an interview saying, 'What would I say to the readers of your three thousand newspapers.' I would say to them to be very careful about believing all they see in those newspapers."

To a fellow who complained about the danger from hatpins in women's hats in the elevated trains and streetcars, Gaynor replied: "Why do you get so close to a woman that her hatpin becomes a threat to you? I hope the next woman uses her hatpin to good effect."

To a letter complaining about a stiff fine for spitting on the platform of the elevated station: "Spitting is a nasty habit and therefore you must be a nasty fellow. You are lucky I wasn't sitting as the Magistrate in your case."

To a Greek Orthodox priest who complained that he was ridiculed when he walked along the street because of his black beard, he wrote: "How is it that they take notice of your beard? Have you trimmed it in some peculiar way, contrary to the Scriptures? . . . Are you certain it is your beard which is the cause of the trouble?"

To a Republican politician who had misquoted him, he wrote: "I am glad to perceive from your letter, just received, that I have already cured you of your propensity to make false statements, that you drop your forged quotation from my letter to Mr. Ridder, and use the correct quotation. While the lamp holds out to burn the vilest sinner may return."

A year after he took office a discharged city employee shot Mayor Gaynor. He came up behind the Mayor on the deck of an ocean liner, where Gaynor stood talking with friends who had come aboard to see him off to Europe. The would-be assassin held the pistol close to the Mayor's head and fired. The bullet entered the back of his right ear, and passed through the throat, and was never extracted. His voice was permanently affected, and the wound hastened his death which occurred a few months after he had finished his term and was running for re-election, as an "independent" this time, of course. Incidentally, the photo of Mayor Gaynor staggering to his feet after the attempt on his life is in every collection of the famous news photos of all time.

Throughout his career as a judge and mayor Gaynor kept his private life strictly to himself. Few people knew that he had been born on a farm, that he had once studied for the priesthood, and that he had been married twice. Photographs of his wife and children were nonexistent as far as the public was concerned. He went home every week-end to a farm on Long Island, at St. James, and tolerated no intrusion except for neighboring farmers with whom he would discuss crops, weather conditions, and purely local affairs. He was a political and mental giant among pygmies. Compared to Gaynor, Jimmy Walker was a department store floorworker; La Guardia, an opportunist whom Gaynor would have given the back of his hand; and Impellitteri would have done well to have been allowed to tie Gaynor's shoelaces. (About La Guardia, I can never forgive him for having withheld the salary of Professor Bertrand Russell when the mob was hounding the British philosopher out of the City College of New York for teaching "advanced" ideas. One may well imagine what Gaynor would have done in this case. He probably would have delivered Russell's pay envelope himself, and with his cane carved a path through the mob of shouting obscurantists.)

But with all of Gaynor's notable achievements, his greatest talent was his remarkable use of the English language. Professor Brander Matthews read Gaynor's letters in his class at Columbia University, and so did the English masters at Oxford and Cambridge. Gaynor was one of the most widely read political figures in our history. His knowledge of the religious, philosophical, and literary classics of the world was phenomenal. Time after time as he delivered a lecture and quoted from Marcus Aurelius, Cervantes, Shakespeare, and the Bible, he would turn to the reporters and give them the volume and the chapter of his quoted reference so that their account of the occasion would be complete.

His written opinions as a judge were full of references and quotations from the great minds of our civilization. One of his decisions is known to this day as the "Pater Noster Case." It was a divorce case against a man. The evidence showed that he met the woman at a railroad station, that they came together in a hack with their baggage to the hotel, that the man registered them as man and wife, and that they went to the bedroom assigned to them. One of the judges wrote an opinion that this evidence was not sufficient. Gaynor wrote an opinion that the legal inference of misconduct could and should be drawn from it, that they did not go there to say their prayers, and he cited that passage from Burton's *Anatomy of Melancholy*, which says of a man under such conditions, "It is presumed he saith not a Pater Noster."

One of the best Gaynor episodes concerned the Protestant clergyman, Dr. Charles H. Parkhurst, and the "Leapfrog Dance" in a New York brothel. Dr. Parkhurst felt that the city had too many prostitutes and that Gaynor wasn't doing anything about getting rid of them. So to gather evidence, he hit upon one of the most interesting experiments ever initiated by a man of the cloth. He went out to gather the evidence himself. He hired a private detective companion. Dr. Parkhurst, head of the fashionable Madison Square Presbyterian Church, trimmed his fine beard, put on old waterfront clothing, a turtle-neck sweater, and off he went. Dr. Parkhurst insisted on "a full investigation." The companion, a Mr. Gardner, wrote a book about it in later years. First they visited some Bowery saloons, but each time Dr. Parkhurst said, "This is bad, but I want to see worse." Then Gardner steered the doctor to the five-cent lodging houses where the reek of perspiration from the naked sleepers was enough to knock you down. A few more lodging houses, but the clergyman still wasn't satisfied. "I want to see the worst." Gardner finally got the point. He and the doctor then made a round of the brothels, plus a few opium houses as a bonus. Dr. Parkhurst was all the time taking notes, and, on the third night, says companion Gardner, he took the clergyman to the one and only Hattie Adams House, where Gardner says he arranged with the madam for her girls to perform their famous "dance of nature" for the edification of Dr. Parkhurst.

Gardner records that they first had to blindfold the "professor" as they called the piano player in these places, because the girls were shy and would perform only for strangers. The "dance of nature" included a "leapfrog" sequence during which Gardner writes he was the frog and the others jumped over him, with Dr. Parkhurst taking it all in.

This was where the clergyman made a serious blunder. When he made his report from his pulpit and demanded that the district attorney close all the places he had visited, Dr. Parkhurst, to emphasize the degradation he had seen, mentioned this "leapfrog" sequence in the "dance of nature" up at the Hattie Adams House. Well, don't ask! The newspapers immediately picked that up, and the whole town was buzzing—jokes by the million and saloons were advertising special leapfrog concoctions. So by the time Dr. Parkhurst appeared before the Society for the Prevention of Crime, the dignity had gone out of the whole thing and the opposition papers called it "Dr. Parkhurst's Leapfrog Investigation." It blew up in ribaldry and jest.

In the end, however, the brothels and joints were closed by the reform Mayor John Purroy Mitchel. But to this day no one has adequately answered Mayor Gaynor's original statement to Dr. Parkhurst: "If you secured for me the authority to take the prostitutes down to the river and drown them all, I would see a point to your demands, but you don't want that. What you want me to do is to chase them out of New York and you would feel better, I suppose, if they were walking the streets of Philadelphia, New Haven, and Jersey City."

† Suggestions for Reading and Writing

1. In what ways does the opening paragraph of this sketch prepare the reader for what follows?
2. What elements of style here may account for the wide popularity of Golden's writings? Do you find his style and approach folksy? Explain.
3. Would Mayor Gaynor be a more likely political candidate today than in 1912? Were he alive today, would you want him for governor of your state?
4. Golden here refers negatively to two former New York mayors, Walker and La Guardia. To determine the validity of his comments, read Gene Fowler's *Beau James: The Life and Times of Jimmy Walker* (1949) and either Arthur Mann's *La Guardia, A Fighter Against His Times* (1959) or Bella Rodman and Philip Sterling's *Fiorello La Guardia* (1962). If you wish to pursue this subject, see also La Guardia's *The Making of An Insurgent: An Autobiography: 1882–1919* (1948).
5. For a book-length biographical study by Harry Golden, see his *Carl Sandburg* (1961).

from

CITIZEN
HEARST

W. A. Swanberg

Having written well-received biographies of railroad magnate
Jim Fisk and the Civil War's colorful General Dan Sickles,
William Andrew Swanberg (1907–   ) tackled the life of
William Randolph Hearst (1863–1951). Easily one of this
century's most complex and extraordinary individuals, Hearst
dominated, as much as one man could, American life for almost
six decades. His newspapers were being read by about one of
every four American families at the time many were agreeing
with a critic's charge that Hearst himself was "the most deeply
hated single individual in his nation."

   In Citizen Hearst (1961), Swanberg sought not to judge but
to know his fascinating, many-sided hero. Working under a
Guggenheim Fellowship, Swanberg went through mountains of
material and interviewed scores of individuals who knew Hearst.
His completed study is an engrossing narrative of the age and a
rich but carefully balanced portrait of the man—too balanced
for some critical tastes.

   Hearst once said that he wanted to read no biography of
himself. "If it doesn't tell the truth, it will make me mad," he
declared, "and if it tells the truth it will make me sad." Evidently
Swanberg's book both angered and saddened the trustees of
Columbia University; they rejected flatly the Pulitzer Prize
Advisory Board's recommendation that Citizen Hearst be
designated the best biography of 1961.

   In the following selection footnotes have been omitted.

I . ATTRACTING THE CHIEF'S ATTENTION

In 1923, Hearst, who disliked to grow old, reached sixty. In point of energy expended and scope of activities, he had already outstripped a score of average lifetimes. In his mastery of journalistic techniques he was unrivaled. In his observance of the best standards of journalism, he was precisely what the *North American Review* had called him years earlier, "a blazing disgrace to the craft."

Al Smith had touched the root of the evil when he said of the *Journal*, "you cannot look for truth in this paper." Others had tried in their own way to describe the peculiar delinquencies of the Hearst press. Will Irwin had said that in it "the music of the spheres became a screech." R. L. Duffus said it "reduced everything to the common denominator of two or three instincts and passions." Arthur James Pegler, a Hearst writer and the father of Westbrook Pegler, remarked, "A Hearst newspaper is like a screaming woman running down the street with her throat cut." Oswald Garrison Villard described Hearst journalism as "gathering garbage from the gutters of life."

The trouble with Hearst's newspapers was to be found in the deep-seated flaws in his own character—his instability, his hunger for power, his insatiable need for money, his vein of cruelty.

His papers were seldom indecent. He forbade indecency. They merely "plugged" crime and scandal for circulation. It had to be said that from Ambrose Bierce and Mark Twain to Kipling and Shaw, they printed an enormous amount of quality material. They had fought many good fights. They were pre-eminent in features, in their ownership of Barney Google, Jiggs and other cartoon characters loved by the millions. They were deficient in the newspaper's first requisite—news. The faking of news stories and photographs was brought to a high art by the romancers of the Hearst press. Truth, the touchstone of news value, was unimportant to Hearst because circulation, money and power were his goals. He had—always with startling exceptions—sold out his own newspapers to his own weaknesses.

For years they had been used unblushingly as personal publicity organs for Hearst. Now they were employed, with equal impudence, to advance the career of Miss Davies.

But the fearsome thing about this big, soft-voiced man who liked nothing better than a good joke, was his occasional hatreds. He specialized in attack, and in attack he was pitiless. He loved political cartoonists who could inspire hatred. He had preached hatred of Huntington, Mark Hanna, McKinley, Boss Murphy, Archbold and Standard Oil, Wilson,

England, and Al Smith, to name only a few. The insinuating, venomous quality of his appeals to hatred were unmatched. There was a diabolic strain of abnormality in the man who could accuse Wilson, who wrecked his own health in a trip to Europe to fight for his cherished League, of going there merely to receive honors and gifts; and in the man who could suggest that Al Smith was the murderer of tenement babies.

Hearst's streak of sadism warred constantly with his kindly impulses and sometimes won out. It generally was brought to bear on enemies, but occasionally it impaled employes. There were times when he seemed to enjoy the squirmings of two of his executives who were placed in an irreconcilable position that a word from him would have dissipated. The business of putting two men on the same job also occurred frequently, and some felt the reason was not so much to determine the best man as to afford the Chief a malicious amusement. One of the marvels of the whole Fourth Estate was the fantastic salaries he paid his executives. Some of them such as Brisbane, Goddard, Merrill, Carvalho and Kobler became wealthy men or millionaires in their own right. A much larger and lower echelon were, if not quite rich, far more prosperous than they had ever dreamed of being. Walter Howey, for example, was making $8000 a year as city editor of the Chicago *Tribune* when he was lured away by a Hearst offer of $35,000. The big-pay Hearst men knew that they could get no such salaries elsewhere, and they knew that Hearst knew they knew it. While they respected him, admired him, and in some cases came close to loving him, they were also in terror of him, for on any whim he could cast them into darkness. This inevitably inculcated a kind of groveling which Hearst, always the king, seemed to enjoy. Executive messages to him were usually couched in flattering and cautious terms, replete with phrases such as "with the greatest respect," and "if I may be so bold as to suggest." As the first buildings of his *palazzo* complex were completed, he began holding occasional conferences of executives at San Simeon. It became *de rigueur* for each of them to take him some gift, knowing they would be entertained royally during their stay.

The question of what gift to select was known to give Hearst men gray hairs. It had to be costly, rare or distinctive. But what could one give Hearst, who had everything? Albert Kobler, like his chief, had become a collector of letters and autographs, owning a fine collection of Napoleon letters which he had promised his son. Kobler solved one of the what-to-give-Hearst problems by presenting him with a real rarity, a letter Napoleon wrote from Moscow—a gift his son still regrets.

The absolute, dynastic power Hearst reserved for himself, and his refusal to delegate real authority to his subordinates, placed them in the position of courtiers vying for his favor. This sometimes had the effect of elevating those who were the more skilled courtiers and of downgrading able men who refused to curry favor. Great scorn was exhibited in the

Organization for men who worked to "attract the attention of Mr. Hearst," although most of the executives were guilty of that very thing to some degree. This created one of the most appalling jungles of office politics ever seen. There was jealousy, suspicion, intrigue. There was a constant jockeying for position, with editors in Atlanta, Rochester or Los Angeles lying awake nights to perfect schemes for gaining elevation in the hierarchy, sometimes at the expense of a colleague. The stakes were high, with salaries of $100,000, $200,000 or more waiting those who climbed. Hearst undoubtedly encouraged this feeling of competition, knowing that it stimulated his men to strain every nerve for circulation and revenue. It also inspired them in some cases to resort to dubious methods of gaining circulation or advertising. A number of executives became known as favorites of the Chief, among them Brisbane, Carvalho, Bradford Merrill, the irrepressible Walter Howey, and Clarence Lindner in San Francisco. Some of them wielded enormous influence, and there were those less favored who were pulling strings to displace them. In the Organization, an executive had to watch his step and watch his colleagues.

Running contrary to Hearst's subtle cruelty was his unswerving loyalty to his employes if they were assailed from some outside source, or if they were victims of ill luck. His sentimentality was as overwhelming as his brutality. "Tell him a sad story," Frances Marion recalls, "and tears would roll down his face." The instances of his sudden kindnesses, entirely on impulse and without plan, will never be counted. He was one of the most delinquent of millionaires in contributing to organized charity, and one of the most generous when hardship came to his personal attention. He happened to read a pathetic story in his Chicago *Herald-Examiner* of a family whose father was unemployed, the children in rags. They lived in an attic flat and were about to be evicted. Hearst sent a telegram to his Chicago editor ending, "Please give them $10,000 and furnish them with a home." The Chicago staff saved money by finding a good flat and getting the father a job. When Cartoonist Swinnerton came down with tuberculosis, Hearst sent him to Arizona on full salary. When Henri Pene Du Bois, art critic for the New York *American*, developed a heart condition that numbered his days, he wanted to die in Italy. Hearst sent him to write a series about Italian art galleries, and Du Bois' melancholy wish was granted. Numbers of old Hearst employes drew "advances" which they never bothered to repay. In many instances, men facing financial crisis because of wild speculation or gambling, had their debts paid by order of the Chief. In San Francisco, a veteran *Examiner* stereotyping foreman was found to have swindled the company for a long period by padding the payroll and stealing type metal for resale. Hearst let him go but put him on a substantial pension.

Hearst not infrequently defended his employes against arbitrary acts of his own executives. On one occasion, Arthur Brisbane decided to remove all bylines from cartoons and strips—a move calculated to keep the ownership of the cartoon copyright even if the artist should leave the Organization. The angry cartoonists appointed Harry Hershfield, creator of *Abie the Agent*, to present their case to Hearst at the Clarendon. Hearst listened to Hershfield intently. "I didn't know Artie was doing that," he said. "Don't worry. I'll see that you not only get back your signature bylines but that you also get printed bylines." He did.

A showman to the core, Hearst favored men who scored newsbeats by exhibitions of nerve and ingenuity, by striking methods such as climbing fire escapes or donning disguises, or who handled run-of-the-mill stories with a flair that gave them distinction. Many an obscure reporter was delighted to get a bonus of fifty dollars or more along with the Chief's accolade for such a feat. The men in the Organization had the satisfaction of knowing that their boss, however unpredictable, was no rich dilettante but one of the most skilled professionals in the business, a man who could write rings around his best editorialists and was likewise accomplished at all other facets of the game.

When he made one of his rare errors in judgment, it could be a big one, as in his original skepticism about the future of tabloids. Once the innovator, he was badly beaten by the tabloid New York *Daily News*. He grew concerned when the *News* neared a half-million circulation, passing his own *American* and threatening his *Journal*. The *American*, his favorite, was slipping, and Editor Victor Watson got orders to do battle. The *American* announced a circulation-promoting lottery with a grand prize of $1000 and many lesser ones. Next day the *News* launched its own lottery, with a daily prize of $2500. The *American* doubled it to $5000, the *News* countering by going to $10,000. Joseph Patterson, publisher of the *News*, was almost as rich as Hearst and fully as determined. The contest was operated by sending out trucks loaded with coupons, which were distributed to frenzied crowds in such places as Times Square, Columbus Circle and the Battery. Prizes were awarded to lucky persons holding numbers corresponding with those published in the newspaper. The details of the lottery so absorbed the staffs of both papers that the news got little attention. Watson, it was said, collapsed when the *Daily News* raised its grand prize to $25,000 and promised to double any rival. By now the contest was so expensive that both publishers were glad to call it quits, losing most of the circulation gain they had won.

Another paper that passed the *American* was the full-sized *Times*, which had been dying when Hearst entered New York and which he had sometimes scoffed at for its sobriety. It had registered steady gains under Adolph Ochs, who shunned stunts and set a new standard in careful news reporting. Ochs was the tortoise and Hearst the hare. Ochs had been satisfied to build slowly, with a passion for accuracy and fairness. The impatient Hearst wanted circulation fast. Surrounding the title of his *American* were the words, "Character, Quality, Enterprise, Accuracy." Its character was dubious, its quality poor, its accuracy notoriously shaky, and its enterprise, while undeniably vigorous, was prone to exhaust itself in schemes for getting the best pictures in the latest love slaying. Being himself theatrical, exotic and violent, Hearst expected his papers to be that way. A champion rationalizer, he could send out these instructions to his editors:

> Make a paper for the nicest kind of people—for the great middle class. . . .
> Omit things that will offend nice people. Avoid coarseness and slang and a low tone. The most sensational news can be told if it is written properly . . .
> Do not exaggerate.
> Make the paper helpful and kindly. Don't scold and forever complain and attack in your news columns. Leave that to the editorial page.
> Be fair and impartial . . . Make a paper for all the people and give unbiased news of all creeds and parties. . . .

Undoubtedly he believed these precepts and would have resented any suggestion that his newspapers did not live up to them. The great egoist was able to manufacture his own logic. Not surprisingly, some thousands of Hearst city-room underlings, faced by the realities of their jobs, wondered cynically whether the Chief was a mite crazy or just a plain liar. The evidence suggests that Hearst was not an intentional or conscious liar, although the truth was an elastic substance in his hands. He easily believed what he wanted to believe, so much so that his ratiocination sometimes soared into a dream world. Yet when he came down from the clouds, he could be wonderfully practical and even eloquent. When he hired Fremont Older to take charge of the San Francisco *Call*, he knew that Older had felt impelled to leave his cherished *Bulletin* because the publisher had ordered him to stop his campaign for Tom Mooney. The separation had almost broken Older's heart. He was a crusader of great gifts, and Hearst, obviously fearful that Older might go overboard on Mooney to the detriment of other news, wrote him delicate instructions which also illuminate his drift toward conservatism and away from the radicalism of his youth:

> My Dear Mr. Older: I have your letter about the Mooney case. Of course I understand, as you say, that the labor people are not always grateful for the work done for them. Neither is any other class of the community. But our object is not so much to secure the gratitude of this or that element as to do what in our

opinion is essentially just and right, and secure the approval of our own conscience.

The one thing, however, that I want to warn you against becoming in the *Call* is a class newspaper, a newspaper with the limited viewpoint of any faction in the community.

This is not only undesirable because of its inevitable limitation of our objects and ideals, but it is undesirable because of the distinct limitations of our influence and our opportunity to accomplish our objects and ideals.

A newspaper, in order to do great good, in order to convince all the people and secure the general support of the public, must be a paper of all the people, and not of one faction arrayed against the other factions in the community.

A newspaper only gets an open minded hearing when it is generally believed to be a broad minded newspaper, when its policies are liberal and tolerant, when it sees the good in all classes, and the actual need of various factors in our civilization.

Radicalism has its value, but an excessive radicalism is dangerous. Conservatism has its uses. It is only the hide bound conservatism that can see no benefit in new ideas that is a brake on progress. . . .

Out of his long experience in journalism, government and politics, Hearst had formulated a moderate and practical philosophy, however he failed to live up to it.

But Hearst at sixty had lost most of his public following because he so often compromised his own ideals for expediency. Samuel Seabury was the vocal symbol of a public trend. Liberals who once hailed him had lost faith in him. His bewildering political shifts had alienated the steadfast. People were offended by talk of his private life. Many readers of the Hearst papers had come to view Hearst's editorials and crusades as nonsense. They bought the papers for Happy Hooligan, Krazy Kat, and extensive coverage of the Hall-Mills scandal. They decided that Hearst was, after all, a millionaire building a castle in California and that his concern for "the people" was a sham. He had become a political monstrosity. And yet, because he spoke to millions, he remained a powerful voice from the wings.

II. THE ODDITIES OF GENIUS

Hearst's journalistic recklessness, political unintelligibility and personal eccentricities had long since made him a national conversation piece. Over bars, teacups and dinner tables he was an object of discussion, often heated, aimed at disassembling him and isolating that part which was faulty. He provoked a frustration like that caused by a Chinese puzzle that refuses to be solved.

What *was* wrong with Hearst? Certainly there was something wrong with him, as there is something wrong with everyone, but in him the physical or psychological imperfections, joined as they were with genius, produced a combination never seen before in mortal man. Whatever was wrong with him was wrong in a greater degree than customary, or in an uncommon blend of defect. Journalists from Willis Abbot to Oswald Garrison Villard, and politicians from Bryan to Al Smith, had tried and failed to understand him. Those closest to him could agree only on one trait that was itself confusing—his duality, his inconsistency, his unpredictability. He seemed two men rather than one.

It is a truism that every normal person veers somewhat from his average behavior, with moments of selfishness balanced by surges of idealism—a duality Stevenson dramatized in his *Dr. Jekyll and Mr. Hyde.* Dr. Jekyll was a saintly physician until he drank a potion that turned him into Mr. Hyde, suppressing his virtues and unleashing his evil. Hearst was Jekyll and he was Hyde, with no need for chemical draughts. As Jekyll he could rescue an imperiled toad, overwhelm his friends with generosity, fight for "the people." As Hyde he could descend to lies, chicanery and cruelty.

Hearst *was* two men, to such an extent that he rightly should have been equipped with two bodies. In him, the minor deflection of personality seen in ordinary persons became a wild, schizoid plunge from the heights to the depths. If the average swing of the personality pendulum is a modest twenty degrees, Hearst's could swoop a fearful 180. He lacked the psychic brakes that hold normal persons within reasonable limits of behavior so that they can be identified and understood by their unchanging or little-changing traits. He was like an intricate jeweled mechanism, lacking one vital part so that it sometimes whirled out of control.

Any effort to analyze this inscrutable Sphinx has its dangers, but when one sees elements of comedy as well as tragedy in him, the blurred image gains some approach to focus. Hearst was an incurable adolescent. Maturity in normal persons implies the disenchanting realization that many of the desires and fantasies of childhood must be postponed, must be labored for, and that many others can never be achieved even after infinite labor. Maturity, the gradual adjustment to reality, the stoic acceptance of disappointment, never became a part of the Hearst ego. He refused to let it enter. He operated on the pleasure principle. He would admit of no doubt that he could do what he wanted to do, have what he wanted to have. Had he not been gifted with an ability and a drive that enabled him to satisfy most of his wants, he would in all probability have gone insane.

On those occasions when he failed to achieve his aims, as in politics, the blow was so wounding that he would do precisely what a thwarted child would do. He would go into a rage.

As an exhibitionist, he had few peers. Painfully shy, he had to prove his leadership to himself and the world. This need found expression from childhood on in his bent for impact and sensationalism. He would make his presence felt if he had to break windows, corrupt an alligator, touch off rockets, start a war, buy stolen letters, or defame Al Smith to do it. He would gain leadership even at the cost of the personal torture public speaking visited on him. Since early in the century, his desire to be President had led him into so many comic or desperate byways that it had come to be a joke, first to other politicians, then to a growing segment of the public. In his hunger for office, his newspapers, at first his most sacred possessions, had become chiefly weapons, a means to gain power to satisfy his wants.

His childhood was abnormal in the closeness and long duration of his communion with his mother, coupled with his father's absences. His reverence for his mother seemed to color his adult relationships. He had been almost equally devoted to his grandmother. Annie Laurie, Mrs. Logan and Louella Parsons were only three in a long line of Hearst women employes who considered him the personification of kindliness. Women occupied a special niche in his regard. When Miss Davies entered his life, she became the fulfillment of his childish, romantic dream of womanly perfection. Whatever minor flaws she might have, he would correct with the best of tutors. With affectionate selfishness, he would mold her to fit his dream. He loved her in romantic roles, in rich period costumes, with a background of portcullises, tapestries or other symbols of queenliness and luxury. He would not permit her to take any role that even verged on realism or sordidness. Miss Davies, who could rule him in almost every other way, had no authority over her own screen activities. Artistically she was his property.

In his childhood he had been paraded through castles and art galleries until his busy imagination was fired by visions of medieval and Renaissance magnificence which he never lost. Certainly he pictured himself as a Tudor, a Bourbon, a Hapsburg, a prince of absolute power, surrounded by beauty and luxury. To him, maturity did not mean the surrender of this roseate dream, but merely a skillful adaptation so that the dream could be achieved within the realities of twentieth-century life. An atavist, a medieval character transplanted out of his time, he was determined to cling to the imperial ideal even if it had to be done on Riverside Drive, at Palm Beach and San Simeon, determined to gain power even if it had to be done in the unsatisfactory way of asking people for their votes instead of taking power by succession. If he never quite succeeded in reconciling his medievalism to the twentieth century, he never stopped trying and he came closer than anyone else ever got or ever will get. At sixty, Hearst was the nearest approach to a Lancaster or a

Burgundy in the democratic United States. He was kingly in his power, in his possessions, in the way he did, with few limitations, what he wanted to do. But he was beginning to encounter certain democratic curbs on his kingliness that would plague him for the rest of his life.

Emotionally, he was a jumble of contradictions, afflicted by the polarity that often accompanies genius. Some of his whims and postures were too fantastic for normal understanding. He lived in a dream world which he turned into near reality through sheer force of will, ability and energy. It is significant that he became fascinated by the stage and then by the screen, where his fantasies could be acted out just as he wished them to be and he could avoid the hurtful jolts of reality. He forever hopefully regarded the real world as one vast stage where he would write the script, serve as producer and director, shift the scenes, manipulate the actors and produce a cosmic drama utterly enchanting because he created it to suit himself. He failed in this because of his own political ineptitude. But he did not fail in his cut-down version of the dream—iron control over a great chain of newspapers and thousands of employes, and possession of his own duchy in the West, complete with castle and lovely duchess.

As a husband and father, he was kindly but delinquent because he was too preoccupied with his ambitions to give himself to his family. He was devoted to his sons, but they seldom saw him. When he felt remorse about this, he tried to rectify it by giving the boys lavish gifts of money or motorcars.

For all his kindness, he lacked the essence of friendship, the ability to unbend, to confide, to reveal himself. He must have been aware of deep flaws of personality, for he concealed them from outsiders.

His inconsistency, which so puzzled observers, was in reality a key to his personality. He could vary from day to day and from hour to hour. His closest colleagues never were sure how he would react to a situation. He took pride in this as proof that he was not hidebound in opinion. He was fond of paraphrasing Emerson by saying, "Consistency is the hobgoblin of little minds." This was an evasion. When a problem arose, he judged it not from any immovable standards or moral values, since he had few of these, but from the impulse or advantage of the moment. He could, and did, argue on both sides of a question with equal facility and apparent conviction, depending on which of his two selves was in charge. He was forever taking positive stands on public questions, grounding his arguments on "principle," which he doubtless believed at the time. It was his capacity to shift diametrically in opinion, sometimes apparently for his own advantage, that caused critics to damn him for insincerity, cynicism and downright demagoguery. He had brilliant powers of reasoning and persuasion without any solid inner ground to anchor them on.

Traditionally, great men are remembered in part for their principles but more for the manner in which they fought for them. History lays down basic rules of fair play which public men are expected to observe in fighting for their principles. While Hearst for decades had a sympathy for "the people" and for progressive measures beneficial to them, he so often violated the amenities of the game that the referees—the politicians and eventually the public—threw him out bodily. His ideas were often wonderful. His methods were often deplorable. The mistaken suspicion grew that he was utterly selfish and would sacrifice any principle to gain power and office.

In the end, it is futile to attempt to analyze him as one man, since he was two. General conclusions about him must always be qualified as referring to Hearst in his Jekyll aspect or to Hearst as Hyde. The true story of Hearst must be what Hearst was himself—a riot of incongruity. He could only be described in contradictions. He was true, and he was false. He was a puritan, and he was a libertine. He was democratic, and he was kingly. He was immovable, and he was fickle. He was kindly, and he was cruel. He was great, and he was contemptible.

✔ Suggestions for Reading and Writing

1. Would this section of *Citizen Hearst* have made Hearst glad, mad, or sad? Would his reaction change with a reading of the entire book? Explain.

2. Compare a Hearst newspaper with the same issue of the New York *Times*. Are the differences indicated by Swanberg still evident?

3. Does the longevity of his newspaper empire prove Hearst gave the people the newspapers they wanted? In other words, do you agree we always get the newspapers we deserve?

4. An interesting term paper should result from a comparison of Swanberg's *Citizen Hearst* and one or more of the earlier studies of Hearst. See, for instance, Mrs. Fremont Older's *William Randolph Hearst, American* (1936), Oliver Carson and E. S. Bates's *Hearst, Lord of San Simeon* (1936), John Tebbel's *The Life and Good Times of William Randolph Hearst* (1952) or John K. Winkler's *William Randolph Hearst—A New Appraisal* (1955).

5. An equally challenging essay should result from a comparison of Hearst's life and that of his major early journalistic competitor, Joseph Pulitzer. For this, see Don C. Seitz's *Joseph Pulitzer: His Life and Letters* (1924) or J. W. Barrett's *Joseph Pulitzer and His World* (1941).

6. For a broader view of Swanberg as biographer, read *Citizen Hearst* entire and compare its style and structure with those of his *Sickles the Incredible* (1956), *Jim Fisk* (1959), or *Dreiser* (1965).

[THORSTEIN
VEBLEN]

John Dos Passos

After Harvard, study in Spain, and war service in the French ambulance corps, John Dos Passos (1896–   ) emerged as one of America's major novelists of the twenties and the thirties. He drew upon his war experiences for his first novels, of which Three Soldiers (1921) was the most significant. Critical recognition came with the appearance of Manhattan Transfer (1925), a novel interweaving many loosely related episodes into a sprawling collective panorama of New York City life.

Dos Passos has remained an active writer to this day, producing a long series of novels, travel books, biographies, and works of political and social commentary. But his literary reputation rests primarily on his U. S. A. trilogy: The 42nd Parallel (1930), 1919 (1932), and The Big Money (1936). Focusing on America's social processes during this century's first three decades, these novels trace a fiercely materialistic and competitive society's effects upon the individual.

To capture and sustain reader interest, Dos Passos employs a series of striking narrative devices. He introduces a number of varied characters whose lives intersect occasionally or merely run parallel. He pinpoints each episode in time by a "Newsreel" panorama of contemporary songs, advertisements, and news events. He then adds a second dramatic dimension by "The Camera Eye," in which he conveys his own attitude toward the material through impressionistic stream-of-consciousness passages. He stresses throughout the corrosive futility and corruption of American life. (Dos Passos has since greatly modified his social views.)

Linking the narrative episodes are short, pointed biographies of Americans who helped shape the age and whose lives offer a dramatic counterpoint to those of the narrative's little people. One such biography is that of the flamboyant political economist Thorstein Veblen (1857–1929), whose ideas have remained influential to the present. The biography appeared in The Big Money.

↗ ↗ ↗ ↗ ↗

Veblen,
a greyfaced shambling man lolling resentful at his desk with his cheek on his hand, in a low sarcastic mumble of intricate phrases subtly paying out the logical inescapable rope of matteroffact for a society to hang itself by,

dissecting out the century with a scalpel so keen, so comical, so exact that the professors and students ninetenths of the time didn't know it was there, and the magnates and the respected windbags and the applauded loudspeakers never knew it was there.

Veblen
asked too many questions, suffered from a constitutional inability to say yes.

Socrates asked questions, drank down the bitter drink one night when the first cock crowed,

but Veblen
drank it in little sips through a long life in the stuffiness of classrooms, the dust of libraries, the staleness of cheap flats such as a poor instructor can afford. He fought the boyg all right, pedantry, routine, timeservers at office desks, trustees, collegepresidents, the plump flunkies of the ruling businessmen, all the good jobs kept for yesmen, never enough money, every broadening hope thwarted. Veblen drank the bitter drink all right.

The Veblens were a family of freeholding farmers.

The freeholders of the narrow Norwegian valleys were a stubborn hardworking people, farmers, dairymen, fishermen, rooted in their fathers' stony fields, in their old timbered farmsteads with carved gables they took their names from, in the upland pastures where they grazed the stock in summer.

During the early nineteenth century the towns grew; Norway filled up with landless men, storekeepers, sheriffs, moneylenders, bailiffs, notaries in black with stiff collars and briefcases full of foreclosures under their arms. Industries were coming in. The townsmen were beginning to get profits out of the country and to finagle the farmers out of the freedom of their narrow farms.

The meanspirited submitted as tenants, daylaborers; but the strong men went out of the country

as their fathers had gone out of the country centuries before when Harald the Fairhaired and St. Olaf hacked to pieces the liberties of the northern men, who had been each man lord of his own creek, to make Christians and serfs of them,

only in the old days it was Iceland, Greenland, Vineland the northmen had sailed west to; now it was America.

Both Thorstein Veblen's father's people and his mother's people had lost their farmsteads and with them the names that denoted them free men.

Thomas Anderson for a while tried to make his living as a traveling carpenter and cabinetmaker, but in 1847 he and his wife, Kari Thorsteinsdatter, crossed in a whalingship from Bremen and went out to join friends in the Scandihoovian colonies round Milwaukee.

Next year his brother Haldor joined him.

They were hard workers; in another year they had saved up money to preempt a claim on 160 acres of uncleared land in Sheboygan County, Wisconsin; when they'd gotten that land part cleared they sold it and moved to an all-Norway colony in Manitowoc County, near Cato and a place named Valders after the valley they had all come from in the old country;

there in the house Thomas Anderson built with his own tools, the sixth of twelve children, Thorstein Veblen was born.

When Thorstein was eight years old, Thomas Anderson moved west again into the blacksoil prairies of Minnesota that the Sioux and the buffalo had only been driven off from a few years before. In the deed to the new farm Thomas Anderson took back the old farmstead name of Veblen.

He was a solid farmer, builder, a clever carpenter, the first man to import merino sheep and a mechanical reaper and binder; he was a man of standing in the group of Norway people farming the edge of the prairie, who kept their dialects, the manner of life of their narrow Norway valleys, their Lutheran pastors, their homemade clothes and cheese and bread, their suspicion and stubborn dislike of townsmen's ways.

The townspeople were Yankees mostly, smart to make two dollars grow where a dollar grew before, storekeepers, middlemen, speculators, moneylenders, with long heads for politics and mortgages; they despised the Scandihoovian dirtfarmers they lived off, whose daughters did their wives' kitchenwork.

The Norway people believed as their fathers had believed that there were only two callings for an honest man, farming or preaching.

Thorstein grew up a hulking lad with a reputation for laziness and wit. He hated the irk of everrepeated backbreaking chores round the farm. Reading he was happy. Carpentering he liked or running farmmachinery. The Lutheran pastors who came to the house noticed that his supple mind slid easily round the corners of their theology. It was hard to get farmwork out of him, he had a stinging tongue and was famous for the funny names he called people; his father decided to make a preacher out of him.

When he was seventeen he was sent for out of the field where he was working. His bag was already packed. The horses were hitched up. He was being sent to Carleton Academy in Northfield, to prepare for Carleton College.

As there were several young Veblens to be educated their father built them a house on a lot near the campus. Their food and clothes were sent to them from the farm. Cash money was something they never saw.

Thorstein spoke English with an accent. He had a constitutional inability to say yes. His mind was formed on the Norse sagas and on the matteroffact sense of his father's farming and the exact needs of carpenterwork and threshingmachines.

He could never take much interest in the theology, sociology, economics of Carleton College where they were busy trimming down the jagged dogmas of the old New England bibletaught traders to make stencils to hang on the walls of commissionmerchants' offices.

Veblen's collegeyears were the years when Darwin's assertions of growth and becoming were breaking the set molds of the Noah's Ark world,

when Ibsen's women were tearing down the portieres of the Victorian parlors,

and Marx's mighty machine was rigging the countinghouse's own logic to destroy the countinghouse.

When Veblen went home to the farm he talked about these things with his father, following him up and down at his plowing, starting an argument while they were waiting for a new load for the wheatthresher. Thomas Anderson had seen Norway and America; he had the squarebuilt mind of a carpenter and builder, and an understanding of tools and the treasured elaborated builtupseasonbyseason knowledge of a careful farmer,

a tough whetstone for the sharpening steel of young Thorstein's wits.

At Carleton College young Veblen was considered a brilliant unsound eccentric; nobody could understand why a boy of such attainments wouldn't settle down to the business of the day, which was to buttress property and profits with anything usable in the debris of Christian ethics and eighteenthcentury economics that cluttered the minds of collegeprofessors, and to reinforce the sacred, already shaky edifice with the new strong girderwork of science Herbert Spencer was throwing up for the benefit of the bosses.

People complained they never knew whether Veblen was joking or serious.

In 1880 Thorstein Veblen started to try to make his living by teaching. A year in an academy at Madison, Wisconsin, wasn't much of a success. Next year he and his brother Andrew started graduate work at Johns Hopkins. Johns Hopkins didn't suit, but boarding in an old Baltimore house with some ruined gentlewomen gave him a disdaining glimpse of an etiquette motheaten now but handed down through the lavish leisure of the slaveowning planters' mansions straight from the merry England of the landlord cavaliers.

(The valleyfarmers had always been scornful of outlanders' ways.)

He was more at home at Yale where in Noah Porter he found a New England roundhead granite against which his Norway granite rang in clear dissent. He took his Ph.D. there. But there was still some question as to what department of the academic world he could best make a living in.

He read Kant and wrote prize essays. But he couldn't get a job. Try as he could he couldn't get his mouth round the essential yes.

He went back to Minnesota with a certain intolerant knowledge of the amenities of the higher learning. To his slight Norwegian accent he'd added the broad a.

At home he loafed about the farm and tinkered with inventions of new machinery and read and talked theology and philosophy with his father. In the Scandihoovian colonies the price of wheat and the belief in God and St. Olaf were going down together. The farmers of the Northwest were starting their long losing fight against the parasite businessmen who were sucking them dry. There was a mortgage on the farm, interest on debts to pay, always fertilizer, new machines to buy to speed production to pump in a halfcentury the wealth out of the soil laid down in a million years of buffalograss. His brothers kept grumbling about this sardonic loafer who wouldn't earn his keep.

Back home he met again his college sweetheart, Ellen Rolfe, the niece of the president of Carleton College, a girl who had railroadmagnates and money in the family. People in Northfield were shocked when

it came out that she was going to marry the drawling pernickety bookish
badlydressed young Norwegian ne'erdowell.

Her family hatched a plan to get him a job as economist for the
Santa Fe Railroad but at the wrong moment Ellen Rolfe's uncle lost
control of the line. The young couple went to live at Stacyville where
they did everything but earn a living. They read Latin and Greek and
botanized in the woods and along the fences and in the roadside scrub.
They boated on the river and Veblen started his translation of the
Laxdaelasaga. They read *Looking Backward* and articles by Henry
George. They looked at their world from the outside.

In '91 Veblen got together some money to go to Cornell to do
postgraduate work. He turned up there in the office of the head of the
economics department wearing a coonskin cap and grey corduroy trousers and said in his low sarcastic drawl, "I am Thorstein Veblen,"

but it was not until several years later, after he was established at the
new University of Chicago that had grown up next to the World's Fair,
and had published *The Theory of the Leisure Class*, put on the map by
Howells' famous review, that the world of the higher learning knew who
Thorstein Veblen was.

Even in Chicago as the brilliant young economist he lived pioneer-
fashion. (The valleyfarmers had always been scornful of outlanders'
ways.) He kept his books in packingcases laid on their sides along the
walls. His only extravagances were the Russian cigarettes he smoked and
the red sash he sometimes sported. He was a man without smalltalk.
When he lectured he put his cheek on his hand and mumbled out his
long spiral sentences, reiterative like the eddas. His language was a mixture of mechanics' terms, scientific latinity, slang and Roget's Thesaurus.
The other profs couldn't imagine why the girls fell for him so.

The girls fell for him so that Ellen Rolfe kept leaving him. He'd
take summer trips abroad without his wife. There was a scandal about a
girl on an ocean liner.

Tongues wagged so (Veblen was a man who never explained, who
never could get his tongue around the essential yes; the valleyfarmers had
always been scornful of the outlanders' ways, and their opinions) that his
wife left him and went off to live alone on a timberclaim in Idaho and
the president asked for his resignation.

Veblen went out to Idaho to get Ellen Rolfe to go with him to
California when he succeeded in getting a job at a better salary at Leland
Stanford, but in Palo Alto it was the same story as in Chicago. He
suffered from woman trouble and the constitutional inability to say yes
and an unnatural tendency to feel with the workingclass instead of with
the profittakers. There were the same complaints that his courses were
not constructive or attractive to big money bequests and didn't help his

students to butter their bread, make Phi Beta Kappa, pick plums off the
hierarchies of the academic grove. His wife left him for good. He wrote
to a friend: "The president doesn't approve of my domestic arrangements; nor do I."

Talking about it he once said, "What is one to do if the woman
moves in on you?"

He went back up to the shack in the Idaho woods.

Friends tried to get him an appointment to make studies in Crete, a
chair at the University of Pekin, but always the boyg, routine, businessmen's flunkeys in all the university offices . . . for the questioner the
bitter drink.

His friend Davenport got him an appointment at the University of
Missouri. At Columbia he lived like a hermit in the basement of the
Davenports' house, helped with the work round the place, carpentered
himself a table and chairs. He was already a bitter elderly man with a
grey face covered with a net of fine wrinkles, a vandyke beard and yellow
teeth. Few students could follow his courses. The college authorities
were often surprised and somewhat chagrined that when visitors came
from Europe it was always Veblen they wanted to meet.

These were the years he did most of his writing, trying out his ideas
on his students, writing slowly at night in violet ink with a pen of his own
designing. Whenever he published a book he had to put up a guarantee
with the publishers. In *The Theory of Business Enterprise, The Instinct
of Workmanship, The Vested Interests and the Common Man,*

he established a new diagram of a society dominated by monopoly
capital,

etched in irony

the sabotage of production by business,

the sabotage of life by blind need for money profits,

pointed out the alternatives: a warlike society strangled by the
bureaucracies of the monopolies forced by the law of diminishing returns
to grind down more and more the common man for profits,

or a new matteroffact commonsense society dominated by the needs
of the men and women who did the work and the incredibly vast
possibilities for peace and plenty offered by the progress of technology.

These were the years of Debs's speeches, growing laborunions, the
I.W.W. talk about industrial democracy: these years Veblen still held to
the hope that the workingclass would take over the machine of production before monopoly had pushed the western nations down into the
dark again.

War cut across all that: under the cover of the bunting of Woodrow
Wilson's phrases the monopolies cracked down. American democracy
was crushed.

The war at least offered Veblen an opportunity to break out of the airless greenhouse of academic life. He was offered a job with the Food Administration, he sent the Navy Department a device for catching submarines by trailing lengths of stout bindingwire. (Meanwhile the government found his books somewhat confusing. The postoffice was forbidding the mails to *Imperial Germany and the Industrial Revolution* while propaganda agencies were sending it out to make people hate the Huns. Educators were denouncing *The Nature of Peace* while Washington experts were clipping phrases out of it to add to the Wilsonian smokescreen.)

For the Food Administration Thorstein Veblen wrote two reports: in one he advocated granting the demands of the I.W.W. as a wartime measure and conciliating the workingclass instead of beating up and jailing all the honest leaders; in the other he pointed out that the Food Administration was a businessman's racket and was not aiming for the most efficient organization of the country as a producing machine. He suggested that, in the interests of the efficient prosecution of the war, the government step into the place of the middleman and furnish necessities to the farmers direct in return for raw materials;

but cutting out business was not at all the Administration's idea of making the world safe for Democracy,

so Veblen had to resign from the Food Administration.

He signed the protests against the trial of the hundred and one wobblies in Chicago.

After the armistice he went to New York. In spite of all the oppression of the war years, the air was freshening. In Russia the great storm of revolt had broken, seemed to be sweeping west, in the strong gusts from the new world in the east the warsodden multitudes began to see again. At Versailles allies and enemies, magnates, generals, flunkey politicians were slamming the shutters against the storm, against the new, against hope. It was suddenly clear for a second in the thundering glare what war was about, what peace was about.

In America, in Europe, the old men won. The bankers in their offices took a deep breath, the bediamonded old ladies of the leisure class went back to clipping their coupons in the refined quiet of their safedeposit vaults,

the last puffs of the ozone of revolt went stale

in the whisper of speakeasy arguments.

Veblen wrote for the *Dial*,

lectured at the New School for Social Research.

He still had a hope that the engineers, the technicians, the nonprofiteers whose hands were on the switchboard might take up the fight where the workingclass had failed. He helped form the Technical Alliance. His last hope was the British general strike.

Was there no group of men bold enough to take charge of the magnificent machine before the pigeyed speculators and the yesmen at office desks irrevocably ruined it

and with it the hopes of four hundred years?

No one went to Veblen's lectures at the New School. With every article he wrote in the *Dial* the circulation dropped.

Harding's normalcy, the new era was beginning,

even Veblen made a small killing on the stockmarket.

He was an old man and lonely.

His second wife had gone to a sanitarium suffering from delusions of persecution.

There seemed no place for a masterless man.

Veblen went back out to Palo Alto

to live in his shack in the tawny hills and observe from outside the last grabbing urges of the profit system taking on, as he put it, the systematized delusions of dementia praecox.

There he finished his translation of the *Laxdaelasaga*.

He was an old man. He was much alone. He let the woodrats take what they wanted from his larder. A skunk that hung round the shack was so tame he'd rub up against Veblen's leg like a cat.

He told a friend he'd sometimes hear in the stillness about him the voices of his boyhood talking Norwegian as clear as on the farm in Minnesota where he was raised. His friends found him harder than ever to talk to, harder than ever to interest in anything. He was running down. The last sips of the bitter drink.

He died on August 3, 1929.

Among his papers a penciled note was found:

It is also my wish, in case of death, to be cremated if it can conveniently be done, as expeditiously and inexpensively as may be, without ritual or ceremony of any kind; that my ashes be thrown loose into the sea or into some sizable stream running into the sea; that no tombstone, slab, epitaph, effigy, tablet, inscription or monument of any name or nature, be set up to my memory or name in any place or at any time; that no obituary, memorial, portrait or biography of me, nor any letters written to or by me be printed or published, or in any way reproduced, copied or circulated;

but his memorial remains

riveted into the language:

the sharp clear prism of his mind.

1 Suggestions for Reading and Writing

1. Discuss the ways in which Dos Passos communicates by means of style and tone. Pay special attention to the poetic devices embodied in his prose.
2. Summarize as specifically as possible Dos Passos' social views as revealed here. Compare this attitude with that conveyed in his profile of "The House of Morgan" in *1919*.
3. Critics have made much of Dos Passos' altered political views since the thirties. Analyze this shift by comparing the views conveyed in *U. S. A.* with those of a recent novel, such as *Midcentury* (1961).
4. Does the "Norway" passage here add to or detract from the total portrait? Why?
5. Does this seem a full, well-rounded portrait of Veblen? Does a different figure emerge from J. A. Hobson's *Veblen* (1936)?
6. Can you explain the references here to Darwin, Ibsen, Marx, and Spencer?
7. What is Dos Passos' attitude toward Veblen the man? Do you agree with it? Explain.
8. After a careful sampling of *The Portable Veblen* (1948), ed. Max Lerner, write a concise précis of Veblen's political ideas. (For a detailed analysis of Veblen's thought, see either David Riesman's *Thorstein Veblen: A Critical Interpretation* [1953] or Bernard Rosenberg's *The Values of Veblen: A Critical Appraisal* [1956].)

[NIELS BOHR]

Time Magazine

No American publication is more familiar to American readers of all ages—at home or abroad—than Time, "The Weekly News Magazine." Its bright-banded cover, vividly breezy prose style, and neat division of all life's aspects into clearly labeled categories are eagerly awaited by the faithful who look to Time for a compact journalistic overview of the week's events. Almost *every issue contains a capsule profile of an individual prominent in business, science, education, culture, or entertainment.*

But a Time profile differs from most of the others in this anthology in that it is a composite, rather than an individual, effort. Reporters, researchers, writers, and editors all contribute to the final tightly compressed portrait that appears. Occasionally such a portrait takes the form of an obituary—as does this one of the late Danish scientist Niels Bohr.

↗   ↗   ↗   ↗   ↗

He was a gentleman who helped create the world's most deadly weapon; a humble man who collected as many honors as almost any man of his time. Before he died of a heart attack last week at 77, Danish Physicist Niels Bohr left an unmistakable imprint on the 20th century.

For a boy who always wanted to be a physicist, Niels Henrik David Bohr could have chosen no better age in which to live. By the time he was in college, physics was in fascinating chaos. Blow after blow had shattered its foundations: Albert Einstein proved that matter is energy, Max Planck proved that energy comes in indivisible packets he called quanta, Lord Rutherford proved that though the very name atom means "indivisible" in Greek, atoms are not indivisible. Nothing seemed certain. One physicist declared that all students should be warned: "Caution! Dangerous structure! Closed for reconstruction!"

Chewing on Stubs. In this chaos Bohr found his own future. In 1912, he went to Rutherford's laboratory at Manchester, England, just after Rutherford had advanced the theory that atoms are miniature solar systems with electrons revolving like planets around a sunlike nucleus. The idea had serious faults, which Bohr, then 27, spotted promptly; he corrected them by applying the unfamiliar principles of Planck's new quantum theory.

Bohr's atomic model answered dozens of questions that had the physicists of the time chewing their pencil stubs. It won him a Nobel Prize, but it, too, had faults which were gradually corrected by mathematical abstractions that seemed to grow more and more bizarre. Bohr himself did much of the correcting, and even the most recent concepts of atomic structure reflect his genius for inventive analysis.

Golden Age. In 1920, Bohr organized the University of Copenhagen Institute for Theoretical Physics, which quickly became a kind of scientific shrine, attracting students from all over the world. "The unique

"A Man of the Century," *Time,* LXXX (November 30, 1962), 56–57. Reprinted by permission from *Time* The Weekly Newsmagazine; copyright Time Inc. 1962.

and exciting feature of Copenhagen," wrote Professor John A. Wheeler of Princeton, "lies in the stimulus that Bohr gives. I know of nothing with which to compare it except the school of Plato." J. Robert Oppenheimer, who was later to head the atom-bomb-making Los Alamos Scientific Laboratory, said about physics in the 1920s: "It was a heroic time. It was not the doing of any one man; it involved the collaboration of scores of scientists from many different lands. But from first to last, the deeply creative, subtle and critical spirit of Niels Bohr guided, restrained, deepened, and finally transmuted the enterprise." He never dogmatized. "Every sentence I utter," Bohr liked to tell his students, "must be understood not as an affirmation but as a question." Once he defined truth as "something that we can attempt to doubt, and then perhaps, after much exertion, discover that part of the doubt is unjustified."

Niels Bohr deeply resented any restrictions that hindered the search for scientific truth. When the Nazis began to harass the great German universities, he wrote to physicists who he thought might be in danger of persecution and invited them to Copenhagen. Many came, and whenever any of them arrived, Bohr always made certain that he or one of his colleagues was at the railroad station to welcome them to his pleasant refuge.

Terrible Secret. The Nazis were not the only terror loose in the world. There was something else that only the physicists suspected. With their new mathematical tools they had been delving deep into atomic secrets, and they had come to realize that atomic nuclei hold enormous stores of potentially destructive energy.

Early in 1939, before the start of World War II, Bohr made a trip to the U. S. Just as his ship was about to leave Copenhagen, two German refugee physicists, Lise Meitner and O. R. Frisch, rushed aboard with a dismaying report. They had just heard that German Chemists Otto Hahn and Fritz Strassmann in Berlin had split the uranium atom. This was atomic fission, and with it the Nazis might soon be able to build an atomic bomb.

Bohr took the terrible news with him to New York and passed it along to U. S. physicists whom he trusted. By then the U. S. was well supplied with first-rank physicists, many of them Bohr's former students; they understood only too well the implications of his message. Soon confirming experiments were in full swing. Bohr himself worked for a while at Princeton. And there, one snowy night as he walked from his club to a laboratory, a problem that he had been puzzling over was unexpectedly resolved and the facts fell into place. Bohr realized that it was the rare uranium isotope U-235 that fissions. That knowledge was a signal contribution to further U. S. research.

He returned to Copenhagen before the Nazis overran Denmark in April 1940. At first they did not bother Bohr, despite his part-Jewish ancestry. Then, in 1943, he learned that he was slated for arrest. That same night Bohr, his wife and his son Aage sneaked aboard the fishing boat *Sea Star* and escaped to Sweden. (He was the kind of man about whom absent-minded professor stories are told, and legend has it that he had kept a bottle of heavy water, then important for atomic research, hidden in his refrigerator; in his hasty departure he left the heavy water behind and rescued an ordinary bottle of beer.)

Soon after Bohr reached Sweden, a British bomber arrived to pick him up. During the dangerous flight, while the bomber dodged German fighters, he almost died of asphyxiation from a faulty oxygen mask. From England he went on to the U. S., where the news that he had brought in 1939 had already mushroomed into the enormous Manhattan Project for constructing the first atom bomb.

First Bomb. At Los Alamos, Bohr, whose face was familiar to just about every physicist alive, was introduced with transparent secrecy as Mr. Nicholas Baker. Though he probably did as much as any other man to ensure the success of the Manhattan Project, once the first bomb was built, he would not wait to see the first test explosion at Alamogordo. For the rest of his life, all nuclear weapons were objects of horror to him. His fondest hope was to find a way to abolish them.

After the Nazi defeat, Niels Bohr returned home to Copenhagen; soon his own institute was open for business once more. Bohr was recognized as the leading citizen of Denmark, but to the end of his life he never quite believed that he was really a famous man. Once he went into the office of Scandinavian Airlines and asked diffidently whether he might cash a small check. When the manager offered to cash any amount he wanted, he was amazed that his name had been recognized.

Though creative theoretical physics is for younger men, Bohr did extraordinary work in getting European science on the track again after the war. He pleaded tirelessly for the peaceful uses of atomic energy, was one of the leading backers of CERN, Europe's cooperative research center at Geneva. Honors came so thickly that he could not have worn all his medals at the same time.

Last summer Bohr suffered a slight cerebral hemorrhage. After an autumn vacation in Italy, he seemed to recover, and he began writing his eagerly awaited history of quantum physics. But he spoke of a growing concern: Who would carry on his work when he was gone? One afternoon last week, while talking with a colleague, he felt dizzy. He went to bed with a slight headache, lost consciousness and died.

✓ Suggestions for Reading and Writing

1. *Time*'s use of language (*"Time*style" it has been called) has been much debated. What stylistic devices are evident here?
2. Does Professor Bohr emerge as public man, private man, both, neither? Explain. (For a more detailed treatment of Bohr, see Robert Jungk's *Brighter Than A Thousand Suns* [1958], especially pp. 37–47, 99–104, 120–123, and 172–174.)
3. Do you feel that *Time*'s writers have been strongly influenced here by the traditional stereotype of the modest, humble, absentminded genius? If you do, could you reshape the basic details into a differently toned profile?
4. How does this portrait differ in style and tone from the New York *Times*'s brief biography-obituary of actor Monty Woolley that follows?

[MONTY WOOLLEY]

New York Times

Any comprehensive poll probably would find the century-old New York Times the nation's leading daily. Recent statistics reveal that its daily wordage is five times that of the New Testament and that its Sunday edition frequently exceeds four pounds and 450 pages. As dependable as it is exhaustive, the Times is the only "newspaper of record" in the United States, publishing as it does the complete text of all historically significant documents and speeches. It also has a foreign staff of fifty correspondents, with an international edition based in Paris.

Among its many interesting features is a daily profile of a newsworthy figure. As with Time magazine, this profile often takes the form of an obituary. The Times, in any event, is not likely to be caught off-guard; material on almost any person of consequence can be gathered from its huge "morgue" and assembled in a matter of minutes.

The following sketch of the actor Monty Woolley offers a representative example.

Monty Woolley, Actor, 74, Dies; 'Man Who Came to Dinner' Star

Stage-Screen Player Noted for Sheridan Whiteside Role—Director Taught at Yale

ALBANY, May 6 (UPI)—Monty Woolley, the bearded actor known for his portrayal as "The Man Who Came to Dinner," died today in Albany Medical Center Hospital. He was 74 years old.

Mr. Woolley had been on the critical list since April 6 with a heart ailment. He was moved to the medical center from Saratoga Hospital about 30 miles north of here. He had lived in Saratoga Springs for the last few years.

Mr. Woolley's funeral was scheduled tentatively for Wednesday at Saratoga Springs. The service will be held in Bethesda Protestant-Episcopal Church, with the Rev. W. Benjamin Holmes officiating. Burial will be in Greenridge Cemetery.

Memorable Role
Special to The New York *Times*.
NEW YORK.

It was as the arrogant waspish, murderously comic and strangely lovable Sheridan Whiteside in "The Man Who Came to Dinner" that Monty Woolley achieved a probably enduring theatrical fame.

Making only his third Broadway appearance, he starred for two seasons in the George S. Kaufman-Moss Hart comedy about a world-famous lecturer, resembling the late Alexander Woollcott, immobilized by a leg fracture in a small town in Ohio.

Mr. Woolley went on to play the same role in the highly successful film version in 1941. He confined his activities to Hollywood for several years thereafter, and emerged as a first-rate performer in films as diverse as "Life Begins at 88," in which he played the leading role of a drunken old actor, "The Bishop's Wife," "Miss Tatlock's Millions" and "When Irish Eyes Are Smiling."

But it was as Whiteside that he remained in the national consciousness. In 1949, in fact, when he arrived at Cambridge, Mass., to appear in a revival of the play, he was greeted by members of the Harvard Dramatic Club, faculty members and even a few Radcliffe girls wearing false beards.

Most people found it difficult, if not impossible, to think of the performer without his splendid white Van Dyke and flaring mustaches. Mr. Woolley, who throughout his life had a deserved reputation as a wit, often spoke in defense of beards. In an article he wrote in 1942 for The Times he termed the beard "the historic trademark of genius."

"Take the beards off Santa Claus and Bluebeard and what have you?" he went on. "Nothing but a pair of middle-aged, overstuffed bores."

Edgar Montillion Woolley became a member of the fashionable world at birth, which took place in the old Bristol Hotel at Fifth Avenue and 42nd Street. The hotel was owned by his father, who was also the proprietor of the fabled Grand Union Hotel in Saratoga Springs, N. Y.

In the elaborate dining rooms and salons of the two establishments the boy met Lillian Russell, Victor Russell, Sarah Bernhardt and just about every other theatrical and social celebrity of the era.

Mr. Woolley attended the MacKenzie School in Dobbs Ferry, N. Y., and entered Yale in 1907. One of his classmates was Cole Porter, the composer, with whom he formed a lifelong friendship. This was depicted in the 1946 screen biography of Mr. Porter, "Night and Day," in which Mr. Woolley played himself.

Around the two undergraduates formed a group of admirers of the theater and high life in general that specialized in elaborate parties and frequent trips from New Haven to Manhattan.

Mr. Woolley became president of the Yale Dramatic Association and remained after graduation to get his master's degree. He then went to Harvard for further study under Prof. George Lyman Kittredge, the Shakespearean scholar, before returning to Yale as an instructor in English.

In 1916 he enlisted in the National Guard for service in the Mexican border campaign but got no further than a remount station at Toby-hanna, Pa. Later he served in France as a lieutenant in intelligence on the General Staff.

After the war he went back to the Yale faculty as an assistant professor of drama. Under his influence student theatricals blossomed. But in 1927, when the Yale experimental theatre was established, Prof. George Pierce Baker of Harvard was brought in to head it, and Mr. Woolley resigned.

For a while he rusticated in his family's Victorian mansion in Saratoga Springs—the home he returned to late in life—and grew his beard, which originally had a pinkish tinge. Then he headed for Broadway. With Mr. Porter's help he soon established himself as a successful director. Among his credits were Mr. Porter's "Fifty Million Frenchmen," the second "Little Show" and "Jubilee."

↑ MAN ABOUT TOWN

Meanwhile Mr. Woolley was making a reputation as a wit, party-goer and man about town that kept many persons, perhaps including himself, from taking his theatrical career seriously.

In 1937 he went to Hollywood for the first time, and appeared in several films, including the notable "Nothing Sacred," starring William Powell and Carole Lombard, "Man About Town" and "Dancing Co-Ed."

In recent years Mr. Woolley curtailed his activities. Among his final films were "As Young as You Feel," in 1951, which The Times's critic described as "a vastly superior entertainment."

His television appearances were infrequent and not notably success-ful. More than a decade ago he said, "For five minutes on a Fred Allen show I rehearsed for nine or 10 days. I was nervous and watched the clock constantly. I thought it was all terrible."

Mr. Woolley never married. He leaves no immediate survivors.

↑ Suggestions for Reading and Writing

1. Does the capsule outline preceding the main section strengthen or weaken the total profile? Why?
2. The people, titles, and events mentioned here would indicate that this article is slanted toward which reader-group?
3. What are the strong and weak points of this biographical approach? Is there as much information and insight as the general reader cares to receive? Does he have reason to feel cheated?
4. Did Mr. Woolley lead a life to be envied? Explain. Do you here gather that he played himself on stage and screen? Or did he mold himself to fit his public image? Are you given any hints?
5. What similarities and differences are there between this sketch and such other journalistic pieces as *Time*'s on Niels Bohr and Golden's on Mayor Gaynor? Which of the three is the most effective as biography?
6. Other interesting brief life-summaries are occasionally to be found in the *New Yorker*'s "Talk of the Town" section. See, for example, the article on the death of Grandma Moses, *New Yorker* (December 23, 1961), p. 17.

ON BIOGRAPHY

The following is a selected list of twentieth-century books and essays dealing with biography. Far from exhaustive, this list is meant only as a guide to further reading. The sources listed tend to be general; however, they will lead the interested student to more specialized studies. Several of them have extensive bibliographies of their own.

BOOKS

Balch, Marston, ed. *Modern Short Biographies*. New York, 1935.
Bowen, Catherine D. *Adventures of a Biographer*. Boston, 1959.
———. *The Writing of Biography*. Boston, 1951.
Bowerman, G. F. *The New Biography*. Washington, 1929.
Burr, Anna R. *The Autobiography: A Critical and Comparative Study*. Boston, 1909.
Clark, Arthur M. *Autobiography: Its Genesis and Phases*. Edinburgh, 1935.
Clark, Barrett H., ed. *Great Short Biographies of the World*. New York, 1928.
Clifford, James L., ed. *Biography as an Art: Selected Criticism 1560–1960*. New York, 1962.
Connely, Willard. *Adventures in Biography*. London, 1956.
Cross, Wilbur L. *An Outline of Biography: From Plutarch to Strachey*. New York, 1924.
Dargan, Marion, ed. *Guide to American Biography: 1607–1933*. 2 vols. Albuquerque, 1949, 1952.
Dunn, Waldo H. *English Biography*. London, 1916.
Durling, Dwight and William Watt, eds. *Biography: Varieties and Parallels*. New York, 1941.
Edel, Leon. *Literary Biography*. New York, 1959.
Garraty, John A. *The Nature of Biography*. New York, 1957.
Hyde, Marietta A., ed. *Modern Biography*. New York, 1934.
Johnson, Edgar. *One Mighty Torrent: The Drama of Biography*. New York, 1937.
———, ed. *A Treasury of Biography*. New York, 1941.
Johnston, James C. *Biography: The Literature of Personality*. New York, 1927.
Kendall, Paul Murray. *The Art of Biography*. New York, 1965.
Lillard, R. G. *American Life in Autobiography*. Stanford, 1956.
Longaker, Mark. *Contemporary Biography*. Philadelphia, 1934.
———. *English Biography in the Eighteenth Century*. Philadelphia, 1931.

Matthews, William, ed. *American Diaries: An Annotated Bibliography*. Berkeley, 1945.

———, ed. *British Autobiographies: An Annotated Bibliography*. Berkeley, 1955.

———, ed. *British Diaries: An Annotated Bibliography*. Berkeley, 1950.

Maurois, André. *Aspects of Biography*. New York, 1929.

Merrill, Dana K. *Development of American Biography*. Portland, 1932.

Metcalf, John C., ed. *The Stream of English Biography: Readings in Representative Biographies*. New York, 1930.

Misch, Georg. *A History of Autobiography in Antiquity*. Cambridge, 1951.

Nicolson, Harold. *The Development of English Biography*. London, 1927.

O'Brien, Kate. *English Diaries and Journals*. London, 1947.

Pascal, Roy. *Design and Truth in Autobiography*. London, 1960.

Pearson, Hesketh. *Ventilations: Being Biographical Asides*. Philadelphia, 1930.

Pinto, V. de Sola, ed. *English Biography in the Seventeenth Century*. London, 1951.

Ponsonby, Arthur. *English Diaries*. London, 1922.

———. *More English Diaries*. London, 1927.

Rowse, A. L. *The Use of History*. London, 1946.

Shumaker, Wayne. *English Autobiography: Its Emergence, Materials, and Form*. Berkeley, 1954.

Stauffer, Donald A. *The Art of Biography in Eighteenth-Century England*. Princeton, 1941.

———. *English Biography Before 1700*. Cambridge, Mass., 1930.

Stephen, Leslie. *Studies of a Biographer*. London, 1898–1902.

Thayer, William R. *The Art of Biography*. New York, 1920.

Trevelyan, G. M. *Biography: A Reader's Guide*. London, 1947.

Valentine, Alan C. *Biography*. New York, 1927.

ESSAYS

Adams, James T. "New Modes in Biography" and "Biography as an Art," *The Tempo of Modern Life*, pp. 171–199. New York, 1931.

Adcock, St. John. "The Gentle Art of Biography." *Bookman*, LXXV (October 1928), 24–25.

Alexander, Holmes M. "Wrong Ways to Write Biography," in *The Writer's Handbook*, ed. A. S. Burack, pp. 271–279. Boston, 1936.

Anthony, Katharine. "Writing Biography," in *The Writer's Book*, ed. Helen Hull, pp. 220–226. New York, 1950.

Benson, A. C. "The Art of the Biographer," in *Essays by Divers Hands*, pp. 139–164. London, 1926.

Bentley, G. E. et al., "The Critical Significance of Biographical Evidence," in *English Institute Essays: 1946*, pp. 3–101. New York, 1947.

Bowerman, George F. "The New Biography." *Wilson Bulletin*, IV (November 1929), 107–111, 153–159.

Boyd, Ernest. "Sex in Biography." *Harper's*, CLXV (November 1932), 752–759.

Bradford, Gamaliel. "The Art of Biography." *Saturday Review of Literature*, I (May 23, 1925), 769–770.

———. "Confessions of a Biographer," *Wives*, pp. 3–14. New York, 1925.

———. "Psychography," *A Naturalist of Souls*, pp. 3–25. Boston, 1926.

Brooks, Van Wyck. "Thoughts on Biography," *Sketches in Criticism*, pp. 105–116. New York, 1932.

Bruce, Harold L. "Biography," in *Essays in Criticism by Members of the Department of English, University of California*, pp. 77–87. Berkeley, 1929.

Bryant, Arthur. "The Art of Biography." *London Mercury*, XXX (July 1934), 236–243.

Burdett, Osbert. "Experiment in Biography," *Tradition and Experiment in Present-Day Literature*, pp. 161–178. London, 1929.

Chamberlain, John. "Walking the Tightrope: An Inquiry into the Art of Political Biography." *Modern Monthly*, VII (1933), 105–109.

Clifford, James L. "Biography: Craft or Art?" *University of Toronto Quarterly*, XXVII (April 1959), 301–309.

———. "The Complex Art of Biography or All the Doctor Johnsons," in *Academic Discourse*, ed. John J. Enck, pp. 189–197. New York, 1964.

———. "Speaking of Books." *New York Times Book Review*, January 29, 1956, p. 2.

Cook, Edward T. "The Art of Biography," *Literary Recreations*, pp. 1–33. London, 1918.

Cross, Wilbur L. "From Plutarch to Strachey." *Yale Review*, XI (October 1921), 140–157.

Crothers, Samuel M. "Satan Among the Biographers," *The Cheerful Giver*, pp. 76–104. Boston, 1923.

Davies, Godfrey. "Biography and History." *Modern Language Quarterly*, I (March 1940), 79–94.

Dobrée, Bonamy. "Modern Biography." *National Review*, XCIX (July 1932), 121–129.

Drew, Elizabeth. "Biography," *The Enjoyment of Literature*, pp. 78–108. New York, 1935.

Field, Louise M. "Biographical New Dealing." *North American Review*, CCXXXVIII (December 1944), 546–552.

Flexner, J. T. "Biography as a Juggler's Art." *Saturday Review of Literature*, XXVI (October 9, 1943), 3–4, 9.

Frenkel, Else. "Studies in Biographical Psychology." *Character and Personality*, V (1936), 1–34.

Fuess, Claude M. "The Biographer and His Victims." *Atlantic Monthly*, CXLIX (January 1932), 62–73.

———. "Debunkery and Biography." *Atlantic Monthly*, CLI (March 1933), 347–356.

Garraty, J. A. "Biographers Are Only Human." *Saturday Review*, XXXVI (March 20, 1954), 11–13, 55–57.

———. "How Should You Tell a Man's Story?" *New York Times Book Review*, July 5, 1959, pp. 1, 10.

———. "How to Write a Biography." *South Atlantic Quarterly*, LV (1956), 73–86.

———. "The Interrelations of Psychology and Biography." *Psychological Bulletin*, LI (November 1954), 569–582.

Gelber, Lionel M. "History and the New Biography." *Queen's Quarterly*, XXXVII (January 1930), 127–144.

Gosse, Edmund. "Biography." *Encyclopaedia Britannica*. 11th ed., III, 952–954.

Guedalla, Philip. "The Method of Biography." *Journal of the Royal Society of Arts*, LXXXVII (July 21, 1939), 925–935.

Handlin, Oscar. "History in Men's Lives." *Virginia Quarterly*, XXX (Summer 1954), 534–541.

Hart, Albert B. "The Modern Historical School for Scandal." *Current History*, XXXI (February 1930), 968–970.

Hergesheimer, Joseph. "Biography and Bibliographies," in *Breaking into Print*, ed. Elmer Adler, pp. 75–83. New York, 1937.

Howe, Mark A. De Wolfe. "Biography Drifts Toward the Novel." *Independent,* CXV (September 26, 1925), 359–361.

Hughes, Rupert. "Pitfalls of the Biographer." *Pacific Historical Review,* II (March 1933), 1–33.

Johnson, Edgar. "American Biography and the Modern World." *North American Review,* CCXLV (June 1938), 364–380.

Johnston, George A. "The New Biography." *Atlantic Monthly,* CXLIII (March 1929), 333–342.

Jones, Howard Mumford. "Introduction," *The American Plutarch,* ed. Edward T. James, pp. xiii–xxiii. New York, 1964.

———. "Methods in Contemporary Biography." *English Journal,* XXI (January–February 1932), 113–122.

Josephson, Matthew. "Historians and Mythmakers." *Virginia Quarterly,* XVI (January 1940), 92–109.

Lee, Sidney. "Principles of Biography" and "The Perspective of Biography," in *Elizabethan and Other Essays,* ed. Frederick S. Boas, pp. 31–82. Oxford, 1929.

Lynd, Robert. "Fictitious Biography," *Books and Writers,* pp. 312–316. London, 1952.

Malone, Dumas. "Biography and History," in *The Interpretation of History,* ed. J. R. Strayer, pp. 121–148. Princeton, 1943.

Marcu, Valeriu. "Biography and Biographers," *Men and Forces of Our Time,* pp. 3–17. London, 1931.

Maurois, André. "The Modern Biographer." *Yale Review,* XVII (January 1928), 227–245.

Mumford, Lewis. "The Task of Modern Biography." *English Journal,* XXIII (January 1934), 1–9.

Nevins, Allan. "The Biographer and the Historian," in *Humanities for Our Time,* ed. Walter R. Agard, pp. 45–66. Lawrence, Kansas, 1949.

———. "Biography and History," *The Gateway to History,* pp. 318–341. New York, 1938.

Nichols, R. F. "The Dictionary of American Biography." *Pennsylvania Magazine of History and Biography,* LX (1936), 323–328.

Nicolson, Harold. "Biography Old and New." *Living Age,* CCCLII (1937), 265–268.

———. "How I Write Biography." *Saturday Review of Literature,* X (May 26, 1934), 709–711.

———. "The Practice of Biography." *American Scholar,* XXIII (1954), 151–161.

Nock, Albert J. "The Purpose of Biography." *Atlantic Monthly,* CLXV (March 1940), 340–346.

Notestein, Wallace. "History and the Biographer." *Yale Review,* XXII (March 1933), 549–558.

Partin, Robert. "Biography as an Instrument of Moral Instruction." *American Quarterly,* VIII (Winter 1956), 303–315.

Partington, Wilfred. "Should a Biographer Tell?" *Atlantic Monthly,* CLXXX (August 1947), 56–63.

Pearson, Hesketh. "About Biography," in *Essays by Divers Hands,* ed. E. V. Rieu, pp. 55–72. London, 1958.

———. "Warts and All." *Saturday Review of Literature,* XXIX (October 12, 1946), 13–14.

Plumb, J. H. "The Interaction of History and Biography." *Times Literary Supplement,* January 6, 1956, p. xxi.

Riegel, R. E. "Changing Fashions in American Biography." *New England Social Studies Bulletin,* IX (1953), 8–14.

Schelling, Felix E. "The Art of Biography," *Appraisements and Asperities*, pp. 50–55. Philadelphia, 1922.

Smith, Bradford. "Biographer's Creed." *William and Mary Quarterly*, X (April 1953), 190–195.

Smith, Samuel S. "The Art of Framing Lies" and "The Criticism of Biography," *The Craft of the Critic*, pp. 92–119. New York, 1931.

Stern, Madeleine B. "Approaches to Biography." *South Atlantic Quarterly*, XLV (July 1946), 363–371.

Stewart, J. I. M. "Biography," in *The Craft of Letters*, ed. John Lehmann, pp. 6–25. London, 1956.

Symons, A. J. A. "Tradition in Biography," *Tradition and Experiment in Present-Day Literature*, pp. 149–160. London, 1929.

Tolles, Frederick B. "The Biographer's Craft." *South Atlantic Quarterly*, LIII (October 1954), 508–520.

Tozzer, Alfred M. "Biography and Biology." *American Anthropologist*, XXXV (July–September 1933), 418–432.

Trueblood, Charles K. "Biography." *Dial*, LXXXIII (August 1927), 128–136.

Van Doren, Carl. "Biography as a Literary Form." *Columbia University Quarterly*, XVII (March 1915), 180–185.

Weedon, William S. "Concerning Biography," *Humanistic Studies in Honor of J. C. Metcalf*, pp. 247–267. Charlottesville, Va., 1941.

Whibley, Charles. "The Indiscretions of Biography." *English Review*, XXXIX (December 1924), 769–772.

White, Newman I. "The Development, Use, and Abuse of Interpretation in Biography," in *English Institute Annual, 1942*, pp. 29–58. New York, 1943.

Williams, Orlo. "The Subject of Biography." *National Review*, C (May 1933), 693–702.

Wingfield-Stratford, Esmé. "Biographers and Their Victims." *Fortnightly*, CXXXVII (April 1932), 444–451.

ALTERNATE TABLE OF CONTENTS

Critical Articles, Biography, Autobiography

CRITICAL ARTICLES

John A. Garraty	Biography in the Ancient World	3
W. S. Lewis	The Difficult Art of Biography	59
Leon Edel	[The Subject Matter of Biography]	116
Virginia Woolf	The Art of Biography	164

Edward Hayes O'Neill   from The New Biography   191
Bernard De Voto   The Skeptical Biographer   276
Iris Origo   Biography, True and False   368

BIOGRAPHY

Bible   The Book of Ruth   18
Plutarch   from The Life of Julius Caesar   24
William Roper   from *Life of Sir Thomas More*   39
John Foxe   Bishop Ridley and Bishop Latimer 52
John Aubrey   Shakespeare · Suckling · Dave-
                             nant   67
Samuel Johnson   Gray   132
James Boswell   from *Life of Johnson*   143
John Gibson Lockhart   from *Life of Sir Walter Scott* 172
Lytton Strachey   Florence Nightingale   207
André Maurois   from *Disraeli*   250
Catherine Drinker Bowen   [Oliver Wendell Holmes]   321
Gertrude Stein   [Ernest Hemingway]   380
Robert Rice   [Mort Sahl]   388
Louis Untermeyer   [Amy Lowell]   404
James Thurber   My Friend McNulty   419
Deems Taylor   The Monster   428
Harry Golden   Mayor William J. Gaynor   433
W. A. Swanberg   from *Citizen Hearst*   439
John Dos Passos   [Thorstein Veblen]   450
Time Magazine   [Niels Bohr]   459
New York *Times*   [Monty Woolley]   463

AUTOBIOGRAPHY

John Bunyan   from *Grace Abounding*   77
Samuel Pepys   from *Diary*   87
William Butler Yeats   from *Autobiographies*   199
H. G. Wells   from *Experiment in Autobiography* 262
Thomas Sancton   The Silver Horn   293
Dylan Thomas   from *Portrait of the Artist as a
                            Young Dog*   303
Alfred Kazin   from *A Walker in the City*   313
James Baldwin   Notes of a Native Son   339
Moss Hart   from *Act One*   355